Paul and Economics

Paul and Economics

A Handbook

Thomas R. Blanton IV and Raymond Pickett,
editors

Fortress Press
Minneapolis

PAUL AND ECONOMICS

A Handbook

Cover image: Roman civilization, fresco portraying baker, from Pompeii / De Agostini Picture Library / A. Dagli Orti / Bridgeman Images

Cover design: Tory Herman

Print ISBN: 978-1-5064-0603-9

eBook ISBN: 978-1-5064-0604-6

The paper used in this publication meets the minimum requirements of American National Standard for Information Sciences — Permanence of Paper for Printed Library Materials, ANSI Z329.48-1984.

Manufactured in the U.S.A.

This book was produced using Pressbooks.com, and PDF rendering was done by PrinceXML.

Contents

Contributors

Thomas R. Blanton IV is auxiliary professor in New Testament studies at the Lutheran School of Theology at Chicago. He is the author of *A Spiritual Economy: Gift Exchange in the Letters of Paul of Tarsus* (New Haven, CT: Yale University Press, 2017) and *Constructing a New Covenant: Discursive Strategies in the Damascus Document and Second Corinthians* (Tübingen: Mohr Siebeck, 2007). Blanton is currently a cochair of the SBL Early Christianity and the Ancient Economy program unit.

Ward Blanton is reader in biblical cultures and European thought in the department of religious studies at the University of Kent. He is the author of *A Materialism for the Masses: Saint Paul and the Philosophy of Undying Life* (New York: Columbia University Press, 2014) and *Displacing Christian Origins: Philosophy, Secularity, and the New Testament* (Chicago: University of Chicago Press, 2007).

Timothy A. Brookins is assistant professor of classics at Houston Baptist University and the author of *Corinthian Wisdom, Stoic Philosophy, and the Ancient Economy* (Cambridge: Cambridge University Press, 2014) and "The (In)frequency of the Name 'Erastus' in Antiquity" (*NTS* 59 [October 2013]: 496–516).

Cavan Concannon is assistant professor of religion at the University of Southern California and the author of *Assembling Early Christianity: Trade, Networks, and the Letters of Dionysios of Corinth* (Cambridge: Cambridge University Press, 2017) and *"When You Were Gentiles": Specters of Ethnicity in Roman Corinth and Paul's Corinthian Correspondence* (New Haven, CT: Yale University Press, 2014), and editor (with Lindsey

Mazurek) of *Across the Corrupting Sea: Post-Braudelian Approaches to the Ancient Eastern Mediterranean* (London: Routledge, 2016).

Zeba A. Crook is professor of religious studies at Carleton University and the author of "Matthew, Memory Theory and the New No Quest" (*HTS Teologiese Studies / Theological Studies* 70, no. 1 [2014]: 1–11. doi: 10.4102/hts.v70i1.2716), *Parallel Gospels* (New York: Oxford University Press, 2012), and *Reconceptualising Conversion* (Berlin: de Gruyter, 2004).

Neil Elliott teaches biblical studies at United Theological Seminary and Metropolitan State University and is acquiring editor in biblical studies at Fortress Press. He is the author of *The Arrogance of Nations: Reading Romans in the Shadow of Empire* (Minneapolis: Fortress Press, 2008), *Liberating Paul: The Justice of God and the Politics of the Apostle* (Maryknoll, NY: Orbis, 1994), and *The Rhetoric of Romans: Argumentative Constraint and Strategy and Paul's Dialogue with Judaism* (Sheffield: JSOT Press, 1990), and coauthor (with Mark Reasoner) of *Documents and Images for the Study of Paul* (Minneapolis: Fortress Press, 2010).

John T. Fitzgerald is professor of New Testament and early Christianity at the University of Notre Dame and the author of numerous works dealing with Paul, including "Paul, Wine in the Ancient Mediterranean World, and the Problem of Intoxication," in *Paul's Graeco-Roman Context* (ed. Cilliers Breytenbach [Leuven: Peeters, 2015]), (with Wayne A. Meeks) *The Writings of St. Paul: Annotated Texts, Reception, and Criticism* (New York: W. W. Norton, 2007), and *Cracks in an Earthen Vessel: An Examination of the Catalogues of Hardships in the Corinthian Correspondence* (Atlanta: Scholars Press, 1988). He is currently preparing a commentary on the Pastoral Epistles for the Hermeneia series.

David B. Hollander is an associate professor of history at Iowa State University and the author of *Money in the Late Roman Republic* (Boston: Brill, 2007) as well as articles on Roman coinage, agriculture, and trade. He also served as the area editor for economy for *The Encyclopedia of Ancient History* (ed. Roger Bagnall et al., 13 vols. [Malden, MA: Wiley-Blackwell, 2012]). Hollander is currently cochair of the SBL Early Christianity and the Ancient Economy program unit and serves on the editorial boards of the *Ancient History Bulletin* and *The Encyclopedia of Ancient History* (online edition).

Richard A. Horsley is Distinguished Professor of Liberal Arts and the Study of Religion at the University of Massachusetts Boston (Emeritus), and author or editor of numerous works including *1 Corinthians* (ANTC [Nashville: Abingdon, 1998]) and *Paul and Empire: Religion and Power in Roman Imperial Society* (Harrisburg, PA: Trinity Press International, 1997).

John S. Kloppenborg is a professor in the department for the study of religion at the University of Toronto and author of numerous works, including (with Richard Ascough) *Attica, Central Greece, Macedonia, Thrace*, vol. 1 of *Greco-Roman Associations: Texts, Translations, and Commentary* (Berlin: de Gruyter, 2011), *Q, the Earliest Gospel: An Introduction to the Original Sayings and Stories of Jesus* (Louisville, KY: Westminster John Knox, 2008), and *The Tenants in the Vineyard: Ideology, Economics, and Agrarian Conflict in Jewish Palestine* (Tübingen: Mohr Siebeck, 2006).

Jinyu Liu is associate professor of classical studies at DePauw University and Shanghai "1000 Plan" Distinguished Professor at Shanghai Normal University, and the author of "Professional *Collegia*," in *The Cambridge Companion to Ancient Rome* (ed. Paul Erdkamp [Cambridge: Cambridge University Press, 2013]) and Collegia centonariorum: *The Guilds of Textile-dealers in the Roman West* (Leiden: Brill, 2009).

Raymond Pickett is professor of New Testament at the Lutheran School of Theology at Chicago. He is the author of "Conflicts at Corinth" in vol. 1 of *Christian Origins: A People's History of Christianity* (ed. Richard A. Horsley [Minneapolis: Fortress Press, 2005]) and *The Cross in Corinth: The Social Significance of the Death of Jesus* (Sheffield: Sheffield Academic Press, 1997).

Ulrike Roth is senior lecturer in ancient history at the University of Edinburgh. She is the author of *Thinking Tools: Agricultural Slavery between Evidence and Models* (London: University of London, 2007) and numerous articles on Roman slavery. She has also published on (early) Christian slavery, including her article on the role of Onesimus in Paul's letter to Philemon, "Paul, Philemon, and Onesimus: A Christian Design for Mastery," in the *Zeitschrift für die Neutestamentliche Wissenschaft* 105 (2014), and on slavery and manumission in the donation and will of the deacon Vincent of Huesca in sixth-century Spain, "Slavery and the Church in Visigothic Spain: The Donation and Will of Vincent of Huesca," in *Antiquité Tardive* 24 (2016).

L. L. Welborn is professor of New Testament and early Christianity at Fordham University and the author of *Paul's Summons to Messianic Life: Political Theology and the Coming Awakening* (New York: Columbia University Press, 2015), *An End to Enmity: Paul and the "Wrongdoer" of Second Corinthians* (Berlin: de Gruyter, 2011), and *Paul, the Fool of Christ: A Study of 1 Corinthians 1–4 in the Comic-Philosophical Tradition* (London: T&T Clark, 2005). Welborn serves as editor of the book series Synkrisis, published by Yale University Press.

Annette Weissenrieder is professor of New Testament at the Graduate Theological Union, Berkeley, and San Francisco Theological Seminary. Her main areas of research include the Corpus Hellenisticum, with an emphasis on Greco-Roman medicine and philosophy, ancient architecture, and numismatics (especially of temples); she is preparing a new edition of the Vetus Latina Beuron Luke and Matthew (together with Thomas Bauer from the University of Erfurt).

Preface

In the wake of the global financial crisis of 2007–2008, economic issues have taken a more central role not only in public discussion but also in the field of biblical studies. A number of recent studies have addressed the topics of inequality and the distribution of resources, while others have addressed important theoretical issues relevant to the contemporary framing of the economies of ancient Israel, Hellenistic and Roman Judea, Greece, and the Roman Empire. In the area of New Testament studies, Paul of Tarsus and his epistles have played a central role in discussions of patronage and commensality. The image of Paul has also been taken up by religious leaders, community organizers, and political theorists who seek ways to both reconceptualize and reconfigure what is increasingly viewed as a dysfunctional economic system in the globalized corporate capitalism that characterizes the early twenty-first century. For these reasons, a close examination of Paul's letters has become a pressing need.

This book attempts to fill that need. The volume is far from a haphazard collection of loosely connected essays; on the contrary, it consists of carefully selected topics on the main economic issues relevant to the study of the Pauline epistles. Since the early Christian assemblies associated with Paul constituted part of a larger economic system within the Roman Empire, the task has necessarily been interdisciplinary. The essays collected in this volume have been written by classicists and economic historians as well as by New Testament scholars. Moreover, the essays herein tend to follow a particular format. The contributors to this volume—all experts in their fields who have made significant contributions with regard to the topics about which they have written—have been invited not only to survey the recent history of scholarship to orient readers quickly to the present state of research on a given topic, but also, in cases in which there is good reason to do so, to break new ground by introducing methods, approaches, and data to catalyze future studies in the area. Because the articles both incorporate broad overviews of each topic and suggest avenues of further research, this volume aims to be useful to students, researchers, and general readers interested in the economic aspects of the early Christian assemblies associated with Paul. The chosen format renders this book perfect for use as a course textbook, as a reference work for students and researchers in the areas of Biblical studies, classics, and economic history, and as a guide for interested general readers.

The majority of the essays presented in this volume were first presented in abbreviated form at a conference entitled "Paul and Economics" that was held at the Lutheran School of Theology at Chicago on September 18–19, 2015. The interdisciplinary discussion that took place provided the researchers with common points of reference that were helpful not only in refining the final versions of articles but also by providing a level of coherence and integration to the volume that otherwise would not have been possible. The editors thank Esther Menn, Dean and Vice President for Academic Affairs, and James Nieman, the president of the Lutheran School of Theology at Chicago, for their generous support of the "Paul and Economics" conference. In addition, we would like to thank Neil Elliott, the acquiring editor in biblical studies, and the staff at Fortress Press for enthusiastically endorsing the publication of this volume and for their expert guidance through the various stages of the book's production.

Thomas R. Blanton IV
Raymond Pickett

Introduction

Raymond Pickett

The study of Paul's letters has undergone a great deal of change in recent decades. An important paradigm shift occurred in the 1970s as scholars began to reassess Paul and the messianic movement he played a significant role in shaping in the light of the more variegated picture of Judaism that was emerging. The work of Krister Stendahl, E. P. Sanders, and others fundamentally changed the landscape of Pauline studies by exposing the extent to which interpretations of Paul's letters were influenced more by Reformation theology and constructions of subjectivity than the Jewish context of the first century in which Paul was formed.[1] The new perspective on Paul, as it came to be known, was followed by studies that appropriated models and methods from the social sciences to explore the social history and dynamics of the Pauline communities. Gerd Theissen's essays in *The Social Setting of Pauline Christianity* were a groundbreaking attempt to provide a social analysis of the Corinthian assembly. His essay on 1 Corinthians 11:17–34 was an early attempt to consider economic disparity as an underlying issue in the dispute over the Lord's Supper in Corinth.[2]

---

1. Krister Stendahl, "The Apostle Paul and the Introspective Conscience of the West," *Harvard Theological Review*, 56, no. 3 (1963): 199–215. E. P. Sanders, *Paul and Palestinian Judaism: A Comparison of Patterns of Religion* (Philadelphia: Fortress Press, 1977). Stendahl's classic article argued that the emphasis on individual conscience and sin characteristic of most interpretations of Paul reflected a primarily Lutheran and Augustinian lens that is not entirely aligned with Paul's concerns. Only 120 pages of Sanders 552-page book are devoted to Paul, with the bulk devoted to a description of what Sanders terms "normative Judaism."

Wayne Meeks's book *The First Urban Christians* was a thoroughgoing social description of Pauline Christianity that continued Theissen's emphasis on social stratification and status.[3] Meeks and Abraham Malherbe, his colleague at Yale, challenged the prevailing viewpoint since Deissmann at the turn of the twentieth century that the Pauline assemblies were comprised predominantly of the poor and dispossessed of the Roman provinces.[4] They declared a new "emerging consensus," which maintained that the communities Paul established reflected a cross-section of urban society with the extreme top and bottom of the Greco-Roman social scale absent from the picture.

Several studies using a variety of social and anthropological models to provide a thick description of the social location and dynamics of the Pauline assemblies followed in subsequent years. Bruce Malina and others appealed to anthropological models to call attention to cultural dynamics, especially honor and shame.[5] Other scholars poured over ancient texts to analyze Paul's rhetoric and connections with Greco-Roman literary topoi and philosophy. In most of this scholarship during the 1980s and 1990s, economic aspects of Paul's mission and the communities he established received little attention. Moreover, the view proposed by Meeks that there were people from several different social levels in the assemblies, with the "typical Christian" being a free artisan or small trader, some of whom owned slaves, houses, and exhibited other signs of wealth, persisted.[6] The profile of the preponderance of these Christ believers was, for the most part, uncritically accepted until the late 1990s. A strong rebuttal to the so-called "new consensus" appeared on the scene in 1998 with Justin Meggitt's book entitled *Paul, Poverty and Survival.*[7] Meggitt reiterated Deissmann's thesis, arguing that "Paul and his followers should be located amongst the 'poor' of the first century, that they faced the same anxieties over subsistence that beset all but the privileged few in that society."[8] Although Meggitt's work was criticized for dividing the Roman world into two

2. Gerd Theissen, *The Social Setting of Pauline Christianity: Essays on Corinth* (Philadelphia: Fortress Press, 1982), 145–74.
3. Wayne A. Meeks, *The First Urban Christians: The Social World of the Apostle Paul* (New Haven, CT: Yale University Press, 1983).
4. Ibid., 51–73. Meeks refers to Abraham J. Malherbe, *Social Aspects of Early Christianity* (Baton Rouge: Louisiana State University Press, 1977).
5. Bruce J. Malina, *The New Testament World: Insights from Cultural Anthropology* (Atlanta: John Knox, 1981).
6. Meeks, *First Urban Christians*, 73.
7. Justin J. Meggitt, *Paul, Poverty and Survival* (Edinburgh: T&T Clark, 1998).
8. Ibid., 179.

groups, the wealthy elite and the poor nonelites, it served to reopen the debate about the economic levels of the Pauline communities.[9]

In 2004, Steven Friesen developed what he called a "poverty scale" for Greco-Roman urbanism as a model for estimating the economic level of the urban communities Paul established.[10] His poverty scale included seven economic levels, which are listed below:

Scale	Description	Includes	%
PS1	Imperial elites	Imperial dynasty, Roman senatorial families, a few retainers, local royalty, a few freed persons	0.04
PS2	Regional or provincial elites	Equestrian families, provincial officials, some retainers, some decurial families, some freed persons, some retired military officers	1
PS3	Municipal elites	Most decrial families, wealthy men and women who do not hold office, some freed persons, some retainers, some veterans, some merchants	1.76
PS4	Moderate surplus	Some merchants, some traders, some freed persons, some artisans (especially those who employ others), and military veterans	7 (?)
PS5	Stable near subsistence level (with reasonable hope of remaining above the minimum level to sustain life)	Many merchants and traders, regular wage earners, artisans, large shop owners, freed persons, some farm families	22 (?)
PS6	At subsistence level (and often below minimum level to sustain life)	Small farm families, laborers (skilled and unskilled), artisans (especially those employed by others), wage earners, most merchants and traders, small shop/tavern owners	40
PS7	Below subsistence level	Some farm families, unattached widows, orphans, beggars, disabled, unskilled day laborers, prisoners	28

In 2009, Friesen teamed with Roman economic historian Walter Scheidel to produce a revised poverty scale based on size of the Roman econ-

---

9. See Dale B. Martin, "Review Essay: Justin J. Meggitt, *Paul, Poverty and Survival*," *JSNT* 24, no. 2 (December 2001): 51–64. Note that all abbreviations in this volume follow *The SBL Handbook of Style*, ed. Billie Jean Collins, Bob Buller, and John F. Kutsko, 2nd ed. (Atlanta: SBL Press, 2014).
10. Steven J. Friesen, "Poverty in Pauline Studies: Beyond the So-Called New Consensus," *JSNT* 26, no. 3 (March 2004): 323–61.

omy in the mid-second century.[11] Developing a more complex method, they maintained Friesen's 3 percent elites, estimated that 10 percent of the entire population belongs to what they term the "middling" group (PS4), with the remainder of the population (approaching 87 percent) near, at, or below subsistence level. In his book *Remember the Poor: Paul, Poverty and the Greco-Roman World*, Bruce Longenecker critically engaged the work of Friesen and Scheidel, and slightly enlarged the PS4 and PS5 groups while decreasing the combined levels of PS6 and PS7 from 68 percent to 55 percent. Although Longenecker's version has more people in the "middling" group, his analysis still has more than half of the population at or below subsistence level.[12]

Longenecker's 2010 book is the latest full-scale treatment of economic aspects of Paul's letters and communities. As the title suggests, he is mostly interested in describing the approach to caring for the poor in the Pauline communities in relation to Greco-Roman and Jewish initiatives. He focuses much of his attention on the Jerusalem collection and the christological rationale for a charity model of relief. John Kloppenborg's essay in this volume revisits the issue of the Jerusalem collection, which is one of the economic topics in Pauline scholarship that has received a fair amount of attention. There are, however, many other economic aspects of the Pauline mission and assemblies that have escaped the attention of Pauline scholarship because it has been more interested in Paul's theology and rhetorical argumentation than in the practical matters of economic relations and practice. Yet it should be evident from the contemporary cultural landscape that the existence and viability of religious communities cannot be separated from questions of financial resources and sustainability along with other economic factors.

The lack of attention paid to these matters likely has something to do with the social location of biblical scholarship in a middle-class academic setting, which until recently has tended to be insulated from economic stress. It is difficult not to see some correlation between the social location of biblical scholarship and the so-called "new consensus" that prevailed throughout the 1980s and 1990s. So it is no coincidence that the concern surrounding economic conditions in recent years, globally and in the United States, has sparked a renewed interest

---

11. Walter Scheidel and Steven J. Friesen, "The Size of the Economy and the Distribution of Income in the Roman Empire," *JRS* 99 (2009): 61–91.
12. Bruce W. Longenecker, *Remember the Poor: Paul, Poverty and the Greco-Roman World* (Grand Rapids: Eerdmans, 2010), 53.

in the Bible and economics. Since the ascendancy of neoliberalism and critical awareness of capitalism as a totalizing ideology, new questions are being raised about how the realities and assumptions of capitalism have shaped the interpretation and use of the Bible. The essays in this reference volume serve to orient readers to the present state of research on a given economic topic in the study of Paul but also to break new ground by introducing methods, approaches, and data to catalyze future studies. Some essays address issues that have not been dealt with, and many, if not most, raise new questions and suggest avenues of exploration that might serve to inspire future research on selected topics.

In the opening essay, David B. Hollander provides an overview of the Roman economy in the early empire. He uses a macroeconomic lens to look at the machinations and efficiency of the Roman economy as a whole. Hollander raises at the outset the topic of method and notes that among Roman historians, there is an increased reliance on modern economic theory. At issue in the debate between "primitivists" and "modernists" is whether the ancient economy is fundamentally different from the modern market economy and therefore not susceptible to analysis with the tools of economics. He claims that more recently, ancient historians have been influenced by the New Institutional Economics (NIE), developed by Douglass North, which describes economic history as the examination of "the structure and performance of economies through time," with "performance" meaning things like production, distribution, output, and income, and "structure" referring to the institutions (political and economic), "technology, demography, and ideology"[13] that are understood to determine performance. From this perspective, the state emerges as the dominant force regulating several aspects of the Roman economy, including production and distribution. In terms of efficiency, it is judged to be a robust economy.

The New Institutional Economics provides a wide-angle lens and a useful frame of reference for examining several aspects of the Roman economy. Hollander considers broader issues such as the rate of growth and the level of integration. Although there was no imperial economic policy per se, he focuses on the role of the state in the economy. But what is less clear is who exactly benefits from the Roman Empire's economic development. He looks at the role and rate of taxes,

---

13. Douglass C. North, *Structure and Change in Economic History* (New York: Norton, 1981), 3.

the state's involvement in trade and various industries, lending practices, the regulation of markets, coinage and institutions of exchange, agriculture, slavery, and the military. The claim that the army accounted for as much as half of the Roman budget and played a significant impact on trade and economic expansion would, for example, be an important factor to consider in an examination of any of the provinces in which Pauline communities were located. While conquest and annexation opened up new markets and catalyzed a robust economy, Hollander emphasizes that it was Roman citizens who benefited most from the economic expansion and growth. Economic conditions for provincials would have been less favorable.

In her essay on urban poverty in the Roman Empire, Jinyu Liu focuses on the other end of the economic spectrum. She points out that one of the challenges of assessing the levels and impact of poverty in Roman society is that we know more about the perceptions of poverty from elite texts than the lived experience of the poor. Since both literary and archaeological resources reflect a more privileged perspective in which the poor are stigmatized, attempts to understand the effects of poverty have relied on a variety of factors, including material conditions and popular oral and literary forms such as fables, proverbs, and curse tablets. The picture that emerges from a more multidisciplinary approach to the sources is one of large-scale deprivation characterized by inequality, hostility, and fear.

The contrast between the essays by Hollander and Liu reflect the complexity and divergent perspectives on the economic context of Paul's letters and assemblies. The term "economy" comes from the Greek word *oikos*, meaning household. The Greek term *oikonomia* referred originally to "household management" and only by extension to political economy or what is called economics in modern English usage. In focusing on the regulation of the economy by the Roman Empire, Hollander's broad overview of the Roman political economy provides an important framework but does not indicate its impact on the lives of common people any more than the GDP or stock market in the present-day economy sheds light on economic struggles of families and communities. Moreover, in addition to an economy regulated by the empire, there was also a commercial economy and other local exchange economies that operated outside of the control of the state.

What Liu's essay highlights is that a large sector of the population of the Roman Empire lived with some symptoms of material deprivation. She identifies informal strategies for poverty alleviation and survival, but there is a paucity of information about the function of household and community economies—that is, with the acquisition, distribution, use, and sharing of the basic necessities of life. Along with the question of the correlation between the political economy of the Roman Empire and the economic lives of the masses, questions about the actual practices of the Pauline households and assemblies should be kept in view. The other issue that needs to be explored is that of ideology. There is always an ideological component in any economic theory or policy. Terry Eagleton defines ideology as "the ways in which what we say and believe connects to the power-structure and power-relations of the society we live in. . . . Those modes of feeling, valuing, perceiving and believing which have some kind of relation to the maintenance and reproduction of social power."[14] Economic realities both shape and are shaped by patterns of social relations, and consideration of the economy's impact on social relations raises questions of class and power.

The question of how economic issues impacted social relationship within the Pauline assemblies as well as the larger social context is important both for practical reasons and because social status and power relations are, to a large extent, predicated on material resources. How people from different socioeconomic and ethnic backgrounds interacted in a community organized around the event of a crucified Galilean Jew believed to be vindicated by the God of Israel is a central concern in understanding the dynamics of community life and structure, especially since the ethos of the assemblies is ostensibly set in contrast to certain Greco-Roman values and norms in the letters. In his essay "Economic Profiling of Early Christian Communities," Timothy A. Brookins critically reviews the scholarship on the economic levels in the Roman Empire and their implications for the Pauline assemblies. He shows how the debate has moved beyond the binary model of elites (*honestiores*) and the poor (*humiliores*) to a more differentiated economic scale that posits a majority (55–65 percent) at or around subsistence level with estimates of 20–30 percent at a middling level, 10–20 percent below subsistence, and about 2 percent elites. This indicates that while the presence of elites was unlikely, the other economic levels were represented in some, if not all, of the *ekklēsiai*. In such small communities, the resulting social stratification required ongoing negotiation of power and material resources.

As Brookins's essay demonstrates, the issue of social stratification

14. Terry Eagleton, *Literary Theory: An Introduction*, 2nd ed. (Malden, MA: Blackwell, 1996), 13.

has been the focus of much of the scholarship on economic aspects of the Pauline assemblies, especially with regard to Corinth. His review of work on economic profiling of the communities claims that the differences in perspective over the decades have been exaggerated largely due to terminology. The more sophisticated models and measurements being used more recently provide a more nuanced account. Although the various economic levels have been quantified with greater precision, Brookins raises a number of questions in need of further exploration. He also calls for more attention to the epistemological aspect of this kind of historical investigation, which includes not only criteria for selecting and interpreting data but also self-awareness about assumptions, predilections, and the significance of the interpreter's social location. The empire-wide focus of work done on economic levels does not take into account geographical differences. For example, the most elaborate economic profile is of the Corinthian community, but Corinth was a port city with a thriving commercial economy that distinguished it from the other urban centers. There is much less specific data about the other cities where Paul established communities. Brookins also notes the significant difference between the city and the countryside, with approximately 90 percent of people living in the countryside. The rural-urban divide further complicates the economic landscape of the sociopolitical and communal context of the Pauline assemblies.

Another complicating factor of the economic context of the Pauline assemblies was slavery. The Roman Empire was a full-scale slave society, which meant that the economy was dependent on slavery. Walter Scheidel has estimated between 1 and 1.5 million slaves in the first century BCE, representing 8–10 percent of the total population of 50–60 million inhabitants.[15] Some estimates are as high as 30–40 percent in some places. We know that there were slaves in the Pauline assemblies, and recent works by Jennifer Glancy and J. Albert Harrill, among others, have emphasized the place of slaves in these communities and the implications of total domination by masters, including subjection to physical and sexual abuse.[16] However, the economic implications and impact of slavery on the Pauline mission has received little consideration. In her essay "Paul and Slavery: Economic Perspectives," Ulrike Roth contends that "slavery was first and foremost an institution of

---

15. Walter Scheidel, "Human Mobility in Roman Italy, II: The Slave Population," *JRS* 95 (2005): 64–79.
16. Jennifer A. Glancy, *Slavery in Early Christianity* (Minneapolis: Fortress Press, 2006). J. Albert Harrill, *Slaves in the New Testament: Literary, Social, and Moral Dimensions* (Minneapolis: Fortress Press, 2006).

coerced labor" and maintains that slave exploitation was an economically relevant element of Paul's modus operandi.

Paul uses the language of slavery figuratively throughout the letters, including referring to himself as a "slave of Christ." As Roth points out, to a large extent the theological implications of slave/slavery as a metaphor have overshadowed interest in the economic demands and opportunities that shaped slaves' experiences. In contrast to a previous debate about whether in 1 Corinthians 7:21 Paul encouraged the manumission of slaves, she maintains that slave exploitation was integral to the Pauline mission. Roth's essay challenges some basic assumptions that have been operative in New Testament scholarship regarding slavery, and reframes the discussion in terms of slave labor power. Elites and other dominant social and political groups relied on slave labor to generate surplus that served to maintain their dominance. However, according to Roth, it was not uncommon for slaves to have access to funds that belonged to their masters, and even to receive allowances (*peculium*) for their own personal use. This skews the recent economic scales, which either do not account for slaves or erroneously posit that they lived in poverty.

Roth draws on evidence of slaves' cultic activity and slave sponsorship in *collegia* to suggest that slaves were economic agents in the Pauline mission. She argues that not only did slaves provide financial support for Paul's mission but that Paul was strategic, even opportunistic, in seeking out slave labor to support his mission. Although she deals with several Pauline texts, Onesimus serves as the prime example of a slave who continued to be a source of labor for Paul. Based on legal connotations of the partnership (κοινωνία) Paul had with Philemon, Roth contends that Paul shared joint ownership of Onesimus. By highlighting the inherently economic and exploitative aspects of slave labor, Roth has offered an alternative reading and raised new questions about the role of slaves in the Pauline assemblies. What was the particular attraction of slaves to this messianic movement, and how did their economic agency affect relationships with masters and others in the communities?

An interesting component of the profiles of the Pauline communities that has not received much attention but has socioeconomic implications is meeting space. Based on certain passages, especially in 1 Corinthians, Pauline scholarship has operated on the assumption that the assemblies gathered in houses. The implication was that there were people who owned houses large enough to host gatherings of the entire community. Given the supposition that the gatherings took place in houses owned by a person of some means and status, the debate has been focused on the configuration and uses of space. In her essay "Architecture: Where Did Pauline Communities Meet?," Annette Weissenrieder reconsiders the Corinthian assembly in the light of what that term signified in Greco-Romans political use and what is known about houses in Corinth. Based on the evidence from Corinth, she contends that there were not houses that were exclusively available to wealthy members of the Corinthian assembly. The operative word here is "exclusively" because a more variegated and complex picture of the housing situation becomes apparent from her research. The *insula* where the majority of people lived were inhabited by a cross-section of people and not just "nonelites." So while the unequivocal markers of socioeconomic status in Greco-Roman society were reflected in a hierarchical configuration of space, there was more social interaction across class lines than often imagined. Just as recent scholarship has problematized the bifurcation of economic level into rich and poor, or "elites" and "nonelites," Weissenrieder maintains that the dichotomy between the villa and the *insula* did not exist in first-century Corinth.

The most significant and potentially influential suggestion in Weissenrieder's essay is that a particular house in Corinth that may have been a *bouleutērion* where the Corinthian political assembly would have met was also the place where the Corinthian assembly met. Her proposal is based in part on an interpretation of 1 Corinthians 11:18, where "your coming together *en ekklēsia*" indicates that they meet not in a house but rather in the space of an assembly. In 1 Corinthians, Paul uses the term *ekklēsia* to define the shape of the gathering as political while simultaneously differentiating "the assembly of God" from the civic assembly. This is somewhat paradoxical and could have been the cause of some tensions, including some of the conflicts Paul deals with in the letter, inasmuch it calls attention to both the public character of an "assembly" founded on the Roman execution and subsequent vindication of a Galilean Jew even as it was organized structurally according to the rubrics of the civic *ekklēsia*. If shown to be persuasive, Weissenrieder's account would raise a number of questions about the economic implications of such a public and political organization and witness of the Pauline assembly. Would the assemblies have been similar to other civic groups or voluntary associations who paid dues and rented space, or would they have been regarded as a deviant group that paid a price socially and economically for being an outlier?

In his essay "Economic Location of Benefactors in Pauline Communities," Zeba A. Crook maintains that voluntary associations provide an analogous social group for evaluating the socioeconomic location and generosity of those involved in the assemblies of Christ. Benefaction was an important, if not the main, source of economic sustainability for all social groups in antiquity. The question of how the community generated material and financial resources is central to the question of how they survived, and also has implications for economic relations within the assemblies. Crook notes that benefactors in the Pauline communities are easy enough to identify because they are named and described as having done something of value. They are Gaius, Phoebe, Prisca and Aquila, Erastus, Crispus, and Stephanas, and possibly also Lydia, Jason, and Chloe. However, in reviewing previous scholarly attempts to describe their economic location and status, he consistently finds a lack of precision. For example, what does it mean to say that Gaius was "a man of some wealth," as Meeks does, or that he and others hosted the assembly in his house if we don't know where they lived?

In the absence of concrete evidence and criteria in Paul's letters, Crook proposes that the benefaction in the Pauline assemblies of Christ would be most similar to the voluntary association model and examples of benefaction. Although there was a good deal of diversity among voluntary associations, they are the most prominent type of social group in antiquity, and ample epigraphic evidence provides a nuanced and illuminating picture of benefaction practices. Crook notes that acts of generosity came from within and without the association. Since there is no indication from Paul's letters of outside benefaction, which is not to say there were no outside benefactors, Crook focuses on benefactions from within. The inscriptions Crook considers indicate both considerable socioeconomic diversity and a variety of types of giving. Honor was the driving force of benefaction, so anyone with some surplus could have been motivated to contribute. The lower range of acts of generosity is particularly interesting and important for understanding benefaction in the Pauline assemblies. Even slaves gave as little as five denarii.

Crook maps the picture that emerges from the epigraphic data about benefaction within the voluntary associations onto the economy scales of Friesen and Longenecker. He infers that since there are no elites in the community (PS1–3) and since people living at or below subsistence level have no surplus, most of the acts of generosity came from people with moderate surplus or those remaining above minimum level to sustain life (PS4–5). He suggests that Christ believers in Corinth might have contributed to such things as meeting space, travel, service, and the Jerusalem collection. At the end of the essay, Crook urges scholars to be more open to the idea that entry into the Pauline assemblies required a membership fee. Kloppenborg in his essay also argues for the assemblies being organized on the voluntary association model with membership fees, as do scholars like Harland and Ascough.[17] If this trend proves to be compelling to more scholars, what is known about voluntary associations could shed a good deal of light on the social and economic arrangements of the Pauline communities. Indeed, this model converges nicely with Weissenrieder's claim that the *ekklēsia* met in public spaces. It would suggest that more than a few patrons with moderate surplus would have been involved in providing financial support, even if at varying levels.

John Fitzgerald takes up the topic of "Food and Drink in the Greco-Roman World and in the Pauline Communities" in his essay. Food is an important dimension of any discussion of economics at any level. From a macroeconomic perspective it constitutes a large percentage of an economy's GDP, but it also plays a major part in the economies of households as well as social and religious organizations. However, as Fitzgerald points out, food and drink cannot be reduced to the matter of economics. Food served as a marker of social status and identity and was an essential part of social relationships and gatherings in antiquity. However, in addition to economic factors, religious and ethical considerations also influenced dietary preferences and dining practices. The connection between the economic and religious aspects of eating and drinking figures prominently in treatments of Paul's discussions of food and drink in 1 Corinthians and Romans, and is dealt with by Fitzgerald toward the end of the essay.

Fitzgerald presents a richly detailed description of eating patterns and practices in the Greco-Roman world based on the most recent scholarship and supported with numerous quotes from primary sources. His overview of the Mediterranean diet notes the staples of cereals, legumes, and oil and wine, and challenges longstanding assumptions that fish and meat were not financially accessible to people from the lower classes. Geography determined to some extent what

---

17. Philip A. Harland, *Associations, Synagogues, and Congregations: Claiming a Place in Ancient Mediterranean Society* (Minneapolis: Fortress Press, 2003). Richard S. Ascough, "The Thessalonians Christian Community as a Professional Voluntary Association," *JBL* 119, no. 2 (2000): 311–28.

kind of food was available, though Fitzgerald states that "what one ate in Rome was limited almost exclusively by one's culinary preferences, dietary restrictions, and finances." Fitzgerald's nuanced discussion of food in the ancient world connects social relations and issues in general, and in the Pauline communities in particular, to habits of eating. There is less emphasis on drink except to underscore that wine was the most common beverage of the Greco-Roman world, and Paul deals with it in his letters primarily out of concern for the problem of intoxication.

The consumption of meat is a source of contention in Corinth and also in Paul's letter to the Romans. Scholarship on 1 Corinthians has typically related the controversy surrounding eating to socioeconomic factors in the assembly. Fitzgerald reviews three different treatments of the problem that interpret it in terms of social location. He contributes to the discussion by dispelling the notion that most people were functional vegetarians and only the wealthy ate meat. He shows that while wealthier people ate more expensive meat, often meat that was sacrificed, other less expensive kinds of meat were more widely available even to the poor. One of the key contributions of Fitzgerald's essay is his argument that the strife surrounding the eating of meat in Corinth was more an issue of religious conviction and practice than of economic disparity.

Questions about where and how the assembly gathered are relevant to the interpretation of the controversy surrounding the Lord's Supper in 1 Corinthians 11:17–34. As noted, most scholarship has surmised that the meal occurred in a home of one of the wealthier members, and that the situation Paul addresses reflects a class conflict of sorts. In his essay "Socioeconomic Stratification and the Lord's Supper (1 Cor 11:17–34)," Neil Elliott acknowledges the challenge posed by the paucity of information about the social patterns and practices in Corinth. Toward the end of his essay, he too imagines that the convivial meals characteristic of the voluntary associations provide the best frame of reference for the gathering of the assembly of Christ in Corinth. However, he is primarily interested in the underlying ideology of social-scientific interpretations of 1 Corinthians 11:17–34 that have been preoccupied with the issue of status rather than poverty.

Elliott begins by contrasting recent sociopolitical interpretations of the Eucharist, which engage questions of global hunger and social inequities and emphasize praxis with more sober treatments of the conflict surrounding the Lord's Supper by New Testament scholars in which Paul is depicted as a social conservative who compromises core convictions and ideals in order to stabilize tensions between the haves and have nots. Reconstructions that have Paul responding to a conflict in which some poor members of the community go hungry by exhorting those with more than enough to "eat at home" before gathering, he points out, betray either an inherent contradiction or what he terms "an apostolic failure of nerve." It would indicate that Paul addressed but did not resolve what he regarded as a problem of the offense of some going hungry at the Lord's Supper because he did not want to offend higher-status believers who were simply acting according to accepted Greco-Roman social norms and customs.

Two important hermeneutical insights central to discussions of economic relations in Corinth can be gleaned from Elliott's essay. First, his claim that "we cannot understand Paul's rebuke in this part of the letter without setting it in the larger context of his endeavor to promote a communal practice in his assemblies" is consistent with Paul's focus on the integrity of the corporate body throughout the letter. This would signal that Paul was dealing with this and other issues in Corinth on a structural level, and therefore that he regarded it as a matter of justice. The second hermeneutical insight is related to the first. To those who, in the name of objectivity, would suggest that reading this passage through a social justice lens are imposes contemporary concerns on an ancient text, Elliott counters with the claim that prioritizing social status and stratification over economic concern about poverty and hunger in the text betrays the ideological influence of late capitalism. Essays by L. L. Welborn and Ward Blanton will also address the influence of capitalist ideology in this volume. At this juncture, it is good to be reminded that the pretense of objectivity in historical investigations of economic issues in antiquity and in Paul should be counterbalanced by critical self-awareness about the influence of social location and embedded ideological assumptions.

Richard Horsley also critiques the emphasis on stratification and social status that has characterized the sociological approach because it has overshadowed the economic exploitation that was a significant part of the context of the Jesus movement and the Pauline mission. His essay "Paul's Shift in Economic 'Location' in the Locations of the Roman Imperial Economy" is shaped more by a sociology of movements perspective, which discerns a convergence between the Jesus movement's response to the "political-economic-religious impact of the Roman conquest and rule of Palestine" and Paul's efforts to implement an alternative social vision to ameliorate the socioeconomic consequences of Roman rule. Whereas most treatments of the economic context of Paul's mission are descriptive of some aspect or implications of the economic environment, Horsley asks questions about the generative forces of the movement that began in Galilee and spread throughout the major cities of the empire. He claims that while the movement evolved as it moved from agrarian Galilee to a more urban setting, a constant feature was ongoing innovative changes in social-economic relations that challenged the dominant power relations.

Horsley is critical of recent neoclassical constructions of the Roman economy that he considers "proto-capitalist" in that they abstract economy from society. Rather than an economy based on "supply and demand," he maintains that it was a political economy driven by what the imperial state and the wealthy elites who mediated it coerced from subject peoples. In Galilee, Jesus was leading a covenant renewal movement aimed at bolstering village communities suffering the effects of taxes, debt, and dispossession. While much scholarship has highlighted the ostensible disjunction between the Jesus movement and Paul's mission, Horsley links them by situating Paul as a diaspora Judean deeply influenced by a counter-imperial scribal vision, which he learned in a Jerusalem scribal circle. The apocalyptic visions of 1 Enoch 85–90, the Testament of Moses, and especially Daniel 7–12 provided the framework for Paul's apocalyptic interpretation of the crucifixion and resurrection of the Messiah as God's judgment of imperial rule and the hope of the restoration of God's people. Horsley accounts for the shift Paul made from persecutor of to participant in the Jesus movement in terms of transitioning from initially seeing it as a threat to the Jewish security in Jerusalem to gradually realizing that it was embodying the social and economic practices of his ancestral traditions.

Explaining the shift in Paul's own economic location, he is described as someone initially with enough economic resources to study in Jerusalem, which are diminished as he devoted himself to establishing messianic communities comprised of displaced people. Paul's own downward economic mobility was evidenced in the fact that he depended in part on manual labor, which was disdained by elite culture, to support himself. Just as Roman rule in Palestine ran through the Jerusalem aristocracy, so in the provinces it was administered by local elites competing for honors to Caesar. Horsley is reluctant to generalize about the Roman economy because it looked different in each city, but in different ways in each of the letters, Paul attempts to persuade his readers to disengage from the local political-economic-religious order characterized by patronage, benefaction, temples, rituals, images, and games managed by wealthy elites

Readers of these essays will likely notice a tension or perhaps a dialectic between a macroeconomic perspective and a view that emphasizes how economics are embedded in social relationships. The macroeconomic approach seeks to describe the behavior and performance of the Roman economy in terms of how it operated, but it is not concerned with its impact on people's lives. Included are questions about poverty and economic levels, control and flow of resources, even cultural institutions such as patronage and benefaction. This involves a more abstract conceptualization of the economy, and yet these realities shaped even the most mundane affairs of daily life. An important question in any attempt to ascertain economic relations within the Pauline assemblies concerns the extent to which communal practices reflected or resisted cultural economic norms or, as Thomas R. Blanton IV proposes, adapted available forms of economic exchange.

Thomas Blanton begins his essay "The Economic Functions of Gift Exchange in Pauline Assemblies" by pointing out that *oikonomia* denoted the ordering of social relations and the division of labor within the *oikos* until the late eighteenth century, when the locus of economic activity shifted from the household to the nation-state. He notes that it wasn't until the late nineteenth century that "economics" came to be used interchangeably with "political economy," which then also became associated with the emerging notion of autonomous self-regulating markets. This modern view of economics is anachronistic for examining macroeconomic practices in the Roman Empire and economic relations in the Pauline assemblies, and yet it continues to shape perspectives on the ancient economy. The Roman economy was a "political economy" inasmuch as it controlled the production and allocation of resources that it extracted from the provinces, but an empire functions differently than a nation-state. On the most basic level, markets are places where people exchange goods and services, so there were markets in Greco-Roman society as there are in most societies. Hollander uses the market construct in his overview of the Roman economy, but it was not a "market economy" per se.

In his exploration of how gift exchange performed economic functions in the Pauline assemblies, Thomas Blanton takes his cue from Karl Polanyi, who maintained that market exchanges are typically embedded in social networks established by kinship, religion, and other forms of sociopolitical relations.[18] Blanton makes use of the three modes of the transmission of goods and services Polanyi identifies to look at economic relations in Paul, namely market exchange, redistribution, and reciprocity. While many of the resources used in the Pauline assemblies may have come from market transactions, Blanton construes reciprocity and redistribution as forms of gift exchange. The Jerusalem collection and possibly the Lord's Supper are examples of redistribution. Paul uses the word *charis* to denote the gift character of the collection. But underlying Paul's appeal for generosity in the Corinthian correspondence was the intimation that the Achaeans were competing with the Macedonians for honor. References to reciprocity in Paul's letters include hospitality and donations of travel funds and labor time.

The main argument of Thomas Blanton's essay is that currency from market exchanges was transformed into gift, and that though both forms of gift exchange (redistribution and reciprocity) were means of obtaining honor in accordance with Greco-Roman norms of gift exchange, Paul conceives of it as a "spiritual economy" in the letters. As Blanton puts it, "religion" and "economy" were two sides of a single coin. This is evident in the conflict surrounding the Lord's Supper in Corinth, where Jesus's gift of himself is memorialized in a ritual meal that "constitutes its participants as a living memorial to their heavenly benefactor," but the material neglect of those who go hungry at the meal exposes a disparity that is incommensurate with the gift character of the meal. In his discussion of the situation reflected in 1 Corinthians 11:17–34, Blanton follows the consensus view that the meal operated according to principles of reciprocity and patronage, though he acknowledges an article by Kloppenborg that proposes that the Lord's Supper may have been financed by regular dues paid by members of the Pauline assembly, as was the case in other collegia.[19] If the Pauline assemblies followed the pattern of the Greco-Roman voluntary associations, as some in this volume propose, it would be interesting to reconsider the role of patronage vis-à-vis the practice of gift exchange.

Paul's collection for the Jerusalem assembly of Christ is the economic endeavor that has received the most attention. Kloppenborg briefly reviews five different views of the reasons for and significance of the collection. However, his interest is not so much the purpose of

---

18. Karl Polyani, *Origins of Our Time: The Great Transformation* (London: Victor Gollancz, 1945).
19. John S. Kloppenborg, "Precedence at the Communal Meal in Corinth," *NovT* 58, no. 2 (2016): 167–203.

the collection, which has been the focus of the majority of scholarship. Rather, he aims to understand the collection and the challenges it posed in relation to how other groups in Greco-Roman society collected and dispersed funds. There are only a few passing references to the collection in Paul's letters (1 Cor 16:1–4; Gal 2:10; 2 Corinthians 8–9; and Rom 15:25–28), which raise as many questions as they answer, but there is a good deal of literary evidence describing the financial practices of various groups. Kloppenborg notes just how little we know about the Jerusalem collection and proposes that well-established and documented Hellenistic fiscal practice provides a useful frame of reference for interpreting the issues surrounding the collection.

Paul provides directions to the Corinthians regarding the collection in 1 Corinthians 16:1–4 not because they do not know how to collect funds but rather because they had concerns about collecting funds for another ethnic group that was nonlocal. They had questions about the security and accounting in its delivery. According to Kloppenborg, inscriptions from private associations indicate that detailed records were kept to insure against theft and misuse. This converges with how Paul addressed the issue of the security and delivery of the collection in 1 Corinthians 16:1–4. His exhortation to put funds aside weekly not only served to prevent a last-minute appeal when he arrived but also provided occasion to keep records of contributions, as was the practice of most voluntary associations. Paul also makes reference to envoys who would deliver the collection with letters to assure the Corinthians that it would arrive safe and secure, and that proper recognition would be given to those who contributed. Both of these were also common concerns in voluntary associations.

Kloppenborg proposes that the practice of voluntary contributions or subscriptions (*epidoseis*) is a better model for understanding how donors were recognized than the patronage model. Donative inscriptions typically honored the benefactor or donor, and such public recognition was a primary motive for giving. Although Paul recognized people by naming them in the letters as a way of honoring them, there is debate about whether patronage was operative in the Pauline assemblies. In contrast to patronage, the *epidoseis* called on all resident citizens, not just the wealthy, to contribute to a common project as a way of performing their membership in the *polis*. This was more of a collective approach to benefaction that allowed people to give various amounts, some very small. It also served a formational function that galvanized people around a shared project and appealed to certain civic virtues. Kloppenborg suggests that this is what Paul is doing in 2 Corinthians 8:7, where he praises the Corinthians for "faith, speech, knowledge, total commitment, and the love we inspired in you," and adds χάρις to that. In this respect, Paul's approach to the Jerusalem collection would have been very similar to other voluntary subscriptions. According to Kloppenborg, the novel aspect of the Jerusalem collection was that it was nonlocal, for a specific group of the poor who came from a different ethnicity. For this reason, Kloppenborg characterizes Paul's collection for the Jerusalem saints as "transgressive."

One of the more impressive aspects of Paul's mission was the frequency and geographical scope of his travels. Cavan Concannon's essay "Economic Aspects of Intercity Travel among the Pauline Assemblies" points out that while Paul's travels have received a fair amount of attention in Pauline studies, it has mostly revolved around questions of chronology, missional organization, the psychology of travel, and the discourse of travel. The accounts in Acts have played a large role in the reconstruction of chronologies and itineraries of Paul's travels. Scholars have long debated the historicity of Acts in the light of its rhetorical and theological agenda, but along with Paul's letters it is all scholars have had to work with. Concannon takes a different approach that features "a historiography of contingent and fragile possibilities" and proposes that "early Christianity was comprised of tenuous and shifting networks, rather than a single, if at times fractious, 'movement.'"

Concannon asserts that the tendency of Pauline scholarship to focus so much on the meaning of what Paul says in his letters has resulted in a lack of attention to the logistical practicalities, financial costs, and social institutional networks that had to be negotiated by Paul and the assemblies. This is a central theme in most of the essays in this volume. Concannon argues that the ostensibly linear picture that emerges from traditional scholarship, which imagines a movement that spreads throughout the empire, betrays an underlying anti-Semitism that renders Judaism as "an abrogated form of national, particular religion." Moreover, he says that this portrait of Paul's mission and its theological underpinnings "become a mirror of a constructed theology and mission of the Roman Empire by virtue of Paul's negotiation of geographic space." Concannon would prefer to replace the preoccupation with facticity and objectivity that has characterized studies of Paul's travel and chronology with a more speculative but realistic description of Paul's dealings with these assemblies.

Concannon is influenced by the work of Peregrine Horden and

Nicholas Purcell, who describe Mediterranean geography as microregions that were knit together.[20] In this world, connectivity was about stringing together a multitude of short distances. Using Philippi as a case study, he finds forty-eight places of connectivity and then maps them onto Paul's movements to and from Philippi in the letters. He uses a variety of maps to paint a very different picture than the accounts of Paul's journeys found on most New Testament maps. Instead, what becomes manifest are a number of "tenuous and shifting networks, made up of people, letters, boats, and wind patterns, and the work, cost, and contingency that made them possible." He emphasizes the amount of resources and effort needed to sustain connections between these networks and suggests that the exigent conditions and circumstances that affected travel to and from these networks shaped how and even whether they were sustained or not. A thoroughgoing appropriation of Concannon's method and insight highlighting what he calls the "struggle against distance" would contribute to a revised conception of the expansion of the Pauline mission.

L. L. Welborn revisits the tendency to construe the conflicts in the Corinthian community in terms of status rather than economics, as raised by some of the other essays in this volume, in his essay "Marxism and Capitalism in Pauline Studies." He brings to the task an explicitly Marxist lens "in which history is conceived as a struggle between the classes" and contrasts it with what he terms "capitalist interpretation," which ignores the category of class as relevant to the study of Paul and prefers the less precise category of status. By looking at a representative sampling of interpretations of Paul, Welborn examines why Paul has not been a resource for Marxist theory and revolutionary practice. He begins with the foundational works of Theissen and Meeks, which have already been discussed. His contribution to the discussion is identifying Max Weber's sociology of religion, which he describes as seeking to rationalize the relation between social stratification and religious ideas, as a major influence on both Theissen and Meeks. Meeks's "moderate functionalist" approach was concerned with the stabilizing role of religion in society. In Theissen's case, this was mediated through Ernst Troeltsch's idea of love-patriarchalism, which legitimated acceptance of given equalities. These studies and the consequent "new consensus" reflect a capitalist zeitgeist more than the social reality of the Pauline assemblies.

---

20. Peregrine Horden and Nicholas Purcell, *The Corrupting Sea: A Study of Mediterranean History* (Oxford: Wiley-Blackwell, 2000).

In his discussion of more recent interpreters, Welborn notes the irony that Dale Martin, who was Meeks's student and successor, provides the most thorough Marxist interpretation of Paul because he posits that class is an essential concept for understanding the conflicts in Corinth. He points out, however, that Martin does not meet the second criteria of Marxist interpretation, which is contesting the inevitability of the exploitative relation between the classes. Indeed, this acquiescence to existing structures of exploitation is a hallmark of Pauline interpretation. What Welborn shows is that the pretense of neutrality and disinterested historical description notwithstanding, the triumph of capitalism as a totalizing economic system lies behind the persistent view that Paul and other Christ believers were not interested in structural change. Even Meggitt's book *Paul, Poverty and Survival* eliminates class struggle by maintaining that all of the people in the assemblies were among the poor and practiced a "mutualism" as a survival strategy.[21] Welborn suggests that he fell sway to the despair of many Leftist thinkers after the collapse of communism.

Welborn is most critical of Bruce Longenecker's book *Remember the Poor* because he interprets the reference to the "poor" in Galatians 2:10 as a reference to poor people in general rather than "the poor among the saints in Jerusalem," and on that basis argues that Paul advocates for generosity and charity rather than a structural strategy that would offset poverty.[22] It is in response to Longenecker that Welborn offers his own counterclaim based on 2 Corinthians 8 that Paul articulates a "rudimentary theory of economic relations between Christ believers" predicated on the idea of "equality" (ἰσότης) in 2 Corinthians 8:14. It is the hope that real structural change is possible and the commitment to engage in the struggle for social transformation that distinguishes Marxist interpretation and Welborn's own approach to Paul. Even the more political readings of Paul, such as those of David Briones and Neil Elliott, suppose, for different reasons, that Paul's vision is constrained by the dominant imperial ideology and power structure. Welborn's strongest affirmation of a Marxist approach is reserved for an article on 1 Corinthians by Laura Nasrallah who says that Paul, in addressing the issues of slaves in the community, asks slave and owner alike to imagine themselves potential slaves, as commodities.[23] Contra the ten-

---

21. Meggitt, *Paul, Poverty and Survival*.
22. Longenecker, *Remember the Poor*.
23. Laura Salah Nasrallah, "'You Were Bought with a Price': Freedpersons and Things in 1 Corinthians," in *Corinth in Contrast: Studies in Inequality*, ed. Steven J. Friesen, Sarah A. James, and Daniel N. Schowalter (Leiden: Brill, 2014), 54–73.

dency to refer real structural transformation to the eschaton, Nasrallah does not believe that an emphasis on an imminent end made Paul and his fellow believers accepting of social inequalities.

Welborn acknowledges that he has been influenced by recent political readings of Paul by mostly European philosophers, some of whom are post-Marxist, but limits his discussion of Paul to the exegetical tradition. Ward Blanton takes up the political readings of Paul by philosophers in his essay "A New Horizon for Paul and the Philosophers: Shifting from Comparative 'Political Theology' to 'Economic Theology,'" but as the title suggests he marks the shift in focus from political to economic theology. Both Welborn and Ward Blanton emphasize the impact of the economic crisis of 2008 on philosophy, especially those engaged with Marxist critiques of political economy. In this era of globalization, politics has become so dominated by economics that the shift seems inevitable. Although this phenomenon is complex and multifaceted, Ward Blanton concentrates primarily on the problem of debt. He points out that the migration of "political theology" into "economic theology" is the consequence of the new geopolitical mode of governing by debt.

Philosophical examinations of Paul's political theology were initiated by Jacob Taubes's interaction with the political theology of Carl Schmitt, who claimed that all political theories were secularized theologies.[24] Schmitt's political theology was organized around the theme of sovereignty and the authority to claim exception to the rule of law. Ward Blanton tracks the transformation of political theology into economic theology via the migration of sovereignty from the political to the economic. He adopts Roberto Esposito's phrase "debt sovereignty," which refers to the transfer of sovereignty from the national government to global finance.[25] In a time when, as he puts it, representative democratic leaders have been reduced to debt managers, critical reflection on Paul serves the dual purpose of understanding the present situation through the religious constructs of sacrifice, sin, and debt and also the possibility of a "messianic" suspension from the structural violence of contemporary capitalism.

The notion of debt has deep roots in the tradition of biblical Judaism and is inextricably connected with theologies of sin and sacrifice. How

---

24. Jacob Taubes, *The Political Theology of Paul*, ed. Aleida Assmann and Jan Assmann, trans. Dana Hollander (Stanford: Stanford University Press, 2004). Carl Schmitt, *Political Theology: Four Chapters on the Concept of Sovereignty*, trans. George Schwab (Chicago: University of Chicago Press, 2005).

25. Roberto Esposito, *Two: The Machine of Political Theology and the Place of Thought*, trans. Zakiya Hanafi (New York: Fordham University Press, 2015).

do the theological constructs of debt and sacrifice, read austerity, function in global capitalism? For example, Ward Blanton wonders with Esposito whether students have become "sin for us" on our behalf, "as if being sacrificed such that other forms of economic accumulation can normalize themselves through this sacrificial ritual?" However, the main interest in Paul is not so much a genealogy of the concepts as an example of and hope for an alternative to or break from the economic theology of the current regime. Ward Blanton calls for biblical scholars to become more involved in the larger interdisciplinary and international discussions about economics. What study of the Pauline assemblies might contribute to the discussion is a case study that could be used in a comparative analysis of minority communities that experienced "temporal newness or breaks in temporal continuities in relation to transformations or intensifications of certain economic practices." The philosophical function of Pauline references, he says, will be "an explicit invitation to take up a dramatic stance in relation to that open question: will we, in the end, have continued to maintain our current economic order, or will some other order break through?"

The study of Paul's letters has historically been most attentive to Paul's communication of the significance of the messianic event for the communities to which he wrote. The operative assumption of the exegetical tradition in Pauline scholarship is that it is ideas, theological constructs, or rhetorical arguments that shape social reality and relationships. In recent years there has been more emphasis on the cultural context of Paul's letters, that is, on the interaction between Paul's gospel and communities and Greco-Roman and Jewish cultural norms and practices. But as we know from our own experience in the contemporary world, economic reality has a profound impact on almost every aspect of cultural and community life. Taken together, the essays in this volume aim to lay a foundation and a framework for further exploration of the role of economic factors in the interpretation of Paul's letters and the formation and development of the assemblies. Building on earlier work that has foregrounded previously neglected issues such as social stratification and patronage, these essays situate Paul's letters squarely in the context of material resources and economic structures to raise new questions about how political economy, economic location and class, funding of community life, slavery, meeting space, travel, food, and other economic matters may have shaped Paul's work with these communities and the dynamics within them. The more complex and grounded picture that emerges may also lead to new insights about

Paul's gospel and the motivations, behavior, relationships, and challenges of those who embraced it.

1

———

The Roman Economy in the Early Empire: An Overview

David B. Hollander

The century between Octavian's victory over Antony and Cleopatra at Actium in 31 BCE and the civil wars of 69 CE was a time of great prosperity for the Roman people, if not for some of their subjects. This "happy period" of (relative) peace facilitated a substantial expansion of long-distance trade and, thanks to the immense revenues at their disposal, permitted Augustus and his Julio-Claudian successors to devote considerable sums to the Empire's infrastructure (and self-aggrandizement). If you were a Roman citizen, it was a great time to be alive.[1]

1. My thanks to Tom Blanton and Ray Pickett for organizing the Paul and Economics conference at which I first presented this chapter and to my fellow panelists and the audience for many useful questions and comments. For comments on a later draft, I am also grateful to Jinyu Liu and Rachel Meyers. Justin Ott and Kim King provided valuable research assistance. All remaining errors are, of course, my own.

The Study of the Roman Economy

The last twenty-five years have been a similarly prosperous time for the study of the Roman economy, but the entrance barriers to the field have become substantial. The sheer volume of scholarship, a mountain of publications since 1990, is the largest obstacle. Pride of place among them must go to the relevant chapters of *The Cambridge Economic History of the Greco-Roman World*, a monumental work whose bibliography alone is 150 pages long.[2] In addition, there are the many volumes published in Bowman and Wilson's Oxford Studies on the Roman Economy series, Lo Cascio's Pragmateiai series, the monographs and articles of a host of both well-established and up-and-coming scholars, as well as the essential "classics" of the field, such as the writings of Moses Finley, Keith Hopkins, and Richard Duncan-Jones.

Unfortunately, despite all the new work, there is still considerable debate over fundamental issues. The oldest debate, which began in the nineteenth century, is that between the "primitivists" and "modernists," despite the fact that, as Peter Garnsey and Richard Saller have recently noted, "no one self-identifies as part of either camp."[3] At issue is whether the ancient economy is fundamentally different from the modern, market economy and therefore not susceptible to analysis with the tools of economics.[4] A second major debate centers on demography. Although much information about the Roman census survives, there is no agreement on the empire's population. While once the argument was between the "high count" and the "low count," there is now a middle count as well. Currently we can be reasonably sure only that the population of Augustan Italy was between five million and fourteen million.[5] As for the population of the empire as a whole, Walter Scheidel suggests it was approaching sixty million in the mid-first century CE.[6] A third area of debate concerns economic growth. There seems to be general agreement that some growth (i.e., increase in per capita GDP) took place during the Roman period, but the details—its

2. Walter Scheidel, Ian Morris, and Richard Saller, eds., *The Cambridge Economic History of the Greco-Roman World* (Cambridge: Cambridge University Press, 2007).
3. Peter Garnsey and Richard Saller, *The Roman Empire: Economy, Society and Culture* (Oakland: University of California Press, 2015), 89.
4. Some would distinguish between the primitivism-modernist debate and a (closely related) formalist-substantivist debate. See Paul Cartledge, "The Economy (Economies) of Ancient Greece," in *The Ancient Economy*, ed. Walter Scheidel and Sitta von Reden (New York: Routledge, 2002), 15.
5. Alessandro Launaro, *Peasants and Slaves: The Rural Population of Roman Italy (200 BC to AD 100)* (Cambridge: Cambridge University Press, 2011), 21.
6. Walter Scheidel, "Demography," in Scheidel, Morris, and Saller, *Cambridge Economic History*, 48.

extent, the main beneficiaries, and precisely when it occurred—remain hazy and subject to considerable dispute.[7] A fourth question concerns the level of integration enjoyed by the Roman Empire. Economic integration, "the synchronised and parallel variation of prices, wages and interest rates in different markets,"[8] improves the performance of an economy, but levels of integration can vary considerably by commodity. While some deny Rome had a "single integrated economy,"[9] Peter Temin has argued for a unified wheat market in the Mediterranean and William V. Harris suggests that the markets for several goods, including papyrus and fine pottery, were highly integrated.[10] Some Romans thought the empire's financial market was already highly integrated in the late Republic.[11] A related issue is the relative importance of the state and private traders in distribution—that is, whether the market or redistribution (and reciprocity) was the main force behind the movement of goods. With respect to Rome, Paul Erdkamp has argued that "free trade . . . operated in the margins of a system that was characterised by public supply channels," but others see private trade playing a more central role.[12]

Three other obstacles confront those who would understand the Roman economy. First, there is the lack of fine resolution. It is often difficult to get detailed information about the specific times and places we would like to know better. A macroeconomic focus predominates except in certain exceptional instances. Secondly, there is the need to understand a broad array of economic jargon, such as Gini index, elasticity, the low equilibrium trap, satisficing decisions, liquidity preference theory, "bounded rationality," human capital, comparative advantage, rent seeking, and HALE (Health Adjusted Life-Expectancies). Finally, there is the imposing amount of primary evidence to

---

7. As Peter Temin (*The Roman Market Economy* [Princeton: Princeton University Press, 2013], 218) notes, "we are just at the beginning of any measurement of ancient economic growth."

8. Scheidel and Reden, *The Ancient Economy*, 133–34.

9. David Mattingly, "The Imperial Economy," in *A Companion to the Roman Empire*, ed. David S. Potter (Malden, MA: Blackwell, 2006), 286.

10. Temin, *Roman Market Economy*, 46; William V. Harris, "Prolegomena to a Study of the Economics of Roman Art," *AJA* 119, no. 3 (2015): 408–10. See also, Gilles Bransbourg, "Rome and the Economic Integration of Empire," *ISAW Papers* 3 (2012): http://tinyurl.com/gt8tu5z.

11. See Cicero's discussion of the financial connections between Asia Minor and Rome in *Pro Lege manilia* 17–19. Note also, for the empire, Dominic Rathbone, "Earnings and Costs: Living Standards and the Roman Economy," in *Quantifying the Roman Economy: Methods and Problems*, ed. Alan Bowman and Andrew Wilson (Oxford: Oxford University Press, 2009), 310.

12. Paul Erdkamp, *The Grain Market in the Roman Empire: A Social, Political and Economic Study* (Cambridge: Cambridge University Press, 2005), 244–57. For a contrasting view, see Peter Temin, "A Market Economy in the Early Roman Empire," *JRS* 91 (2001): 169–81; and Rathbone, "Earnings and Costs," in Bowman and Wilson, *Quantifying the Roman Economy*, 309.

which even the briefest consultation of the secondary literature quickly points one: literary texts of various genres, inscriptions, papyri, coins, ceramics, survey data, and shipwrecks. And, of course, one must always keep in mind the array of texts and objects (such as textiles) that have *not* survived in any significant quantities.

Navigating through these barriers is difficult, but a few major trends in the study of the Roman economy provide some guidance. First, there is the increased reliance on modern economic theory. In 2002, Reden could plausibly claim that most scholars considered modern economic theory "unhelpful for understanding money in the ancient world,"[13] but this sort of attitude is no longer widespread (at least in the study of the Roman economy). While some still reject it (the substantivists from the old formalist versus substantivist debate), they tend to be rejecting a simplistic and outmoded version of economics (that is, neoclassical economics). As economist Takeshi Amemiya noted in 2005, "Modern economists may give the impression that they believe that every consumer maximizes utility and every producer maximizes profit, but they are actually much more pragmatic."[14] Within economics, the New Institutional Economics (NIE), developed by Douglass North, has been particularly influential with ancient historians. North described economic history as the examination of "the structure and performance of economies through time," with "performance" meaning things like production, distribution, output, and income, and "structure" referring to the institutions (political and economic), technology, demography, and ideology.[15] In essence, NIE suggests that we can learn more about the performance of the Roman economy by studying its institutions and their impact on transaction costs.[16] Though some doubt its value,[17] it is safe to say that NIE is currently far more influential than Finley's *The Ancient Economy*. Finley's pessimistic views on the economic significance of ancient technology and innovation have also fallen out of favor. Listing the ancient innovations of which he was aware, he commented that "it adds up to not very much for a great civ-

---

13. Sitta von Reden, "Money in the Ancient Economy: A Survey of Recent Research," *Klio* 84, no. 1 (2002): 142.

14. Takeshi Amemiya, "Comment on Davies," in *The Ancient Economy: Evidence and Models*, ed. J. G. Manning and Ian Morris (Stanford: Stanford University Press, 2005), 157.

15. Douglass C. North, *Structure and Change in Economic History* (New York: Norton, 1981), 3.

16. Elio Lo Cascio, "The Early Roman Empire: The State and the Economy," in Scheidel, Morris, and Saller, *Cambridge Economic History*, 626.

17. See, for example, Francesco Boldizzoni, *The Poverty of Clio: Resurrecting Economic History* (Princeton: Princeton University Press, 2011).

ilization over fifteen hundred years,"[18] but more recent work suggests he was overly pessimistic.[19]

Keith Hopkins's "taxes-and-trade" model for the Roman economy, first developed in a 1980 *Journal of Roman Studies* article, has fared much better than Finley's conception of the Roman economy.[20] Hopkins suggested that Roman taxes in coinage generated increased trade in the empire as taxpayers needed to earn money to pay them. Though garnering its share of criticism, scholars have continued to propose modifications and elaborations to his model.[21] Comparative history is another area of increased emphasis. Peter Bang uses Mughal India (sixteenth through early eighteenth centuries CE) for comparison with Rome in *The Roman Bazaar*[22] while Temin in *The Roman Market Economy* compares Rome to early modern European economies, suggesting that "Roman Italy was comparable to the Netherlands in 1600."[23]

Another important development concerns statistics: scholars now pursue quantification much more vigorously. Shipwreck data, the results of survey archaeology, coin production estimates, and ceramic distribution figures all contribute. Alessandro Launaro, for example, analyzed the data from twenty-seven Italian survey projects to make a persuasive argument concerning Roman population estimates. Analysis of the shipwreck data continues to offer tantalizing insights. While the overall distribution of wrecks may indicate an increase in seaborne commerce in the late republic and early empire, there seems to have been "a marked dip [in wrecks] in the early Augustan period."[24]

In what follows, I will describe the constituent elements of the Roman economy in the time of Paul and note key developments.

18. Moses Finley, "Technical Innovation and Economic Progress in the Ancient World," *Economic History Review* 18, no. 1 (August 1965): 29.
19. For general discussion, see Kevin Greene, "Technological Innovation and Economic Progress in the Ancient World: M. I. Finley Re-Considered," *Economic History Review* 53 (2000): 29–59.
20. Keith Hopkins, "Taxes and Trade in the Roman Empire (200 B.C.–A.D. 400)," *JRS* 70 (1980): 101–25. Hopkins developed his ideas further in "Rome, Taxes, Rents and Trade," *Kodai* 6/7 (1995/96): 41–75; and "Rents, Taxes, Trade and the City of Rome," in *Mercati Permanenti e Mercati Periodici nel Mondo Romano: Atti degli Incontri Capresi di Storia dell'Economia Antica (Capri 13–15 ottobre 1997)*, ed. Elio Lo Cascio (Bari, ITA: Edipuglia, 2000), 253–67.
21. See, for example, Hans-Ulrich von Freyberg, *Kapitalverkehr und Handel im romischen Kaiserreich (27 v. Chr.–235 n. Chr.)* (Freiburg: Rudolf Haufe, 1988).
22. Peter F. Bang, *The Roman Bazaar* (Cambridge: Cambridge University Press, 2008).
23. Temin, *Roman Market Economy*, 259.
24. Andrew Wilson, "Approaches to Quantifying Roman Trade," in Bowman and Wilson, *Quantifying the Roman Economy*, 224.

Institutions of Exchange

Given the importance of NIE, I will first examine the institutions of exchange in the Roman world with an emphasis on general developments during the first century of the empire. In this period, a wide range of developments lowered transaction costs, promoted or at least facilitated trade, and increased the integration of the economy. I will pay particular attention to the role of the state, the "dominant force" in the Roman economy.[25] Though it may be anachronistic to speak of imperial economic policy,[26] the Romans were aware of basic economic phenomena. To cite just one example, Suetonius is able to connect a drop in interest rates and an increase in real estate prices with an increase in the supply of coinage following Augustus's Alexandrian triumph (Suetonius, *Divus Augustus* 41).

Let us begin with taxation since, as Hopkins suggested, it probably had a profound effect on the Roman economy. Rome's subjects paid both direct taxes (*tributum*) and indirect ones (*vectigalia*) albeit with considerable regional variation. There are many unresolved (and perhaps unresolvable) questions particularly with respect to the direct taxes: What proportion of them were collected in coin rather than in kind (i.e., agricultural produce)? To what extent was *adaeratio* (conversion of an in-kind tax into a cash payment or vice versa) an option for taxpayers? Were taxes relatively low, as many scholars think?[27] What people and property were exempt? Beginning in Egypt, Augustus established a new poll tax on the basis of a census,[28] but how quickly and systematically did this practice expand to other provinces?[29]

In the late republic, the question of rewards for Roman veterans had regularly generated strife. To deal with this issue, Augustus created a new treasury, the *aerarium militare*, in 6 CE to pay veterans' retirement bonuses and provided it with 170 million sesterces (*Res Gestae* 17.2).[30]

---

25. Neville Morley, "Economy and Economic Theory, Roman," in *The Oxford Encyclopedia of Ancient Greece and Rome*, ed. Michael Gagarin and Elaine Fantham, 7 vols. (Oxford: Oxford University Press, 2010), 3:12.

26. Walter Scheidel, "The Roman Economy," *Classical Review* 55, no. 1 (2005): 252.

27. See, for example, Hopkins, "Taxes and Trade," 116; Garnsey and Saller, *The Roman Empire*, 126; and Dominic Rathbone and Peter Temin, "Financial Intermediation in First-Century AD Rome and Eighteenth-Century England," in *Pistoi dia tèn technēn: Bankers, Loans and Archives in the Ancient World. Studies in Honour of Raymond Bogaert*, ed. Koenraad Verboven, Katelijn Vandorpe, and Véronique Chankowski (Leuven: Peeters, 2008), 416.

28. Dominic Rathbone, "Egypt, Augustus and Roman Taxation," *Cahiers du Centre Gustave Glotz* 4 (1993): 86–99.

29. Peter Brunt, "The Revenues of Rome," *JRS* 71 (1981): 163–66.

30. The main Roman treasury was the *aerarium Saturni*.

To fund its continuing operation, he instituted a 5 percent tax on certain inheritances (the *vicesima hereditatium*) (Dio 55.25) and a 1 percent tax on sales at auctions (the *centesima rerum venalium*) (Tacitus, *Annales* 1.78). Augustus also instituted a 2 percent tax on slaves sold at auction to fund the *vigiles*, a firefighting and police force at Rome (Dio 55.31). Later emperors made adjustments. Tiberius cut the auction sales tax in half, at least for a while (Tacitus, *Ann.* 2.42; Dio 58.16), and Caligula abolished it (Suetonius, *Gaius Caligula* 16; Dio 59.9.6). Caligula introduced a variety of "new and strange" taxes and fees on everything from food sales to prostitution (Suetonius, *Cal.*, 40), but Claudius abolished at least some of them (Dio 60.4.1).[31] By 43 CE, the tax on slave sales had risen to 4 percent.[32]

The *publicani*, whose role in the collection of direct taxes had already diminished by the end of the republic,[33] continued to collect indirect taxes such as customs dues (*portoria*) and pasturage fees (*scripturae*) under the empire.[34] While dissuaded from the idea of abolishing these taxes, Nero did undertake several reforms to curb the collectors' notorious abuses.[35] Provincial communities were generally responsible for collecting the *tributum* owed to Rome and would have used other taxes, liturgies, and the revenue from municipal properties to pay their own local expenses. The rule that cities could not levy new taxes without permission from the emperor may date to the reign of Augustus.[36] Taxes were only one of the state's sources of revenue. It also derived profit from booty, legacies, rents, and the auction of confiscated property. In addition, the property of some who died intestate apparently escheated to the *fiscus*, the emperor's private treasury (Tacitus, *Ann.* 2.48).

The state became involved in several industries. Augustus and his successors took control of some mines and quarries,[37] and they proba-

31. Dominic Rathbone, "Nero's Reforms of *Vectigalia* and the Inscription of the *Lex Portorii Asiae*," in *The Customs Law of Asia*, ed. M. Cottier et al. (Oxford: Oxford University Press, 2008), 254–55.

32. *Inscriptiones Latinae Selectae*, ed. Hermann Dessau, 3 vols. (Berlin: Weidmann, 1892–1916), no. 203; and William V. Harris, "Towards a Study of the Roman Slave Trade," MAAR 36 (1980): 136n44.

33. Julius Caesar deprived the *publicani* of responsibility for collecting tribute in Asia Minor in 48 BCE (Dio Cassius, *Hist. rom.* 42.6). For discussion of earlier measures by A. Gabinius in Syria, see Ernst Badian, *Publicans and Sinners: Private Enterprise in the Service of the Roman Republic* (Ithaca, NY: Cornell University Press, 1972), 109.

34. P. A. Brunt, "Publicans in the Principate," in *Roman Imperial Themes* (Oxford: Clarendon Press, 199), 354–432; D. Rathbone, "The Imperial Finances," in *The Cambridge Ancient History*, vol. 10, *The Augustan Empire, 43 B.C.-A.D. 69*, ed. Alan K. Bowman, Edward Champlin, and Andrew Lintott, 2nd ed. (Cambridge: Cambridge University Press, 1996), 309–23; and Onno van Nijf, "The Social World of Tax Farmers and Their Personnel," in Cottier et al., *Customs Law of Asia*, 279–311.

35. Tacitus, *Annales*, 13.50–51 and 15.18. For discussion, see Rathbone, "Nero's Reforms," 251–78.

36. Garnsey and Saller, *The Roman Empire*, 50.

bly profited from the sale of building stone and sarcophagi produced in state-owned workshops.[38] By the reign of Tiberius, there were imperial *figlinae* (potter's workshops) producing bricks.[39] The emperors became owners of large amounts of agricultural land as well. Octavian confiscated much land in Egypt.[40] Suetonius (*Tiberius* 49) reports that Tiberius confiscated the property of many wealthy men in Spain, Gaul, Syria, and Greece, while Nero probably acquired large amounts of land in Africa (Pliny the Elder, *Naturalis historia* 18.35). The imperial family had estates in Egypt from the reign of Augustus on.[41] The produce of such real estate probably ended up on the market along with some of the goods collected as in-kind taxes.[42] Tenney Frank estimated annual state income by the end of the reign of Augustus at 450 million sesterces, while Hopkins suggested it was over 800 million in the first century CE.[43]

The biggest single expense of the Roman state, it is generally agreed, was the army, accounting for as much as half of the annual budget. Ordinary Roman soldiers earned a salary of 900 sesterces per year (minus various deductions) supplemented by occasional donatives. The soldiers' spending money and the money spent to equip and supply the armies undoubtedly had a major impact on the regions where armies were stationed. Trade followed the legions, and communities sprung up around them.[44] The grain distributions at Rome were another major expense. Under Augustus, the *annona* distributed free grain to over two hundred thousand Romans (*Res Gestae* 15). The Romans seem to have relied heavily on private traders and shippers for their supply networks, promoting trade and effectively subsidizing the transport of some private merchandise.[45] Outlays for building projects, specta-

---

37. Ben Russell (*The Economics of the Roman Stone Trade* [Oxford: Oxford University Press, 2013], 53) argues convincingly against the prevailing assumption that the emperors essentially "nationalized" mines and quarries.
38. Lo Cascio, "Early Roman Empire," 645.
39. Paul Weaver, "Imperial Slaves and Freedmen in the Brick Industry," *ZPE* 122 (1998): 239.
40. Livia Capponi, *Augustan Egypt: The Creation of a Roman Province* (New York: Routledge, 2005), 97–122.
41. Dorothy J. Crawford, "Imperial Estates," in *Studies in Roman Property*, ed. Moses I. Finley (Cambridge: Cambridge University Press, 1976), 35–70.
42. For some discussion, see Erdkamp, *Grain Market*, 221–23.
43. Tenney Frank, *An Economic Survey of Ancient Rome*, vol. 5, *Rome and Italy of the Empire* (Baltimore: Johns Hopkins Press, 1940), 7; Hopkins, "Taxes and Trade," 119.
44. As William V. Harris ("Roman Terracotta Lamps: The Organization of an Industry," *JRS* 70 [1980]: 126–45) notes, traders would be "attracted by the massed buying power which a legion represented."
45. Giuseppe Pucci, "Pottery and Trade in the Roman Period," in *Trade in the Ancient Economy*, ed. Peter Garnsey, Keith Hopkins, and C. R. Whittaker (Berkeley: University of California Press, 1983), 111–12.

cles, and the salaries of provincial governors would also have constituted a regular and substantial portion of the overall budget. With the exception of Tiberius (Suetonius, *Tib.* 47), the Julio-Claudian emperors all undertook ambitious building projects at Rome and provided various shows.

In addition to producing, distributing, and selling goods, the state also, of course, regulated certain aspects of the economy, albeit in a fairly inconsistent manner. In physical markets, *aediles* or *agoranomoi* might be present to monitor the activities of merchants and maintain official weights and measures. The Romans also regulated lending and borrowing, probably capping interest rates at 12 percent (except for maritime loans) in the early empire.[46] Augustus lent money without charging interest (although it is unclear on what scale; Suetonius, *Aug.* 41), burnt records of debts owed to the treasury at Rome (Suetonius, *Aug.* 32),[47] and even cancelled provincial debts at some point (Dio Chrysostom, *Or.* 31.66–67). Inconsistent enforcement of lending regulations led to the credit crisis of 33 CE, which was only resolved when Tiberius provided banks with 100 million sesterces for interest-free loans (Tacitus, *Ann.* 6.16–17). Claudius felt it necessary to regulate loans to minors (Tacitus, *Ann.* 11.13.2).

There were at least intermittent attempts to regulate the grain market. Intriguingly, Suetonius (*Aug.* 42) claims that, with respect to the *annona*, Augustus took thought for farmers and traders in addition to the urban populace. Tiberius fixed grain prices in Rome in 19 CE, providing compensation to merchants (Tacitus, *Ann.* 2.87). Claudius, to secure Rome's food supply, provided incentives to those who would finance ship construction and essentially insured merchants against losses due to storms (Suetonius, *Divus Claudius* 18–19).[48] Nero fixed grain prices in Rome in 62 CE after the loss of hundreds of ships to storm and fire (Tacitus, *Ann.* 15.18.2) and again in 64 CE in the wake of the great fire (Tacitus, *Ann.* 15.39.2). Assuming the state sold surplus grain on the market, it may have always had an influence on the price. Outside of Rome, the picture is less clear. Germanicus reduced Egyptian grain prices in 19 CE by releasing grain from government storehouses (Tacitus, *Ann.* 2.59), but most communities probably had to rely on local initiatives.[49]

---

46. Matt Gibbs, "Interest Rates," in *The Encyclopedia of Ancient History*, ed. Roger S. Bagnall et al., 13 vols. (Malden, MA: Wiley-Blackwell, 2013), 6:3471–73.

47. Nero also destroyed such records on one occasion (Tacitus, *Ann.* 13.23).

48. Erdkamp (*Grain Market*, 245–46) argues that Claudius's initiative was directed at those who had contracted to supply grain to Rome, not at traders more generally.

Ordinarily, the Romans probably let the market price for goods prevail, but there were exceptions. A shortage of papyrus under Tiberius led to state control of its distribution (Pliny the Elder, *Nat* 13.27.89), while Nero fixed rates for lawyers (Suetonius, *Nero* 17). He also regulated the food that *popinae* could serve (Suetonius, *Nero* 16) and banned the sale of Tyrian purple (Suetonius, *Nero* 32). In addition to direct intervention, many of the state's activities had substantial, if perhaps unintentional, effects on the economy of the empire. The gradual (if uneven) spread of Roman law and legal institutions, for example, would tend to reduce transaction costs.[50]

Developments in the Roman money supply also decreased transaction costs and improved the overall performance of the imperial economy. Augustus's reforms were especially salutary after the "chaotic currency situation" of the triumviral period.[51] With Lugdunum serving as his main mint for denarii from 12 BCE, Augustus produced both new coins (for example, *dupondii* and *sestertii* in orichalcum, an alloy of copper and zinc) and more coins, most notably large quantities of gold *aureii*.[52] Roman silver coins remained pure until the reign of Nero.[53] The use of Roman coinage spread and monetization continued but, as with Roman legal institutions, these developments were patchy.[54] The Romans were uninterested in creating a uniform, empire-wide monetary system. Egypt, for example, maintained a separate currency.[55] Many provincial cities produced their own coinage, while the Romans sometimes minted provincial issues.[56]

Government spending on infrastructure had a salutary effect on the imperial economy by improving the transportation network, promoting agriculture, and ameliorating urban living conditions. The Romans built many roads and bridges as well as canals, harbors, and light-

---

49. For discussion of municipal grain funds, see ibid., 268–83.
50. Dennis Kehoe, "The Early Roman Empire: Production," in Scheidel, Morris, and Saller, *Cambridge Economic History*, 543; Andrew M. Riggsby, *Roman Law and the Legal World of the Romans* (Cambridge: Cambridge University Press, 2010), 221; and David Johnston, *Roman Law in Context* (Cambridge: Cambridge University Press, 1999), 11.
51. William Metcalf, "Roman Imperial Numismatics," in Potter, *Companion to the Roman Empire*, 36.
52. Ibid., 37.
53. Kevin Butcher and Matthew Ponting, "The Roman Denarius under the Julio-Claudian Emperors: Mints, Metallurgy and Technology," *OJA* 24, no. 2 (May 2005): 163–97.
54. Richard Duncan-Jones, "The Monetization of the Roman Empire: Regional Variations in the Supply of Coin Types," in *Roman Coins and Public Life under the Empire: E. Togo Salmon Papers II*, ed. George M. Paul and Michael Ierardi (Ann Arbor: University of Michigan Press, 1999), 61–82.
55. Dominic Rathbone, "Prices and Price Formation in Roman Egypt," in *Économie Antique: Prix et Formation des Prix dans les Économies Antiques*, ed. Jean Andreau, Pierre Briant and Raymond Descat (Saint-Bertrand-de-Comminges: Musée Archéologique Départemental, 1997), 187.
56. Metcalf, "Roman Imperial Numismatics," 39–40.

houses. Claudius built a new harbor and lighthouse at Ostia and created new farmland in Italy by draining the Fucine Lake (Suetonius, *Claud.* 20). There was an increase in the construction of aqueducts in Italy and the provinces in the early empire as well.[57] David Mattingly argues that there was a substantial increase in the "scale and volume" of road, river, and maritime traffic in this period.[58] Finley and others stressed "the prohibitive cost of land transport,"[59] but new research suggests they overestimated the difficulties.[60] Georges Raepsaet argues that in terms of efficiency, transportation reached "a very exceptional peak during the Roman Empire."[61] In addition to the improvements to infrastructure, better harnesses allowed horses to play a greater role in transportation.[62] Maritime technology also improved. There were advances in ship construction, including the use of the newly invented chain pump and wooden force pump for emptying bilges.[63] Changes to the rigging, sails, and hulls of vessels may have made sea travel safer and more efficient.[64] The adoption of barrels for wine transport beginning in the early empire made the wine trade less visible archaeologically but conferred advantages over the use of amphorae.[65]

Private institutional infrastructure also facilitated trade in the early empire. In the realm of finance, bankers, pawnbrokers, endowments, associations, and others lent money, and traders could enlist the aid of *intercessores* and *proxenetae* to arrange loans. Interest rates seem (usually) to have been non-usurious.[66] Temin suggests that Roman financial institutions were "better than those of eighteenth-century France and Holland" and "similar to those in eighteenth-century London."[67] A

57. Andrew Wilson, "Hydraulic Engineering and Water Supply," in *The Oxford Handbook of Engineering and Technology in the Classical World*, ed. John Peter Oleson (Oxford: Oxford University Press, 2008), 297–98.
58. Mattingly, "The Imperial Economy," 285.
59. M. I. Finley, *The Ancient Economy* (Berkeley: University of California Press, 1985), 32.
60. See, for example, Ray Laurence, *The Roads of Roman Italy: Mobility and Cultural Change* (London: Routledge, 1999); and Colin Adams, "Transport," in *The Cambridge Companion to the Roman Economy*, ed. Walter Scheidel (Cambridge: Cambridge University Press, 2012), 237.
61. Georges Raepsaet, "Land Transport, Part 2: Riding, Harnesses, and Vehicles," in Oleson, *Oxford Handbook of Engineering*, 602.
62. Ibid., 595.
63. Richard Stein, "Roman Wooden Force Pumps: A Case-Study in Innovation," *JRA* 17 (2004): 221–50; and Andrew Wilson, "The Economic Influence of Developments in Maritime Technology in Antiquity," in *Maritime Technology in the Ancient Economy: Ship-Design and Navigation*, ed. W. V. Harris and K. Iara (Portsmouth, RI: Journal of Roman Archaeology, 2011), 223.
64. For a review of developments, see William V. Harris, introduction to Harris and Iara, *Maritime Technology*, 13–19; and Wilson, "Economic Influence," 211–33.
65. Greene, "Technological Innovation," 48.
66. Columella (*De re rustica*, 3.3.9) and Pliny the Elder (*Naturalis historia*, 14.55–57) both imply that 6 percent was the prevailing interest rate in the first century CE.

vast array of specialists engaged in the empire's commerce. Shipowners, captains, pilots, porters, and ballast experts (*saburrarii*) facilitated the movement of goods while moneychangers, *interpretes*, and auctioneers worked in the markets.[68] Many traders specialized in particular commodities (from pigs to wine) and formed associations (*collegia*, *koina*, etc.) with their colleagues. Once viewed as almost exclusively social and religious organizations,[69] recent work shows that occupational associations sometimes provided loans, set prices, suppressed would-be competitors, assigned territory, and dealt collectively with government authorities on behalf of their members.[70] One could also, of course, conduct business through a partnership (*societas*), the *familia* (by means of slaves, freedmen, and clients), or friends.[71]

Supply and Demand

Turning from distribution to production, here again there were substantial developments in the early empire, including improvements in agricultural and food processing technology, construction methods, and manufacturing. In agriculture, what has been called the "villa system" spread.[72] This entailed, as Dominic Rathbone puts it, "the concentrated cultivation of the vine and olive as cash crops and the massed use of slave labour."[73] Farmers and landowners did not pursue self-sufficiency but cultivated at least part of their land with a view to market opportunities. For precisely this reason, Columella (*De re rustica*, 1.2.3), the early imperial agricultural writer, emphasized access to transportation when describing the ideal farm. Slave-run estates did

67. Temin, *Roman Market Economy*, 189.
68. David Hollander, "Risky Business: Traders in the Roman World," in *Traders in the Ancient Mediterranean*, ed. Timothy Howe (Chicago: Ares, 2015), 147–48.
69. See, for example, Finley, *The Ancient Economy*, 138.
70. Matt Gibbs, "Collegia," in Bagnall et al., *The Encyclopedia of Ancient History*, 4:1649–52; and Jinyu Liu, "Associations, Greek and Roman," in Bagnall et al., *The Encyclopedia of Ancient History*, 2:846–49. The association of salt merchants of Tebtunis, for example, paid taxes for its members, assigned territory, and set prices (P.Mich. 657).
71. See, for example, Aaron Kirschenbaum, *Sons, Slaves and Freedmen in Roman Commerce* (Washington, DC: Catholic University of America Press, 1987); Jean-Jacques Aubert, "The Fourth Factor: Managing Non-Agricultural Production in the Roman World," in *Economies beyond Agriculture in the Classical World*, ed. David J. Mattingly and John Salmon (London: Routledge, 2001), 90–111; and Huib Lirb, "Partners in Agriculture: The Pooling of Resources in Rural *Societates* in Roman Italy," in *De Agricultura: In memoriam Pieter Willem De Neeve*, ed. Heleen Sancisi-Weerdenburg et al. (Amsterdam: J. C. Gieben, 1993), 263–95.
72. Annalisa Marzano, *Roman Villas in Central Italy: A Social and Economic History* (Leiden: Brill, 2007), 223–33.
73. Dominic Rathbone, "The Development of Agriculture in the 'Ager Cosanus' during the Roman Republic: Problems of Evidence and Interpretation," *JRS* 71 (1981): 12.

not drive out the smallholders but instead relied on the part-time, seasonal labor of such farmers (as well as, in some instances, migrant workers and nearby urban residents) to achieve profitability.[74] Another critical trend was the spread of convertible husbandry, "a method of intensive mixed farming," which improved yields.[75] Viticulture and olive cultivation expanded in Italy and elsewhere. North Africa and southern Spain increased their production of olive oil, while Gallic viticulture grew. The use of crushed terracotta improved the drainage of orchards,[76] and the Romans introduced many new crops into Italy and other parts of Europe, including the plum, jujube, tuber apple, pistachio, and cherry.[77] Pliny the Elder (*Nat.* 15.57) feared that arboriculture had been exhausted in terms of potential for innovation. Horticulture saw the invention of greenhouses, while market gardens remained important, although rampant theft may have reduced their presence in some urban areas (Pliny the Elder, *Nat.* 19.59).

Beyond the well-known "Mediterranean triad" of grain, olive oil, and wine, a vast array of goods were produced and traded within and beyond the borders of the empire: perfumes, honey, cheese, figs, *garum* (fish sauce), wax, amber, textiles, timber, dyes, incense, spices, and medicinal plants, to list just a few. Some of these commodities merit further attention, while others have already prompted fascinating work.[78]

The tremendous demand for seafood spurred developments in pisciculture. By the late republic, large-scale fish processing facilities were appearing along the shores of the Mediterranean,[79] and Roman maritime villas had begun to feature vast artificial fishponds.[80] The Romans improved and standardized fish hooks,[81] began to raise oysters, and even invented heated fish tanks (Pliny the Elder, *Nat.* 9.168–74). The production and consumption of meat, especially pork, also increased

74. Dennis Kehoe, "Contract Labor," in Scheidel, *Cambridge Companion to the Roman Economy*, 115.
75. Geoffrey Kron, "Roman Ley-Farming," *JRA* 13 (2000): 277–87.
76. Geoffrey Kron, "Agriculture, Roman Empire," in Bagnall et al., *Encyclopedia of Ancient History*, 1:221.
77. Pliny the Elder, *Nat.*, 15.46–47 (plums, jujubes, tuber apples), 15.102 (cherries); for pistachios, see Daniel Zohary, Maria Hopf, and Ehud Weiss, *Domestication of Plants in the Old World: The Origin and Spread of Cultivated Plants in West Asia, Europe, and the Nile Valley*, 4th ed. (Oxford: Oxford University Press, 2012), 152.
78. On perfumes, see Gary Reger, "The Manufacture and Distribution of Perfume," in *Making, Moving and Managing: The New World of Ancient Economies, 323-31 BC*, ed. Zofia H. Archibald, John K. Davies, and Vincent Gabrielsen (Oxford: Oxbow Books, 2005), 253–97.
79. A. I. Wilson, "Fishy Business: Roman Exploitation of Marine Resources," *JRA* 19 (2006): 534.
80. James Higginbotham, *Piscinae: Artificial Fishponds in Roman Italy* (Chapel Hill: University of North Carolina Press, 1997), 39.
81. Geoffrey Kron, "Animal Husbandry, Hunting, Fishing, and Fish Production," in Oleson, *Oxford Handbook of Engineering*, 205.

under the empire. Roman cattle grew in stature and weight.[82] Game farming, developed in the late republic, continued to be of considerable importance.[83]

The production of higher-quality iron tools had a beneficial effect on many aspects of agriculture.[84] Furthermore, in cereal cultivation, Pliny the Elder (*Nat.* 18.48.172–73) mentions the recent invention of a wheeled plow in Raetia Galliae, and the *vallus*, a machine for reaping grain, apparently saw considerable use in Gaul (Pliny the Elder, *Nat.* 18.72).[85] In the sphere of food processing, the Romans began to exploit the potential of waterpower to grind grain and, for grapes and olives, screw presses, which were lighter and used space more efficiently.[86] In Rome, water and animals powered high-capacity mixers producing dough for large beehive ovens.[87]

Mining expanded under the Romans, especially in Spain. Pliny the Elder (*Nat.* 33.78) records the claim that Asturia, Callaecia, and Lusitania produced twenty thousand pounds of gold per year. Lead and copper concentrations increase dramatically in ice core samples from Greenland dating to the late republic and early empire; these elevated levels probably stem mainly from large-scale Roman mining and smelting operations.[88]

Along with better iron tools, brass began to play a major role in the early empire.[89] The Romans also popularized "antiquity's plastic," leather.[90] Carol van Driel-Murray observes that tanning spread with the Roman conquests.[91] M. C. Bishop and J. C. N. Coulston estimate that

---

82. Geoffrey Kron, "Archaeozoological Evidence for the Productivity of Roman Livestock Farming," *Münstersche Beiträge zur Antiken Handelsgeschichte* 21, no. 2 (2002): 53–73.

83. On game farming, see Kron, "Animal Husbandry," 186.

84. Kron, "Agriculture, Roman Empire," 1:219.

85. Greene, "Technological Innovation," 36.

86. On presses, see Pliny the Elder, *Nat.*, 18.317; Andrew Wilson, "Machines in Greek and Roman Technology," in Oleson, *Oxford Handbook of Engineering*, 359; Jeremy Rossiter, "Olives and Olive Oil," in Bagnall et al., *Encyclopedia of Ancient History*, 9:4890–94; and Helmuth Schneider, "Technology," in Scheidel, Morris, and Saller, *Cambridge Economic History*, 158. On the use of water power to grind grain, see Örjan Wikander, "The Water-Mill," in *Handbook of Ancient Water Technology*, ed. Örjan Wikander (Leiden: Brill, 2000), 398.

87. On dough mixers, see Wilson, "Machines in Greek and Roman Technology," 358; on kneading, see David L. Thurmond, *A Handbook of Food Processing in Classical Rome: For Her Bounty No Winter* (Leiden: Brill, 2006), 64–72.

88. Sungmin Hong et al., "Greenland Ice Evidence of Hemispheric Lead Pollution Two Millennia Ago by Greek and Roman Civilizations," *Science* 265 (1994): 1841–43; Sungmin Hong et al., "History of Ancient Copper Smelting Pollution during Roman and Medieval Times Recorded in Greenland Ice," *Science* 272 (1996): 246–49.

89. Kevin Greene, "Inventors, Invention, and Attitudes toward Innovation," in Oleson, *Oxford Handbook of Engineering*, 809.

90. Carol van Driel-Murray, "Tanning and Leather," in Oleson, *Oxford Handbook of Engineering*, 483.

91. Ibid.

a single legion would require more than forty-six thousand goat hides just for its tents.[92]

There were no technological developments in ceramics in the early empire, but Arretine ware (also known as *terra sigillata*) became quite popular in the late first century BCE, perhaps thanks to the connections of Maecenas, a native of Arretium and a close associate of Augustus.[93] Production spread from Italy to southern Gaul, with large workshops appearing at Lyon, La Graufesenque, and elsewhere.[94] Probably through the use of agents (*institores*), the Italian terracotta lamp industry also expanded to the provinces.[95] Glassblowing, invented in the first century BCE, developed quickly in the early empire, leading to cheap glassware, windows, and glass mirrors.[96] The glass industry never, however, rivaled ceramic production.[97]

Roman textiles do not, of course, survive in any great quantities, but they were undoubtedly of considerable economic importance. Willem Jongman suggests that clothing may have been the average person's largest expense after food and shelter.[98] It is not clear that there were any technological improvements in textile production in the early empire, but the two-beam vertical loom, used for "patterned fabrics," became more popular.[99] Roman demand for flax products may have provided Galilean peasants with an attractive cash crop in the early empire.[100] Papyrus production flourished: a new "brand" called *Fanniana* entered the market, and Claudius is credited with an improved type called *Augusta* (Pliny the Elder, *Nat.* 13.24.74–80). With respect to the scale of papyrus production, William V. Harris proposes that "we should think of tens of thousands of rolls a year being exported from Egypt."[101]

Concrete, developed in the second century BCE,[102] permitted some significant changes in construction practices in the early empire. The

92. M. C. Bishop and J. C. N. Coulston, *Roman Military Equipment: From the Punic Wars to the Fall of Rome* (Oxford: Oxbow Books, 2006), 247.
93. Andrew Wallace-Hadrill, *Rome's Cultural Revolution* (Cambridge: Cambridge University Press, 2008), 415–16.
94. Kevin Greene, *The Archaeology of the Roman Economy* (London: B. T. Batsford, 1986), 157–62.
95. Harris, "Roman Terracotta Lamps," 126–45.
96. E. Marianne Stern, "Roman Glassblowing in a Cultural Context," *AJA* 103, no. 3 (1999): 441–84.
97. E. Marianne Stern, "Glass Production," in Oleson, *Oxford Handbook of Engineering*, 541.
98. Willem Jongman, "Wool and the Textile Industry of Roman Italy: A Working Hypothesis," in Lo Cascio, *Mercati Permanenti*, 188.
99. John P. Wild, "Textile Production," in Oleson, *Oxford Handbook of Engineering*, 471.
100. Patrick Scott Geyer, "Flax," in Bagnall et al., *Encyclopedia of Ancient History*, 5:2698.
101. William V. Harris, "Trade [70–192 AD]," in *Rome's Imperial Economy: Twelve Essays* (Oxford: Oxford University Press, 2011), 174.
102. Marcello Mogetta, "A New Date for Concrete in Rome," *JRS* 105 (2015): 1–40.

Romans were able to build larger cisterns and waterproof them more effectively.[103] Hydraulic concrete was important for harbor construction throughout the Mediterranean.[104] The "building boom" of the early empire made brick production highly lucrative, and the use of *opus testaceum* (brick-faced concrete) began in the first century CE.[105] Standardized bricks made construction more efficient, and brick-faced walls obviated the need for formwork for the concrete.[106] Trusses and iron tie bars improved vaults, and *tegulae mammatae* allowed for heated walls in baths.[107]

Any discussion of the Roman economy must also take the "service sector" into account. Fulling and prostitution have both received thorough study in recent years.[108] The "entertainment industry" encompassed a wide range of activities from athletics and gladiatorial spectacles to chariot racing and theatrical productions. Baths were a major feature of most Roman towns, usually charging admission and consuming large amounts of wood and charcoal. In Britain, coal was sometimes used for heating and forges.[109] Gambling, not apparently an organized business, was nevertheless quite popular.[110]

While consumption is, of course, closely related to production, there has been considerably less work on the nature of demand in the Roman economy. Cultural, ethnic, and religious factors would have a profound effect on economic decisions (and not exclusively with respect to demand).[111] As early as 1993, William V. Harris noted the potential

---

103. Wilson, "Hydraulic Engineering," 288; Lynne Lancaster, "Roman Engineering and Construction," in Oleson, *Oxford Handbook of Engineering*, 261.
104. Wilson, "Economic Influence," 225–26.
105. Helmuth Schneider, "Technology," in Scheidel, Morris, and Saller, *Cambridge Economic History*, 169; on *opus testaceum*, see Lancaster, "Roman Engineering and Construction," 263–64.
106. Andrew Wilson, "The Economic Impact of Technological Advances in the Roman Construction Industry," in *Innovazione tecnica e progresso economico nel mondo romano*, Atti degli Incontri capresi di storia dell'economia antica (Capri, 13-16 aprile 2003), ed. Elio Lo Cascio, Pragmateiai 10 (Bari, ITA: Edipuglia, 2006), 227–29.
107. For trusses and iron tie bars, see Lancaster, "Roman Engineering and Construction," 266–70, 273 (*tegulae mammatae*). See also Fikret Yegül, *Baths and Bathing in Classical Antiquity* (Cambridge, MA: MIT Press, 1992), 383.
108. On prostitution, see Thomas A. J. McGinn, *The Economy of Prostitution in the Roman World: A Study of Social History and the Brothel* (Ann Arbor: University of Michigan Press, 2004). On *fullones*, see Miko Flohr, *The World of the Fullo: Work, Economy, and Society in Roman Italy* (Oxford: Oxford University Press, 2013).
109. John Robert Travis, *Coal in Roman Britain*, British Archaeological Reports (Oxford: John & Erica Hedges, 2008).
110. For some discussion of gambling, see Nicholas Purcell, "Literate Games: Roman Urban Society and the Game of *Alea*," *Past and Present* 147, no. 1 (1995): 3–37; and J. P. Toner, *Leisure and Ancient Rome* (Cambridge: Polity Press, 1995).
111. Susan E. Alcock, "The Eastern Mediterranean," in Scheidel, Morris, and Saller, *Cambridge Economic History*, 696.

insights to be had from examining Roman "consumption choices," but it is still an understudied topic.[112] The final chapters of Andrew Wallace-Hadrill's *Rome's Cultural Revolution*, which discuss the "consumer revolution" of the late republic and early empire, show what is possible in this sphere.[113] Roman economic historians need to pay more attention to early Christian sources but also to consider more fully the economic implications of Roman religious practices. Temples throughout the empire acted as banks, controlled lands, attracted pilgrims (and offerings), and generated markets.[114] Marc Kleijwegt, for example, has demonstrated the tremendous importance of the religious textile market.[115] The riot of the silversmiths at Ephesus, recorded in Acts 19, is another indication of how important the religious market could be.

The Romans and Greeks may not have had economic thought in anything like the modern sense of the phrase, but they had plenty of opinions about economic subjects. Wealth and poverty, the relative respectability of various professions, patronage and gift-giving, and household management are prominent topics of discussion. We can also learn more about how they conceived of risks and rewards.

Labor

With separate chapters in this volume devoted to slaves and the poor, I will keep my discussion of labor brief. There is broad agreement that the Roman economy relied heavily on the slave mode of production in the early empire, but it is not clear just how many slaves there were. Scheidel estimates that slaves made up roughly 10 percent of the overall population of the empire, while Harris suggests it may have been twice that.[116] Both agree, however, that the evidence—except with respect to Egypt—permits only very rough approximations. There were certainly regional variations, with more slaves in Italy than the

---

112. William V. Harris, "Between Archaic and Modern: Some Current Problems in the History of the Roman Economy," in *The Inscribed Economy: Production and Distribution in the Roman Empire in the Light of Instrumentum Domesticum: The Proceedings of a Conference Held at the American Academy in Rome on 10–11 January, 1992*, ed. William V. Harris (Ann Arbor: University of Michigan, 1993), 28.

113. Wallace-Hadrill, *Rome's Cultural Revolution*, 315–55.

114. See, for example, Beate Dignas, "Sacred Revenues in Roman Hands: The Economic Dimension of Sanctuaries in Western Asia Minor," in *Patterns in the Economy of Roman Asia Minor*, ed. Stephen Mitchell and Constantina Katsari (Swansea, UK: Classical Press of Wales, 2005), 207–24.

115. Marc Kleijwegt, "Textile Manufacturing for a Religious Market, Artemis and Diana as Tycoons of Industry," in *After the Past: Essays in Ancient History in Honour of H. W. Pleket*, ed. Willem Jongman and Marc Kleijwegt (Leiden: Brill, 2002), 81–134.

116. Walter Scheidel, "Slavery," in Scheidel, *Cambridge Companion to the Roman Economy*, 92; Harris, *Rome's Imperial Economy*, 93.

provinces and more urban slaves than rural ones.[117] Though free workers were the majority everywhere, we must be sensitive to the ways in which even "free" laborers were constrained by various forces. Freed slaves might owe work to their former owners or have limitations placed on their ability to compete in the market.[118] Debtors might be obligated to work for their creditors and clients for their patrons. Some public works were built or maintained by means of *corvée*,[119] and soldiers, finally, engaged in much work only tangentially related to the security of the empire. On the other hand, it is important to remember that many slaves, particularly in urban areas, fulfilled roles (e.g., cupbearer) designed to enhance the status of their owners rather than to be productive. While slavery was probably profitable for most Roman slave owners, profitability was not necessarily always the main goal.[120]

Because, as John Bodel has put it, "there was no peculiarly slave labor,"[121] we must consider to what extent slaves and free workers competed in the labor market. In agriculture, as noted earlier, slave and free labor could complement one another. No doubt this was also true in other sectors of the economy where demand was seasonal (e.g., construction). Temin has argued that the distinctive elements of Roman slavery (an open system with frequent manumission) allowed slaves to be "part of an integrated labor force" with free workers.[122] Attitudes toward labor nevertheless influenced the hiring decisions of employers. Since upper-class Romans viewed most forms of work other than farming as slavish,[123] if they wanted to invest in business, they preferred to employ their slaves and freedmen. This allowed them "to maintain a respectable distance ... while yet retaining full control over profits"[124] and, through the institution of *peculium*, limit their liabil-

---

117. Walter Scheidel, "The Roman Slave Supply," in *The Cambridge World History of Slavery*, vol. 1, *The Ancient Mediterranean World*, ed. Keith Bradley and Paul Cartledge (Cambridge: Cambridge University Press, 2011), 289.

118. On competing with one's freedman, see Hollander, "Risky Business," 164.

119. For canal maintenance and other *corvées* in Egypt, see Capponi, *Augustan Egypt*, 75–76. The *Lex Coloniae Genetivae Iuliae* XCVIII (*CIL* II 5439 = *ILS* 6087) allowed the decurions of Urso to make use of up to five days of labor per year from every adult male in the colony.

120. John Bodel, "Slave Labour and Roman Society," in Bradley and Cartledge, *Cambridge World History of Slavery*, 314; and Scheidel, "Slavery," 98.

121. Bodel, "Slave Labour and Roman Society," 312.

122. Temin, *Roman Market Economy*, 130.

123. Cicero, *De officiis*, 1.150–51. Numerous inscriptions, however, demonstrate that many artisans and traders took pride in their occupations. See Sandra R. Joshel, *Work, Identity, and Legal Status at Rome: A Study of the Occupational Inscriptions* (Norman: University of Oklahoma Press, 1992).

124. Bodel, "Slave Labour and Roman Society," 316. See also John H. D'Arms, *Commerce and Social Standing in Ancient Rome* (Cambridge, MA: Harvard University Press, 1981); and Neville Morley, "Markets, Marketing and the Roman Elite," in Lo Cascio, *Mercati permanenti*, 211–21.

ity.[125] These practices, of course, prevented free workers from obtaining employment in elite households and businesses.[126] Wage labor was especially important in the building industry, and it is here that many poorer urban residents would have found employment (Suetonius, *Vespasianus* 18). Janet DeLaine estimates that construction employed between forty and sixty thousand workers in Rome in this period.[127] There would also have been consistent and considerable demand for porters and stevedores as day laborers in major cities.[128] Our limited evidence for wages in the first century of the empire suggests they remained stable.[129] Many fundamental questions concerning Roman labor are intractable and likely to remain so. However, approaching the Roman economy from the perspective of human capital, "the education, training, and health of the labor force," may offer new insights.[130] As Richard Saller points out, human capital has "non-trivial implications" for the Roman economy and its potential for growth.[131] High mortality rates, for example, would prevent many fathers from passing on valuable skills to their sons.

Conclusion

On balance, the Roman economy was doing remarkably well in Paul's time *for Roman citizens*. Conquest and annexation added to the imperial revenue and opened up new markets. The annexation of Egypt was especially important in this regard, allowing for a massive expansion of trade with India. Strabo (*Geographica* 2.12) reports that more than one hundred merchant vessels sailed between Myos Hormos and India, far more than under the Ptolemies. Pliny the Elder (*Nat.* 12.84) complained that the empire spent 100 million sesterces per year on goods from India, China, and the Arabian Peninsula.[132] Roman citizens were best positioned to exploit the new territory, roads, bridges, canals, and harbors they had built, as well as to take advantage of the increased safety of travel. There were new opportunities to supply Rome and Roman

125. Kirschenbaum, *Sons, Slaves and Freedmen*, 200–201.
126. Scheidel, "Slavery," 107.
127. Janet DeLaine, "Bricks and Mortar: Exploring the Economics of Building Techniques at Rome and Ostia," in Mattingly and Salmon, *Economies beyond Agriculture*, 231.
128. P. A. Brunt, "Free Labour and Public Works at Rome," *JRS* 70 (1980): 81.
129. On the stability of wages, see Dennis Kehoe, "Contract Labor," in Scheidel, *Cambridge Companion to the Roman Economy*, 114, 126.
130. Richard P. Saller, "Human Capital and Economic Growth," in Scheidel, *Cambridge Companion to the Roman Economy*, 71.
131. Ibid., 74.
132. For discussion of this passage, see Harris, "Trade [70–192 AD]," 175.

armies with a wide range of goods. Imperial building programs offered much potential profit for the wealthy through building contracts or the sale of construction materials, while the urban poor could earn money as day laborers. Citizens were also best able to take advantage of the spread of Roman law and money as well as the new markets created by the veterans settled in colonies throughout the empire. Neville Morley suggests the average Roman simply had more and better stuff than other people in antiquity, including better diet and health.[133] Things were not, to be sure, uniformly good. Many a wealthy Roman lost his fortune during the credit crisis of 33 CE (Tacitus, *Ann.* 6.17), and informers were always ready to seize upon any sign of disloyalty. Floods, fires, earthquakes, storms, and epidemics sometimes struck, but the damages were rarely widespread. There are, however, some signs that by the reign of Nero, the Roman government had overextended itself financially. Tacitus (*Ann.* 15.18.3) reports that Nero criticized previous emperors for overspending and gave HS 60 million to the *aerarium* each year, but vanity projects like the *Domus Aurea* cannot have helped matters. As noted earlier, Nero's reign saw the beginning of the debasement of the *denarius*. The senate's vote, early in 70 CE, to borrow HS 60 million from private lenders also suggests difficulties—no doubt the wars of the previous year were the main culprit—but ultimately the plan was not carried out (Tacitus, *Historiae* 4.47).

For provincial subjects, economic conditions may have been far less favorable. Strabo (*Geogr.* 17.1.53) notes that Roman taxes caused a revolt in Egypt under Augustus, and Josephus (*B.J.* 2.118, *A.J.* 18.1) reports similar events in Judaea. Debt, high interest rates, and taxation prompted the Gallic revolt of Florus and Sacrovir in 21 CE (Tacitus, *Ann.* 3.40). Taxation also triggered the revolt in 28 CE of the Frisii, who specifically targeted the soldiers involved in tax collection (Tacitus, *Ann.* 4.72). There was Thracian resistance to conscription, and a disgruntled peasant in Spain assassinated the praetor L. Piso, apparently

---

133. Neville Morley, "Economy and Economic Theory," in Gagarin and Fantham, *Oxford Encyclopedia of Ancient Greece and Rome*, 3:8. However, some studies of skeletal remains have found a decline in stature during the Roman period. Such results may indicate that the average Roman was less well-off than has been supposed. See, for example, Geoffrey Kron, "Anthropometry, Physical Anthropology, and the Reconstruction of Ancient Health, Nutrition, and Living Standards," *Historia* 54, no. 1 (2005): 68–83; Monica Giannecchini and Jacopo Moggi-Cecchi, "Stature in Archeological Samples from Central Italy: Methodological Issues and Diachronic Changes," *American Journal of Physical Anthropology* 135, no. 3 (March 2008): 284–92; Rebecca Gowland and Peter Garnsey, "Skeletal Evidence for Health, Nutritional Status and Malaria in Rome and the Empire," in *Roman Diasporas: Archaeological Approaches to Mobility and Diversity in the Roman Empire*, ed. Hella Eckardt (Portsmouth, RI: Journal of Roman Archaeology, 2010), 131–56; and Walter Scheidel, "Physical Well-Being," in Scheidel, *Cambridge Companion to the Roman Economy*, 321–33.

because of his efforts to collect public revenue (Tacitus, *Ann.* 4.45). Caratacus, the son of a British king, appealed to the burden of Roman taxes to generate support for resistance to Rome in 50 CE (Tacitus, *Ann.* 12.34), and many communities requested tax relief.[134]

Rome did, however, provide substantial benefits to the provinces. The Roman army cleared irrigation canals in Egypt (Suetonius, *Aug.* 18). Under Tiberius, we hear of soldiers building roads and bridges at Nauportus (Tacitus, *Ann.* 1.20), and in the wake of the 17 CE earthquake that seriously damaged twelve cities in Asia Minor, the emperor not only remitted taxes but also provided funds for rebuilding (Tacitus, *Ann.* 2.47; Suetonius, *Tib.* 48.2; and Dio 57.17). Caligula financed building projects at Syracuse, Samos, and Ephesus (Suetonius, *Cal.* 21), while Claudius remitted taxes to Apamaea after an earthquake (Tacitus, *Ann.* 12.58). And Nero provided Lugdunum with HS 4 million for rebuilding after a devastating fire (Tacitus, *Ann.* 16.13). Nevertheless, it seems reasonable to assume that the Roman economy disproportionally benefited Roman citizens rather than the population of the empire more broadly.

Select Bibliography

Andreau, Jean. *L'économie du monde romain.* Paris: Ellipses, 2010.

Aubert, Jean-Jacques. *Business Managers in Ancient Rome: A Social and Economic Study of Institores, 200 B.C.–A.D. 250.* Leiden: Brill, 1994.

Bang, Peter F. *The Roman Bazaar: A Comparative Study of Trade and Markets in a Tributary Empire.* Cambridge: Cambridge University Press, 2008.

_____., Mamoru Ikeguchi, and Harmut G. Ziche, eds. *Ancient Economies, Modern Methodologies: Archaeology, Comparative History, Models and Institutions.* Pragmateiai 12. Bari, ITA: Edipuglia, 2006.

Bowman, Alan, and Andrew Wilson, eds. *Quantifying the Roman Economy: Methods and Problems.* Oxford Studies on the Roman Economy. Oxford: Oxford University Press, 2009.

Burnett, Andrew M., Michel Amandry, and Pere Pau Ripollès, eds. *Roman Provincial Coinage.* 9 vols. London: British Museum Press, 1992.

D'Arms, John H. *Commerce and Social Standing in Ancient Rome.* Cambridge, MA: Harvard University Press, 1981.

Duncan-Jones, Richard. *Money and Government in the Roman Empire.* Cambridge: Cambridge University Press, 1994.

---

134. For example, Syria and Judaea in 17 CE (Tacitus, *Ann.*, 2.42). On resistance to Rome and its causes, see Martin Goodman, "Enemies of Rome," in Garnsey and Saller, *The Roman Empire*, 55–67.

_____. *Structure and Scale in the Roman Economy*. Cambridge: Cambridge University Press, 1990.

Erdkamp, Paul. *The Grain Market in the Roman Empire: A Social, Political and Economic Study*. Cambridge: Cambridge University Press, 2005.

Frayn, Joan M. *Markets and Fairs in Roman Italy: Their Social and Economic Importance from the Second Century B.C. to the Third Century A.D.* Oxford: Clarendon Press, 1993.

Garnsey, Peter, and Richard Saller. *The Roman Empire: Economy, Society and Culture*. Oakland: University of California Press, 2015.

Greene, Kevin. *The Archaeology of the Roman Economy*. London: B. T. Batsford, 1986.

Harris, W. V. *Rome's Imperial Economy: Twelve Essays*. Oxford: Oxford University Press, 2011.

Holleran, Claire. *Shopping in Ancient Rome: The Retail Trade in the Late Republic and the Principate*. Oxford: Oxford University Press, 2012.

Hopkins, Keith. "Taxes and Trade in the Roman Empire (200 B.C.–A.D. 400)." *Journal of Roman Studies* 70 (1980): 101–25.

Horden, Peregrine, and Nicholas Purcell. *The Corrupting Sea: A Study of Mediterranean History*. Oxford: Blackwell, 2000.

Lo Cascio, Elio, ed. *Mercati permanenti e mercati periodici nel mondo romano: Atti degli Incontri capresi di storia dell'economia antica (Capri 13-15 ottobre 1997)*. Pragmateiai 2. Bari, ITA: Edipuglia, 2000.

Morley, Neville. *Metropolis and Hinterland: The City of Rome and the Italian Economy, 200 B.C.–A.D. 200*. Cambridge: Cambridge University Press, 1996.

Russell, Ben. *The Economics of the Roman Stone Trade*. Oxford: Oxford University Press, 2013.

Scheidel, Walter, ed. *The Cambridge Companion to the Roman Economy*. Cambridge: Cambridge University Press, 2012.

_____, and Sitta von Reden, eds. *The Ancient Economy*. New York: Routledge, 2002.

Temin, Peter. *The Roman Market Economy*. Princeton: Princeton University Press, 2013.

Wallace-Hadrill, Andrew. *Rome's Cultural Revolution*. Cambridge: Cambridge University Press, 2008.

2

———

Urban Poverty in the Roman Empire:
Material Conditions

Jinyu Liu

The increasing attention to the issue of poverty and the poor in the Greco-Roman world is emblematic of a historiographical trend that steers away from the elite perspective and from a top-down approach to writing ancient history.[1] This trend both necessitates and is enriched by recovering the experiences of the historically marginalized and invisible.[2] It is significant that *Roman Social History: A Sourcebook* includes a sizable section specifically devoted to poverty.[3] Both the materials included in the sourcebook and the content of the impor-

1. I thank Tom Blanton and David Hollander for sharing with me unpublished materials, and Nahyan Fancy, David Gellman, Keith Nightenhelser, Nick Rauh, Manu Raghav, and Rebecca Schindler for helpful insights and suggestions. I greatly appreciate the helpful comments of the editors.
2. Jerry Toner, *Popular Culture in Ancient Rome* (Cambridge: Polity, 2009); Robert C. Knapp, *Invisible Romans* (Cambridge: Harvard University Press, 2011).
3. Tim G. Parkin and Arthur J. Pomeroy, *Roman Social History: A Sourcebook* (London: Routledge, 2007), 205–43.

tant contribution *Poverty in the Roman World*,[4] however, also point to the plight of ancient historians—that is, in regard to poverty and the poor in the Roman Empire, we know more about the classical writers' perceptions of poverty and the poor than the actual lived experience of the poor,[5] more about Rome and Egypt than elsewhere, and more about people far above the subsistence level than those at or below it, the latter being the convenient and conventional definition for the poor in the Roman world.[6] In the introduction to *Poverty in the Roman World*, Robin Osborne states that poverty was an "under-explored territory."[7] Nevertheless, encouraging advancements—methodological and conceptual—have since been made. Drawing on these advancements, this chapter provides a critical synthesis, identifies gaps, and suggests ways of conducting further research with a primary chronological focus on the first three centuries of the Roman Empire.

Studies of Poverty in the Roman Empire: An Overview

Developments along three main directions—that is, critical approaches to the textualized poverty in ancient literature, a nuanced understanding of economic stratification in the Roman Empire, and bioarchaeological research on living conditions in the Roman world—can be clearly identified.

First, a number of discourse-centered studies have highlighted "poverty" and "the poor" as heuristic, rhetorical, or philosophical constructs in the ancient literary sources, constructs that were indicative of the elite preoccupation with maintaining wealth and status. Asking

4. Margaret Atkins and Robin Osborne, eds., *Poverty in the Roman World* (Cambridge: Cambridge University Press, 2006).

5. For copious bibliography, see, most recently, L. L. Welborn, "The Polis and the Poor: Reconstructing Social Relations from Different Genres of Evidence," in *The First Urban Churches 1: Methodological Foundations*, ed. James R. Harrison and L. L. Welborn (Atlanta: SBL Press, 2015), 189–244; see also Mik R. Larsen, "The Representation of Poverty in the Roman Empire" (PhD diss., University of California, Los Angeles, 2015).

6. Peter Garnsey and Greg Woolf, "Patronage of the Rural Poor in the Roman World," in *Patronage in Ancient Society*, ed. Andrew Wallace-Hadrill (London: Routledge, 1990), 153.

7. This is not to say that there had been no studies prior. E.g, ibid., 153–70; C. R. Whittaker, "The Poor," in *The Romans*, ed. Andrea Giardina (Chicago: University of Chicago Press, 1993), 272–99; Marcus Prell, *Sozialökonomische Untersuchungen Zur Armut Im Antiken Rom: Von Den Gracchen Bis Kaiser Diokletian* (Stuttgart: Steiner, 1997), with bibliography; Justin J. Meggitt, *Paul, Poverty and Survival* (Edinburgh: T&T Clark, 1998); Anneliese Ruth Parkin, "Poverty in the Early Roman Empire: Ancient and Modern Conceptions and Constructs" (PhD diss., Cambridge University, 2001). Also see Evelyne Patlagean, *Pauvreté économique et pauvreté sociale à Byzance, 4e-7e siècles* (Paris: Mouton, 1977). For further bibliography, especially on poverty in the Christian context, see Pauline Allen, Bronwen Neil, and Wendy Mayer, *Preaching Poverty in Late Antiquity: Perceptions and Realities* (Leipzig: Evangelische Verlagsanstalt, 2009), 15–16.

the question of why poverty and the poor entered the elite discourses at all, Greg Woolf emphasizes: "poverty was evoked as a vantage point from which to scrutinize wealth."[8] "For those who produced and consumed this texualised poverty, the poor must have seemed a distant and largely undifferentiated mass, the diachrony of their individual tragedies blurring into a static background of endemic misery."[9] Stigmatization and pathologization of poverty were prevalent within the political and moral discourses in the Greco-Roman world. In the eyes of Seneca, who preached practicing "poverty," poverty itself was a bad thing, classed with grief (*luctus*), disgrace (*ignominia*), distress (*dolor*), illness (*morbum*), exile (*exilium*), and death (*mors*).[10] Poverty was often associated with untrustworthiness.[11] Being poor was understood as an evil, symptomatic of being forsaken by fortune.[12]

One should note, however, that even before the episcopal "invention of the poor,"[13] certain philosophical and moral functions were sometimes allocated to poverty. It was a trope, for example, to link (alleged) poverty, especially that of the Roman nobles in the republican period, to such traditional, long-lost values and virtues as simplicity, frugality, diligence, incorruptibility, and lack of greed.[14] It was also familiar to construe poverty as an antidote to the dependence on material goods and the accompanying anxieties.[15] The goddess Pauperies (*dea Pauperies*) can be described as *obnoxia, immunda,* or *importuna*,[16] but it was possible to use *proba* as a qualifier for her.[17] Dio Chrysostom even suggested thinking about poverty as offering "innumerable opportunities from earning a living to those who want to work independently that are neither dishonourable nor harmful."[18] Yet, all of these represented people of means looking at poverty and the poor from a safe distance. Not only did this "texualized poverty" bear little on the lived experience of the poor, but, more significantly, it trivialized real poverty.[19]

8. Greg Woolf, "Writing Poverty in Rome," in Atkins and Osborne, *Poverty in the Roman World,* 91.

9. Woolf, "Writing Poverty in Rome," 84; see also Parkin, "Poverty in the Early Roman Empire," vi, contra "blanketing approaches" taken by Prell and Meggitt.

10. Vincent J. Rosivach, "Seneca on the Fear of Poverty in the *Epistulae Morales,*" *L'Antiquité Classique* 64, no. 1 (1995), 93, with note 8.

11. Valerius Maximus, 2.3.

12. Dio Chrysostom, *Or.* 63.1.

13. Peter Brown, *Poverty and Leadership in the Later Roman Empire* (Hanover, NH: University Press of New England, 2002).

14. Valerius Maximus 4.2; 8.7. ext. 11; Knapp, *Invisible Romans,* 251–52.

15. Rosivach, "Seneca on the Fear of Poverty," 91–98.

16. *AE* 1916.7 = *AE* 1916.8 (Sitifis, Mauretania Caesariensis); Horace, *Epistulae* 2.2.199; Horace, *Carmina* 3.16.37.

17. Horarce, *Carm.* 3.29.55.

18. Dio Chrysostom, *Or.* 7.103, trans. Parkin and Pomeroy, *Roman Social History,* 220.

For the wealthy who at times practiced "poverty" in Seneca the Younger's writings, for example, it meant having a few slaves, downgrading silverware to earthenware, and the like. The humorous and/or ironic intent of Martial and Juvenal, who wrote copiously about poverty, misery, and mistreatment, also cautions us not to take their writings at face value.[20] While distancing ourselves from the stylized poverty in the Roman literature is a crucial step toward a sophisticated investigation into real poverty in the Roman world, it also raises the question of where we can turn for sources. Methodologically speaking, there has been a shift from primarily text-based examination to multidisciplinary studies informed by and integrating demographic, bioarchaeological, and comparative approaches. It should also be noted that L. L. Welborn argues against a dismissive tendency toward ancient texts and calls for a closer look at the glimpses of "realities" that they reveal.[21]

Second, the past decade has seen an outpouring of effort on quantifying and modeling the stratification of Roman society (see Timothy A. Brookins's chapter in this volume).[22] In 2004, Steven Friesen suggested a seven-layer "poverty scale," in which about 68 percent of the population in the urban contexts belonged to the two lowest strata, where people lived at or below the subsistence level. This scheme was further refined in the 2009 *Journal of Roman Studies* (*JRS*) article coauthored by Friesen and Scheidel, in which the nonelite income scale was minutely divided into nine levels ranging from the highest level, estimated at 8.4 to 10 times subsistence, to the lowest level (starvation).[23] Taking into consideration their results, Bruce Longenecker suggests that in the urban contexts, the elite, the middling groups, the vulnerable, and those at or below the subsistence level constituted 3 percent,

19. Rosivach, "Seneca on the Fear of Poverty," 95–96. Also see Steven M. Beaudoin, *Poverty in World History* (London: Routledge, 2007), 27.
20. Neville Morley, "The Poor in the City of Rome," in Atkins and Osborne, *Poverty in the Roman World*, 26.
21. Welborn, "Polis and the Poor," 189–244.
22. Steven J. Friesen, "Poverty in Pauline Studies: Beyond the So-Called New Consensus." *JSNT* 26, no. 3 (2004): 323–61; Walter Scheidel, "Stratification, Deprivation and Quality of Life," in Atkins and Osborne, *Poverty in the Roman World*, 40–59; Walter Scheidel and Steven J. Friesen, "The Size of the Economy and the Distribution of Income in the Roman Empire," *JRS* 99 (2009): 61–91; Bruce W. Longenecker, "Exposing the Economic Middle: A Revised Economy Scale for the Study of Early Urban Christianity," *JSNT* 31, no. 3 (2009): 243–78; Bruce W. Longenecker, *Remember the Poor: Paul, Poverty, and the Greco-Roman World* (Grand Rapids: Eerdmans, 2010); Ben-Zion Rosenfeld and Haim Perlmutter, "The Poor as a Stratum of Jewish Society in Roman Palestine 70–250 CE: An Analysis," *Historia* 60, no. 3 (2011), 273–300; Travis B. Williams, "Benefiting the Community through Good Works? The Economic Feasibility of Civic Benefaction in 1 Peter," *JGRChJ* 9 (2013): 147–95.
23. Scheidel and Friesen, "Size of the Economy," 61–91, esp. table 7 on p. 83.

15 percent, 27 percent, and 55 percent respectively of the population.[24] Despite the differences in the estimations, these scholars all place the majority of the population at or below the subsistence level, although they also apportion niches for the middling groups. The scaling of the Roman economy contributes to deconstructing the binary model that "reflects the rhetorical differentiation that is common in Greco-Roman literature, in which the respectable elite are contrasted with the ordinary poor."[25] Although the elite authors sometimes differentiated the respectable (in their view) part of the common people (*pars populi integra*) from the rest of the common people,[26] the nonelite were usually collectively referred to as *plebs, populus, multitudo,* οἱ πολλοί, τὸ πλῆθος, δῆμος, and so on and characterized in a negative way. A wide range of pejorative qualifiers, such as lazy, ignorant, insolent, violent, useless, credulous, dirty, seditious, and so on, were often applied to the masses.[27] The political dimension was thus embedded in the socioeconomic stratification.[28]

The effort to explore the economic gradation of the Romans not only brings out the complexity of the composition of the *plebs* but also serves to highlight that the understanding of the poor is closely intertwined with larger socioeconomic and political issues, such as the scale of the Roman economy vis-à-vis distribution of wealth, the Malthusian checks and the margin of growth of Roman economy, the structure and level of taxation, and the elite perceptions of the place of the *plebs*. In recent years, a series of articles have also explored Roman living standards by looking at the purchasing power of the earnings of the Roman workers.[29] Some are more optimistic than others in their estimation of the quality of life in the Roman Empire. The dearth and the frag-

---

24. Longenecker, *Remember the Poor*, 53.

25. Ibid., 40; Morley, "Poor in the City," 21–27.

26. E.g., Tacitus, *Historiae* 1.4.

27. Morley, "Poor in the City," 26–27; Suzanne Said, "Plutarch and the People in the Parallel Lives," in *The Statesman in Plutarch's Works*, vol. 2, *The Statesman in Plutarch's Greek and Roman Lives*, ed. Lukas de Blois, Jeroen Bons, Ton Kessels, and Dirk M. Schenkeveld (Leiden: Brill, 2005), 7–25.

28. Morley, "Poor in the City," 27.

29. Morris Silver, "*Roman Economic Growth and Living Standards: Perceptions versus Evidence*," Ancient Society 37 (2007): 191–252; Robert C. Allen, "How Prosperous Were the Romans? Evidence from Diocletian's Price Edict (AD 301)," in *Quantifying the Roman Economy: Methods and Problems*, ed. Alan Bowman and Andrew Wilson (Oxford: Oxford University Press, 2009), 327–45; Dominic W. Rathbone, "Earnings and Costs: Living Standards and the Roman Economy (First to Third Centuries AD)," in Bowman and Wilson, *Quantifying the Roman Economy*, 299–326; Walter Scheidel, "Real Wages in Early Economies: Evidence for Living Standards from 1800 BCE to 1300 CE," *Journal of the Economic and Social History of the Orient* 53, no. 3 (2010): 425–62; Walter Scheidel, "Roman Real Wages in Context," in *Quantifying the Greco-Roman Economy and Beyond*, ed. François de Callataÿ (Bari, ITA: Edipuglia, 2014), 209–18.

mentary state of data on wages and prices make quantification a risky endeavor, however. More often than not, the margin of error is also increased rather than minimized by methodological difficulties.

Third, the application of scientific techniques to the analysis of archaeological materials, especially the organic remains such as skeletons, waste, and so on from the Roman world, has made important contributions to expanding our overall knowledge of health, hygiene, disease, and diet across social classes and through the life cycle of individuals, and will continue to do so.[30] One should heed the caveats that archaeometry is not immune from interpretative challenges and that it does not hold the keys to all of our questions. For example, while overall "skeletal lesions or features . . . are considered good indicators of health and nutritional status, causes for them are numerous and range from infectious diseases . . . to malnutrition and physiological traumas. Many of these skeletal lesions and features are nonspecific to a particular disease or stressor, so diagnosis is often difficult or impossible on the basis of osteological data alone."[31] In the area of anthropometry, not only is it highly challenging to estimate height based on skeletal remains—the stature estimates for the Roman period have diverged from 164.4 cm (male) and 152.1 cm (female) to 168.4 cm or higher—the correlation between stature, nutritional status, and life expectancy is also complex.[32] In terms of paleodietary studies, isotopic analysis of

30. E.g., Tracy Prowse, Henry P. Schwarcz, Shelley Saunders, Roberto Macchiarelli, and Luca Bondioli, "Isotopic Paleodiet Studies of Skeletons from the Imperial Roman-Age Cemetery of Isola Sacra, Rome, Italy," *Journal of Archaeological Science* 31, no. 3 (2004): 259–72; Tracy Prowse, Henry P. Schwarcz, Shelley Saunders, Roberto Macchiarelli, and Luca Bondioli, "Isotopic Evidence for Age-Related Variation in Diet from Isola Sacra, Italy," *American Journal of Physical Anthropology* 128, no. 1 (2005): 2–13; O. E. Craig, M. Biazzo, T. C. O'Connell, P. Garnsey, C. Martinez-Labarga, R. Lelli, L. Salvadei et al., "Stable Isotopic Evidence for Diet at the Imperial Coastal Site of Velia (1st and 2nd Centuries AD) in Southern Italy," *American Journal of Physical Anthropology* 139, no. 4 (2009), 572–83; R. L. Gowland and P. Garnsey, "Skeletal Evidence for Health, Nutritional Status and Malaria in Rome and the Empire," in *Roman Diasporas: Archaeological Approaches to Mobility and Diversity in the Roman Empire*, ed. Hella Eckhardt (Portsmouth, RI: Journal of Roman Archaeology, 2010), 131–56; Tracy L. Prowse, "Diet and Dental Health through the Life Course in Roman Italy," in *Social Bioarchaeology*, ed. Sabrina C. Agarwal and Bonnie A. Glencross (Oxford: Wiley-Blackwell, 2011), 416; Martin Pitts and Rebecca Griffin, "Exploring Health and Social Well-Being in Late Roman Britain: An Intercemetery Approach," *AJA* 116, no. 2 (2012): 252–55; Patrick Denis Beauchesne, "Physiological Stress, Bone Growth and Development in Imperial Rome" (PhD diss., University of California, Berkeley, 2012); Kristina Killgrove and Robert H. Tykot, "Food for Rome: A Stable Isotope Investigation of Diet in the Imperial Period (1st–3rd centuries AD)," *Journal of Anthropological Archaeology* 32, no. 1 (2013): 28–38; Peter Garnsey and Richard Saller, *The Roman Empire: Economy, Society and Culture*, 2nd ed. (Oakland: University of California Press, 2015), 33, with bibliography; for a survey and bibliography of isotopic studies of materials from Roman Britain, see Gundula Müldner, "Stable Isotopes and Diet: Their Contribution to Romano-British Research," *Antiquity* 87, no. 335 (2013): 137–49.

31. Michael MacKinnon, "Osteological Research in Classical Archaeology," *AJA* 111, no. 3 (2007): 480–81.

the thermally altered bones, such as those found in cremation burials, which were prevalent before the third century CE, are less useful than the analysis of inhumed skeletons.[33]

One should also note that while archaeologies of poverty have become increasingly significant in the archaeologies of the later periods and in other regions, classical archaeology in general is lagging behind in this area.[34] While it is granted that studies of *insulae* and the *puticuli* directly concern the conditions of the poor in the city of Rome in life and death, classical archaeology has been predominantly "an elitist archaeology focused on public monuments and upper-class life style" until very recently.[35] As a fast-growing field, the archaeology of sanitation has confirmed what we have learned from the literary sources about the squalor of the Roman cities and the omnipresence of a wide range of parasites.[36] Social differentiation of morbidity and mortality, however, is not always easy to achieve based on the epigraphic and osteological materials that we have. Cases have been made for seasonal patterns of death under the influence of infectious diseases, especially malaria,[37] but questions about whether there might

32. Laura Ottini, S. Minozzi, W. B. Pantano, C. Maucci, V. Gazzaniga, L. R. Angeletti, P. Catalano, and R. Mariani-Costantini, "A Subject with Abnormally Short Stature from Imperial Rome," *Journal of Endocrinological Investigation* 24, no. 7 (2001): 546–48; Geoffrey Kron, "Anthropometry, Physical Anthropology, and the Reconstruction of Ancient Health, Nutrition, and Living Standards," *Historia* 54, no. 1 (2005): 68–83; Simona Minozzi, Paola Catalano, Carla Caldarini, and Gino Fornaciari, "Palaeopathology of Human Remains from the Roman Imperial Age," *Pathobiology* 79, no. 5 (2012): 268–83. Gowland and Garnsey, "Skeletal Evidence," 151, disagree with Kron's calculation of mean stature of "late Iron Age and Roman era Italian males" and his optimistic assessment of the health status of the Romans.
33. Christopher W. Schmidt and Steve A. Symes, *The Analysis of Burned Human Remains* (Amsterdam: Elsevier, 2008), 106–7.
34. There was no contribution from classical archaeology to the second thematic issue of *Historical Archaeology* in 2011 devoted to "Archaeologies of Poverty." See also Charles E. Orser, "The Archaeology of Poverty and the Poverty of Archaeology," *International Journal of Historical Archaeology* 15, no. 4 (2011), 533–43.
35. Stephen L. Dyson, *Rome: A Living Portrait of an Ancient City* (Baltimore: Johns Hopkins University Press, 2010), 241.
36. Gemma C. M. Jansen, Ann Olga Koloski-Ostrow, and Eric M. Moormann, eds., *Roman Toilets: Their Archaeology and Cultural History* (Leuven: Peeters, 2011); Ann Olga Koloski-Ostrow, *The Archaeology of Sanitation in Roman Italy: Toilets, Sewers, and Water Systems* (Chapel Hill: University of North Carolina Press, 2015); Piers D. Mitchell, "Human Parasites in the Roman World: Health Consequences of Conquering an Empire," *Parasitology*, 2016, 1–11. Cf. Alex Scobie, "Slums, Sanitation and Mortality in the Roman World," *Klio* 68 (1986): 399–433.
37. Brent D. Shaw, "Seasons of Death: Aspects of Mortality in Imperial Rome," *JRS* 86 (1996): 100–138; Brent D. Shaw, "Seasonal Mortality in Imperial Rome and the Mediterranean: Three Problem Cases," in *Urbanism in the Preindustrial World: Cross-Cultural Approaches*, ed. Glenn R. Storey (Tuscaloosa: University of Alabama Press, 2006) 86–109; Walter Scheidel, "Germs for Rome," in *Rome the Cosmopolis*, ed. Catharine Edwards and Greg Woolf (Cambridge: Cambridge University Press, 2003), 158–76; Walter Scheidel, "'Germs for Rome' 10 Years After," in *Les affaires de Monsieur Andreau: économie et société du monde romain*, ed. Catherine Apicella, Marie-Laurence Haack, and

have been alternative patterns of death for the very poor cannot be readily addressed since they left no epitaphs to mark the months of their death.[38]

Although physical marks or expressions of poverty can now be traced through osteological studies, it is a much greater challenge to probe into the psychological dimension of poverty. In the fields of psychology, neuroscience, social work, and so on, there has emerged over the past few decades a large body of literature on the psychological effects of poverty.[39] Importantly, this literature brings out not only the negative impact of poverty but also the resilience of the poor.[40] For the ancient world, these topics are necessarily difficult to pursue and have only recently incurred scholarly attention. Scholars have turned to fables, proverbs, curse tablets, dream literature, and medical writings to recover oral traditions and the psychological world of the nonelite, especially slaves and the poor.[41] What emerges from these sources is the theme of the world perceived as a harsh and unforgiving place dominated by inequality, hostility, and fear. On the other hand, as Sara Forsdyke notes, "fables often simultaneously inculcate strategies for managing relations with the powerful in ways that optimize gains for the weak."[42]

As the study of poverty moves toward a more integrated mode of inquiry, it becomes important to revisit the taxonomy and terminologies that have been customarily used in the field. The conventional taxonomy of poverty differentiates "structural, conjunctural, and occasional poverty, also known as endemic, epidemic and episodic poverty."[43] The usefulness of such differentiation for the Roman world,

François Lerouxel (Bordeaux: Ausonius Éditions, 2014), 281–91; Gowland and Garnsey, "Skeletal Evidence." For changing patterns of seasonal death, see Kyle Harper, "A Time to Die: Preliminary Notes on Seasonal Mortality in Late Antique Rome," in *Children and Family in Late Antiquity. Life, Death and Interaction*, ed. Christian Laes, Katariina Mustakallio, and Ville Vuolanto (Leuven: Peeters, 2015), 15–34.

38. For a study of differential mortality due to diet and status in later periods, see Susan E. Klepp, "Seasoning and Society: Racial Differences in Mortality in Eighteenth Century Philadelphia," *William and Mary Quarterly* 51, no. 3 (1994): 473–507.

39. Mical Raz, *What's Wrong with the Poor? Psychiatry, Race, and the War on Poverty* (Chapel Hill: University of North Carolina Press, 2013).

40. Karen Seccombe, "'Beating the Odds' versus 'Changing the Odds': Poverty, Resilience, and Family Policy," *Journal of Marriage and Family* 64, no. 2 (2002): 384–94.

41. Teresa Morgan, *Popular Morality in the Early Roman Empire* (Cambridge: Cambridge University Press, 2007); Toner, *Popular Culture*; Knapp, *Invisible Romans*, 97–124; Sara Forsdyke, *Slaves Tell Tales: And Other Episodes in the Politics of Popular Culture in Ancient Greece* (Princeton: Princeton University Press, 2012); William V. Harris, *Mental Disorders in the Classical World* (Leiden: Brill, 2013), esp. Jerry Toner's chapter, "The Psychological Impact of Disasters in the Age of Justinian."

42. Forsdyke, *Slaves Tell Tales*, 59, 60–61; cf. Knapp, *Invisible Romans*, 118.

43. Peter Garnsey, "Mass Diet and Nutrition," in *Cities, Peasants and Food in Classical Antiquity: Essays*

however, has already been (mostly mildly) doubted.[44] The distinction between structural and conjunctural poverty, or permanent and temporary poverty, is often difficult to maintain. Although at the micro level, poverty was by no means static, it was structural factors that caused and exacerbated poverty and rendered episodic poverty irremediable. These structural factors or variables included land-owning patterns, modes of resource allocation, (lack of) mechanisms of social mobility, gender relations dominated by patriarchal hierarchy, and so on. It is precisely because of the institutionalized inequality and limited space of structural chances that we hear more about episodic poverty, caused by individual, circumstantial "misfortunes" including bad harvests / high grain prices, unemployment, sudden illness, debt/ insolvency, absent husbands, death of bread-earning spouses, divorce, and so on. In these scenarios, poverty was associated with personal failure or circumstances, and the blame or onus of alleviating it fell on the allegedly "conjunctural" poor themselves rather than the structural, artificial factors. Some of the ancient authors did recognize Roman imperialism, injustice, economic exploitation, and so on as causes of poverty,[45] although even those who condemned these factors as sources of vulnerability did not propose or advocate changes at the structural level.[46]

To understand urban poverty in the Roman world, it is necessary to look at what "urban" meant, how many people were urban dwellers, and what, if anything, distinguished urban poor from rural poor. Different estimations of the number of cities in the Roman Empire and of the population of urban centers of various sizes have resulted in varying estimations of the percentage of urban population in the Roman world.[47] High and low counts have both been proposed, and regional variations have not escaped notice. Scheidel and Friesen suggest that

in *Social and Economic History* (Cambridge: Cambridge University Press, 1998), 226–27; Parkin, "Poverty in the Early Roman Empire," 26; Morley, "Poor in the City," 36.

44. William V. Harris, "Poverty and Destitution in the Roman Empire," in *Rome's Imperial Economy: Twelve Essays* (Oxford: Oxford University Press, 2011), 29, 33, 50–51; Claire Holleran, "Migration and the Urban Economy of Rome," in *Demography and the Graeco-Roman World: New Insights and Approaches*, ed. Claire Holleran and April Pudsey (Cambridge: Cambridge University Press, 2011), 175–77; Welborn, "Polis and the Poor," 197–98.

45. Steven J. Friesen, "Injustice or God's Will? Early Christian Explanations of Poverty," in *Wealth and Poverty in Early Church and Society*, ed. Susan R. Holman (Grand Rapids: Baker Academic, 2008), 18–26, citing Revelation and James (Jacob in Friesen's view).

46. Longenecker, *Remember the Poor*, 107.

47. The bibliography is extensive, see Luuk de Ligt and Simon Northwood, *People, Land, and Politics: Demographic Developments and the Transformation of Roman Italy 300 BC–AD 14* (Leiden: Brill, 2008); Paul Erdkamp, "Urbanism," in Walter Scheidel, *The Cambridge Companion to the Roman Economy* (Cambridge: Cambridge University Press, 2012), 241–65.

15 percent of the Greco-Roman population lived in urban contexts. For Roman Britain, Millett's calculation is that the urban population may have only been a little over 6 percent of the overall population.[48] For Italy, Morley is willing to assign 25 percent to cities excluding Rome, and almost 40 percent if Rome is included.[49] Despite the disparities in estimations, there are general consensuses on two points: that the majority of the Roman population lived in nonurban contexts and that many Roman cities had no more than a few thousand inhabitants.[50] These points are important because they complicate the understanding of "urban" as well as the sources and structures of income for the urban dwellers. Paul Erdkamp has rightly emphasized "that the division between town and countryside does not completely overlap with the division between agricultural and non-agricultural sectors of the economy."[51] Compared with the countryside, the urban centers may be characterized with higher population density, more restricted access to natural resources, higher concentration of skilled laborers, and volatile job opportunities, but better access to benefactions as well as certain amenities such as baths, fountains, and entertainment facilities. Yet, a city and countryside divide may not have been particularly salient for smaller urban centers where "a significant part of their residents were part of the agricultural sector."[52] The urban and country divide is also complicated by immigration of country dwellers into cities,[53] which means the same person may have different experiences at different stages of their life. It is, therefore, difficult to speak of normative experiences of the "urban" poor.

Subsistence Living: The Quantitative and Qualitative Aspects

Greek and Latin have a rich collection of words that refer to poverty and the poor, including *paupertas, pauper, inopia, inops, egens, tenuis,*

48. Martin Millett, *Roman Britain* (London: Batsford, 2005), 21; cf. Michael J. Jones, "Cities and Urban Life," in *A Companion to Roman Britain*, ed. Malcolm Todd (London: Historical Association, 2004), 187.
49. Neville Morley, *Metropolis and Hinterland: The City of Rome and the Italian Economy, 200 B.C.–A.D. 200* (Cambridge: Cambridge University Press, 1996), 182.
50. Erdkamp, "Urbanism," 246.
51. Ibid. Cf. J. A. North, "Religion and Rusticity," in *Urban Society in Roman Italy*, ed. Tim Cornell and Kathryn Lomas (New York: St. Martin's Press, 1995), 145.
52. Erdkamp, "Urbanism," 246.
53. Holleran, "Migration and the Urban Economy," 155–80; Paul Erdkamp, "Seasonal Labour and Rural-Urban Migration in Roman Italy," in *Migration and Mobility in the Early Roman Empire*, ed. Luuk de Ligt and Laurens E. Tacoma (Leiden: Brill, 2016), 33–49; Seth Bertrand, "Food Distributions and Immigrations in Imperial Rome," in Ligt and Tacoma, *Migration and Mobility*, 50–71.

indigens, mendicans, ptochos, penia, penes, deomenos, and so on. At the semantic level, these are all terms indicative of wanting, lacking, and absence. Ancient writers often, but not always, differentiated poverty and destitution.[54] The exact economic sense of poverty and destitution, however, was much more nebulous.[55] A small number of epitaphs, either self-commemorative or put up by relatives or friends, for both genders and for people of freeborn, freed, or servile status, specifically used the word *pauper* to refer to the deceased.[56] Yet, these self-styled paupers were by no means penniless or homeless. In the commemorative context, the term *pauper* was not only collocated with terms of virtue but itself was often presented as a virtue or certain praiseworthy, recommendable quality. Even when *pauper* or *paupertas* were used in the economic sense on these epitaphs, they were represented as constituting a non-obstacle to integrity or respectability. This corpus of epitaphs informs us more of the sub-elite's aspiration to respectability and dignity than poverty itself.[57]

Much effort has been made to quantify subsistence living in absolute terms for the Roman world. The absolute measure usually uses indicators of basic biological and physiological needs, such as calorie intake, to define poverty. Since the minimum calorie intake is measured in balance with energy expenditure, there is considerable variation in the calorie requirement of individuals depending on their workload, age, sex, activity level, body mass, climate, and so on, and scholarly opinions differ as to the benchmark for calorie needs in the Roman period. Based on the GU Nährwert Tabelle 1994,[58] for men in the age range between nineteen and twenty-five, Marcus Prell uses 2,600, 3,800, and 4,200 calories per capita per day for light, ordinary, and heavy manual laborers respectively, 2,200 calories for women, and 2,000 calories for the others. In his calculation, a family comprising a male manual laborer, his wife, and three children would need 11,800 calories a day (or an average of 2,360 calories per person/day).[59] Based on the Food

---

54. Morley, "Poor in the City," 29. Cf. Whittaker, "The Poor"; Harris, "Poverty and Destitution"; Welborn, "Polis and the Poor," 198–99.

55. Longenecker, *Remember the Poor*, 37.

56. In particular, *CIL* I.1212 = *ILS* 7602; *CIL* IX. 5659=*AE* 2001. 921; *CIL* II. 4315= *ILS* 5301; *AE* 1957. 3a= *RIT* 441= *AE* 1962.189; *CIL* VI 2489 = VI 32649 = *ILS* 2028; *CIL* III. 2835 = *ILS* 2257; Haidra 6. 16 = EDCS-65600177; *ILAlg* II–III 8467 = *AE* 1966. 539 = *AE* 1992. 1880; *AE* 2003. 567. See also *CIL* VI 8012 = *ILS* 8436; *CIL* IX. 3358.

57. Paul Veyne, "La 'plèbe moyenne' sous le Haut-Empire romain," *Annales* 55, no. 6 (2000), 1170; Peter Brown, *Through the Eye of a Needle: Wealth, the Fall of Rome, and the Making of Christianity in the West, 350–550 AD* (Princeton: Princeton University Press, 2012), 342–44.

58. Ibrahim Elmafda, *Die große GU-Nährwert-Tabelle: Kalorien/Joule- und Nährstoffgehalte unserer Lebensmittel auf einen Blick*, 2nd ed. (Munich: Gräfe und Unzer, 1994).

and Agriculture Organization of the United Nations (FAO) / World Health Organization (WHO) joint report on energy and protein requirements from 1971, Travis Williams postulates that a hypothetical Anatolian household composed of a senior female, a couple, a teenage boy, and a teenage girl would need a total of 13,305 calories per day (or 2,661 calories per person/day).[60] William Harris criticizes the tendency to overstate the average Roman caloric intake influenced by the standard of modern industrialized countries and prefers the 2,000 calories benchmark proposed by Keith Hopkins. Hopkins uses a rounded figure of 250 kg (37 *modii*) of wheat equivalent as the minimum survival ration, which covers food intake of 2,000 calories per person per day, 15 kg wheat-equivalent per person per year for clothing, and an equal amount for heat and housing. But he does note: "At this rate of consumption, many/most people would feel hungry and lethargic."[61] Harris is in favor of an even lower average survival ration on the grounds that only adult males were subject to poll-tax, a large percentage of the population (perhaps 35 percent) was children, low calorie intake does not lead to immediate death, and so on.[62] In a more elaborate scheme, Scheidel and Friesen use wheat-equivalent of 164 kg as the benchmark for the starvation level, 164–327 kg as below subsistence level, and 327–491 kg as "at or close to subsistence," where ca. 390 and 335 are used as the minimal gross and net subsistence incomes respectively—both include clothes, fuel, and shelter.[63]

The estimation of 390 kg of wheat equivalent as the minimal gross subsistence income—that is, tax inclusive income—is arguably still on the low side. It leaves little room for sickness or any emergency situation. Nor does it allow for costs associated with death and burial. In addition, both calorie intake and wheat equivalent are crude measurements for poverty in that they flatten food composition and obscure the nutritional values of food intake. Even if the McKeown thesis, which gives primacy to nutrition as the factor explaining modern mor-

59. Prell, *Sozialökonomische Untersuchungen Zur Armut*, 103, 189.
60. Williams, "Benefiting the Community," 173.
61. Keith Hopkins, "Rome, Taxes, Rent, and Trade," in *The Ancient Economy*, ed. Walter Scheidel and Sitta von Reden (New York: Routledge, 2002), 197–98; see also Scheidel and Friesen, "Size of the Economy," 65, citing Colin Clark and Margaret Haswell, *The Economics of Subsistence Agriculture*, 4th ed. (London: Macmillan, 1970), 59–64.
62. Harris, "Poverty and Destitution," 41–42.
63. Scheidel and Friesen, "Size of the Economy," 83; Clark and Haswell, *Economics of Subsistence Agriculture*, 64–65. Data from the Auschwitz Concentration Camp also indicate that ca. 1,700 calories per day for those engaged in hard labor and ca. 1,300 calories per day for the others are dangerous starvation-level rations.

tality decline,[64] has been challenged, there is a large amount of literature on the intricate relationship between malnutrition, morbidity, and mortality.[65] Insufficient or unbalanced intake of calories, protein, and vitamins adversely affects child development, impairs the immune system, and reduces resistance to bacteria, parasites, and viral infections. Parasites and infectious diseases, in turn, obstruct absorption of nutrients from food, exacerbating malnutrition and obstructing restoration of the immune system. The synergistic relationship between malnutrition and infectious diseases is particularly pertinent, especially since the last few decades have brought the crowdedness, squalor, and infectious diseases that were omnipresent in the city of Rome and other bigger cities into sharp focus.[66] It is true that all urban social strata shared the larger living environment and that parasites and infectious diseases do not respect socioeconomic status. It is also true that certain groups, especially infants and pregnant and lactating women across classes, tended to be more vulnerable.[67] Yet, disease is not a physical or biological experience alone, but involves social and economic consequences. The poor were not only exposed to greater risk factors but would also experience more difficulty with recuperation and suffer more serious economic consequences due to reduced or lost work capacity or productivity, all of which would feed into each other and form a vicious cycle.[68] In addition, the wealthy were more mobile than the poor. In the high season of malaria, the Senate adjourned to allow the senators to escape from the city.[69] In 289 CE,

---

64. John M. Kim, "Nutrition and the Decline of Mortality," in *The Cambridge World History of Food*, ed. Kenneth F. Kiple and Kriemhild Coneè Ornelas (Cambridge: Cambridge University Press, 2000), 1383.

65. E.g., Peter Garnsey, *Food and Society in Classical Antiquity* (Cambridge: Cambridge University Press, 1999), 43–61; S. J. Ulijaszek, "Relationships between Undernutrition, Infection, and Growth and Development," *Human Evolution* 11, no. 3–4 (1996): 233–48; Philip C. Calder, Catherine J. Field, and Harsharnjit S. Gill, eds., *Nutrition and Immune Function* (New York: CABI Publishing, 2002); Michael L. Latham, *Human Nutrition in the Developing World* (Rome: Food and Agriculture Organization of the United Nations, 1997).

66. Scobie, "Slums, Sanitation and Mortality," 399–433; Valerie M. Hope and Eireann Marshall, eds., *Death and Disease in the Ancient City* (London: Routledge, 2000); Scheidel, "Germs for Rome," 158–76; Scheidel, "'Germs for Rome' 10 Years After," 281–91; Walter Scheidel, "Disease and Death," in *The Cambridge Companion to Ancient Rome*, ed. Paul Erdkamp (Cambridge: Cambridge University Press, 2013), 45–59; Neville Morley, "The Salubriousness of the Roman City," in *Health in Antiquity*, ed. Helen King (London: Routledge, 2005); Rena van den Bergh, "The Plight of the Poor Urban Tenant," *Revue Internationale des droits de l'Antiquité* 50 (2003): 443–77 (at 444); Koloski-Ostrow, *Archaeology of Sanitation*, 53; Mitchell, "Human Parasites."

67. Garnsey, *Food and Society*, 49.

68. World Health Organization, *Global Report for Research on Infectious Diseases of Poverty* (Geneva: World Health Organization, 2012).

69. Scheidel, "Germs for Rome," 66. Cf. Seneca, *Epistulae morales* 104.

when two thousand people died daily in the city of Rome, the emperor and his court were at the Villa Quintiliana near Laurentum.[70]

Poverty takes a heavy toll on infants and children. While suspecting that acute childhood illness rather than poor nutrition was responsible for the stature of the population, because illness prevented children from growing as fast in antiquity, Ray Laurence not only acknowledges but also emphasizes the point that nutrition and wealth may dramatically affect health and illness, based on a comparison of the skeletal remains of two males aged 46 years from Herculaneum in terms of height and conditions of bones and teeth.[71] Differential growth in infancy and childhood can indeed be seen in the bioarchaeological data with high-status children being larger than their poorer counterparts.[72] Circumstances may also have hampered the poorer children from achieving catch-up growth before skeletal maturation. If they survived infancy, children of the poorer families belonged to the labor force.[73] Prolonged stress signifying labor activity (such as lifting heavy loads, rowing, and farm work) from childhood has been observed in skeletal remains.[74] The apprentices for weaving and other trades in the papyrological evidence tended to be twelve to fourteen (*aphēlikes*) years old, many of whom were freeborn boys. Formally arranged apprenticeship involved expenses such as sharing the maintenance cost of the child with the master, as well as the taxes levied on the apprentice, and a small registration fee at the notary office.[75] The free children whose parents could not afford to invest in their vocational training would be unskilled laborers, street peddlers, and so forth.

---

70. Herodian 1.12.2; Dio Cassius (Xiphilinus) 72.14.4; Whittaker, "The Poor," 285.
71. Ray Laurence, "Health and the Life Course at Herculaneum and Pompeii," in King, *Health in Antiqutiy*, 87, 90.
72. Rebecca C. Redfern and Rebecca L. Gowland, "A Bioarchaeological Perspective on the Pre-Adult Stages of the Life Course," in *Families in the Roman and Late Antique World*, ed. Mary Harlow and Lena Larsson Lovén (London: Continuum, 2012), 119.
73. Keith R. Bradley, *Discovering the Roman Family: Studies in Roman Social History* (New York: Oxford University Press, 1991), 103–24; Christian Laes, "Child Slaves at Work in Roman Antiquity," *Ancient Society* 38 (2008): 235–83 (includes information about free children); Christian Laes, *Children in the Roman Empire: Outsiders Within* (Cambridge: Cambridge University Press, 2011), ch. 5, "Roman Children at Work."
74. See Laurence, "Health and the Life Course," for bibliography. Luigi Capasso and Luisa Di Domenicantonio, "Work-Related Syndesmoses on the Bones of Children Who Died at Herculaneum," *Lancet* 352, no. 9140 (November 14, 1998), 1634.
75. *P. Wisc.* 1.4; *P. Oxy.* 2.275; *P. Oxy.* 2.310; *P. Mich.* 2.121 recto 2, 8; *P. Oxy.* 275, 2875, 2971; *P. Oxy. Hels.* 29; *P. Tebt.* 385. Sabine R. Huebner, *The Family in Roman Egypt: A Comparative Approach to Intergenerational Solidarity and Conflict* (Cambridge: Cambridge University Press, 2013), 62; Jinyu Liu, "Group Membership, Trust Networks, and Social Capital: A Critical Analysis," in *Work, Labour, and Professions in the Roman World*, ed. Koenraad Verboven and Christian Laes, Impact of Empire 23 (Leiden, Brill, 2016), 203–26.

Due to the seasonality of a wide range of jobs including construction, dock work, pottery production, and so on,[76] unemployment or shortage of orders was one of the major concerns for laborers and craftsmen. Robert Allen assumes 250 days of work per year for a Roman laborer, while Scheidel and Friesen use 225 days, both of which may have been too optimistic.[77] In the so-called "Parable of the Good Employer" (Matt 20:1–16),[78] the theological symbolism apart, the story is also a good illustration of the unpredictability that characterized the life of the laborers. Men waited in the marketplace (ἐν τῇ ἀγορᾷ) to be hired as day laborers or for odd jobs. Employers—in this particular case, a master of a household looking for helping hands for his vineyard—went to find laborers at the agora. Supply exceeded demand, which meant that not everyone would be picked and that choices were made at the employer's whim. The agreed payment was one denarius per person per day, which was paid at the end of the day. If employed every day, the man would be able to live at subsistence level.[79] But employment the next day was not guaranteed. Chronic irregularity of income was a source for not only economic but also psychological stress. In Artemidorus's *Oneirocritica* (*Book of Dreams*), dreams were interpreted in accordance to the status, gender, occupation, age, health state, and so on of the dreamers. Terms such as πένης, πενία, πενόμενος, ἐν ἐνδείᾳ, and ἀπορία were often collocated with σχολή, ἀπραξία, and ἀργία. Desire for business or employment and threat of unemployment were frequent themes.[80] To have a greater number of ears was interpreted as a good sign for an artisan (*andri cheirotechnēi*), for he was to hear many people "placing orders" (*ergodotōn*, literally "giving work").[81] For the purpose of dream interpretation, non-nutritious food, illness, and employment

---

76. Frontinus, *De Aquis* 2.123; Greg S. Aldrete and David J. Mattingly, "Feeding the City: The Organization, Operation, and Scale of the Supply System for Rome," in *Life, Death, and Entertainment in the Roman Empire*, ed. D. S. Potter and David J. Mattingly (Ann Arbor: University of Michigan Press, 1999), 171–204; Cameron Hawkins, "Contracts, Coercion, and the Boundaries of the Roman Artisanal Firm" in Verboven and Laes, *Work, Labour, and Professions*; Seth Bertrand, "Workers in the Roman Building Industry" in Verboven and Laes, *Work, Labour, and Professions*; Elisabeth Murphy, "Roman Workers and Their Workplaces: Some Archaeological Thoughts on the Organization of Workshop Labour in Ceramic Production," in Verboven and Laes, *Work, Labour and Professions*.

77. Allen, "How Prosperous?," 337; Scheidel and Friesen, "Size of the Economy," 70; Bertrand, "Food Distributions," 50–52.

78. Parkin and Pomeroy, *Roman Social History*, 215–16.

79. Cf. Scheidel and Friesen, "Size of the Economy," 12.

80. A. J. Pomeroy, "Status and Status-Concern in the Greco-Roman Dream-Books," *Ancient Society* 22 (1991): 62–65.

81. Artemidorus, *Oneirocritica* 1.24.

were closely linked.[82] Goat meat, therefore, indicated scanty work or business due to its boniness.[83]

Theories concerning how a "good" diet ensured "good" health were not lacking in antiquity, often informed by a humoral theory and with a philosophical emphasis on moderation, balance, and self-control in the background.[84] As Veronika Grimm has recently emphasized, with a moralizing agenda and a tendency to show off erudition, the ancient medical and literary sources on food are not particularly helpful with the question of "who ate what?"[85] Glimpses of the diets of the rural and urban poor, nevertheless, are present. In discussing properties of foodstuffs, as well as preparation methods he did not approve of, Galen provided us with information concerning food and dietary practices down the social scale, especially among the peasants and urban poor in Asia Minor.[86] Wheat was of supreme importance among cereals and could be consumed in the form of bread, flat-cake, and porridge. When describing pancakes made of wheaten flour and mixed with honey or sea salt, Galen also made a side note that country folks and very poor town dwellers made many other such flat-cakes.[87] Even in the form of bread, it is noted that, regarding unleavened and under-sieved bread flours especially associated with the diets of the poor, "unless baked in very thin sheets the resulting 'bread' is unpalatable and difficult to chew."[88]

Coarse and abrasive food is known from written sources and can also be traced in the archaeological record.[89] Apart from wheat, millet, barley, emmer, and rye were also consumed. Consumption of millet seems to be of greater extent in the rural areas than in the urban contexts.[90] At times of extreme hunger, the poor may have been forced to make

82. Pomeroy, "Status and Status-Concern," 66.
83. Artemidorus, *Oneirocritica* 1.70.
84. Vivian Nutton, *Ancient Medicine* (London: Routledge, 2004), 47, 58, 33–34; Mark Grant, *Galen on Food and Diet* (London: Routledge, 2000); Owen Powell, *Galen on the Properties of Foodstuffs: De Alimentorum Facultatibus* (Cambridge: Cambridge University Press, 2003); Joan P. Alcock, *Food in the Ancient World* (Westport, CT: Greenwood Press, 2006), esp. ch. 6, "Concepts of Diet and Nutrition."
85. Veronika Grimm, "On Food and the Body," in *A Companion to the Roman Empire*, ed. David S. Potter (Malden, MA: Blackwell, 2006), 354–68.
86. Garnsey and Woolf, "Patronage of the Rural Poor," 155.
87. Galen, *De alimentorum facultatibus* 1.3 (6.492K).
88. David L. Thurmond, *A Handbook of Food Processing in Classical Rome: For Her Bounty No Winter* (Leiden: Brill, 2006), 16.
89. Prell, *Sozialökonomische Untersuchungen Zur Armut*, 82; T. Braun, "Barley Cakes and Emmer Bread," in *Food in Antiquity*, ed. John Wilkins, David Harvey, and Mike Dobson (Exeter: University of Exeter Press, 1995), 25–37; Alastair Small, Carola Small, Richard Abdy, Alessandra De Stefano, Roberta Giuliani, Martin Henig, Kathryn Johnson et al., "Excavation in the Roman Cemetery at Vagnari, in the Territory of Gravina in Puglia, 2002," *Papers of the British School at Rome* 75 (2007): 159.
90. Killgrove and Tykot, "Food for Rome," 28–38.

bread from oats, which was "food for draught animals, not for men."[91] An urban diet was likely less varied than a rural diet.[92] But any diet that is heavily reliant on cereals has at least two issues. The first is that the consumption of this fiber-rich food, which also contains phytate, may interfere with absorption of iron and other nutrients. The second is that although wheat contains protein and a rich array of vitamins, it is deficient in vitamins A, C, D, and B12.[93] A diet that is composed of predominantly cereals and little else could easily result in eye diseases, rickets, and so on. The redress relies on diversifying the basket of food.

Papyrological materials point to the availability of various inexpensive legumes, including lentils, beans, chickpeas, flat beans, fenugreek, lupines, arakos, and so on, even for the poor.[94] In Roman Palestine, fruits and vegetables included legumes, olives, grapes, figs, dates, beets, cabbages, and squashes.[95] Root crops may have played an important role in the survival of the poor.[96] The nutritious values of these vegetables and fruits vary.[97] More importantly, their availability in most of the regions in the Roman Empire was subject to seasonal fluctuations. Fermented, cured, pickled, and dried goods were created for off-season consumption and for food that spoils easily.[98] Robert Allen has envisioned a "Mediterranean respectability basket" (per year), which is composed of bread (182 kg), beans/peas (52 L), meat (26 kg), olive oil (5.2 L), cheese (5.2 kg), eggs (52), wine (68.25 L), soap (2.6 kg), linen (5 m), candles (2.6), lamp oil (2.6 L), and fuel (5.0 MBtu).[99] For a similar respectability basket, Travis Williams has come up with an annual expense of approximately 557 denarii for a mid-level Anatolian household of five, or HS 445.6 per person per year.[100] Such a "respectability basket" or even its downgraded version was beyond the reach of the overwhelming majority of the Romans.[101]

91. Galen, *Alim. fac.* 1.14 (6.523); Powell, *Galen on the Properties of Foodstuffs,* 56. For fodder as food in time of dearth, see also Paul Erdkamp, *The Grain Market in the Roman Empire: A Social, Political and Economic Study* (Cambridge: Cambridge University Press, 2005), 149.

92. Paul Erdkamp, "The Food Supply of the Capital," in Erdkamp, *Cambridge Companion to Ancient Rome,* 262.

93. Alcock, *Food in the Ancient World,* 234; Garnsey, *Food and Society,* 19–22.

94. Roger S. Bagnall, *Egypt in Late Antiquity* (Princeton: Princeton University Press, 1993), 26–28.

95. Gildas Hamel, *Poverty and Charity in Roman Palestine, First Three Centuries C.E.* (Berkeley: University of California Press, 1990), 9.

96. Thurmond, *Handbook of Food Processing,* 169.

97. For beans, see Peter Garnsey, "The Bean: Substance and Symbol," in Garnsey and Scheidel, *Cities, Peasants and Food,* 214–25.

98. Thurmond, *Handbook of Food Processing,* passim.

99. Allen, "How Prosperous?," 334.

100. Williams, "Benefiting the Community," 184.

101. Scheidel, "Real Wages in Early Economies," 434.

The general consensus that the popular diet in the Roman Empire was largely grain and vegetable based has yet to be significantly challenged.[102] As W. Jongman notes, "Man's tragedy is that his most favoured food, meat, competes with himself for resources."[103] Except for pigs, animals such as sheep or cattle were not raised mainly for their meat. Recent research has not yielded conclusions that go much beyond what Mireille Corbier stated in 1989: "Meat remained an expensive food, but it was not a rarity reserved for a small number of occasions and for a small elite."[104] Cookshops and street food seemed prevalent in the urban contexts.[105] Peddlers sold a wide range of food including sausages, pastries, and all kinds of hot food on the street and at such open-access facilities as baths, as we learned from Seneca's complaint about the noise coming from these peddlers hawking their goods with different intonations.[106] Some of this food may have been refreshments of portable size such as chicken joints, mutton chops, and shellfish, which have been found at the drain of the baths inside the legionary fortress at Caerleon (Wales).[107] Yet, all this information only indicates the availability of meat in small chunks for sale to ordinary people. How much of it was consumed by the very poor cannot be answered.[108] Cribra orbitalia, or an increase in the porosity of the roof of the orbit, or eye socket, may be associated with anemia caused by parasitic infections or deficiency in vitamin B12 or folic acid.[109] It is important to note that B12 can only be obtained from animal sources.

102. Garnsey, "Mass Diet and Nutrition"; Garnsey, "Food and Society," 16; for bibliography, see Grimm, "Food and the Body," 360; Michael Beer, *Taste or Taboo: Dietary Choices in Antiquity* (Totnes, UK: Prospect Books, 2010). Michael MacKinnon, *Production and Consumption of Animals in Roman Italy: Integrating the Zooarchaeological and Textual Evidence* (Portsmouth, RI: Journal of Roman Archaeology, 2004); H. E. M. Cool, *Eating and Drinking in Roman Britain* (Cambridge: Cambridge University Press, 2006); Christophe Chandezon, "Animals, Meat, and Alimentary By-Products," in *A Companion to Food in the Ancient World*, ed. John Wilkins and Robin Nadeau (Chichester, UK: Wiley-Blackwell, 2015).

103. W. Jongman, "Adding It Up," in *Pastoral Economies in Classical Antiquity*, ed. C. R. Whittaker (Cambridge: Cambridge Philological Society, 1988), 212; Hamel, *Poverty and Charity*, 33; Grimm, "Food and the Body," 368.

104. Mireille Corbier, "The Ambiguous Status of Meat in Ancient Rome," *Food and Foodways* 3, no. 3 (1989): 224; Meggitt, *Paul, Poverty and Survival*, 109–12.

105. Steven J. R. Ellis, "The Distribution of Bars at Pompeii: Archaeological, Spatial and Viewshed Analyses," *JRA* 17 (2004): 371–84; Steven J. R. Ellis, "The Pompeian Bar: Archaeology and the Role of Food and Drink Outlets in an Ancient Community," *Food and History* 2, no. 1 (2004): 41–58.

106. Seneca, *Ep.* 56.2.

107. Lea Stirling, "Art, Architecture, and Archaeology in the Roman Empire," in Potter, *Companion to the Roman Empire*, 83.

108. Grimm, "Food and the Body."

109. Danny A. Milner, Jacqui Montgomery, Karl B. Seydel, and Stephen J. Rogerson, "Severe Malaria in Children and Pregnancy: An Update and Perspective," *Trends in Parasitology* 24, no. 12 (2008): 590–95, cited in Gowland and Garnsey, "Skeletal Evidence," 134, 147.

Meat can also counteract inhibition of absorption of iron caused by the phytate in the bran.[110] The high occurrence of cribra orbitalia at multiple sites may be suggestive, although not conclusively, of a low level of meat consumption.[111]

How much fish contributed to the nutrition of the Roman population remains a question that isotopic studies have only started to help settle.[112] It is not surprising that isotopic studies have detected consumption of seafood among the ordinary people at coastal sites such as Herculaneum, Isola Sacra, and Poundbury.[113] As the researchers have rightly noted, both Poundbury and Isola Sacra represent biased samples of Romans, the former being a prosperous port town and the latter being a military camp site. The researchers did not find significant correlation between isotopic values and burial type at Isola Sacra. But this may not lead to any definitive conclusion concerning dietary differentiation among different socioeconomic statuses, especially since the studies have relied on the skeletal remains, although many of the burials were of the cremation type, which are not easy to use for paleodietary studies because heat causes shifts in isotopic composition.[114] In Poundbury, social differentiation of food and dietary patterns has in fact been identified: the different isotopic values in high-status individuals (in lead coffins and mausoleums) and simple inhumations in earth graves or wooden coffins suggest that marine products were an elite food in Roman Britain.[115] As Annalisa Marzano has amply shown, "consumption of seafood, especially fresh fish, was both a status marker and a cultural signifier in the Roman world." In addition, not all the fish were the same: "marine fish were prized more than freshwater ones, and large species more than smaller ones."[116] Small fish and fry were for more modest consumption.[117] Processed, especially salt-cured, fish

110. Tom Brody, *Nutritional Biochemistry*, 2nd ed. (Amsterdam: Academic Press, 1999), 749–50.
111. L. Salvadei, F. Ricci, and G. Manzi, "Porotic Hyperostosis as a Marker of Health and Nutritional Conditions during Childhood: Studies at the Transition between Imperial Rome and the Early Middle Ages," *American Journal of Human Biology* 13, no. 6 (2001): 709–17; Mitchell, "Human Parasites in the Roman World," 2–3.
112. For bibliography on fish, see Garnsey and Saller, *The Roman Empire*, 33.
113. Peter Garnsey, "Bones and History: New Approaches to the Study of Diet and Health in the Ancient Mediterranean," trans. Yang Huang and Ying Xiong, *Historical Research* 5 (2006): 3–11; Prowse et al., "Isotopic Paleodiet Studies," 269–70.
114. Schmidt and Symes, *Analysis of Burned Human Remains*, 106–7.
115. M. P. Richards, R. E. M. Hedges, T. I. Molleson, and J. C. Vogel, "Stable Isotope Analysis Reveals Variations in Human Diet at the Poundbury Camp Cemetery Site," *Journal of Archaeological Science* 25, no. 12 (1998): 1247–52.
116. Annalisa Marzano, *Harvesting the Sea: The Exploitation of Marine Resources in the Roman Mediterranean* (Oxford: Oxford University Press, 2013), 300.
117. Galen, *Alim. fac.* 3.29 (6.721–22).

(*salsamenta*) probably represented a significant portion of a poor urban Roman's consumption of animal protein. Rich in glutamate, fish sauce, which seemed to be consumed at all levels, can be a good source of amino acids.

The Roman jurists defined "*vivere*" (to live) as pertaining not only to food (*cibum*), but also to clothing (*vestimenta* and *stramenta*), without which one cannot live.[118] It should be noted that clothing was not cheap. Making one's own clothing may not have even been an option for those poorer families who may not have owned a loom. The majority of the Romans would have possessed very few pieces of clothing. Mending was common.[119] Clothes were worn until they were worn out, and the parts that were still usable were recycled. Secondhand clothing was apparently circulated.[120] Pawnshops carrying stolen clothing, among other items, supplied the sources for the secondhand clothing market. Theft of clothing was frequent, as indicated by sources from legal discussions to curse tablets.[121] The beggars were invariably described as wearing torn rags.

Housing conditions are an important social determinant of health. As far as the housing conditions of the Roman poor are concerned, much attention has been given to the *insulae* of Rome. These apartment blocks suffered from structural defects arising from walls too thin to support the height of the building, the use of poor building materials, and so on. While collapse and fire threatened these buildings, the rooms were dark, damp, small, poorly ventilated, and crowded, which was conducive to the reproduction of parasitic microorganisms, cross infection, and spread of disease.[122] Cesspits full of human waste at the bottom floor of the apartment buildings and lack of running water in these *insulae* certainly did not help.[123] Lodging in the larger urban centers was expensive.[124] In Ostia, like in Rome, the very poor may

---

118. *Dig.* 50.16.234.2 (Gaius).

119. Cato, *De agricultura* 59; *P. Oxy.* 4.736; *T. Vindol.* 3.607; U. Mannering, "Roman Garments from Mons Claudianus," in *Archéologie des Textiles: Des origines au Ve siècle: Actes du colloque de Lattes, octobre 1999,* ed. Dominique Cardon and Michel Feugère (Montagnac: Editions Monique Mergoil, 2000), 288–89; J. P. Wild, "The Textile Industries of Roman Britain," *Britannia* 33 (2002): 23.

120. For secondhand clothing, see Jinyu Liu, *Collegia Centonariorum: The Guilds of Textile Dealers in the Roman West* (Leiden: Brill, 2009), 70–74; Petronius, *Satyricon* 12–13.

121. Alexandra Croom, *Roman Clothing and Fashion* (Stroud, UK: Tempus, 2000), 24.

122. Strabo, *Geographica* 5.3.7; Vitruvius, *De Architectura* 2.8.17; Pliny the Elder, *Naturalis historia* 35.173. On fire, see Tacitus, *Annales* 15.38; Suetonius, *Nero* 6.38; Juvenal, *Satirae* 3; Martial, *Epigramma* 7.61. See also Scobie, "Slums, Sanitation and Mortality," 405–6, 427; van den Bergh, "Plight of the Poor," 467; Gregory S. Aldrete, *Floods of the Tiber in Ancient Rome* (Baltimore: Johns Hopkins University Press, 2006), 106; Morley, "Salubriousness of the Roman City," 195–98.

123. Koloski-Ostrow, *Archaeology of Sanitation*, 19, 82.

have rented rooms in cheap lodging houses, which may have housed a mixture of temporary and permanent residents.[125] Shops functioned not only as manufacturing and commercial spaces but also as living spaces for the shopkeeper's family,[126] who crammed into the limited space of the (often one-room) shops. In Pompeii, there is evidence that the poorer inhabitants may have suffered in the urbanization process, some of whom "were being squeezed out in the face of the rapacious expansion of its richer inhabitants."[127] The alternative to not being able to live even in flimsily built structures would be to find shelter under bridges or in porticoes, basements, temple porches, storerooms under the stairs of apartment buildings, tombs, public lavatories, kitchens, baths, or wherever shelter were available.[128] The living conditions of the poor meant that they had increased susceptibility to suffering damage in floods and vulnerability to diseases or famine following disasters.[129]

To meet the "standard of dying" was costly.[130] Proper burial and commemoration, which could include a funeral, cremation, interment, tomb, epitaph, and repeated commemorative rituals, would incur considerable cost. Nerva reportedly introduced a burial grant (*funeraticium*) of HS 250 to the *plebs* in the city of Rome.[131] In 136 CE, the association of the worshippers of Diana and Antinous (*cultores Dianae et Antinoi*) at Lanuvium stipulated HS 250 for a member's funeral and

124. For classic treatment, see Bruce W. Frier, *Landlords and Tenants in Imperial Rome* (Princeton: Princeton University Press, 1980).

125. Van den Bergh, "Plight of the Poor," 453.

126. M. Flohr, "Working and Living under One Roof: Workshops in Pompeian Atrium Houses," in *Privata Luxuria: Towards an Archaeology of Intimacy*, ed. Anna Anguissola (Munich: Utz, 2012), 51–72.

127. Rick Jones and Damian Robinson, "Intensification, Heterogeneity and Power in the Development of Insula VI.1 389," in *The World of Pompeii*, ed. John J. Dobbins and Pedar W. Foss (London: Routledge, 2007), 397.

128. Van den Bergh, "Plight of the Poor," 454; Holleran, "Migration and the Urban Economy," 179; Claire Holleran, *Shopping in Ancient Rome: The Retail Trade in the Late Republic and the Principate* (Oxford: Oxford University Press, 2012), 155.

129. Tacitus, *Hist.* 1.86; Aldrete, *Floods of the Tiber*, 106, 172; Jerry Toner, *Roman Disasters* (Malden, MA: Polity, 2013), 20.

130. N. Purcell, "Tomb and Suburb," in *Römische Gräberstraßen: Selbstdarstellung, Status, Standard: Kolloquium in München Vom 28. Bis 30. Oktober 1985*, ed. Henner von Hesberg and Paul Zanker (Munich: Verlag der Bayerischen Akademie der Wissenschaften, 1987), 25–41. For death and commemoration, see also G. J. Oliver, ed., *The Epigraphy of Death: Studies in the History and Society of Greece and Rome* (Liverpool: Liverpool University Press, 2000), 9–11; Maureen Carroll, *Spirits of the Dead: Roman Funerary Commemoration in Western Europe* (Oxford: Oxford University Press, 2006); Valerie M. Hope, *Death in Ancient Rome: A Source Book* (London: Routledge, 2007); Laurie Brink and Deborah Green, eds., *Commemorating the Dead: Texts and Artifacts in Context: Studies of Roman, Jewish, and Christian Burials* (Berlin: de Gruyter, 2008).

131. A. Degrassi, "Nerva funeraticium plebi urbanae instituit," *Bullettino dell' Istituto di Diritto Romano "Vittorio Scialoja"* 63, no. 2 (1960): 233–79; Keith Hopkins, *Death and Renewal* (Cambridge: Cambridge University Press, 1983), 211.

HS 50 to be distributed to the mourners.[132] HS 250 could support a person to live at subsistence level for more than a year. But this number is at the lowest end of the attested funeral costs.[133] Dying as a poor person who could only make ends meet during their lifetime meant a lack of (ritualized) commemoration or lasting memory being passed down to posterity. Not all of them necessarily ended up in *puticuli*, which, as Emma-Jayne Graham has shown, may not have been used as a regular form of disposal by the poor.[134] Modest, simple graves and cremations in amphorae interspersed with larger, more elaborate burial structures seem to become more common practices after the latter half of the first century CE,[135] although we should be wary not to associate a simple grave automatically with poverty in the life of the deceased.[136] A niche in the collective burial compound such as a *columbarium* or the patron's tomb may also be a possibility,[137] although as John Bodel has reminded us, structures such as *columbaria* were expensive.[138] Upon death, therefore, those with 390 kg wheat-equivalent income would quickly, if not instantly, become voiceless and faceless. Poverty as deprivation would complete its full circle.

Poverty Alleviation and Survival Strategies

Cross-cultural studies of poverty in premodern societies have identified four broad categories of mechanisms that address and prevent deprivation—namely, "state-run establishments and practices, private institutions, family-based arrangements, and informal strategies."[139] This section briefly examines all four categories in the Roman context. It will become clear over the course of the discussion that systematic, top-down poverty relief was not in place in the Roman world, although

---

132. *CIL* XIV.2112 = *ILS* 7212.

133. Richard Duncan-Jones, *The Economy of the Roman Empire: Quantitative Studies* (Cambridge: Cambridge University Press, 1974), 131.

134. Emma-Jayne Graham, *The Burial of the Urban Poor in Italy in the Late Roman Republic and Early Empire* (Oxford: Archaeopress, 2006), 63–84, 111.

135. Hopkins, *Death and Renewal*, 211; Hope, *Death in Ancient Rome*, 133; Graham, *Burial of the Urban Poor*, 111–13; Andrew Lintott, *The Romans in the Age of Augustus* (Malden, MA: Wiley-Blackwell, 2010), 91–92.

136. R. F. J. Jones, "Rules for the Living and the Dead: Funerary Practice and Social Organisation," in *Römerzeitliche Gräber als Quellen zu Religion, Bevölkerungsstruktur und Sozialgeschichte*, ed. Manuela Struck (Mainz: Institut für Vor- und Frühgeschichte, 1993), 247–54.

137. Dorian Borbonus, *Columbarium Tombs and Collective Identity in Augustan Rome* (New York: Cambridge University Press, 2014).

138. John Bodel, "From Columbaria to Catacombs: Communities of the Dead in Pagan and Christian Rome," in Brink and Green, eds., *Commemorating the Dead*, 180. Cf. Hope, *Death in Ancient Rome*, 132.

139. Beaudoin, *Poverty in World History*, 30.

imperial and elite benefactions with restricted scopes and uneven chronological and regional distributions were available. It is therefore particularly important to look at informal survival strategies. Meggitt defines a survival strategy as "a coping mechanism whereby a person living close to subsistence attempts to ensure adequate access to the necessities of existence."[140] This section shows that the survival strategies may take the forms of seeking, reducing consumption of, and pooling resources. Most of these arrangements, however, can be characterized as preventive or security mechanisms rather than mechanisms to reduce or lift people out of poverty.

Ravallion notes, "For the bulk of history, governments have played little direct role in reducing poverty, beyond dealing with transient, destabilizing, sources of poverty, such as famines."[141] Rome is no exception to this general observation. A good deal of care went into ensuring the grain supply of the city of Rome by measures such as imposing taxation in kind from grain-producing provinces and providing incentives to private shippers and bakers.[142] In the early empire, the *plebs frumentaria*, which numbered 150,000 to 320,000, were entitled to receive a dole of unmilled wheat at the rate of 5 *modii* (ca. 407.73 kg/year) per person per month. Although this was slightly more than the subsistence ration, the dole was by no means sufficient to support a family, especially if the high rent at Rome is taken into consideration. Although how the *plebs frumentaria* was chosen is not entirely clear, immigrants, children, and women seemed to be regularly excluded.[143] Nevertheless, the large number of dole receivers meant that there must have been poor citizens, to whose families the doles constituted a significant subsidy. Looking at the Roman Empire globally, however, a question arises as to whether the grain supply to Rome meant poverty elsewhere. It may be telling that according to Scheidel's calculation, unskilled laborers in Roman Egypt would have been unable to generate sufficient income on their own to maintain their families at even a bare-bones subsistence level, let alone aspiring to a "respectability

140. Meggitt, *Paul, Poverty and Survival*, 164.
141. Martin Ravallion, *The Economics of Poverty: History, Measurement, and Policy* (New York: Oxford University Press, 2016), 19.
142. Erdkamp, *Grain Market*, esp. 211–37; Adriaan J. B. Sirks, *Food for Rome: The Legal Structure of the Transportation and Processing of Supplies for the Imperial Distributions in Rome and Constantinople* (Amsterdam: J. C. Gieben, 1991).
143. Denis van Berchem, *Les distributions de blé et d'argent à la plèbe romaine sous l'Empire* (New York: Arno Press, 1975); Peter Garnsey, *Famine and Food Supply in the Graeco-Roman World: Responses to Risk and Crisis* (Cambridge: Cambridge University Press, 1988), 265; Carlos Machado, "The Epigraphy of the *plebs frumentaria*," *JRA* 25 (2012): 599–602.

basket."[144] The *plebs frumentaria* could also expect to receive irregular but sizable cash distributions (*congiaria*) from the emperors.[145] Grain doles are also attested in Oxyrhynchus, Antinoopolis, Hermopolis, and Alexandria.[146] For Peter Garnsey, these grain doles "were meant to benefit a privileged section of the citizen population rather than all citizens or the poor," even more so elsewhere than at Rome.[147] In some places, measures were also taken to ensure oil supply at appropriate prices.[148]

Following Paul Veyne's work foregrounding the civic nature of euergetism, few people nowadays would characterize *sportulae* or the *alimenta* schemes, whether established with imperial support or not, as forms of charities that primarily aimed at aiding the poor, although the poor might have benefitted incidentally.[149] The alimentary schemes, with or without imperial involvement, often stipulated the number of boys and girls to receive allowances.[150] In Tarracina, Italy, for example, an alimentary scheme supported one hundred boys up to sixteen years of age at the monthly rate of 5 denarii each, and one hundred girls up to fourteen years of age at the monthly rate of 4 denarii each.[151] In Sicca Veneria, Africa Proconsularis, P. Licinius Papirianus of equestrian rank established a private alimentary program with the stipulation that three hundred boys aged three through fifteen and two hundred girls aged three through thirteen were to receive monthly allowances of HS 10 and HS 8 per person, respectively.[152] Although citizen status rather than poverty seems to be the basic qualification, considering the small population size of most of the Roman urban cen-

---

144. Scheidel, "Real Wages in Early Economies," 427–36.
145. E.g., seventy-five denarii in 44 BCE; one hundred denarii in 29 BCE, 24 BCE, and 12 BCE respectively; sixty denarii in 5 BCE and 2 BCE respectively; seventy-five denarii, 13 CE; sixty-five denarii in 15 CE; seventy-five denarii in 17 CE; sixty denarii in 20 CE and 23 CE respectively; two distributions at the rate of seventy-five denarii in 37 CE. Cf. Greg Rowe, *Princes and Political Cultures: The New Tiberian Senatorial Decrees* (Ann Arbor: University of Michigan Press, 2002), 87; Peter M. Swan, *The Augustan Succession: An Historical Commentary on Cassius Dio's Roman History, Books 55-56 (9 B.C.-A.D. 14)* (Oxford: Oxford University Press, 2004), 365–66.
146. *P. Oxy.* 40.2892–2940, 2941–42; *W. Chr.* 425; Eusebius, *Historia ecclesiastica* 7.21. Richard Alston, "Trade and the City in Roman Egypt," in *Trade, Traders and the Ancient City*, ed. Helen Parkins and Christopher J. Smith (London: Routledge, 1998), 182.
147. Garnsey, *Famine and Food Supply*, 267.
148. Alston, "Trade and the City," 182, citing *P. Oxy.* 12.1455; cf. *PUG* 1.21, 22.
149. Harris, "Poverty and Destitution," 52; Longenecker, *Remember the Poor*, 72.
150. For *alimenta*, see, Richard Duncan-Jones, "The Purpose and Organisation of the Alimenta," *Papers of the British School at Rome* 32 (1964): 123–46; Greg Woolf, "Food, Poverty and Patronage: The Significance of the Epigraphy of the Roman Alimentary Schemes in Early Imperial Italy," *Papers of the British School at Rome* 58 (1990): 197–228.
151. *CIL* 10.6328 = *ILS* 6278.
152. *CIL* 8.1641= *ILS* 6818 (c. 175–80).

ters, a few hundred children must have been a large percentage of the total number of local children. Duncan-Jones has also made the point that the allowances were too insignificant for the elite and most likely served their inferiors.[153] Sometimes the designated beneficiaries were boys and girls of the entire urban *plebs*, such as that established by Pliny the Younger.[154] We also occasionally encounter need-based gifts. An inscription from Letoon of Xanthos records an anonymous benefaction:

> He educates and supports all the children of the citizens, having accepted their charge in person for 16 years, and having for this purpose made over to the city properties and moneys together with initial capital for a year, so that from the interest his charity is preserved for ever. He gives a funeral fund for the dead and provides for the dowries of needy daughters, and he nourishes the poor.[155]

Such alimentary projects, however, were not set up everywhere in the empire. As far as Lycia and Pamphylia are concerned, where there was a concentration of epigraphic evidence for private *alimenta*, C. P. Jones has suggested that "both were very productive of grain, and their urban elites, being highly Romanised, might have been receptive to a type of benefaction favoured by Nerva and his successors."[156] In poorer regions, such benefactions may have been much less frequent. In addition, proper execution of the programs, steady returns, or continued, long-term operation could not be guaranteed. The potential mismanagement or ineffective execution was certainly a concern to the donors, as shown by Pliny the Younger's carefully planned scheme to ensure the success of his endowments.

The urban poor may have also expected to have the opportunities to receive distributions including (bath) oil and cash handouts at places and facilities such as baths and theaters.[157] One inscription from Comum, for example, stipulated that oil (for cleansing purpose) was to be given "to the people in the Campus and in all the *thermae* and *balineae* that are in Comum."[158] The Roman baths were remarkably open.

153. Duncan-Jones, *Economy of the Roman Empire*, 318.
154. *CIL* 5.5262 = *ILS* 2927, aliment(a) pueror(um) / et puellar(um) pleb(is) urban(ae).
155. The translation is that of Garnsey's (*Famine and Food Supply*, 262). The benefactor, however, may not have been the famous Opramoas of Oenoanda. See J. J. Coulton, "Opramoas and the Anonymous Benefactor," *JHS* 107 (1987): 171–78.
156. C. P. Jones, "Eastern Alimenta and an Inscription of Attaleia," *JHS* 109 (1989): 191.
157. *Mart.* 3.7, 10.90; Garrett G. Fagan, *Bathing in Public in the Roman World* (Ann Arbor: University of Michigan Press, 1999), 207, 217.
158. *CIL* 5.5279 = *ILS* 6728; Fagan, *Bathing in Public*, 306.

The admission fees, if there were any, to baths were low, and offers of free bathing were a form of benefaction.[159] The baths must have provided some comfort for the poor on cold days. But as Fagan has reminded us, the baths were far from equalizing places; rather, they were places where the rich showed off their wealth and distinctions of status were expressed in a variety of ways.[160]

Patronal assistance of the clients may take the form of legal help, monetary support, food provision, and so on, and could be crucial to prevent middling group families from slipping into poverty, especially in times of crisis.[161] Yet, as Verboven has argued, the institution of patronage may have played an insignificant role in alleviating poverty for the poorest, who usually did not have patrons.[162]

To what extent did private associations, variously called collegia, familia, synodoi, thiasoi, koina, and so on contribute to community self-help, especially with respect to poverty?[163] Upon joining a collegium, a member would receive a package deal, which offered access to feasts, communal funeral service, connection with patrons through collegium, possible low-interest loans, aid in times of difficulty or financial crisis, or at least a combination of some of these.[164] Yet, it has long been recognized that being a collegium member was costly, involving various expenditures including entrance fees, periodic fees, ad hoc contributions, and so on.[165] The entrance fees to the collegium of the worshippers of Diana and Antious (cultores Dianae et Antinoi) at Lanuvium, for example, was set at HS 100 in 136 CE,[166] which could purchase 224 kg

159. Fagan, Bathing in Public, 160–62, 196–206.
160. Ibid., 216–19.
161. Koenraad Verboven, The Economy of Friends: Economic Aspects of Amicitia and Patronage in the Late Republic (Brussels: Editions Latomus, 2002), 114.
162. Ibid., 114, 333.
163. Cf. Beaudoin, Poverty in World History, 33: "Perhaps the best known form of community self-help, however, was a product of urban society: the guild."
164. Nicholas Tran, Les Membres des Associations Romaines: Le Rang Social des Collegiati en Italie et en Gaules sous le Haut-Empire (Rome: École Française de Rome, 2006), 105–9; Jinyu Liu, "The Economy of Endowments: The case of Roman associations," in Pistoi Dia Tèn Technèn: Bankers, Loans and Archives in the Ancient World. Studies in Honour of Raymond Bogaert, ed. Koenraad Verboven, Katelijn Vandorpe, and Véronique Chankowski (Leuven: Peeters, 2008), 231–56, with bibliography; Philip F. Venticinque, "Family Affairs: Guild Regulations and Family Relationships in Roman Egypt," GRBS 50, no. 2 (2010): 273–94; Philip F. Venticinque, "Matters of Trust: Associations and Social Capital in Roman Egypt," CHS Research Bulletin 1, no. 2 (2013): http://tinyurl.com/j9jouq8.
165. Onno van Nijf, The Civic World of Professional Associations in the Roman East (Amsterdam: J. C. Gieben, 1997), 31–69; Tran, Les Membres des Associations Romaines; John R. Patterson, Landscapes and Cities: Rural Settlement and Civic Transformation in Early Imperial Italy (Oxford: Oxford University Press, 2006), esp. 260–63); Koenraad Verboven, "The Associative Order, Status and Ethos of Roman Businessmen in the Late Republic and Early Empire," Athenaeum 95 (2007): 861–93; Liu, "Economy of Endowments," with bibliography. For ad hoc contributions, see P.Mich. 5.243 (BL 9.160).

of wheat at the rate of HS 3 per modius. Lower entrance fees have also been attested. The *thiasos* of the worshippers of Dionysos at Physkos in the second century CE seemed to have only charged 14 obols, although other contributions were also required.[167] The associations represent a resource-pooling mechanism, but the option of joining an association was simply not available to the overwhelming majority of the Roman population, who had no surplus to spare. It would, however, be rash to dismiss the relevance of associations to poverty studies. In fact, there are two sides to this relevance. On one hand, associations may have had the effect of obstructing the poorest from accessing support networks, resources, and work opportunities;[168] on the other hand, the associations can be understood as preventive strategies that could help the members with poverty alleviation in times of difficulty. The regulation of an association in Egypt in the first century stipulated that if a member ignored another member who was in distress (ἐν ἀηδίᾳ) and did not help him out of his trouble, he should pay 8 drachmas.[169] The association of *apolysimoi* of Tebtynis (43 CE) made it a rule to stand surety for a period of sixty days for any member who was arrested for a debt up to 100 drachmas.[170]

Collegia were not a substitute for but intertwined and interacted with the networks of family, friends, and neighbors, which could be an important source of support and which seemed particularly significant in rural contexts.[171] Parents-in-law could accommodate a poverty-stricken son-in-law, although conflict may have been hard to avoid.[172] Among craftsmen, borrowing money from relatives was frequent, although data become scarce further down the social scale.[173] Family-based arrangements such as taking in orphaned relatives were by no means unusual. In 58 CE, Helen and her husband petitioned to register Amoitas, the minor son of her deceased brother, as apprentice to

166. *CIL* 14.2112 = *ILS* 7212; Duncan-Jones, *Economy of the Roman Empire*, 131; higher entrance fees: *ILS* 9100; *P.Lond* 1178; *P.Oxy.* 2476.
167. *IG* IX/12.670 = *AGRW* no. 30.
168. Liu, "Group Membership."
169. *P.Mich.* 5.243 = *ARGW* no. 300.
170. *P.Mich.* 5.244 = *ARGW* no. 301.
171. Venticinque, "Family Affairs," 273–94; Garnsey and Woolf, "Patronage of the Rural Poor," 154–55; Garnsey, *Famine and Food Supply*, 55–63; Morley, "Poor in the City," 34–35.
172. *P. Oxy.* 2.281 (20–50 AD); Judith Evans Grubbs, *Women and the Law in the Roman Empire: A Sourcebook on Marriage, Divorce and Widowhood* (London: Routledge, 2002), 212.
173. Cf. for Tryphon as debtor, see *P. Oxy.* 2.304, 318, and 320; as creditor, see *P. Oxy.* 2.269, 319. Loans and repayments made by Pausiris Jr.: *P.Mich. inv.* 84–92 (AD 73–74). Dominic Rathbone and Peter Temin, "Financial Intermediation in First-Century AD Rome and Eighteenth-Century England," in Verboven, Vandorpe, and Chankowski, *Pistoi Dia Tèn Technèn*, 417.

Pausiris.[174] There is no mention of the boy's mother. It seems very likely that Helen may have taken in the fatherless boy.[175] Apprenticing children to friends, neighbors, or relatives was by no means rare.[176] I have argued elsewhere that the Roman apprenticeship was not simply an economic institution aiming at enhancing the productivity and specialized skills of the apprentices but, more importantly, a social institution that was closely intertwined with other existing networks in which both parties were involved and had intragenerational and intergenerational dimensions. It was far from uncommon for the master's family and the apprentice's family to share the disciplinary obligations as well as the obligations to "nourish" the apprentice. In a way, therefore, apprenticeship can be seen as a cost-sharing strategy among craftsmen in launching the occupational careers of their children. These craftsmen may have been above subsistence level of living, which put them in a position to make arrangements for their children to increase the prospect of economic security for not only the children themselves but also the parent(s) in old age.

Adaptive strategies to prevent downward slippage may also be represented in patterns of marriage and household formation. Economic consideration may have been behind the late male marriage, which allowed a man more opportunities to "accumulate sufficient resources or income to establish a neolocal marriage."[177] In terms of household sizes and structures, Bagnall and Frier's study of the Egyptian case shows that the proportion of solitary families, conjugal families, and no families was higher in the metropolises than in the villages, but the proportion of extended- and multiple-family households was much lower in the metropolises. Families were, on average, somewhat larger in villages than in metropolises.[178] In so far as extended- and multiple-family household arrangements can be understood as "a social risk management strategy that enabled distribution of resources across more people," the lower proportion of these types in the metropolises

174. *P.Mich.* 3.171.
175. For fostering by relatives, see Paul Veyne, "The Roman Empire," in *From Pagan Rome to Byzantium*, ed. Paul Veyne, trans. Arthur Goldhammer, A History of Private Life 1 (Cambridge, MA: Belknap Press, 1987), 10.
176. Lucian (*Somnium* 1–5) was apprenticed to his uncle; *P.Wisc.* 1.4; *P. Oxy.* 2.275. Liu, "Group Membership."
177. Saskia Hin, "Family Matters: Fertility and Its Constraints in Roman Italy," in Holleran and Pudsey, *Demography and the Graeco-Roman World*, 99–116 (at 112).
178. Roger S. Bagnall and Bruce W. Frier, *The Demography of Roman Egypt* (Cambridge: Cambridge University Press, 2006), 67–68.

may be associated with factors ranging from the non-farming-based occupations to restricted living space in the cities.[179]

In Anneliese Parkin's study of poverty in the early Roman Empire, she lists decapitalization, or the shedding of mouths to feed, as a strategy of poor families to combat poverty. The relationship between poverty, reproduction, and child rearing, however, is a complex one. The causes for infanticide or child exposure are often difficult for us to trace. A wide range of factors including discernable deformity of the neonate, extramarital procreation, procreation as a result of prostitution, gender preference, and the desire to increase prospects to remarry may all lead to infanticide or child exposure.[180] It is risky to assume that poverty was the primary cause or motivation. This leads to a highly relevant question of the dynamics of fertility and poverty. Under extreme conditions, "biological mechanisms respond to food crises and severe distress by preventing reproduction."[181] Malnourishment and certain diseases such as malaria and tuberculosis may also affect fecundity. But poverty does not necessarily lead to decreased fertility. While the early Malthusian theory argues for high fertility as a cause of poverty, later economists have pointed out that causality may point in the opposite direction: "poverty could be the cause of high fertility: Poor people often want more children because children represent wealth, provide household labor and are the only form of social security available to parents in their old age."[182] Morris Silver has argued to see high fertility among the poor as a reaction to the collective mode of taxation that limits their "ability to accumulate productive capital, human and material." For him, "People in a poverty-stricken commune may well choose to have larger families

179. Sabine Huebner, "*Household Composition in the Ancient Mediterranean: What Do We Really Know?*" in *A Companion to Families in the Greek and Roman Worlds*, ed. Beryl Rawson (Chichester, UK: Wiley-Blackwell, 2011), 83.

180. Seneca the Elder, *Controversiae* 10.4.16; Hin, "Family Matters," 110; Parkin, "Poverty in the Early Roman Empire," 161n787; Judith Evans Grubbs, "Infant Exposure and Infanticide," in *Oxford Handbook of Childhood and Education*, ed. Judith Evans Grubbs and Tim Parkin (Oxford: Oxford University Press, 2013); Rebecca Gowland, A. Chamberlain, and R. C. Redfern, "On the Brink of Being: Re-Evaluating Infanticide and Infant Burial in Roman Britain," in *Infant Health and Death in Roman Italy and Beyond*, ed. Maureen Carroll and Emma-Jayne Graham (Portsmouth, RI: Journal of Roman Archaeology, 2014). Cf. Cynthia Patterson, "'Not Worth the Rearing': The Causes of Infant Exposure in Ancient Greece," *Transactions of the American Philological Association* 115 (1985): 103–23. Gender preference: Artemidorus, *Oneirocritica* 1.15; *P.Oxy.* 4.744; Bagnall and Frier, *Demography of Roman Egypt*, 151–53.

181. Hin, "Family Matters," 111; see also Sabine R. Huebner, *The Family in Roman Egypt: A Comparative Approach to Intergenerational Solidarity and Conflict* (Cambridge: Cambridge University Press, 2013), 59.

182. Thomas W. Merrick, "Population and Poverty: New Views on an Old Controversy," *International Family Planning Perspectives* 28, no. 1 (2002): 41–46.

than residents in wealthy communities. The consumption of children and even their investment returns are beyond the reach of tax collectors and commune busybodies."[183] Bagnall and Frier indeed have reported a total fertility rate (TFR) of 6.0 in Roman Egypt,[184] which showed characteristics of a natural fertility pattern. Opinions differ as to whether a high-pressure regime or a low-pressure regime prevailed in Roman Egypt, with Rathbone holding a different view than Frier and Scheidel in arguing for a low-pressure regime, which would lead to a more optimistic estimation of population pressure on available resources.[185]

To what extent did migration play a role in the survival strategies of poor families? Although there has been disagreement as to the extent of the "graveyard effect" of major cities, especially Rome, and their roles as "population sinks," very few have doubted the need for constant immigration to maintain the sizes of the major urban centers.[186] Scholarly opinions differ, however, as to whether the major cities needed large sizes of population to function or, on the contrary, the cities became large as a result of immigration, and whether migration was driven by "pull" factors—ranging from rising prices for urban goods and urban amenities to ethnic groups elsewhere—or "push" factors—such as population growth, dispossession, and falling grain prices in the countryside.[187] Lacking the resources to move, however, the very poor may have been less mobile than "the moderately prosperous households."[188] Nor did moving to the cities necessarily lead to a more promising life. Supported by comparative materials from the developing world, Claire Holleran has argued that in the case of Rome, the immigrants tended to be trapped in absolute poverty and that migration had a negative impact upon the employment market, which did

---

183. Silver, "Roman Economic Growth," 234–35.

184. Bagnall and Frier, Demography of Roman Egypt, 150–51.

185. Dominic Rathbone, "Poverty and Population in Roman Egypt," in Atkins and Osborne, Poverty in the Roman World, 100–114.

186. Morley, Metropolis and Hinterland, 39–54; Walter Scheidel, "Progress and Problems in Roman Demography," in Debating Roman Demography, ed. Walter Scheidel (Leiden: Brill, 2001), 31–32; Scheidel, "Disease and Death," 55–56; Saskia Hin, The Demography of Roman Italy: Population Dynamics in an Ancient Conquest Society, 201 BCE–14 CE (Cambridge: Cambridge University Press, 2013), 221–28.

187. Ryan M. Geraghty, "The Impact of Globalization in the Roman Empire, 200 BC–AD 100," Journal of Economic History 67, no. 4 (2007): 1036–61; for a good summary of these debates, see Holleran, "Migration and the Urban Economy," 155–63; Hin, Demography of Roman Italy, 215–21.

188. Erdkamp, "Seasonal Labour," 37.

not help with increasing wage levels.[189] Yet, led by (often false) perceptions of opportunities, immigrants may still have moved to the *urbs*.[190]

Joining the army may also have been a way out of poverty. In Aquileia, a nicely carved epitaph marking a decently sized tomb commemorated a navy veteran who said he was born in deepest poverty (*natus summa in pauperie*).[191] The recruitment of soldiers, however, did not target the poorest segment of the population. As Michael Alexander Speidel has reminded us, Tacitus's references to soldiers as mostly from "the destitute and the vagrant" (*inopes ac vagi*) may have been a projection of his aristocratic prejudice.[192] Quantitatively, perhaps only a small percentage of the Roman population may have hoped to change their lives through military service in the first two centuries of the empire.

The desperately destitute may have resorted to begging and relied on the generosity of the passers-by to delay starvation.[193] Poverty may also have led parents to sell (to pimps) or prostitute their children.[194] The freeborn may even have sold themselves into slavery to avoid starvation. Despite the inalienability of freedom according to the principle of Roman law, "life threatening poverty" provided an acceptable reason for a freeborn person's self-sale into slavery.[195] Reactions to uneven distribution of means may also have taken the form of anomic behaviors such as violence and crime, "in order to obtain through force what society withholds."[196] Petty theft was widespread in urban contexts, although organized banditry seemed less of an urban phenomenon.

Conclusion

The influential *Despouy Report on Human Rights and Extreme Poverty* underscores a "vicious circle of poverty," which comprises a "hori-

189. Holleran, "Migration and the Urban Economy," 175–80.
190. Ibid., 177–78; Erdkamp, "Seasonal Labour," 33–49; Bertrand, "Food Distributions," 50–71.
191. *CIL* 5.938 = *ILS* 2905 (Aquileia).
192. Tacitus, *Ann.* 4.4; Michael Alexander Speidel, "Das römische Heer als Kulturträger," in *Heer Und Herrschaft Im Römischen Reich Der Hohen Kaiserzeit* (Stuttgart: Steiner, 2009), 530, with n. 82.
193. A. Parkin, "'You Do Him No Service': An Exploration of Pagan Almsgiving," in Atkins and Osborne, *Poverty in the Roman World*, 60–82; Longenecker, *Remember the Poor*, 74.
194. Thomas A. J. McGinn, *The Economy of Prostitution in the Roman World: A Study of Social History and the Brothel* (Ann Arbor: University of Michigan Press, 2004), 56.
195. W. V. Harris, "Demography, Geography and the Sources of Roman Slaves," *JRS* 89 (1999): 73. Sometimes, however, self-sale into slavery was motivated by the hope to have a management career in a rich family.
196. Werner Riess, "The Roman Bandit (Latro) as Criminal and Outsider," in *The Oxford Handbook of Social Relations in the Roman World*, ed. Michael Peachin (Oxford: Oxford University Press, 2011), 697.

zontal vicious circle" with mutually reinforcing conditions creating a cumulative, compound effect of deprivations, and a "vertical vicious circle," or intergenerational perpetuation of poverty.[197] This may effectively summarize the broad-stroke discussion of poverty in the Roman cities above. From lack of stable employment to coarse diet and poor housing conditions, the lives of the poor in the Roman cities can be characterized by multidimensional deprivations—of resources, capabilities, choices, security, and power.[198] This deprivation was embedded in the sociopolitical systems that organized the ownership of land, the ultimate form of wealth in the premodern, agrarian economy that was Rome. The profits from the land were channeled to the state in the form of taxation; to the emperor, who had immense land holdings; and to the large landowners, including the senatorial, equestrian, and local elites to support their social and cultural status and political careers. These were also the privileged and powerful who made laws and dominated the public discourse that criminalized and marginalized the poor. These sociopolitical systems supported rigid status differentials and allowed verbal, physical, and psychological abuse of the poor in a top-down direction.[199] Under this structure, both mobility paths and formal ways of poverty alleviation were limited. In sickness, old age, and other situations, the poor had little to rely on except for family-based arrangements.

Although upward mobility was more prominently (re)presented in the epigraphic records, especially those from former slavers, the anxiety over downward mobility may have been more constantly on the minds of many people than the aspiration to upward mobility. Preventive strategies, such as joining a *collegium* and arranging vocational training for the children, were not even available to the truly poor, who lived at or below the subsistence level and often could not even leave marked tombstones to refer to themselves as *pauperes*, a term that some of the "middling group" members used in a positive sense. In this light, I invite attention to the lack of a full-scale study of the relationship between the "middling group" and the poor, especially the mechanisms of mobility between these conditions at the micro and macro levels, as well as what, if any, culturally speaking, marked them

197. "Report of the Special Rapporteur on Human Rights and Extreme Poverty," E/CN.4/Sub.2/1996/13, 28 June 1996.
198. Cf. "Poverty and the International Covenant on Economic, Social and Cultural Rights," E/C.12/2001/10, 10 May 2001.
199. Garrett G. Fagan, "Violence in Roman Social Relations," in Peachin, *Oxford Handbook of Social Relations*, 467–91, esp. 481.

apart from the poor. This is a lacuna that has not been filled by two of the recent publications, *The Oxford Handbook of Social Relations in the Roman World* and *The Ancient Middle Classes: Urban Life and Aesthetics in the Roman Empire, 100 BCE–250 CE.*[200]

Select Bibliography

Atkins, Margaret, and Robin Osborne, eds. *Poverty in the Roman World.* Cambridge: Cambridge University Press, 2006.

Bowman, Alan, and Andrew Wilson, eds. *Quantifying the Roman Economy: Methods and Problems.* Oxford Studies on the Roman Economy. Oxford: Oxford University Press, 2009.

Garnsey, Peter. *Food and Society in Classical Antiquity.* Cambridge: Cambridge University Press, 1999.

Garnsey, Peter, and Richard Saller. *The Roman Empire: Economy, Society and Culture.* 2nd ed. Oakland: University of California Press, 2015.

Garnsey, Peter, and Walter Scheidel. *Cities, Peasants and Food in Classical Antiquity: Essays in Social and Economic History.* Cambridge: Cambridge University Press, 1998.

Hamel, Gildas H. *Poverty and Charity in Roman Palestine, First Three Centuries C.E.* Berkeley: University of California Press, 1990.

Harris, William. V. "Poverty and Destitution in the Roman Empire." In *Rome's Imperial Economy: Twelve Essays,* 27–54. Oxford: Oxford University Press, 2011.

Holleran, Claire, and April Pudsey, eds. *Demography and the Graeco-Roman World: New Insights and Approaches.* Cambridge: Cambridge University Press, 2011.

Knapp, Robert. *Invisible Romans.* Cambridge: Harvard University Press, 2011.

Longenecker, Bruce W., *Remember the Poor: Paul, Poverty, and the Greco-Roman World.* Grand Rapids, MI: Eerdmans, 2010.

Meggitt, Justin J. *Paul, Poverty and Survival.* Edinburgh: T&T Clark, 1998.

Parkin, Anneliese Ruth. "Poverty in the Early Roman Empire: Ancient and Modern Conceptions and Constructs." PhD diss., Cambridge University, 2001.

Parkin, Tim G., and Arthur J. Pomeroy. *Roman Social History: A Sourcebook.* London: Routledge, 2007.

---

200. Emanuel Mayer, *The Ancient Middle Classes: Urban Life and Aesthetics in the Roman Empire, 100 BCE–250 CE* (Cambridge, MA: Harvard University Press, 2012).

Patlagean, Evelyne. *Pauvreté économique et pauvreté sociale à Byzance, 4e-7e siècles*. Paris: Mouton, 1977.

Prell, Marcus. *Sozialökonomische Untersuchungen Zur Armut Im Antiken Rom: Von Den Gracchen Bis Kaiser Diokletian*. Stuttgart: Steiner, 1997.

Scheidel, Walter. "Real Wages in Early Economies: Evidence for Living Standards from 1800 BCE to 1300 CE." *Journal of the Economic and Social History of the Orient* 53, no. 3 (2010): 425–62.

Scheidel, Walter, and Steven J. Friesen, "The Size of the Economy and the Distribution of Income in the Roman Empire." *JRS* 99 (2009): 61–91.

Scobie, Alex. "Slums, Sanitation and Mortality in the Roman World." *Klio* 68 (1986): 399–433.

Silver, Morris. "Roman Economic Growth and Living Standards: Perceptions versus Evidence." *Ancient Society* 37 (2007): 191–252.

Toner, Jerry. *Popular Culture in Ancient Rome* (Cambridge, UK: Polity, 2009).

Welborn, L. L. "The Polis and the Poor: Reconstructing Social Relations from Different Genres of Evidence." In *The First Urban Churches 1: Methodological Foundations*, edited by James R. Harrison and L. L. Welborn, 189–244. Atlanta: SBL Press, 2015.

Whittaker, C. R. "The Poor." In *The Romans*, edited by Andrea Giardina, 272–99. Chicago: University of Chicago Press, 1993.

3

Economic Profiling of Early Christian Communities

Timothy A. Brookins

Three decades into the first century of the Common Era, a new sect of Judaism sprang to life in a remote corner of the Roman Empire. By the end of the first century, "Christians" had captured the public eye far and wide. Judging from the sources, the socioeconomic status of these newcomers became an absorbing interest. The book of Acts, written near the turn of the second century, exhibits an almost defensive posture in its earnestness to demonstrate that Christianity had penetrated into the higher circles of society. A few years later, Pliny the Younger, governor of Pontus and Bithynia, remarked with curiosity that Christians could be found of "every age, every rank, and also of both sexes" (*Epistulae* 10.96). Others, however, looked the Christians over and found them uniformly unimpressive. Celsus, to whom Origen would later issue a response (*Contra Celsum* 3.48), dismissed them as "wool-workers, cobblers, laundry-workers, and the most illiterate and bucolic yokels" (cited in Origen, *Cels.* 3.55).[1] Likewise, Lucian's description no doubt represented the opinion of many when he called them, in short, "simple folk" (ἰδιῶται ἄνθρωποι; *De morte Peregrini* 13). By the end of the second century, it seems, there was no circle of society where Christians were not found, although their "lower-class" constituency apparently remained most conspicuous.

Today the question of the socioeconomic status of early Christians continues to fascinate (as we shall see, for reasons that are not the same for everyone). Among the earliest Christians, Pauline communities are better documented than any, and for that reason have remained the focus of a long, winding, and, in many respects, controversial discussion about the socioeconomic constituency of the earliest Christian groups. Locating Pauline Christians on the ancient economy scale has proved difficult for at least two reasons: first, because of the fragmentary state of the evidence, and second (as more recent discussions have brought further to the fore), because of the unavoidable issues of method, and with it ideology, that play into the interpreter's orientation toward that evidence.

The purpose of the following essay is to trace roughly the last century of discussion on the economic location of Pauline Christians. Rather than beginning there, however, we should like to begin by identifying some of the critical methodological issues that confront interpreters as they approach the evidence and that help to explain why discussion of the economic issues has been, and continues to be, so fraught with disagreement.

Epistemological Issues

Just as it is with other historical investigations, so it is with investigating the economic status of early Christians: no matter how close one gets to an "objective" description of things, it is impossible to escape the influence of the subjective horizon of the interpreter. The relevant issues here are methodological, ideological, or—in a word—epistemological.

Selection of Evidence

In closing his 1982 collection of essays, Gerd Theissen identified three sources of evidence available for use in sociological interpretation of

---

1. Translation from Henry Chadwick, *Origen: Contra Celsum* (Cambridge: Cambridge University Press, 1965), 165–66.

ancient religious traditions: (1) *constructive* evidence, including both (a) sociographic evidence (where texts describe groups) and (b) prosopographical evidence (where texts describe individuals); (2) *analytic* evidence, or evidence drawn from inference from historical events, social norms, or religious symbols; and (3) *comparative* evidence, or evidence that utilizes similarities in behavioral patterns observed in one religious group to illuminate practices observed in another group.[2]

When it comes to the selection of data, then, at least two problems stand out. The most fundamental problem concerns which data to regard and which to exclude. In his assessment of early Christian economic status, for instance,[3] E. A. Judge drew freely and, some might say, uncritically from the canonical book of Acts. Most since Judge, however, have utilized Acts only with caution,[4] and others—because of its tendency to highlight the permeation of Christianity into the highest circles of society against the evidence of Paul's letters—have rejected it as altogether unreliable.[5] Gerd Theissen has struck a middle position in suggesting that we "cannot exclude it" in the course of investigation.[6]

A corollary to the problem of selectivity is the problem of which evidence to prioritize as the "key" to the remaining evidence. Insofar as individuals may be recorded to history precisely because of their atypicality, prosopographical evidence may mislead the interpreter into supposing that what are actually anomalies in the historical record were instead representative phenomena (one might suppose, for example, that because individuals about whom Paul's letters provide testimony may have been "wealthier," the average Christian must also have been such).[7] Insofar as sociographic, analytic, and comparative evidence, on the other hand, ask us to deduce particular conclusions from more generalized data, excessive reliance on these sorts of data

---

2. Gerd Theissen, *The Social Setting of Pauline Christianity: Essays on Corinth*, ed. and trans. John H. Schütz (Philadelphia: Fortress Press, 1982), 177–95.

3. See also Justin Meggitt's warning against indiscriminate use of elite sources: "Sources: Use, Abuse, Neglect. The Importance of Ancient Popular Culture," in *Christianity at Corinth: The Quest for the Pauline Church*, ed. Edward Adams and David G. Horrell (Louisville, KY: Westminster John Knox, 2004), 241–55.

4. Wayne A. Meeks, *The First Urban Christians: The Social World of the Apostle Paul* (New Haven, CT: Yale University Press, 1983), 61; Theissen, *Social Setting*, 68–69.

5. Justin Meggitt, *Paul, Poverty and Survival* (Edinburgh: T&T Clark, 1998), 9; Steven J. Friesen, "Poverty in Pauline Studies: Beyond the So-Called New Consensus," *JSNT* 26, no. 3 (2004): 323–61, esp. 348; Bruce W. Longenecker, *Remember the Poor: Paul, Poverty, and the Greco-Roman World* (Grand Rapids: Eerdmans, 2010), 249–51.

6. Gerd Theissen, "The Social Structure of Pauline Communities: Some Critical Remarks on J. J. Meggitt, *Paul, Poverty and Survival*," *JSNT* 24, no. 2 (2001): 65–84, esp. 68–69.

7. Though this is a pitfall that the leading voices in the conversation have avoided falling into; see comments in Theissen, *Social Setting*, 73.

could lead to a problem of "sweeping generalization" (for example, the premise that because most people in the ancient world were "poor," there must have been no exceptions to this description in Paul's churches either).

Interpretation of the Facts

Facts do not "speak for themselves," but interpreters speak for the facts (as well as identify them). The element of "interpretation" (*hermēneia*) can be especially problematic in cases involving archaeological data, which few biblical interpreters have been specifically trained to handle.[8] The perennial debate over the Corinthian inscription referring to an *aedile* named Erastus (is this the man Paul referred to in Rom 16:23?), including controversy over the inscription's original location, its dating, and even whether it in fact refers to an individual named "Erastus,"[9] demonstrates just how thorny issues of interpretation related to specific pieces of data can be.

Theory and Models

The unavoidable necessity of interpretation in the handling of socioeconomic data raises the question of validity in using "models" or "theories" in analysis of socioeconomic issues. As Bengt Holmberg has observed, "Data are mute, until made to talk by being inserted in an interpretive framework."[10] That is, models can provide a benchmark that helps control interpretation and handling of the facts by providing an initial, abstract description of social or behavioral patterns. A "model," then, serves as "an abbreviated form of probability judgment about what might have occurred," thus turning guesses about the meaning of data into "educated" guesses.[11]

In other words, models frame the sociohistorical context in which particular events come into meaningful focus. For example, "analytic"

---

8. On this concern, see Peter Oakes, "Methodological Issues in Using Economic Evidence in Interpretation of Early Christian Texts," in *Engaging Economics: New Testament Scenarios and Early Christian Reception*, ed. Bruce W. Longenecker and Kelly D. Liebengood (Grand Rapids: Eerdmans, 2009), 9–34, esp. 20; Richard E. Oster, "Use, Misuse and Neglect of Archaeological Evidence in Some Modern Works on 1 Corinthians (1 Cor 7,1–5; 8, 10; 11, 2–16; 12, 14–26)," *ZNW* 83, no. 1–2 (1992): 52–73.

9. For recent bibliography, see Timothy A. Brookins, "The (In)frequency of the Name 'Erastus' in Antiquity: A Literary, Papyrological, and Epigraphical Catalog," *NTS* 59 (October 2013): 496–516, esp. 497–98.

10. Bengt Holmberg, "Methods of Historical Reconstruction," in Adams and Horrell, *Christianity at Corinth*, 270.

11. Ibid.

data such as those indicating the prevalence of patronage practices in Roman culture might be used as a framework for reading the somewhat more (to us) obscure data provided by Paul in 1 Corinthians regarding divisions in the Corinthian church. Here the patronage "model" would be applied as a sort of key to interpretation of the church's problems as adumbrated in the text.[12]

Despite their helpfulness, however, models cannot "substitute for evidence," for they are based on evidence.[13] As such, models are tentative and revisable, and the interpreter must exercise the discipline not to force particularized data through too generalized a grid.[14]

Ideology

"Ideology" is a loaded word, with manifold connotations. For present purposes, let the term be used with reference to the configuration of ideas or values that drive an interpreter—that is, the underlying body of thought that gives the interpreter a vested interest in the outcome of investigation.[15] Discussion of early Christian economic issues over the last twenty years has reflected an increasing awareness of both the positive and negative roles that ideologies play in interpretation. Negatively, hidden ideologies and their accompanying biases or prejudices may be used to predetermine conclusions;[16] positively, ideologies may be used openly to resist what are perceived to be either misapprehensions of the evidence or what runs counter to modern value systems.[17]

---

12. For this approach, see John K. Chow, *Patronage and Power: A Study of Social Networks in Corinth*, JSNTSup 75 (Sheffield: JSOT Press, 1992).
13. Holmberg, "Methods of Historical Reconstruction," 270.
14. On such methodological issues, see David G. Horrell, "Whither Social-Scientific Approaches to New Testament Interpretation? Reflections on Contested Methodologies in the Future," in *After the First Urban Christians: The Social-Scientific Study of Pauline Christianity Twenty-Five Years Later*, ed. Todd D. Still and David G. Horrell (New York: T&T Clark, 2009), 6–20.
15. On the relationship between ideology and methodology, see Margaret Y. MacDonald, "The Shifting Centre: Ideology and the Interpretation of 1 Corinthians," in Adams and Horrell, *Christianity at Corinth*, 273–94.
16. Meggitt, *Paul, Poverty and Survival*, 96. Similarly to Meggitt, Friesen suggested that the current "consensus" reflects a "modern, Western, male fascination with upward mobility, and a determination to find signs of wealth in the early churches." Steven J. Friesen, "The Wrong Erastus: Ideology, Archaeology, and Exegesis," in *Corinth in Context: Comparative Studies on Religion and Society*, ed. Steven J. Friesen, Daniel N. Schowalter, and James C. Walters (Leiden: Brill, 2010), 235.
17. As Friesen says, "There is no disentangled knowledge, only a choice of entanglements." For his part, he chooses to "foreground economic inequality" and to undertake historical work from an "ideology of inequality"—that is, with the realization that most people in the Roman Empire lived near subsistence level. Friesen, "The Wrong Erastus," 231–32, 235. Bruce Longenecker makes a more qualified appeal for attention to economic issues in "Exposing the Economic Middle: A Revised Economy Scale for the Study of Early Christianity," *JSNT* 31, no. 3 (2009): 243–78, esp. 269–70.

In a recent article treating the use of economic evidence in interpretation of early Christian texts, Peter Oakes puts the matter in helpfully balanced perspective: on the one hand, where the economic dimensions of early Christian issues have been ignored, a little more ideological drive could help inject missing perspective back into the discussion; on the other, using economics as an overall analytic framework, that is, treating economic issues as inherently the fundamental ones, could collapse into economic reductionism.[18]

Rhetoric

All language "reduces" reality as it attempts to render or, if one likes, to "construct" it. Thus, it is important to recognize the role of rhetoric not only as it relates to the interpretation of ancient texts but also as it relates to its role as a vehicle of the interpreter's ideology.

On the first count, for instance, the stark line between rich and poor, drawn with the distinction between the *honestiores* (elites) and *humiliores* (the poor) in ancient elite sources, can hardly be taken as an accurate representation of ancient distribution of wealth, although interpreters have often taken the language at face value.[19] Indeed, Bruce Longenecker has demonstrated that ancient writers employed little consistency in their use of economic language. The terms πένης and πτωχός, for example, were used interchangeably with reference to a broad band of people intended to be depicted in the sources as nonelite—that is, as "poor." Equally, this terminology could be used with reference to those who were, by virtually any other standard, quite wealthy.[20] Thus, Longenecker has pointed out that the debate over the nature of stratification "is itself the result of a lack of conceptual clarity, as interpreters engage in argumentation without first having established a stable discursive context."[21]

One must, of course, also take into account the role of rhetoric on the part of the interpreter. Particularly where interpreters have been overtly ideologically driven, data can be presented as one-sidedly rosy or gloomy, as the interpreter may be inclined. This we shall see below.

---

18. Oakes, "Methodological Issues," 10–13.
19. As Meggitt (*Paul, Poverty and Survival*, 50) does (but cf. ibid., 103).
20. Longenecker, "Exposing the Economic Middle," 244–47.
21. Longenecker, *Remember the Poor*, 40.

Probability in Historiography

Historiographical conclusions are not founded on discrete, bedrock facts but hang together from interdependent arguments based, at least purportedly, on the evidence viewed cumulatively. Dale Martin puts the matter concisely: "normal historiography need not demonstrate what *must* be the case. It need only show what *probably* is the case—which is *always* accomplished by cumulative and complicated evidence."[22] In short, in the practice of historiography, it is responsible for the interpreter neither to present questionable conclusions as certain ones nor to treat merely possible conclusions as the preferred ones. With historiography, we are concerned rather with probabilities, as estimated through careful consideration of the full breadth of available evidence.

Economic Profiling

The purpose of the brief survey of epistemological issues just covered is to help provide some explanation for the winding and often very charged nature of discussion that has taken place concerning economic status in Pauline communities over roughly the last century. We now turn to the issue of economic profiling itself. Our purposes here will be not only to trace the various stages of scholarship on the topic but also to offer some synthetic remarks about the current state of the discussion.

Early Socioeconomic Approaches

By all accounts, the modern conversation about the economic status of early Christian groups began with the work of the great papyrologist Adolf Deissmann (1866–1937). Highly influential throughout the first half of the twentieth century, Deissmann compared the authors of the New Testament to the artisans, peasants, and slaves who produced the documentary papyri.[23] Thus, Deissmann declared, in words now well known: "The New Testament was not a product of the colourless refinement of an upper class. . . . On the contrary, it was, humanly

---

22. Dale Martin, "Review Essay: Justin J. Meggitt, *Paul, Poverty and Survival*," *JSNT* 84 (2001): 62; Martin's italics.
23. Adolf Deissmann, *Light from the Ancient East: The New Testament Illustrated by Recently Discovered Texts of the Graeco-Roman World*, trans. Lionel R. M. Strachan (Peabody, MA: Hendrickson, 1995).

speaking, a product of the force that came, unimpaired and strengthened by the Divine Presence, from the lower class."[24] As we shall see, Deissmann also acknowledged the presence of the well-to-do in Christian circles, but it was for his emphasis on the lower classes that he would be remembered.

Others in Deissmann's era also emphasized Christianity's humbler origins. Karl Kautsky and Shirley Jackson Case portrayed Christianity as a revolutionary movement of the anti-Roman proletariat.[25] Compared to Deissmann, however, Kautsky and Case made far less impact on later discussions. At bottom, all later reconstructions of early Christian socioeconomic constituency would represent a response in some way to Deissmann's focus on the lower classes.

The "New Consensus"

E. A. Judge is credited with inaugurating a new stage in the discussion with his publication of a small but highly influential volume titled *The Social Pattern of Christian Groups in the First Century* (1960). In a reassessment of the social constituency of early Christian groups, Judge concluded in chapter 5 that although Christians did not break into the upper orders of the Roman ranking system, they were still "dominated by a socially pretentious section of the population of the big cities."[26] A few years earlier (1954), A. T. Robertson had articulated similar views in *The Origins of Christianity*.[27]

Between 1974 and 1975, Gerd Theissen published a series of essays examining social dynamics in the earliest church at Corinth.[28] Theissen argued that while a majority of the church's members belonged to the "lower classes," the church also contained a dominant minority drawn from the "upper classes."[29] This stratification of members accounted for a number of the problems addressed in 1 Corinthians. Although Theissen's analysis focused on the Corinthian church, he surmised that the Corinthian congregation may have been "characteristic of the Hel-

24. Ibid., 144.
25. Karl Kautsky, *Der Ursprung des Christentums: eine historische untersuchung* (Stuttgart: Dietz, 1908); Karl Kautsky, *Foundations of Christianity* (New York: Russell & Russell, 1953); Shirley Jackson Case, "The Nature of Primitive Christianity," *AmJT* 17, no. 1 (1913): 63–79.
26. E. A. Judge, *The Social Pattern of Christian Groups in the First Century: Some Prolegomena to the Study of New Testament Ideas of Social Obligation* (London: Tyndale, 1960), 60.
27. A. T. Robertson (*The Origins of Christianity*, rev. ed. [New York: International Publishers, 1962], 132) said that Paul and his companions were "at least of the middle class and middling education."
28. Later translated into English by John Schütz and collected into *The Social Setting of Pauline Christianity*.
29. Theissen, *Social Setting*, 69.

lenistic congregations as such."[30] Accordingly, Theissen concluded that "Hellenistic primitive Christianity was neither a proletarian movement among the lower classes nor an affair of the upper classes," but that it rather "encompassed various strata."[31]

It was the work of Gerd Theissen and others in his stream that Abraham Malherbe held in mind when, in 1977, he announced the emergence of a "new consensus":[32] the social status of early Christians was perhaps "higher than Deissmann had supposed"; the church comprised rather a "cross section of most of Roman society."[33] In 1983—the same year that the second edition of Malherbe's volume went to press—Wayne Meeks would ratify this claim: "The 'emerging consensus' that Malherbe reports seems to be valid: a Pauline congregation generally reflected a fair cross-section of urban society."[34] Although not everyone accepted the conclusions of these interpreters (John Gager was a notable example),[35] their views gained wide acceptance in the guild and gave impetus to a burgeoning trend of scholarship focused on the supposed wealthier constituents of Pauline churches.

Primary representatives of the "new consensus" (as it came to be called), including Judge, Theissen, and Meeks, qualified their claims by noting that no evidence existed for Christians among the highest orders of the elite. As Meeks remarked, "the extreme top and bottom of the Greco-Roman social scale are missing" from the cross section: we find neither senators, equestrians, or decurions, nor agricultural slaves or day laborers in the first-century church.[36] Judge and others were equally explicit about the absence of elites.[37] Yet, during the 1990s, a number of studies, representing what might be called the "new guard" of so-called new-consensus scholarship, did begin to employ, less critically, the terminology of "elites" in describing those of higher stand-

30. Ibid., 70.
31. Ibid., 106.
32. Abraham J. Malherbe, *Social Aspects of Early Christianity*, 2nd ed. (Philadelphia: Fortress Press, 1983), 31, 87. The volume was based on a lecture series presented at Rice University in 1975.
33. Ibid., 87.
34. Meeks, *First Urban Christians*, 73.
35. John G. Gager, *Kingdom and Community: The Social World of Early Christianity* (Englewood Cliffs, NJ: Prentice-Hall, 1975); John G. Gager, review of *Social Aspects of Early Christianity*, by Abraham Malherbe, *RelSRev* 5, no. 3 (1979): 174–80.
36. Meeks, *First Urban Christians*, 73.
37. Judge, *Social Pattern*, 52; Dale B. Martin, *Corinthian Body* (New Haven, CT: Yale University Press, 1995), xvi–xvii; Jerome Murphy-O'Connor, *St. Paul's Corinth*, Good News Studies 6 (Collegeville, MN: Liturgical Press, 2002); even Theissen's ("Social Structure," 73, 75) language of the "upper classes" seems appropriately qualified.

ing in Pauline communities.[38] This development would later give rise to criticism against "new-consensus" scholarship as a whole.

Binary Models of the Ancient Economy

In 1998, Justin Meggitt published a volume utilizing a binary economic schema drawn from the work of Géza Alföldy.[39] This schema depicted the Roman Empire as a sharply divided society consisting of a poor majority (99 percent) and a tiny elite minority (1 percent). According to Meggitt, Paul and his churches found themselves among the impoverished 99 percent, and like most everyone else "could expect little more from life than abject poverty."[40] A "wide gulf" separated the two economic levels, and there were "few economic differences between those that found themselves outside of the rarefied circles of the elite."[41] In highlighting the prevalence of poverty both in Paul's churches and in Roman society at large, Meggitt presented his study as a challenge to the conclusions of the "new consensus."[42]

Meggitt's study drew criticism from multiple quarters. Theissen responded in an effort to provide further substantiation for his claim that social stratification existed within Christian communities, pointing out that significant stratification could exist even among the sub-elite groups.[43] Moreover, in a scathing review of Meggitt's book published in the *Journal for the Study of the New Testament*, Dale Martin pointedly summed up what still seems to be a common reaction to Meggitt's work: "As a corrective to some exaggerations of a popular consensus it may be welcome, but as a challenge to the consensus itself and as an alternative proposal, it fails."[44]

Steven Friesen, however, estimated that Meggitt's binary schema, despite its shortcomings, accomplished a "necessary polemical task" in waking up modern Westerners to the prevalence of poverty in the

---

38. Andrew D. Clarke, *Secular and Christian Leadership in Corinth: A Socio-Historical and Exegetical Study of 1 Corinthians 1-6* (New York: Brill, 1993); David W. J. Gill, "In Search of the Social Elite in Corinth," *TynBul* 44, no. 4 (1993): 323–37; Bruce W. Winter, *After Paul Left Corinth: The Influence of Secular Ethics and Social Change* (Grand Rapids: Eerdmans, 2001), 120.
39. Géza Alföldy, *Die römische Sozialgeschichte: ausgewählte Beiträge* (Stuttgart: Steiner Verlag Wiesbaden, 1986); Géza Alföldy, *The Social History of Rome* (Totowa, NJ: Barnes & Noble, 1985).
40. Meggitt, *Paul, Poverty and Survival*; for his dependence on Alföldy, see ibid., 50n49.
41. Ibid., 50, 7, respectively.
42. Ibid., 99–153.
43. Theissen, "Social Structure"; Gerd Theissen, "Social Conflicts in the Corinthian Correspondence: Further Remarks on J. J. Meggitt, *Paul, Poverty and Survival*," *JSNT* 25, no. 3 (2003): 371–91.
44. Martin, "Review Essay," 54. Meggitt responded to both Theissen and Martin in "Response to Martin and Theissen," *JSNT* 84 (2001): 85–94.

ancient world.[45] Thus Meggitt's work provided the stimulus to bring the conversation to its next stage.

Scalar Models of the Ancient Economy

The last two decades of work on Paul and economics have witnessed the development of considerably more nuanced tools of analysis and, as a result, much greater precision in situating early Christians along the economic spectrum. Specifically, analysis at this stage has centered around the development of differentiated economic "scales" and estimation of population percentages at each level.

A formidable advance in the discussion came in 2004 with a seminal article by Steven Friesen.[46] While Friesen lauded Meggitt's attention to the problem of poverty in the ancient world, he also issued a call to move beyond Meggitt's (Alföldy's) binary model of the ancient economy. Building on data supplied by C. R. Whittaker for European economies between the fifteenth and eighteenth centuries CE,[47] Friesen devised a seven-tiered economic scale, or "poverty scale" (PS), differentiated according to variation in individual economic resources measured in relation to subsistence level (as defined by caloric intake).[48] "Elites," comprising the highest three levels (PS1–3), constituted only 3 percent of society. Another 7 percent enjoyed a "moderate surplus" of resources (PS4). The remaining 90 percent sat near or below subsistence level (PS5–7). Friesen utilized his scale as a benchmark for reevaluating social descriptions of Pauline assemblies. Based on evidence from the Pauline letters, he concluded that there were no "wealthy saints" in the Pauline assemblies; the "vast majority" were poor, living at or below subsistence level, although a few found themselves hovering safely above the threshold of poverty, at the PS4 level.[49]

---

45. Friesen, "Poverty in Pauline Studies," 339. Meggitt, of course, anticipated Friesen's assessment of his work on both counts. He showed awareness on the one hand that his analysis "appears at times somewhat undifferentiated," but he insisted at the same time that this is "a necessary price to pay in order to bring out such an important and neglected aspect of the lives of the Pauline Christians." Meggitt, *Paul, Poverty and Survival*, 5.

46. Friesen, "Poverty in Pauline Studies."

47. C. R. Whittaker, "The Poor in the City of Rome," in *Land, City, and Trade in the Roman Empire* (Aldershot, UK: Variorum, 1993), ch. 7.

48. As Friesen ("Poverty in Pauline Studies," 343) states, "'subsistence level' is here defined as the resources needed to procure enough calories in food to maintain the human body. The calorific needs of humans are gauged in various ways by scholars, but they usually range from 1,500 to 3,000 calories per day, depending on gender, age, physical energy required for occupation, pregnancy, lactation and so on."

Friesen's article has ranked among the most important contributions for stimulating discussion on the economic status of early Christians. However, it now seems that Friesen also exaggerated the importance of his article somewhat in each of the areas where he claimed to advance the discussion.[50] First, Friesen (rightly) pointed out that there never was a "new consensus," since Deissmann had acknowledged the presence of some fairly well-to-do Christians alongside the peasant and artisan majority. Three years earlier, however, Theissen had already anticipated Friesen on this point, in words clear and concise: "The 'new consensus' is neither new nor is it a consensus."[51] Second, although like Meggitt, Friesen presented his work as a challenge to the findings of the so-called new consensus, Judge, Theissen, and Meeks in fact all agreed that no evidence existed for Christians among the senatorial, equestrian, and perhaps even decurial orders of society.[52] Third, despite Friesen's intent to devise a more differentiated economic scale, the resulting percentages (distorted somewhat further by his rhetoric, as we shall see below) ultimately collapsed his model into little more than a binary construction.[53]

Shortly after Friesen's article, Peter Oakes independently devised an economic scale of his own.[54] In contrast to Friesen, who had based his scale on subsistence level, Oakes based his scale on income as correlated with domestic space occupied. By assessing differences in house size observable in housing remains left at Herculaneum and Pompeii in southern Italy, Oakes was able to show that among the first-century nonelite, "there was a diversity that involved social stratification." Notably, the record disclosed a middling group that was neither abjectly poor nor distinctly elite (30.5 percent).[55] Flanking this group were elites (2.5 percent) and the poor (67 percent). Although Oakes's scale included a total of ten distinct economic bands, he pointed out

---

49. Friesen, "Poverty in Pauline Studies," 357.
50. See Peter Oakes, "Constructing Poverty Scales for Graeco-Roman Society: A Response to Steven Friesen's 'Poverty in Pauline Studies,'" *JSNT* 26, no. 3 (2004): 367–71; and John M. G. Barclay, "Poverty in Pauline Studies: A Response to Stephen Friesen," *JSNT* 26, no. 3 (2004): 363–66.
51. Friesen, "Poverty in Pauline Studies," 325; Theissen, "Social Structure," 66.
52. Friesen, "Poverty in Pauline Studies," 358; on the others, see nn. 36–37 above.
53. Prior to Friesen's work, Ekkehard W. Stegemann and Wolfgang Stegemann (*Urchristliche Sozialgeschichte: Die Anfänge im Judentum und die Christusgemeinden in der mediterranen Welt* [Stuttgart: Kohlhammer, 1995; *The Jesus Movement: A Social History of Its First Century* [Minneapolis: Fortress Press, 1999]) had also proposed subdividing the elite and nonelite groups, but their work also seemed to reduce to a binary schema.
54. Peter Oakes, *Reading Romans in Pompeii: Paul's Letter at Ground Level* (Minneapolis: Fortress Press, 2009). See also Oakes's earlier work *Philippians: From People to Letter*, SNTSMS 110 (Cambridge: Cambridge University Press, 2001).
55. Oakes, *Reading Romans*, xi.

that his percentages could be correlated rather evenly with Friesen's.[56] Table 3.1 represents Oakes's "very tentative model of income distribution in Pompeii and Herculaneum, based on equivalent urban space occupied":

Table 3.1: Oakes (2009)[57]

Equivalent space occupied (m^2)	Percentage of population
above 1,000	2.5
900–999	0.2
800–899	0.3
700–799	0.5
600–699	1
500–599	2.5
400–499	4
300–399	4
200–299	7
100–199	11.0
0–99	67

A 2009 article by Bruce Longenecker represented an important step toward addressing some of the shortcomings of Friesen's scale.[58] Drawing from the work of Walter Scheidel—who, using census data from property owners in the late republic, had argued for a "middling" percentage of 20–25 percent—Longenecker substantially revised Friesen's PS4 and PS5 percentages, raising them respectively from 7 to 17 percent and from 22 to 25 percent. He further proposed relabeling Friesen's "Poverty Scale" (PS) an "Economic Scale" (ES) in an attempt to be more value neutral, and subdividing PS4 into ES4a (closer to elite status) and ES4b (closer to stable subsistence status). Thus, Longenecker elongated the middle section of Friesen's scale, exposing a more sizeable space between the "rich" and "poor" and taking another important step toward breaking apart the old binary construct.

Longenecker's revisions were short-lived, however. That same year,

---

56. Ibid., 66.
57. Reproduced from ibid., 61, table 2.2.
58. Longenecker, "Exposing the Economic Middle," 243–78.

Friesen collaborated with Scheidel in an impressive effort to create a maximally fine-tuned economy scale. Their aims were to establish "a convergent range of estimates" of the size of the economy of the Roman Empire at its peak (second century CE), and from these data to develop a "model of income distribution and inequality."[59] In this model, as in Friesen's earlier work, income translates to subsistence level. Table 3.2 provides a summary of their findings. Moving from top to bottom of the table, brackets 6–600 represent elites; ~1 [1.44]–5 represent middling groups; 0.5–0.99 represent those at, close to, or not far above subsistence; and 0.25–0.49 represent below-subsistence groups. Percentages for each bracket are bounded by "pessimistic" and "optimistic" estimates. In short, the proposed elite group population is fixed at approximately 1.5 percent, the middling percentage accounts for "roughly one-tenth" of the population, 70–75 percent are close to subsistence, and 10–22 percent sit beneath subsistence.[60]

Table 3.2: Scheidel and Friesen (2009)

Level	Proportion according to assessment of non-elite income share	
	"pessimistic"	"optimistic"
600	0.0008	0.0006
300–599	0.002	0.001
150–299	0.005	0.003
75–149	0.01	0.01
45–74	0.04	0.03
24–44	0.1	0.1
12–23	0.4	0.3
6–11	1.1	0.8
5	0.4	0.8
4	0.6	1.2
3	1	1.8
2	1.5	2.7
1	4.8	8.3

59. Walter Scheidel and Steven J. Friesen, "The Size of the Economy and the Distribution of Income in the Roman Empire," *JRS* 99 (2009): 61–91.
60. Table reproduced from ibid., 85, table 10; the language "roughly one-tenth" comes from ibid., 88.

0.75–0.99	8	19
0.5–0.74	60	55
0.25–0.49	22	10

Longenecker took these developments into account in his 2010 monograph, *Remember the Poor*. Taking a more optimistic perspective, but respecting the complexity of Scheidel's and Friesen's study, Longenecker marginally lowered his percentages for the middling group, deducting 2 percent from ES4 and awarding it to the ES5 group.

The percentages from Friesen (2004), Longenecker (2009), and Longenecker (2010) are summarized in Table 3.3. ES1–3 represent the elite, ES4–5 represent middling groups, ES6 represents those *at* subsistence, and ES7 represents those *below* subsistence.

Table 3.3: Friesen (2004), Longenecker (2009), Longenecker (2010)[61]

	Friesen 2004	Longenecker 2009	Longenecker 2010
ES1–ES3	3	3	3
ES4	7	17	15
ES5	22	25	27
ES6	40	30	30
ES7	28	25	25

The State of the Question

In the last century of dialogue on economic distribution under the Roman Empire, summarized above, considerable progress seems to have been made.

(1) The development of finely differentiated economic scales has injected much greater precision of language into the discussion. The old binary model that distinguished only between "elites" and "poor" can no longer be regarded as accurate (if it was ever so regarded). Likewise, the "cross section" model, while much more differentiated, has been exposed as being somewhat unstable, due to a lack of consistency in the use of labels and often a lack of explicit definition. What is meant by "the wealthy"? The "well-to-do"? The "upper-classes"? The "poor"?

---

61. Reproduced from Longenecker, *Remember the Poor*, 53.

The multitiered scales proposed since Friesen's in 2004 have made important steps in clarifying these potential obscurities. For example, in speaking of the "wealthy" church members, the interpreter might now specify that he or she refers to members with a "moderate surplus of funds," belonging to ES4 (or even ES4a or ES4b), but not those among the highest "elite," represented by ES1–3. Likewise, by defining the "poor" as those belonging to levels ES6 or 7, the interpreter could avoid conflating those struggling to survive (ES6–7) with those who found themselves nonetheless in a stable (ES5) or relatively comfortable position (ES4), even if they did not enjoy membership in the ruling class (ES1–3). Likewise, the work of Scheidel and Friesen (2009) has qualified measurements of economic levels relative to subsistence with hairsplitting precision: for example, they distinguish those "below subsistence" (10–22 percent) and "at or close to subsistence" (55–65 percent) from those "¼ to ⅔ above subsistence" (8–19 percent). Because Friesen's and Longenecker's scales have lacked mathematical precision of the same order, it becomes difficult to correlate their tiers with those of Scheidel and Friesen. Yet, it seems reasonable to suppose that "below," "at or close," and "¼ to ⅔ above subsistence" (Scheidel and Friesen) could be roughly correlated, respectively, with PS/ES7, PS/ES6, and at least a percentage of PS/ES5.

In sum, scalar models such as these have begun to offer sufficient nuancing to account for diversity in ancient experiences and, in addition, have helped to control against the skewing of data, and thus can help to stabilize the academic discourse.[62] They have also revealed that alleged differences in perspective from Theissen to the present have often been overdrawn and have had more to do with particular nuances and terminological variation than with substantial disagreement.[63]

(2) Current models involve a great deal of conjecture, but it is "tightly controlled conjecture," nonetheless (this is particularly true of Scheidel and Friesen's study).[64] Moreover, rough consistency in assessments of early Christian economic profiles over a period of some forty or fifty years confirms that we have been headed in the right direction: the "typical" Christian may have been, as Meeks said, the "free artisan or small trader,"[65] but there must also have been some Christians fur-

---

62. Longenecker, "Exposing the Economic Middle," 249.
63. Longenecker, *Remember the Poor*, 228–31.
64. Scheidel and Friesen, "Size of the Economy," 63.
65. Meeks, *First Urban Christians*, 73.

ther down (Longenecker's ES6), and an upper middling minority (Longenecker's ES4) also found representation, not least in Corinth. (We shall look at some of the evidence for economic profiles of Pauline Christians below.) If it is correct to say that there "never was a 'new consensus,'" this is because this diversity in Christian communities has generally always been acknowledged. As Longenecker points out, "a simple trawl through three prosopographic analyses from the last three decades (i.e., those of Meeks in 1982, Horrell in 1996, and Friesen in 2004)" illustrates that prosopographical analyses have been relatively stable, "even across the 'consensus' divide."[66]

(3) The extent of ancient economic diversity found at the sub-elite levels, exposed by Theissen, Oakes, and others, has revealed that there was ample space for social stratification within the first Christian assemblies. It is not difficult to imagine, for instance, what difference the gap between those "moderate surplus" persons who stood on comfortably high ground (ES4b) and those who struggled to keep their heads above water (ES6) might have made to social relations in Christian communities. And how much greater the distance between those who stood on the threshold of elite status (ES4a)—if indeed these were to be found in the church—and those truly impoverished individuals who were withering away daily (ES7).

(4) Longenecker's sensitivity to Christian communal practices alerts us to the fact that the economic positions of individual Christians are unlikely to have remained static. In the Greco-Roman *collegia* (associations), and probably to an even greater extent in Paul's churches, benefaction shown by the more fortunate was sure to have played a role in helping to elevate those of lower status or at least to mitigate their challenges. This need not mean that communities altogether "leveled out," but Paul's letters provide evidence that he expected the more fortunate to at least help "offset" the needs of those individuals who found themselves mired in greater difficulties.[67]

(5) One thing that has remained common to studies conducted after Friesen (2004) is an increasing tendency toward the middle and "near-subsistence" populations in the estimated percentages. Based on elite consumption of GDP resources, Scheidel and Friesen (2009) concluded that most people had to be close to subsistence (perhaps 70–75 percent, it would appear, adding together the groups closest to subsistence in their scale), and that this pattern was "inflexible" because there

---

66. Longenecker, *Remember the Poor*, 251–52.
67. Ibid., 259–97, esp. 288.

could not be too many poor households "without paralyzing society."[68] Accordingly, they proposed a range of some 10 to 22 percent for those below subsistence—which is substantially lower than the 28 percent for the PS7 group proposed by Friesen in 2004. This change also resonates with the conclusion reached by Guy Sanders in his recent study of Roman Corinth. Sanders estimates an elite population of 2 percent, a middling population of 20 percent, and more than 65 percent living "close to or at subsistence level."[69] This leaves less than 13 percent living below subsistence (see table 3.4).

Table 3.4: Sanders (2014)

Population	Percentage of population
Elites	2
Middling population	20
Close to or at subsistence	>65
[Below subsistence]	[<13]

Correlating these findings with Friesen's original tiers, this means that the vast majority of those belonging to what Friesen called PS5–7 would better be categorized as being "*near* subsistence," with some of them bobbing at the surface, and others in fact skimming above it. Only roughly 10 to 20 percent of this majority could be categorized as falling indefinitely below subsistence. This, of course, is not to minimize the plight of this still quite substantial sector of the population, but it does provide some much-needed qualification to Friesen's originally far more pessimistic estimate of 28 percent.

Alongside these advances, made really only in the last ten years, a number of issues where disagreement remains call for further discussion.

(1) Ambiguities over definition still threaten to throw discussion into confusion. Friesen (2004) performed a valuable service in redistributing the old binary categories of "rich" and "poor" into seven distinct socioeconomic strata. However, his rhetoric at that point still exhibited some potentially misleading tendencies. In his discussion, for example, PS5 was routinely lumped together with PS6 and 7:

---

68. Scheidel and Friesen, "Size of the Economy," 88.
69. Guy D. R. Sanders, "Landlords and Tenants: Sharecroppers and Subsistence Farming in Corinthian Historical Context," in *Corinth in Contrast: Studies in Inequality*, edited by Steven J. Friesen, Sarah A. James, and Daniel N. Schowalter, NovTSup 155 (Leiden: Brill, 2014), 121–24.

> The overwhelming majority of the population under Roman imperialism lived near the subsistence level, that is, categories PS5–7.
>
> There was an enormous difference in financial resources between the few people in the top three categories and the majority who lived near the subsistence level (PS5–7).[70]

These remarks are true from one perspective. But one must not forget how Friesen defined PS5: these people were "*stable* near subsistence."[71] While such people must have remained conscious of their proximity to the truly impoverished, manifestly their "stability" above the subsistence level, by definition, also secured them safely above the realities of poverty in personal experience. Those of this class could, with at least equal warrant, have been grouped together with those among PS4 ("moderate surplus resources"). Moreover, those of PS6, "*at* subsistence level," no doubt lived hand to mouth, but Friesen's added parenthetical description, "and often *below* minimum level to sustain life," seems patently one-sided; with these living "at" subsistence level, could we not equally have added, "and *usually above* the minimum level"? Friesen's presentation of the data, it seems, paints a gloomier picture of things than a more holistic representation of the data would seem to require.

But Scheidel and Friesen also place an additional 8–19 percent "¼ to ⅔ above subsistence." Do they mean to include this latter group when they refer to (and here I use their exact language) "the vast majority of the population" that lived "close to subsistence"?[72] Or is the group of 8–19 percent included when Scheidel and Friesen say that "most households" had to be concentrated "relatively close to subsistence"?[73] Expressions like these suggest that when talking about the "vast majority of the population" living "close to subsistence" alongside the 55–65 percent "at or close to subsistence," Scheidel and Friesen mean also to subsume at least some from the level just above: adding the 8–19 percent "¼ to ⅔ above subsistence" would yield roughly 65–80 percent "relatively close to subsistence."

(2) For some interpreters, the language of the discussion has continued to approximate the old binary construct not only because of the distortions inherent to their rhetoric but also because of a tendency

---

70. Friesen, "Poverty in Pauline Studies," 343, 345, respectively.
71. Ibid., 341.
72. Scheidel and Friesen, "Size of the Economy," 62.
73. Ibid., 88.

to inflate percentages conjectured at the more impoverished levels. The reasons for downward distortion in Friesen's (2004) figures can be discerned by tracking them back to their source(s).[74] Friesen openly acknowledged his debt to Whittaker's study (1993) for his percentages, but Whittaker had drawn his numbers from Stuart Woolf's *The Poor in Western Europe in the Eighteenth and Nineteenth Centuries* (1986), who in turn had relied on Brian Pullan's article "Poveri, mendicant e vagabondi (secondi XIV–XVII)" (1978).[75] Whittaker distinguished between the disabled poor (4–8 percent of society), the "crisis" poor (20 percent), and the "conjunctural" poor (30–40 percent).[76] The legitimacy of Friesen's decision to fix his percentage amounts at the upper end of Whittaker's estimates is itself open to question.[77] But equally serious problems become evident once we trace the data back to Pullan. Pullan had subsumed his figures within three concentric circles, together comprising 50–70 percent of society. The innermost circle contained 4–8 percent "structural poor" (*pauvres structurels*) or "permanently poor" (*permanentemente povere*). Circumscribing this circle was 20 percent "conjunctural" (*pauvres conjoncturels*) or "crisis poor" (*poveri della crisi*), describing people who were sufficiently employed at times, but at others had to take recourse to alms. The remaining portion consisted of artisans, low-ranking employees, and small shopkeepers, who possessed modest properties (*modestissime riserve di proprietà*) and were sufficiently resourced to sustain themselves without outside assistance, except in the event of prolonged crisis, illness, or accident.[78]

A comparison of Pullan, Whittaker, and Friesen exposes discrepancies in their terminology (i.e., compare Pullan's "conjunctural" poor with Whittaker's "conjunctural" poor):

74. For this point, I am indebted to Luke Ming-Mou Tsai's recently defended dissertation, "Brothers in Dispute: A Socio-Economic and Legal Analysis of the Litigants in the Church of Corinth" (PhD diss., Dallas Theological Seminary, 2016), 86–87.

75. Stuart Woolf, *The Poor in Western Europe in the Eighteenth and Nineteenth Centuries* (London: Methuen, 1986), 5–6; Brian Pullan, "Poveri, Mendicanti e Vagabondi (Seconli XIV–XVII)," in *Storia d'Italia. Annali 1. Dal feudalesimo al capitalismo*, ed. Ruggiero Romano and Corrado Vivanti (Torino, ITA: Einaudi, 1978), 981–1047. For Whittaker's reliance on Woolf, see Whittaker, "The Poor," ch. 7, pp. 4, 25.

76. Whittaker, "The Poor," ch. 7, p. 4.

77. Friesen ("Poverty in Pauline Studies," 338–39) justifies his decision by appealing to his pessimistic "Finleyan" model of the ancient economy, although Longenecker (*Remember the Poor*, 258–59) notes that the appropriateness of Finleyan economics has been called into serious question by a number of studies.

78. Pullan, "Poveri, Mendicanti e Vagabondi," 988–89.

Table 3.5: A Comparison of Pullan, Whittaker, and Friesen

Pullan (50–70%)	Whittaker (approximately 50–70%)	Friesen (70%)
20% (conjunctural or crisis poor)	20% (crisis poor)	28% (8% 20%) at PS7
4–8% (structural or permanently poor)	4–8% (disabled)	
[22–46%] (other artisans, etc.)	30–40% (conjunctural poor)	40% at PS6

The chief problem, however, is not only that Friesen's percentages exhaust the upper end of the range of Pullan's outermost circle (approximately 70 percent rather than 50 percent), but in fact that the entire 70 percent consists of those "at" or "below" subsistence level (PS6–7) and contains no one at the "stable" level (PS5). As just indicated, Pullan's second circle describes those who wavered between PS6 and 7, not those who remained stagnant at PS7; Pullan's outermost circle seems to describe those at the bottom half of Friesen's PS5 level ("stable near subsistence"), who only sometimes dipped below its threshold, not those permanently fixed "at subsistence (and often below minimum level to sustain life)," or PS6. Thus, Friesen has manifestly downshifted his groups by at least a half-category from where Pullan, on whom he ultimately depends, had placed them. In short, the difference is between having, at the extremes, 50 percent making up PS5, 6, and 7, and having 70 percent making up PS6 and 7 alone.

(3) It will be crucial for any future research to take into account fluctuation in the strength of the economy in diverse geographical and temporal contexts. (a) Undeniably, the importance of Scheidel's and Friesen's (2009) work as an attempt to plot the size of the ancient economy and its distribution of wealth is without parallel. However, theirs is not ultimately the most suitable scale available for those in early Christian studies concerned with the "first urban Christians" since their scale presents economic averages across all areas of the Roman Empire, mixing together, among other things, urban and rural data. Friesen's earlier work (2004), as well as its revision in Longenecker (2009; 2010), is more helpful in that it focuses estimates on urban contexts, where economies were undoubtedly more robust. (b) While Scheidel and Friesen (2009) did recognize that middling-income groups may have been "disproportionately present in urban contexts" (because of the attractions that the city offered this group) and per-

haps double their representation elsewhere, they concluded that any substantially higher degree of concentration of middling groups there "would imply that rural areas were almost entirely populated by subsistence-level households, which seems unrealistic."[79] This, however, is mistaken. In a dissertation defended in 2016, Luke Tsai pointed out that elevated middling percentages in the city do not in fact substantially impact overall percentages for this group elsewhere, since 90 percent of people lived in the countryside.[80] For example, doubling the size of the middling group in urban areas, from, say, 9 to 18 percent, would result in a final decrease of only one percentage point (for a total of 8 percent) for the middling group in the countryside and does not in fact result, as Friesen and Scheidel presume, in a rural area "almost entirely populated by subsistence-level households."

Excursus: Urban vs. Rural Middling Percentages

Tsai does not show the work for his calculation, but my calculations reveal that he is correct.

If we doubled the middling slice in urban areas from 9 percent to 18 percent, and the population in urban areas constituted 10 percent of the total population, then this should be represented as:

$(0.1)(0.18)$

The remaining 90 percent of the population resided in rural areas. Our variable, moreover, is "What percentage does the middling group comprise overall?" This we therefore represent by:

$(0.9)(x)$

In the end, we want, hypothetically, an empire-wide figure of 9 percent for the middling group. This should be represented as 0.09. This will be the sum of the other calculations.

Our formula, then, is:

$(0.1)(0.18) + (0.9)(x) = 0.09$

x therefore equals 0.08, or 8 percent. In other words, the *rural* middling share is reduced by only one percent if we double the size of the middling population in *urban* areas.

---

79. Scheidel and Friesen, "Size of the Economy," 90.

80. Tsai, "Brothers in Dispute," 113, citing Andrew Wilson, "City Sizes and Urbanization in the Roman Empire," in *Settlement, Urbanization, and Population*, ed. Alan Bowman and Andrew Wilson (Oxford: Oxford University Press, 2011), 182–91; and Elio Lo Cascio, "Urbanization as a Proxy of Demographic and Economic Growth," in *Quantifying the Roman Economy: Methods and Problems*, ed. Alan Bowman and Andrew Wilson (Oxford: Oxford University Press, 2013), 88.

This point has tremendous implications for assessments of the urban economic situation in which Paul's churches were situated. (c) It is crucial also to account for the unique differences exhibited between one urban center and another. When it comes to the economy of Roman Corinth, Guy Sanders has emphasized the importance of evidence localized to Greece.[81] Longenecker cites studies suggesting that Roman Corinth experienced substantial economic growth within the first two centuries of our era, as demonstrated by growth in commerce, manufacturing, and technological development;[82] moreover, Corinth was comparatively very prosperous among cities of its time.[83] However, there is equally a danger of "overlocalizing" evidence, for example, by focusing strictly on housing at Corinth (or Herculaneum and Pompeii for that matter).[84] Oakes suggests that the solution is "to keep in mind all levels from the most local to the most general."[85] (d) Notwithstanding the structural similarity of all pre-Industrial economies, one needs to distinguish as much as possible between the Roman Empire on the one hand and medieval and late pre-Industrial economies on the other; Friesen's study (2004) of the former was based on the latter.

(4) While wealth or income (correlated with subsistence) continues to emerge in analysis as the most important economic variable, the legitimacy of this move continues to be questioned (and there continue to be questions about what constitutes "subsistence"). Oakes submits that a behavior-based poverty scale, perhaps articulated along the lines of "socially perceived necessities" (which vary between societies or groups), might introduce more nuance than income-based considerations. Necessities could be defined against "deprivation lists," that is, by observing prioritization in the remedying of deprivations.[86] Oakes's concern is to provide as much control as possible to definition, by including as many variables as possible (elsewhere he refers to wealth, in addition to "house size, quality of wall and floor decoration, quantity of loose finds of types relating to discretionary expenditure, frequency of access to expensive medical care as indicated in skeletal remains, degrees of variety in diet as indicated by study of food remains, and estimated expense of funerary monument").[87]

81. Sanders, "Landlords and Tenants," 107.
82. Longenecker, "Exposing the Economic Middle," 255–57.
83. For evidence based on rises in urbanization and consumption, see Tsai, "Brothers in Dispute," 55–78.
84. For the former, see Murphy-O'Connor, *St. Paul's Corinth*, 178–85; for the latter, Oakes, *Reading Romans*, 61.
85. Oakes, "Methodological Issues," 26.
86. Oakes, "Constructing Poverty Scales," 369–71.

(5) All of our models face difficulties in confronting the complexities of the Greco-Roman household. Were all slaves positioned at the ES6 or 7 level? Or did some enjoy greater "stability" (ES5) of subsistence than many freedmen, peasants, or artisans? A different set of problems faces non-subsistence models. Oakes's household-based model accounts only for householders, which, he notes, accounts only for roughly one-eighth of society.[88] Adding a spouse and two children, houses containing families of four would still account for only one-half of society. To what level do we assign the missing half? In all models, filling in the unknowns requires considerable guesswork. If more "scientific" means of calculation can be extrapolated from the evidence, it is to this level of detail that we would need to advance in order to sharpen our precision any further.

(6) Interpreters have reached wide agreement that Christian communities in the first century represented a broad cross section of society (see below). Most have suggested that we have little if any solid evidence for Christians among the "elite" (ES1–3). But this must be regarded as an open question. In an impressively thorough study, Alexander Weiss has recently argued anew that decuriones—including specifically Erastus (Rom 16:23)—as well as senators were indeed already represented among Christians in the first century.[89] Weiss's work is sure to provoke renewed discussion concerning the question of the presence of true "elites" among the first urban Christians.

Summary

The following summary is offered not as a fresh constructive attempt to devise a socioeconomic scale of the Roman Empire but as an attempt to highlight, at a glance, where the preceding decades of discussion have led us. This summary takes into account relevant criticisms of recent studies as well as the fact of basic geographical and local variation in economic circumstances, especially between city and countryside. Because most New Testament scholars have focused their interests on urban Christian groups, and chiefly Pauline assemblies, numbers reflect urban environments rather than rural ones. Two principles, often locked in tension with each other in the preceding studies,

---

87. Oakes, "Methodological Issues," 31.
88. Oakes, *Reading Romans*, 59–62.
89. Alexander Weiss, *Soziale Elite und Christentum: Studien zu ordo-Angehörigen unter den frühen Christen*, Millennium Studies 52 (Berlin: de Gruyter, 2015).

are here resolved in a slight adjustment of ranges: (1) as the laws of ancient economies dictated (see above), most people had to be near subsistence (anywhere from barely reaching the surface to resting just above it) to maintain social and economic stasis; and (2) urban environments exhibited superior economic strength and possessed more attraction for middling and elite groups than rural ones. Equally, it has been shown that the middling percentage represented empire-wide could be—and because of the opportunities afforded by the city, almost certainly should be—doubled in many urban areas without significantly depleting percentages for that group elsewhere; this in turn reduces percentages at other levels proportionately, having its greatest impact on the large, near-subsistence group. In keeping with the dominant approach, brackets are described relative to wealth, as correlated with subsistence:

Table 3.6: Adjusted First-Century Urban Populations at a Glance

Population	Percentage of population
Elite	3
Moderate surplus	15–25
Near (at or above) subsistence	60–70
Below subsistence	10–20

By simplifying things in this way, of course, we lose the fine gradations of difference that we know existed around the middle two levels. What this breakdown is intended to demonstrate, however, is that (1) the "middling" group (here described in terms of "moderate surplus") was in fact, in cities, probably larger than our studies in general have indicated with their percentages; (2) correspondingly, the bottom, "below subsistence" group was notably smaller than the scales of Friesen and Longenecker indicated; and (3) a vast majority of people were concentrated neither comfortably above nor definitely below subsistence, but rather "near" it.

It must be said that these numbers probably do not mirror the constituency of the first Christian assemblies exactly, as Christianity seems to have drawn somewhat disproportionately from society's lower tiers.[90] Nonetheless, these figures provide a probable point of depar-

---

90. See Oakes, *Reading Romans*, 83, table 3.3; and Longenecker, *Remember the Poor*, 295.

ture for the socioeconomic breakdown of the average city of the first-century empire.

The Economic Level of Pauline Christians

As matters regarding ancient economic realities have come into clearer focus, interpreters of the New Testament have reassessed earlier analyses of the economic level of Pauline communities. Meeks had calculated that we know nearly eighty names of individuals associated with Pauline Christianity, about thirty of whom are described in sufficient detail in available sources to give us some clue about their status. Theissen assigned to the "upper classes" no less than nine of the seventeen known members of the Corinthian church: Aquila, Prisca, Stephanas, Erastus, Sosthenes, Crispus, Phoebe, Gaius, and Titius Justus.[91] Meeks thought he found evidence for wealth and prestige for most of the same individuals.[92]

Interpreters since Theissen have continued to work with the same prosopographical, sociographic, analytic, and comparative evidence.[93] With regard to prosopographical evidence, Theissen had considered "statements about holding office, about 'houses,' about assistance rendered to the congregation, and about travel" made in association with Pauline church members.[94] Additionally, as a piece of sociographic data, 1 Corinthians 1:26 has often been taken as a representation, *in nuce*, of the socioeconomic constituency of the Corinthian church.[95] Theissen's remarks on this text have become proverbial: "If Paul says that there were not many in the Corinthian congregation who were wise, powerful, and wellborn, then this much is certain: there were some" (although noneconomic interpretations of this text are at least equally plausible).[96] Prosopographical analyses have tended to focus on this confessedly small "wise, powerful, and wellborn" group. Discus-

91. Theissen, *Social Setting*, 95.
92. Meeks, *First Urban Christians*, 55–63.
93. Studies of note include: Theissen, *Social Setting*, 73–96; Meeks, *First Urban Christians*, 55–63; Clarke, *Secular and Christian Leadership*; Chow, *Patronage and Power*; Alan Mitchell, "Rich and Poor in the Courts of Corinth: Litigiousness and Status in 1 Cor 6:1–11," *NTS* 39, no. 4 (1993): 562–86; David G. Horrell, *The Social Ethos of the Corinthian Correspondence: Interests and Ideology from 1 Corinthians to 1 Clement* (Edinburgh: T&T Clark, 1996); Friesen, "Poverty in Pauline Studies," 348–58; Longenecker, *Remember the Poor*, 220–58; L. L. Welborn, *End to Enmity: Paul and the "Wrongdoer" of 2 Corinthians* (Berlin: de Gruyter, 2011), 230–82; Timothy A. Brookins, *Corinthian Wisdom, Stoic Philosophy, and the Ancient Economy*, SNTSMS 159 (Cambridge: Cambridge University Press, 2014), 107–24.
94. Theissen, *Social Setting*, 73.
95. Brookins, *Corinthian Wisdom*, 47–48, 48n92.
96. Theissen, *Social Setting*, 72.

sion has focused on this group despite its small size not only because of the socioeconomic atypicality of the individuals comprising this group but also because it is almost exclusively these kinds of people for whom Paul supplies prosopographical data. Why these individuals received more attention than others in Paul's letters is not known for certain, but in all likelihood, it is because they wielded disproportionate influence in their respective communities. At least some of them seem to have been installed by Paul as leaders precisely because of their influence (Stephanas in 1 Cor 16:15–16).

The problem with locating Pauline church members on our now more refined economic scales is that the evidence still remains fragmentary and often ambiguous. However, it bears repeating that even if we are not working with certainties, in many cases the evidence remains sufficient to establish prosopographical probabilities. Our scales, moreover, have definitely helped to qualify the language of "wealth" used in earlier studies, in some cases without nuance, as well as to define more precisely the "cross section" of society most probably represented in Paul's churches. Putting things in terms of Longenecker's "Economy Scale," analyses suggest that Pauline Christians spanned at least levels ES4–6. Moreover, Longenecker has shown that while Paul's descriptions of his communities gravitated toward ES5 language (stable near subsistence), a number of individuals mentioned in his letters by name fit the profile described by the higher tier of ES4 (moderate surplus resources).[97] It is to this latter category, ES4, not the elite level of ES1, 2, or 3, that the "wealthy" of Paul's communities most likely belonged. Longenecker places several individuals at this level: Erastus, Gaius, Stephanas, Crispus, and Phoebe, with Erastus falling at the higher end, at ES4a. Friesen (2004) placed Gaius and Erastus at the same level (PS4) but also identified Chloe, Prisca, and Aquila as potential candidates.[98]

Debate, however, has continued to swirl around the figure of Erastus. Among the "wealthier" Christians possible to identify in the earliest Christian communities, Erastus has a better chance than anyone of qualifying for "elite" status. If Weiss is right that Erastus was the *aedile* (οἰκονόμος) of Corinth, this would place him among the city's municipal elite, and thus at the ES3 level. A flurry of publications addressing the

97. Longenecker, *Remember the Poor*, 253.
98. From Friesen, "Poverty in Pauline Studies," 348–58; and Longenecker, *Remember the Poor*, 220–58.

status of Erastus has appeared since 2010.[99] No doubt, we have not yet heard the last word.

Conclusions

Attempts to locate Pauline Christians on the socioeconomic spectrum have revealed a significant degree of agreement among interpreters of the last half-century. However, assessments have not agreed on all points, and even where agreement has existed beneath the surface, differences in presentation have sometimes still served to maximize the appearance of divergence. As in all historiographical matters, differences of opinion here are at bottom "epistemological" in origin. Most fundamentally, the interpreter must decide what kinds of data count as evidence. She must also decide how the individual pieces are to be interpreted, and then how these pieces fit together, and finally how findings are to be most honestly presented.

In closing, let us return, then, to the issue of epistemology.

The interplay alluded to at several points above—that between the overall picture abstracted from the evidence and data unique to specific people or situations—emerges in analysis in a number of what we might call "epistemological polarities."

(1) One's orientation toward the economic situation in the first century could be plotted along a spectrum from "optimistic" to "pessimistic" with respect to the prevalence of poverty. Generalization here prioritizes, probably necessarily, sociographic over prosopographical data—although in this one also runs the risk of allowing the former to smother the latter. At this point, "comparative" sociological data also become a necessary tool for helping situate the economy of the early Roman Empire against other pre-Industrial economies; as we have seen, for instance, Friesen (2004) stressed similarity and virtual uniformity here, whereas Longenecker (2009; 2010) has emphasized the exceptional strength of the Roman Empire among other economies of its kind.

(2) A second underlying polarity is that between "skepticism" and "positivism" as an orientation toward the evidence. Extreme skepticism, on the one hand, selectively disregards particular pieces of evidence on the grounds that they are insufficient to establish anything,

---

99. See n. 9 above.

whereas positivism regards as certifiable fact what might have multiple plausible interpretations.

(3) A third polarity falls along the axis between "minimalism" and "maximalism" in one's use of evidence in profiling. The minimalist might suggest, for instance, that some Christian indicated in the sources as having had a "house" and "slaves" (e.g., Crispus, Stephanas), and about whom no other firm economic indicators are given, *must* be placed at the PS5/ES5 level (stable near subsistence). However, evidence of this extent, logically, would suggest only a minimum possibility: such evidence could describe anyone from PS5/ES5 *and up*. At the other extreme, the maximalist might prefer, without specific evidentiary warrant (thus, apparently arbitrarily or based on ideological preference) to locate such individuals at perhaps the upper end of PS4/ES4, or Longenecker's ES4a, when in fact the individual could be placed lower.

At this juncture, it seems fitting to close discussion with Cicero's remarks on the laws of historiography. He identifies two: first, that the historian must tell only the truth, and second, that he must tell the whole truth (Cicero, *De Oratore* 2.62). These laws describe something profoundly more far-reaching in their philosophical complexity than Cicero perhaps foresaw, for they describe what is endemic to all attempts at human expression, namely the use of language not only as the vehicle for the "truth" but also as a means of reducing, or at any rate simplifying, the "whole" of our chaotic existence into some kind of intelligible representation. Speaking in "Bakhtinian" terms, we are dealing with the inevitably "dialogistic" nature of all historical work. That is, historical claims arise out of tension between "polyphonic" voices—the voices of stubbornly divergent data, as well as of often very contentious interpreters of those data.

In this historical sphere of inquiry, positivism does not apply. Every claim is a probability judgment, and no judgment stands immutable. Fortunately, the "dialogistic" impetus at work in roughly the last century of interpretation has served as a slow but, by all signs, sure corrective mechanism on shots made wide of the mark. If early reconstructions highlighted Christianity as a "movement of the lower classes," and later reconstructions the prominent role of the "well-to-do" in this movement, more recent voices have opened up a noticeable space for a sizeable "middling" group. At present, it seems safe to say that Christianity in the first century represented (almost) a complete "cross section" of society but nonetheless also mirrored the rest of society in its predominant "near subsistence" constituency.

It is the very nature of dialogism for tensions of voices to be smoothed out over time by greater refinement of perspective, by taking account of more evidence, or by revising definitions. But it is equally the nature of dialogism for closure never to be final. Just as each voice in the conversation responds to earlier ones, so later voices will respond to these. The conversation continues.

Select Bibliography

Barclay, John M. G. "Poverty in Pauline Studies: A Response to Stephen Friesen." *JSNT* 26, no. 3 (2004): 363–66.

Deissmann, Adolf. *Light from the Ancient East: The New Testament Illustrated by Recently Discovered Texts of the Graeco-Roman World.* Translated by Lionel R. M. Strachan. New York: Harper & Brothers, 1927.

Friesen, Steven J. "Poverty in Pauline Studies: Beyond the So-Called New Consensus." *JSNT* 26, no. 3 (2004): 323–61.

Judge, E. A. *The Social Pattern of Christian Groups in the First Century: Some Prolegomena to the Study of New Testament Ideas of Social Obligation.* London: Tyndale, 1960.

Longenecker, Bruce W. "Exposing the Economic Middle: A Revised Economy Scale for the Study of Early Christianity." *JSNT* 31, no. 3 (2009): 243–78.

_____. *Remember the Poor: Paul, Poverty, and the Greco-Roman World.* Grand Rapids: Eerdmans, 2010.

Malherbe, Abraham J. *Social Aspects of Early Christianity.* 2nd ed. Philadelphia: Fortress Press, 1983.

Martin, Dale B. "Review Essay: Justin J. Meggitt, *Paul, Poverty and Survival.*" *JSNT* 84 (2001): 51–64.

Meeks, Wayne. *The First Urban Christians.* New Haven: Yale University Press, 1983.

Meggitt, Justin. *Paul, Poverty and Survival.* Edinburgh: T&T Clark, 1998.

Oakes, Peter. "Methodological Issues in Using Economic Evidence in Interpretation of Early Christian Texts." In *Engaging Economics: New Testament Scenarios and Early Christian Reception,* edited by Bruce W. Longenecker and Kelly D. Liebengood, 9–34. Grand Rapids: Eerdmans, 2009.

_____. *Reading Romans in Pompeii: Paul's Letter at Ground Level.* Minneapolis: Fortress Press, 2009.

_____. Review of *Corinth in Context: Comparative Studies on Religion and Society*, by Steven J. Friesen, Daniel N. Schowalter, and James C. Walters. *JSNT* 33, no. 5 (2011): 97–98.

Sanders, Guy D. R. "Landlords and Tenants: Sharecroppers and Subsistence Farming in Corinthian Historical Context." In *Corinth in Contrast: Studies in Inequality*, edited by Steven J. Friesen, Sarah A. James, and Daniel N. Schowalter, 103–25. NovTSup 155. Leiden: Brill, 2014.

Scheidel, Walter. "Stratification, Deprivation and Quality of Life." In *Poverty in the Roman World*, edited by Margaret Atkins and Robin Osborne, 40–59. Cambridge: Cambridge University Press, 2006.

Scheidel, Walter, and Steven J. Friesen. "The Size of the Economy and the Distribution of Income in the Roman Empire." *JRS* 99 (2009): 61–91.

Still, Todd D., and David G. Horrell, eds. *After the First Urban Christians: The Social-Scientific Study of Pauline Christianity Twenty-Five Years Later*. New York: T&T Clark, 2009.

Theissen, Gerd. "Social Conflicts in the Corinthian Community: Further Remarks on J. J. Meggitt, *Paul, Poverty and Survival*." *JSNT* 25, no. 3 (2003): 371–91.

_____. *The Social Setting of Pauline Christianity: Essays on Corinth*. Edited and translated by John H. Schütz. Philadelphia: Fortress Press, 1982.

_____. "The Social Structure of Pauline Communities: Some Critical Remarks on J. J. Meggitt *Paul, Poverty and Survival*." *JSNT* 84 (2001): 65–84.

4

———

Paul's Shift in Economic "Location" in the Locations of the Roman Imperial Economy

Richard A. Horsley

The apostle Paul's economic "location" kept shifting with the remarkable sequence of his life. Saul had sufficient means to journey from the diaspora Judean community of his origin in Tarsus to Jerusalem, where Herod had massively rebuilt the temple. As a pilgrim there, he became zealous for "the traditions of his ancestors," evidently influenced by scribal circles (perhaps Pharisees), and joined in efforts to suppress the nascent movement of Jesus-loyalists (Gal 1:13–14; Phil 3:5–6). Within a few years, however, he suddenly joined the movement he had at first been persecuting, a movement that began with poor villagers, whose leaders had left their economic base in farming and fishing villages to expand the movement in Jerusalem and beyond. Commissioned by the exalted Christ with his own gospel, Paul worked tirelessly to catalyze new communities of Jesus-loyalists who were economically marginal. Yet, he declined the economic support that was supposedly due to the apostles of the rapidly expanding movement. How might we understand the shifting economic "location" of Paul in the different locations of the Roman imperial order in which he moved from being a pilgrim from a diaspora Judean community to being a persecutor of a nascent movement of Israelite villagers to becoming a principal catalyst of new communities in that expanding movement?

How Should We Proceed? Perspectives and a Proposal

Since there are so many differing viewpoints on what constitutes "the economy" or "economics" in the Roman Empire, the first step surely is some critical attention to what we are seeking to understand with a focus on "Paul and Economics." Brief reviews of scholarly estimates of the relative socioeconomic status of the Pauline congregations and of the ways classical historians have presented the Roman economy may be suggestive.

Beyond Social Stratification to Political-Economic Power Relations

Thirty some years ago, in what quickly became a touchstone for further investigation of Paul and his mission, Wayne Meeks presented as a "new consensus" that Paul's congregations were socially stratified, reflecting "a fair cross-section of urban society."[1] He argued that free artisans and small traders were especially prominent, described several of Paul's converts as wealthy, and claimed that we hear nothing of those who lived at the subsistence level. Meeks relied heavily on the exegesis and sociology of Gerd Theissen, who argued that while most members of the Corinthian community were from "the lower classes," some members were from the upper classes and were still interacting with the wealthy elite of the city.[2]

Meeks and others interested in "the social world" were following the structural-functional sociology that had dominated North American

1. Wayne A. Meeks, *The First Urban Christians* (New Haven, CT: Yale University Press, 1983), 51–73. Meeks ventures the generalization that the most active and prominent members of Paul's circle were individuals of "high status inconsistency" ("achieved status" higher than their "attributed status") and suggests that the rise and success of early Christianity was due to their drive and abilities.

2. Gerd Theissen, "Soziale Schichtung in der korinthischen Gemeinde," *ZNW* 65, no. 3–4 (1974): 232–72; collected with related articles in Gerd Theissen, *Studien zur Soziologie des Urchristentums*, WUNT 19 (Tübingen: Mohr Siebeck, 1979); Gerd Theissen, "The Social Stratification in the Corinthian Community," in *The Social Setting of Pauline Christianity: Essays in Corinth* (Philadelphia: Fortress Press, 1982), 69–119.

and, to a degree, Western European social science in the previous generation. This approach viewed society as a coherent system in which individuals of different socioeconomic locations, roles, occupations, and interests all fit together into a cohesive whole. Focusing on social stratification enabled such sociologists to ignore or downplay historical change and political-economic conflict. Critical analysis from within the field of sociology itself explained that part of the agenda of structural-functional sociology was to provide an alternative to Marxist analysis, which appeared all the more threatening to the Western academic establishment after the Russian Revolution in 1917.[3] Ironically, New Testament interpreters began borrowing the method only after structural functionalism had been widely abandoned in sociology itself (by around 1970). Its influence spread in New Testament studies, especially through the influential work of Gerd Theissen on the "itinerant radicalism" of Jesus's followers as well as on Paul's congregations, despite some sharp criticism.[4] The functionalist sociological focus on "stratification" and "social status" enabled New Testament scholars interested in "the social world" to avoid recognizing economic conflict and economic exploitation, both then and now.

In the critical review in 2002 by the SBL Paul and Politics Group of how analysis of Paul's mission and letters had changed in the twenty years since Meeks's work, Steven Friesen pointed out that the consensus that made poverty "disappear" in Pauline studies was not so new. He pointed out that early in the twentieth century, Adolf Deissmann had argued that while most of the Corinthian community consisted of lower class folks, the leaders who supposedly hosted the church in their houses were "middle class."[5] More explicit in their motives, perhaps, than the later structural-functional sociologists, Deissmann and the distinguished, elderly theologian Adolf von Harnack, in speeches to an important German church conference, used such a description of the Pauline communities to counteract recent successes of the Marxist Social Democratic Party. They explained, reported Friesen, that social inequality and poverty were not a serious problem in German society since the gospel could bring inner enlightenment and argued that by

---

3. See esp. the thorough criticism in Alvin W. Gouldner, *The Coming Crisis in Western Sociology* (New York: Basic Books, 1970), which was based on a self-study of the field led by Gouldner.

4. Gerd Theissen, *Sociology of Early Palestinian Christianity* (Philadelphia: Fortress Press, 1978); criticism by John H. Elliott, "Social-Scientific Criticism of the New Testament and Its Social World," *Semeia* 35 (1986): 1–33; Richard A. Horsley, *Sociology and the Jesus Movement* (New York: Crossroad, 1989), 1–64, 147–65.

5. Adolf Deissmann, *St. Paul: A Study in Social and Religious History*, trans. Lionel R. M. Strachan (London: Hodder & Stoughton, 1912), 216–17.

better caring for souls, the church could win back the hearts and minds of the working class.[6] The "consensus" in established New Testament studies had not changed at all but merely found a legitimating (if, by then, outmoded) "social scientific" facade. It also perpetuated the separation of religion from political-economic relations, assuming that differences in socioeconomic status could be mitigated or resolved by religion. In Theissen's construction, differences in the political-economic order were accepted but were ameliorated in the Pauline congregations by the "love-patriarchalism," which expected concern and responsibility from the wealthy, and respect and subordination from the poorer members.[7]

To provide an alternative to Meeks and Theissen, Friesen developed a "poverty scale" of the population of the Roman Empire, which found 3 percent extremely wealthy, 7 percent with a small cushion, and 90 percent living at or near subsistence.[8] On this scale, the women and men mentioned in Paul's letters or in Acts were almost all at or near subsistence. This "poverty scale" evoked some pushback in the field, such as an attempt to relocate a greater percentage of the population of the Roman Empire and of the membership of the Pauline communities back up into the middle level of an "economic scale."[9] Friesen's "poverty scale" in the Roman Empire calls attention to the vast "income gap" between the extremely wealthy and the vast majority of people who lived at or near subsistence. The recognition of this yawning gulf between the few extremely wealthy families and the vast majority is surely relevant to the dawning awareness of the increasing income gap in today's world of global capitalism, the current context of our interpretation of Paul and his letters.

Estimating the scale of relative economic levels, however, does not yet move toward an analysis of the historical power relations between the tiny hyper-wealthy elite and the mass of people living near subsistence—that is, of who had power over whom. Understanding Saul's change of economic "location" in joining the movement of Jesus-loyalists would entail a sense of the economic power relations that gave

---

6. Steven J. Friesen, "Poverty in Pauline Studies: Beyond the So-Called New Consensus," *JSNT* 26, no. 3 (2004): 330–31.

7. Theissen, *Social Setting*, esp. 107–9.

8. Friesen, "Poverty in Pauline Studies," 323–61. With access to fuller "economic data," Friesen produced a revised version of the "poverty scale" in collaboration with the Roman economic historian Walter Scheidel, "The Size of the Economy and the Distribution of Income in the Roman Empire," *JRS* 99 (2009): 61–91.

9. Bruce W. Longenecker, "Exposing the Economic Middle: A Revised Economy Scale for the Study of Early Christianity," *JSNT* 31, no. 3 (2009): 243–78.

rise to the movement in Roman Palestine and to the suppression of the movement in which he participated. Understanding Paul's working to support himself and his refusal or acceptance of support during his intensive mission to generate new communities requires a sense of the economic power relations involved in the various locations where he worked. Addressing these power relations will require a multifaceted analysis that can shed some light on the political-economic-religious structure and dynamics of the Roman imperial order.

Beyond a Synthetic Overview to Historically Distinctive Power Relations in Greek Cities

Interpreters of Paul have been heavily dependent on scholars of the Hellenistic-Roman world for their understanding of the context of Paul's mission and letters. This has become all the more evident with the increasingly wider recognition that the imperial order the Romans established in the eastern Mediterranean set the conditions in which the movement of Jesus-loyalists emerged and spread.[10] Brief reflection on how classical historians have conceptualized "economics" leads to what we are after in two further connections and how we might proceed.

Western European classical historians have tended to present the ancient Greek and/or Roman economy somewhat synthetically and synchronically, as suggested in the titles of important and influential books, such as *The Ancient Economy* (M. I. Finley) and *The Roman Economy* (A. H. M. Jones). Synthetic overviews do contribute much to our understanding, but ancient Rome had a long and changing history. Already in the second century BCE Roman warlords and their armies were building an empire around the eastern Mediterranean. The "restoration" of the republic by Octavian/Augustus following his victory at Actium brought a significant consolidation of the Roman imperial order of "Peace and Security," at least for the powerful wealthy urban and provincial elite. Yet there are many indications that this meant further economic difficulties for ordinary people in both city and countryside.

Investigations of the mission of Paul and his coworkers and the communities they organized have a particular interest in the significant

---

10. Laid out, in reliance on key works of Roman historians, in Richard A. Horsley, ed., *Paul and Empire: Religion and Power in Roman Imperial Society* (Harrisburg, PA: Trinity Press International, 1997). Attentive to economic relations in the extensive subsequent discussion is Neil Elliott, *The Arrogance of Nations: Reading Romans in the Shadow of Empire* (Minneapolis: Fortress Press, 2008).

historical changes in the cities of Greece and other areas of the eastern Mediterranean under the impact of Roman conquest and imperial rule. These changes further contributed to the distinctive features, such as demography and political-economic power relations, of each of the cities or areas to which Paul and his coworkers took their mission. About thirty years ago, historians of the Roman Empire began ferreting out some of these historical changes and distinctive features, thus complicating the general features of "the Roman world"—and by implication "the Roman economy."[11] Accordingly, it is important now for investigations of the mission of Paul and his coworkers to reformulate an agenda that takes into account the distinctive history and resulting political-economic patterns in Galatia, Philippi, Thessalonica, Corinth, and Ephesus.[12]

Not an Abstracted Market Economy but an Embedded Imperial Political Economy

A generation ago, Moses Finley and others had laid out how ancient cities were economically dependent on the countryside, increasingly on the land controlled by the wealthy but farmed by tenants or slaves. Informed by how Karl Polanyi was rethinking premodern economies, Finley also recognized that the ancient economy was not dominated by "the market" and "trade"—that is, it was not proto-capitalist. In the last twenty-five years, as neoliberal economic theory and practice have come to dominate not only in the West but in a globalized economy, a new generation of Roman historians has revived neoclassical economic theory, as exemplified in recent books such as *The Roman Market Economy* and *The Ancient Middle Classes.*[13] While balanced by more critical articles, many of the essays in the synchronic *Cambridge Companion to the Roman Economy*[14] work with the controlling concepts of "market," "supply and demand," "money and prices," and even "eco-

---

11. On Anatolia, for example, see Stephen Mitchell, *Anatolia: Land, Men, and Gods in Asia Minor*, 2 vols. (Oxford: Clarendon Press, 1993).
12. Examples of how such investigations of particular locations might be further pursued are Neil Elliott on Rome/Romans in *Arrogance of Nations*; Brigitte Kahl on Galatia/Galatians in *Galatians ReImagined: Reading with the Eyes of the Vanquished* (Minneapolis: Fortress Press, 2010); and Jorunn Øklund on Corinth/Corinthians in *Women in Their Place: Paul and the Christian Discourse of Gender and Sanctuary Space*, JSNTSup 269 (London: T&T Clark, 2004).
13. Peter Temin, *The Roman Market Economy* (Princeton: Princeton University Press, 2013); Emanuel Mayer, *The Ancient Middle Classes: Urban Life and Aesthetics in the Roman Empire, 100 BCE–250 CE* (Cambridge, MA: Harvard University Press, 2012).
14. Walter Scheidel, ed., *The Cambridge Companion to the Roman Economy* (Cambridge: Cambridge University Press, 2012).

nomic integration through the expansion of trade and markets." In these neoclassical constructions, the Roman economy appears to have been proto-capitalist after all.

Neoclassical economics abstracts "the economy" from society. Indeed it assumes that "the economy" is something in and of itself, an independent entity operating according to its own laws, such as that of "supply and demand."[15] In the Roman Empire, however, as in any empire or society in any historical circumstances, concrete economic realities were embedded in networks of social-political-religious relations that were often complex and full of conflict, whether in the Roman Empire as a whole or in the particular cities where Paul and his coworkers generated new communities.

The recent focus on Rome as having had a market economy that achieved a degree of integration through "the expansion of trade" imagines the state as somehow separate from the economy, on which it admittedly had significant effects. But this analysis ignores the historical reality that the Roman imperial state stood not only at the apex but at the center of the Roman imperial economy.[16] It is puzzling to read an argument (based on a limited set of data) that Rome had a "unified wheat *market*"[17] when, according to extensive historical sources, the Roman imperial state was extracting huge quantities of grain from Egypt and other areas of the empire. One of the central concerns of the imperial state was the food supply for the Roman populace and army, which would have been a significant part of the imperial economy.[18] More than one emperor fixed food prices and subsidized the shipping enterprises contracted to transport grain from Egypt and elsewhere, whether in the building of ships or in compensation for losses (Tacitus, *Annales* 2.59, 2.89, 15.18.2, 15.39.2; Suetonius, *Divus Claudius* 18–19). Augustus had even established a grain dole for the citizens of the metropolis (*Res Gestae* 15), many of whom had previously been pushed off the land by their wealthy creditors, who replaced their labor with the slaves that the indebted legionnaire-farmers had helped capture, per orders of their warlord commanders (such as Pompey and Varus

---

15. For the intellectual history that defined the economy as an independent entity, see now Roland Boer and Christina Petterson, *Idols of Nations: Biblical Myth at the Origins of Capitalism* (Minneapolis: Fortress Press, 2014).

16. "The dominant force in the Roman economy," as explained by Neville Morley, "Economy and Economic Theory, Roman," in *The Oxford Encyclopedia of Ancient Greece and Rome*, ed. Michael Gagarin and Elaine Fantham (Oxford: Oxford University Press, 2010), 3:12.

17. Temin, *Roman Market Economy*, 46 (emphasis added).

18. Peter Garnsey and Richard Saller, *The Roman Empire: Economy, Society, and Culture*, 2nd ed. (Berkeley: University of California Press, 2015), ch. 5.

in Judea and Galilee).[19] Much of the grain supply was expropriated in the form of taxes. But Augustus also simply took over temple lands in Egypt, and Tiberius confiscated some of the large landholdings of wealthy men in Syria and Greece as well as in Gaul and Spain.[20] There may well have been an expansion of long-distance trade as well as of local trade in commodities such as fine pottery in the early empire. Such trade, however, was for the lifestyle of the wealthy in Rome and the other cities of the empire. The economy of the Roman Empire was not a market economy but a political economy, which was based not on "supply and demand" but on demand and supply, that is, demand by the imperial state and its wealthy local elite, and supply coerced from subject peoples, tenants, and slaves. To understand the Pauline mission, we want to understand economic relations in particular, but we cannot understand them as separate from the broader structure and networks of social-political-religious relations in which they were embedded.

Vision, Challenge, and Innovation, and Principles for a Procedure

Finally, considering that Paul's shift in economic "location" was occasioned by a new (political-economic-religious) movement, yet another factor must be taken into account. New social movements, particularly movements that are "catching on" among the people and spreading rapidly, often initiate innovative changes in local socioeconomic relations and challenge the dominant power relations. Such changes and challenges may be responses to intensification (or other changes) in the dominant power relations. Such new social movements, moreover, may be associated with or be driven by a vision of a dramatically different political-economic-religious life, an alternative to the dominant system.

In sum, these reflections suggest that investigation of "Paul and Economics" should be guided by four interrelated principles.

(1) *What have become separated in modern (and still in postmodern) academic discourse and division of labor as "economic," "political," and "religious/cultural" were not separable in concrete historical life.* While this and other essays here are interested particularly in the economic dimension, it

---

19. Keith Hopkins, *Conquerors and Slaves* (Cambridge: Cambridge University Press, 1978).
20. Besides taking control of the mines, the state also became involved in production of building materials such as stone and bricks. All of these matters are mentioned, with references, by David Hollander, "The Roman Economy in the Early Empire," ch. 1 in this volume.

will be important to remember that the texts, institutions, and relations investigated and discussed were inseparably political-economic-religious.[21]

(2) *Roman conquest and rule of different subject peoples and cities wrought significant historical changes and developments in the generations prior to Jesus and Paul, so that each location had its distinctive features, such as its demography and its pattern of power relations.*

(3) *In the different locations of the Roman imperial order, we are particularly interested in the structure and dynamics of the historical power relations.* The requisite multifaceted analysis of historical power relations in different locations of the Roman imperial order can build on the work of critical Roman historians Peter Garnsey and Richard Saller, *The Roman Empire: Economy, Society, and Culture.*[22] As their title indicates, they recognize that economic relations were embedded in sociopolitical and cultural relations. While favoring a Weberian approach focused on status, they also look for the political-economic structure that generated and maintained economic inequality, drawing on the Marxian analysis of G. E. M. de Ste. Croix.[23] They recognize that the Roman Empire was an agrarian society in which the wealth and power of the (tiny) ruling groups depended on their control over productive land and dependent labor (slaves, tenants, wage-workers), which they managed by their control of the legal system and use of coercive sanctions.

(4) Partly in response to the intensification of the dominant power relations during the preceding generations, *the movement(s) of Jesus-loyalists sought innovative changes in local socioeconomic relations* and, perhaps influenced by them, *Saul/Paul acted out of a vision of an alternative social life.*

Moving to More Appropriate Concepts and Procedures

Ever more critical and precise investigations of ancient texts in historical contexts are raising our awareness that some of the central synthetic constructs of New Testament studies have been obscuring historical realities. For example, the different communities or movements of Jesus-loyalists addressed in Paul's letters or the Gospels of

---

21. The rest of this essay will assume this important recognition that economic relations are embedded in social-political-religious relations and only will only occasionally use the cumbersome hyphenated concept "political-economic-religious" relations and context.

22. See esp. their analysis of class as power-relations, Garnsey and Saller, *The Roman Empire*, 109–12.

23. G. E. M. de Ste. Croix, *Class Struggle in the Ancient Greek World: From the Archaic Age to the Arab Conquests* (London: Duckworth, 1981).

Mark or John had not yet developed into what is labeled "early Christianity." Informed by these recent investigations, this complex investigation of Paul's economic location in the broad context of the locations of the Roman imperial order will involve assumptions, approaches, concepts, and historical analysis and information that differ from some of those previously standard in New Testament studies.[24]

With regard to the use of Paul's letters as sources, once it is clear that these are ad hoc compositions of arguments in response to what Paul sees as problems in particular assemblies, then rhetorical criticism of the arguments is the appropriate first step.[25] Otherwise statements will be taken out of (the all-important) context. In a crucial example for this investigation, much of the discussion of social stratification in the "Pauline" communities is rooted in the misreading of a few key passages, such as 1 Corinthians 1:26 and 4:8, which ignores the issue that Paul is arguing in 1 Corinthians 1–4, as well as the diverse and complex possible meaning of some key terms in the wider culture in which both Paul and the Corinthians were embedded. Particularly influential has been Theissen's literalistic reading of 1:26, "if Paul says that there were not many in the Corinthian congregation who were wise, powerful, and wellborn, then this much is certain: there were some."[26] Terms such as "wise, powerful, and wellborn," however, had long since become widely used metaphorically as standard discourse among philosophers—particularly the Stoics, as well as shared by the Wisdom of Solomon and elaborated by Philo of Alexandria—that not the political-economic power holders but (only) the wise person (*sophos*) was truly "wise," "powerful," and "nobly born"—and, to go on to 1 Corinthians 4:8, also "rich," "king," and "honored." Paul's argument (from 1 Cor 1:10 to 4:21) is laced with steps that are loaded with irony and/or sarcasm (e.g., 1 Cor 1:26–31, 4:8–13). Paul is mocking people of low socioeconomic status who were suddenly claiming exalted spiritual status.[27] References to particular passages in the discussion

---

24. Analysis will also take into account the elite perspective and interests of nearly all literary sources for the Roman world and the kyriarchal perspective of Paul's letters as well as Greek and Roman sources.

25. Instructive rhetorical analyses of 1 Corinthians and Philippians respectively in Antoinette Clark Wire, *The Corinthian Women Prophets: A Reconstruction through Paul's Rhetoric* (Minneapolis: Fortress Press, 1990); and Cynthia Briggs Kittredge, *Community and Authority: The Rhetoric of Obedience in the Pauline Tradition*, HTS 45 (Harrisburg, PA: Trinity Press International, 1998). For a consideration of the role of rhetoric in power-relations in the Roman imperial order, particularly as it bears on rhetoric in 1 Corinthians, see Richard A. Horsley, "Rhetoric and Empire—and 1 Corinthians," in *Paul and Politics: Ekklesia, Israel, Imperium, Interpretation: Essays in Honor of Krister Stendahl*, ed. Richard A. Horsley (Harrisburg, PA: Trinity Press International, 2000), 72–102.

26. Theissen, "Social Stratification," 72.

below presuppose previous efforts of rhetorical criticism of Paul's arguments in particular situations.[28]

From Pilgrim to Persecutor to Apostle:
Saul's Dramatic Change in "Location"

Why would diaspora Judeans such as Saul of Tarsus, who had sufficient economic resources to travel and live for a time in another city, have gone to Jerusalem in the 20s or 30s CE? What political-economic circumstances would have given rise to the Jesus movement(s) and other popular movements among the Galilean and Judean villagers? Why would the high-priestly heads of the Roman imperial order in Jerusalem have attempted to suppress the movement of Jesus-loyalists? Why would Saul have participated in such suppression? And why would he have suddenly joined the movement he had been persecuting, and with what economic implications? All of these interrelated conflicts and events were rooted in the political-economic-religious impact of the Roman conquest and rule of Palestine.[29]

Intensifying Conflict in Roman Palestine and
Origins of the Jesus Movement

Roman conquest and Roman imperial rule intensified the structural political-economic-religious conflict based in the fundamental divide between rulers and ruled in Palestine. After the Romans had conquered the area and laid the people under tribute, the sustained military conflict between rival Hasmonean high priests and the Roman civil wars repeatedly devastated the countryside. To impose order on Palestine, the Roman Senate installed the military strongman Herod as "King of the Judeans." He established an extensive network of military

---

27. All investigated in a series of articles in the late 1970s (based on a 1971 dissertation), later collected in Richard A. Horsley, *Wisdom and Spiritual Transcendence in Corinth: Studies in First Corinthians* (Eugene: Cascade Books, 2008).

28. For example, on 1 Corinthians, see Richard A. Horsley, *1 Corinthians*, ANTC (Nashville: Abingdon, 1998); on Philippians, see Kittredge, *Community and Authority*.

29. The brief historical sketch in the following paragraphs depends on my attempts at a more precise as well as comprehensive history of Roman Palestine, particularly in Richard A. Horsley, *Galilee: History, Politics, People* (Valley Forge, PA: Trinity Press International, 1995), and on my attempts to understand the Gospels' portrayal of the movement of renewal and resistance generated by Jesus in the intensifying political-economic conflict in Roman Palestine, laid out in Richard A. Horsley, *Jesus and the Spiral of Violence: Popular Jewish Resistance in Roman Palestine* (San Francisco: Harper & Row, 1987) and, with further research and refinement, in Richard A. Horsley, *Jesus and the Politics of Roman Palestine* (Columbia: University of South Carolina Press, 2014).

fortresses to ensure his security and set up a lavish royal court. After Octavian's consolidation of his imperial power (as Augustus), Herod launched the massive building projects of two cities in honor of "Augustus" (Caesarea and Sebaste) and temples dedicated to the emperor, and made lavish gifts to the imperial family and benefactions to cities of the empire. He also massively rebuilt the Jerusalem Temple, the central economic as well as political-religious institution in Palestine, and over the years expanded the high-priestly aristocracy with his own appointees. To support these extraordinary expenditures, he taxed his subjects intensively, letting up the pressure only when he had nearly destroyed his "tax base."[30]

In their vengeful reconquest following the widespread revolts after Herod's death in 4 BCE, Roman troops devastated villages and enslaved people, including in the area of Nazareth in Galilee. The Romans appointed Herod's son Antipas as ruler over Galilee. His building of two new capital cities in the course of the next twenty years would have added appreciably to the economic burden of the Galileans, his location directly in Galilee making the collection of revenues more efficient. The Romans placed Judea under the control of the priestly aristocracy that Herod had expanded, reimposed the tribute, and charged the high priests with its collection. As indicated in the accounts of the Judean historian Josephus and in later rabbinic recollections, the high-priestly families became increasingly predatory on the people. In both Galilee and Judea, village communities and their constituent families, the fundamental socioeconomic forms of agrarian life, were evidently disintegrating under the impact of Roman conquest and Herodian and high-priestly rule, compounded by the manipulation of needy villagers into spiraling debt.[31]

It would be hard to imagine that it was only coincidental that the movement that Jesus catalyzed in villages, as portrayed in the Gospels, emerged in lower Galilee following the impact of the Roman conquests and the Herodian client rulers.[32] In the standard theological scheme of

---

30. Herod's taxation and other sources of "income" are critically detailed, in relation to the Roman tribute, etc., in Fabian E. Udoh, *To Caesar What Is Caesar's: Tribute, Taxes, and Imperial Administration in Early Roman Palestine (63 B.C.E.–70 C.E.)*, BJS 343 (Providence, RI: Brown Judaic Studies, 2005).

31. Further discussion in Horsley, *Jesus and the Politics*, 26–40, drawing upon an array of previous studies.

32. The following is a brief summary of a reconstruction of Jesus's mission in historical context, laid out initially in Horsley, *Jesus and the Spiral*, and further developed and refined in Richard A. Horsley, *Jesus and Empire: The Kingdom of God and the New World Disorder* (Minneapolis: Fortress Press, 2003); Richard A. Horsley, *Jesus and the Powers: Conflict, Covenant, and the Hope of the Poor* (Minneapolis: Fortress Press, 2011); and, most recently, in Horsley, *Jesus and the Politics*.

"Christian" origins from "Judaism," Jesus is an individual redeemer-figure and teacher unengaged in political-economic life, not the leader of a movement. A movement ("the church") was started by the disciples only after they were inspired by the "resurrection faith." By contrast, the Gospels portray Jesus as a Moses- and Elijah-like prophet generating a movement of the renewal of Israel among subsistence Galilean villagers, many of whom were evidently hungry and in debt. In addition to extensive healing, Jesus insists upon renewal of traditional covenantal customs of mutual aid and cooperation in village communities. Such a program would presumably have strengthened local socioeconomic communities against the further disintegrating effects of the Roman imperial order in Palestine with its multiple demands on villagers for revenues by multiple layers of rulers—although it would not appear to have been a direct threat to the Herodian or high-priestly rulers, much less to Roman rule.

In the Gospels' portrayals, however, Jesus's mission as a prophet of renewal climaxed in demonstrative opposition to the Roman-appointed high-priestly rulers based in the temple, for which he was crucified by the Roman governor as "king of the Judeans"—that is, a leader of insurrection. Many of his loyalists, moreover, were convinced that the martyred prophet was then vindicated by God as the messiah-designate (e.g., Acts 2:32–36, 3:20–21). Some who were convinced of his now exalted role in the renewal of Israel remained in Jerusalem to recruit new members in the public space of the huge new temple complex. The leaders of the Jesus-loyalists and probably others in the movement were rustic peasants now displaced from their socioeconomic base in the villages of Galilee. They were poor and, according to the idealized account in Acts (2:43-45, 4:32-37), "held all things in common," an extreme form of mutual economic support probably informed by covenantal village customs. Whether in the renewal of covenantal community in the villages of Galilee or in the Jerusalem commune, Jesus had generated an expanding movement that had political-economic as well as religious implications.

This rapidly expanding movement focused on one whom the Romans had crucified as a leader of insurrection was evidently threatening to the high priests, who took repressive action (Mark 8:34–38; 13:9; Luke 12:2–9; Acts 4:1–4, 13–21; etc.). While the Gospels give no indication that the Jesus movement(s) showed any signs of insurrection, Josephus (A.J. 17.271–83) offers accounts of several insurrectionary or other resistance movements led by popularly acclaimed "kings" or popular prophets that the Romans suppressed with their military forces.[33] Popular protests and even a peasant "strike" also contributed to the escalating political-economic disorder that the Romans expected the high priests and their scribal representatives to contain (Josephus, *A.J.* 18.261–84). Although we cannot take the account at face value, the Gospel of John understands the position/role of the high-priestly rulers in maintaining the Roman imperial order in Judea: they supposedly took action against Jesus as a way of stopping the movement of Jesus-loyalists before it evoked another punitive reconquest of Judea by the Romans (John 11:45–53).

From Diaspora Judean Pilgrim to Persecutor: Probing His Traditions of Elders

The intensifying but tenuous power relations of the Roman imperial order in Judea were also the context of the sudden move of Saul of Tarsus, a diaspora Judean pilgrim to Jerusalem, to begin persecuting Jesus-loyalists. For information on this, we depend primarily on statements in the letters of Paul, sometimes in apologetic contexts, supplemented from accounts in Acts that cannot be taken at face value but that may offer historical hints.

As evident in the early chapters of Acts, Herod's massively constructed temple became a pilgrimage destination for Judeans from the diaspora, the symbolic center of worldwide Jewry (as a subset of the Roman imperial order). Even while construction was still being completed in the first century CE, Judeans from many diaspora communities came to Jerusalem as pilgrims. Some of them, such as Stephen and Saul of Tarsus, settled in for longer stays, evidently enamored of their new-found collective identity centered in the temple. Saul thus appears to have possessed sufficient economic resources for travel to and a prolonged stay in Jerusalem.

Constructions of Saul's high status and economic privilege have appealed mainly to his sudden claim in Acts (22:22–29, 25:6–12) that he is a Roman citizen. We should be suspicious of this account both because it is integral to Acts' apologetic narrative that the movement of Jesus-loyalists is not a political threat to the imperial order and espe-

---

33. Richard A. Horsley, "Popular Messianic Movements around the Time of Jesus," *CBQ* 46, no. 3 (1984): 471–93; Richard A. Horsley, "Popular Prophetic Movements at the Time of Jesus, Their Principal Features and Social Origins," *JSNT* 9, no. 26 (July 1986): 3–27. Fuller discussion of the escalating political-economic disorder in Roman Palestine in Horsley, *Jesus and the Spiral*, ch. 4.

cially because it is a way for the narrative to bring the hero-apostle Paul finally to Rome, the center of the empire.[34] The key indicators of Saul's economic location may be that he was a Judean from the diaspora living in Jerusalem *and* that he evidently had the leisure (economic resources) to spend several years there learning the traditions of the ancestors. A critical consensus still holds that Saul probably was originally from Tarsus ("I am a Judean, born in Tarsus in Cilicia," Acts 22:3). Given his proficiency in Greek, familiarity with Greek rhetorical forms, and knowledge of the Judean scriptures in Greek, it is clear that he was "at home" in the Hellenistic culture of such a city.

That Saul was himself a Pharisee (Acts 23:6, 26:4) seems doubtful since in his letters Paul himself does not claim to have been a Pharisee. Yet, he claims that he was educated in the ancestral laws in phrases that suggest this training must have been in circles of Pharisaic or other Jerusalem scribes. He boasts in Philippians 3:5-6 that he was "an Israelite of the tribe of Benjamin, Hebrew born of Hebrews, as to the law, a Pharisee, . . . as to righteousness under the law, blameless." And in Galatians 1:14 he says that he had "advanced in *ioudaismos* beyond many among my people of the same age, for I was far more zealous for the traditions of my ancestors."[35] While he does not say that he was/is a Pharisee, his formulation "as to the law, a Pharisee," probably indicates that he knew and followed the Pharisees' understanding (version) of the law (according to which temple affairs were conducted, according to Josephus, *A.J.* 18.15). With "Hebrew born of Hebrews," he seems to be indicating that his education in (particular versions of) the law was in Hebrew/Aramaic (that is, as cultivated in Jerusalem scribal circles and not in a Greek-speaking synagogue in Tarsus). Whatever the particulars of his training after coming to Jerusalem from the diaspora, he evidently had the leisure to learn torah and other ancestral traditions, without having to labor as did artisans or farmers (Sir 38:25–39:4).[36]

In Paul's own key account of the turning point in his own life, when suddenly he received his commission as an apostle in an *apokalypsis* of Christ, he declares that it was his zeal for the ancestral traditions that was driving him to persecute the "assembly" of Jesus-loyalists (Gal

---

34. On further doubts about the credibility of this claim in Acts (e.g., that the granting of Roman citizenship to Judeans in the East was rare), see the critical review in Calvin Roetzel, *Paul: The Man and the Myth* (Minneapolis: Fortress Press, 1999), 19–22.

35. Since the connotations of *ioudaismos* beyond its being synonymous with "the traditions of the ancestors" are not clear, it may be best to leave the term untranslated. The translation "Judaism" in NRSV and other versions is anachronistic.

36. Investigation of the role and training of scribes in Richard A. Horsley, *Scribes, Visionaries, and the Politics of Second-Temple Judea* (Louisville, KY: Westminster John Knox, 2007), chs. 3–6.

1:14–16). So we should expect that it was "the traditions of the ancestors," which he could have learned in Jerusalem scribal circles, that were in or behind the broader pattern of thought evident in his letters, the fanatical conviction of which could have led him to persecute the movement of Jesus-loyalists (but then suddenly to join them).

Once we have moved beyond the standard old Protestant theological construction of Paul, there is no reason to imagine that the *ioudaismos* (the traditions of the ancestors) about which he had been fanatical was an obsession with observance of the law. Also, the Acts narrative indicating that in persecuting Jesus-loyalists, Saul and others were collaborating closely with the high priests is not credible: it is inseparably linked with Acts' distinctive "road to Damascus" story of Saul's "conversion" (Acts 9:1–2; cf. 26:10–11), which can hardly be squared with his own account of his *apokalypsis* (Gal 1:15–16). The high priests were client rulers who collaborated closely with their Roman patrons to maintain order by suppressing popular unrest and by collecting the tribute to Caesar (as Josephus's histories generally make clear). Pharisaic and other scribes, however, had their own reasons to attack the Jesus-loyalists. They were personally dedicated to maintaining the Judean ancestral traditions as what defined their own collective identity distinct from or in opposition to the imperial order in which they were forced to live. It is in what Paul may have been learning in scribal circles that we should seek for those traditions of the elders that led him first to persecute and then to join the movement of Jesus-loyalists.[37]

The Traditions of the Ancestors about Which Saul Was Zealous

The appropriate approach may be to begin with clues in Paul's letters about his broader understanding of his mission in the context of the Roman imperial order. These clues indicate that his mission was to implement a vision of an alternative to the empire. And that vision appears to have been broadly similar to and rooted in a prominent Judean scribal view opposed to the empire, which Saul could easily have learned from a Jerusalem scribal circle in which it was being cultivated.

---

37. The term *ioudaismos* that Paul uses as synonymous with the ancestral traditions may have been formulated pointedly in opposition to *hellenismos*, the long-dominant imperial ideology in the East. This was the imperial political ideology that the dominant high priestly faction was following in transforming the Jerusalem temple-state into the Hellenistic city of Antioch in 169 BCE.

Paul claims to be commissioned to bring the gospel of Jesus Christ to the other peoples of the world (parallel to Simon's/ Peter's mission to "the circumcised," the Israelites) and to catalyze new assemblies in the wider movement of renewal of Israel (Galatians 1–2). His gospel focuses on a sequence of three events: the crucifixion of Jesus, which had happened in the recent past; Jesus Christ's vindication/exaltation by God, which Paul understood as the beginning ("first fruits/down-payment") of the general resurrection that would happen in the imminent future; and the *parousia* of Christ in "the day of the Lord." These events, moreover, are the fulfilment not only of Israelite tradition but of history generally, running through the history of Israel since the promise to Abraham. That promise included that all peoples would receive blessings through the seed of Abraham. It had now been revealed that that seed is Christ, so that all those who trust in / have become loyal to Christ have become heirs of Abraham by adoption, by promise (see the argument in Galatians 3–4; cf. Romans 9–11). If that sounds like a direct challenge to the empire and its assumption that history was running through Rome, it was. In crucifying (the one who became) "the Lord of Glory" (i.e., vindicated Christ, exalted to be the true *Kyrios* of the world), the "the rulers of this age" (i.e., the Romans) had touched off the sequence of events of fulfilment that would continue as Christ was subjected "every ruler and every authority and power" prior to the final fulfilment at his *parousia* in "the day of the Lord" (1 Cor 2:8, 15:24; 1 Thess 4:14–18; etc.). Meanwhile, the fledgling assemblies that Paul and his coworkers were catalyzing had become an alternative nonhierarchical, multiethnic society based in local communities, whose *politeuma* was "in heaven" and was to be fulfilled at the coming of the true (imperial) Savior (Phil 3:17–21). That was, ideally at least, an alternative society directly opposed to the imperial order in which the Romans dominated through the propertied urban elite who funded and presided over honors to the emperor as the central divine power that held the whole system together.

Where did Paul come by his grandiose gospel? The standard answer has been that the perspective and some of the principal concepts came from "Jewish apocalypticism." The latter, however, can now be recognized as a modern scholarly construct. The apocalyptic scenario articulated influentially by Schweitzer and summarized in what became standard form by Bultmann is not attested in Judean texts prior to Paul.[38] The fundamental framework of Paul's gospel, however, can be found in the historical visions in Daniel 7–12, the animal vision in 1

Enoch 85–90, and the Testament of Moses.[39] These historical visions, composed at the time of the invasion of Judea by the Seleucid emperor Antiochus IV Epiphanes, all portray the sequence of foreign empires that had conquered and/or ruled over Israel/Judah. The sequence of events had come to a crisis for the subjected people with the escalation of imperial violence by Antiochus, a crisis in which some of those who resisted had become martyred. The visions end with God's judgment of the imperial rulers, the restoration of the people (Israel/the Judeans) to independence of imperial rule, and, in Daniel 12 at least, the vindication of the martyrs.[40] In these historical visions produced in scribal circles that were engaged in resistance, imperial domination and exploitation stood under the judgment of God, who would restore (the independence of) the people.

The remarkable parallel between the historical framework (sequence) of Paul's gospel and the historical visions in Daniel and Enoch texts suggest that the latter decisively influenced Paul's gospel. The notable difference, of course, is that for Paul the crucifixion, resurrection, and return of Christ and the expansion of the movement had become the new form of the martyrdom of the faithful leader(s), the vindication of the martyrs, and the renewal of the people. The composition of the Parables of Enoch (1 Enoch 37–71) in the first century suggests this ancestral tradition of historical visions was still being cultivated in some scribal circles. From Saul's time of learning in Jerusalem, he had adopted a continuing scribal conviction that God would act to judge the Roman empire and renew the people. From the brutal Roman reconquest of Galilee and Judea in response to the revolt in 4 BCE, scribal circles would likely have had a sober sense that any resistance that might provoke Roman retaliation would be suicidal. And the Jesus movement's recruitment and expansion may well have seemed to be a threat to the scribal *modus vivendi* with the Roman order in Judea. Scribes working from the perspective of these traditions of the ancestors, along with their students from the diaspora, may well have been calling for its suppression lest it evoke Roman intervention.

38. See further Richard A. Horsley, *The Prophet Jesus and the Renewal of Israel: Moving beyond a Diversionary Debate* (Grand Rapids: Eerdmans, 2012), chs. 1–4.
39. See the critical rereading and analysis of these texts in Horsley, *Scribes, Visionaries*, chs. 7–9; and Richard A. Horsley, *Revolt of the Scribes: Resistance and Apocalyptic Origins* (Minneapolis: Fortress Press, 2010), chs. 4–5.
40. What these historical visions do not exhibit is any central hero figure, such as a prophet or messiah. The "one like a human being" in Daniel 7 is not such a figure but a symbol of "the holy ones of the Most High," who represent the people as a whole who receive the sovereignty/restoration.

How Saul Was Set Up for the Move to the Jesus Movement

If Saul had learned about and become zealous for this particular tradition of the scribal ancestors, moreover, it could also have been an enabling factor in his move to join the movement he had been persecuting. This eager expectation of an end to imperial domination and renewal of the people (Israel) could have combined with other factors of Saul's political-economic-religious location to make such a move conceivable for him rather than for scribal teachers who were dependent on their high-priestly patrons. The eager expectation of judgment and renewal that Saul had gained from the traditions of the ancestors could easily have "set up" the crisis that precipitated the vision that led to his dramatic move.

If this was what had shaped Saul's convictions, then he had come to share many of the basic concerns of the Jesus movement. From the conquest in 63 BCE on, Roman domination, including the imposition of tribute and client rulers, posed a continuing crisis for Judeans and Galileans. As sketched above, village communities were disintegrating under the economic pressures of multiple layers of rulers. In key scribal texts as well as in the Jesus movement, Roman and Roman client rule were denounced, both on the basis of prophetic tradition and in prophetic terms (compare, e.g., the sequence of confrontations in Mark 11–12 and Stephen's speech in Acts 7 with the Parables of Enoch): God's judgment was certain. In both this scribal view and in the Jesus movement, moreover, the renewal of Israel in opposition to and by the rulers was certain, the significant difference being that the Jesus movement understood the renewal to be underway already. Both the key scribal circles and the Jesus movement trusted that God would vindicate or had vindicated those who became martyrs in the struggle. These are parallel concerns and the same or similar agendas.

If Saul had learned in scribal circles, he would presumably have been influenced by their attitudes toward villagers and urban artisans and others. The urban poor and especially villagers were suspicious and distrustful of "scribes and Pharisees" because of the role they played as representatives of the temple-state.[41] On the other hand, while scribal sages and teachers may have looked down their noses at farmers and artisans, they were sympathetic with the poverty of the people. And although the people did not welcome their initiative, scribes were

---

41. As readily evident in the Gospel woes and controversy stories of Jesus (see esp. Mark 7:1-13; 12:38–13:2; Luke 11:39–52).

sometimes eager to make common cause with the people (see Josephus's accounts of the Sicarii in the summer of 66, *B.J.* 2.425–27). Saul himself, as a Judean from a diaspora community, was not a scribe dependent on the high priests for his livelihood and was hence much freer to make common cause with a popular movement.

Amidst this broader conflict between the Roman imperial order in Palestine and the Israelite resistance, both scribal and popular, we may be zeroing in on the parallel agendas between Saul's traditions of the ancestors and the Jesus movement that set up Saul's personal yet also political-economic crisis leading him to join the movement he had been persecuting.

As a Judean from the city of Tarsus, Saul may have had little acquaintance with village life in Cilicia or Judea-Galilee or with the way in which popular Israelite tradition functioned in village communities. He may well have gotten caught up in the opposition to the Jesus movement as a potential threat to the uneasy public order in Jerusalem and only gradually become aware of what the Jesus movement was all about. They were practicing what he had learned were the socioeconomic principles and other traditions of the ancestors; they were already implementing the renewal of Israelite society in resistance to the Roman order in Palestine, a renewal that his scribal teachers had anticipated only in the future; and they were not really so disruptive as to bring the Romans down on their heads. Is it possible that as Paul recognized that the movement of Jesus-loyalists was implementing the renewal of Israel in independence from the imperial order that he was fervently hoping for, he began to question his attacks on them? This could be the personal crisis that set him up to receive his own vision, his gospel, through an *apokalypsis* of Jesus Christ (Gal 1:12–16).

Paul's Labor and the Assemblies' Support of the Apostles

Not only did Saul abandon his position of relative economic privilege when he joined the movement of Jesus-loyalists but he declined the support that was due to him as an apostle, as he insists at key points (1 Corinthians 9; 1 Thess 2:9). The support of the apostles, who were organizing new communities and maintaining communications and ties between them, was evidently part of the economics of the movement from its beginnings. Judging from Paul's letters, the economics of the movement were formulated in the context of and in response to the power relations in the cities where he and his coworkers carried out their mission.

The Political-Economic-Religious Context(s) of Paul's and His Coworkers' Mission

Rome conquered or otherwise came to dominate Greek cities in the second century BCE. Most famous for its brutality was the Romans' ruthless destruction of the classical city of Corinth in 146 BCE. For the next century and right on through the Roman civil war, the Romans made war in and beyond Greece, draining local economies to support their expeditions. Among the major changes effected by Roman domination of Greece that had a direct relation to the later Pauline mission were the Roman colonies established in Corinth and Philippi by Roman warlords. Julius Caesar established a large colony of army veterans and surplus population from Rome, including many freedpersons, at the site of Corinth. As the principal hub of shipping and communications between Italy and the Aegean and eastward, Corinth grew in size with displaced people from diverse backgrounds. At Philippi, two successive colonies of Roman army veterans were established in 42 and 30 BCE. The indigenous Thracians (and/or "Greeks") were pushed off their lands by the Roman colonists and subordinated to the now predominantly Roman politics and political culture of the city. Slaves (or other dependents) were brought in to work the expanded estates of the Roman veteran families.

Distinctive as they were in their origins as Roman colonies in the first century BCE, Philippi and Corinth generally shared many of the key developments of the political-religious economy of Greece (and Asia). The economy of the empire remained overwhelmingly agricultural, with each city (with the notable exception of Rome itself) largely dependent on its own *chōra* (countryside) for food.[42] But exploitation of agricultural producers and urban populations by the wealthy urban elite was intensified and consolidated under Roman domination. That change was directly related to the developing relation between the wealthy urban elite and the emperor (and imperial family) under the early principate.

Rome always encouraged rule by the "better sort" and an ever

---

42. "Agricultural production must always have constituted the lion's share of ancient activity." Susan E. Alcock, *Graecia Capta: The Landscapes of Roman Greece* (Cambridge: Cambridge University Press, 1993), 109.

sharper juridical and political demarcation of rich and poor.[43] The wealthy urban elite were placed in charge of the collection of taxes. Through whatever means—probably foreclosure on debts that people had incurred to pay local and Roman taxes—they were able to gain control of more and more land, steadily expanding their own wealth and local power. Archaeological surface surveys show a severe drop in the number of rural farmsteads as small sites were abandoned, land tenure became less secure, and small-scale cultivators disappeared.[44]

As farmers could no longer support themselves on their land, they worked for wages or became tenants of the wealthy, both of which involved some belt-tightening. In the generations immediately preceding the Pauline missions in Macedonia and Achaia, many people were evidently being forced off their land and into the cities in hopes of eking out a living, as the wealthy further consolidated their holdings.[45] Some wound up far from their origins in search of a living. A goodly portion of the people in any of these cities, but particularly in Corinth, would have been displaced people, uprooted from their ancestral homes and homelands, losing supportive family and village community with their familiar customs.

Some of the people on the land and certainly in the cities would also have been slaves—who were totally subject to their owner—or freedmen/women (or their descendants)—who remained dependent on their former owners. Most freedmen/women would have been in positions similar to marginal free people whose income was dependent on the wealthy for whom they made goods or the "building contractors" for whom they labored on projects sponsored by wealthy benefactors.

With increasing numbers of displaced people dependent on low-paid work, many were regularly hungry. As an antidote to the hunger of the poor, and probably with an eye to preventing social unrest, the wealthy mounted regular acts of euergetism, such as public banquets or other distribution of food (which of course had been produced by the low-paid labor of the rural poor). Such actions, memorialized in decrees honoring local *euergetai*, consolidated the rule of the wealthy in city life and contributed to the acceptance of the new political-economic order. The wealthy urban elite also "donated" buildings in the cities,

---

43. A common historical observation; see recently ibid., 77.

44. For results from archaeological surface surveys that have confirmed textual indications, see ibid., 71–72.

45. Many references in Apuleius, *Metamorphoses*; see further Alcock, *Graecia Capta*, 107.

such as monuments, temples, and tombs, with appropriate inscriptions indicating their largesse. This flow of expenditure (on buildings, services, luxuries, and other conspicuous consumption) in turn generated much of the work on which the population had become increasingly dependent.[46] Some of the urban poor would have been pulled into the patronage networks of wealthy figures, thus increasing their political-economic power.[47] But we should not imagine that the extensive pyramids of patronage that developed in Rome, filled with people forced off the land or otherwise socially and economically adrift, were duplicated in Corinth and other Greek cities.[48]

What held the Roman imperial economy together and maintained the imperial political order were not an imperial bureaucracy and the army, but the elaborate honors to Caesar, especially in the Greek East: temples, rituals, images, and games funded and headed by the wealthy elite of the cities. These elite became a network of patronage pyramids headed by the emperor.[49] Cities such as Ephesus, Philippi, Thessalonica, Athens, and Corinth accumulated many temples, monuments, and shrines dedicated to the emperor. Temples and shrines to gods of the city were grouped around the imperial temple at the center of the public area. Statues of the emperor were placed in those temples, and rituals to the emperor were performed in other public arenas such as the theaters. Festivals and games were held in honor of the emperor. The presence of the emperor came to pervade public space, and honors to the emperor came to structure the annual calendar.

These elaborate honors to the emperor were funded and led by the wealthy men of each city, who held not only the city priesthoods and civic offices but also the highly coveted imperial priesthoods in those cities. Benefactions from the emperor, of course, had to be "earned." So wealthy prominent citizens also bestowed lavish gifts on the emperor, perhaps thus bringing good fortune to their hometown by attracting imperial favor.[50]

Corresponding to how economic power relations were embedded

---

46. Alcock, *Graecia Capta*, 114.

47. Ibid., 112–13.

48. Richard P. Saller, *Personal Patronage under the Early Empire* (Cambridge: Cambridge University Press, 1982). For how the patronage pyramids held the imperial order together but probably extended into the general populace much less than in Rome, see Horsley, *Paul and Empire*, part 2, esp. pp. 94–95.

49. See esp. S. R. F. Price, *Rituals and Power: The Roman Imperial Cult in Asia Minor* (Cambridge: Cambridge University Press, 1984); and Paul Zanker, *The Power of Images in the Age of Augustus* (Ann Arbor: University of Michigan Press, 1988), summarized and abridged in Horsley, *Paul and Empire*, chs. 3–5, 7.

50. Alcock, *Graecia Capta*, 163.

with and inseparable from religion/culture as well as politics, economic resistance by subject peoples was embedded with political-religious attitudes, protests, and movements. As in Galilee and Judea, village communities might provide mutual aid for hungry peasants who had become impoverished from taxes and debts owed to predatory landlords.[51] While such customary mutual aid by fellow villagers may have enabled at least temporary resistance to the loss of control over ancestral land and labor, their limited resources could not stem the disintegration of village communities for long. In contrast to areas of Spain and Gaul, as well as Galilee and Judea, where subject people were still able to mount insurrections against the taxes and debts that drained away the resources they needed to support themselves,[52] people in the cities of Greece had been displaced and become more fully "integrated" into the imperial economic order and thus did not form active resistance movements. Yet, among those displaced from their social roots, indigenous language, culture, and even social structure persisted underneath the dominant Hellenistic-Roman political-economic-religious forms in some of the cities around the eastern Mediterranean. The formation and persistence of religious-ethnic communities in the Greek cities was one possible form of resisting assimilation into the local and wider imperial order, while also involving degrees of adjustment.[53]

Support of the Apostles and Paul's Inconsistency: Living from His Own Labor and/or from Gifts

An instrumental aspect of the economics of the movement of Jesus-loyalists was the support of the "organizers" (envoys/apostles/"missionaries"), who proclaimed the gospel, performed healings, and renewed or organized local communities (assemblies). The movement had begun in village communities in Galilee and evidently spread into villages and small towns of nearby areas in Syria as well as in Judea and Samaria. This is the political-economic context presupposed in the well-known "mission" discourses of Jesus in Luke (Q) 10:1–16 and in Mark 6:8–13 (Luke 9:3–6; Matt 10:1–15 combines the two). The village

---

51. Garnsey and Saller, *The Roman Empire*, 98.
52. Hollander, "Roman Economy," mentions several such revolts against Roman economic extraction (taxes and debts).
53. This possibility, exemplified perhaps by the Jewish/Judean communities/synagogues in Alexandria or Rome, has not been adequately investigated, perhaps largely because of the lack of sources.

communities and their component households in which the movement began lived at a subsistence level. Accordingly, the mission speeches instruct the envoys, who are no longer supporting themselves by farming and/or fishing, to stay in whatever household takes them in and to eat (be content with) whatever the family offers—and not to go from house to house looking for more (Luke 10:5-7; Mark 6:10).

Paul's most extensive discussion of the economic support of apostles comes in a personal illustration he uses as part of an argument that even though one has the authority to do certain things, there may be important reasons (mainly community considerations) not to do them (1 Corinthians 9). Most of the analogies and customs Paul cites that authorize the apostles' right to economic support come from agrarian village life: the principle included in the law of Moses that "you shall not muzzle an ox while it is treading out the grain" (1 Cor 9:9; Deut 25:4) and the custom that whoever plows and threshes should share in the crop (1 Cor 9:8-11). These agrarian analogies suggest continuity in the practice of the movement from its origins in Galilean village communities to the mission of Paul and his coworkers in the cities of Greece.[54] Paul, or perhaps the apostles working in Jerusalem, added the authorizing analogy of those who work in the temple receiving their food from the temple (1 Cor 9:13). The rationale in Jesus's mission speech, "the laborer deserves to be paid" ("the worker deserves his food/wages," Luke 10:7), becomes the Lord's command that "those who proclaim the gospel should get their living from the gospel." It was evidently the practice in the movement that Cephas, the Lord's brothers, and the other apostles (and their wives) were supported by the assemblies (1 Cor 9:4-6). This was their right in return (and this gave them the freedom) for their work in expanding the movement.

What Paul and his coworkers were engaged in was a far more difficult undertaking than what their predecessors were doing in the villages of Galilee and nearby areas. The latter were going to already existing communities, albeit weakened and perhaps disintegrating from the economic demands of multiple layers of rulers and creditors. The envoys sent out as "laborers in the harvest" were on a mission of renewal of village community through healing and preaching hope and, in the covenantal renewal teaching of Jesus, pressing the people to renewed mutual aid and cooperation.[55] Paul and his coworkers, on

---

54. In contrast to the dichotomy often posited in New Testament studies between the Jesus movement in Palestine and "the Christ cult" among "the Gentiles."
55. Discussed in Horsley, *Jesus and the Powers*, chs. 5-6.

the other hand, were creating communities "from scratch." The cities of Greece were filled with displaced people of different backgrounds whom the apostles, outsiders from distant Jerusalem or Antioch, brought together perhaps for the first time. It would have taken some time for local support and solidarity to materialize.

The nascent communities that Paul catalyzed in the cities of Greece were probably not that much better-off economically than the village communities in which the movement had begun. Paul, moreover, was not working alone; he mentions many coworkers in his letters, often multiple coworkers involved in particular assemblies and/or moving between them, such as Timothy, Epaphroditus, Barnabas, and Prisca and Aquila (Rom 16:3; 1 Cor 9:6, 16:19; Phil 2:22-25). In addition to Paul's coworkers, there were other, sometimes rival, apostles traveling through, engaged in preaching and teaching (1 Cor 3:5, 22; 16:12; 2 Cor 11:4-6). For local assemblies whose members lived near or at subsistence level, supporting an apostle plus one or more coworkers may well have been a considerable burden. Supporting multiple apostles and coworkers would have been a serious problem, even if they stayed only a few months. As the movement expanded, of course, there would have been more people to shoulder the burden. By the time the "instruction" later included in the Didache was being developed (in Syria?) a few decades after Paul's mission, the number of apostles and prophets and teachers either traveling through or wishing to settle in communities had become a serious problem requiring regulation about testing, criteria of authenticity, and length of stay (Didache 11-13). Only "the true" prophet/ teacher "is worthy of his food" (Did. 13:1-2), and an itinerant "who comes in the name of the Lord" is allowed to stay only two or three days; if he wishes to settle and has a craft, however, then "let him work for his bread" (Did. 12:1-3).

This is the context for the mission of Paul and his coworkers in which he declines to accept the support due an apostle, on the one hand, yet does accept support from some communities in some circumstances, on the other. In his argument to the Corinthian "spirituals" that they should not make use of their newfound freedom from their enlightened knowledge that "all things are authorized for me" (*panta moi exestin*, one of their slogans; 1 Cor 6:12), he offers an illustration from his own "apostolic" practice. Although Paul is an apostle, like Cephas and others, and hence has the "authority" (their term, *exousia*) to receive economic support, he has not made use of this "authority" (1 Corinthians 9). He is evidently arguing that he has made it a general principle in his mission to decline economic support from the assemblies in which he was working and to work to support himself. His reflection on his mission among the Thessalonians, in what was probably his earliest known letter, suggests that this was his preferred practice and that its motive was concern about the Thessalonians' economic circumstances.[56] "You remember our labor and toil; we worked night and day so that we might not burden any of you while we proclaimed to you the word of God" (1 Thess 2:9). References in other letters indicate that there was poverty among the assemblies of Macedonia (2 Cor 8:1–2). In a later defensive argument to the Corinthians, he again insists that the reason he proclaimed the gospel free of charge was to not burden them (2 Cor 11:7–9).

On the other hand, Paul also indicates that he had accepted aid the Philippians had sent him when he was working in Thessalonica (Phil 4:15–16). If not accepting support from a community in which he was working was a matter of principle for him, that apparently did not mean that he would not accept support from a community where he had worked previously. This would address the problem of a mission that entailed coming to a new city and generating a new community "from scratch." As Paul says, the Philippians sent him aid "in the early days" of his work in Thessalonica (Phil 4:15–16). In the same defensive argument to the Corinthians cited just above, he also indicates that he had been able not to burden them because some of the Macedonians were helping supply his needs (2 Cor 11:7–9).

Paul says several times that he "worked (for a living) with his hands" (1 Cor 4:12, 9:6; 1 Thess 2:9), although he never mentions at what. On the basis of the reference to his long and close association with Prisca and Aquila (Acts 18:3) it is generally accepted that he, like them, was a tentmaker (or more broadly, a leatherworker; *skēnopoios*).[57] He reminds the Thessalonians that he had worked night and day in exhausting "labor and toil" during the time he was preaching to and working with them (1 Thess 2:9). That fits descriptions of ancient rhetors and other (elite) sources that it was necessary for artisans among the urban poor to work long and hard in order to earn enough to live on (e.g., Dio Chrysostom, *Or.* 7:103–53). It would not have been surprising that at

---

56. Richard S. Ascough, "The Thessalonian Christian Community as a Professional Voluntary Association," *JBL* 119, no. 2 (2000): 314–15, pulls together the indications that the Thessalonians Paul addresses were manual laborers, with extensive references to other scholarship.

57. Ronald F. Hock, *The Social Context of Paul's Ministry: Tentmaking and Apostleship* (Philadelphia: Fortress, 1980), 20–21.

points Paul would indeed have been hungry, cold, and poorly clothed (1 Cor 4:11; 2 Cor 6:5, 11:27).[58]

Because Paul uses such terms in describing his working with his hands, it has been supposed that he had a negative view of manual labor that derived from his own supposedly "upper class" background.[59] In the dominant cultural ethos, the wealthy elite viewed manual labor as demeaning and slavish.[60] This was reflected to a degree in the elite culture of philosophy and public rhetoric, which had in turn influenced the more elite Hellenistic Jewish culture, for example, of Philo of Alexandria.[61] In assessing Paul's arguments in sections of 1 and 2 Corinthians, however, it is necessary to take the rhetorical situation into account, since he is emphasizing his own lowliness in order to oppose what he sees as a spiritual elitism ("wealthy," "nobly born," etc.). It may well be that some in the Corinthian assembly were criticizing him for not accepting the patronage of the better-off community members (1 Cor 9:1).[62] Paul, however, digs in his rhetorical heels all the more in boasting of the afflictions involved in his hard labor in order to make the gospel free and not burden them (2 Cor 6:4; 11:7–11, 27). He knew very well that manual labor was despised in the dominant elite culture, and he played on this rhetorically. His arguments indicate that if anything, he is proud of his manual labor as instrumental to, indeed a necessary aspect of, his mission. He has been "entrusted with a commission" (note the Greek term, *oikonomia*) to proclaim the gospel free of charge (1 Cor 9:17–18). A good indicator of his own affirmation of manual labor—in which nearly all of the people he reached were engaged—is his understanding of his and his coworkers' work in

---

58. See further ibid., 34–35.

59. Hock, *Social Context*; his argument is effectively criticized by Todd D. Still, "Did Paul Loathe Manual Labor? Revisiting the Work of Ronald F. Hock on the Apostle's Tentmaking and Social Class," *JBL* 125, no. 4 (2006): 781–95. Unaffected by the burgeoning rhetorical criticism, Jerome Murphy-O'Connor reaffirms Hock's arguments in *Paul: A Critical Life* (Oxford: Clarendon Press, 1996), 85.

60. One regularly finds uncritical statements about "the generally negative attitude toward manual labor in antiquity," for example, in the references listed by Ascough, "Thessalonian Christian Community," 314n19. The view that manual labor was demeaning and slavish that may have been prominent in the cultural ethos was articulated especially by those whose life of privilege depended on others' labor. More critical studies might inquire how artisans understood their own work and how workers felt about having to work for the wealthy and powerful.

61. As suggested above, if Saul had been associating with Jerusalem scribal circles, he may have picked up their pride in their leisure (from manual labor). But following his "revelation," he joined a movement of people engaged in manual labor. On the question of motivation, see further below.

62. While it may be helpful for comparing and contrasting to know the different ways in which philosophers found support, as laid out by Hock (*Social Context*, 50–65), Paul and his mission are hardly reducible to an individual philosopher.

building the movement as *labor* (e.g., Rom 16:6; 1 Cor 3:13–15; 15:10, 58; 16:16; Phil 1:6; 2:16; 1 Thess 1:3; 3:5; 5:12).

Paul's Declining or Accepting Support and His Working as Aspects of His Overall Vision/Mission

Paul's decline of support from communities he was working in appears to be related not simply to their severely limited resources but also to his overall agenda. His mission was not just *located* in the Roman Empire. Judging from the way he articulates key aspects of his gospel and of his vision of the fulfillment of history, he understood his mission as *opposition* to the Roman Empire. As sketched above, in Paul's vision, history had been running not through Rome, as the prevailing imperial ideology had it, but through Israel. Although Israel, along with other peoples, had been subjected by the Romans (as by earlier empires), God's promises to Abraham would eventually be fulfilled. In ignominiously crucifying Jesus, the "rulers of this age" had killed "the Lord of glory" (1 Cor 2:8), who was now exalted on high as the true Lord, with authority over the imperial powers and rulers (Phil 2:5–11). Paul's own mission was to expand the movement of Jesus-loyalists among other subject peoples who were now heirs of the promise to Abraham and whose new constitution/citizenship was already prepared in heaven. With the parousia of Christ in "the day of the Lord" (and the completion of the general resurrection), the rule of God would finally be fully established. Paul borrowed some key images and titles from the Roman imperial ideology in articulating his anti-imperial gospel: his "gospel" itself was an alternative message of "salvation" to that of Caesar; Jesus had been exalted as the new "Lord" and "Savior." But Paul was catalyzing communities, local assemblies in a wider intercultural assembly, whose political-economic-religious relations were to be virtually the opposite of those prevailing in the Roman imperial order.

Paul's vision seems utopian, and that would be a fair characterization. But it is not a narrowly religious or disembodied spiritual vision. He does not imagine reality as bifurcated into bodies that live in the political-economic world and separable souls that can live in a separate spiritual sphere. He and his assemblies are living *in* the Roman imperial order. But they are not *of* the Roman imperial order in their respective cities. Comments in nearly every letter indicate some of the ways they are still embedded in "the world" (that is passing away) in various contingencies, some in various forms of direct or indirect dependency and vulnerability. But in key passages in nearly every letter, some previously taken as counsels of mere quietism, he presses the newly established assemblies to disengage from the local political economic-religious order, with the resulting persecutions and negative economic effects. And his own declining of economic support and laboring to support himself seems to be related to this disengagement.

The clearest cases are in 1 Thessalonians and Philippians, with the Corinthian situation more complicated by conflict within the assembly and between (some) Corinthians and Paul.

In 1 Thessalonians 5:1–11, Paul points directly to the conflict of the assembly with the Roman imperial (political-economic-religious) order, particularly to the honors to the emperor, whose celebrations included the central symbols and slogan "Peace and Security"—that is, at least for the wealthy elite who sponsored the imperial cult. Presumably because the assembly seemed to pose a threat to the local social order (because its members quit serving the "idols," that is the gods, including Caesar), the assembly, like Paul himself, had suffered persecution. Their perseverance through this persecution evidently became an example to all the Jesus-loyalists in Macedonia and Achaia (1 Thess 1:6–9).

It is not surprising, then, that when Paul comes to exhortation of the community (1 Thess 4:9–12), he advises them to "keep their heads down" as well as to actively love one another "more and more." Might we surmise that this "love" included mutual aid for each other in difficult circumstances of persecution and its negative economic effects? This may well have been necessary, judging from Paul's later reference to "the assemblies in Macedonia" as living in "extreme poverty," as well as undergoing a "severe ordeal of affliction," which would only have made it worse (2 Cor 8:1–4). Particularly striking is the complex ensuing exhortation: "Aspire to *live quietly, to mind your own affairs,* and to *work with your hands,*" as he had previously directed them, so that you may "behave properly toward outsiders and be *dependent on no one*" (1 Thess 4:11–12). This sounds like a direct (and resistant) response to the Roman imperial order in Thessalonica, pulling back from and not participating in the political-economic-religious life of the city. As Hock points out, the language Paul uses, *hēsychazein kai prassein ta idia* (to live quietly and attend to one's own affairs) is unmistakably political, the opposite of *prassein ta koina* (attending to public affairs).[63]

---

63. Hock, *Social Context*, 46, and 90–91nn191–92, where he cites references from Plutarch and Epictetus and particularly the late-first-century *Letters of Chion* 13.3, 14.5, 16.5–8.

As explained above, however, this also involved an inseparable economic dimension, considering that many or most people in a city such as Thessalonica were involved in indirect or even direct economic dependency on the wealthy elite, whose position was maintained by their leadership of local "civil religion" now centered in honors to the emperor (that is the local religious political economy). In these difficult circumstances of persecution with its likely negative economic effects on the Thessalonians it would only be fitting that Paul would "labor and toil" so as not to burden them (1 Thess 2:1–12), whether or not we judge him inconsistent in following his stated principle of declining to accept the support due to an apostle.

When Paul composed Philippians, he was in prison, presumably for pressing his mission. Seeing the Philippians in a similar situation, under attack, he urges them to persist in their loyalty to the gospel in solidarity with one another and to "in no way be intimidated by those who oppose them" (presumably in Philippi; Phil 1:27–30). The key verb in his exhortation is *politeuesthe*, which should be translated in political terms as "carry out your political-economic-religious affairs" or "conduct your self-government." That Paul, at least, understands the assembly of Philippians as an alternative community over against the Roman imperial order is further suggested by the conclusion of his argument in Philippians 3:1b–21 that "our constitution/politics" (*citizenship* is too weak) "is in heaven" (and is about to be implemented on earth—cf. the Lord's prayer) "whence we are awaiting a Savior" (the alternative to the emperor), "who has the power to subject all things" (including the imperial order in which they are still living). Again, the economic, religious, and political dimensions are inseparable, as exemplified in the Romans' expropriation of the Philippians' land, conduct of civil affairs, and imposition of colonies of army veterans three generations earlier. Only in his concluding expression of thanks to the Philippians for their gifts of economic aid does Paul discuss his own poverty, making it sound like periodic destitution (Phil 4:10–19). He expresses appreciation for the aid, but insists that he could have managed without it; he has known what it is like to have plenty and at other times to go hungry. Here he says that (to that point) no assembly other than theirs had shared with him in giving and receiving in earlier years.

Paul's correspondence and relationship with the Corinthians did not go well for him. His later letters to the community are either extremely defensive (2 Corinthians 10–13) or devoted to the collection for the poor in Jerusalem (2 Corinthians 8–9). 1 Corinthians is probably the best indication of how he wanted the community to relate to the broader political economic religious order in Corinth. His arguments in this letter deal with a succession of issues, from claims of high spiritual status to "immorality" in the community, members in conflict with one another, and sexual asceticism, to "eating meat offered to idols" in an ethical freedom based on theological knowledge. His arguments begin with reference to "the rulers of this age" outsmarting themselves by crucifying the Lord of glory and conclude with a reference to the exalted Christ handing over the kingdom to God after destroying "every ruler and every authority and power"—a vivid reminder of how his gospel was directly opposed to the Roman imperial order. The arguments in between urge the assembly to conduct its own disciplinary affairs, resolve conflicts within the community without appealing to local authorities, and generally to maintain solidarity and even care for one another as a community—that is, as a collective body of cooperative members (1 Corinthians 5, 6, and 12–14, respectively). The end of his response to asceticism seems to sum up the stance he urges the community to take to the established order: "the appointed time has grown short; from now on . . . let those who buy be as though they had no possessions, and those who deal with the world as though they had no dealings with it. For the present form of this world is passing away" (1 Cor 7:29–31). He is urging the members of the community to have as little dealings with "the world" (the established order) as possible, except perhaps for their recruiting (1 Cor 5:10), but to act as an alternative society.[64]

The argument in 1 Corinthians 8–10 fits the same general stance toward the Roman imperial order in Corinth. In this argument, as in others in the letter, he is trying to persuade the Corinthian spirituals by using some of their own language.[65] Ostensibly agreeing with their enlightenment theology that there is only one God, he warns that "there are many gods and many lords" (such as those being served in the temples and shrines in Corinth; 1 Cor 8:1–6). He then urges those who possess knowledge not to use their new-found freedom of action based on their knowledge, specifically not to eat meat offered to

---

64. Explored more fully in Horsley, "1 Corinthians: A Case Study of Paul's Assembly as an Alternative Society," in *Paul and Empire*, 242–52; and Richard A. Horsley, "Paul's Assembly in Corinth: An Alternative Society," in *Urban Religion in Corinth: Interdisciplinary Approaches*, ed. Daniel N. Schowalter and Steven J. Friesen (Cambridge, MA: Harvard University Press, 2005), 371–95.

65. Fuller exploration in Horsley, *Wisdom and Spiritual Transcendence*, chs. 4 and 6; and Horsley, *1 Corinthians*, on 1 Corinthians 8–10.

idols (which those who possessed knowledge claimed did not symbolize gods) out of consideration for the members who do not possess such a liberated consciousness/knowledge. He is pleading with them not to participate, even indirectly by eating meat that may have been sacrificed in the imperial and related cults. It may not be coincidental that in the middle of the argument, he uses as an illustration using his own "freedom/authority" not to work.

Conclusion

In conclusion, in view of the complexities of Paul's economic "location" and locations, we can consider the possible complexities of his motivation in declining support and working with his hands yet accepting at least supplementary support in his mission. We may even speculate about the personal-psychological aspects of his motivation. He may well have felt uncomfortable about his more comfortable origins and unworthy as a Johnny-come-lately to the ranks of the apostles, as one who had not known or been called by Jesus himself (cf. 1 Cor 15:8–10). He insists more than once that he was concerned not to be "burdening" the people in the assemblies, most of whom were themselves economically marginal. More broadly in the agenda of his mission, he claims that his not using his right/freedom and working to support himself was not of his own free will because he had been entrusted with a stewardship (as he declares in 1 Cor 9:17–18). Picking up on the "pragmatism" of his inconsistency of behavior that he articulates in the next step of his argument (1 Cor 9:19–23), we can explain his acceptance of support in some cases from the same sense of commission with the gospel and community formation.

Among his later letters to the Corinthians, 2 Corinthians 10–13 is a desperate defense of his apostleship, with sharp polemic against the "superapostles." His claim that he did not burden the Corinthians is now almost sarcastic. He desperately claims that what makes him a better servant/minister of Christ are the countless beatings from Judean and Roman officials, the dangerous situations he had endured, and the hunger, thirst, and cold he had regularly suffered in the course of his mission. The tone is painfully defensive, and his self-pity would not have endeared him to the Corinthians any more than it does to us. For his plea to have had any credibility, however, his catalogue must have referred to at least some serious persecutions and other sufferings that resulted from the activities of his mission. That is, Paul's defense provides reference to the political-economic repression that resulted from the political-economic-religious challenge that local officials sensed in the movement, its communities, and particularly its leaders as they engaged with the Roman imperial order in its various locations.

Select Bibliography

Alcock, Susan E. *Graecia Capta: The Landscapes of Roman Greece*. Cambridge: Cambridge University Press, 1993.

Ascough, Richard S. "The Thessalonian Christian Community as a Professional Voluntary Association." *JBL* 119, no. 2 (2000): 314–28.

Boer, Roland, and Christina Petterson. *Idols of Nations: Biblical Myth at the Origins of Capitalism*. Minneapolis: Fortress Press, 2014.

De Ste. Croix, G. E. M. *Class Struggle in the Ancient Greek World: From the Archaic Age to the Arab Conquests*. London: Duckworth, 1981.

Elliott, Neil. *The Arrogance of Nations: Reading Romans in the Shadow of Empire*. Minneapolis: Fortress Press, 2008.

Friesen, Steven J. "Poverty in Pauline Studies: Beyond the So-Called New Consensus," *JSNT* 26, no. 3 (2004): 323–61.

Garnsey, Peter, and Richard Saller. *The Roman Empire: Economy, Society, and Culture*. 2nd ed. Berkeley: University of California Press, 2015.

Hock, Ronald F. *The Social Context of Paul's Ministry: Tentmaking and Apostleship*. Philadelphia: Fortress Press, 1980.

Horsley, Richard A. *1 Corinthians*. ANTC. Nashville: Abingdon, 1998.

_____. *Jesus and the Politics of Roman Palestine*. Columbia: University of South Carolina Press, 2014.

_____, ed. *Paul and Empire: Religion and Power in Roman Imperial Society*. Harrisburg, PA: Trinity Press International, 1997.

_____. "Paul's Assembly in Corinth: An Alternative Society." In *Urban Religion in Corinth: Interdisciplinary Approaches*, edited by Daniel N. Schowalter and Steven J. Friesen, 371–95. Cambridge, MA: Harvard University Press, 2005.

Judge, E. A. "St. Paul as a Radical Critic of Society." In *Social Distinctives of the Christians in the First Century: Pivotal Essays*, 99–115. Edited by David M. Scholer. Peabody, MA: Hendrickson, 2008.

Longenecker, Bruce W. "Exposing the Economic Middle: A Revised Economy Scale for the Study of Early Christianity." *JSNT* 31, no. 3 (2009): 243–78.

Morley, Neville. "Economy and Economic Theory, Roman." In *The*

Oxford Encyclopedia of Ancient Greece and Rome, edited by Michael Gagarin and Elaine Fantham, 3:8–13. Oxford: Oxford University Press, 2010.

Saller, Richard P. *Personal Patronage under the Early Empire*. Cambridge: Cambridge University Press, 1982.

Scheidel, Walter, ed. *The Cambridge Companion to the Roman Economy*. Cambridge: Cambridge University Press, 2012.

Still, Todd D. "Did Paul Loathe Manual Labor? Revisiting the Work of Ronald F. Hock on the Apostle's Tentmaking and Social Class." *JBL* 125, no. 4 (2006): 781–95.

5

———

Architecture: Where Did Pauline Communities Meet?

Annette Weissenrieder

In a recently published article, "Citizenship, the Citizen Body, and Its Assemblies," Josine Blok has demonstrated that an ancient political assembly *ekklēsia* was as much tied together by democratic principles as by venerating cults,[1] families, and houses (*oikoi*). Members of the *ekklēsia* honored the same gods at home and in the public sphere of the *ekklēsia*. She speaks of a "perceived covenant of the community of mortals and the immortal gods" in which the *ekklēsia* and the *oikos* played an important role.[2]

All members of the *polis* (men and women), who honored the same gods and goddesses at home and in public, were required to take on public duties in the citizen-state. One of the main verbs here is the term for "participation," *metechein*, μετέχειν, which can be translated as

---

1. Josine Blok, "Citizenship, the Citizen Body, and Its Assemblies," in *Companion to Ancient Greek Government*, ed. Hans Beck (West Sussex: Wiley-Blackwell, 2013), 161–75.
2. Ibid., 161.

"to partake of something common with another," "have a share with others," or "to participate."[3] Blok makes clear that this participation refers to "belonging to a group and participating in all it did," which is connected with a second term, *timē* (honor), entailing "giving honor to the community." Honors were granted "based on birth, wealth and/ or gender."[4] These honors may have been fulfilled by participation in a procession, in a cult festival, or in cult sacrifices, which were also performed in the houses. These duties were recognized by the *polis* community. Therefore, the concept of honor (*timē*, τιμή) was seen as reciprocal. It connected house, *ekklēsia*, and *polis*. A person who had fallen into disgrace was declared *atimos* and, vice versa, a citizen who felt treated with injustice could also file a complaint against his or her *atimia*. It may be important to mention that these terms (*metechein*, *timē*, *atimos*) are referred to in Paul's letters only in 1 Corinthians, as will be shown below.

Another close connection between house and *ekklēsia* occurs in epistolary greetings in 1 Corinthians 16:19, Romans 16:3–5, Philemon 2, and Colossians 4:15, however, not surprisingly, with a different emphasis in these early Christian letters. In the *Handbook of Early Christianity*, Caroline Osiek refers to patrons "who hosted meetings of the Christian assembly regularly in their house,"[5] and according to M. Bruce Button and Fika J. van Rensburg, this refers to the so-called "house-church formula" (τῇ κατ' οἶκον αὐτῶν ἐκκλησίᾳ), which is, in these letters, associated with names like Stephanus or Prisca and Aquila.[6] This is deepened by a second phrase that refers to Gaius in Romans 16:23 and 1 Corinthians 14:23; in Greek we read: ὁ ξένος μου καὶ ὅλης τῆς ἐκκλησίας, which is very often translated in scholarship as Gaius, the "host of the whole church/assembly."[7] Whereas some scholars assume that Gaius hosted the Christian *ekklēsia* in a meeting hall, the majority suggest that he invited the whole *ekklēsia* into his house. In addition, we hear that the Christian assembly met in houses (*en oikō*) as well as in the assembly (*en ekklēsia*), where they were sitting together and not reclining (*kathēme-*

---

3. Henry George Liddell, Robert Scott, and Henry Stuart Jones, *A Greek-English Lexicon*, 9th ed. with revised supplement (Oxford: Clarendon, 1996), 1120. See for this esp. Lysias 6.48, 30.15; Aristotle, *Politica* 1282a29.

4. Blok, "Citizenship," 168.

5. Carolyn Osiek, "Archaeological and Architectural Issues and the Question of Demographic and Urban Forms," in *Handbook of Early Christianity: Social Science Approaches*, ed. Anthony J. Blasi, Jean Duhaime and Paul-André Turcotte (Walnut Creek, CA: AltaMira Press, 2002), 98.

6. M. Bruce Button and Fika J. van Rensburg, "The 'House Churches' in Corinth," *Neotestamentica* 37, no. 1 (2003): 1, 3, 9–10.

7. The late Latin tradition (e.g., ar b vgcl) provides a correction to "all the churches."

nai; 1 Cor 14:30). What kind of houses do we imagine for "the *ekklēsia* throughout the *oikos*" and for the whole *ekklēsia* in Gaius's house? And how is the *ekklēsia* related to the house? And does this finally lead to assuming that a portion of the Corinthian church belonged to the "prosperous/elite,"[8] that is, wealthy people (as Marlis Gielen, Gerd Theissen, Wayne Meeks, and Peter Lampe argue),[9] or to the "nonelite," as Justin Meggitt and others recently proposed?[10]

In this paper, I wish to demonstrate possible meeting places of Pauline communities, with an emphasis on Corinth, based on ancient visual and literary sources. First, I start with an overview of various houses as meeting spaces in Corinth. My main argument is concerned with the question of differences in the functions of houses and wealth of the owners, as well as the possibility of sitting together. As has been shown by Janet DeLaine for the study of Roman housing in Ostia,[11] it is too simple to draw a dichotomy between the single rich family *domus*, typified in Pompeii, and the rented apartments of the multi-occupancy *insulae* for the nonelite in Corinth. This will be deepened by a brief overview of sitting/reclining, and I will show that the *ekklēsia* should be taken seriously as another meeting space. This will be amplified in a final part, in which I contend that reading 1 Corinthians in light of *ekklēsia* discourses in antiquity provides new insights into Paul's definition of *ekklēsia* as the embodied assembly of God. The goal of this paper is to form an understanding of the conceptual models of meeting spaces available in Corinth and to integrate these models with a new understanding of the so-called "house formulas," which will be reconsidered grammatically in the conclusion.

---

8. On the discussion of the terms *elite/nonelite, wealthy, prosperous,* or *poor,* see several papers in this volume.

9. Marlis Gielen, "Zur Interpretation der paulinischen Formel ἡ κατ' οἶκον ἐκκλησία," ZNW 77, no. 1-2 (1986): 109-25; Gerd Theissen, "Soziale Integration und sakramentales Handeln. Eine Analyse von 1 Cor. XI 17–34," in *Studien zur Soziologie des Urchristentums,* WUNT 19 (Tübingen: Mohr Siebeck, 1983), 290–317; Wayne A. Meeks, *The First Urban Christians: The Social World of the Apostle Paul* (New Haven, CT: Yale University Press, 1983); Peter Lampe, "Das korinthische Herrenmahl im Schnittpunkt hellenistisch-römischer Mahlpraxis und paulinischer Theologia Crucis (1Kor 11,17–34)," ZNW 82, no. 3–4 (1991): 183–213.

10. Justin Meggitt, *Paul, Poverty and Survival* (Edinburgh: T&T Clark, 1998), 66–67.

11. Janet DeLaine, "Housing Roman Ostia," in *Contested Spaces: Houses and Temples in Roman Antiquity and the New Testament,* ed. David L. Balch and Annette Weissenrieder (Tübingen: Mohr Siebeck, 2012), 327–51.

Houses in Corinth

There is a semantic intersection of *oikos*/*domus* both in Greek and in Latin. Three connotations should be mentioned. First, the concepts refer to a circumscribed space: a *domus* in a Campanian style is an atrium house including the garden, an *insula*, a cellar room or a separate room in a house, a tavern, and even a grave. They also refer to the household, which may include cognate as well as agnatic kinship; the concept includes family in a narrower sense but also the household, which includes slaves. And finally, *oikos* and *domus* can signify the social status of a house and thereby its property.[12]

The Atrium House

Numerous passages in the New Testament (Acts 2:46, 5:42; most often in 1 Corinthians 11–14) indicate that communal gatherings took place in the house. The fact that the issue of architectural typology dominates so much of the debate among New Testament scholars about the Lord's Supper is certainly due to the concept of the house (*oikos*) introduced by Paul in 1 Corinthians 11:22 and 34, which allows scholars to infer that a private house was the space in which the celebration of the feast of remembrance and the gatherings of the *ekklēsia* took place.

Ancient architectural typology was first brought into the debate by the New Testament scholar and archaeologist Jerome Murphy-O'Connor.[13] In his well-known book *St. Paul's Corinth*, he looks at examples of archaeological specimens from Corinth and Pompeii. In the section "House Churches and the Eucharist," he connects the Corinthian house congregation with the Villa Anaploga (a villa that has since become inaccessible because of an olive grove that has been planted there), which he believes belonged to a wealthy member of the congregation. Murphy-O'Connor locates the meeting place of the house congregation in the *triclinium* of the Villa Anaploga, which he identifies as a specific room for meeting and eating. Murphy-O'Connor, Lampe, and many other scholars following their lead see the physical structure of the Roman house and specifically the limited space in the *triclinium* as problematic because guests who arrived late would not have been able

---

12. There are no inscriptions preserved for associations in Corinth. For associations outside Corinth, see the contribution by Kloppenborg in this volume.
13. Jerome Murphy-O'Connor, *St. Paul's Corinth: Texts and Archeology*, 3rd ed., Good News Studies 6 (Collegeville, MN: Liturgical Press, 2002).

to find any more places on the couches (*klinē*), in the *triclinium*.[14] Peter Lampe views this archaeological evidence in the framework of a normal "eranos meal." The break between the main dish, the main course for wealthy Corinthians, and the *secundae mensae*, the dessert with a blessing of the bread and a blessing of the wine, is of fundamental importance for Lampe, since this interruption represents, he says, a pause in the ceremony that would have allowed newly arrived guests to join the company. These latecomers, however, did not find any more space in the *triclinium*.[15] Lampe therefore analyzes the structural features, the wealth of the owner, and limitations of space and its use as the cause of conflict in Corinth.

But compared to houses that are well known to us from Pompeii or Ostia, Villa Anaploga lacks certain features of a typical *domus* of a Campanian standard, such as a cistern beneath the *impluvium*. Absent are also the *tablinum* and an *alae*, as well as typical symmetry around the atrium, which is common in Pompeian houses. Also, the typical alignment of vestibule and atrium, which would make the *impluvium* visible to passersby, is missing. Rooms are arranged asymmetrically around the atrium, which is often a characteristic even for "lower" classes (as John Clarke calls them).[16] The house may be compared to simple country villas or farmhouses that fit into the category that Andrew Wallace-Hadrill calls a "modest house";[17] in addition, rooms 9–11 have a different entrance and may be the space for slaves. Whereas there is no doubt that the Villa Anaploga itself was built in the first century CE, recent scholarship suggests that the mosaic composed of stone and glass tesserae should not be dated before the third century CE since there is nothing comparable until then.[18]

---

14. For atrium or peristylum see Gordon D. Fee, *The First Epistle to the Corinthians*, NICNT (Grand Rapids: Eerdmans, 1987), 533; Raymond F. Collins, *First Corinthians*, Sacra Pagina 7 (Collegeville, MN: Liturgical Press, 1999), 418; Lampe, "Das korinthische Mahl," 197; Murphy-O'Connor, *St. Paul's Corinth*, 129–38; Theissen, "Soziale Integration," 297.

15. Lampe, "Das korinthische Mahl," 183–213 and Peter Lampe, "The Corinthian Eucharistic Dinner Party: Exegesis of a Cultural Context (1 Cor. 11:17–34)," *Affirmation* 4 (Fall 1991): 1–15.

16. John R. Clarke, *The Houses of Roman Italy 100 B.C.–A.D. 250: Ritual, Space and Decoration* (Berkeley: University of California Press, 1991), 25.

17. Wallace-Hadrill, "Houses and Households: Sampling Pompeii and Herculaneum," in *Marriage, Divorce, and Children in Ancient Rome*, ed. Beryl Rawson (Oxford: Clarendon, 1991), 191.

18. An early dating can be found also by Stella Grobel Miller, "A Mosaic Floor from a Roman Villa at Anaploga," *Hesperia* 41 (1972), 332–54, which is questioned in recent times; see for further considerations Katherine M. D. Dunbabin, *Mosaics of the Greek and Roman World* (Cambridge: Cambridge University Press, 1999); S. E. Waywell, "Roman Mosaics in Greece," *AJA* 83, no. 3 (1979): 297; Maria Papaioannou, "The Roman Domus in the Greek World," in *Building Communities: House, Settlement and Society in the Aegean and Beyond*, ed. Ruth Westgate, Nick Fisher, and James Whitley, British School at Athens Studies 15 (London: British School at Athens, 2007), 354. See also Murphy-O'Connor, *St. Paul's Corinth*, 178; David G. Horrell, "Domestic Space and Christian Meetings at Corinth:

This villa is indeed very different from the *domus* in Panayia field from the third century CE,[19] which has beautiful mosaics,[20] marble fountains, and sculptures and paintings showcasing the owner's status in Roman Corinthian society.

There is also the Shear Villa in Kokkinovrysi (also in the northwestern section of Corinth), whose original plan has been destroyed.[21] The first room is marked by Shear as an atrium with an *impluvium*; its ground is decorated with marble in different color shadings and its walls are decorated with marble and a Meander mosaic.[22] Northwest of this atrium is where Shear supposes the *triclinium* was located, a space decorated with simple mosaics because of *klinē* being placed in this room.[23] There is a consensus that the house went through several constructions. Shear argues on the basis of some findings like lamps and coins that the mosaic was already installed in the year 146 BCE and could have been reinserted in the year 44 CE with the renewed settlement in a new house structure. This suggestion was taken up recently by L. L. Welborn.[24] Whereas Shear formulates the dating of the villa in a cautious manner, it is described in New Testament scholarship as a fact.[25] Sharing Shears's careful analysis, S. E. Waywell argues that the *triclinium* and two other rooms are from the third century.[26] Because the plan of the house was decisively changed after the new settlement, an assumption that all researchers share, no statements about either the settlement of the house or the social standing of the residents in the first century CE can be made.

To summarize this point: The atrium houses from Corinth known to us from the first century CE do not have separate entrances for private guests and clients, large reception rooms, or a hierarchy of decoration,

Imagining New Contexts and the Buildings East of the Theatre," *NTS* 50, no. 3 (2004): 350–51; L. L. Welborn, *An End to Enmity: Paul and the "Wrongdoer" of Second Corinthians*, BZNW 185 (Berlin: de Gruyter, 2011), 338–39 (also with cross-reference to Robinson).

19. Saul S. Weinberg, *The Southeast Building, the Twin Basilicas, the Mosaic House*, Corinth 1, pt. 5 (Princeton: American School of Classical Studies at Athens, 1960), 116.

20. Ibid., 115.

21. Theodore Leslie Shear, *The Roman Villa*, Corinth 5 (Cambridge, MA: Harvard University Press, 1930); Theodore Leslie Shear, "Excavations at Corinth in 1925," *AJA* 29, no. 4 (1925): 381–88; Theodore Leslie Shear, "Excavations in the Theatre District and Tombs at Corinth in 1929," *AJA* 33, no. 4 (1929): 515–36; Charles Kaufmann Williams II and Orestes H. Zervos, "Corinth, 1981: East of the Theater," *Hesperia* 51, no. 2 (1982): 115–63; Charles Kaufmann Williams II and Orestes H. Zervos, "Corinth, 1982: East of the Theater," *Hesperia* 52, no. 1 (1983): 1–47.

22. Shear, "Excavations at Corinth in 1925," 391–92.

23. So in any case, Shear, "Excavations at Corinth in 1925," 394 and Shear, *The Roman Villa*, 17.

24. Welborn, *An End to Enmity*, 342–48.

25. Ibid., 342–48.

26. Shear, "Excavations at Corinth in 1925," 395, and Shear, *The Roman Villa*, 26; Waywell, "Roman Mosaics in Greece," 297.

privileging the visitors admitted to the innermost heart of the house, and they may not have belonged to the elite. The few examples from Corinth that are available to us up to now do not provide sufficient evidence for houses that were exclusively available to wealthy members of the Corinthian *ekklēsia*.

The *Insulae*

Particularly in the later first and early second century, other forms of higher-status houses emerged as part of the residential and commercial multistory *insulae*. D. G. Horrell has taken a closer look at the supposed limited space in the *triclinium*, seeking to prove that even the houses of lower-class people had room for many participants at meals and worship services.[27] Horrell focuses on the houses in the East Theater Street, a street with numerous small businesses, where he assumes the residents were "non-elite, not the most impoverished urban residents."[28] He raises the question of whether the buildings may have been shops, taverns, or *popinae*. Although we find in the ground floor of building 1 a window counter that opened to the street to sell food to passersby, there is no evidence that these buildings could have served people inside the houses, because no standard equipment like wine counters has been found yet, as Charles K. Williams II and Orestes H. Zervos argue.[29] Buildings 1 and 3 consisted of two large rooms along East Theater Street with smaller rooms in the back and an upper floor. In building 3, dry-sieved bones and 171 sheep/goat horns have been preserved in the ground floor, but there is no window and no standard equipment for inns and taverns.[30] Though these buildings seem to be in accord with Horrell's assessment, building 3 is not as it has painted decorations in the ground floor and "must have had rooms decorated with a quite presentable fresco program" in the upper floor,[31] and the

---

27. D. G. Horrell, "Domestic Space and Christian Meetings at Corinth: Imagining New Contexts and the Buildings East of the Theatre," *NTS* 50 (2004): 349–69; Edward Adams and David G. Horrell, *Christianity in Corinth: The Quest for the Pauline Church* (Louisville, KY: Westminster John Knox, 2004); Peter Oakes, "Contours of the Urban Environment," ch. 2 in *After the First Urban Christians: The Social-Scientific Study of Pauline Christianity Twenty-Five Years Later*, ed. Todd D. Still and David G. Horrell (New York: T&T Clark, 2009); and Peter Oakes, *Reading Romans in Pompeii: Paul's Letter at Ground Level* (Minneapolis: Fortress Press, 2009).
28. Horrell, "Domestic Space," 367f.
29. Charles K. Williams II and Orestes H. Zervos, "Corinth, 1985: East of the Theater," *Hesperia* 55, no. 2 (1986): 129–76; Charles K. Williams II and Orestes H. Zervos, "Corinth, 1987: South of Temple E and East of the Theater," *Hesperia* 57, no. 2 (1988): 93–146.
30. Papaioannou, "The Roman Domus," 354.
31. See Williams and Zervos, "Corinth, 1985," 140.

pottery found was of a fine quality. Not only have good building materials been used, the houses are also built with "superior workmanship."[32] The upper floor must have had at least one large room with paintings in the second Pompeian fresco style (or style of transition). Building 7 (sharing a wall with building 5) has in its lower floor "a moderately impressive room, decorated with frescoes of single birds. It only has a small hearth."[33] The entrance of building 5 on the East Theater Street was framed by painted wall plaster and frescoes and faced the theater of Corinth.[34] On the lower level, an isolated rectangular hearth with a thick bed of gravel was found for holding the heat, a technical feature that is well known in Pompeii and in villas of this area. The room also preserves figures of Hermes, Heracles, or Aphrodite, which give a formal outline to these rooms.[35] This is confirmed by graffiti in Greek written by a more skilled hand, which may preserve the term Ἀντέρω[σ]ωε.[36] The name may either be interpreted as a Roman cognomen, which, however, is not known yet in Corinth, or the name may refer to one of the sons of Ares and Aphrodite, Anteros; therefore the niche can be interpreted as a *lararium*. Countless finds from the Roman Empire confirm the cultic function of the niche as an installation site for altars, incense burners, statuettes of gods, reliefs, and other cult objects. The name written in this niche can therefore also be interpreted as a call to prayer to the son of the gods Anteros.[37] This *insula* is representative of where the majority of the population in Corinth lived, both permanent residents as well as those many from all walks of life who were in transit.[38] One thing is clear: these houses were occupied not only by "nonelite" people. Compared to the Villa Anaploga, the rooms are of similar size and even greater beauty.

There are also houses from 44 BCE that were former shops later reconstructed with very poor stone floors and repaired walls. We have findings in the area west of the *bouleutērion*.[39] We may assume that these areas were occupied by "nonelites" from 44 BCE on. Often work-

---

32. Ibid., 131.
33. See Williams and Zervos, "Corinth, 1987," 128f.
34. See Williams and Zervos, "Corinth, 1985," 129–66; Williams and Zervos, "Corinth, 1987," 128.
35. Williams and Zervos, "Corinth, 1985," 161f.
36. Williams and Zervos ("Corinth, 1987," 128) describe this room as a "moderately impressive room."
37. Ibid.
38. Wallace-Hadrill ("Houses and Households," 217–18) writes: "Alongside the familiar figure of the *paterfamilias* surrounded by his family and slaves, we are invited to imagine widows, freedmen, heirs, and legatees anxious to exploit urban property for the rich range of opportunities it offered: on the one hand habitation, whether for gracious living with frescos, statutes, gardens, and private baths, or as lodging for a motley crowd of dependents, freedmen, employees, clients, and visitors; on the other hand, profit, from lodgers, shops, fulleries, warehouses, and baths to let."

ing spaces must have supplied living quarters for those employed there, in back of single spaces. Williams also mentions a terracotta factory, which is located in a house in the Potters' Quarter with a court surrounded by several rooms. Firing in this building is unattested. That these were indeed living spaces as well as commercial space is suggested by remaining evidence for latrines.[40] Larger apartment blocks are also mentioned in an official letter written by the governor of Achaea approving Priscus (P. Licinius Priscus Juventianus) to buy *ager publius* to erect fifty buildings. The list of donations starts with construction of buildings for athletes. The letter mentions two different terms for the suggested accommodations, οἴκους and ξενίας. Each of these rooms was called a "room," *oikos*. The suggested accommodations were to be erected at a place identified as "ruins of the marble stoa."

Gardens

In his book *Roman Domestic House and Early House Churches*, David Balch refers several times to the possibility of retiring to the *peristylum*, should problems of space arise.[41] Dining while sitting occurred in the open and in peristyle gardens, as Balch recently convincingly showed. For the sake of comparison, he refers to the "munificence meals," which involve public meals and large ancient gardens. However, the gardens, although an important meeting point for (opulent) meals, are not directly mentioned in Paul.[42]

---

39. Oscar Broneer, *The South Stoa and Its Roman Successors*, Corinth 1, pt. 4 (Princeton: American School of Classical Studies at Athens, 1954), 136f.

40. See Charles Kaufman Williams II, "The City of Corinth and Its Domestic Religion," *Hesperia* 50, no. 4 (1981): 408–21, esp. 419–21.

41. Balch focuses on Pompeiian houses and gardens; see also Oakes, *Reading Romans*; K. M. D. Dunbabin, "*Nec grave nec infacetum*: The Imagery of Convivial Entertainment," in *Das römische Bankett im Spiegel der Altertumswissenschaften: Internationales Kolloquium 5./6. Oktober 2005, Schloss Mickeln, Düsseldorf*, ed. Konrad Vössing (Stuttgart: Franz Steiner, 2008), 13–26.

42. For garden areas, see P. Soprano, "I triclini all'aperto di Pompei," in *Pompeiana: raccolta di studi per il secondo centenario degli scavi di Pompei*, ed. Amedeo Maiuri, Biblioteca della parola del passato 4 (Naples: Gaetano Macchiaroli, 1950), 288–310, which lists thirty-nine outdoor *triclinia*, including five *biclinia*, one *stibadium*, some destroyed, and five visually represented in frescoes. Wilhelmina F. Jashemski, *The Gardens of Pompeii: Herculaneum and the Villas Destroyed by Vesuvius* (New York: Caratzas Brothers, 1979), 1, 346n1, has evidence of fifty-six outdoor garden *triclinia*; Wilhelmina F. Jashemski, "The Campanian Peristyle Garden," in *Ancient Roman Gardens. Dumberton Oaks On the History of Landscape Architecture*, ed. Elisabeth Blair MacDougall (Washington DC: Dumbarton Oaks Research Library and Collection, 1981), 31–48; Wilhelmina F. Jashemski, "Gardens," in *The World of Pompeii*, ed. John J. Dobbins and Pedar W. Foss (New York: Routledge, 2007), 487–98; Eleanor Winsor Leach, *The Social Life of Painting in Ancient Rome and on the Bay of Naples* (Cambridge: Cambridge University Press, 2004), 37–38, mentions several dialogues in Cicero's garden; Giovanni di Pasquale and Fabrizio Paolucci, *Il giardino antico da Babilonia a Roma: Scienze, arte e natura* (Livorno, ITA: Sillabe, 2007) gives an impressive exhibit on sculptors and mosaics in the garden. For literary

Cellars

In recent times, cellars have also been described as one possible meeting space.[43] The room of the cellar close to the forum on the western side of the north-south road is 3.06 x 7.82 meters in size. A stairway gives access to the basement. But there is no evidence that this specific cellar was used as a meeting space. The cellar has been used for drainage and is full of tableware and amphorae from different places. The interesting detail, however, is that the deposit shows mostly vessels and tableware from Syria and the Aegean, as K. W. Slane has shown.[44]

We have seen that the dichotomy between the villa for the elite and an *insula* for the nonelite does not exist in Corinth in the first century CE. The houses mentioned are mostly reconstructed after Corinth was refounded after 44 BCE. The graffiti, the tableware, and building reconstruction are mostly not Roman but either Corinthian, Syrian, or Ephesian in nature. The houses and cellars therefore reflect migration and a reestablished living environment. All of the houses mentioned could be evaluated as potential types of meeting space of the assembly in a house.

Sitting or Reclining?

If space is understood as a social-hierarchical environment, then furniture is certainly a factor that can contribute to that hierarchical environment. Thus 1 Corinthians 14:30 reads: "And if someone sitting down [*kathēmenai*] receives a revelation, the person who is speaking should conclude." An important piece of furniture for the houses mentioned was the *klinē* (couch), from *klinein* (to recline); it served often both as a bed to sleep on at night and as a couch to recline on at meals.[45] Literary sources also mention couches in households of lower status. Very com-

---

evidence, see A. R. Littlewood, "Ancient Literary Evidence for the Pleasure Gardens of Roman Country Villas," in MacDougall, *Ancient Roman Villa Gardens*, 7–30.

43. Edward Adams, *The Earliest Christian Meeting Spaces: Almost Exclusively Houses?* (London: T&T Clark, 2013), 204–5; he refers mainly to an excavation report by Kathleen Warner Slane, "Two Deposits from the Early Roman Cellar Building, Corinth," *Hesperia* 55, no. 3 (1986): 273–318.

44. K. W. Slane, "Two Deposits from the Early Roman Cellar Building, Corinth," *Hesperia* 55.3 (1986): 271-318.

45. Instead of *klinē*, ancient authors refer to terms like *klinarion*, as well as *klintēr*, *klinis*, and *chameuna*, *chian*. For further information on Rome: *lectus*, see G. M. A. Richter, *The Furniture of the Greeks Etruscans and Romans* (London: Phaidon Press, 1966), 52–55 and 105; on Herculaneum, see Stephan T. A. M. Mols, "Houten Meubels in Herculaneum: Vorm, Techniek en Functie" (PhD diss., Katholieke Universiteit Nijmegen, 1994), 174–77.

mon were built-in stone couches whose surface is mostly chamfered to fifteen degrees and therefore not suitable for sitting. Furniture for sitting displayed more variety in its forms; common pieces were a backless stool (*díphros*)[46] and a folding stool (*díphros okladías*).[47] We know of numerous examples of both pieces of furniture from Corinth. Also very common were simple wooden benches and stone benches.

First, it is often claimed that we encounter a gender difference in sitting or reclining in antiquity. We have many images of men reclining on couches. The images sometimes display a typological difference between men and women of the same class. Men are shown holding a drinking vessel while reclining, women are sitting at the end of the couch or holding some toilet articles. But there are exceptions: images of women resting in front of a table set for a meal, which were probably commissioned by craftspeople and freed slaves who were not members of the elite and did not feel bound by aristocratic norms.[48]

Archaeological finds in Corinth should be mentioned: in the so-called Potters' Quarter in Corinth, which was mentioned above, there are terracotta figurines of men and a few of women in a reclining posture.[49] Similar figurines have recently been found in other temples.[50] Women are reclining just like men, supported on their left arms, most likely with a cushion at their backs, right arm free for eating. They demonstrate that a reclining posture for women was not unfamiliar in Corinth.

Secondly, of interest to us is the question of status in sitting and reclining. The majority of images show reclining persons. Most interesting are, therefore, a number of frescoes classified as belonging to the "folk painting" genre; however, none of these can be found in Corinth.[51] Here, we have seemingly realistic representations of every-

---

46. These are well known in both Greek and Roman context. For the Greek context, see Richter, *Furniture of the Greeks*, 38–41; and for the Roman context, see A. T. Croom, *Roman Furniture* (Stroud, UK: Tempus, 2007), 87–105.

47. Of these, too, we have examples from ancient Greece and Rome—for example, in frescoes in private homes, such as the images of Psyche in the Villa of the Vetii, as well as from a great number of images of Zeus, Asclepius, and Dionysos.

48. Cf. H. Wrede, "Stadtrömische Monumente: Urnen und Sarkophage des Klinentypus in den beiden ersten Jahrhunderten n. Chr.," *Archäologischer Anzeiger*, 1977, 424–27; and Rita Amedick, ed., *Die Sarkophage mit Darstellungen aus dem Menschenleben*, vol. 4, *Vita Privata* (Berlin: Mann, 1991), 11–12; for further information, see Carolyn Osiek and Margaret Y. MacDonald, *A Woman's Place: House Churches in Earliest Christianity*, with Janet H. Tulloch (Minneapolis: Fortress Press, 2006), 156, 159–62.

49. Agnes Newhall Stillwell, *The Potters' Quarter: The Terracottas*, Corinth 15, pt. 2 (Princeton: American School of Classical Studies at Athens, 1952), 111, fig. 31.

50. See ibid., 54–55; it is striking that although the figurines are entered in the catalog as female, in the description of the figurines, there is no indication of their gender.

day life, which were found in the taverns that were not frequented by the members of the elite.[52] A series of images relevant to our discussion comes from a back room of a tavern that served as a dining room (Caupona via di Mercurio).[53] The stools are made of wood and probably free of decoration. The company in conversation, the furniture, and the setting shown leads to the conclusion that customers belong more to the lower class, although the frescoes display subtle distinctions in status with different clothes. This is confirmed by the names of innkeepers from antiquity that we know of today, most of whom are identified as *libertus/liberta*. In addition, some of them bear surnames of Greek origin,[54] which probably indicate their slave names.[55]

We have seen so far that sitting at a meal, whether in a house or in public gathering places, was rather unusual and uncommon in antiquity. We have also seen that sitting signified a lowering of status. Are we therefore to suppose that members of the Corinthian community underwent a change in status when they sat while eating and celebrating the Eucharist instead of reclining—a change in status that is, however, not reflected in the text of the first letter to the Corinthians itself? Hardly!

Exegetical scholarship thus far has completely ignored the word that Paul uses only in this place in the text for sitting—*kathēmenai*. *Kathēmenai* is not otherwise used by Paul.[56] An examination of the use of this

51. Thomas Fröhlich, *Lararien- und Fassadenbilder in den Vesuvstädten. Untersuchungen zur 'volkstümlichen' pompejanischen Malerei* (Mainz: Zabern, 1991), 13–20 and 211, takes a rather critical view of this genre classification in general but finds it a likely designation for the table scene.

52. The interpretation of the frescoes has changed recently, now that the pictures can be seen in a restored, cleaned-up state. This makes it possible to identify a kissing couple in the picture as a man and a woman; otherwise they had been identified as a homosexual couple—either two men, as in Fröhlich, *Lararien- und Fassadenbilder in den Vesuvstädten*, 213, or as a lesbian couple, as in F. A. Todd, "Three Pompeian Wall-Inscriptions, and Petronius," *The Classical Review* 53, no. 1 (1939): 5–9. See, therefore, John R. Clarke, *Art in the Lives of Ordinary Romans: Visual Representations and Non-Elite Viewers in Italy, 100 B.C.–A.D. 315.* (Berkeley: University of California Press, 2003), 162–80; especially helpful in this regard is the paper by I. Bragantini, "VI 14.35.36: Caupona di Salvius," in *Pompei: pitture e mosaici*, vol. 5 (Rome: Istituto della Enciclopedia italiana, 1994), 366–71, which presents the old photographs next to the new reproductions from Emil Presuhn, *Pompei: Die neusten Ausgrabungen von 1874 bis 1878* (Leipzig: Weigel, 1879), Abt. V 3-6, plates 6–7; regarding the frescoes, see also August Mau, "Scavi di Pompei," *Bullettino dell'Instituto di Corrispondenza Archeologica* no. 8–9, 1878, 191–94; Tönnes Kleberg, *In den Wirtshäusern und Weinstuben des antiken Rom*, 2nd ed. (Darmstadt: Wissenschaftliche Buchgesellschaft, 1966), 54 and table 10.17; Karl Schefold, *Die Wände Pompejis: Topographisches Verzeichnis der Bildmotive* (Berlin: de Gruyter, 1957), 135–36.

53. Fröhlich, *Lararien- und Fassadenbilder in den Vesuvstädten*, 214.

54. Ibid.

55. Kleberg, *In den Wirtshäusern und Weinstuben des antiken Rom*, 20. See also the thorough description of rights (innkeepers were denied certain civil rights, and hostesses in particular were quasi-prostitutes) in ibid., 20–21.

56. Acts 20:9 is also interesting, where there is mention of a certain Eutychus who fell asleep while

word in ancient literature is revealing. First, it is worth noting that *kathēmenai* is not a typical term for a seated meal; the word is seen much more frequently in descriptions of different cultures and (table) manners, as in Strabo, but in general this use of the word is rare, especially considering its many other uses.[57]

The word is used more often to describe the difference between a speaker who stands up to deliver a speech and the listeners who sit and listen silently in order to be able to follow the argument, and then perhaps rise for listening and attending to what is happening in the *ekklēsia*. Thus 1 Corinthians 14:30 reads: "And if someone sitting down [*kathēmenai*] receives a revelation, the person who is speaking should conclude." Remarkably, ancient Greek and Roman literature mentions only a few spaces in which this kind of silent listening takes place, where the sitting expressed by the word *kathēmenai* is required:[58] primarily in a courtroom[59] or in the political *ekklēsia*.[60] Several texts develop this.[61] Passages by Aeschines and Aristophanes give proof that senators and citizens sat in the *ekklēsia*.[62] Some texts mention, in addition to the *ekklēsia* and the courtroom, other public rooms in which one sat and observed an event, as we read in Plato.[63] The fact that the theater is mentioned here alongside the courtroom is no contradiction, given the context of ancient Greece. We know of many Greek cities that had to move from their original council hall into the theater, the forum, or even temples because of the number of their participants.[64] Corinth was probably one of these cities.

sitting in a gathering of the community. Perhaps the sitting mentioned in Acts 2:2 is also a reference to a gathering of the community.

57. Strabo *Geogr.* 3.3.

58. I have also found a passage describing sitting on a "banking-table"; see Isocrates, *Oratio Trapeziticus* 17.12.

59. See Plato, *Apologia* 35c; Plato, *Respublica* 758d: "For these reasons, this presidential section of the State must always have the control of the summoning and dissolving of assemblies, both the regular legal assemblies and those of an emergency character. Thus, a twelfth part of the Council will be the body that manages all these matters, and each such part shall rest in turn for eleven-twelfths of the year: in common with the rest of the officials, this twelfth section of the Council must keep its watch in the State over these matters continually. This disposition of affairs in the city will prove a reasonable arrangement." (Translation: Bury, LCL). See also Aristophanes, *Vespae* 1.

60. For example, Homer, *Iliad* 76–78.

61. Thucydides 5.85.

62. Aeschines, *In Timarchum* 1.112: "The senators had been sitting with the other citizens as members of the assembly." Cf. Aristophanes, *Acharnenses* 29–32.

63. Plato, *Respublica* 6.492b (Translation: Bury): "the multitude are seated together in assemblies or in court-rooms or theaters or camps or any other public gathering of a crowd, and with loud uproar censure some of the things that are said and done and approve others, both in excess, with full-throated clamor."

64. On the subject of displays of munificence and the so-called *epula* (banquets) of antiquity, see the

Coming Together in the Assembly (*en ekklēsia*)

Among Paul's letters, the word *ekklēsia* appears most frequently in the letters to the Corinthians (thirty-one times in the two letters to the Corinthians), and of these instances, the greatest number occur in chapters 11–14 of 1 Corinthians.[65] The Greek term ἐκκλησία derives from ἐκ- "out" and κλή- "to call," and means the chosen people. The Greek term is sometimes translated as *contio* or *comtia, concilium, conventus,* or *concionem* in Latin,[66] especially in Roman law, where it describes more the way of coming together. However, we also often find a transliteration of the term as *ecclesia,* as, for example, in the letters of Pliny the Younger to Trajan where he uses *bule* next to *ecclesia consentiente.*[67] Especially interesting is a bilingual inscription from Ephesus from around 104 CE that was found in the Ephesian theater. Next to the Greek, the Latin translation can be found.[68] These two Latin sources make clear that the term *ecclesia* could not be translated without losing some of its implicit connotations.

While the house (*oikos*) is seen as a space in New Testament scholarship, the meeting *en ekklēsia* is often interpreted as a house-church or church and is not discussed in the context of space and bodily behavior. It is noteworthy that Paul, in mentioning "coming together" (*synerchomai,* συνέρχομαι),[69] specifically does not write "in the house" (*en oikō*), but rather "in the assembly" or "in the space of an assembly" (*en ekklēsia;* in 1 Cor 11:18). He refers more to the private homes *en oikō* when it comes to eating (1 Cor 11:22, 34).[70] In addition, the *oikos* space

section on the Amiternum. In addition to the seated guests, we know also that there were always reclining guests—a differentiation for which there is no evidence in the letter to the Corinthians.

65. 1 Cor 1:2; 4:17; 6:4; 7:17; 10:32; 11:16, 18; 12:28; 14:5, 12, 19, 23, 33, 34, 35; 15:9.

66. On the political *ekklēsia,* see Marcellinus, *Vita Thucydides* 6.8.72, 6.8.93, 6.32.51; Aristophanes, *Acharnenses* 169; Polybius 4.34.6; Plato, *Politicus* 298c; Plato, *Protagoras* 319b; Plutarch, *Romulus* 27; Xenophon, *Hellenica* 2; Lucian, *Dialogi deorum* 24.1; Isocrates, *De pace* 170, 7.68, 8.130; *IG* 2.945.5; A. Geoffrey Woodhead, *Inscriptions: The Decrees,* Athenian Agora XVI (Princeton, NJ: American School of Classical Studies at Athens, 1997), 102.6; 79.6; 181.6; for Latin sources: Varro, *De lingua latina* 7.10; Pliny the Elder, *Naturalis historia* 35, 7.212; Cicero, *In Catilinam* 1.32.2; Cicero, *In Vatinium* 22; Seneca, *Dialogi* 2.12.2; Calidius *Oratione Fragmentum in Nonius* 208.27; Livy 1.48.3.

67. Pliny the Younger, *Epistulae* 10, 111.

68. *I.Eph* 1.29a lines 9–10 (Latin: *ita ut [om]n[i e]cclesia supra bases ponerentur*), lines 19–20 (Greek: ἵνα τίθηται κατ᾽ ἐκκλησίαν ἐν τῷ θεάτρῳ). For a translation of the dedication, see Rosalinde A. Kearsley, ed., *Greeks and Romans in Imperial Asia: Mixed Language Inscriptions and Linguistic Evidence for Cultural Interaction until the End of AD III,* Inschriften Griechischer Städte aus Kleinasien 59 (Bonn: Rudolf Habelt, 2001), §157.

69. See here also a degree for the Thesmophorion *Inscriptiones Graecae* II 573b, II2 1177; note, too, the coming together in an association of Dionysos: *Inscriptiones Graecae* IX,12 670 pl. IX 20; see also Paul Marie Duval, ed., *Recueil des Inscriptions Gauloises,* Gallia Supplement 45 (Paris: Editions du Centre national de la recherche scientifique, 1985).

in 1 Corinthians 14 is not mentioned at all in the context of the communal gathering.[71] "Coming together in an assembly" (*synerchomai en ekklēsia*) is a *terminus technicus* for the civic assembly as well as for the Corinthian community.[72]

The phrase "in the assembly" (*en ekklēsia*, ἐν ἐκκλησία) occurs five times in 1 Corinthians: as already mentioned, as division of the assembly in 11:18; in 14:19, speaking with mind is discussed; in 14:28, Paul clarifies that each member should be silent *en ekklēsia* if there is no one to interpret; and finally in 14:33, Paul refers to the women who should keep silent. In 12:28, we read *en ekklēsia* with regard to the structure and function of the assembly. To understand the phrase "in an assembly" (*en ekklēsia*), we have to also understand the preposition *en* (ἐν, "in"). *En* is mainly used to connote a static relation topographically; it is that of confinement, to signify crossing borders that are not permeable (one is in or out). εἰς, in contrast, connotes allative or illative orientation,[73] for example, the crossing of rooms and borders that are permeable. The preposition ἐν (*en*) is less connected with the idea of movement than with the idea of the established, of fixedness. The particle ἐν (*en*) connotes a separation of inside and outside. It is used to describe the action of entering a room, moving in, until the entrance is made, and is therefore put in close relationship with this space. Somebody is either inside or outside. By contrast, *eis* (εἰς) is used to describe entering a space, if access is possible. If Paul refers therefore to *en ekklēsia*, he refers to a space that separates one group from another group and one space from another space.

This clear examination brings with it the further issue of the concrete arrangement of the meeting space, *ekklēsia*. However, there is no easy solution for this issue either. For the classical and Hellenistic periods, ancient literary testimoniums mention a few political institutions at Corinth.

In several Greek cities, we find a configuration of a large hall, a *prytaneion* (for the magistrate), a *bouleutērion* (for the council members), and a court house. In Corinth, we find a building similar in a

---

70. See Jorunn Økland, *Women in Their Place: Paul and the Corinthian Discourse of Sanctuary Space* (London: T&T Clark, 2004), 148.

71. Ibid., 138–40.

72. On *synerchomai*, see for example Polybius 4.7.2.

73. Pietro Bortone, *Greek Prepositions: From Antiquity to the Present* (Oxford: Oxford University Press, 2010); Stavros Skopeteas, "Grammaticalization and Sets of Form-Function Pairs: Encoding Spatial Concepts in Greek," in *Studies in Grammaticalization*, ed. Elisabeth Verhoeven, Stavros Skopeteas, Yong-Min Shin, Yoko Nishina, and Johannes Helmbrecht, Trends in Linguistics 205 (Berlin: de Gruyter, 2008), 25–56.

certain way to the Greek *bouleutērion* and *ekklēsiastērion* and the typical Roman council building, but at the same time quite unusual in terms of its architecture and departing from all known types, a manifestation that is not found again in any later buildings.[74] The presence of a *bouleutērion* in a city does not in and of itself provide any information about the city's political organization, since we see examples of *bouleutēria* from monarchies just as often as from oligarchies and democracies. This house, possibly identified as a *bouleutērion* in Corinth, in any case, is from the first century BCE and should not necessarily be interpreted as a sign that the government in Corinth was democratic.[75] The building is oriented toward the north, in the direction of the *agora*, and is in well-preserved condition even today. The largest room of the curia occupies a horseshoe-shaped space (13.5 x 12 m). Of special interest to us here are the well-preserved blocks of porous sedimentary rock that are set into the curved walls. They are of various heights and have inserts for armrests, allowing us to presume with some certainty that this building was a senate house.[76] The statue of an official that has been found under the floor of the entrance gives additional indication that this was probably a public building. It appears that with time this building became too small to be used for meetings of the Corinthian senate, leaving it vacant. Meetings were probably moved from the original meeting building to the theater or the stadium.

For a further differentiation of meeting space in Corinth, scholars have referred to what is known as the Astarita vase, a Corinthian *krater* from the sixth century BCE. Claude Bérard assumes that the vase represents Corinthian society and "la réception d'une ambassade à Corinthe," which refers to the *theatron*: "en effet, les ambassades sont reçues dans l'agora, ou plutôt dans les différents bâtiments qui

---

74. See Henry S. Robinson, *Ancient Corinth: A Guide to the Excavations*, 6th ed. (Athens: American School of Classical Studies at Athens, 1960), 57; Robert L. Scranton, *Monuments in the Lower Agora and North of the Archaic Temple*, Corinth 1, pt. 3 (Princeton: American School of Classical Studies at Athens, 1951), 126; William McDonald, *The Political Meeting Places of the Greeks* (Baltimore: Johns Hopkins, 1943) 177–81; Charles H. Morgan, "Excavations at Corinth, 1935–1936," *AJA* 40, no. 4 (1936): 479–80.

75. *Corinth* 8.3 309 fr. e; see also Plutarch, *Cleomenes* 19.1: "When this happened, Aratus was at Corinth, holding a judicial examination of those who were reputed to favour the Spartan cause. The unexpected tidings threw him into consternation, and perceiving that the city was leaning towards Cleomenes and wished to be rid of the Achaeans, he summoned the citizens into the *bouleutērion*, and then slipped away unnoticed to the city gate." (Translation: Perrin, LCL). Cf. also Plutarch, *Aratus* 40.2–4 and Polybius 5.25.5.

76. It is not certain if the passage in Plutarch's *Cleomenes* (19.1) regarding a *bouleutērion* is meant to be referring to the meeting building; the meeting building is certainly not big enough for a meeting of many people.

entourent celle-ci, prytanée, bouleutérion, ecclésiasterion."[77] This view corresponds to the assertions of Frank Kolb, who demonstrates that the interior furnishing of the *agora* could have been quite minimal. In early times, it primarily provided a space for *agōnes,* or athletic contests, and had an *orchestra,* a space dedicated to a divinity in which sacred dances were performed. A measure of skepticism regarding the aforementioned *ekklēsiastērion* is appropriate. We know of only a few cities in antiquity that had *ekklēsiastēria* of their own. As yet, Corinth does not belong to this number. Admittedly, it is worth noting that in this regard the boundary between *ekklēsiastērion* and the *theatron* was fluid,[78] as Vitruvius describes.[79]

The word *theatron* means first a gathering place, an audience gathered together, and then later a play (an important example of that is 1 Cor 4:9): "*theatron* konnte im Griechischen denn auch stets jede für Zuschauer gedachte Anlage bei jedem beliebigen Anlaß bezeichnen und blieb nie auf das Theatergebäude beschränkt."[80]

More recently, the archaeologist J. C. Donati has argued that the Corinthian assembly met in the Apolloneion, the temple of Apollo on Temple Hill, as Nicolaus of Damascus and Plutarch (*Aratus* 40.2–3; *Cleomenes* 19.1) argue.[81] In the course of the development and expansion of the administration, distinctive buildings were designed and built in the Greek *poleis.* As a rule, these were located near the *agora.*

---

77. Claude Bérard, *Architecture et politique: réception d'une ambassade en Grèce archaïque,* Études de Lettres, series 3, book 10 (Lausanne: Imprimerie des arts et métiers, 1977), 1–25, fig. 4. 15.

78. There are several ancient sources that argue for *ekklēsiai* being held in a theatre; see Frank Kolb, *Agora und Theater, Volks- und Festversammlung,* Archäologische Forschungen 9 (Berlin: Mann, 1981), 88n9. See in addition for Enna: Livy 24.39.3–4 (214 BCE); for Engyion: Plutarch, *Marcellus* 20.3 (212 BCE); Epidauros: *Inscriptiones Graecae* IV 1.84.23–24 (around 40 CE); Katane: Frontinus, *Strategemata* 3.2.6 (around 415 BCE); for Miletos: *Inschriften von Olympia* 52.46 (around 138 BCE; William Dittenberger and Karl Purgold, *Die Inschriften von Olympia* [reprint: Berlin: Asher, 2009]); Rhodes: Polybus 15.23.2. (around 202 BCE); for Samos: *Sylloge Inscriptione Graecarum* 3 976.3–8 (second century BCE); for Skotoussa: Pausanias, *Graeciae descriptio* 6.5.2. (371 BCE); for Taras: Valerius Maximus 2.2.5; for Thebes: Plutarch, *Moralia* 799e–f; for Tralles: Vitruvius, *De architectura* 7.5.5 (first century BCE); for Syrakousai: Plutarch, *Timoleon* 34.6; Justin *Epit.* 22.2.10.

79. Vitruvius, *De architectura* 7.5.5. The term *ekklēsiastērion* is also known by Dionysius of Halicarnassus, *Antiquitates Romanae* 4.38.6 and 10.40.4. A few cities had an *ekklēsiastērion,* which are known to us through written sources and archaeological findings. The most well-known is probably in Athens on the Pnyx; see Homer A. Thompson, "The Pnyx in Models," *Hesperia Supplements* 19 (1982): 141–42; and Mogens Herman Hansen, *The Athenian Ecclesia II: A Collection of Articles 1983–1989* (Copenhagen: Museum Tusculanum Press, 1989), 129–65. In Priene, a building on the *agora* on the south, next to the *prytaneion* is identified as an *ekklēsiastērion*; during a restoration there was an inscription restored on two blocks at the wall outside the building: ΟΡΟΣ Ε[ΚΚΛΕΣΙΑΣ]. But this restoration was questioned.

80. Kolb, *Agora und Theater,* 3n17.

81. Jamieson C. Donati, "Marks of State Ownership and the Greek Agora at Corinth," *AJA* 114, no. 1 (2010): 3–26.

For the fourth century BCE, we can perhaps draw on two passages by Xenophon and Diodorus for evidence for the Corinthian *agora* being a place of political meeting. The *agora* seems to have been built originally for *agōnes* (athletic contests), "deren kultischer Hintergrund offensichtlich Grabstätten, Heroenkulte und Heiligtümer chthonischer Gottheiten (Athena Hellotis, Poseidon) bildeten."[82] This designation appears to be closely tied to its cultic-topographical traditions. Xenophon tells of an attack by various groups on the members of the Corinthian peace party in the year 392 BCE:

> And in the first place they devised the most sacrilegious of all schemes; . . . but these men chose the last day of the Euclea because they catch more people in the *agora*, so as to kill them. Then again, when the signal was given to those who had been told whom they were to kill, they drew their swords and struck men down—one while standing in a social group, another while sitting [*kathēmenon*] in his seat, still another in the theatre, and another even while he was sitting [*kathēmenon*] as judge in a dramatic contest. Now when the situation became known, the better classes immediately fled, in part to the statues of the gods in the *agora*, in part to the altars.[83]

Xenophon goes on to report that many people who were in the *agora* were killed. Diodorus describes the people who were killed as "men who favored a democracy, while contests were being held in the theatre."[84] We can suppose, though not be sure, that these men belonged to the people's assembly, the *ekklēsia*, which probably met in the temple of Apollo located next to the *agora*.[85] This is now deepened by a new evaluation of archaeological material. In a recent article, J. D. Donati evaluates around twenty objects that he counts as "state property" (drinking cups, weights, measurements, and counting tables) and that are related to commercial and civic activity.[86] These objects have all been found on the south side of Temple Hill, adjacent to the Temple of Apollo. These drinking vessels, which declare "I belong to the city" (*damosion emi*), as well as counting tables with the term *damosia Korinthiōn* on the right corner, lamps, and a decree have been found south of Temple Hill. These new insights are of interest for reading 1 Corinthians, which is the only Pauline letter discussing a temple.

---

82. Cf. Kolb, *Agora und Theater*, 81.
83. Xenophon, *Hellenica* 4.4.2–3. (Translation: C. L. Brownson.)
84. Diodorus 14.85.1–2.
85. Kolb, *Agora und Theater*, 81–83, sees this as the only possible interpretation.
86. Donati, "Marks of State Ownership," 20.

The insight we have gained from this investigation may seem at first to be negative: namely, that the question of a space for the *ekklēsia* cannot be answered with certainty. This means that a more meaningful question would be: what significance did the space for the *ekklēsia* have in Corinth? The view of this self-generating space makes one thing clear: this space did exist in Corinth. It was a publicly accessible space. But it is more than this. The *ekklēsia* represents not only the gathering of the Corinthian community and is therefore a symbol of their cohesion, but it is also, by means of the celebration of the Lord's Supper, the projection of a christological self-understanding from inside and outside, which would be reflected in the conduct of people within the space of the *ekklēsia*. In this sense, the Corinthian *ekklēsia* not only possessed a space but rather *was* this space; the gathering place is the remembrance of the humiliating death of Jesus Christ in that it embodies and represents it physically.

Behavior in a Civic *Ekklēsia* and the *Ekklēsia* of God

The question of where exactly the Corinthian assembly (*ekklēsia*) may have met is difficult to answer. It is, however, very likely that the Corinthian *ekklēsia* met not in a building only accessible to a small group of members but at a place where the political assembly also met.[87] However, Dio Cassius mentions several times that Augustus had limited political rights not only in the Greek assemblies but also in the Roman ones: "In the first place, the populace should have no authority in any matter, and should not be allowed to convene in any assembly at all."[88] Does this mean that the *ekklēsia* did not exist in the first century CE? Scholars in classics like Werner Eck[89] or John Ma[90] question the disappearance of *ekklēsia* in the first-century Greek polis, referring

87. This can be supported by the phrase "the assembly *ekklēsia*" in 1 Thess 1:1. See G. van Kooten, "Ἐκκλησία τοῦ θεοῦ: The 'Church of God' and the Civic Assemblies (ἐκκλησίαι) of the Greek Cities in the Roman Empire. A Response to Paul Trebilco and Richard A. Horsley," *NTS* 59 (2012): 522–46. For the use of *ekklēsia* terminology for the Jewish Synagogue see R. J. Korner, *Before 'Church': Political, Ethno-religious, and Theological Implications of the Collective Designation of Pauline Christ-followers as ekklēsiai* (PhD diss., McMaster University, 2014), 176-83.

88. Cassius Dio 52.30.1–3 (translation: Cary, LCL).

89. I would like to acknowledge my gratitude to Prof. Werner Eck, University of Freiburg, for his thought-provoking critical comments and guidance on this point during my sabbatical in Freiburg. W. Eck, „Ämter und Verwaltungsstrukturen in Selbstverwaltungseinheiten der frühen römischen Kaiserzeit," in *Neutestamentliche Ämtermodelle im Kontext*, ed. T. Schmeller, M. Ebner, and R. Hoppe, Quaestiones disputatae 239 (Freiburg: Herder, 2010), 9–33. See also: S. Dmitriev, *City Government in Hellenistic and Roman Asia Minor* (Oxford: Oxford University Press, 2005), 289–328.

90. John Ma, "Public Speech and Community in the Euboicus," in *Dio Chrysostom: Politics, Letters, and Philosophy*, ed. S. Swain (New York: Oxford University Press, 2000), 108–24.

to inscriptions and textual evidence suggesting that cities like Tarsus or Miletus continued to exist in imperial times with Roman approval: Rome led the *poleis* in a framework under Roman administration. The most significant intellectuals of this period who refer to the *ekklēsia* in imperial times are Plutarch, Dio Chrysostom, and Dio of Prusa.[91]

There are several good arguments for seeing the meeting of the political *ekklēsia* as the background of the gathering of the congregation in Corinth, for only in this way can the fact that the members of the congregation are seated in chapters 11–14 be explained.[92]

The administration of a civic *ekklēsia* was usually entrusted to an *epistatēs* (presider, *prytane*),[93] who later also represented the emperor when imperial missives, instructions, and decrees were read aloud to the assemblies.[94] We know from Philippians 1:1 and Romans 16:1 of the *diakonoi* who called the assembly. Dionysus of Halicarnassus talks about the way speakers in civic assemblies attempt to instruct people, just as Paul reminds the Corinthians to become his imitators.[95] An assembly followed a certain "liturgy."[96] Prayers for the *ekklēsia* are also found in the collection of preambles in the *Oratione Fragmenta* by Dinarchus,[97] and they also appear to have been more numerous in the orations of earlier times.[98] Since priests therefore could have had a central role in the assembly, it seems likely that these political meetings also could have taken place in a temple.[99] The *leges sacrae*, the sacred laws, provide some evidence of the way *ekklēsia* may have been related to a temple.[100]

91. For further examples, see H. Halfmann, *Die Senatoren aus dem östlichen Teil des Imperium Romanum bis zum Ende des 2. Jh. n.Ch.* (Göttingen: Vandenhoeck & Ruprecht, 1979), nos. 56, 73, 79, 86.
92. This is by no means to say that one should derive the Pauline concept of *ekklēsia* exclusively from the political concept of a community gathering; I only seek to show that this background allows us to formulate explanations for many choices in the letters to the Corinthians.
93. Philo even names the high priest as *prytane* of the *ekklēsia*; cf. Philo, *De somniis* 2.186; Philo, *De specialibus legibus* 3.131; Diodorus, 40.3.
94. Maurice Holleaux, *Études d'Épigraphie et d'Histoire Grecques*, vol. 1, *Mémoires relatifs à Rhodes et à la Béotie* (Paris: E. de Boccard, 1938); cf. also C. G. Brandis, "Ekklesia," *Pauly's Realencyclopädie der classischen Altertumswissenschaft* 5 (1905): 2193–2200; for Athens, see Margherita Guarducci, *L'epigrafia Greca Dalle Origini al Tardo Impero* (Rome: Libreria dello stato, 1987) 114, 168.
95. See Josephus, *A.J.* 14.149–55 for Athens; *Sylloge Inscriptioum Graecarum* 3 258, 463, and *Orientis Graecae Inscriptiones* 727, 771; regarding crown and inscription, see Philo, *Legatio ad Gaium* 153.
96. Brandis, "Ekklesia," 2199.
97. See for example Dinarchus, *Fragmenta* XXIX (LCL 395, *Minor Attic Orators*); Dionysius Halicarnassensis, *De Dinarcho* 314.6. See also V. de Marco, "Un' orazione attribuita a Dinarco ed un frammento di Istro," *La Parola del Passato* 16 (1961): 81–92.
98. See for example the prayer by Praxagoras: Aristophanes, *Ecclesiazusae* 171–72 (here the speech delivered at an oratory contest); Aristophanes, *Equites* 634–38; 763–68, and Aristophanes, *Ranae* 885–94.
99. See also R. C. T. Parker, *Polytheism and Society at Athens* (Oxford: Oxford University Press, 2005); idem, "The Vocabulary of Religion," in *History of Ancient Greek*, ed. A.-F. Christidis. (Cambridge: University Press, 2007), 1070–73.

Sokolowski mentions in his volumes *Lois sacrées des cités grecques* several inscriptions that list *ekklēsia* in the context of a temple.[101] Important is the reference to "the temple purifying" (τῷ ἱερῷ καθάρσιῳ), which may use the word temple as an instrumental dative: it is the temple that acts as purifier of the assembly as a whole, as can be found in the famous reference to ΚΑΘΑΡΣΙΟΝ (= *purification*) referring to the Athenian assembly that is purified as a whole.[102] This text refers to the ritual purification of the theatre and the streets for the following procession.

The *ekklēsia*, however, has even greater significance than that given by the reading aloud of instructions. The assembly also had the responsibility of making sure the voice of the people was represented.[103] Clearly, various obligations were connected with this, particularly under Roman rule. Therefore participation in an *ekklēsia* was tied to the rights of full citizenship;[104] the right of people of lower status and women to participate in the *ekklēsia* and speak in discussions was disputed.[105] Unsurprisingly, this has led to speculation on the part of exegetes that Paul's law forbidding women to speak was an acknowledgement of an older idea of *ekklēsia*.[106] The idea, however, that generally in a political meeting the right to speak was given to those superior in social standing due to status, age, or gender while those who were inferior listened was an essential one within the framework of Roman society and applied to women of high status as well as to many other social groups of the society.[107]

This is at least true if we look at *ekklēsia* mainly from the political perspective, not including the religious aspect of the *polis*. Here, the idea of "sharing" or "being a member and therefore being entitled to a share," which is expressed in the term *metechein*, is important for the

---

100. See *Leges Graecorum Sacrae* II 46 [abbreviated: LGS]; F. Sokolowski, *Lois sacrées des cités grecques*, École Française d'Athènes 18 (Paris: de Boccard), 51, 62, (in the following LSCG); *Inscriptiones Graecae* 12,9,189; *LGS* II 88; Sokolowski, *Sacrées greques*, *LSCG* 92,27–28 focusing on the Sacred Law of the Artemision; *Inscriptiones Graecae* IX 1,654.

101. Sokolokwski, *Lois sacrées*, *LSCG* 34,14–15: εἰς τὴν πρώτην ἐκκλησίαν προσαγαγεῖν αὐτοὺς; 39,15-16: Εἰς τὴν ἐπιοῦσαν ἐκκλησίαν προσαγαγεῖν τὸν [ο]ἰκεῖον τῆς ἱερείας; 40,5: Temple of Asclepius: ἐκκλησία κυρία.

102. See Valerius Harpocrationis, *Lexicon*, Art. *karthasion*: ἔθος ἦν Ἀθήνησι καθαίρειν τὴν ἐκκλησίαν.

103. The following terms regulate conduct in an *ekklēsia*, according to Paul, in 1 Corinthians: *hermēneia* (14:26); *ana meros* (14:27); *diamēneuetō* (14:28); *kathēmenō* (14:30); *kath hena* (14:31); *sigatō* (14:33); *hypotassesthōsan* (14:34); *aischron [. . .] estin [. . .] lalein* (14:35); *euschēmonōs* (14:40); *kata taxis* (14:40).

104. See e.g. Aristotle, *Politica* 42.

105. See Philo, *De decalogo* 32.

106. Cf. K. Thraede, "Art. Frau," *RAC* 8 (1972), 197–269.

107. See, therefore, Andrew Wallace-Hadrill, *Rome's Cultural Revolution* (Cambridge: Cambridge University Press, 2008), 38–71.

political *ekklēsia*, but it is also present in 1 Corinthians 10:17, where Paul expresses in a parallelism that the Corinthians "partake [*metechein*] of the one bread" and "partake [*metechein*] of the table of the Lord." Sharing the one bread and the table of the Lord is argued as the foundation for being a member of the body of Christ. And it is in this context that Paul refers to the assembly of God in verse 31, which has been often understood as a translation of *qahal El* or *qahal YHWH*.[108] With this, one would assume that the assembly of God would be used in the translation of the LXX; however, with the sole exception of 2 Esdras 23:1, "the assembly of God" never occurs in the LXX. It seems therefore rather unlikely that this assembly of God is "a continuity with the Old Testament assembly." It seems more likely that Paul is using this term to establish and at the same time to distinguish the phrase "the assembly of God" from the civic assembly in a theological way while at the same time using the basic terms and (ideal) behavioral norms to set a parallel with a public meeting.

In any case, a major responsibility of the leader was to ensure the orderly conduct of the meeting (*eukosmia*, εὐκοσμία).[109] Several inscriptions that are preserved as *leges sacrae* show the importance of *eukosmia* in some cults, for example the decree of Demetrias, which is surprisingly not so much interested in details regarding the cult as it is in maintaining orderly behavior and a proper procedure during consultation, even if need be through the aid of security officers (ῥαβδοῦχοι).[110] Despite many differences among the inscriptions, many share basic features with this document: the sanctuary is presented as functioning according to a given set of (behavior) rules and very often mentioned next to the temples and also the ἐκκλησία.[111] Likewise, we are familiar with *euschēmonōs* (εὐσχημόνως)[112] and *taxis* (τάξις) as descriptions of commendable behavior (see 1 Cor 14:40).[113] They belong to the sphere of *dignitas*, that virtue of which Cicero and others repeatedly remind their readers.[114] Many sacred laws preserve τάξις or even εὐταξίς; for

---

108. See the list of scholars mentioned in Paul Trebilco, *Self-Designations and Group Identity in the New Testament* (Cambridge: Cambridge University Press, 2012), 444.

109. Cf. Aeschines 1.34; see also *Sylloge Inscriptionum Graecarum* 3 737; *Leges Graecorum Sacrae* (*LGS*) II 46; *Sylloge Inscriptionum Graecarum* 3 790I; *LGS* II 80; *IG* IX 2.1109 I (Oracle of Apollo).

110. See Louis Robert, *Hellenica*, vol. 5 (Paris: Librairie d'amérique et d'orient, Adrien-Maisoneuve, 1948), 16–48, noting here esp. lines 17 and 51.

111. See also Eran Lupu, *Greek Sacred Law: A Collection of Documents (NGSL)* (Leiden: Brill, 2005), 10–11 [in the following, abbreviated NGSL].

112. Cf. Sokolowski, *Lois sacrées (LSCG)* 48B, 6 and 21.

113. On *taxis* in terms of conduct that takes into consideration status, age, etc., see Xenophon, *Memorabilia* 2.1.7. On the subject of order in general within the *ekklēsia*, see Plato, *Leges* 925b; Plato *Politicus* 305c.

example: "he shall sacrifice . . . three others for command appearance, discipline, and endurance."[115] We also read that "no one should misbehave in the holy houses of Apollo."[116] Even animals are prohibited from the holy houses; another inscription mentions several articles of clothing and other things that people are not allowed to bring into a temple and the *ekklēsia*.[117] Disturbances (*akatastasia, ἀκαστασία*) and wrongdoing (*adikos, ἄδικος*) are often mentioned together. For the order of the *ekklēsia*, a certain behavior is foundational.[118]

The disturbances mentioned in 1 Corinthians 14:33 refer not only—as in non-Christian texts as well—to the disturbances in the assembly of the *ekklēsia* and the confusion and agitation during a conflict (2 Cor 6:2), but also to the physical unrest caused by a *pneuma* in the body that does not allow a person to stay quiet but rather precipitates conflicts, as we see, for example, in the case of Chrysippus.[119] With Chrysippus, Paul shares the view that "negative *pneuma*" should not be given space in the *ekklēsia*.

If the space of the *ekklēsia* also represents the completion of the creation of the space by the subject not only for those who already consider themselves members of the *ekklēsia*, then the reference to *apistos* and *idiōtēs* is crucial.[120] Jorunn Økland refers to the "outsider,"[121] and numerous commentaries speak of the "unlearned" who could join the community. I would like to contradict this interpretation of *idiōtēs*. Numerous inscriptions, including some from Corinth, discuss *ekklēsia* and the behavior in a temple context and mention the term with a connotation that is also relevant for our context.[122] Rather, these sources suggest the distinction between officials and private citizens. Around 330 BCE, the Athenian orator Lykourgos writes, the constitution "rests

---

114. On *euschēmonōs* see, for example, Aristophanes, *Vespae* 1210; Xenophon, *Cyropaedia* 1.3.8; Aristotle, *Ethica nicomachea* 1.10.13.

115. Lupu, *NGSL* 14.44–46: [. . .] εὐεξίας καὶ εὐταξίας φιλοπονίας.

116. SEG L 1037.2–4: μηθεὶς ἐν τοῖς ἱεροῖς οἴκοις τοῦ Ἀπόλλωνος ἀτάκτως ἀναστραφεῖ.

117. SEG XXXVI 1221.

118. SEG XXXI 416.8 and 19; Sokolowski, *Lois sacrées (LSCG)* 75.7.9–10; Sokolowski, *Lois sacrées (LSCG)* 53.26; F. Sokolowski, *Lois sacrées de l'Asie Mineure*. Ecole française d'Athènes. Travaux et mémoires 9. Paris: de Boccard, 1955; abbreviated as *LSAM* 83.61.

119. Stobaeus 2.82 Chrysippus = *SVF* 3.121; see also Polybius 7.4.8 and the reception of Macarius Aegyptus, Migne 34.497C. On this topic, see G. L. Marriott, "Macarii anecdota," *Harvard Theological Studies* 5 (1918): 51–58; and Athanasius Alexandrinus, M. 26.896B; cf. also Manetho 5.57.

120. With regard to *apistis*: *IG* II 610, *IG* II2 1361; Sokolowski, *Asie Mineure (LSAM)* 45, 4. With regard to *idiōtēs*, for the purity laws in the different temples, see: *Sylloge Inscriptionum Graecarum 3* 763; on how to behave in the Artemision, see: *DGE* 808; *LGS* II 88; Sokolowski, *Asie Mineure (LSAM)* 45; *Sylloge Inscriptionum Graecarum 3* 571; *Sylloge Inscriptionum Graecarum 3* 599; *Sammlung der griechischen Dialektinschriften (SGDI)* 5663.

121. Økland, *Women in Their Place*, 195–96.

122. *IG* XII 2.645b refers to *archōn ē idiōtēs*, as do *IG* II 17 and *CIG* 3059.

on three tiers, the official, the judge, and the private citizen" (idiōtēs).[123] These tiers were integral parts of the constitution of an ekklēsia and the polis. In recently found inscriptions, we read: "if a private person brings a charge against a shopkeeper or [vice versa], they shall submit their charges in writing to the neopoiai up to [illegible]."[124] This is deepened by a decree concerning the priesthood (around 400 BCE) where it says: "if a private person performs [a sacrifice], a portion [of meat] shall be given from the victim, so as to be placed in the likon, and the priestly prerogative, and the tongue."[125] The inscriptions make no distinction between behavior in an ekklēsia and in a temple. No distinction was made in the ekklēsia between officials and private citizens, to the extent that both could bring petitions to the ekklēsia; both then needed to convince the ekklēsia of their case in order to argue the matter successfully in a probouleuma. If Paul uses the concept of the idiōtēs as an argument for comprehensible speech, then it must be only in the sense that he already considers the idiōtēs, unlike the unlearned person, as belonging to the ekklēsia to some extent already. The difference between the members, then, does not have to do with inside and outside but refers to the charismata that the idiōtēs may not yet be able to access.

We have evidence that the political assemblies of non-Christian and Jewish ekklēsiai also had executive and legislative functions. No wonder, then, that we find words in Paul's writing that designate points of conflict, dispute, and reconciliation.[126] These words, which we can identify as legal terminology from legal papyri and Roman law, refer without exception to actual circumstances in which, we can imagine, the ekklēsia in pagan antiquity had jurisdiction: situations such as the resolution of disputes (1 Cor 6:1–6), defining the role of Christians in the status quo (1 Cor 7:17–24), or involving vocabulary with legal connotations (1 Cor 14:20, 24, 25).

Therefore, it is noteworthy that within the structural organization and procedural actions Paul oriented himself toward the civic ekklēsia

---

123. Lycurgus, Leocrates 79 (trans. Beck).
124. Lupu, NGSL 18.25.
125. Lupu, NGSL 20 A.
126. Examples from 1 Corinthians are easily cited: pragma (6:1); adikoi (6:1): the word is used if someone is accused unjustly—see Lupu, NGSL 14 B 35; aproskopoi [. . .] ginesthe (10:32); philoneikos (11:16)—see similar Lupu, NGSL 14 B 46–47 and 54–56; haireseis (11:19); krima (11:28); and krinō (6:1)—see the calendar of Cos (LSCG 151) and the calendar of Mycons (LSCG 96.13), where it refers to the choice of the assembly of two sows; dokimazetō (11:28)—see SEG XLV 1508 and W. Blümel, "Ein dritter Teil des Kultgesetzes aus Bargylia," Epigraphica Anatolica 32 (2000): 89–93, with regard to the sacrifice, Lupu, NGSL 5.5; anaxiōs (11:27); enochos (11:27)—see Lupu, NGSL 14 B 39, 14 B 100, 17.9–10; schisma (11:18, 12:25); paraklēsis (14:3); kakía (14:20); phrēn (14:14, 15, 19); eirēnē (14:33).

in terms of behavioral rules for individuals and the community. Is this also connected with the question of space? It is very likely that the Corinthian *ekklēsia* met in an outside space and had to behave in a certain manner, as did other *ekklēsiai*. It is interesting that in chapters 11–14, the discussion of economic background comes up only during the Eucharistic meals when "those who do not have" are mentioned. Otherwise, the behavioral rules are more discussed.

Conclusion: Where Did the Corinthian Community Meet?

We have seen that the Corinthians meeting *en ekklēsia* could have possibly met in the Appolloneion in Corinth, where they would therefore have had to behave in a specific way. How can we evaluate the assembly meeting in a house?

Firstly "the church *kat' oikon*": Most exegetes agree that papyrological evidence has shown that the accusative *kat' oikon* in the formula was equivalent to the dative *en oikō* in Koine Greek, "the church in the house."[127] Nonetheless, this conclusion is based on only two papyrological passages, Zen. Pap. 59659,3 ὄντων ἡμῶν κατὰ τοῦ Νέστου ἐποίκιον ("as we stayed in the cottage of Nestos") and BGU III 993 col. 3.10 τὰ κατ' οἰκίαν αὐτοῦ ἔπιπλα ("the household in his house"). Both passages emphasize, like Gielen, a spatial meaning of the preposition κατά with genitive known only in Koine Greek, which also suggests a person who does not have sufficient knowledge of classical Greek.

At this point, I would urge more caution. Whereas ἐν with dative refers to a specific space or place, as I have just shown, the accusative means an input or an indication of direction "toward," which does not directly apply here because the preposition refers to a space and an indication of "throughout" with an emphasis on space. This latter has been quite well known since Homer, especially with reference to a city, but also to *kat' oikon* "living throughout/between others in the same family community" (Homer, *Iliad* 4.285).[128] Sophocles (*Antigone* 1153; *Trachiniae* 727; *Ajax* 203) refers to this phrase when he mentions domestic affairs that affect all members of the house, as does Josephus (*A.J.* 17.192, 11.50). The preposition is therefore not reduced to a space or place but emphasizes the inclusion of the addressees, which are, in the

---

127. Marlis Gielen, "Zur Interpretation der paulinischen Formel ἡ κατ' οἶκον ἐκκλησία," *ZNW* 77, no. 1–2 (1986): 109–25, here 11–13; see just recently Adams, *Earliest Christian Meeting Places*, 19.

128. Raphael Kühner and Bernhard Gerth, *Ausführliche Grammatik der griechischen Sprache. Bd. 1: Satzlehre.* (Hannover: Hahn, 1966), 480.

Pauline passages, all members of this house. Therefore, the translation should not be rendered as "at home," as Lampe indicates,[129] but could emphasize the circumferential aspect "throughout." This brings us to the translation "the *ekklēsia* which is distributed throughout the house." This does not, of course, refer to a local church, which would assume that the church is based in different houses, but on "the *ekklēsia* throughout an *oikos*." At this point, it seems clear that Paul has experienced a space in which different people participated, be they slaves, widows belonging to the house, or freedman working in this space. Therefore, the phrase "the *ekklēsia* distributed throughout the house" may include slaves, even if they are not mentioned.

We come secondly to the formula "the whole church/*ekklēsia*." What then does the phrase ὅλης τῆς ἐκκλησίας, which is usually translated as "the whole church/*ekklēsia*" mean? In order to understand this phrase, the majority of scholars refer to Gaius as the host of the Corinthian *ekklēsia* for a more precise identification of this person. L. L. Welborn has just recently made a brilliant contribution on the different Gaii and their roles in the Corinthian society in order to locate the one Gaius, the wealthy member.[130] I would like to bring our attention to a small grammatical detail, which does not make a huge difference in English, but it does in Greek. Most of the translations take the adjective ὅλος as an attributive adjective. So Plato writes in the Republic τῇ πόλει ὅλῃ ("the whole city"; 519e), which means that the whole city—all the inhabitants—come together at the same time and the same place. This would be similar to the "whole church" coming together in one house. This attributive position emphasizes the complete process.

If the adjective is prefixed ἐν ὅλῃ τῇ πόλει τοῦτο, the "city as a whole" is meant, represented only by some of its members. This means, in our case, that some members of the city represent the whole. If we transfer this to the Corinthian passages, then that means: "the whole *ekklēsia* comes together at the same time," which means that the *ekklēsia* is represented by some members. Therefore, Gaius invited a network of people into his house; this means that neither his elite or nonelite status outside the *ekklēsia* nor the size of his house would play a role.

Therefore, we may still say that Gaius was the host of the *ekklēsia* as a whole in his house, however, without the implication that he had to

129. Peter Lampe, *From Paul to Valentinus: Christians at Rome in the First Two Centuries* (London: T&T Clark, 2003), 193.
130. L. L. Welborn, *An End to Enmity: Paul and the "Wrongdoer" of Second Corinthians*, BZNW 185 (Berlin: De Gruyter, 2011), 289–381.

host one hundred people or more. He may have just been the host for a network of people. The phrase ἐν οἴκῳ is mostly connected with the Eucharist celebrated in houses. The *ekklēsia* or the phrase *en ekklēsia* is not connected to a concrete meeting space. It is very likely that the *ekklēsia* met outside, and its bodily behavior makes references to the political *ekklēsia* plausible. If we take this shift seriously, then power structures in meetings are more visible, and these are not only related to houses.

At the basis of our result lies the assumption that the inhabitants of the different possible spaces not only structure the space conceptually by means of concrete arrangement of and movement within the space, but that they also perform a physical and concrete structuring. Spaces that host gatherings project not only a certain social order in the way that the inhabitants move within them, but they also represent society's way of thinking in that they symbolize these thoughts through their conduct. The way space is represented through language in texts makes it possible to relate this back to ancient principles of order. These are also called semiotic codes and are not based on an exact reconstruction of the concept of space. Rather these allow a reconstruction that is aimed at the recognition of conceptual representational models and organizations of meaning. If we follow this line of thinking, then the issue of sitting or reclining at a meal is not only a question of a lack of space in a room but rather is instrumental in the creation of a space, just like standing while speaking publicly, attentive silence, gender-specific conduct, and so on. Clearly, the *sōma* of the individual, along with the community as a whole, is also instrumental in constituting the space of an *ekklēsia* (as shown in 1 Cor 6:1–6, 7:17–24, 10:23–11:16, and especially in 11:17–34, where *sōma* is defined christologically).

Select Bibliography

Adams, Edward. *The Earliest Christian Meeting Spaces: Almost Exclusively Houses?* London: T&T Clark, 2013.

Balch, David L. *Contested Ethnicities and Images: Studies in Acts and Art.* WUNT 345. Tübingen: Mohr Siebeck, 2015.

Button, M. Bruce, and Fika J. van Rensburg. "The 'House Churches' in Corinth." *Neotestamentica* 37, no. 1 (2003): 1–25.

Gielen, Marlis. "Zur Interpretation der paulinischen Formel ἡ κατ' οἶκον ἐκκλησία." ZNW 77, no. 1–2 (1986): 109–25.

Horrell, David G. "Domestic Space and Christian Meetings at Corinth: Imagining New Contexts and the Buildings East of the Theatre." *NTS* 50, no. 3 (2004): 349–69.

Jewett, Robert. "Tenement Churches and Communal Meals in the Early Church: The Implications of a Form-Critical Analysis of 2 Thessalonians 3:10." *BR* 38 (1993): 23–43.

Lampe, Peter. "The Corinthian Eucharistic Dinner Party: Exegesis of a Cultural Context (1 Cor. 11:17–34)." *Affirmation* 4 (Fall 1991): 1–15.

_____. "Das korinthische Herrenmahl im Schnittpunkt hellenistisch-römischer Mahlpraxis und paulinischer Theologia Crucis (1Kor 11,17–34)." *ZNW* 82, no. 3–4 (1991): 183–213.

_____. *From Paul to Valentinus: Christians at Rome in the First Two Centuries.* London: T&T Clark, 2003.

Murphy-O'Connor, Jerome. *St. Paul's Corinth: Texts and Archeology.* 3rd ed. Good News Studies 6. Collegeville, MN: Liturgical Press, 2002.

Oakes, Peter. "Contours of the Urban Environment." In *After the First Urban Christians: The Social-Scientific Study of Pauline Christianity Twenty-Five Years Later,* edited by Todd D. Still and David G. Horrell, 21–35. New York: T&T Clark, 2009.

_____. *Reading Romans in Pompeii: Paul's Letter at Ground Level.* Minneapolis: Fortress Press, 2009.

Osiek, Carolyn. "Archaeological and Architectural Issues and the Question of Demographic and Urban Forms." In *Handbook of Early Christianity: Social Science Approaches,* edited by Anthony J. Blasi, Jean Duhaime, and Paul-André Turcotte, 83–104. Walnut Creek, CA: AltaMira Press, 2002.

Papaioannou, Maria. "The Roman Domus in the Greek World." In *Building Communities: House, Settlement and Society in the Aegean and Beyond; Proceedings of a Conference Held at Cardiff University, 17–21 April 2001,* edited by Ruth Westgate, Nick Fisher, and James Whitley, 351–61. British School at Athens Studies 15. London: British School at Athens, 2007.

Theissen, Gerd. *The Social Setting of Pauline Christianity: Essays on Corinth.* Edited and translated by John H. Schütz. Philadelphia: Fortress Press, 1982.

Wallace-Hadrill, Andrew. "Domus and Insulae in Rome: Families and Households." In *Early Christian Families in Context: An Interdisciplinary Dialogue,* edited by David L. Balch and Carolyn Osiek, 3–18. Grand Rapids: Eerdmans, 2003.

Weissenrieder, Annette. "Contested Spaces in 1 Corinthians 11:17–34 and 14:30: Sitting or Reclining in Ancient Houses, in Associations and in the Space of the *Ekklēsia*." In *Contested Spaces: Houses and Temples in Roman Antiquity and the New Testament*, edited by David L. Balch and Annette Weissenrieder, 59–107. WUNT 285. Tübingen: Mohr Siebeck, 2012.

Welborn, L. L. *An End to Enmity: Paul and the "Wrongdoer" of Second Corinthians.* BZNW 185. Berlin: de Gruyter, 2011.

6

Paul and Slavery: Economic Perspectives

Ulrike Roth

Introduction: Locating Christian Slavery

In a seminal intervention in the study of slavery in the Americas, Ira Berlin and Philip D. Morgan called in the early 1990s for a renewed focus on what they termed "the centrality of labour in the slaves' experience":[1]

> Slaves worked. When, where, and especially how they worked determined, in large measure, the course of their lives. The centrality of labour in the slaves' experience seems so obvious that it has often been taken for granted. Recent studies of slavery in the Americas have focused on the slaves' social organization, domestic arrangements, religious beliefs, medical practices, along with music, cuisine, and linguistic and sartorial style

1. I am extraordinarily grateful to Tom Blanton and Ray Pickett for the invitation to participate in the "Paul of Tarsus and Economics" conference at the Lutheran School of Theology at Chicago in the autumn of 2015, and to contribute to the present volume. I am no less grateful to the other participants for engaging discussion at the conference (which made me refocus my chapter contribution).

that gave Afro-American culture its distinctive form during slavery. For the most part these aspects of slave life have been understood as emanating from the quarter, household and church rather than field and workshop. This emphasis has obscured the activities that dominated slave life. After all, slavery was first and foremost an institution of coerced labour. Work necessarily engaged most slaves, most of the time.[2]

Berlin and Morgan sought to refocus attention on "field and workshop"—that is, on the slave's place of work—and away from "household and church" to arrive at a better understanding of slave life. The present contribution seeks to contextualize the role of slave labor in a geographical and chronological context far removed from that of slaves in the modern Americas but nonetheless related to it—slaves put to work in the mid-first century CE by Paul and other Christ devotees. The primary aim of this chapter is to situate Paul's use of slave labor in the wider context of the economic exploitation of slaves in the Roman Empire. I begin with a brief overview of modern approaches to Paul's relationship with slavery before analyzing key evidence to argue for the systematic inclusion of slave owners and slaves amongst the early Christians—for economic reasons. I suggest, moreover, that the product of Paul's hybrid approach to slave exploitation has significantly influenced the development of Christian attitudes to slavery. In conclusion, I argue that the economic exploitation of slaves was at the root of the development and rise of the Christian church: the economics that underpin Paul's missionary success cannot be explained without taking account of the role played by the "peculiar institution."[3] I contend, therefore, that Paul's use of slave labor—like its legacy—is deserving of its own term: Christian slavery.[4]

---

2. Ira Berlin and Philip D. Morgan, eds., *The Slaves' Economy: Independent Production by Slaves in the Americas* (London: Frank Cass, 1991), 1.

3. My use of the term "mission" (*vel sim.*) does not imply the existence of an institutionalized (church) structure; the same applies to my use of the term "church" (*vel sim.*).

4. Despite using the term Christian slavery, my argument is unrelated to Paul Allard's *Les esclaves chrétiens: depuis les premiers temps de l'Église jusqu'à la fin de la domination romaine en Occident* (Paris: Didier, 1876), or to Dimitris J. Kyrtatas's *The Social Structure of the Early Christian Communities* (London: Verso, 1987). Kyrtatas's (*Social Structure*, 19–86) discussion of "Christianity among slaves and freedmen" is directed at disproving earlier theories of the lower-class infiltration of Christianity (including by slaves) and the humanizing effects of Christianity on slavery—rather than at conceptualizing Christian slavery.

Approaching Paul and Slavery

The study of Paul's approach to slaves and slave labor has a long pedigree in modern scholarship. This is largely influenced by the fact that Paul's writings provide abundant reference to slavery. The discussion has focused on what J. Albert Harrill has termed "literary, social, and moral dimensions"—in consequence, the debate has been "less about real slaves."[5] In this sense, the contribution of NT scholarship to the study of slavery as an institution has concentrated on understanding slavery as a "thinking tool"—that is, as a theoretical structuring device (of theological thought).[6] It has been less concerned with practical aspects of slavery, least of all with slavery's economic dimensions and how economic demands and opportunities shaped slaves' experiences amongst the early Christians. This approach to the study of Paul and slavery is also evident outside of NT scholarship: Peter Garnsey, for instance, begins his discussion of Paul's intellectual contribution to slave theory by stating that "Paul, in common with the Stoics and Philo, gives priority to moral/spiritual slavery over slavery according to the law."[7] But socioeconomic aspects have not been ignored altogether. I sketch in the following two sections the main directions that the argument has taken: despite agreement on some core issues, Paul's attitude to and involvement in slave exploitation have attracted quite different treatments and interpretations.

The Dilemma of Christian Slave Ownership

A central strand in the modern discussion of Paul and slavery has focused attention on what John M. G. Barclay has termed "the dilemma of Christian slave ownership."[8] "It is impossible," wrote Barclay, "to imagine someone like Gaius or Philemon offering hospitality to a whole

---

5. J. Albert Harrill, *Slaves in the New Testament: Literary, Social, and Moral Dimensions* (Minneapolis: Fortress Press, 2006), 16.
6. For an in-depth study of Paul's use of the rhetoric of slavery, see Dale B. Martin, *Slavery as Salvation: The Metaphor of Slavery in Pauline Christianity* (New Haven, CT: Yale University Press, 1990). An overview of modern contributions (in the twentieth century) is found in John Byron, *Recent Research on Paul and Slavery* (Sheffield: Sheffield Phoenix, 2008); and a recent survey of key issues and contemporary texts in Karin B. Neutel, *A Cosmopolitan Ideal: Paul's Declaration "Neither Jew nor Greek, Neither Slave nor Free, nor Male and Female" in the Context of First-Century Thought* (London: Bloomsbury T&T Clark, 2015), 144–83.
7. Peter Garnsey, *Ideas of Slavery from Aristotle to Augustine* (Cambridge: Cambridge University Press, 1996), 173.
8. John M. G. Barclay, "Paul, Philemon, and the Dilemma of Christian Slave-Ownership," *NTS* 37, no. 2 (1991): 161–86.

church (Rom 16. 23; Phlm 2) without the aid of slaves: one could not maintain a house sufficient to accommodate a significant number of guests on a regular basis without the assistance of slaves, at least in door-keeping, cooking and serving at table."[9] Notwithstanding the argument presented by Annette Weissenrieder in this volume for a public location for various congregations' meeting places,[10] the essence of Barclay's contention holds irrespective of where the local Christ-groups met: members of these groups are seen as slave owners whose *modus operandi* was based (and reliant) on the exploitation of slaves. And despite attempts at minimizing the economic relevance of slave owning (see the section "Slavery and the Economics of Missionary Success" below), there is widespread agreement that Paul's missionary activity drew, on the one hand, on the support of slave owners and that, on the other hand, it was also directed at slaves, in addition to their masters.

Almost inevitably, modern scholars have been quick at conceptualizing a situation in which both slaves and masters were part of the same cult community as a potential seedbed for status anxiety and conflict: the involvement of both in the early Christian communities has been seen as a latent source of friction. Barclay emphasized the "tension between the realities of slavery and the demands of brotherhood."[11] Logically, given the above described benefits derived from slave owners, Paul is seen as having to strike a careful balance between slaves and masters. Yet, Paul amplified the conflict potential by giving prominence to the figures of master and slave (and freedman) in his constructions of the Christian universe. Some scholars have consequently foregrounded the dichotomous relationship between the developing Christian faith and the practice of slavery, based on an understanding of slavery as a social injustice; in this vein, Allen Dwight Callahan has spoken of "the problematic of Christian relations under the Roman slave regime."[12] Scholars are, however, agreed that "Paul like everyone else accepted legal slavery."[13]

In sum, there exists a significant strand in modern scholarship that recognizes the embeddedness of the Pauline mission in contemporary

---

9. Ibid., 166.
10. See also David G. Horrell, "Domestic Space and Christian Meetings at Corinth: Imagining New Contexts and the Buildings East of the Theatre," NTS 50, no. 3 (2004): 349–69.
11. Barclay, "Paul," 186.
12. Allen Dwight Callahan, "Paul's Epistle to Philemon: Toward an Alternative *argumentum*," HTR 86, no. 4 (1993): 357.
13. Garnsey, *Ideas of Slavery*, 176.

slaveholding practices. At the same time, Paul is seen as carefully responding to the challenge posed by the mix of statuses that the new cult communities attracted, neither questioning the exploitation of slave labor nor actively engaging with it himself on the ground.

A "Living Tool" Caught between Two Masters

In her 2002 monograph *Slavery in Early Christianity*, Jennifer A. Glancy sought to focus "on the impact of the ubiquitous ancient institution of slavery on the emergence and development of Christianity."[14] Glancy explicitly contends that "slaves and slaveholders were more pivotal in early Christian circles than has been generally acknowledged"; she speaks in consequence of "the centrality of slavery" and of slavery's role in "the reconstruction of the social histories of the emerging churches,"[15] concentrating in particular on the body of the slave, its theoretical availability and practical subjection to physical and sexual abuse. Not dissimilarly, Harrill has argued in a number of recent contributions for much greater involvement on Paul's part in the slaveholding practices of his days.[16] Harrill contends that much of the evidence involving real slaves in Paul's letters is not equipped to open a window on the slave experience but, rather, on the perspective of slave owners—thus engaging the master narrative, designed to maintain the power structures that underlie the "peculiar institution." A letter such as the one to Philemon, which deals extensively with a person subjected to slavery, documents, according to Harrill, "Paul's participation and deep implication in ancient slavery."[17] As a result, the slave Onesimus emerges from the letter as "a 'living tool' caught between two 'masters' deciding on the use of his services,"[18] a phrase that has provided the peg for this section.

Taking the notion of mastery in Philemon further, I have myself recently argued that Paul did not just accept what William L. Westermann termed "the going system of labor . . . including the slave structure,"[19] but that what Harrill called "Paul's participation and deep implication in ancient slavery" went far beyond the use of the master

---

14. Jennifer A. Glancy, *Slavery in Early Christianity* (Oxford: Oxford University Press, 2002), 3.
15. Ibid.
16. J. Albert Harrill, "Paul and Slavery," in *Paul in the Greco-Roman World: A Handbook*, ed. J. Paul Sampley (Harrisburg, PA: Trinity Press International, 2003), 575–607; and Harrill, *Slaves*.
17. Harrill, *Slaves*, 16.
18. Ibid.
19. William L. Westermann, *The Slave Systems of Greek and Roman Antiquity* (Philadelphia: American Philosophical Society, 1955), 150.

narrative and extended to the point of actual slave ownership.[20] In Paul's letter to Philemon, I contend, scholarship has at its disposal a cryptic relic of Paul's joint ownership (with Philemon) of the slave Onesimus: the legal framework of the (worldly) κοινωνία that Paul entered with Philemon made the two men co-owners of any goods given into the κοινωνία—human chattels, namely, Onesimus, included. Scholars have long recognized that Paul writes in the letter "als wäre er selbst der Herr des Sklaven Onesimus";[21] and that "the epistle maintains the claim that Onesimus 'belongs' to the apostle":[22] the slave-owning context that I have argued for explains why.

In sum, whilst some regard Paul's dealings with slaves and masters as a challenge that the apostle had to handle with caution (see "The Dilemma of Christian Slave Ownership" just above), recent scholarship has gone a substantial step further in seeing in Paul's writings not just acceptance but active reinforcement of slavery. Indeed, at one extreme end of current thinking, Paul emerges as personally involved in slave exploitation with mastery as an intrinsic element of his missionary activity.

Paul and Slave Exploitation

In this section, I will once more review references to slavery and slaves in Paul's correspondence with Christ devotees who fell into his missionary remit (including letters whose Pauline authorship is not agreed; if deutero-Pauline, these show how others made sense of Paul's example, offering evidence of his impact). The letters document, by themselves, a clear pattern of involvement in slavery, especially in household contexts. Yet, as Glancy has pointed out, "on the basis of these texts, we cannot reach firm conclusions about the size of those households nor the degree to which their slaves specialized in productive, managerial, domestic, or sexual duties."[23] But if the evidence is contextualized more fully in contemporary slaveholding practices, slave exploitation emerges as an economically highly relevant element of Paul's modus operandi and, by extension, the Christian mission.

---

20. Ulrike Roth, "Paul, Philemon, and Onesimus: A Christian Design for Mastery," ZNW 105, no. 1 (2014): 102–30.

21. Peter Arzt-Grabner, Philemon (Göttingen: Vandenhoeck & Ruprecht, 2003), 246.

22. Chris A. Frilingos, "'For My Child, Onesimus': Paul and Domestic Power in Philemon," JBL 119, no. 1 (2000): 101.

23. Glancy, Slavery, 45.

From the "House of Stephanas" to the Emperor's Household

First, there is generic (sometimes merely implied) mention of slaves as part of another's household, such as when Paul refers to "the house of Stephanas" (τὸν Στεφανᾶ οἶκον, 1 Cor 1:16; and τὴν οἰκίαν Στεφανᾶ, 1 Cor 16:15); "Chloe's people" (ὑπὸ τῶν Χλόης, 1 Cor 1:11) might fall into the same category.[24] A similar setup is implied concerning Gaius's capacity as host (Γάϊος ὁ ξένος μου καὶ ὅλης τῆς ἐκκλησίας, Rom 16:23). The "households" of Aristobulus and Narcissus, to whom Paul sent greetings in Rome (ἐκ τῶν Ἀριστοβούλου, Rom 16:10; ἐκ τῶν Ναρκίσσου τοὺς ὄντας ἐν κυρίῳ, Rom 16:11), add further implied mention of slaves. In the letter to Philemon, there is direct mention of a slave—Onesimus—and his exploitation by Paul and Philemon. In Galatians—in which slavery plays a central role throughout—the Pauline rebuke culminates in addressing a real-life situation between slave and freedperson (Gal 3:28). Similarly, in Colossians and Ephesians (often regarded as deutero-Pauline), the admonitions address both real slaves and real masters (Col 3:22—4:6; Eph 6:5-9). In Philippians, the description of Epaphroditus's tasks suggests slave status: like Onesimus, Epaphroditus took care of Paul's daily needs, including acting as courier (Phil 2:25, 4:18).[25] A scribe—Tertius—is explicitly mentioned in Romans (Rom 16:22). Comparable contemporary evidence documenting the specialized employment of slaves for such tasks includes multiple epigraphically attested slave *pedisequi* (foot attendants) in one of the large *columbarium* in Rome; a *silentiarius* (confidant) in the household of the Statilii; *tabellarii* in charge of letter delivery or general couriers; an *act(u)arius* offering short-hand writing; and scribes (*a manu*).[26] In Philippians, greetings are moreover sent from what were potentially the most powerful servile Christ devotees in Paul's orbit—members of the *familia Caesaris*, the Roman emperor's household (τῆς Καίσαρος οἰκίας, Phil 4:22)—denominated in the letter, like others, as "saints" (οἱ ἅγιοι, Phil 4:21-22). Presented as elites in the Roman literary sources, the slaves

---

24. On the inclusion of slaves in an οἶκος/οἰκία, see Gerd Theissen, *The Social Setting of Pauline Christianity: Essays on Corinth* (Edinburgh: T&T Clark, 1982), 83–86 (and 93–96 for "Chloe's people").

25. Slave status does not exclude the assumption of leadership roles, including patronage, in the religious community, nor does access to (one's own) money to further religious goals question or exclude slave status. (See also the discussion in the section "Economic Profiling of Christian Slaves" below.) For a review of the roles suggested for Epaphroditus, and an argument in favor of his role as a patron of sorts, see John Reumann, *Philippians: A New Translation with Introduction and Commentary* (New Haven, CT: Yale University Press, 2008), 424–26 and 442–44.

26. The evidence is assembled in Kinuko Hasegawa, *The Familia Urbana during the Early Empire: A Study in Columbaria Inscriptions*, British Archaeological Reports 1440 (Oxford: Archaeopress, 2005), 35–39.

and ex-slaves in the emperor's service included high-ranking professionals, charged with significant managerial and administrative tasks in the organization of the empire, as well as individuals who served in fairly ordinary support roles, including as guards (*custodes*) and attendants (*pedisequi*)—primarily men[27] (proportionally, only very few female members' occupational titles are known[28]). It is nonetheless "a precious bit of information," as Wayne A. Meeks phrased it, "that some members of this group had found reason to be initiated into Christianity," given their owners' (or patrons') lack of interest in Christianity for a couple of centuries to come.[29]

This overview is not exhaustive, but the chosen examples are characteristic of the kind of information available for Christian slaves (and slave owners) in Paul's letters. But it is only when these sparse details are viewed in the round, including both addresses to real life situations and figurative uses, that a pattern of typical involvement in slavery in the early Christ-groups emerges (table 6.1).[30] Obviously, I have taken a "maximizing" approach to the evidence for slave owning; I return to the reasons below. On a "maximizing" view, then, the "peculiar institution" permeates the real and conceptual spaces of Christ devotees as a matter of fact in the surviving correspondence—with multiple references, allusions, and analogies in all letters (but for 1 and 2 Thessalonians—on which also more below). This is no news: as Meeks already stated, "a typical Pauline congregation would include both slave owners and slaves."[31] But what does this mean for an economic assessment of early Christianity and the Pauline mission?

27. P. R. C. Weaver, *Familia Caesaris: A Social Study of the Emperor's Freedmen and Slaves* (Cambridge: Cambridge University Press, 1972).
28. Ibid., 170–78.
29. Wayne A. Meeks, *The First Urban Christians: The Social World of the Apostle Paul* (New Haven, CT: Yale University Press, 1983), 63.
30. The differentiation between "realistic" and "figurative" uses in the table is weak, allowing for overlaps and transformations of concepts into real-life situations and vice versa. Other terms could be included to enhance the analysis (e.g., uses of κύριος).
31. Meeks, *First Urban Christians*, 64.

Table 6.1: Schematically contextualized key occurrences (in bold) of δουλεία, δουλεύειν, δοῦλος, and οἰκέτης (*vel sim.*) in figurative and realistic usages in (in alphabetical order) Colossians, 1 and 2 Corinthians, Ephesians, Galatians, Philemon, Philippians, Romans, 1 and 2 Thessalonians, 1 and 2 Timothy, and Titus. References in light italics indicate circumstantial occurrences of slaves, masters, and/or slave owning.

	FIGURATIVE USAGE	REALISTIC USAGE A	REALISTIC USAGE B
	including "slave of Christ/God"	mention of real slaves and specific addresses to real life situations concerned with slavery	codifying addresses to real life contexts concerned with slavery
Romans	1:1; 1:9 (λατρεύειν); 6:6; 6:16–20; 6:22; 7:6; 7:25; 8:15; 8:21; 12:11; 14:4 (οἰκέτης); 14:18; 16:18	9:12; *16:10; 16:11; 16:22; 16:23*	
1 Corinthians	7:22–23; 9:19; 9:27	*1:11; 1:16;* 7:21–22; 12:13; *16:15; 16:19*	
2 Corinthians	4:5; 11:20	11:20	
Galatians	1:10; 2:4; 4:1; 4:3; 4:7–9; 4:24–25; 4:30–5:1; 5:13	3:28; 4:1; 4:22–23; 4:30	
Ephesians	6:6–7	6:5–9	
Philippians	1:1; 2:7; 2:22; 3:3 (λατρεύειν)	2:7; *2:25; 4:18; 4:22*	
Colossians	1:7; 3:23–24; 4:7; 4:12	3:11; 3:22–23; 4:1; *4:9; 4:15*	
1 Thessalonians	1:9		
1 Timothy			*3:4–5; 3:12; 5:8; 5:14;* 6:1–2
2 Timothy	1:3 (λατρεύειν); 2:24	*1:16; 4:19*	
Titus	1:1; 2:3; 3:3		2:9–10
Philemon	16	*2; 10–13;* 16; *17–18*	

The recent debate on the socioeconomic study of the first urban Christians has been vigorous. Responding to the "poverty-debate" and its antecedents (reviewed from different angles by Zeba Crook and

Timothy Brookins in this volume), Steven J. Friesen proposed a new approach to assessing the means levels of the early Christ-groups—soon followed by revisions suggested by Bruce W. Longenecker, adding to the structural consideration of "economic scale levels" (so-called ES levels, previously called PS ["poverty scale"] levels by Friesen), as well as more traditional types of analysis, including proso-pography.[32] Slave owners among Christ devotees figure prominently in these studies, even if the proposed categorizations cluster mostly around the subsistence level. Yet, slave owning—including the capacity to dispose of another's labor power—plays a minor role in these assessments. Slaves, moreover, almost disappear. But whilst "enslaved persons" are not listed in the seven PS/ES categories (even if "freed-persons" are included),[33] Friesen at least considers the case of Onesimus. Following the traditional runaway thesis for the letter to Philemon, Friesen puts Onesimus "near the bottom of the profile" because he "could only survive on deception or the mercy of others"; the slave Onesimus therefore figures in PS 6–7, at or below subsistence.[34] Even Philemon, as a clearly attested slave owner,[35] only manages to be placed in PS 4–5, at just above subsistence level or, perhaps, benefitting from a moderate surplus of resources; the justification is that "many poor people owned slaves in the ancient world."[36] What becomes immediately clear when viewed from this angle is that the "pauperizing" approach to the early Christians' socioeconomic standing works to minimize the economic benefits derived from slave exploitation; the poorer the Christ devotees, the less their implication and participation in slavery (despite the explicit notion that poverty does not exclude slave owning)—the early Christians were poor, but they did not break the backs of others. It is important to stress that this corollary is not intended by the poverty debate. But it remains a fact that the emphasis on poverty has nearly erased discussion of the surplus-producing settings typically associated with slavery. By contrast, table 6.1, as stated, is based on a "maximizing" approach to slave exploitation: given the acceptance of slavery as "the going system of labor," the evidence

---

32. Bruce W. Longenecker, "Socio-Economic Profiling of the First Urban Christians," in *After the First Urban Christians: The Social-Scientific Study of Pauline Christianity Twenty-Five Years Later*, ed. Todd D. Still and David G. Horrell (London: T&T Clark, 2009), 36–59; Steven J. Friesen, "Poverty in Pauline Studies: Beyond the So-Called New Consensus," *JSNT* 26, no. 3 (2004): 323–61.

33. Longenecker, "Socio-Economic Profiling," 44; Friesen, "Poverty in Pauline Studies," 341.

34. Friesen, "Poverty in Pauline Studies," 350.

35. A different status identification for Onesimus (i.e., that of Philemon's brother) has been argued for by Callahan ("Paul's Epistle to Philemon") but has not found acceptance.

36. Friesen, "Poverty in Pauline Studies," 341 and 353–54.

for slave exploitation cannot be expected to be conspicuous, requiring great sensitivity in the analysis and interpretation of the possible relics in our source material, such as the casual references to "households" or slave jobs (each of which *could*, of course, be explained differently). But such a "maximizing" approach also demands acknowledgement of enslaved individuals above and beyond the economic resource that they represented to their masters—that is, recognition of the slaves' capacity for their own economic agency. Given my quite different view of Onesimus's situation to that employed by Friesen (see the section "A 'Living Tool' Caught between Two Masters" above), based in itself on preparedness to identify slave exploitation rigorously in the evidence, I explore in the following section, with the help of a comparative perspective, the repercussions of such a "maximizing" approach for understanding Onesimus's economic possibilities in a religious context, before returning to the question of the economic role of masters and slaves in Paul's missionary undertaking.

Economic Profiling of Christian Slaves

"At Rome," slaves are known to have benefitted from so-called *peculium* allowances—that is, assets kept in an account separate from their masters' (even if the latter maintained at all times full ownership over these assets)—and to have transacted business, small and large, on the basis of such funds, both on behalf of their masters and on their own, engaging more widely (in the latter case) in what slavery scholars call "slave personal production," thus contributing to "the slave economy."[37] Animals and land are reported amongst *peculium* in our sources for agricultural slaves; outside of rural contexts, slaves were known to amass considerable fortunes—strikingly exemplified by the *dispensator* Rotundus, slave of the emperor Claudius and financial administrator for Nearer Spain, whom Pliny the Elder reported in the later first century CE to have owned a silver dish of 500 grams that required the establishment of a brand-new workshop for its production, accompanied by eight side dishes weighing each 250 grams.[38] As Catherine

---

37. The discussion is concentrated in modern slavery studies; see Verene A. Shepherd and Hilary McD. Beckles, eds., *Caribbean Slavery in the Atlantic World*, rev. ed. (Kingston, JAM: Ian Randle, 2000), 712–83.
38. Pliny the Elder, *Naturalis historia* 33.145. For modern discussion of *peculium* in Roman slavery, see Ulrike Roth, "Food, Status, and the *peculium* of Agricultural Slaves," *JRA* 18 (2005): 278–92; Aaron Kirschenbaum, *Sons, Slaves and Freedmen in Roman Commerce* (Jerusalem: Magnes Press, 1987), 31–88.

Hezser has shown in her work on Jewish slavery, "although the term *peculium* does not appear in Jewish sources, the phenomenon that slaves would conduct business with their master's property and sometimes be allowed to maintain [*sic*] part of the proceeds was known to rabbis as well."[39] Slaves in Greek cultural contexts, too, abound in our sources in possession of their "own" funds and as engaged in business by and "for themselves"—as the example of the fishermen and fishmongers in Ephesus, cited by both Crook and John Kloppenborg in this volume, shows lucidly. That in the eye of the law (whether Greek, Jewish, or Roman) such slaves did not *own* the money and goods they possessed is immaterial in the context of economic analysis. It is these slaves' capacity to control financial assets, goods, and labor power that matters, rather than their legal capacity to own or dispose of property (as is typically the case with women and minors too). How, then, would one assess Onesimus's economic capacity on the present state of evidence?

As Philemon's slave, Onesimus was considered capable of rendering basic clerical services—such as the running of errands—to Paul (Phlm 11–12), enjoying a considerable level of freedom of movement. Whatever his duties involved in detail, Onesimus was for all practical purposes left to look after himself; there was no master or overseer to keep an eye on him, nor was he queuing up for his daily ration of a cooked meal as envisaged by Paul's contemporary Lucius Junius Moderatus Columella in his treatise on an idealized slave-run rural estate.[40] And Onesimus became a Christ devotee (Phlm 10), demonstrating the slave's engagement in religious activity independent from his master—and irrespective of the fact that Philemon too was converted. What would have prevented Onesimus from consulting instead (or also, cf. 1 Cor 8:1–13, 10:14–22) the oracle of Kareios at Hierapolis across from Colossae (where he might have been known regardless of whether Philemon's household was located there)[41] or from frequenting the temple of Artemis at Ephesus (should he indeed have served Paul in the city)?[42] Following conversion, Paul regarded Onesimus as capable of contributing to missionary activities (Phlm 16–17), implying a social and intellectual aptitude that is most readily associated

---

39. Catherine Hezser, *Jewish Slavery in Antiquity* (Oxford: Oxford University Press, 2005), 386–87 (see also 276–84).

40. Columella, *De re rustica* 11.1.19.

41. Col 4:9; see also Meeks, *First Urban Christians*, 59.

42. A city in western Asia Minor is a likely location for Paul's imprisonment: Philemon 1, 10, and 13; Roth, "Paul, Philemon, and Onesimus," 111–13 and 118.

with what Meeks has called "some education or special skills."[43] Moreover, Onesimus had at his disposal funds that belonged to his master Philemon, which, perhaps, he misused (Phlm 18). Here, the train of information and immediate speculation stops. But what does all this presuppose?

A slave with access to the master's funds, or trusted with money (and potentially financial business), who appears learned and skilled enough to be considered an active contributor to missionary activity, and whose labor duties involve freedom of movement, including independent travelling, recalls more readily the type of slave made famous by Cicero in his *a manu* Tiro, or Gamliel's Tabi, than the slave set to work in the mines who was caricatured by Plautus in the second century BCE as "kept in chains" by his underground workplace.[44] And the greater the level of freedom enjoyed by slaves in their labor duties, the greater their access to the kinds of funds that I referred to above.[45] Obviously, it is impossible to prove that Onesimus, or any other servile Christian, including the abovementioned "saints" from "the household of Caesar" (which later texts viewed as a source of converts),[46] indeed benefitted from the enjoyment of their own funds, or that they could have used such funds at their own discretion, but their cultic activity independent of their owners—in one case, the Roman emperor—is remarkable and suggestive. My interest is, in any case, with creating a "type" that fits the evidence *and* takes account of the workings of slavery. The question that arises next, then, is how to contextualize the potential for slave economic activity in religious contexts.

Beginning with evidence from the *familia Caesaris*, a man called Nemesianus, an imperial slave bookkeeper (*librarius*), is known through an epigraphic votive from the Roman province of Dacia as a powerful religious sponsor: Nemesianus dedicated an entire temple in fulfilment of an earlier vow (*templum a solo pecunia sua ex voto fecit*).[47] But slaves owned privately, with theoretically much smaller purses, were also engaged in cult practices—with other slaves and with the free—and they, too, are known to have acted in leading roles. At Laurion in the mining district of Attica in mainland Greece in the first century CE,

43. Meeks, *First Urban Christians*, 59.
44. Plautus, *Captivi* 729–30.
45. The relationship between *peculium* and skilled and unsupervised slave labor is discussed in Orlando Patterson, *Slavery and Social Death: A Comparative Study* (Cambridge, MA: Harvard University Press, 1982), 182–86.
46. Acts of Paul 11 (NTA 2:383).
47. AE 1913, 50.

inscriptions record the intention of the slave Xanthos, a devotee of the god Men, to found a cult group (ἔρανος) supervised by himself as priest.[48] Whether Xanthos (who by all appearances came from Lycia and was owned by a Roman master) fulfilled his promise is unknown, but the surviving epigraphy is suggestive of the required economic resources. Xanthos, who, like Paul, assumed the role of cult founder on the basis of a divine call, envisaged benefiting from the priest's share of the regular *Opfergaben*, thus further increasing his economic resources.[49] Voluntary associations such as *collegia* provided another outlet for slave sponsorship in a religious context, as is shown by a marble plaque from Rome in which a *collegium* consecrates a cult place to the *numen* of the *domus Augusta* and to Aesculapius and Salus Augusta. The plaque was "signed" by over fifty people—some were slaves of the emperor, some of private individuals, some were men, and some women.[50]

These examples are but the tip of the iceberg of slaves' cultic activities and sponsorship in antiquity (and privilege, by the nature of the evidence, information on conspicuous religious consumption).[51] Given the poor survival of evidence for the early Christ-groups, it is actually safer to assume similarity rather than difference from the documented patterns of slaves' religious practices. (Indeed, if Kloppenborg is right in stressing the embeddedness of the Christ-groups' organization in practices known from voluntary associations, as discussed, *inter alia*, in his chapter in this volume, the "transition" was minimal in structural and cultic-habitual terms.) It is probable, therefore, that some servile Christ devotees supported Paul's efforts through material contributions—that is, that slaves were economic agents in the Christian mission. Onesimus, as suggested, enjoyed the required economic capacity; in the lack of evidence to the contrary, he should be regarded as a potential sponsor. However speculative the proposed assessment of

---

48. Franz Bömer, *Untersuchungen über die Religion der Sklaven in Griechenland und Rom.*, vol. 3, *Die wichtigsten Kulte der griechischen Welt*, 2nd exp. ed. (Stuttgart: Franz Steiner, 1990), 198.

49. *IG* II/III2 1365–66, discussed in Siegfried Lauffer, *Die Bergwerkssklaven von Laureion*, 2nd exp. ed. (Wiesbaden: Franz Steiner, 1979), 128, 177–85, 191–92 (and 180–81 for the cult's location at Laurion, not Sounion). For discussion of Xanthos as cult-founder, see James Constantine Hanges, *Paul, Founder of Churches: A Study in Light of the Evidence for the Role of "Founder-Figures" in the Hellenistic-Roman Period* (Tübingen: Mohr Siebeck, 2012), 304–16 (but note that Xanthos is, oddly, identified as the son of Gaius Orbius in the translation: 307).

50. *CIL* VI 30983.

51. The resulting interpretive issues are discussed (in a Roman context) by John A. North, "The Ritual Activity of Roman Slaves," in *Slaves and Religions in Graeco-Roman Antiquity and Modern Brazil*, ed. Stephen Hodkinson and Dick Geary (Cambridge: Cambridge Scholars Publishing, 2012), 85–87.

this slave, it is not any more conjectural than that of Philemon or Stephanas, two obvious examples amongst the slaveholders.

In his study of the free Christ devotees' socioeconomic standing, Gerd Theissen expressed ambiguity over religious service as a reliable economic indicator by drawing a parallel with slavery—for "even slaves may have been called 'servers' in Christian congregations."[52] Friesen, too, employed evidence for religious dedications by slaves as a means to minimize their economic importance, as did Justin J. Meggitt with slave owning—for "even other slaves . . . owned slaves."[53] Thus, activities known to have been carried out by enslaved persons are minimized in economic terms. Obviously, the capacity to offer labor power or worldly assets need not indicate high social status; Bruce J. Malina has correctly emphasized the methodological dangers in using "wealth" as the sole status indicator in the ancient world.[54] But the quite different examples of Nemesianus and Xanthos should make us hesitate to assign by default slaves' economic activity to at or below subsistence level. Furthermore, social ranking is not my interest here. Rather, I have suggested that *even slaves* were capable of economic support and that slave sponsorship needs to be included in analyses of resource management in the early Christ-groups. To exclude enslaved individuals from economic assessments of the Christian communities or to minimize their contributions on the basis of their legal status means to become subject to participation and deep implication in practices that are characteristic of slaveholding cultures, foremost the acts of silencing and marginalization that are fostered by existing power structures, and that in turn sustain these, whether by accident or by choice.

To sum up: "Onesimus the sponsor" has been modelled here as a "type," taking account of the sparse information available about the man, and giving it meaning through contextualization in the sea of source material for slave "civic" and religious activities that are a widely recognized element of ancient slaveholding practices.[55] I show in the next section why this "type" should be taken as the default where specific evidence is missing. If we do, religious sponsorship, including acting as benefactor on the basis of one's economic

---

52. Theissen, *Social Setting*, 88.
53. Friesen, "Poverty in Pauline Studies," 355; Justin J. Meggitt, *Paul, Poverty and Survival* (Edinburgh: T&T Clark, 1998), 131.
54. Bruce J. Malina, "Social Levels, Morals and Daily Life," in *The Early Christian World*, vol. 1, ed. Philip F. Esler (London: Routledge, 2000), 375.
55. For general discussion on the basis of Roman examples, see North, "Ritual Activity."

resources, is to be added to the basket of the Christian slave experience: "field and workshop" cannot be separated from "household and church" in early Christian slavery—contrary to the approach of Berlin and Morgan in the study of slavery in the modern Americas.

Slavery and the Economics of Missionary Success

While it is impossible to quantify "the slave economy" within the (equally unquantifiable) contribution of slavery to the ancient economy at large, scholars agree, to speak with Moses Finley, that "slaves dominated, and virtually monopolized, large-scale production in both the countryside and the urban sector. It follows that slaves provided the bulk of the immediate income from property . . . of the élites, economic, social and political."[56] More recently, Walter Scheidel has focused attention on the purpose and effect of the use of slave labor in classical antiquity; he emphasized rightly that "dominant groups . . . relied to a significant degree on slave labor to generate surplus and maintain their position of dominance."[57] The early Christians were most certainly not in a position of dominance, yet Christianity developed into one of history's most dominant groups. There cannot be a single answer as to why this was the case. But I suggest in what follows that the issues reviewed in the previous section ought to be given greater weight in attempts to understand the roots of this development. This section, then, seeks to contextualize further the seemingly disconnected information on the use of slave labor by Paul and his addressees to outline a hypothetical sketch of the economic location of slavery in the mission: I contend that slave exploitation was a systematic feature behind Christianity's early success.

In his study of Paul's "survival strategy," Meggitt has demonstrated that "Paul's *modus operandi* did not allow him to combine his labour fully with his ministry."[58] Notwithstanding Paul's own engagement in manual labor, he sought assistance from others on a recurrent basis to free himself for work on the gospel, often expressing an expectation of support (e.g., 1 Cor 9:4–18; 2 Cor 11:7–9, 12:13–18). Moreover, if full account is taken of the logistics behind Paul's efforts at staying connected with the numerous Christ-groups, as discussed by Cavan Con-

---

56. M. I. Finley, *Ancient Slavery and Modern Ideology* (London: Chatto & Windus, 1980), 79–82.

57. Walter Scheidel, "Slavery," in *The Cambridge Companion to the Roman Economy*, ed. Walter Scheidel (Cambridge: Cambridge University Press, 2012), 89.

58. Meggitt, *Paul, Poverty and Survival*, 76.

cannon in this volume, the demand for slaves to undertake some of the legwork—in a literal sense—emerges as very real. The service of slaves for errands or with intergroup communications, tasks that are not in themselves of a religious nature, provided one solution to Paul's needs. As was seen in the previous section, such tasks were widely associated with slave labor, and the provisioning of such labor through the generosity of Christian slaveholders is clearly attested in Paul's letters—once more Onesimus, but probably also Epaphroditus, are suitable examples. It would be naïve, however, to assume that Paul's use of slave labor was a coincidence, even if it is not possible to document why slave labor was made available to him. Yet, it would be rather odd for Philemon, for instance, to provide slave labor to Paul via the κοινωνία arrangement that he entered into with Paul without knowledge of that labor supply's usability or desirability for Paul. It follows that Paul sought out, at the very least in an opportunistic fashion, the availability of slave labor to support the Christian mission.

But as the case of Onesimus documents, Paul's readiness to exploit the labor capacity of slaves did not function as a bar to their being subject to missionary efforts. Nor did conversion function to release the Christian slave from what Berlin and Morgan have called the "centrality of labour in the slaves' experience"; once Christian, Onesimus continued to be regarded by Paul as a source of labor. The only difference mentioned by Paul is a potential shift of duties to include work on the ministry, which he could not have asked of the slave prior to his conversion. The logical consequence of Paul's approach to Onesimus is that upon implementation of a change in Onesimus's duties, a new supply source for the labor duties previously carried out by Onesimus needed to be found. There is little doubt in my mind that Paul would have resorted to precisely the same supply source that had worked well so far—slave labor. The "Onesimus type" is unlikely to reflect a unique individual or the first or only slave who was initiated into Christianity while their labor was exploited by Paul or another Christian missionary. The conversion of a slave hitherto exploited as a source of labor for auxiliary tasks thus functioned to fuel the continued exploitation of slaves. And as with Onesimus, any such "replacement" was a potential Christian in the making—not unlike amongst the Jews, a gentile slave who was circumcised upon purchase or birth into a Jewish home in this period was what Shaye J. D. Cohen has called "a proselyte in the making."[59] Slavery and conversion went hand in hand.

Refocusing on the slave owners, their presence in the Christ-groups is conspicuous, as noted above, but it is also entirely logical. However scholars may come to categorize the means of these early Christians in the future, without the existence of a cult membership that included enough devotees who were economically reasonably secure, many of the situations caught more or less by chance in Paul's letters would not make sense—whatever the proportion of those "whose sins arose from greed and affluence rather than from poverty."[60] But such economic security (however actually fraught in the context of the ancient world) in the societies that Paul encountered and engaged with was for all practical purposes, as Finley, Scheidel, and others have repeatedly reminded us, based on the exploitation of slave labor. This is not to say that slave-owning Christians were all large-scale slaveholders. Rather, their livelihoods were fostered by a slave-owning culture as a matter of course and in excess of the livelihoods of others. How many slaves they owned cannot be known. But minimal ownership of one slave per Christian slaveholder puts these already into a different social and economic category from the nonslaveholders. There is, moreover, no reason to think that because we "meet" the Christian slaveholders "in town," their livelihoods derived entirely from urban undertakings. In some cases, this was probably so, but the close relationship of town and countryside is a well-documented feature of surplus-creating settings (crudely put: civic life in town with productive exploitation in the countryside). This raises much broader questions about conceptualizations of the Christ-groups as "*urban* Christians"—a topic worthy of future investigation. In contrast, a generation or so before the birth of Christ, the Roman aristocrat and scholar Marcus Terentius Varro identified the lack of resources that supported slave owning with poverty: "all agriculture," Varro explained, "is done by men—slaves, free men, or both; by free men when they till the ground themselves, as many poor people (*pauperculi*) do with the help of their families."[61] Those with slaves, such as Philemon, did not fall into Varro's poverty categories—whether or not he owned (or exploited) land in addition to (one assumes) a house in town. That Paul was not blind to present realities is well known. To assume, then, coincidence in the conspicuous presence of slaveholders amongst the early Christians means to deprive Paul of

59. Shaye J. D. Cohen, "The Rabbi in Second-Century Jewish Society," in *The Cambridge History of Judaism*, vol. 3, *The Early Roman Period*, ed. William Horbury, W. D. Davies, and John Sturdy (Cambridge: Cambridge University Press, 1999), 945.

60. W. H. C. Frend, *The Rise of Christianity* (London: Darton, Longman & Todd, 1984), 105.

61. Varro, *De re rustica* 1.17.2.

the capacity of logical thought and forward planning (both of which he was quite plainly capable of). This point can be strengthened.

In their economic study of the origins of Christianity, Robert B. Ekelund Jr. and Robert D. Tollison persuasively argued that Paul pursued his goal of expanding and developing the new religion effectively; more specifically, they showed that Paul's "methods can be seen as an application of the economics of entrepreneurship. In short, Paul was an immensely successful entrepreneur who helped develop a new product in the marketplace for religion and marketed it brilliantly both door-to-door (travels) and through mail order (epistles). Faith drove Paul; economics drove his methods."[62] Personal visits and letters are singled out as the most important elements in Paul's missionary tool kit. What Ekelund and Tollison did not ask is how visits and letters were enabled—economically speaking. The answer lies behind the more readily identified support structures. Thus, the two pillars in Paul's missionary success, "visit" and "letter," are associated with the support of slave owners in the Pauline epistles in the form of offers of accommodation, financial and in-kind travel subventions, and courier services—as Paul's request to Philemon to prepare a guestroom makes most strikingly clear (Phlm 22). In part, slave labor filled the need—as in the case of letter carriers, delivering what Margaret M. Mitchell calls succinctly "Paul's weapon of choice."[63] (And if we think that Phoebe delivered Paul's letter to the Romans—Rom 16:1–2—do we think she travelled alone?) But the real significance of the centrality of "visit" and "letter" lies in the indirect provisioning of resources: the economic basis that generated the surplus required to support the mission's two key elements was built on slave exploitation. As we have seen, Barclay held that offering hospitality to large congregations was not imaginable "without the aid of slaves" (see the section "The Dilemma of Christian Slave Ownership" above); similarly, Glancy emphasized that when Paul accepted hospitality, "domestic slaves would have tended to his needs, from washing his feet upon entering the household to preparing the food for communal meals."[64] But this only captures an almost anecdotal glimpse of the support structures that underpinned the socioeconomic performance of those who were economically more

---

62. Robert B. Ekelund Jr. and Robert D. Tollison, *Economic Origins of Roman Christianity* (Chicago: University of Chicago Press, 2011), 75.

63. Margaret M. Mitchell, "The Emergence of the Written Record," in *The Cambridge History of Christianity*, vol. 1, *Origins to Constantine*, ed. Margaret M. Mitchell and Frances M. Young (Cambridge: Cambridge University Press, 2006), 192.

64. Glancy, *Slavery*, 45.

secure in Paul's orbit. It is, structurally, not possible to explain the documented availability of resources without their reliance on slave exploitation—however much Paul's power of persuasion was stretched at times and irrespective of the support gained from other, economically weaker, groups or the role played by gift exchange (discussed in this volume by Tom Blanton). Indices measuring the "receptiveness to Christianization" that foreground "visit" and "letter" must also include the "presence of slave-owners" as a "Christianization variable" (and, at the micro level, evidence for "slave sponsorship," "slave religious benefaction," and "slave membership in voluntary associations") as a "proxy for ease of Christian conversion"—fully acknowledging Paul's entrepreneurial decisions behind the exploitation of suitable resources, practices, and habitats.[65]

It may never be possible to quantify the relationship of "weaker" and "stronger" contributions—stretched over a vast and complex means range—and their relative economic significance, in the Christian mission, including the contributions of slaveholders and nonslaveholders. A tempting analogy for the envisaged model of the distribution and significance of "weaker" and "stronger" contributions is constituted by the Athenian collection of tribute at the time of the festival of the Great Dionysia in Athens in the mid-fifth century BCE: before the Peloponnesian War, nearly 250 *poleis* are recorded to have contributed, but never more than 190 in any one year. The majority of contributors were small communities with limited resources: the evidence for 442/441 BCE suggests that 86 percent of the total revenue came from 29 percent of the contributing cities, with a dozen *poleis* paying over sixty times as much *each* as sixty eight of the smaller communities *together*.[66] Socially, the league required a high level of participation, unremittingly enforced by Athens; economically, it relied to a significant degree on the contributions of a few. Judging by the various attempts at economic profiling—whether based on a "cumulative" interpretation of the evidence, or made up of 7 or 120 (or however many) economic scale levels—the composition of the Christ-groups, too, was likely characterized by "weaker" and "stronger" contributors (perhaps reflected in such issues as the divisions at the Lord's Supper at Corinth—1 Cor 11:17–34—discussed in Neil Elliott's chapter), and differently so from place to place and across time. All were socially indis-

---

65. Ekelund and Tollison, *Economic Origins*, 197–203.
66. Evidence and discussion is in Robin Osborne, *The Athenian Empire* (London: London Association of Classical Teachers, 2000), 86–105.

pensable for the mission's success, while some few were economically essential: the slave owners that have been the focus of the present chapter characterized the latter group. This does not mean that they belonged to the upper crusts—Friesen's top 2.8 percent; rather, the economic benefits of slave owning need to be taken seriously. Recognizing that the artisans, peasants, soldiers, and slaves mustered by Meggitt as proof of nonelite slave owning hardly removes the capacity for surplus production from slave exploitation, irrespective of individual differences, successes, and failures.[67] To assume that slavery was a sign of poverty, however defined, is a historically unfounded thesis, conceptually reminiscent of the slaveholders' contention that they were engaged in hard labor for the benefit of the slave.[68] That the "stronger" contributors to the tribute at Athens come, at 29 percent, dangerously close to Friesen's 31.8 percent of PS1–5 (and within reach of Longenecker's 45 percent) is surely mere coincidence, but it should make us reflect on the surplus-producing settings enjoyed by those above the subsistence level and the resulting capacity for sponsorship, benefaction, and patronage—without which the bulk of the surviving evidence from antiquity is not comprehensible. Naturally, the Athenian tribute lists are not straightforward evidence for the role of slavery, but, like many (later) associations' inscriptions, they demonstrate the historical possibility of a model of unequal contribution in antiquity in a hugely successful enterprise, with the fringe benefit of affording some statistical insight across a large number of contributors in a society actively engaged in slave exploitation.

Pauline success, then, is not intelligible without recognizing the centrality of slave exploitation in the missionary efforts. Slaveholders and slaves formed part of the early Christ-groups for a purpose; their inclusion can more satisfactorily be explained through systematic effort than by chance, including what Meggitt called "embedded strategies."[69] There is nothing peculiar about this, for to recognize slavery's central role in Paul's undertakings merely means to understand the Christian mission in the historical context in which it belongs: whatever else led to the production of disposable assets that could be turned into benefactions, gifts, or donations, the place of slavery was uncontested in the socioeconomic structures that supported surplus creation, whether in the so-called free Greek cities or those teeming with

---

67. Meggitt, *Paul, Poverty and Survival*, 130–31.
68. See Patterson, *Slavery and Social Death*, 336–37.
69. Meggitt, *Paul, Poverty and Survival*, 164.

citizens of Rome, in the East or the West, in Corinth as in Rome. What would have been peculiar is the omission or avoidance of slaveholders amongst those interested in initiation. But to do so was clearly not on Paul's agenda; economically, he could not have afforded to do so. Instead, Paul ensured adequate access to the necessities of mission.[70] To modify the formulation of Scheidel: Paul relied to a significant degree on slave labor to generate surplus and advance the Christian movement, creating the basis for the cult's future position of dominance (even if a worldly future was not envisaged by him). It is, then, high time to accept that the Christian mission, though fractured at times and held back at others, was economically underpinned by slavery, however unpalatable that proposition might be to modern minds.

Conclusion: A Servile Legacy

Notwithstanding the many questions over their authorship, the instructions to church leaders in the so-called Pastorals include advice on how to deal with slaves (and slave owners) in the Christian community: "Let all who are under the yoke of slavery regard their masters as worthy of all honor, so that the name of God and the teaching may not be defamed. Those who have believing masters must not be disrespectful on the ground that they are brethren" (1 Tim 6:1–2; cf. Titus 2:9–10). These instructions—like the letter(s)—have found much discussion.[71] But the significance of the directive to church leaders to actively sanction slavery so that the cult's religious principles are not defamed is widely understated; in the mind(s) of the author(s), the early Christian community cannot be conceived of *without* slaves and masters, and to manage servile Christ devotees especially (but not only) of masters who were fellow devotees was of paramount importance. Luke T. Johnson wrote that "in this passage, the focus is entirely on the slaves,"[72] but actually, the focus is on those in charge of the cult. And they are told in no uncertain terms that a slave's status is to be maintained lest the Christian movement should take harm. The clearly displayed eagerness to keep the slaveholders happy is paramount, and in the context of cult leadership instruction, the underlying attitude and practical direction are effectively embedded in the cult's modus operandi:

---

70. Modifying the formulation of Meggitt, who discusses "adequate access to the necessities of existence" (ibid.).
71. A recent overview of the issues involved is offered in Luke T. Johnson, *The First and Second Letters to Timothy: A New Translation with Introduction and Commentary* (New York: Doubleday, 2001), 13–99.
72. Ibid., 288.

Christianity cannot be Christianity without slavery—it is a structuring device, conceptual *and* social.

The consensus today is with classifying the Pastorals amongst manuals of church order. Outside of Christian contexts, cult instructions are a well-known feature of religious activity in Greco-Roman society; Xanthos, the aspiring cult-founder at Laurion, is a specific example (see the section "Economic Profiling of Christian Slaves" above), himself author of the cult regulations. In contrast, the cult instructions in the Pastorals were not "invented" by the author(s); rather, these are identified as of divine making—that is, as expressing God's ordering of the world, the *oikonomia* of god (1 Tim 1:4); everything else was fables—μῦθοι—and misguided teaching. Slavery, then, was presented as part of the divine order of things—for now and for the future. Esau had, of course, long paved the way (Gen 25:23), as Paul did not fail to point out (e.g., Rom 9:10–13; Gal 1:15). "Christian teaching," writes David G. Horrell in consequence, "is clearly supporting and sustaining the interests of the socially dominant."[73] But whoever the Pastorals' author(s), the authoritative commands aimed at giving the churches their proper order are not at odds with Paul's (certain) correspondence—however specific and unstructured the latter is.[74] As Michael Wolter has shown, the Pastorals present Paul as an exemplar and norm.[75] Their approach to slavery documents how they understood the attitude and approach of the cult-founder—Paul—to slave exploitation, and how sense was made of it in an ever fuller *parousia*-waiting lounge. And if not written by Paul himself, "their author(s) seem to have understood Paul as founder perhaps more clearly than any of the other pseudo-Pauline authors," as James C. Hanges has put it.[76] The letters' inclusion in the canonical tradition reinforces the point about their role in the establishment of the cult tradition—together with the various elements to be handled according to tradition—slavery fully included. To quote Hanges again: "the preservation of tradition is of the utmost importance."[77] Slave

---

73. David G. Horrell, "The Development of Theological Ideology in Pauline Christianity: A Structuration Theory Perspective," in *Modelling Early Christianity: Social-Scientific Studies of the New Testament in Its Context*, ed. Philip F. Esler (London: Routledge, 1995), 234.

74. Ibid., 232–33. But note Horrell's argument for amelioration of the slave's lot based on notions of fairness, justice, and love in Colossians and Ephesians (Col 4:1; Eph 6:9); for an expanded critique of the "amelioration theory," see Harrill, *Slaves*, 85–117; and Stephan Knoch, *Sklavenfürsorge im Römischen Reich: Formen und Motive* (Hildesheim: Georg Olms Verlag, 2005), for discussion of the forms in which "slave care" took place (in Roman contexts).

75. Michael Wolter, *Die Pastoralbriefe als Paulustradition* (Göttingen: Vandenhoeck & Ruprecht, 1988).

76. Hanges, *Paul, Founder of Churches*, 447.

77. Ibid., 448; similarly, Harrill, *Slaves*, 115, commenting on Colossians: "'tradition' is the only avenue of God's wisdom."

exploitation has, then, been written into the Christian cult regulations in the Pastorals in a very direct sense, following the instructions in earlier letters, and Paul's successors in leadership roles in the emerging church were thus directed to maintain these. It follows that the "peculiar institution" formed part and parcel of the Christian enterprise—of "God's way of ordering things"—by (Pauline) *design*. The economic resource that slavery constituted explains why.

The documented insignificance of slavery in 1 Thessalonians (and its sequel, see table 6.1)—exhibiting just one figurative usage of service to a deity—can now be explained through the apocalyptic nature of the message conveyed in the letter(s): the community "eagerly expected [an] imminent *parousia*."[78] The time had not yet come for Paul to think ahead and to craft a (temporary) future on earth. Ironically, slavery was not yet relevant—a matter of significance given the inclusion of some moral teaching and worldly instruction in 1 Thessalonians.[79] It was only when an extensive, and recurrent, program of "visit" and "letter" was conceived that slavery was allocated a firm place in the Christian universe and, subsequently, in its religious code—as reflected, however crudely, in the threefold division in table 6.1. The fact that a letter regularly regarded as early and concerned with eschatological claims does not mention slavery according to the law reinforces first the early dating and second the proposed interpretation of the later correspondence as providing sustained evidence (however cryptic) for slave exploitation: the changing socioeconomic focus matches the theological evolution (and vice versa). Paul's vision of the ethical and geographical scope for the Christian mission as fundamentally *sine fine* (esp. Rom 10:18, 15:20–21)—to the ends of the earth, as Acts put it (Acts 1:8)—prepared in turn a productive seedbed for the combined spread of religion and slavery on a universal scale, then as later.

In his influential work on the socioeconomic setting of the first Christian communities, Edwin A. Judge stated plainly that "it is of course slavery that is the most fundamental instance of discrimination, and the most difficult to assess."[80] It goes without saying that, as Judge

---

78. Karl P. Donfried, "1 Thessalonians," in *The Blackwell Companion to the New Testament*, ed. David E. Aune (Chichester, UK: Wiley-Blackwell, 2010), 508. The authorship issues over 2 Thessalonians are hairy and well known.

79. 1 Thess 4:1–11. The "omission" of slavery in 1 (and 2) Thessalonians constitutes another aspect of what Donfried ("1 Thessalonians," 510) has called "quite different stages of development and articulation" in Paul's thought.

80. Edwin A. Judge, *The Social Pattern of Christian Groups in the First Century: Some Prolegomena to the Study of New Testament Ideas of Social Obligation* (London: Tyndale, 1960), 28.

also knew, in the light of the sparse and complex nature of the source material, "the interpretation of many of the points is under constant discussion."[81] Much of what has been suggested here will need adjustment and fine-tuning in the future. Nonetheless, I have argued that Paul's approach to the economic exploitation of slaves, and the ways in which the apostle sought to benefit from the slave-system at large, is likely to have been a systematic feature behind his missionary success. The conceptual underpinnings of Paul's developing theology, focused on by Garnsey and others, were heavily dependent on "the going system of labor," just as these underpinnings worked to reinforce that labor system. But beyond the kind of implication in slavery envisaged by Harrill, I contend that the evidence at hand suggests that Paul actively pursued profit from slave owners and from the economic basis of their contribution to the Christian mission—slave exploitation—once *parousia* was relegated to the waiting room. Without acknowledging the role of slave exploitation, the centrality of "visit" and "letter" in Paul's missionary method is unintelligible. Paul's approach to slavery is, then, a good example of the interrelatedness of aspects of life that, for analytical reasons, scholars typically keep apart—especially social, religious, and economic.

When in the late fourth century CE, Ambrose and Augustine grappled in active dialogue with Paul's writings and, in different ways and with different outcomes, with issues that Paul had approached in his correspondence, legal slavery retained its firm location in their theological thought.[82] Is it too far-fetched to think that these clerics, born and raised in a slave-owning culture, understood more readily than modern scholars—and long before the advent of social-scientific and microeconomic approaches on the one hand, and prosopography and close readings on the other—the place of slave exploitation in the Pauline mission, as documented (however evasively) in his letters and as encapsulated (fairly plainly, actually) in the first cult regulations? And that they took Paul's example as their role model in building what we have come to call the Christian church? Unsurprisingly, perhaps, while other Christian voices challenged or demonized slavery, it was possible in the late seventh century CE for a rural church in Visigothic Spain with ownership of less than ten slaves to be regarded

---

81. Ibid., iii.
82. For discussion, see Richard Klein, *Die Sklaverei in der Sicht der Bischöfe Ambrosius und Augustinus* (Stuttgart: Franz Steiner Verlag, 1988); for a shorter discussion in English, see Garnsey, *Ideas of Slavery*, 189–219.

as poor—redefining Varro's dictum cited above and challenging *our* notions of "poverty."[83] Similarly, slaveholders in the world of interest to Berlin and Morgan were able to justify slave exploitation precisely on the basis of Christian doctrine: "the slaveholders' diaries, letters, and other personal papers," wrote Eugene D. Genovese, "show that the Bible and religious tracts held pride of place in their reading."[84]

To advance the modern discussion of the place of the "peculiar institution" in the making of European society, Finley once famously asked whether Greek civilization was based on slave labor.[85] It takes substantially more than a short contribution like the present chapter to argue that one of the dominant religions of the modern world would benefit from being rigorously questioned in similar vein, and that in the light of the religion's extraordinary success, the hybrid combination of economic and religious aspects of slave exploitation that the Pauline mind encouraged, moving swiftly between Greek, Jewish, and Roman contexts (and their various overlapping settings), might more suitably be described—as I have done throughout this chapter—by the emerging creed's name: Christian slavery. But it is a tempting hypothesis for future work on the subject—one that is, naturally, "open to being falsified by data."[86]

Select Bibliography

Many specialized studies on a wide range of topics have been published under the auspices of the Mainz Academy research project on ancient slavery (in German): http://tinyurl.com/h3gkn9f.

Bradley, Keith. *Slavery and Society at Rome.* Cambridge: Cambridge University Press, 1994.

_____. *Slaves and Masters in the Roman Empire: A Study in Social Control.* New York: Oxford University Press, 1987.

_____., and Paul Cartledge, eds. *The Cambridge World History of Slavery.*

83. Concilio de Toledo XVI, *Concilios visigóticos e hispano-romanos*, ed. José Vives (Barcelona: Consejo Superiod de Investigaciones Científicas, 1963), 485 (no. 36). Some critical voices are discussed in Richard Klein, *Die Haltung der kappadokischen Bischöfe Basilius von Caesarea, Gregor von Nazianz und Gregor von Nyssa zur Sklaverei* (Stuttgart: Franz Steiner Verlag, 2000).
84. Eugene D. Genovese, *The Slaveholders' Dilemma: Freedom and Progress in Southern Conservative Thought, 1820-1860* (Columbia: University of South Carolina Press, 1992), 4.
85. Moses I. Finley, "Was Greek Civilization Based on Slave Labour?," *Historia* 8, no. 2 (1959): 145–64.
86. Wayne E. Meeks, "Taking Stock and Moving On," in Still and Horrell, *After the First Urban Christians*, 136.

Vol. 1, *The Ancient Mediterranean World*. Cambridge: Cambridge University Press, 2011.

Finley, M. I., ed. *Slavery in Classical Antiquity: Views and Controversies*. Cambridge: Heffer, 1960.

Fisher, N. R. E. *Slavery in Classical Greece*. London: Bristol Classical, 1993.

Fitzgerald, William. *Slavery and the Roman Literary Imagination*. Cambridge: Cambridge University Press, 2000.

George, Michele, ed. *Roman Slavery and Roman Material Culture*. Toronto: University of Toronto Press, 2013.

Gibson, E. Leigh. *The Jewish Manumission Inscriptions of the Bosporus Kingdom*. Tübingen: Mohr Siebeck, 1999.

Harper, Kyle. *Slavery in the Late Roman World, AD 275–425*. Cambridge: Cambridge University Press, 2011.

Harrill, J. Albert. *The Manumission of Slaves in Early Christianity*. Tübingen: Mohr Siebeck, 1998.

Hopkins, Keith. *Conquerors and Slaves*. Cambridge: Cambridge University Press, 1978.

Hudson, Larry E., Jr. *To Have and to Hold: Slave Work and Family Life in Antebellum South Carolina*. Athens: University of Georgia Press, 1997.

Joshel, Sandra R., and Lauren Hackworth Petersen. *The Material Life of Roman Slaves*. Cambridge: Cambridge University Press, 2014.

Joshel, Sandra R., and Sheila Murnaghan. *Women and Slaves in Greco-Roman Culture: Differential Equations*. London: Routledge, 1998.

Lewis, David Martin. "Greek Slavery in a Near Eastern Context : A Comparative Study of the Legal and Economic Distinctiveness of Greek Slave Systems." PhD diss., University of Durham, 2011.

Luraghi, Nino, and Susan E. Alcock, eds. *Helots and Their Masters in Laconia and Messenia: Histories, Ideologies, Structures*. Cambridge, MA: Harvard University Press, 2003.

Roth, Ulrike, ed. *By the Sweat of Your Brow: Roman Slavery in Its Socio-Economic Setting*. London: Institute for Classical Studies, 2010.

———. *Thinking Tools: Agricultural Slavery between Evidence and Models*. London: Institute for Classical Studies, 2007.

Scheidel, Walter. "Quantifying the Sources of Slaves in the Early Roman Empire." *JRS* 87 (1997): 156–69.

———. "Real Slave Prices and the Relative Cost of Slave Labor in the Greco-Roman World." *Ancient Society* 35 (2005): 1–17.

Thompson, F. Hugh. *The Archaeology of Greek and Roman Slavery*. London: Duckworth, 2003.

Treggiari, Susan M. "Domestic Staff at Rome during the Julio-Claudian Period." *Social History* 6 (1973). 241–55.

Trümper, Monika. *Graeco-Roman Slave Markets: Fact or Fiction?* Oxford: Oxbow Books, 2009.

Zelnick-Abramovitz, Rachel. *Not Wholly Free: The Concept of Manumission and the Status of Manumitted Slaves in the Ancient Greek World.* Leiden: Brill, 2005.

7

Economic Location of Benefactors in Pauline Communities

Zeba A. Crook

Introduction

Serious and careful interest in ancient economy has reemerged among classicists and biblical scholars. The trend in these studies, from their original emergence in the early twentieth century to their reemergence in the early twenty-first century, is somewhat consistent with trends in much of scholarship: movement away from a Marxian focus on poverty and exploitation, movement away from romanticized notions of Christian origins in which "David" overthrows "Goliath" in the guise of Rome, and movement toward reliance on material data and sound social theory. The result of this trend, as Timothy Brookins shows in his essay in this volume, has been the acknowledgement of economic and social diversity within the groups of earliest Christians. However, while Brookins's essay treats the general question of economic profiling of these groups, which I must do briefly too, my primary task is to locate the putative patrons and benefactors of the earliest Christ-following groups in the ancient economy and to speculate on their potential acts of generosity. And "speculate" is the key term here, because Paul's letters do not offer a complete view of the organizational challenges of founding, governing, and sustaining his groups. Being occasional in nature, Paul's letters offer a few glimpses of the challenges or practices, but more often they are silent on them. In order, therefore, to make speculation more potentially fruitful, I shall seek analogies with regard to social and economic stratification and generosity in similar groups, namely voluntary associations. The method, therefore, will be to take data drawn from voluntary association inscriptions and to locate those data within the scalar models that have been developed and refined recently. This seems to me the best way to set a control on the speculation that is an unavoidable part of economic thinking about Paul and patronage.[1]

The Economic Location of Elite Christ Followers

It was Edwin Judge who did the most to alter the long-standing assumption that the first urban followers of Jesus were overwhelmingly drawn from the poor.[2] In a number of publications, Judge argued

1. Outside of political discussions, in modern parlance, patronage is a generally thought to be a positive and friendly phenomenon. A patron is someone who has given generously to an organization (e.g., opera, food bank) or individual (e.g., athlete, artist). In this setting, patron and benefactor are synonymous. In antiquity, on the other hand, patrons and benefactors were different. They were, of course, related, in that in both actions, someone was giving generously to someone else who could not repay and thus reciprocated with honor, gratitude, and public praise. The history of the debate need not be narrated. It is enough to summarize it in this way. Patronage in antiquity required a personal relationship and thus was prone to (I would not be so pessimistic as to say *characterized* by) abuse, extortion, and mistreatment. An example of a patron is Maecenas, the Roman aristocrat who supported Horace. Conversely, benefaction was diffuse and impersonal, in that the recipients of benefactions rarely had a personal relationship with the giver. An emperor who grants a city tax-free status is an example of a benefactor. It is one thing, however, to distinguish the two forms of generosity and quite another always to be able to distinguish between them when looking at actual relationships. For instance, when the wealthy member of an association serves as the *orgeōn* and pays from his own funds for the sacrifices on behalf of his association members, is that an act of patronage or benefaction? I will try to be consistent in my use of this nomenclature, but it is sometimes hard to know how best to categorize relationships of generosity and reciprocity from the available evidence, especially when dealing with actual people and groups (as opposed to literary sources). Let the most recent survey on this question suffice for bibliography: Stephan Joubert, "Patrocinium and Euergetism: Similar or Different Reciprocal Relationships," in *The New Testament in the Graeco-Roman World: Articles in Honour of Abe Malherbe*, ed. Marius Nel, Jan G. van der Watt, and Fika J. van Rensburg (Zürich: LIT Verlag, 2015), 171–96.
2. Abraham J. Malherbe, *Social Aspects of Early Christianity*, 2nd ed. (Philadelphia: Fortress Press, 1983), 31.

not that Pauline groups were *overwhelmingly* drawn from the wealthy and elite but that these groups were *overwhelmed* by the wealthy and elite. Judge concluded an important study by asserting, "Far from being a socially depressed group, then, if the Corinthians are at all typical, the Christians were dominated by a socially pretentious section of the population of the big cities."[3] Elsewhere, Judge elaborated:

> The first churches in the Gentile cities visited by the mission of St. Paul were societies sponsored to a socially heterogeneous membership by local notabilities. It cannot, of course, be proved that this amounts to a patronal system of the Roman kind, but it is plain that the Christian groups rested for their security on the maintenance of some sort of social hierarchy under whose auspices they met.[4]

Judge's assertions were unpopular until the work of Meeks and Theissen made them nearly unassailable.[5] The respective contributions of Meeks and Theissen on the social constitution of Pauline groups helped to cement two interrelated positions among scholars of earliest Christianity. The first position accepts that if not many of the Corinthians, and by short extension, Christ followers in general, were wise, powerful, and of noble birth (1 Cor 1:26), then some of them must have been. This observation has generated much fruitful debate about personal status inconsistency, about congregational problems generated by such social stratification, about the significance of the several female figures among them, and about the economic location of the first Christ followers. It has also led to speculation about those at the higher end of this social spectrum and to the adoption of social-scientific categories for describing and situating those figures: if they provided anything, and they certainly did, then they must have been patrons.

The second position relates to the identity of those elite or patronal figures. Typically, they are easy to identify because they are named (which is likely a significant indication of status on its own) and because they are usually described as having provided or done something of value. They are Gaius, Phoebe, Prisca and Aquila, Erastus, Crispus, Stephanas, and possibly also Lydia, Jason, and Chloe.

---

3. Edwin A. Judge, *The Social Pattern of Christian Groups in the First Century* (London: Tyndale, 1960), 60.

4. E. A. Judge, "The Early Christians as a Scholastic Community," *Journal of Religious History* 1, no. 1 (1960): 7.

5. For an excellent summary and methodological assessment of this consensus, see Richard L. Rohrbaugh, "Methodological Considerations in the Debate over the Social Class of Early Christians," *Journal of the American Academy of Religion* 52, no. 3 (1984): 519–46.

Much of the discussion about these figures is quite colorful. Consider Meeks's and Theissen's descriptions of these figures: Erastus was "a person of both wealth and high civic status";[6] Gaius was "a man of some wealth,"[7] and may have viewed himself "very much in the way that the wealthy patron of a private association for a pagan cultic society might do";[8] Phoebe was an "independent" patron with "some wealth";[9] Stephanas was "fairly high on the scale of wealth";[10] Crispus was "probably well to do"[11] and of "high social status."[12] Finally, Prisca and Aquila had "relatively high" wealth.[13]

These descriptions of leading Pauline figures were deeply significant because they stressed the reality of stratification within Pauline groups and the force of their contribution to scholarship is not to be underestimated. But in sober hindsight, one realizes that these descriptions, while colorful, lack rigor. To refer to Gaius as "a man of some wealth" (Meeks) tells us only that his wealth (and therefore his status) was likely higher than some others in the group. Disconcertingly, this lack of rigor pertains despite the obvious care Theissen takes in attempting to measure social status, which he does in four areas: whether a person holds a civic or associative office, whether they are in a position to render services of any kind, whether they have or manage a house, and

---

6. Wayne A. Meeks, *The First Urban Christians: The Social World of the Apostle Paul* (New Haven, CT: Yale University Press, 1983), 59. There is much debate about Erastus, particularly whether Paul's Erastus is the same Erastus who some years later became an *aedile* of Corinth, and whether the office of *oikonomos tēs poleōs* is equivalent to or lesser than that of *aedile*. Theissen argued that Erastus became *aedile* later, but at the time of Paul's letter was in a lesser office on his way up; see Gerd Theissen, "Social Stratification in the Corinthian Community: A Contribution to the Sociology of Early Hellenistic Christianity," in *The Social Setting of Pauline Christianity: Essays on Corinth*, ed. Gerd Theissen, ed. and trans. John H. Schütz (Philadelphia: Fortress Press, 1982), 75–83. However, it is now clear that the two Erasti are different people. See Steven J. Friesen, "The Wrong Erastus: Ideology, Archaeology, and Exegesis," in *Corinth in Context: Comparative Studies on Religion and Society*, ed. Steven J. Friesen, Daniel N. Schowalter, and James C. Walters, NovTSup 134 (Leiden: Brill, 2010), 231–56. For a recent contrary view, see Timothy A. Brookins, "The (In)frequency of the Name 'Erastus' in Antiquity: A Literary, Papyrological, and Epigraphical Catalog," *NTS* 59 (October 2013): 496–516. How one resolves these questions, however, is irrelevant: even if Paul's Erastus was never later *aedile*, and even if city treasurer was a position that could be held by a city slave, it was still an honorable office and Meeks's observation likely still holds.

7. Meeks, *First Urban Christians*, 57.

8. Ibid., 67.

9. Ibid., 60; so too E. A. Judge, "The Early Christians as a Scholastic Community: Part II," *Journal of Religious History* 1, no. 3 (1961): 128–30.

10. Meeks, *First Urban Christians*, 58.

11. Ibid., 57.

12. Gerd Theissen, "The Social Structure of Pauline Communities: Some Critical Remarks on J. J. Meggitt, Paul, Poverty and Survival," *JSNT* 24, no. 2 (2001): 75; See also John K. Chow (*Patronage and Power: A Study of Social Networks in Corinth* [Sheffield: Sheffield Academic Press, 1992], 89), who describes Crispus as "a person of wealth."

13. Meeks, *First Urban Christians*, 59.

whether they can travel. While, he readily admits, none of these alone is necessarily a marker of high social status, one or more together surely do indicate high status. And in several instances, the people whose names we know in Corinth register on at least two of these measures, and thus, he concludes, must surely have belonged to the "upper classes": Prisca, Aquila, and Stephanas own and offer their homes, provide something for the association, and can travel. Erastus has an office and a house, Crispus has an office and a house, and Phoebe renders services and travels, so they also have "high social status."[14]

The lack of rigor in these colorful descriptions limited their ability to advance scholarship. An alternative approach to thinking about the wealth of the higher end of the Christian spectrum turned to archeology with a focus on living space. Gaius is said to have hosted the "whole" church in his home (Rom 16:23). This invites two closely related questions, both of which would inform our thinking on wealth and status: how many Christians were hosted and how large was the home?[15] Jerome Murphy-O'Connor offers a model of what he claims to have been a "typical" home, the sort Gaius might have lived in. It is, in fact, a fairly impressive "villa" of eleven rooms and a courtyard. Thus, Murphy-O'Connor certainly imagines Gaius in an upper social echelon.[16] Carolyn Osiek and David L. Balch go even further, preferring Pompeian houses as the exemplar, which could hold considerably more people.[17] They make no explicit remarks concerning the elite status of Christian patrons, but the implication must be that it was quite high.[18]

Of course, archeology cannot provide more rigorous ways of locating patrons or benefactors of the first Christ followers because we do not know where they lived. The attempts at imagining the economic stratification of the earliest urban Christ followers in general and the eco-

---

14. Theissen, "Social Structure," 95.

15. A third, much more recent question threatens to upend the entire debate: did Gaius host the entire community or was he a guest of the entire community? On this, see Richard Last, *The Pauline Church and the Corinthian Ekklēsia: Greco-Roman Associations in Comparative Context* (Cambridge: Cambridge University Press, 2015), ch. 2.

16. Murphy-O'Connor makes the point that translating both *oikos* and *oikia* as "home" rather than "house" is to be preferred to avoid the impression that just because someone has an *oikos* means they are a householder. *Oikos* might just as easily refer to the rental of a tenement apartment. See Jerome Murphy-O'Connor, *St. Paul's Corinth: Texts and Archaeology*, 3rd rev. exp. ed. (Collegeville, MN: Liturgical Press, 2002), 183.

17. Carolyn Osiek and David L. Balch, *Families in the New Testament World: Households and House Churches* (Louisville, KY: Westminster John Knox, 1997), 201–3.

18. David Horrell rejects the claim that the Anaploga Villa was at all typical. Horrell argues that the better analog for typical Christian homes is to be found in the upper rooms of shops east of the theatre district; see David G. Horrell, "Domestic Space and Christian Meetings at Corinth: Imagining New Contexts and the Buildings East of the Theatre," *NTS* 50, no. 3 (2004): 356–57.

nomic location of its most elite in particular received a much-needed injection of precision from Steve Friesen.[19] Friesen introduced a seven-tiered "poverty scale" in which the truly elite in status and wealth comprised 3 percent of the ancient world (PS1–3); 7 percent comprised those with moderate surplus, that is, people who lived close to the subsistence level but were safely above it (PS4); 90 percent of ancient people lived precariously at (PS5: 22 percent), slightly below (PS6: 40 percent), or hopelessly below (PS7: 28 percent) subsistence level.[20]

Friesen's important contribution was refined by Bruce Longe-necker.[21] Despite its perceived nuance, Friesen's model essentially reproduced the same binary model assumed (without Friesen's nuance) by Deissmann and more recently by Justin Meggitt.[22] On this binary model, there is tiny band of elites (3 percent) at the top of the socioeconomic pyramid, a mammoth base of the very poor (90 percent) at the bottom, with a small percentage of people in between with moderate surplus but with poverty always lurking on the horizon (the 7 percent that comprise Friesen's PS4). Granted, Friesen did not present the bottom of that pyramid as an undifferentiated mass, but nonetheless, the pyramid was extremely bottom-heavy.

Longenecker's refinement is to introduce a more robust "middling" group. Rewording Friesen's "poverty scale" to something less biased, Longenecker presents a seven-tiered "economy scale." At the top was the same elite 3 percent. Those who lived below subsistence comprised 55 percent of society: ES6 at 30 percent (at or below subsistence) and ES7 at 25 percent (those who were "permanently in crisis"). Longenecker's middling groups, ES4 and ES5, account for 42 percent of society. Those in ES4 (originally 17 percent, later lowered to 15 percent) enjoyed moderate surplus, and those in ES5 (originally 25 percent, later

---

19. Steven Friesen, "Poverty in Pauline Studies: Beyond the So-Called New Consensus," *JSNT* 26, no. 3 (2004): 323–61.

20. Friesen based subsistence on the amount of money it would require to consume 1,500–3,000 calories a day. Though he admits the limitations of this, Peter Oakes goes further in explaining the problems with defining "subsistence"; see Peter Oakes, "Constructing Poverty Scales for Graeco-Roman Society: A Response to Steven Friesen's 'Poverty in Pauline Studies,'" *JSNT* 26, no. 3 (2004): 368–70.

21. Bruce W. Longenecker, "Exposing the Economic Middle: A Revised Economy Scale for the Study of Early Urban Christianity," *JSNT* 31, no. 3 (2009): 243–78; Bruce W. Longenecker, *Remember the Poor: Paul, Poverty, and the Greco-Roman World* (Grand Rapids: Eerdmans, 2010), 36–59. The discussion here concerning Longenecker's initial and subsequent assessments of wealth stratification can be found in these two works, though a summary of both stages in his thinking is available in *Remember the Poor*, 53.

22. Justin J. Meggitt, *Paul, Poverty and Survival* (Edinburgh: T&T Clark, 1998).

raised to 27 percent) could reasonably expect to remain above subsistence level.

Longenecker's adjustments reveal his indebtedness to Friesen, of course, and the changes may appear to be modest, but they do alter our perception of the economic composition of the ancient world. First of all, while Longenecker's "middling" groups (ES4 and ES5) were not among the imperial elite *ordines*, they nonetheless sat atop 55 percent of the rest of society and are thus, in a way, wealthy and elite. In this regard, categories like "wealthy" and "elite" prove themselves to be unhelpful, because any group that is better off than 55 percent of society *is* wealthy and elite, even if not *as* wealthy and elite as some. Put differently, Longenecker's scale is more helpful than the descriptive categories (wealthy, elite, of some means, well-off) that preceded it (e.g., Meeks and Theissen). At the same time, Longenecker's revised model does not, as Meggitt lamented of earlier scholarship, pretend that the poor do not exist.[23] Poverty and the threat of destitution still loom large for most people in this model, but at the same time, this was not the case for a considerable percentage of society.[24]

Naturally, Friesen and Longenecker locate possible patrons of the first Christ followers in ES4 and ES5, agreeing that there were no Christ followers or sympathizers among those in ES1–3 and that those in ES6–7 would be in no position to act as patrons or benefactors. The differences between Friesen and Longenecker on locating these figures are therefore insignificant. They argue for minor adjustments but mostly agree.[25] Yet, those minor adjustments reveal something significant about the debate, namely that the precision they achieve is largely an illusion. Categories such as ES4 or PS6 might sound more precise than "a person of means" or "the poor," but these categories are still mired in ambiguity. For instance, there are merchants to be found in ES3, ES4, ES5, and ES6. Thus, to acknowledge that Prisca and Aquila

---

23. Ibid., 40.
24. Longenecker, *Remember the Poor*, 57.
25. For example, for Friesen, Gaius is the only Christ follower who can be placed with certainty in PS4; Erastus he places in PS4–5. And although Friesen rejects the translation of *prostatis* as "patron" or "benefactor," he still claims that Phoebe was "a leader and authority figure" within the community, and thus he places her in PS4–5. Longenecker, in contrast, places Erastus securely in ES4, which he does also with Gaius and Phoebe. When it comes to Stephanas, Friesen stresses what Paul does *not* say: that he ever stayed with Stephanas, or what precisely Stephanas gave as "service"; he thus places Stephanas in PS5–6. Longenecker places him in ES4–5. Longenecker places Crispus in ES4–5 based on his status as an *archisynagōgos*. Friesen and Longenecker are nearly in agreement on the location of Prisca and Aquila: PS4–5 for Friesen and ES5–6 for Longenecker. Friesen shows that too little is known about Prisca and Aquila, and too much of the evidence is ambiguous to be confident of a higher economic location.

may have been "merchants" tells us nothing concrete about their economic location, save for the fact that they are not ES1, ES2, or ES7, which we certainly knew already.

In addition, the debate on the minor adjustments reveals how little evidence can be presented. Indeed, the cases they mount for situating these figures in or straddling particular locations on their scales amount to little more than plot summary of Pauline texts (sometimes in concert with Acts). And there is so little material to summarize. Longenecker's case for placing Gaius in ES4 relies on Paul's description of him hosting the whole church of Corinth, and nothing else. No less, that case is made in eleven sentences and exhausts all the available evidence.[26]

I stress that these criticisms are meant to draw attention to the limitations of the data, not to the limitations of Friesen's or Longenecker's theoretical frameworks. But the limitations do suggest a strong need for more data to supplement the economy scales and our placement of the Pauline figures within them. A reasonable and potentially fruitful place to look for such data would be other associations that were similar in social status and stratification and likewise relied on patronage and peer benefaction. The suggestion is not that the limitations just expressed will be entirely overcome by the consideration of such data, but that the precision of the economy scales can perhaps be supplemented. Put in the form of a question: can we learn what patrons of Christ-following associations in Corinth may have provided when we see what patrons of other associations supplied to their groups?

Associative Beneficence

Though it has obvious social and political aspects, patronage is at root an economic act. The closest analogy of patronage to Christ-groups would be patronage to other voluntary associations. One inscription in particular illustrates the raw economic nature of acts of patronage or benefaction to voluntary associations—or better, to "elective social formations."[27] *IG* XII Suppl. 365 (= *AGRW* 263) sets out the expectations of

---

26. Longenecker, *Remember the Poor*, 239.

27. The colloquial nomenclature "voluntary association," though widespread, suffers from a number of problems, first and foremost among which is the difficulty of using "voluntary" for any activity in a collectivistic setting such as the ancient Mediterranean. Richard Ascough's more social-scientific language "elective social formation" is better because it is more precise but is awkward for repeated use; see Richard S. Ascough, "'Map-Maker, Map-Maker, Make Me a Map': Redescribing Greco-Roman 'Elective Social Formations,'" in *Introducing Religion: Essays in Honor of Jonathan Z. Smith*, ed. Willi Braun and Russell T. McCutcheon (London: Equinox, 2008), 68–84. Throughout this

the "purchaser" of the position of "eponymous official": he must pay the annual installments on behalf of the group in a particular pattern, and in return, he will receive prescribed benefits.[28] Most inscriptions are not as explicit as this, but it surely only makes explicit the common implicit assumptions: one *purchased* these offices, and in return one expected to receive certain things for it.[29] *IG* II2 1328 (= *AGRW* 19; Piraeus, second century BCE) implies that members are elected, that they cannot decline for fear of being expelled, and that nonetheless they are expected to give generously. This is also likely reflected in a letter of resignation (which survives in papyrus, not stone) that a Fayum patron had to submit to an association because he had lost his wealth (*PMich* IX 575 = *AGRW* 289; 184 CE) and was no longer able to provide for the group from his resources.[30]

The most critical issue for associations was survival, and survival depended on the ability to achieve and maintain financial solvency. Financial solvency was assisted in two ways: costs carried by and levied against membership, and acts of generosity. Costs carried by membership commonly included inaugural fees, monthly or annual fees, contributions made to banquets and to the execution of sacrifices or services, and a variety of fines and levies.[31] There were no pan-Mediterranean practices in this regard, only considerable variation.[32] *IDelta* I

---

work, I shall use "associations" and "groups" to refer in shorthand to ancient elective social formations, which naturally includes the groups and associations established by Paul of Tarsus.

28. Most of the following inscriptions referred to below have been published in many locations in the last 150 years. They are referred to in this paper by their most traditional and, until recently, their most easily accessible location of publication. Many of them, however, also appear in several more recent collections (with translation and commentary) by Richard S. Ascough, Philip A. Harland, and John S. Kloppenborg. When that is the case, the location of the inscription is also indicated: *GRA* I refers to John S. Kloppenborg and Richard S. Ascough, *Greco-Roman Associations: Texts, Translations, and Commentary I. Attica, Central Greece, Macedonia, Thrace* (Berlin: de Gruyter, 2011); *GRA* II refers to Philip A. Harland, *Greco-Roman Associations: Texts, Translations, and Commentary II. North Coast of the Black Sea, Asia Minor* (Berlin: de Gruyter, 2014); and *AGRW* refers to Richard S. Ascough, Philip A. Harland, and John S. Kloppenborg, *Associations in the Greco-Roman World: A Sourcebook* (Waco, TX: Baylor University Press, 2012). This latter work comes with a companion website (http://tinyurl.com/z639faa) consisting of several hundred additional inscriptions, a scholarly bibliography of over one thousand works, and a powerful search tool.

29. *AGRW* 162–63.

30. That the writer is a patron of the group is to be inferred from the choice of verb found in the letter to describe what it is the writer can no longer accomplish: *nemō*. The verb carries the fairly imprecise meaning "to dispense"; it is its fairly common use in the context of what the gods do for humans that the term can be said to carry the connotation of patronage. It also seems unlikely that a mere member would need to resign so formally, so that the writer is a patron is reasonable. Yet, *PLond* VII 2193 (Fayum, 69–58 BCE) shows clearly that resignation from members was conceivable. Nonetheless, the grounds are sufficient therefore to conclude that the writer of *PMich* IX 575 was a patron. So Ascough, Harland, and Kloppenborg in *AGRW* 172.

31. Fines: *IG* II2 1339 (= *GRA* I 46; Athens, first century BCE); *IG* II2 1368 (= *GRA* I 51; Athens, second century CE); *SEG* 31.122 (= *GRA* I 50; Athens, 100 CE).

446 (= *AGRW* 287; Delta region in Egypt, 67, 64 BCE) lists the sort of costs members and patrons might incur: contributions to the banquets, monthly dues, *leitourgia*, and levies. A few times, membership dues are indicated specifically: *PMich* V 243 (= *AGRW* 300; Tebtynis, 14–37 CE) indicates twelve silver drachmas as the monthly fee for an association of sheep and cattle owners.[33] *PLond* III 1178 (= *AGRW* 303; Upper Egypt, 194 CE) indicates one hundred denarii for admission to an association of athletes. Other sources, such as *PMich* V 245 (= *AGRW* 302; Tebtynis, 47 CE), refer to dues but do not indicate the amount.

Two inscriptions in particular are interesting with respect to membership fees. The well-known *CIL* XIV 2112 (= *AGRW* 310; dedicated to Diana and Antinous at Lanuvium in 136 CE) charges plebs 100 sesterces with an amphora of wine to join, with 5 asses (= 1.25 sesterces) for monthly membership maintenance (manumitted slaves paid only one amphora of wine). The minutes and bylaws from a Bacchic association (*IG* II2 1368 = *GRA* I 51 = Danker, *Benefactor* 22; Athens, 164 CE) refers to entrance fees of twenty-five denarii, fifty denarii for applicants without fathers in the association. In addition, monthly contributions of wine are expected from all members. Failure to meet monthly or annual dues results in expulsion.

Ideally, generosity to a group might make member contributions (fees, support, fines) unnecessary, but until then, or in the absence of benefactions, costs carried by members were the only thing between viability and dissolution.[34] Generally, therefore, one needed to be concerned with membership numbers, for when membership numbers became low, the burden on remaining members was naturally increased. A number of associations reached the breaking point because of low member numbers. An association of Tyrian settlers in

---

32. *GRA* I 251. See also ibid., 449.

33. According to the US Department of Health and Human Services, the 2014 income level below which one is living in poverty was $23,850 for a family of four (US Department of Health and Human Services, "2014 Poverty Guidelines," Office of the Assistant Secretary for Planning and Evaluation, December 1, 2014, http://tinyurl.com/zsojg6o). According to Steven Friesen ("Poverty in Pauline Studies," 344), subsistence in a city other than Rome requires at least 600 denarii. As difficult as comparison is on this matter, let us imagine that the two amounts referring to poverty level and subsistence are comparable: if so, 12 drachmas would be the equivalent 480 USD monthly (assuming that 12 drachmas is worth 10.5 denarii), quite a high amount. The Bacchic association behind *IG* II2 1368 (see in the following paragraph) refers to entrance fees of 25 denarii for the sons of members, which is also quite a high amount. It is hard to know if these amounts represent an average amount, but interestingly *CIL* XIV 2112 names 100 sesterces (also worth 25 denarii) membership (*plus* some wine). These values were drawn from Kenneth W. Harl ("Roman Currency of the Principate," accessed January 24, 2016, http://tinyurl.com/hnxrcm2).

34. Franciszek Sokolowski, "Fees and Taxes in the Greek Cults," *Harvard Theological Review* 47, no. 3 (1954): 153.

Italy (*OGIS* 595 = *AGRW* 317; Puteoli, 174 CE) comes from an association that had become so small it could no longer afford to conduct its sacrificial obligations, which cost 250 denarii annually. Likewise, a Dacian association of Jupiter (*ILS* 7215a = *AGRW* 69; 167 CE) comes from an association that had to dissolve itself when its membership dropped to seventeen.[35]

Clearly, the ability of an association to attract acts of generosity had implications for its survival. Nonetheless, while associations had to be concerned with finances, honor and influence mattered far more. The result was a scenario in which men and women actively sought to become patrons or benefactors of associations, and associations sometimes aggressively sought patrons, in some cases naming someone as a patron before even asking that person. Here, clearly, the association hoped to capitalize on the cultural thirst for honor. We have no reason to imagine that financial solvency was any less a concern for the gatherings of Christ followers than for other associations.

The most common form of inscription makes it impossible to specify precisely what people gave to associations. Many of the inscriptions are no more specific than to name the patron and to make explicit the discharge of reciprocity in gratitude for the "generosity" or "benefactions" of said person. Naming a person, sometimes alone and sometimes offering the title of patron or *euergetēs*, appears to have been sufficient, and clearly it was not considered necessary to be more precise about what was provided.[36]

The inscriptions also reveal the sheer variety of services that could be considered an act of generosity by an association. Some of them revolve around service and others around material goods. Acts of generosity can come from within or without the association. Those from within, which Kloppenborg calls "peer benefaction," commonly take the form of administrative support.[37] Members could be elected or might be appointed cyclically, but either way, declining was rarely an option (*IG* II2 1328 = *GRA* I 34; Piraeus, second century BCE) because the associations relied on them to accept.

---

35. Naphtali Lewis and Meyer Reinhold, *Roman Civilization: Selected Readings* (New York: Columbia University Press, 1990), 188–89. In stipulating that no fewer than twelve members can use interest from a bequest for an annual banquet, does *CIL* XI 5047 (= *AGRW* 317; Italian, date uncertain) imply how small the benefactor felt this particular association was allowed to become?

36. Holland Lee Hendrix, "Thessalonians Honor Romans" (ThD diss., Harvard Divinity School, 1984), 22.

37. John S. Kloppenborg, "Graeco-Roman Thiasoi, the Ekklesia at Corinth, and Conflict Management," in *Redescribing Paul and the Corinthians*, ed. Ron Cameron and Merrill P. Miller, Early Christianity and Its Literature 5 (Atlanta: Society of Biblical Literature, 2011), 212.

One common form of associative generosity was to hold an administrative office within an association. There are three reasons to conclude that holding such offices was an act of generosity to the group, since this is not obviously the case at first consideration. First, when Stephanas is honored for performing sacrifices (*IG* II2 1261 = *GRA* 9; Attica, fourth century BCE), surely we are to assume that he was paying for this (or supplementing it) at his own expense, otherwise how would it be worth public honoring?[38] Secondly, that care was so frequently taken to show potential benefactors the honor with which they would be treated if they too gave generously (column C of the same inscription, early third century CE) also indicates that these positions involved benefaction to the group. Finally, while few inscriptions say so explicitly, perhaps *IG* II2 1262 (= *GRA* 10; Attica, 300 BCE), from the same year as column C in *IG* II2 1261, reflects a broader sentiment when it thanks some administrators it names as "supervisors," but whom the inscription describes as conducting sacrifices and "other" duties, referring to these acts as *euergetēmatōn* (line 15).[39]

Another common form of peer benefaction is for a member of the group to cover the cost of the honorary inscription. Thus, several inscriptions mention the person who paid for the stele, pillar, altar, or votive plaque: *SEG* 36.228 (= *GRA* I 38; Attica, second century BCE); *IBeroia* 22 (= *AGRW* 35; Beroea, 7 BCE); *SEG* 35.714 (= *AGRW* 36; Beroea, second century CE); *IPerinthos* 56 (= *GRA* I 87; Perinthos, second century CE); *SEG* 47.1089 (= *GRA* I 89; Thrace, second/third century CE); and *IG* II2 1263 (= *GRA* I 11; Pireaus, third century BCE).[40]

Sometimes, the material support that office holders were expected to give is clearly demarcated in the rules of membership. For instance, *IG* II2 1368 (= *GRA* I 51 = Danker, *Benefactor* 22; Athens, 164 CE) states that for the two-year term, a treasurer must provide lamp oil from his own supply for monthly meetings, for the annual celebration (a meal?), for feast days of the god, and for any extraordinary session (admission of new members, bestowal of honors, recognition of member milestones).

In other places, the office holder is thanked for a clearly specified material support, but it is not clear whether the amount was dictated

---

38. Conversely, anyone in control of money, whether a secretary (*grammateus*) or treasurer (*tamias*), could be honored for having executed his duties responsibly and honestly (using the term *dikaiosynē*), not in a cavalier, profligate, or fraudulent manner. Another possible term was *aprophasistōs* (*IG* II2 1323 = *GRA* 1.31; Athens, second century BCE). Yet surely honesty, while appreciated, was not so rare that it was sufficient cause for public honoring.

39. This same language is reflected in *IG* II2 1263, line 31 (third century BCE).

40. *IG* II2 1263 helpfully states that the votive plaque cost fifty drachmas.

by the parameters of the office or whether it is solely a description of what the office holder elected to give. For example, *IG* II2 1323 (= *GRA* 31; Athens, second century BCE) honors Theon not only for being a treasurer for many years but for doing so "without evasion"[41] and for paying members' burial expenses immediately (perhaps with the expectation of being reimbursed eventually, but that is not stated). Similarly, the treasurer of an Egyptian association (*PRyl* IV 586 = *AGRW* 304; 99 BCE; nothing is known about the identity of the association) advanced the group fifty-three talents and some thousand silver drachmas (with interest, however).

IG II2 1227 (= *GRA* I 15; Athens, 278 BCE) thanks three supervisors and a secretary for benefactions of sixty-five drachmae and the donation of a silver vessel worth fifty-six drachmae, as well as unspecified care of the group. In *IG* II2 1327 (= *GRA* 1.35 = Danker, *Benefactor* 20; Piraeus, 178 BCE), Hermaios gave his services administratively (as treasurer to a Demetrian association), helped financially with necessary sacrifices to the gods, helped defray member burial costs when the association ran short, and donated money for repairs.[42] *IG* X/2.1 4 (Thessalonica, 95 BCE) honors a gymnasiarch for serving as a broker between the association of youths and the Roman gods by providing oil.

Material generosity could come from members. Some inscriptions reflect contributions to the maintenance or renovation of existing association building, or to the construction of new buildings entirely. Part of a long second-century CE Latin inscription (*CIL* III 633 I = *GRA* I 68; Philippi) names eight men who contributed to the construction materials and decoration of a Temple of Silvanus: a bronze statue of Silvanus; four hundred roofing tiles; two marble statues; 265 denarii (for concrete and a painted board of Olympus); 50 denarii towards the building of the temple; and so on. It is difficult to know the value of the materials listed in the inscription, but the references to money are possibly easier to interpret. If a denarius is approximately one day's wages for a manual laborer, then the amounts above range from one or two months' salary to nearly a year's salary.

---

41. *GRA* I 157.
42. Other illustrative examples of members being honored for holding administrative offices abound: Being overseer or leader: *IG* II2 1256 (= *GRA* I 5; Piraeus, fourth century BCE); *IG* II2 1261 (= *GRA* I 9; Piraeus, third century BCE); *IG* II2 1262 (= *GRA* I 10; Piraeus, third century BCE). Being secretary: *IG* II2 1263 (= *GRA* I 11; Piraeus, third century BCE); *IG* II2 1284 (= *GRA* I 22; Piraeus, second century BCE). Being sacrifice maker: *IG* II2 1261 (= *GRA* I 9; Piraeus, third century BCE); *IG* II2 1327 (= *GRA* I 35; Piraeus, second century BCE); *IG* II2 1261 (= *GRA* I 9; Piraeus, third century BCE). Being priest: *IByzantion* 31 (=*GRA* I 90; Thrace, first century CE); *IG* XI4 1061 (= Danker, *Benefactor* 23; Delos, second century BCE).

More commonly, material benefits came from people outside the association. Aelius Alcibiades (*IEph* 22 = *AGRW* 184, Ephesus, second century CE) gave stabling facilities to an association of Dionysiac performers, from which they were able to earn perpetual rent. *ILS* 6469 (second century CE) from the southern Italian town of Petelia records that Megonius Leo gave a vineyard to the Augustales of the town in order to make taking that office more affordable. Other material benefactions include land (*IDelta* I 446 = *AGRW* 287; Egypt, 67, 64 BCE. *CIL* VI 10234 = *AGRW* 322; Rome, 153 CE),[43] a building (*IT* 133; Thessalonica, second century BCE),[44] thrones or silver ornaments (*IG* II2 1328 = *GRA* I 34; Piraeus, second century BCE), shrines (Jaccottet no. 35 = *GRA* I 83; Abdera, third century CE), a dining room (*IGLSkythia* I 167; Skythia, second century CE), books (*IEph* 22a = *AGRW* 184; Ephesus, second century CE), meals (*CIL* V 7906 = *AGRW* 309; Italian, unknown date. *CIL* XIV 246 = *AGRW* 313; Ostia, 140–172 CE. *IEph* 951; Ephesus, unknown date), and finally, cash.[45]

It is also extremely important to register that acts of generous giving in return for honor and recognition were not solely the domain of the aristocratic elite. That is seen in a first-century Ephesian inscription (*IEph* 20 = *GRA* II 127; Ephesus, 54–59 CE). Approximately one hundred members of an association of fishers and fish dealers are honored for their benefactions toward the building of a toll office near the harbor. They are, as one would expect, ranked from most to least generous. Column 1 starts with a benefaction of four columns and ends with a benefaction of thirty denarii. Column 2 begins with twenty-five denarii and ends (except to draw special attention to one benefaction in particular) with fifteen denarii. The back of the inscription, which is in very poor condition, reveals sums as low as five denarii.

Of particular interest is the presence of slaves among the benefactors: these slaves give as little as five denarii (which, while small, must still have been significant enough to warrant being included among

---

43. The patron of this inscription, Salvia Marcellina (a woman), also gave 50,000 sesterces for the sixty members. The inscription also shows an imperial freedman and his brother giving 10,000 sesterces to the association.

44. At least, that is the interpretation of H. L. Hendrix, "Benefactor/Patron Networks in the Urban Environment: Evidence from Thessalonians," in *Social Networks in Early Christian Environment: Issues and Methods for Social History*, ed. L. Michael White, Semeia 56 (Atlanta: Society of Biblical Literature, 1991), 47.

45. *IG* II2 1326 (= *GRA* I 36; Piraeus, second century BCE) refers to a treasurer who gave 1,500 drachmas to the association from his own resources. Another inscription from the same association and same inscriber (*IG* II2 1325 = *GRA* I 33; Piraeus, 185/4 BCE) refers to Dionysus, who gave 1,000 denarii so that the interest from it could pay for sacrifices.

the honorands) and as much as two thousand bricks (worth approximately forty to fifty denarii). That is, while the slave members are among those contributing the least, it is noteworthy that even their contributions are worth mentioning (there were certainly members of the association who were poorer than they were) and, in addition, that some of the slave members, at least, are among those more capable of philanthropy.

SEG 17.823 (= *AGRW* 307; Cyrenaica, 55 CE) lists those who contributed to the renovation of a synagogue. Ten "leaders" and a priest give ten drachmas each; two men, one of whose name is lost, give twenty-five drachmas; and one man, twenty-eight drachmas. Others are listed at the end as giving five drachmas. Here we see a ranking that considers both status within the association as well as amount given: the leaders and the priest are honored first despite giving less than some others honored below. Additionally, those honored below have indisputably Gentile theophoric names.[46] They were perhaps God-fearers or proselytes, and clearly people of some wealth.

The ranking of peer benefactors on honorary inscriptions reflects the internal stratification of many associations. *CIL* XIV 2112 (= *AGRW* 310; dedicated to Diana and Antinous at Lanuvium in 136 CE) states that *plebs* were charged 100 sesterces with an amphora of wine to join, with 5 asses (= 1.25 sesterces) for monthly membership maintenance (manumitted slaves paid only one amphora of wine). According to Fagan, this would have "put membership well within the financial range of many commoners."[47] Looking at the expectations of various official roles within the Lanuvium association, Fagan concludes that the stratification within associations was such that it was expected that "some members faced the burden of provisioning for the rest."[48] The Lanuvium association was not exclusively made up of those of more modest means, but the association did have status variety.[49] In fact, it is inconceivable that the association would have received Senate representation and support had its membership been even predominantly (let alone exclusively) of lower status people (for more on stratification see D'Arms and van Nijf).

46. John M. G. Barclay, *The Jews in the Mediterranean: Diaspora from Alexander to Trajan (323 BCE–117 CE)* (Edinburgh: T&T Clark, 1996), 236.
47. Garrett G. Fagan, "Social Life in Town and Country," in *The Oxford Handbook of Roman Epigraphy*, ed. Christer Bruun and J. C. Edmondson (Oxford: Oxford University Press, 2014), 498.
48. Ibid., 498.
49. Andreas Bendlin, "Associations, Funerals, Sociality, and Roman Law: The Collegium of Diana and Antinous in Lanuvium (CIL 14.2112) Reconsidered," in *Apostdekret und antikes Vereinswesen: Gemeinschaft und ihre Ordnung*, ed. Markus Öhler (Tübingen: Mohr Siebeck, 2011), 265.

CIL XIV 246 (= *AGRW* 313; Ostia, 140–172 CE) lists donors to a temple, among them 11 patrons, a president for life as well as 9 presidents (*quinquennalis*), a benefactor, and 181 other members. *CIL* XIV 250 and 251 (= *AGRW* 314; both Ostian second century inscriptions from an association of sailors and accountants) lists in the first instance 9 patrons (one of whom is a freedman of Augustus), a president for life, 2 presidents, and 125 *plebian* members. The later inscription (*CIL* XIV 251) lists several members of senatorial rank, 5 of equestrian rank, 7 presidents for life, and 259 plebian members.

Christ-Following Patrons

The inscriptions above reveal that the form any act of generosity might take is limited only by the needs of potential recipients and the resources a potential giver can access. That is to say, beneficence took the form of any good or service and was limited only by a person's wealth. We ought, therefore, to be able to map generosity approximately onto the economy scales encountered above.

The first obvious conclusion one can draw here is that only those with financial surplus can be generous, and the greater the surplus the greater the potential generosity. In the inscriptions surveyed above, the range of generosity was considerable: clearly those who gave 5 denarii (*IEph* 20) have less surplus than the one who gave 256 denarii (*CIL* III 633 I). It is, I would speculate, likely that a gift of 256 denarii is possible only for someone in ES1–3 (top 3 percent) of the economy scale. Other benefactions are certainly possible for people at the top of the economy scale: the third-century CE Ephesian patron M. Fulvius Publicianus Nikephoros was a *prytany* and Asiarch, which places him at ES2–ES3.[50] His generosity benefitted a dozen associations and included the construction of buildings and columns in the agora as well as the renovation of the harbor.[51] Conversely, the person who can give five denarii (and who is a member) must have *some* surplus and therefore cannot be living below subsistence. That person therefore cannot be placed at ES6–7. The obvious inference then is that many of the acts of generosity surveyed above are coming from people in ES4–5, which is also the most likely location of those who showed generosity to the

---

50. For a description of Publicianus's career, see Onno van Nijf, *The Civic World of Professional Associations in the Roman East* (Amsterdam: J. C. Gieben, 1997), 83–86.
51. A benefit is direct when, for example, permanent shop space is built for an association of *askomisthoi* in the market. A benefit might be indirect when the harbor is refurbished, attracting tourists on whom an association of silversmiths rely. See ibid., 85.

Pauline associations: Erastus, Gaius, and Phoebe for certain, and possibly also Crispus, Stephanas, and Chloe.

The cultural thirst for honor is what motivated generosity, and this applies to every level of the economy scale, save those with no surplus. That is, ES1–3 can make grander benefactions, but ES4–5 are just as motivated also to act generously when they can.[52] In the inscriptions surveyed above, we find presumably ES4 people (possibly also ES3, but certainly not ES2) giving administrative services (treasurer, sacrificer, priest, secretary). We also see peer benefaction such as erecting honorary steles, pillars, and votive plaques, lamp oil, silver vessels and other ornaments, building supplies, and unspecified cash.

There are also a number of examples of cash benefactions. For instance, the Ephesian fish cartel discussed above (*IEph* 20 = *GRA* II 127; Ephesus, 54–59 CE) honored on the front of a stele some members who gave as little as 15 denarii and on the back those who gave 5 denarii (equivalent to 191–575 USD?). This was to pay for the building of a toll booth; perhaps a modern analogy might be found in parishioners who contribute to build a new church or members of a community raising money for a school, in which case there would be many people capable of contributing those amounts. Along these lines, SEG 17.823 (= *AGRW* 307) records peer-benefactions of 6–28 drachmae (160–1120 USD?) in order to build a synagogue in Egypt in the first century CE.

What might we speculate about benefactions to Pauline associations? Obviously, Pauline associations almost certainly did not receive benefactions sufficient to fund the erection or renovation of buildings (along with bricks, columns, patios, etc.), or the execution of sacrifices (the office of *orgeones*, the execution of *leitourgiai*). A reading of the Corinthian letters reveals four areas in which Pauline associations could conceivably have benefited from acts of generosity, whether from members or not: meeting space, travel, service as treasurer, and meals.[53]

---

52. On the cultural thirst for honor, manifested in a wide variety of ways, see Carlin A. Barton, *Roman Honor: The Fire in the Bones* (Berkeley: University of California Press, 2001); Zeba A. Crook, "Honor, Shame, and Social Status Revisited," *Journal of Biblical Literature* 128, no. 3 (2009): 591–611; Jerome H. Neyrey, *Honor and Shame in the Gospel of Matthew* (Louisville, KY: Westminster John Knox, 1998); Peregrine Horden and Nicholas Purcell, *The Corrupting Sea: A Study of Mediterranean History* (Oxford: Wiley-Blackwell, 2000); Bruce J. Malina, *The New Testament World: Insights from Cultural Anthropology* (Louisville, KY: Westminster John Knox, 1993); Unni Wikan, "Shame and Honour: A Contestable Pair," *Man (New Series)* 19 (1984): 635–52.

53. It is sometimes claimed that Paul rejected the honor-based agonistic conventions of patronage and that patrons of Christ-associations would have found their expectations of the standard expressions of reciprocity frustrated by Paul's egalitarian tendencies. See L. W. Countryman, "Patrons and Officers in Club and Church," in *Society of Biblical Literature 1977 Seminar Papers*, ed.

Obviously, Christ followers in Corinth needed places to meet. Romans 16.23 suggests that Corinthian Christ followers met regularly in several small locations and occasionally in a larger place hosted by Gaius. Phoebe's association in Cenchreae is another association with a patron (*prostatis*) providing space. Stephanas's household is also named: is this because Stephanas also hosted meetings? After all, we are told that Stephanas devoted himself "to the service of the saints" (1 Cor 16:15). Perhaps hosting meetings in his home was one of those services.[54] Acts also contains several references to people sharing their homes with Christ followers: Lydia (Acts 16:14–15); Jason (Acts 17:5–7); Prisca and Aquila (Acts 18:2–3; 1 Cor 16:19; Rom 16:3–5). Providing space for meeting was therefore an act of generosity to the group.

In addition, a good deal of travel happens to and from Corinth, not least of which is Paul's own travel. It is possible that he was always able to make enough money in locations in which he stopped to work to pay his own expenses for travel to his next destination, yet he does express gratitude to people: to Phoebe, whom he identifies as a patron (Rom 16:2), and to Prisca and Aquila, who risked their necks (Rom 16:3–4). It is not inconceivable that Paul's travel was subsidized by acts of patronage.

Yet, Paul was not the only one who traveled. Consider Stephanas: he appears in Ephesus with Fortunatus and Achaicus (1 Cor 16:17). It is unclear who these latter two men are, what their relationship is to Stephanas, and why they came along, but it is clear that Paul is happy to see them all since he names them all. There are many possibilities for imagining how this travel fits within the framework of generosity, and on all of them, someone benefits: Stephanas if his travel was funded by a benefactor of the group, Fortunatus and Achaicus if Stephanas paid their way, and Paul benefits regardless of who paid because of his delight at the visit. Likewise, Chloe's "people" travel to find Paul in Ephesus, surely at Chloe's expense (1 Cor 1:11). Phoebe carries the letter to the Romans from Corinth to Rome, surely at her own expense and much to the benefit of Paul. Paul, and perhaps in some

---

Paul J. Achtemeier, SBLSP 11 (Atlanta: Scholars Press, 1977), 135–43; Longenecker, *Remember the Poor*, 266–67; David G. Horrell, *The Social Ethos of the Corinthian Correspondence: Interests and Ideology from 1 Corinthians to 1 Clement* (Edinburgh: T&T Clark, 1996), 155; Meeks, *First Urban Christians*, 78; Peter Lampe, "Paul, Patrons, and Clients," in *Paul in the Greco-Roman World: A Handbook*, ed. J. Paul Sampley (Harrisburg, PA: Trinity Press International, 2003), 495. Such a claim is, however, simply not consistent with the evidence, namely that Paul *does* use the language of patronage and reciprocity.

54. Peter Lampe ("Paul, Patrons, and Clients," 496) thinks space for meetings was provided by Stephanas, as well as (more speculatively) Titius Justus and Crispus.

shape the Christ associations, benefits from all this travel. Thus, the funding and self-funding of travel in support of Paul and in support of communication between Paul and the associations ought to be considered a benefaction. Perhaps this is what inspires Paul to request that Stephanas be given due recognition (1 Cor 16:17).

Thirdly, there is the matter of the collection. Treasurers were highly valued by associations, and their honesty even more so. Paul was conducting a collection for Jerusalem, so it seems almost certain that someone was serving as treasurer, as much to monitor as to protect the money that was collected. We cannot, of course, know for certain whether the collection was monitored by a treasurer, and if so, whether the treasurer worked *gratis*, but there is evidence that Paul was aware of the need to assure people that the money was being adequately overseen.[55]

Finally, there is the question of the meals. John Kloppenborg's recent analysis of the inscriptions and papyri concludes that it is extremely unlikely that food for meals was provided by a single benefactor. There is no evidence that a single benefactor ever provided regular meals for an association, and this is so despite the fact that these meals could involve only very simple fare (e.g., the Lanuvium association for Diana and Antinous offered bread that cost two asses, as well as four sardines and warm water; *CIL* XIV 2112). Two aspects of early Christian meals all but rule out the possibility of a single benefactor: that Christ-followers met far more often than did other associations, and that there was enough food and wine for members to be drunk and full (1 Cor 11:21). Taken together, the cost of providing weekly meals this large would have been prohibitive and "has no historical analogy" in antiquity.[56]

Conclusion and Future Questions

The conclusions we can draw at this point are necessarily nuanced and qualified: the possibly ES4–5 members of the Pauline associations in Corinth possibly gave to the groups in the arenas of space, travel, and service but probably not meals. Perhaps these people also contributed the most generously to the collection. We cannot know for certain, but there seems sufficient material in the letters to support reasonable

55. John S. Kloppenborg, "Early Christian Occupations: Rethinking Pauline Poverty," in *Gender, Social Roles and Occupations in the New Testament World*, ed. Antti Marjanen (Leiden: Brill, forthcoming).

56. John S. Kloppenborg, "Precedence at the Communal Meal in Corinth," *Novum Testamentum* 58, no. 2 (2016): 13.

speculation, and the analogy provided to other associations supports such speculation.

On the question of generosity and reciprocity to the Pauline associations, particularly as these intersect with economy, there are two areas that invite consideration in future work: the way Paul names members and calls for them to be honored, and the question of membership fees. Calling attention to certain people by name functions as a form of honor, even when it is not accompanied by the call to honor those people (1 Cor 16:17). It is certain that Paul does not name *all* the members of his associations; it is also certain that many of the people he does name he names because they have done or provided something worth acknowledging. Therefore, it is clear that naming people, drawing attention to them among members, and in addition asking, as he often does, that those people be acknowledged, all function as an ascription of honor and the discharge of reciprocity.

This practice appears to function analogously to the erection of public inscriptions, at least in so far as it functions in the domain of distributed honor.[57] Many of those named in Paul's letters are obviously the more elite members of the associations, signified by their possessions: they have a house and/or slaves, they provide service, they travel, or they were/are in possession of an office. There are some people who are named and about whom we know nothing (like Fortunatus and Achaicus who come to Ephesus with Stephanas, or many of those named in Romans 16), but for the most part, Paul names the people of import in his communities. It is likely safe to say that Paul uses naming in order to draw honorable attention to people who in his estimation deserve it. In fact, 1 Corinthians 16:15–20 reads like an honorary inscription in which those named are ranked in order of elite status or honor accrued.

A second fruitful line of inquiry concerns fees paid for membership in the Pauline associations. Scholars should be more open than ever to the idea that entry into Paul's associations required a membership fee. In the older, romantic portrait of the first Christians as the poorest of the poor, a notion like membership fees was unimaginable. There is also much theological currency and investment in the notion that Paul's groups were universal and that membership fees would work against that identity. This is not, however, a reason to reject thinking about membership fees. Rather than assume that Paul's groups were

---

57. I prefer the term "distributed honor" over Malina's "acquired honor" because it emphasizes the agency and control of the public court of reputation; see Crook, "Honor, Shame," 591–611.

entirely *sui generis*, which one must assume in order to reject out of hand a conversation about membership fees, we should work with the available evidence, which suggests that membership fees for associations were universal and that they were not much of a limiting factor for membership.

The inscriptions reveal that membership fees were often low enough to allow those who were far from wealthy to join, and some associations had different fee levels depending on one's social status and economic means. Nor is it reasonable any longer to assume that members of Christ-following associations could never have afforded a membership fee. We know that members of the Pauline associations enjoyed some degree of financial surplus, otherwise the collection could not have been a possibility, let alone resulted in contributions that apparently pleased Paul. This is a second reason we cannot discount out of hand the possibility of membership fees for Paul's associations.

Select Bibliography

Arnaoutoglou, Ilias. "Associations and Patronage in Ancient Athens." *Ancient Society* 25 (1994): 5–17.

Ascough, Richard S., Philip A. Harland, and John S. Kloppenborg. *Associations in the Greco-Roman World: A Sourcebook*. Waco, TX: Baylor University Press, 2012.

Barclay, John M. G. "Money and Meetings: Group Formation among Diaspora Jews and Early Christians." In *Vereine, Synagogen und Gemeinden im Kaiserzeitlichen Kleinasien*, edited by Andreas Gutsfeld and Dietrich-Alex Koch, 113–28. Tübingen: Mohr Siebeck, 2006.

Bendlin, Andreas. "Associations, Funerals, Sociality, and Roman Law: The Collegium of Diana and Antinous in Lanuvium (CIL 14.2112) Reconsidered." In *Aposteldekret und antikes Vereinswesen: Gemeinschaft und ihre Ordnung*, edited by Markus Öhler, 207–96. Tübingen: Mohr Siebeck, 2011.

Danker, Frederick W. *Benefactor: Epigraphic Study of a Graeco-Roman Semantic Field*. St. Louis, MO: Clayton Publishing House, 1982.

Duncan-Jones, Richard. *The Economy of the Roman Empire: Quantitative Studies*. Cambridge: Cambridge University Press, 1982.

Friesen, Steven. "Poverty in Pauline Studies: Beyond the So-Called New Consensus." *JSNT* 26, no. 3 (2004): 323–61.

Garnsey, Peter, and Richard P. Saller. *The Roman Empire: Economy, Society, and Culture*. Berkeley: University of California Press, 1987.

Harland, Philip A. *Greco-Roman Associations: Texts, Translations, and Commentary II. North Coast of the Black Sea, Asia Minor.* Berlin: De Gruyter, 2014.

Kloppenborg, John S., and Richard S. Ascough. *Greco-Roman Associations: Texts, Translations, and Commentary I. Attica, Central Greece, Macedonia, Thrace.* Berlin: De Gruyter, 2011.

Longenecker, Bruce W. *Remember the Poor: Paul, Poverty, and the Greco-Roman World.* Grand Rapids: Eerdmans, 2010.

_____., and Kelly D. Liebengood, eds. *Engaging Economics: New Testament Scenarios and Early Christian Reception.* Grand Rapids: Eerdmans, 2009.

MacMullen, Ramsay. *Roman Social Relations, 50 B.C. to A.D. 284.* New Haven, CT: Yale University Press, 1974.

Nijf, Onno van. *The Civic World of Professional Associations in the Roman East.* Amsterdam: J. C. Gieben, 1997.

Saller, Richard P. *Personal Patronage under the Early Empire.* New York: Cambridge University Press, 1982.

Scheidel, Walter, and Steven J. Friesen. "The Size of the Economy and the Distribution of Income in the Roman Empire." *JRS* 99 (2009): 61–91.

Wallace-Hadrill, Andrew, ed. *Patronage in Ancient Society.* London: Routledge, 1989.

Zuiderhoek, Arjan. *The Politics of Munificence in the Roman Empire: Citizens, Elites, and Benefactors in Asia Minor. Greek Culture in the Roman World.* Cambridge: Cambridge University Press, 2009.

8

Food and Drink in the Greco-Roman World and in the Pauline Communities

John T. Fitzgerald

Inasmuch as eating and drinking are activities typically associated with daily life, it is hardly surprising that references to food and drink occur frequently in the Bible and in literature from the ancient Mediterranean world.[1] The same is true of related activities, such as the planting and harvesting of crops, the collecting of honey, the hunting of game, the breeding and tending of domesticated animals, the catching of fish and other marine life, the pressing of oil, the baking of bread, the making and marketing of wine, the selling and purchasing of food items in the market, cooking, the preparation and serving of meals, and the consumption of a wide array of foodstuffs in family meals as

---

1. For a general survey of food and drink in world history, see Maguelonne Toussaint-Samat, *A History of Food*, trans. A. Bell (Oxford: Blackwell, 1992). See also Jean-Louis Flandrin and Massimo Montanari, eds., *Food: A Cultural History from Antiquity to the Present*, English ed. Albert Sonnenfeld, trans. Clarissa Botsford et al., European Perspectives (New York: Columbia University Press, 1999).

well as at banquets. The scarcity of food and drink in certain situations, such as famine or invasion by a hostile foreign power, can be noted, as well as the voluntary abstinence from food when fasting. Conversely, an abundance of consumable items often appears in descriptions of feasts and in apocalyptic visions and prophetic depictions of renewal and restoration.

Food and drink have many different connotations. Food is often an important marker of social status, with certain prestige foods associated with the elite and other foods associated with the poor.[2] Whereas the rich in the ancient world could dine on "elegant eatables" (*epulasque lautiores*; Statius, *Silvae* 1.6.32), drink the "finest wines" (*lautissima vina*; Pliny, *Naturalis historia* 14.92), and enjoy other expensive food items that had snob appeal, "a poor man's dinner," as the legend on a decorated lamp from Aquileia puts it, consisted of "bread, wine, and black radish."[3] Yet the beggar's food was even more meager. In Aristophanes's *Plutus*, Beggary (Πτωχεία) and Poverty (Πενία) are depicted as sisters (*Plut.* 549), and begging here involves eating "not bread, but mallow shoots, not cake but withered radish leaves" (*Plut.* 543–44 [Kovacs, LCL]). Begging was "the most socially stigmatized form of poverty" and was widespread, being "an everyday occurrence" in cities like Rome.[4] It also was common in places like Roman Palestine, with the *tamhui* (soup kitchen) and the *quppa* (charity fund) being rabbinic institutional responses to the problems of poverty and the hunger associated with it.[5]

Food and drink were also features of identity in the ancient world. What one ate and drank, as well as what one refrained from eating and drinking, contributed to how individuals and groups defined and understood themselves, how they viewed others, and how they were perceived by other individuals and groups. In certain cases, commensality restrictions related to food and drink also served to create and maintain social boundaries that heightened ethnic, philosophical, and religious identity. Food in antiquity functioned conspicuously in identity formation, in the maintenance of social boundaries, and in shaping images of otherness in early and rabbinic Judaism; it played an impor-

---

2. On food as indicative of social status, see Peter Garnsey, *Food and Society in Classical Antiquity* (Cambridge: Cambridge University Press, 1999), 5–7, 113–38.

3. Mireille Corbier, "The Broad Bean and the Moray: Social Hierarchies and Food in Rome," in Flandrin and Montanari, *Food*, 128.

4. Johannes Hahn, "Beggars," in *Brill's New Pauly: Encyclopaedia of the Ancient World*, ed. Hubert Cancik, 22 vols. (Leiden: Brill, 2002–11), 2:578–80.

5. See esp. Gregg E. Gardner, *The Origins of Organized Charity in Rabbinic Judaism* (New York: Cambridge University Press, 2015), 84–138.

tant role in ancient Christianity and early and medieval Islam as well.[6] Furthermore, food can also function within a given religion or group to create and maintain socioeconomic differences. For instance, Gregg Gardner has shown how Tannaitic texts "create and maintain social distance between the poor and the non-poor" in that "the texts advocate commensality *among the poor*, but not commensality *between the poor and non-poor*."[7]

Dining was a conspicuous feature of social life in the Greco-Roman world, not only of family life but also the various voluntary associations, with members eating and drinking together on various occasions.[8] Food was also closely associated with friendship at all social levels, with friends not only dining together but also exchanging gifts that consisted of items of food and drink. In relationships involving patronage, the *sportulae*, or gifts that patrons gave to clients, often consisted of food items placed in a small basket (*sportula*). Eating and drinking also played a prominent role in the ancient economy, with food and drink sold in markets, purchased at bakery shops and other food outlets, and consumed at pubs, bars, and temples with dining facilities, and with various occupations associated with food and drink. In imperial Rome, for example, there were at least fourteen non-slave occupations that involved the selling of food and drink, including green grocers, fruit salesmen, fishmongers, meat dealers, and wine merchants, and those involved in the food industry included the small vendor operating a booth as well as shopkeepers with considerable stock.[9]

Biblical scholarship is increasingly giving attention to both food and drink and the contexts in which they are consumed, and this will doubtless continue to be the case for the foreseeable future.[10] Given

---

6. Jordan D. Rosenblum, *Food and Identity in Early Rabbinic Judaism* (New York: Cambridge University Press, 2010), and David M. Freidenreich, *Foreigners and Their Food: Constructing Otherness in Jewish, Christian, and Islamic Law* (Berkeley: University of California Press, 2011).

7. Gregg E. Gardner, "Let Them Eat Fish: Food for the Poor in Early Rabbinic Judaism," *JSJ* 45, no. 2 (2014): 267–68 (emphasis his), and see also 270: "Thus, the rabbinic prescriptions reinforce the signs of poverty, stigmatizing the poor and reinforcing social separation between the haves and the have-nots. On the Sabbath, distinction and division are created and maintained by separate seating, so to speak. The well-off rabbis eat the requisite foods at the requisite three meals at their own tables, while the poor eat among themselves, consuming the food given to them by the soup kitchen."

8. See the index in Richard S. Ascough, Philip A. Harland, and John S. Kloppenborg, *Associations in the Greco-Roman World: A Sourcebook* (Waco, TX: Baylor University Press, 2012), 379.

9. Susan Treggiari, "Urban Labour in Rome: *Mercenarii* and *Tabernarii*," in *Non-Slave Labour in the Greco-Roman World*, ed. Peter Garnsey (Cambridge: Cambridge Philological Society, 1980), 48–64.

10. For brief surveys of food and drink in scholarship devoted to the Hebrew Bible, early Judaism, and classical rabbinic literature, see Andrew T. Abernethy, *Eating in Isaiah: Approaching the Role of Food and Drink in Isaiah's Structure and Message*, BibInt 131 (Leiden: Brill, 2014), 1–10; and David Kraemer, "Food, Eating, and Meals," in *The Oxford Handbook of Jewish Daily Life in Roman Palestine*, ed.

the breadth of food and drink as a topic in the ancient world and the burgeoning scholarly literature on it, any essay dealing with food and drink in the Greco-Roman world and in the Pauline communities must necessarily be selective, and this treatment is no exception. The following discussion is divided into five unequal parts. The first part is a general introduction to the economics of food and drink in antiquity. The second part provides an overview of drink in the Greco-Roman world and in the Pauline churches, and the third part does the same for food. The fourth part focuses on meat as a religious and economic issue and profiles how three different New Testament scholars have viewed it as a subject in Paul's letters, especially 1 Corinthians. The fifth and final part offers twelve observations and suggestions regarding meat as an economic issue in the Greco-Roman world and in Paul's communities.

The Economics of Food and Drink

As is the case today, there were economic aspects of all foodstuffs in the ancient Mediterranean world, and Columella, who flourished in the mid-50s of the first century CE, claimed that food was more expensive in his own time than it had been previously, when "the poor had a more generous diet" (*De re rustica* 10.1.1 [Ash, LCL]). The increase in wealth, especially in expendable cash, and the pursuit of culinary pleasures had impacted the price of foodstuffs in the market, and this escalation in prices had adversely affected the diet of the poor:

> Very soon, when subsequent ages, and particularly our own, set up an extravagant scale of expenditure on the pleasure of the table, and meals were regarded as occasions not for satisfying men's natural desires but for the display of wealth, the poverty of the common people, forced to abstain from the more costly foods, is reduced to an ordinary fare (*Rust.* 10.1.2 [Ash, LCL]).

Even apart from the impact of conspicuous consumption on market prices, some foods had long been luxury items and thus were quite expensive. As early as the mid-fourth century BCE, the culinary poet Archestratus of Gela wrote his *Life of Pleasure* (ἡδυπάθεια) after conducting a culinary tour of the Mediterranean.[11]

Catherine Hezser (Oxford: Oxford University Press, 2010), 403–19. A recent addition to this area of research is by Kurtis Peters, *Hebrew Lexical Semantics and Daily Life in Ancient Israel: What's Cooking in Biblical Hebrew?*, BibInt 146 (Leiden: Brill, 2016).

11. Athenaeus, *Deipnosophistae* 728d–e (Olson, LCL). On Archestratus, see esp. S. Douglas Olson and Alexander Sens, eds./trans., *Archestratos of Gela: Greek Culture and Cuisine in the Fourth Century BCE:*

Driven by his love of pleasure, this Archestratus made a careful circuit of the entire earth and sea because, it seems, he wanted to inquire painstakingly into matters associated with the belly; and just like individuals who write accounts of their travels by land or sea, he wishes to furnish accurate information about everything as to "where each item of food and drink is best."[12]

This work was the epicure's guide to luxurious food, with an emphasis on highly prized fish, which were to be prepared in simple ways that are suggestive of modern *nouvelle cuisine*.[13] At the same time, the close connection between luxurious dining and sexual activity that appears in a number of Greco-Roman texts was also a conspicuous aspect of the work and made it notorious.[14] The Stoic philosopher Chrysippus identified it as a work that encouraged "sex and partying,"[15] and he was clearly not the only one who thought so.[16]

In that connection, it should be noted that certain kinds of foods had the reputation of being what Menander (frg. 351.11) called ὑποβινητιῶντα βρώματα (aphrodisiac foods).[17] Hyacinth bulbs and oysters were among the foods believed to be aphrodisiacs (Athenaeus, *Deipnosophistae* 2.63e–64a, 8.356c), whereas other foods, such as chaste-tree seeds or the red mullet fish, were thought of as anaphrodisiacs and were consumed to prevent or curb sexual desire.[18] Theophrastus, for example, devotes a section of his *Historia plantarum* (*Enquiry into Plants*) to fertility and antifertility plants and herbs (9.18.3–11) and notes that some items, such as orchid bulbs, could have both effects, functioning either to arouse or to diminish sexual urges (*Hist. plant.* 9.18.4). Needless to say, owing to male fantasizing, some plants achieved notoriety as an aphrodisiac, even when they were not consumed:

Text, Translation, and Commentary (Oxford: Oxford University Press, 2000). The work, commonly translated as the *Life of Luxury*, was also known by the titles *Gastronomy* and the *Science of Dining* (Athenaeus, *Deipn.* 1.4e).

12. Athenaeus, *Deipn.* 7.278d; the line quoted by Athenaeus is from Archestratus, frg. 3, Olson-Sens.

13. For this point, see esp. John Wilkins and Shaun Hill, trans., *Archestratus: Fragments from the Life of Luxury: A Modern English Translation with Introduction and Commentary*, rev. ed. (Totnes, UK: Prospect Books, 2011).

14. Athenaeus, *Deipn.* 8.335b, 9.384b.

15. *SVF* 3.199 = Athenaeus, *Deipn.* 8.335d.

16. Even mentioning his name could provide an incentive to questionable conduct. See, for example, Athenaeus, *Deipn.* 8.335e (Olson, LCL): "But you, by repeatedly mentioning this Archestratus, filled our party with ugly behavior. For what possible source of ruin was omitted by this noble epic poet, the most notorious aspirant to the life-style of Sardanapallus?"

17. See also Athenaeus, *Deipn.* 4.132f, 12.517a.

18. Andrew Dalby, *Food and Drink in the Ancient World from A to Z* (London: Routledge, 2003), 14.

> Most marvelous is the plant which Indos had; they said that it keeps the penis hard, not by ingesting the plant, but using it for anointing; the power of this plant is so great that one can have sex with as many women as one likes—those who use it say as many as twelve. Indos himself—he was big and strong—actually said that he once had sex seventy times, but his semen came out drop by drop, and finally he drew out blood. Besides, women are considerably more eager when they use this drug (Theophrastus, *Hist. plant.* 9.18.9).[19]

Other foods, by contrast, had no sexual connotations and were relatively cheap and thus often served as staple items in the diet of the poor. Products made from cereal grains, especially breads, porridges, and cakes, were such staple items, and they likely supplied anywhere from 50 to 75 percent of the average Mediterranean diet.[20] That bread played a major role in the ancient diet (where the consumption of animal proteins was minimal for most people) is in keeping with the high probability that "a large proportion of the population of ancient Italy throughout Roman times must have been engaged in small-scale or even subsistence farming."[21] The same is true for many other areas of the ancient Mediterranean world and for other societies throughout history where subsistence agriculture is involved.[22]

19. The translation is that of John Scarborough, "Drugs and Drug Lore in the Time of Theophrastus: Folklore, Magic, Botany, Philosophy and the Rootcutters," *Acta Classica* 49 (2006): 20. Theophrastus himself was quite skeptical of such putative effects, saying, "This power, if true, is excessive." It should be noted that A. F. Hort did not include a translation of this section (Theophrastus, *Historia plantarum* 9.18.3–11) in his LCL translation of the work. Athenaeus, *Deipn.* 1.18d, refers to this passage.

20. Magen Broshi ("The Diet of Palestine in the Roman Period: Introductory Notes." in *Bread, Wine, Walls and Scrolls,* JSPSup36 [Sheffield: Sheffield Academic Press, 2001], 123) suggests 50–53 percent, whereas L. Foxhall and H. A. Forbes ("Σιτομετρεία: The Role of Grain as a Staple Food in Classical Antiquity," *Chiron* 12 [1982]: 41–90, esp. 74) suggest 70–75 percent for the Roman Empire as a whole. The higher percentages suggested by Foxhall and Forbes correspond to the findings of G. Fornaciari and F. Mallegni ("Palaeonutrional Studies on Skeletal Remains of Ancient Populations from the Mediterranean Area: An Attempt to Interpretation," *Anthropologischer Anzeiger* 45, no. 4 [December 1987]: 367–68), who characterize Athens as having an agricultural economy from the early Iron Age through the Roman Age (more than a millennium) and only developing a mixed economy and diet in the Byzantine period. For problems with Broshi's figure of 50 percent, see Kraemer, "Food, Eating, and Meals," 405. For the argument that "the common view that the Roman diet largely consisted of cereals is incompatible with prevailing estimates of oil and wine consumption" and thus needs to be lowered, see Willem M. Jongman, "The Early Roman Empire: Consumption," in *The Cambridge Economic History of the Greco-Roman World,* ed. Walter Scheidel, Ian Morris, and Richard Saller (Cambridge: Cambridge University Press, 2007), 604.

21. Joan M. Frayn, "Subsistence Farming in Italy during the Roman Period: A Preliminary Discussion of the Evidence," *Greece and Rome* 21, no. 1 (1974): 11. See also Joan M. Frayn, *Subsistence Farming in Roman Italy* (London: Centaur, 1979).

22. On agricultural progress measured in grain equivalents, see Colin Clark and Margaret Haswell, *The Economics of Subsistence Agriculture,* 3rd ed. (London: Macmillan, 1967), 53–77. Wheat yields in ancient Greece appear to have been less than those in Babylon, Egypt, and Sicily (ibid., 87).

Some food items were produced primarily as feed for animals but could also be consumed by humans, especially the poor and the more affluent who found themselves in desperate circumstances.[23] A biblical example of this would be "carob pods," which came from the carob tree (χεράτιον).[24] The pods were typically "thick and flat (about five or six inches long and one inch wide)" and had a "sweet-tasting pulp."[25] They were often used for medicinal purposes,[26] and in rabbinic Judaism, the consumption of carob pods was sometimes symbolically associated with repentance.[27] One of their main uses was as feed to fatten swine.[28] The latter usage appears in the parable of the "prodigal son," who, accustomed to the more appealing and nutritious fare of his father's table, became so famished that he desired to gorge himself with carob pods (Luke 15:16).

In short, the price of food and drink spanned the economic spectrum, with luxurious and exotic items being the most expensive and items belonging to the staples of the Greco-Roman diet being less expensive. What people ate and drank depended on a plethora of factors, including their financial resources, their dietary preferences and restrictions, the various occasions when they dined, and the kind of lifestyle that they voluntarily or involuntarily led. As such factors suggest, economic factors were only one aspect of food and drink. There were many other aspects, such as the religious and ethical. Some people (such as Pythagoras) and groups (such as the Jewish community) refrained from the consumption of certain foods because of philosophical or religious considerations. But even among those who had no such dietary restrictions, eating and drinking were often viewed from an ethical or hedonistic standpoint.

For example, Alexis, a poet of middle and new comedy, in one gnome celebrates eating, drinking, and sex as the three key activities that

---

23. The cost of fodder was also a factor in what was used to feed animals; see Columella, *De re rustica* 7.3.22, 8.5.25.

24. In Latin, the carob tree is called the *Siliqua Graeca* or sometimes simply *siliqua* (Pliny the Elder, *Naturalis historia* 15.95). The Greek word is also sometimes transliterated into Latin as *ceratium* (Columella, *De arboribus* 25).

25. Ceslas Spicq, "χεράτιον," in *Theological Lexicon of the New Testament*, trans./ed. by J. D. Ernest, 3 vols. (Peabody, MA: Hendrickson, 1994), 2:311. See also Pliny, *Nat.* 15.95 (Rackham, LCL, slightly modified): "The extremely sweet carob . . . is no longer than a man's finger, and occasionally curved like a sickle, and it has the thickness of a man's thumb."

26. Pliny, *Nat.* 23.151, and Spicq, "χεράτιον," 2:312.

27. Lev. Rab. 35:6 (132c). For other rabbinic symbolism connected with the carob, see Judith Z. Abrams, *A Beginner's Guide to the Steinsaltz Talmud* (Northvale, NJ: Aronson, 1999), 30; and for the story of Honi the Circle-Maker and the carob, b. Ta'an. 23a.

28. On carob pods as feed for pigs, see Columella, *Rust.* 7.9.6.

are conducive to pleasure.[29] Over against this understanding, Plutarch, who condemned this viewpoint as the kind of licentiousness (ἀκολασία) that encouraged self-indulgence, quotes Socrates to the effect that "base men live to eat and drink, and good men eat and drink to live."[30] A similar saying is also attributed to Socrates by Diogenes Laertius, who quotes it in a *chreia* about a dinner hosted by Socrates and his wife Xanthippe:

> He had invited some rich men and, when Xanthippe said she felt ashamed of the dinner, "Never mind," said he, "for if they are reasonable they will put up with it, and if they are good for nothing, we shall not trouble ourselves about them." He would say that the rest of the world lived to eat, while he himself ate to live.[31]

Clement of Alexandria endorsed this same sentiment, attributing it to Christ as the Instructor: "Some men, in truth, live that they may eat, as the irrational creatures, 'whose life is their belly, and nothing else.' But the Instructor enjoins us to eat that we may live" (*Paedagogus* 2.1 [Coxe, ANF]).[32] And it was on this basis that Clement gave extended advice on eating (2.1), drinking (2.2), the vessels to be used when dining (2.3), and conduct when dining (2.4), including laughter (2.5), language (2.6), and other matters. Food and drink were never simply economic matters but entailed a variety of other issues.

Drink in the Greco-Roman World and the Pauline Churches

Wine was the most common beverage of the Greco-Roman world, ideally sipped mixed with water and frequently artificially flavored so as to correspond to preferences in regard to taste and to the kind of food that was served or consumed. It belonged on the average shopper's "grocery list" in antiquity, with many people beginning to consume it even as young children. The chief economic issue concerning

---

29. Alexis, frg. 273 Kock = frg. 271 Arnott. See W. Geoffrey Arnott, ed., *Alexis, The Fragments: A Commentary*, CCTC 31 (Cambridge: Cambridge University Press, 1996), 762–64. See Plutarch, *Quomodo adolescens poetas audire debeat* 21d–e and *De virtute morali* 445e.
30. Plutarch, *Adol. poet. aud.* 21e (Babbitt, LCL). See also Musonius Rufus (frg. 18): "Therefore it is fitting for us to eat in order to live, not in order to have pleasure, if, at all events, we wish to keep in line with the wise words of Socrates, who said that the majority of men live to eat but that he ate in order to live." The translation is that of Cora E. Lutz, *Musonius Rufus: "The Roman Socrates"* (New Haven, CT: Yale University Press, 1947), 119.
31. Diogenes Laertius, *Vit. phil.* 2.34 (Hicks, LCL).
32. Inasmuch as Clement used Musonius Rufus as an unacknowledged source of material, he likely derived this saying from Musonius (frg. 18) but transferred it from Socrates to Jesus. See note 30 above.

wine was its price, which ranged from very expensive to cheap. People's choice of wine reflected both their pocketbook and the occasion on which it was to be consumed. Cheaper wines were abundantly available, so price was not a deterrent to the consumption of wine. Serving a lower-grade wine to a wealthy person or patron accustomed to finer wines might be socially awkward, but it was certainly done. Corinthian wine had a horrible reputation, with Alexis (frg. 290 Kock) claiming that drinking wine from Corinth was "torture," by which Athenaeus (*Deipn.* 1.30f) understood him to mean that it was "harsh" to drink.

Most Jews drank wine, especially at functions such as weddings (John 2:1–11) and on holy days such as the Sabbath (Persius, *Satirae* 5.183–84; Plutarch, *Quaestionum convivialum libri IX* 4.6.2, 671e–672c), and its consumption at Passover is certain as early as the Book of Jubilees (49:6). "Beer," by contrast, "was little known and generally disliked in Greece and Rome," though it is also clear that it was popular in ancient Mesopotamia and Egypt and that Roman soldiers enjoyed drinking it.[33] In the Greco-Roman world, it was often viewed as barbaric, with the modern contrast between refined connoisseurs of wine and beer-guzzling barbarians thus having its roots in antiquity. Another drink enjoyed by Roman soldiers was *posca*, a cheap vinegar-based beverage mixed with water that one scholar has dubbed "the Coca-Cola of the Roman army."[34]

Milk was chiefly used in making cheese (which sometimes functioned as a meat substitute; Martial, *Epigrammata* 13.31) and was never a major beverage in its own right in the cities of the Greco-Roman world, largely because of the problems posed by the need for refrigeration to prevent it from spoiling. As a consequence, "the drinking of fresh milk was a luxury shared by farmers and nomadic shepherds with those in cities and royal courts who were rich enough to pay for express delivery."[35] That those in the country did indeed drink milk is stated explicitly by Columella:

> Then, too, it is the sheep which not only satisfies the hunger of the country folk with cheese and milk in abundance but also embellishes the tables of people of taste with a variety of agreeable dishes. Indeed to some tribes, who have no corn, the sheep provides their diet; hence most

---

33. Dalby, *Food and Drink*, 50.
34. Corbier, "Broad Bean," 131. This is the ὄξος (sour or vinegar wine) offered to Jesus in the passion narratives of the canonical gospels (Matt 27:48 and parallels).
35. Ibid., 217.

of the nomadic tribes and the Getae are called the "Milk-Drinkers" (*Rust.* 7.2.1 2).[36]

There is, however, some evidence to suggest that milk was occasionally hawked on the streets of Rome. Calpurnius Siculus, a pastoral poet usually dated to the time of Nero, refers to the shepherd Corydon giving instructions to his brother, "Loud in the cry through your city carry your milk for sale" (*Eclogues* 4.25–26 [Duff and Duff, LCL]). But this commercial activity is depicted as being unusual and untraditional, prompted by hunger and financial desperation. This "materialistic concern" was new, influenced by georgic interests, and "alien to Theocritean, Greek post-Theocritean, and Vergilian pastoral idealism."[37]

In any event, when it was consumed as a beverage, the milk came chiefly from sheep, goats, and cows, and occasionally from asses and mares.[38] The major exception to the preceding statements about milk is breast milk from a human mother or nurse, which was readily given to infants. Those whose drinking habits did not conform to the cultural norm of wine usually restricted themselves to the drinking of water, with Demosthenes the most famous "water-only" drinker from the Greek world, and he makes it clear that his rejection of wine was viewed by his peers as antisocial (*Or.* 19.46; *Philippica ii* 2.29).

Not unexpectedly, we have evidence for the consumption of wine by members of the Pauline churches (1 Cor 11:21), but not for beer or for other drinks. Milk is mentioned twice in Paul's letters, once in conjunction with his depiction of the Corinthians as infants still being nursed and not yet ready for solid food (1 Cor 3:2). Milk here is breast milk, not milk from animals. In the other reference, he speaks of the person tending a flock getting some of the milk produced (1 Cor 9:7). This reference permits the possibility that his argument presupposes the consumption of milk as a beverage, but using the milk for the making of cheese would be another option.

In the genuine letters of Paul, the chief issue concerning wine was mainly the problem of intoxication, which was linked to an array of vices (such as sexual immorality) and social problems (such as lawsuits). Abstinence from wine arises only in Romans 14:21, where Paul says that if one's consumption of wine causes a fellow believer to stum-

---

36. On the use of milk in the making of cheese, see Columella, *Rust.* 7.8.1–3, 6–7; on the making of sour milk, see 12.8.1–3. See also 5.12.–2, 7.12.12–13, etc.
37. Evangelos Karakasis, *Song Exchange in Roman Pastoral*, Trends in Classics 5 (Berlin: de Gruyter, 2011), 250.
38. Dalby, *Food and Drink*, 217.

ble spiritually, it is good to refrain from doing so. The problem of intoxication was a continuing one for his churches after Paul's death and is thus addressed in the Deutero-Pauline letters of Ephesians and the Pastoral Epistles, with those prone to drunkenness debarred from holding ecclesiastical office (Titus 1:6–7), and the author of Titus (2:3–5) using the cultural stereotype of the "old drunken woman" in offering instruction to older women. In addition, drink along with food arises as an issue in Colossians (2:16), where at least some types of foods and drinks are prohibited (2:23). In 1 Timothy, the author warns against heretics who demand "abstinence from foods" (4:3), which apparently includes wine. Timothy, who is abstaining from wine, is encouraged to switch to wine for medicinal purposes (1 Tim 5:23), a directive that would have been seconded by physicians, who often recommended the consumption of wine to their patients.[39]

Food in the Greco-Roman World and in Pauline Communities

As the New Testament suggests and subsequent early Christian literature confirms, issues of food and drink were an ongoing concern for various groups in the Roman Empire. There were also practices related to foods, such as fasting, which Acts attributes to both Paul and churches in the Pauline orbit, including Antioch (Acts 13:2–3, 14:23, see also 27:9), but it is not mentioned in the Pauline corpus, unless 2 Corinthians 6:5 ("hunger") is so understood.

As far as food is concerned, the ancient Mediterranean "diet was based on cereals, legumes, oil, and wine."[40] Cereals, which provided carbohydrates, were the core of the diet, with wheat and barley (except in Egypt) the most popular of the cereals (Herodotus, *Historiae* 2.36) and emmer also used. Cereals were consumed in the form of breads (eaten principally at the main meal), porridges, cakes (eaten at symposia and for dessert), and other grain products.

One Attic choenix of wheat (0.839 kg) a day, which Herodotus (*Hist.* 7.187.2) gives as the standard military grain ration, has 2,803 calories. Eating that amount of wheat "would provide 84% of the energy required by a 'very active' adult male, 73% of the energy required by an 'exceptionally active' adult male, and 98% of the energy required

---

39. For a more detailed treatment, see John T. Fitzgerald, "Paul, Wine in the Ancient Mediterranean World, and the Problem of Intoxication," in *Paul's Graeco-Roman Context*, ed. Cilliers Breytenbach, BETL 277 (Leuven: Peeters, 2015), 331–56.
40. J. Robert Sallares, "Food and Drink," in *The Oxford Classical Dictionary*, ed. Simon Hornblower and Antony Spawforth, 3rd ed. (Oxford: Oxford University Press, 1996), 603.

by a 'moderately active' adult male."[41] As these caloric counts indicate, carbohydrates formed the foundation for the ancient diet.[42] As Andrew Dalby notes:

> Wheat was the preferred staple food of the classical world; club wheat and durum wheat for flat cakes, flat breads and eventually for pasta; bread wheat for raised bread. The two obvious alternative cereals, barley and emmer, were suitable for some types of cakes and biscuits, and made a better basis for broths and gruels than does wheat, but they were little use for bread. However, wheat did not grow well in central and southern Greece, nor in most of central Italy. As cities grew and demand for bread wheat grew, Greek cities, if they did not make do with barley, imported their wheat from north or south. Rome's wheat arrived in big grain ships, much of it from Egypt.[43]

All socioeconomic groups ate bread, which meant that it could be cheap but also that certain types of bread could be more expensive, depending on the price of flour (see, for example, Pliny, *Nat.* 18.80, and Rev 6:6). In general, white bread made from wheat flour was preferred to darker varieties and to that made from barley flour (John 6:9, 13):

> Fine, high-rising, white bread made from the flour of bread wheat, a free-threshing hexaploid wheat that is more sensitive to drought than other wheats and is therefore more difficult to grow in Mediterranean climates, was associated with the upper classes. On the other hand, coarse, brown breads made from emmer wheat or barley, both of which are easier to grow and more common than bread wheat, were associated with the lower classes.[44]

In addition to providing nourishment, bread also served the function of dining utensils. As is well known, the ancient preference was to eat while reclining, not sitting at table (see John 13:23). "If the reclining posture were to be maintained, the easiest tool to supplement the human hand was bread; and if the bread was to act as a kind of scoop, then a flat bread like modern pitta appears eminently suitable, while a

---

41. Foxhall and Forbes, "Σιτομετρεία," 56, using data on energy and protein requirements from the United Nations' Food and Agriculture Organization. See also Jongman, "Consumption," 598–99, who estimates 2,000 kilocalories as the average daily requirement.
42. Clark and Haswell (*Economics of Subsistence Agriculture*, 7) contend that "a community at the lowest level of agricultural productivity, living predominately on cereals, . . . if they have enough calories, will also receive enough protein" to meet human food requirements.
43. Dalby, *Food and Drink*, 349.
44. Kimberly B. Flint-Hamilton, "Legumes in Ancient Greece and Rome: Food, Medicine, or Poison?," *Hesperia* 68, no. 3 (1999): 371.

raised bread might be better for absorbing soups."[45] Indeed, the standard Greek word for "spoon" is μύστρον, which "commonly denotes a hollow piece of bread in the shape of a spoon; this was served with stews and soups."[46]

Legumes (*legumina*), pod-bearing plants whose seeds, pods, and other edible parts were used as food, were another staple of the ancient Greco-Roman diet and an important source of protein. Easily stored, the legumes most commonly used for food were lentils, chickpeas, lupins (favored by Diogenes the Cynic),[47] and the broad or fava bean (which Pythagoras assiduously avoided).[48] Other legumes included black-eyed peas, garden peas, grass peas, lablab beans, and even bitter vetch, which was sold as food in times of famine.[49] Some legumes needed to be carefully cooked to get rid of toxins,[50] but others were often incorporated into breads (e.g., Pliny, *Nat.* 18.117), made into soups (Martial, *Epig.* 5.78.21), or eaten separately, sometimes as a snack (Athenaeus, *Deipn.* 4.138a, 139a). As a staple item, they were typically fairly cheap. "Chickpea soup," for instance, "was a common and cheap street food in classical Rome; a helping cost one *as*" (Martial, *Epig.* 1.103.10).[51] The Mishnah says that dried lupines are a "food for poor people" (m. Šabb. 18:1 [Neusner]), and beans have been called "the poor man's meat."[52] Some legumes even appear to have been used for medicinal purposes, with Augustus testifying that he was cured of an ailment by bitter vetch (Pliny, *Nat.* 18.139) and Pliny the Elder, as well as Hippocratic works, extolling the effectiveness of lentils as a remedy for various bodily conditions.[53] Legumes were generally regarded as less desirable than cereals,[54] and "in literature they nearly always seem to have been considered the food of the lower classes."[55]

Olive oil was the main oil and source of fats in the diet, with sesame

---

45. Wilkins and Hill, *Archestratus*, 17–18.
46. Dalby, *Food and Drink*, 310.
47. Diogenes Laertius, *Vit. phil.* 6.48.
48. Diogenes Laertius, *Vit. phil.* 9.33–34. For lists of legumes (pod-bearing plants), see Columella, *Rust.* 2.7.1–2 and Pliny, *Nat.* 18.117–136.
49. Demosthenes, *Adversus Androtionem* 15.
50. Flint-Hamilton, "Legumes," 374.
51. Dalby, *Food and Drink*, 84.
52. So Peter Garnsey, "The Bean: Substance and Symbol," in *Cities, Peasants and Food in Classical Antiquity: Essays in Social and Economic History*, ed. with addenda by Walter Scheidel (Cambridge: Cambridge University Press, 1998), 225.
53. Flint-Hamilton, "Legumes," 376 nn. 31, 33, citing Pliny, *Nat.* 22.142; Hippocrates, *De haemorrhoidbus*, part 2, and *De ratione victus in morbis acutis* 9.
54. Dalby, *Food and Drink*, 162, 195.
55. Flint-Hamilton, "Legumes," 374; see also 135: "According to Aristophanes, then, lentils are the food of the lower classes."

oil sometimes used as a substitute in Egypt and Mesopotamia. In contrast to cereals and legumes, "olive oil is never a cheap product."[56] Indeed, "olive oil is, and always has been, an expensive commodity," and like wine, is high in calories.[57] It had multiple uses as a food:

> It was a medium for marinating meat and fish before cooking. It was a cooking medium. It was used as a dressing both for cooked food when served, and for fresh green vegetables; for this purpose it was sometimes used alone, sometimes mixed with vinegar and aromatic herbs. Finally it was used in conserving.[58]

That olive oil appears, along with wine, wheat, and flour, in the list of merchants' cargo brought to Rome (and many other places) in Revelation 18:13, reflects the centrality of all these foodstuffs to the ancient Mediterranean diet.

Finally, fruits (such as apples and figs), nuts (including acorns and almonds), and vegetables (especially lettuce, which was served as one of the hors d'oeuvres) formed an important part of the ancient Mediterranean diet, though they receive far less literary attention than other food sources.[59] Galen, however, devotes book 2 of his *De alimentorum facultatibus* to an extensive treatment of various fruits, nuts, and vegetables. Under "autumn fruits," he discusses large gourds, watermelons, melons, and cucumbers. Under "fruits that grow on trees," he treats figs, grapes, raisins, mulberries, cherries, blackberries, rose hips, the fruit of the juniper tree, the fruit of the Syrian cedar, pine nuts, myrtle berries, apricots, apples, quinces, pears, pomegranates, medlars, sorb apples, dates, olives, walnuts, almonds, pistachios, plums, jujubes, carobs, capers, sycamore figs, persea, and citrons. Under "fruits of wild plants," he focuses on acorns. Next, he moves to a treatment of lettuce, endives, mallow, beets, cabbage, orache, blite, purslane, patience dock, curled dock, and black nightshade. He then concludes by discussing celery, alexanders, water parsnip, Cretan alexanders, rocket, stinging nettles, *daucus gingidium*, wild chervil, basil, fennel, asparagus, shoots, turnips, cuckoopints, edder-wort,

---

56. Dalby, *Food and Drink*, 239.
57. Foxhall and Forbes, "Σιτομετρεία," 69, 75.
58. Dalby, *Food and Drink*, 239.
59. "Vegetables" (*[h]olera*) in the Greco-Roman world both included leafy vegetables such as cabbage and lettuce as well as herbs such as dill, mustard, and parsley. Depending on the vegetable, the root or green stem, or both, were eaten. For a list, see Pliny, *Nat.* 19.52–189. Syria was especially famous for vegetables, which were heralded in a Greek proverb, "Syrians have lots of vegetables" (Pliny, *Nat.* 20.33).

asphodel, hyacinth, carrots, caraway, truffles, fungi, onions, garlic, and leeks.[60] As should be obvious, some of the preceding food items were cultivated, whereas others were gathered from the wild.

If one had an orchard or garden, fruits and vegetables might be picked fresh from it, and a garden was known as a "poor man's farm" (*hortus ager pauperis*; Pliny, *Nat.* 19.51), enabling the plebeians of Rome to get their market (*macellum*) supplies very cheaply from the garden (*Nat.* 19.52). If one did not have a garden, vegetables could be bought in the market from a local source or gathered from the wild. The latter was especially important to the lower classes. Indeed, "especially in times of famine and food shortage, the contribution made by wild foods to the diet, especially that of poorer people, was significant."[61]

Most vegetables were cheap and their consumption associated with the lower classes, but there were significant exceptions. Large specimens of kale and asparagus could be quite expensive, prompting Pliny the Elder to say, "The ordinary public declares that even among the vegetables some kinds are grown that are not for them, even a kale being fattened up to such a size that there is not room for it on a poor man's table" (*Nat.* 19.54). Leaving aside those few instances where such enormous vegetables were associated with the gluttony of the rich elite, a vegetable diet was usually synonymous with a simple, unostentatious way of life, whether forced on the poor because of financial circumstances or chosen deliberately by philosophers committed to living in accordance with nature. Such a life could have its advantages. When accompanied by love, a meal consisting only of vegetables was clearly preferable to a carnivore's delight attended with hatred: "Better is a dinner of vegetables where love is than a fatted ox and hatred with it" (Prov 15:17 NRSV).[62]

Turning to the letters of Paul, one can see that Paul and the members of his communities certainly ate bread, particularly at the Eucharist (1 Cor 10:16–17; 11:26–28), and in 2 Corinthians 9:10 Paul even paraphrases Isaiah 55:10 by referring to God as "He who supplies . . . bread for food." Second Thessalonians continues this theme of consumption of bread, with the author saying that he paid for the bread he ate (3:8).

60. For translations of Galen's treatise, see Mark Grant, trans., *Galen on Food and Diet* (London: Routledge, 2000), esp. 109–53; and Owen Powell, trans., *Galen: On the Properties of Foodstuffs (De alimentorum facultatibus)* (Cambridge: Cambridge University Press, 2003), esp. 70–114. Some of their translations for the various food items differ. I have used Grant's translation.

61. Dalby, *Food and Drink*, 350.

62. According to t. Pe'ah 4:8, the weekday soup kitchen provided bread, beans, and oil, and on the Sabbath, vegetables and fish were also provided to the poor. See Gardner, "Let Them Eat Fish," 255.

Olive oil, which could be economically problematic if one owed some-one for one hundred jugs of oil and had not paid the bill (as in the parable of Luke 16:6), is not mentioned in the Pauline corpus, and "veg-etables" appears only in Romans 14:2, where the weak are depicted as restricting their food consumption to "vegetables" (λάχανα)—that is, edible garden herbs and leafy garden vegetables. Taken as literally as possible, this would also exclude the consumption of any cereal-based foods, all legumes (not simply beans), and oils. Since such a restriction would be truly extraordinary, the text is most often inter-preted as a rejection of meat and, in light of Romans 14:21, of wine as well. The identity of the weak and the strong (who by contrast eat everything) is a long-standing crux. Suffice it to say that in the Greco-Roman world, the closest analogy would be the Neopythagoreans, who accepted Pythagoras's well-known rejection of red meat, which was so famous that a *chreia* about it was even used in secondary education, with students asked to decline it as one of their exercises.[63] Accord-ingly, they restricted their diet to vegetables, dried fruit, loaves, sea-sonal morsels, and water (Diogenes Laertius, *Lives of Eminent Philoso-phers* 8.38; Philostratus, *Vita Apollonii* 1.8; 1.21.3; 3.27.2; 6.15), with meat deemed "unclean." Wine, which was similarly rejected, was classified as "clean" in the same way as were fruits and vegetables, but it was rejected because of the problem of intoxication (Philostratus, *Vit. Apoll.* 1.8).

Fish of various kinds were eaten fresh, dried, and pickled, but the degree of fish consumption depended partly on the place of one's resi-dence. Fish enjoyed a place of prominence in Athens and in areas such as the Galilee, where fishing played an important role in the economy and fish was commonly consumed. But in other places and regions, fish may have been scarcer, at least in the view of some scholars. As Andrew Dalby notes, "the proportion of fish in the Greek diet and its availability to poorer people are controversial."[64] Thomas W. Gallant has argued that fish and seafood played a minimal, "subordinate and supplementary" role in not only the Roman diet but also the Roman economy, arguing, *inter alia*, that fish were in short supply, that fish-ing was seasonal in many areas, and that supplies of salt were insuf-ficient to preserve large quantities of fish.[65] Similarly, Robert Sallares

---

63. Ronald F. Hock and Edward N. O'Neil, trans./eds., *The Chreia and Ancient Rhetoric: Classroom Exer-cises*, WGRW 2 (Atlanta: Society of Biblical Literature, 2002), 62–66. The nominative form of the *chreia* was, "Pythagoras the philosopher, when he had disembarked and was teaching letters, used to advise his students to abstain from red meat." Ibid., 65.

64. Dalby, *Food and Drink*, 144.

observes, "Fish are scarce in the Mediterranean because of the absence of large stretches of continental shelf off the coast. They probably did not make a major contribution to the diet."[66]

Their views have been attacked by various scholars, including Tønnes Bekker-Nielsen, Alain Bresson, and Annalisa Marzano,[67] who have convincingly demonstrated that Roman fish farming and fish consumption were indeed widespread and of significant importance to the Roman economy. The same is true of processed fish in the form of fish sauce. As the amphorae show, "during the first century AD, fish sauce in some places played a role in the consumer economy comparable to that of oil."[68] Bekker-Nielsen observes:

> Taking fresh fish, salted fish and fish sauce together, then, it is not an unreasonable estimate that at the height of *garum* production and consumption in the early centuries of the Roman Empire, fish were nearly as important as olives in the ancient economy. If fish never ranked among "the big three," it must have been a strong candidate for fourth place.[69]

At the same time, the degree of fish consumption was doubtless influenced to a certain degree by various geographical and economic factors. People who lived in important cities that were located on the coast or on a major river undoubtedly had greater and more recurring access to fish than those who lived inland or who were far removed from any fishing lakes.[70] Nevertheless, there is archaeological and textual evidence that suggests that even those who did not live close to the water had access to fresh fish. "Distribution of fresh fish was not impossible in antiquity, notwithstanding the lack of refrigeration, for there is sufficient evidence . . . to suggest that fish were often transported to market alive."[71]

65. Thomas W. Gallant, *A Fisherman's Tale: An Analysis of the Potential Productivity of Fishing in the Ancient World* (Gent: Belgian Archaeological School in Greece, 1985), esp. 43.

66. Sallares, "Food and Drink," 603.

67. Tønnes Bekker-Nielsen, "The Technology and Productivity of Ancient Sea Fishing," in *Ancient Fishing and Fish-Processing in the Black Sea Region*, ed. Tønnes Bekker-Nielsen, Black Sea Studies 2 (Aarhus, DNK: Aarhus University Press, 2006), 83–95; Alain Bresson, *The Making of the Ancient Greek Economy: Institutions, Markets, and Growth in the City-States*, trans. Steve Rendall (Princeton: Princeton University Press, 2016), 175–87; and Annalisa Marzano, *Harvesting the Sea: The Exploitation of Marine Resources in the Roman Mediterranean*, Oxford Studies on the Roman Economy (Oxford: Oxford University Press, 2013).

68. Tønnes Bekker-Nielsen, "Fish in the Ancient Economy," in *Ancient History Matters: Studies Presented to Jens Erik Skydsgaard on His Seventieth Birthday*, ed. Karen Ascani, Vincent Gabrielsen, Kirsten Kvist, and Anders Holm Rasmussen, Analecta Romana Instituti Danici, Supplementum 30 (Rome: L'Erma di Bretschneider, 2002), 35.

69. Ibid.

70. Ibid.

Three key factors that affected the price of fish were their provenance, quality, and size. The smaller and lower grades of fish were probably financially accessible to many consumers, whereas the larger specimens and top grades of fish were relatively expensive, often comparable to nicer cuts of meat and sometimes even to exotic game birds.[72] In short, while fish was certainly a part of the actual or potential diet for many people in the Greco-Roman world, the top grades of fish were luxury items.[73]

The Pauline corpus mentions fish only once (1 Cor 15:39) and birds, another Mediterranean food source, just twice (Rom 1:23; 1 Cor 15:39), with none of these references concerned with consumption. Nevertheless, given the location of Pauline communities in cities with nearby ports, such as Corinth and Rome, fish was generally accessible to them at a variety of prices. The Pauline corpus's silence about other food items, such as poultry, eggs, wild game, and wild birds, makes any statements about these as foods mere conjecture, though if one takes Paul's characterization of the strong as eating "everything," these all become possibilities. That would also include grapes, a food item that Paul explicitly mentions in 1 Corinthians 9:7, where he assumes that people have the right to eat grapes from the vineyards they have planted. One thing is clear: "everything" was quite literally available in Rome in a way that it was not in most places, so what one ate in Rome was limited almost exclusively by one's culinary preferences, dietary restrictions, and finances.

Meat in the Greco-Roman World and in New Testament Scholarship

As far as Paul's undisputed letters are concerned, the chief economic issue regarding food that is debated by modern scholars concerns the consumption of meat, and that debate is in turn related to the disputes about the socioeconomic profile of the Pauline communities. In what follows, the views of three New Testament scholars with quite different perspectives will be highlighted.

---

71. Marzano, *Harvesting the Sea*, 13.
72. As John Wilkins ("Introduction: Part Two," in *Food in Antiquity*, ed. John Wilkins, David Harvey, and Mike Dobson [Exeter: University of Exeter Press, 1995], 105) observes, "Communities ate the cheap fish caught off shore and sold any valuable items."
73. For this emphasis, see James N. Davidson, *Courtesans and Fishcakes: The Consuming Passions of Classical Athens* (London: HarperCollins, 1997). On the price of fish, see Marzano, *Harvesting the Sea*, 281–95.

The first is Adolf Deissmann (1866–1937), the most important biblical scholar in the late nineteenth and early twentieth century to do pioneering work on the social history of early Christianity. Deissmann believed that at least "the overwhelming majority" of Paul's followers "were men and women of the middle and lower classes,"[74] with some of the apostle's converts in Corinth coming from "the holes and the corners of the slums" of the city.[75] Yet Deissmann appears to have given very little attention to the complex issue of food, simply declaring that in Paul's world, "the possibilities of life, especially for a poor man, were everywhere very similar, as regards food and drink, clothing, lodging, and labour."[76] Furthermore, he was convinced of the ubiquity of the olive tree, which was for him "the living symbol of the unity of the Mediterranean coast-world."[77] That Paul himself ate olives he had no doubt.

Without provision of olives, moreover, the world-wide journeyings of St.

74. Adolf Deissmann, *St. Paul: A Study in Social and Religious History*, trans. Lionel R. M. Strachan (London: Hodder & Stoughton, 1912), 214–15, see also 7. Elsewhere Deissmann also speaks of early or "primitive" Christianity as a phenomenon of both the middle and the lower classes; see, for example, his *Light from the Ancient East: The New Testament Illustrated by Recently Discovered Texts of the Graeco-Roman World*, trans. Lionel R. M. Strachan (London: Hodder & Stoughton, 1927), 7, 251, 396. This broader description, which intentionally excludes the "upper classes," corresponds to his view that the papyri and ostraca provide evidence for the middle and lower classes (*Light from the Ancient East*, 9, 55, 359; *St. Paul*, 7, 48). For example, he views Nearchus, the author of a papyrus letter to Heliodorus (Papyrus 854 in F. G. Kenyon and H. I. Bell, eds., *Greek Papyri in the British Museum*, 5 vols. [London: British Museum, 1893–1917], 3:205–6) as "a man of the middle class" whose letter was "on the whole non-literary" (*Light from the Ancient East*, 176–77). It was to such "undistinguished non-literary persons" that Paul wrote his letters," which were themselves non-literary (*Light from the Ancient East*, 251, 246). Deissmann's use of "middle class" language reflects his awareness that certain Christians mentioned in the Pauline corpus "cannot have been poor" and his assessment that Gaius (Rom 16:23; 1 Cor 1:14) and Erastus (Rom 16:23) of Corinth were members of "the middle class" (*St. Paul*, 216). He places Paul himself "below the literary upper class and above the purely proletarian lowest classes"; in short, "St. Paul belonged to the middle and lower classes" (*St. Paul*, 53, 110). In the United States, Deissmann's views were echoed by the foremost scholar of New Testament grammar, Archibald T. Robertson (1863–1934), who similarly argued that though "most of his converts were poor," the live wires of the Pauline churches" were people like Gaius, Stephanus, Erastus, Aquila, and Philemon, who were "at least of the middle class and middling education." Archibald Robertson, *The Origins of Christianity*, rev. ed. (New York: International, 1962), 132.

75. This characterization corresponds to the fact that Deissmann very often refers to early Christianity as simply a "movement of the lower classes," with Paul and other missionaries drawing their recruits "from the masses of the ancient world" (*Light from the Ancient East*, 9; see also 144, 246, 312, 328, 338, 395–96). Inasmuch as these "lower orders . . . in the time of the Roman Empire made up the bulk of the population in the great cities of the Mediterranean coast and the interior" (*Light from the Ancient East*, 67), the sociological profile of early Christianity corresponded to that of the empire's population as a whole. For Deissmann's awareness of the difficulty of making clear distinctions between the various social classes, see *Light from the Ancient East*, 7–8n1.

76. Deissmann, *St. Paul*, 42.

77. Ibid., 40.

Paul would be inconceivable; on his journeys especially the fruit of the olive tree must have played the same part as it does still to-day on the Levantine steamers and sailing ships, particularly for the sailors and deck passengers. A handful of olives, a piece of bread, a drink of water—the Levantine requires nothing more.[78]

As for Paul's communities, the apostle's discussion of the Eucharist in 1 Corinthians 11 indicated that "some of the poor saints of Corinth occasionally 'had nothing' whatever."[79] Other Corinthians, who did have food, neither shared it with their fellow believers nor waited until all had been served before beginning to eat. As a consequence, "many devoured their own supplies with greedy haste, and those who had nothing were obliged to hunger."[80]

In regard to meat, Deissmann mentions "the bazaar of the butchers" in the *macellum* (meat market) at Corinth, "where the different kinds of meat cause anxious Christians terrible scruples of conscience," and "the embarrassment" a Christian dinner guest might suffer "when meat, which perhaps came from a pagan offering to idols, is served as roast in the house of a pagan" (1 Cor 10:25, 27).[81] In this connection, he also uses the *macellum* at Pompeii to imagine "the poor Christians buying their modest pound of meat in the Corinthian Macellum (1 Cor. 10:25)," comparing it to the "life-like reality . . . of the picture of the Galilean woman purchasing her five sparrows" in the Gospels,[82] and contrasting this humble depiction with the "abyss of degradation in the higher classes" as evidenced by "the obscene Pompeian bronzes, costly in material and execution."[83]

From the preceding discussion of Deissmann, it becomes clear that he viewed the vast majority of Pauline communities as comprised of people from the lower classes, with some of these from the city's "slums" and occasionally having nothing whatsoever to eat, and a few

78. Ibid. Deissmann's three items (bread, water, and olives) are a slight variation of the common Mediterranean dietary triad of bread, wine, and olive oil. For his treatment of the word ἐλαιών (olive grove) from a lexical standpoint, see his *Bible Studies: Contributions Chiefly from Papyri and Inscriptions to the History of the Language, the Literature, and the Religion of Hellenistic Judaism and Primitive Christianity*, trans. Alexander Grieve (Edinburgh: T&T Clark, 1901), 208–12.
79. Deissmann, *St. Paul*, 215.
80. Ibid.
81. Ibid., 74.
82. Deissmann, *Light from the Ancient East*, 157. Just before this comparison (155–57), Deissmann discusses the cost of sparrows as food in relation to Matthew 10:29–31 and Luke 12:6–7. He uses inscriptions of Diocletian's law regarding maximum tariffs to argue that not only are sparrows "a very cheap article sold in the market as food for the poor" (155) but "of all birds used for food sparrows are the cheapest" (156).
83. Ibid., 157.

others from the middle classes. At the same time, even the poor normally had access to olives, water, and bread and, more importantly, could even afford to buy a "pound of meat" in the *macellum*. The barriers to the poor's consumption of meat were erected by religious scruples of the conscience, not by financial factors. The real economic contrast lay with the elite, whose ostentatious display of wealth demonstrated the social and monetary distance between the aristocracy and the Christians.

This understanding of both the socioeconomic profile of early Christianity and the financial accessibility of meat was challenged by the second scholar whose work is profiled here, Gerd Theissen, one of the leading post-World War II scholars who renewed research into the sociological aspects of early Christianity. Whereas Deissmann had emphasized that "not many" of the first Christians were wise, powerful, or of noble birth according to the standards of Greco-Roman society (1 Cor 1:26), Theissen highlighted the logical implication that at least some of them, "if only a few," did fall into these categories.[84] He placed Paul, Barnabas, Cornelius (Acts 10), and Lydia (Acts 16:14–15) into these "higher strata of society," as well as "the protagonists of the various parties" at Corinth, who "were members of the upper classes." This was especially true of the key adherents of the "Paul party," who occupied "a relatively high social position."[85] Indeed, of the seventeen persons from Corinth known to us by name, "nine belong to the upper classes."[86] Statistically, they constituted a minority, but "a dominant minority."[87] In short, as the evidence from Corinth implies, early Hellenistic Christianity was a socially and economically diverse phenomenon, "encompassing various strata."[88] Pliny the Younger's (*Epistulae* 10.96.9) observation that Christians came from "all ranks" (*omnis ordinis*) of society was thus already true of Pauline Christianity.[89]

In regard to meat as discussed in 1 Corinthians 8–10, Theissen works

---

84. Gerd Theissen, *The Social Setting of Pauline Christianity: Essays on Corinth*, ed. and trans. John H. Schütz (Philadelphia: Fortress Press, 1982), 36, 69, and esp. 70–73. Other scholars from the same general time period who also gave heed to this implication of Paul's statement were Edwin A. Judge, whose pertinent essays are now collected in *Social Distinctives of the Christians in the First Century: Pivotal Essays* (Peabody, MA: Hendrickson, 2008); and Abraham J. Malherbe, *Social Aspects of Early Christianity*, 2nd ed. (Philadelphia: Fortress Press, 1983).

85. Theissen, *Social Setting*, 36–37, 54–57, 95, 102. It should be noted that Theissen's inclusion of evidence from Acts affects his assessment, since Acts gives a more elevated sociological impression of early Christianity than can be inferred simply from Paul's undisputed letters.

86. Ibid., 94–95.

87. Ibid., 73.

88. Ibid., 106.

89. Ibid., 37.

with "the hypothesis that the socially weak of 1:26–27 are identical with those who are weak in the face of consecrated meat."[90] Whereas the strong were financially able to purchase meat in the market on a regular basis, the weak ate meat rarely and in special circumstances. These occasions included public distributions of meat following a military victory or as benefactions made by the rich, "public sacrificial meals," "great religious feasts," banquets held by some voluntary associations, and "private invitations to a temple."[91] He summarizes his conclusion as follows:

> Members of the lower classes seldom ate meat in their everyday lives. For that they were largely dependent on public distributions of meat which were always organized around a ceremonial occasion. The community meals of the *collegia* were also religious feasts. As a result, those from the lower classes knew meat almost exclusively as an ingredient in pagan religious celebrations, and the acts of eating meat and worshipping idols must have been much more closely connected for them than for members of the higher strata who were more accustomed to consuming meat routinely. For the poorer classes meat was truly something "special." It belonged to a sacred time segregated from the everyday world. It has a "numinous" character.[92]

Given the disparity in socioeconomic status of the strong and weak, Theissen thought it unlikely that they would be guests at the same dinner party. Consequently, he identified the speaker in 1 Corinthians 10:28 ("But if someone says to you, 'This has been offered in sacrifice'") as a pagan, not a Christian with a weak conscience. "Only a pagan could describe ritually slaughtered meat this way,"[93] that is, as something ἱερόθυτον (devoted/sacrificed to a divinity).[94] A weak Christian presumably would have referred to it as something εἰδωλόθυτον (devoted/sac-

---

90. Ibid., 125.
91. Ibid., 127–28.
92. Ibid., 128.
93. Ibid., 131. This is also the view, *inter alia*, of BAGD 221 (s.v., εἰδωλόθυτος) and BDAG 280 (s.v., εἰδωλόθυτος).
94. As MM 309 notes, ἱερόθυτον is a late term derived from the classical formulation ἱερεῖα θεόθυτα. See esp. Pollux, *Onomasticon* 1.29: "meat [τὰ κρέα] from sacrificial animals [τῶν ἱερείων] is called 'offered to the gods' [θεόθυτα]." For ἱερόθυτον, see Pseudo-Aristotle, *De mirabilibus auscultationibus* 123, 842a35–37 (Hett, LCL): "They also say that there are kites among them which seize pieces of meat [τὰ κρέα] from those who are carrying them through the market-place, but they do not touch those which are offerings to the gods [τῶν ἱεροθύτων]." See also Plutarch, *Quaest. conv.* 8.3 (Minar, LCL) (cf. *Moralia* 729c), where Sulla is credited with saying that if the Pythagoreans "tasted flesh, it was most often that of sacrificial animals [τῶν ἱεροθύτων], and after a preliminary offering to the gods."

rificed to an idol), the term Paul uses elsewhere in 1 Corinthians in regard to sacrificial meat (8:1, 4, 7, 10; 10:19).

As for 1 Corinthians 11, Theissen viewed it as "a conflict between poor and rich Christians."[95] According to his reconstruction, wealthier members provided the bread and wine that served as the Christians' common meal, thus making it possible for those who had no food (1 Cor 11:22: "those who have nothing") to participate in the meal. But the rich, in addition to sharing in the common meal, also had their own private meal (1 Cor 11:21), which they began eating prior to the congregational meal. This private meal may have included meat. Theissen opines:

> It is possible that 1 Cor 10.14–22 and 11:17ff. deal with the same problem—the problem of eating meat in the congregational gatherings—from different perspectives. In both passages the issue is whether the Lord's Supper is incompatible with any additional meal. There it is a matter of εἰδωλόθυτον (10:19), here of ἴδιον δεῖπνον. It is possible that the two issues are in part identical, that in Corinth one could never absolutely exclude the possibility that a piece of meat was already ritually "implicated." Every piece of meat purchased could be meat sacrificed to idols, possibly even that which was consumed by some Christians at the Lord's Supper.[96]

In 1994, Justin J. Meggitt, the third scholar in this profile, attacked Theissen's reconstruction of the conflict in Corinth by correctly pointing out that Theissen had failed to consider an important source for meat in the Greco-Roman world.[97] This was the meat that was available in the "cookshops" (*popinae* and *ganeae*). These shops, along with the "wine shops" (*tabernae* and *cauponae*), were primarily the domain of the "lower strata'" of society.[98] Indeed, they were at the heart of "'lower-class culture' in the Graeco-Roman world."[99] Juvenal (*Satirae* 8.173), for example, "describes a *popina* in Ostia as filled with gangsters, runaway slaves, sailors, thieves, coffin-makers, butchers, and eunuch priests."[100] These establishments, which were viewed with a jaundiced eye by the elite, were either avoided entirely or frequented by them at a significant risk to their reputations.[101] Meat was served in these shops, but

---

95. Theissen, *Social Setting*, 151.
96. Ibid., 159.
97. Justin J. Meggitt, "Meat Consumption and Social Conflict in Corinth," *JTS* 45, no. 1 (1994): 137–41.
98. Ibid., 138.
99. Ibid., 139.
100. Ibid., 138.
101. Ibid., 139.

given its secular context, such meat—typically sausages, blood puddings, and tripe—had a decidedly non-sacral character.[102] Although meat was relatively expensive,[103] the price of the lower grades of meat served in these shops had to be sufficiently low to be within the budgets of those who patronized them. "The actual quantity eaten would also have been modest, no doubt in many cases akin to the 'ofella', the 'bite' of meat mentioned in Juvenal's eleventh satire" (*Sat.* 11.144).[104]

In 1998, Meggitt repeated his arguments about meat consumption in a book challenging Theissen's work and the so-called "new consensus" about the important role played by a few affluent members of Pauline communities.[105] Adopting an essentially "primitivist" approach to the economy of the Greco-Roman world,[106] he asserted that "the non-élite" constituted "over 99% of the Empire's population" and "could expect little more from life than abject poverty."[107] That same economic profile was correspondingly true of both Paul himself and Pauline Christianity, so that Pauline communities were socially homogenous rather than stratified.[108] That meant that they, like the pagan nonelites, commonly experienced hunger and that most of them only obtained sustenance "under great duress."[109] In addition, he offered interpretations of two key verses in 1 Corinthians that differed from Theissen's reconstruction of the situations addressed. First, he objected to Theissen's contention that the speaker in 1 Corinthians 10:28 is a pagan. Like many other exegetes, he understood the speaker to be a Christian.[110] Second, he argued that the phrase "those who have nothing" in 1 Corinthians 11:22 has an implicit direct object—namely, the Eucharistic bread and wine.[111] In short, for Meggitt, no meal at Corinth was held in conjunction with the Eucharist, and the problem addressed in 1 Corinthians 11 is that "some consumed all the bread and wine quickly (v. 33), leaving others who were less fast on the uptake, with nothing (v. 22)."[112] In 1 Corinthians 11:34, Paul is advising the Corinthians who

102. Ibid., 138–39.
103. Ibid., 138.
104. Ibid., 140.
105. Meggitt's article on meat consumption was incorporated, with minor changes, into his *Paul, Poverty and Survival* (Edinburgh: T&T Clark, 1998), 107–12.
106. Ibid., 42. This approach was made famous by Moses Finley, *The Ancient Economy* (London: Chatto & Windus, 1973).
107. Meggitt, *Paul, Poverty and Survival*, 50.
108. Ibid., 75.
109. Ibid., 59.
110. Ibid., 112–13.
111. Ibid., 118–22, 189–93, esp. 120, 190.
112. Ibid., 190.

were tempted to view the Eucharistic elements as food "to consume a real meal" at home prior to the communal gathering.[113]

Naturally, in addition to Deissmann, Theissen, and Meggitt, many other scholars have contributed to scholarly discussions about the role of food and drink in Pauline communities, but for the purposes of this essay, the contributions of these three scholars are sufficient to illustrate the different approaches and assessments that have been offered. In the final, following part of this chapter, an assessment of food and meat will be offered, along with a number of other observations.

An Assessment of Food and Meat in the Greco-Roman World and in Paul's Letters

The issue of meat in Paul's world and communities is far more complicated than is generally recognized, in part because in various philosophical, social, and religious circles it had an ambiguous status.[114] In what follows, twelve major points will be made that have implications for how Paul's assumptions and arguments are to be understood, but no attempt will be made at exegesis per se.

First, in terms of cost, the price of various foodstuffs in the market was not fixed but varied, partly as a function of supply and demand. As a result, shoppers could sometimes purchase items for a bargain, but at other times they had to pay an inflated price for the same items. This sometimes happened when two shoppers wanted the same item and got involved in a bidding war. One instance of a bidding war in Rome over a fish is reported in Genesis Rabbah:

> R. Tanhuma said: It once happened in Rome on the eve of the great fast [sc. The Day of Atonement] that a certain tailor went to buy a fish, and it fell out that he and the governor's servant began bargaining for it. Each overbid the other until it reached twelve dinars, at which price the tailor

---

113. Ibid. The problematic nature of Meggitt's exegesis of 1 Corinthians 11:17–34 was already pointed out by James Carleton Paget, review of *Paul, Poverty and Survival*, by Justin J. Meggitt, *JTS* 51, no. 1 (2000): 276–82, esp. 281. Theissen responded twice to Meggitt, and Meggitt in turn responded at least once directly to both Theissen and Dale Martin. See Gerd Theissen, "The Social Structure of Pauline Communities: Some Critical Remarks on J. J. Meggitt, *Paul, Poverty and Survival*," *JSNT* 84 (2001): 65–84; Gerd Theissen, "Social Conflicts in the Corinthian Community: Further Remarks on J. J. Meggitt, *Paul, Poverty and Survival*," *JSNT* 25, no. 3 (2003): 371–91, esp. 377–89 (where the Lord's supper, idol meat, and the *popinae* are discussed, and the importance of the latter as a meat source is minimized); Dale Martin, "Review Essay: Justin J. Meggitt, *Paul, Poverty and Survival*," *JSNT* 84 (2001): 51–64; and Justin J. Meggitt, "Response to Martin and Theissen," *JSNT* 84 (2001): 85–94.

114. Mireille Corbier, "The Ambiguous Status of Meat in Ancient Rome," *Food and Foodways* 3, no. 3 (1989): 223–64.

bought it. At dinner the governor demanded of the servant, "Why have you not served fish?" "I will tell you the truth, sir," he replied. "A certain Jew did thus to me: did you really want me to bring you a single fish for twelve dinars!" "Who was it?" inquired he. "So-and-so, the Jew," he answered. He had him summoned and said to him, "A Jewish tailor can eat a fish at twelve dinars!" "Sir," replied he, "we have one day when all our sins of the year are forgiven, and we honour it greatly." When he produced proof of his words, he dismissed him. (Gen. Rab. 11.4)[115]

Excessively high prices for market items evoked occasional imperial efforts to regulate prices; Tiberius, for example, outraged by three mullets having been sold for thirty thousand sesterces, proposed "that the prices in the market should be regulated each year at the discretion of the senate" (Suetonius, *Tiberius* 34.1 [Rolfe, LCL]).[116]

Second, there is a broad scholarly consensus that meat was not a staple food item in the ancient Mediterranean world and played only a minor role in the diet of most people, especially the nonelite who resided in cities. According to this *communis opinio*, which is based largely on literary evidence, many if not most people were functional vegetarians in their everyday lives, eating meat only occasionally.[117] This consensus does recognize, however, that some individuals did eat meat on a more customary basis. Soldiers sometimes had an abundance of meat to eat (e.g., Ammianus Marcellinus, *Hist.* 22.12.6),[118] and priests at times of religious festivals and other sacrificial occasions had more meat at their disposal than they could consume. Hunters of wild game certainly ate meat when the hunt was successful (e.g., Gen 27:3–5, 7, 19, 25, 31, 33), athletes ate meat (Pliny, *Nat.* 23.22), and people with an abundance of livestock butchered them for food on occasion (for example, 1 Sam 25:11), but even if such individuals did eat meat more frequently than most others, they were the exception. No one should be misled by the Homeric depiction of the heroes, suitors, and others feasting almost exclusively on roast meat. That literary scenario with its artificial diet is not grounded in the social reality of any time period in the ancient Mediterranean world.[119]

---

115. The translation is from H. Freedman and Maurice Simon, trans., *Midrash Rabbah*, 3rd impression, 10 vols. (London: Soncino, 1961), 1:84.
116. According to Suetonius, *Divus Claudius* 38.1 (Rolfe, LCL), Claudius "took from the aediles the regulation of the cook-shops [*popinarum*]."
117. For discussion of this issue, see the eleventh point below.
118. See R. W. Davies, "The Roman Military Diet," *Britannia* 2 (1971): 122–42, esp. 138.
119. As Wilkins, "Introduction: Part Two," 105, observes, the Homeric texts "construct a special diet that does not for the most part reflect what people ate in the prehistoric Aegean as far as we understand it from archaeology." For the penchant for the consumption of meat in Homer, see

Third, the rich could afford to make meat one of the staple items in their diet if they chose to do so, but in the Greco-Roman world, the epicure's luxury meal par excellence was large and exotic fish, not meat. That culinary preference appears already in Archesratus's *Life of Pleasure*, with forty-two of the book's preserved fragments devoted to fish and only three to meat.[120] The total absence of fish from the diet of Homer's heroes caught the attention of Greco-Roman writers, who noted it precisely because it contrasted so starkly with the preferences and dietary practices of their own times (Athenaeus, *Deipn.* 1.9d).

Fourth, when the rich did dine on meat, especially at a dinner party with guests, the meal was likely to be prepared by a professional chef who either had been hired for the occasion or was a member of the host's slave staff. When hired (as was typically the case in classical Athens), he might bring assistants with him or simply supervise the host's domestic slaves in the preparation and serving of the meal. Whereas in classical Athens the cook (μάγειρος) was typically a free man,[121] in late republican and early imperial Rome the cook (*coquus*) was usually a slave and played an important role in enhancing a wealthy individual's reputation as a gourmet.

Fifth, when meat was served at dinner, it was not like eating steak in a modern restaurant, where diners sit at a table with plates on which the steak is served, with knives used by diners to cut the meat and forks utilized to hold the meat while it is being cut into pieces and then to transfer the meat from the plate to the diner's mouth. In the ancient dining context, tables were small and portable, like modern TV trays. Knives were used principally to carve the meat into portions, and forks functioned primarily as serving utensils. "Solid food," including meat, "if not eaten directly from the serving tray, was placed on one's table, which thus served the function of a modern dinner plate."[122] Further-

---

Ilias 4.345; 7.313–18; 8.162; 9.205–17; 24.621–26; *Odyssea* 9.162; 14.26–28, 80–82, 418–38; 15.140, 323; 17.258, 269–71, 330–32, 412; 22.21; 24.364. In the case of the suitors, feasting on the roast meat of Odysseus is part of Homer's depiction of their outrageous, extravagant behavior. Interest in the food eaten by the heroes in Homer began in antiquity, with Athenaeus, for example, devoting a section of his *Deipnosophistae* to "The Life of the Heroes in Homer" (1.8e–14d). The explanation for the artificial meat-heavy diet of the heroes is unclear. Athenaeus observes that Homer "presents his heroes as eating nothing but meat" (*Deipn.* 1.18a), mostly beef (*Deipn.* 1.9a), because of his concern for "propriety" (πρέπον; *Deipn.* 1.18a). For other suggestions, see Wilkins, "Introduction: Part Two," 105.

120. The three meats are hare (frg. 57), goose (frg. 58), and sow's womb as a relish (frg. 62).
121. On the *mageiros*, see esp. Guy Berthiaume, *Les rôles du mágeiros: Étude sur la boucherie, la cuisine et le sacrifice dans la Grèce ancienne*, Mnemosyne 70 (Leiden: Brill, 1982); and also John Wilkins, *The Boastful Chef: The Discourse of Food in Ancient Greek Comedy* (Oxford: Oxford University Press, 2000), 369–414.
122. Dalby, *Food and Drink*, 118.

more, food was typically placed on the table "in bite-size portions,"[123] so that, in the case of pieces of meat, diners would simply use their hands to place the pieces directly in their mouth. In Latin, "*offellae* is a name which frequently occurs for small pieces of meat served as individual portions."[124]

Sixth, those who were not affluent had better grades of meat on special occasions, such as birthdays and religious festivals. In his *Satirae*, Juvenal describes what was true in the "good old days" and continued to be the case for the nonelite who lived in the country: "In those times, it was their custom to keep a back of dried pork hanging from the wide-barred rack for festivals, and to serve their relatives a birthday treat of bacon, along with fresh meat, if a sacrificial offering made it available" (*Sat.* 11.81–85 [Braund, LCL]). As this text and other sources indicate, "pork is the characteristic meat of the ordinary people of Rome"[125] and also the meat that was often deemed the most nutritious (Galen, *Alimen. facult.* 3 [6:661.3 Kühn]). Juvenal depicts here sides of pork as being set aside for festivals and birthdays, with the possibility of some sacrificial meat being consumed, if available. Whereas the bacon was salted to preserve it, the sacrificial meat would be fresh (*nova*; *Sat.* 11.85).

Seventh, as this text from Juvenal also shows, people ate both sacrificial meat and unsacrificed meat (sometimes called ἄθυτος [not accompanied by sacrifice]),[126] and they sometimes did so on the same occasion. Ancient Israelites ate both types of meat, as the list of consumable animals in Deuteronomy 14:4–5 shows, and the same is true of Second Temple and Hellenistic Jews and their pagan neighbors. Two medical texts establish this fact. First, the Hippocratic treatise on diet gives a list of animals that may be eaten, which includes cattle, goats, pigs, sheep, donkeys, horses, dogs, wild boars, deer, hare, foxes, and hedgehogs (*De victu* 2.46).[127] Galen provides a more extensive list in his *On the*

123. Wilkins and Hill, *Archestratus*, 17.
124. Joan Frayn, "The Roman Meat Trade," in Wilkins, Harvey, and Dobson, *Food in Antiquity*, 111.
125. E. Courtney, *A Commentary on the* Satires *of Juvenal* (London: Athlone Press, 1980), 501.
126. See esp. the *Suda*, s.v., ἄθυτους (Alpha 773 Adler), which defines ἄθυτους as "without sacrifices" (ἄνευ θυσιῶν) and quotes Damascius of Damascus (the last head of the Neoplatonic school in Athens), *Life of Isidore*, frg. 216 Zintzen (133 Asmus) as follows: "His body needed to eat meat [κρεοφαγίας], but he could not endure partaking [of it] without [it] being sacrificed [ἀθύτου]." See also Hierocles of Alexandria, *In aurem carmen* (*Commentary on the Golden Verses*) 26.14: "the injunction to keep away from carcasses [θνησιμαίων] as completely prohibiting us . . . even from partaking of unoffered [ἀθύτων] and unhallowed [ἀνιέρων] meats [σαρκῶν]." The translation is that of Hermann S. Schibli, *Hierocles of Alexandria* (Oxford: Oxford University Press, 2002), 314. The word ἄθυτος can also have the sense of an animal that is "not fit to be sacrificed," as in Lev 19:7 LXX. On the word ἄθυτος, see Berthiaume, *Les rôles du mágeiros*, 82–83.
127. A list of edible birds is given in Hippocrates, *De victu* 2.47. For the occasional consumption of dog meat, see James Roy, "The Consumption of Dog-Meat in Classical Greece," in *Cooking Up the Past:*

Properties of Foodstuffs, where he mentions pork, beef, lamb, hare, venison, wild ass, donkey, horse, camel, bear, lion, leopard, dog, panther, and fox (*Aliment. facult.* 3 [6:660.1–665.5 Kühn]). Some of these animals (such as bear) were eaten very rarely, but others were eaten with regularity, and this includes non-sacrificial animals, such as hares, which were a favorite target for hunters.

Eighth, the importance of hunting as a source for meat should not be neglected. Xenophon in his *Cynegeticus* (*On Hunting*; 2.1) emphasizes the importance of hunting in a young man's education, arguing that it is the first pursuit he should take up once he is no longer a boy, spending as much on it as his financial means permit. As to what to hunt, particular importance is attached to the hare (λαγώς),[128] which was abundant and could be hunted on foot with hounds and nets. Unlike large game animals, which often could be hunted successfully only with the resources of the affluent, hares could be hunted by people of all socioeconomic classes.[129] Hares were certainly hunted at Corinth from early times, with depictions of dogs chasing hares appearing as a motif on both proto-Corinthian and archaic Corinthian vase paintings. Indeed, "one of the Late Protocorinthian painters [is] designated the Corinthian Hare Hunt Painter."[130]

Ninth, financial considerations influenced the kind of meat that one ate. Domesticated animals, such as cows, sheep, and goats, "were too valuable as sources of milk and wool to be recklessly slaughtered for meat."[131] Long-term fiscal prudence, therefore, dictated that meat eaters should consciously elect to eat cheaper types of meat. The mid-

---

Food and Culinary Practices in the Neolithic and Bronze Age Aegean, ed. Christopher Mee and Josette Renard (Oxford: Oxbow Books, 2007), 342–53.

128. See Xenophon, *Cynegeticus* 3.3, 6, 8; 4.4, 6, 9–10; 5.1, 7–33; 6.5–6, 8, 10–13, 16–18, 23–25; 7.7–10; 8.1 8.

129. On the hare as a popular animal hunted in both Greece and Rome, see Kenneth F. Kitchell Jr., *Animals in the Ancient World from A to Z* (London: Routledge, 2014), 82–85. Inasmuch as the hare was an unclean animal in Jewish thought (Lev 11:6), it was not pursued by Jewish hunters, though the motif of the hare hunt appears in medieval Jewish haggadah. Marc Michael Epstein (*Dreams of Subversion in Jewish Medieval Art and Literature* [University Park: Pennsylvania State University Press, 1997], 16–38) interprets it as a symbolic of the oppression of ancient Israel by Egypt and other nations.

130. Mikhail Y. Treister, *Hammering Techniques in Greek and Roman Jewellery and Toreutics*, ed. James Hargrave, Colloquia Pontica 8 (Leiden: Brill, 2001), 52. See also T. J. Dunbabin and M. Robertson, "Some Protocorinthian Vase-Painters," *ABSA* 48 (1953): 172–81, esp. 178. Fragments of pottery decorated by the Corinthian Hare Hunt Painter are preserved in the Corinth Archaeological Museum (C-32-139). See also Helen M. Johnson, "The Portrayal of the Dog on Greek Vases," *The Classical Weekly* 12, no. 27 (1919): 209–13, esp. 210: the motif of a dog chasing a hare "is extremely popular with the so-called Proto-Corinthian artists."

131. Courtney, *Juvenal*, 501.

dle comedy poet Antiphanes in his play *The Seamstress* has this exchange in a dialogue between two speakers.

> (A.) What kind of meat's your favorite (he says)?
> (B.) What kind?
> The cheap kind! The type of sheep that doesn't produce
> any wool or cheese, which is to say a lamb, my friend.
> Likewise the type of goat that doesn't produce any cheese,
> that is, a kid. Since there's money to be made from the full-grown ones,
> I don't mind eating lousy food like this (frg. 21).[132]

Cheap food also had philosophical backing. Vegetables, of course, were relatively cheap, and Plato famously depicted his ideal city-state as vegetarian (*Respublica* 2.372c). Teles (frg. 2) tells the story of how Diogenes the Cynic heard a man complaining about how expensive it was to live in Athens, where a food item like pig's feet cost three drachmas. In response, he took him to a stall where a choenix of lupine seeds were sold for one copper and to stalls where figs and myrtle berries were sold for two coppers, doing so to show that living in the city was cheap if you bought the right kind of food. Musonius Rufus mounted a vigorous philosophical argument that the purpose of food was not pleasure but "health and strength." Cheaper foods were the most conducive for good health and therefore should be preferred, for "people who eat the cheapest food are the strongest." "Furthermore, even if expensive and cheap food strengthened the body equally well, nevertheless one ought to choose the cheaper food because it is more conducive to temperance and more fitting for a good man" (frg. 18).[133]

Tenth, despite occasional governmental efforts to prohibit the sale of any cooked items in the *popinae* and similar places,[134] cheap meat

---

132. The fragment is preserved by Athenaeus, *Deipn.* 9.402d–e, and the translation is that of Olson (LCL).
133. The translation is that of Lutz, *Musonius Rufus,* 119, 121. Arguments against meat consumption also included health factors, such as that it made one lethargic (Clement of Alexandria, *Stromateis* 7.6).
134. Suetonius, *Tib.* 34.1; Suetonius, *Nero* 16.2; Dio Cassius, *Hist. Rom.* 60.6.7 (Claudius), 65.10.3 (Vespasian); cf. Suetonius, *Claud.* 38.1. On the καπηλεῖον (often a tavern) in ancient Greece, see Clare F. Kelly-Blazeby, "*Kapeleion:* Casual and Commercial Wine Consumption in Classical Greece" (PhD diss., University of Leicester, 2008); and for a possible precursor to such Roman bans, see James Davidson, "A Ban on Public Bars in Thasos?," *The Classical Quarterly* 47, no. 2 (1997): 392–95. Yet it is not clear that in the case of Rome, all these were permanent bans. The selling of hot water in these places was also prohibited (Dio Cassius, *Hist. Rom.* 59.11.6, 60.6.7), but it appears quite likely that at least some of these were temporary measures instituted at times of public mourning. Earnest Cary says, "Both hot water and hot viands were regarded by Caligula and Claudius as being inappropriate to a season of public mourning, and their sale was therefore prohibited at such times." Dio Cassius, *Roman History*, trans. Earnest Cary, 9 vols., LCL (Cambridge: Harvard University Press, 1914–1927), 7:149n2. The governor Ampelius similarly issued restrictions concerning the selling

was usually readily available in these shops, which were ancient bars and grills and sometimes functioned as the "fast-food joints" of the Roman Empire, with the additional attraction for some customers that they routinely offered opportunities for gambling and occasionally prospects for sex with prostitutes.[135] For the lower classes, such places were popular places offering occasions for social interaction and conviviality,[136] but they were despised by the elite, who only visited them surreptitiously or at the risk of their reputations, and whose condemnation had significant symbolic value in highlighting their social and moral superiority to the masses.[137] The meat (typically sausages) served in these establishments was cheap "pub food," with one bar in Pompeii (located in the atrium at 9.7.24–25) charging one *as* for a small sausage, which was exactly how much it charged for dates and a serving of leeks.[138]

In an urban world in which many residences did not have kitchens and thus any place to prepare a cooked meal, the *popinae* served a vital function by providing prepared meals, especially hot meals, which for the urban poor were "the ultimate dining pleasure."[139] Their physical location in cities (especially Pompeii) has been disputed, with some scholars contending that they were subjected to "moral zoning" ordinances that placed them away from the larger houses of the rich,[140] so that aristocrats could "shelter their wives and children from contact with deviants."[141] Other scholars have argued that this claim is contradicted by archaeology, showing that in Pompeii "many bars can

of wine and cooked meat, but these had to do with the time of the day when such sales were forbidden (Ammianus Marcellinus, *Hist.* 28.4.4). Yet even if these prohibitions were designed to be absolute, they were largely ineffective, as the repeated efforts at regulation demonstrate. See Garrett G. Fagan, "Leisure," in *A Companion to the Roman Empire*, ed. David S. Potter, Blackwell Companions to the Ancient World (Oxford: Blackwell, 2006), 369–84, esp. 376. On the taverns (*tabernae*), see Claire Holleran, *Shopping in Ancient Rome: The Retail Trade in the Late Republic and the Principate* (Oxford: Oxford University Press, 2012), 99–158.

135. Fagan, "Leisure," 373–76 ("Drinking, Gambling, and Hired Sex: Fun at the Roman Tavern").
136. J. P. Toner, *Leisure and Ancient Rome* (Cambridge: Polity, 1995), 65–88; and Steven J. R. Ellis, "The Pompeian Bar: Archaeology and the Role of Food and Drink Outlets in an Ancient Community," *Food and History* 2, no. 1 (2004): 41–58, esp. 52.
137. Fagan, "Leisure," 376: "Their function was as much symbolic as pragmatic, in that they staked out the elite's position on morality and public display in opposition to a perceived plebian culture centered on the taverns and cook-shops that stood outside elite norms." See also Toner, *Leisure and Ancient Rome*, 79–83.
138. *CIL* IV 5380. For a translation, see Alison E. Cooley and M. G. L. Cooley, *Pompeii: A Sourcebook* (New York: Routledge, 2004), 163. See also Ellis, "Pompeian Bar," 48.
139. Corbier, "Broad Bean," 134, see also 136.
140. John DeFelice, *Roman Hospitality: The Professional Women of Pompeii*, Marco Polo Monographs 6 (Warren Center, PA: Shangri-La Publications, 2001), 129.
141. Ray Laurence, *Roman Pompeii: Space and Society* (London: Routledge, 1994), 87.

be found nearby, opposite, neighbouring, and structurally attached to several of the large and grand homes in Pompeii."[142] Instead of being "dive bars" located away from pedestrian traffic, "food and drink outlets occupied commercially viable and high-rent street-fronts."[143]

Wherever their location, they were extremely popular eating establishments, accessible to many of the lower classes, both slave and free. Juvenal depicts a slave doing hard labor in a gang of ditchdiggers as eschewing fresh vegetables and dreaming of the tripe (typically pig's stomach) that he once enjoyed in the city at one of its numerous *popinae*: "These days, a filthy ditchdigger in his huge shackles would turn up his nose at such vegetables, all the while reminiscing about the taste of tripe in the steaming diner [*popinae*]" (Juvenal, *Sat.* 11.79–81 [Braund, LCL]).

Eleventh, archaeological and especially osteological evidence poses a significant challenge to the *communis opinio* that the poor ate meat only on rare occasions and thus were functional vegetarians. Veronika Grimm, one of the scholars who has challenged this consensus, states the objection as follows:[144]

> Analysis of food remains from around human habitations in recent archaeology seems also to contradict the vegetarian argument. Reports of the excavation in Rome, at the *Schola Praeconum*, indicate the systematic production of animals of standard age—young animals—for the Roman market, suggesting that the main meat consumed by the urban population was pork, followed by beef and lamb. The bone sample found that all parts of the body were represented for all three species. The authors write: "the inference is that some at least of the urban population whose food refuse was dumped in the *Schola Praeconum* had purchased even the poorest cuts of meat."[145]

Furthermore, Anthony King's study

of regional comparison of mammal bones in the Roman world further showed that domestic quadrupeds were butchered for food all around the Roman world; the ranking of preference for the meat of these animals

---

142. Ellis, "Pompeian Bar," 51–52.
143. Ibid., 50.
144. Veronika E. Grimm, "On Food and the Body," in *A Companion to the Roman Empire*, ed. David S. Potter, Blackwell Companions to the Ancient World (Oxford: Blackwell, 2006), 368.
145. The reference is to David Whitehouse, Graeme Barker, Richard Reece, and David Reece, "The *Schola Praeconum* I: The Coins, Pottery, Lamps, and Fauna," *Papers of the British School at Rome* 50 (1982): 53–101, esp. 81–89 ("Animal Bones"), with the quotation found on p. 89. It should be noted that the *Schola Praeconum* finds reflect meat consumption in Rome in the first half of the *fifth* century CE, not the first.

varied across different regions of the empire. In the light of the literary evidence supported by these studies the vegetarian argument is hard to maintain.[146]

Michael MacKinnon's study of the production and consumption of animals in Roman Italy added to the case for a greater consumption of meat in the Roman Mediterranean world, suggesting that meat "was consumed in greater quantities than among earlier Greek cultures, with a far greater percentage deriving from non-ritual contexts."[147] This osteological evidence is compelling and, as Willem Jongman has argued, "suggests that meat consumption rose dramatically during the late Republic, to reach a peak in the early empire."[148] In addition, advances in Roman animal husbandry "resulted in the introduction of significantly larger livestock, with perhaps twice as much meat per animal."[149] Meat was by no means a staple, and the consumption of the nicer and more expensive types of meat was still an occasional treat for carnivores. But the consumption of cheaper and tougher cuts of meat was not uncommon, and "meat consumption seems to have reached a level where it made a meaningful contribution to the diet of quite a few people."[150] That level of consumption has implications for the economic profile of the standard of living for the mass of the population, indicating that "per capita incomes were increasing,"[151] and in keeping with this "intermediate prosperity,"[152] "significant numbers of quite ordinary people attained standards of living above bare subsistence."[153] To put the point in modern terms involving beef: the lower classes rarely if ever ate meat like filet mignon, but they did eat the "hamburgers and hot dogs" available to them and occasionally enjoyed a sirloin steak.

Twelfth, in addition to price, another factor that often influenced the choice of meat to be eaten was whether the animal had been offered in sacrifice, which was "the principal act of Greek religion."[154]

146. The reference is to Anthony C. King, "Diet in the Roman World: A Regional Inter-Site Comparison of the Mammal Bones," *JRA* 12 (1999): 168–202.
147. Michael MacKinnon, "Meat, consumption of," *The Encyclopedia of Ancient History*, ed. Roger S. Bagnall, 13 vols. (Malden, MA: Wiley-Blackwell, 2013), 8:4370–72, summarizing the results of his monograph *Production and Consumption of Animals in Roman Italy: Integrating the Zooarchaeological and Textual Evidence* (Portsmouth, RI: Journal of Roman Archaeology, 2004).
148. Jongman, "Consumption," 614, see also 604.
149. Ibid., 614.
150. Ibid., 605.
151. Ibid., 616.
152. Ibid., 604.
153. Ibid.

Sacrificial meat was undoubtedly the religious and culinary preference of ancient Greeks. In an important study of the μάγειρος, Guy Berthiaume has demonstrated that he functioned as sacrificer, butcher, salesman, and cook.[155] That the same person played these four different but interconnected roles shows how even secular banquets retained an important association with ritual sacrifice in Greek thought and practice. As one reviewer of the book remarked,

> it is salutary to be shown how inseparable the art of cooking was from religion in ancient Greece. B[erthiaume] might well have quoted at length the speech of a cook in New Comedy (Athenion fr. 1K), claiming that the cook's art has contributed most to piety, by teaching men how to sacrifice and eat animals![156]

In an appendix to his study, Berthiaume has also demonstrated that the majority of Greeks preferred sacrificial meat to unsacrificed meat.[157] In this connection, he constructs a grid of preferences, with meat from animals that have been immolated in sacrifice (ἱερόθυτα) at the top. Next in terms of preference are animals that were ritually slaughtered but not sacrificed.[158] At the bottom of the list are animals that were not sacrificed or were not fit to be sacrificed, including the meat of animals who had died from natural causes (χενέβρεια).[159] Some refused to eat such meat at all; indeed, in Berthiaume's opinion, "the majority of the Greeks . . . would have preferred to forego meat rather than to eat of the *athutos*,"[160] meat that is unsacrificed or unfit for sacrifice.

Even if it is true that the majority avoided unsacrificed meat, a substantial minority consumed it, at least on some occasions. Some Greeks did eat food that was ἄθυτος, and this "infraction" was sometimes noted by others who disapproved. An early instance of this appears in the

---

154. Gunnel Ekroth, "Meat in Ancient Greece: Sacrificial, Sacred or Secular?" *Food and History* 5, no. 1 (2007): 250. Osteological evidence indicates that cattle, sheep, goats, and pigs were the principal animals that were sacrificed, but occasionally other animals were sacrificed and eaten at Greek sanctuaries (256, 260). The meat could be roasted, but it seems mostly to have been boiled (266–68).

155. Berthiaume, *Les rôles du mágeiros*, 1–80.

156. N. J. Richardson, review of *Les rôles du mágeiros*, by G. Berthiaume, *JHS* 104 (1984): 235.

157. Berthiaume, *Les rôles du mágeiros*, 81–92.

158. See Ekroth, "Meat," 263–66, on animals not sacrificed but slaughtered and/or consumed at sanctuaries for alimentary purposes.

159. Ibid., 92. Other terms for this meat were θνησείδιον, νεκριμαῖα, and in the LXX, θνησιμαῖα. Ekroth, "Meat," 255, agrees: "A diversified sacredness scale for meat can therefore be imagined, ranging from the meat deriving from the full-scale *thysia* [sacrifice] to the opposite end, presumably the meat from an animal that had died of natural causes."

160. Berthiaume, *Les rôles du mágeiros*, 91. See also Ekroth, "Meat," 266.

infamous poem regarding women by Semonides, a Greek iambic poet who flourished in the mid-seventh century BCE. In this poem, Semonides delineates ten different types of women, seven of which are made from animals, one from an insect, and two from matter. In regard to the woman made from a weasel, he says, "She does much harm to her neighbours by her thieving and she often eats up sacrifices left unburned [ἄθυστα]" (Gerber, LCL).

Others who ate unconsecrated food felt that the gods punished them for this consumption. For example, one of the so-called "confession texts" from Asia Minor has the following account of how a certain Meidon offended the divine because his servants consumed unconsecrated meat in a cultic setting, how he was punished for this religious offense, and how he was ultimately healed:

> Mediôn son of Menandros held a drinking party in the Temple of Zeus Trôsou, and his servants ate unsacrificed meat [ἄθυτα], and he (i.e., the god) made him dumb for three months and appeared to him in his dreams (to bid him) set up a stele and inscribe on it what had befallen him, and (only) then did he begin to speak (again).[161]

A similar text was found in the village of Ortakeui in Phrygia:

> [I] honored the Lord with purifications and burnt sacrifices, that he might rescue my body, and at length he healed me in my body: wherefore I recommend that none eat a sacred [ἱερόν] goat-steak that has not been sacrificed [ἄθυτον]; for he will suffer my afflictions (if he does so).[162]

At the same time, it is abundantly clear that many Greeks did eat meat that was neither sacrificed nor ritually slaughtered, as well as meat from animals that had died of natural causes.[163] Pseudo-Aristotle speaks explicitly of the owners of sheep and cattle offering them as sac-

---

161. Georg Petzl, *Die Beichtinschriften Westkleinasiens*, Epigraphica Anatolica 22 (Bonn: R. Habelt, 1994): 1–2, no. 1. The translation is that of Richard Gordon, "Raising a Sceptre: Confession-Narratives from Lydia and Phrygia," *JRA* 17 (2004): 189. The precise sense in which the food was ἄθυτα is unclear. Gordon ("Raising a Sceptre," 189) thinks the sin involved "the eating of meat that had not been duly sacrificed." For other options and pertinent texts, see Peter Hermann and Kemal Ziya Polatkan, *Das Testament des Epikrates und andere neue Inschriften aus dem Museum von Manisa* (Vienna: Böhlaus, 1969), no. 15, 58–63, esp. 61; and Jeanne Robert and Louis Robert, "Bulletin épigraphique," *Revue des Études Greques* 83 (1970): 362–488, no. 511, 437–38. For a photograph of the stele with its inscription, see James B. Rives, "Religion in the Roman Provinces," in *The Oxford Handbook of Roman Epigraphy*, ed. Christer Bruun and Jonathan Edmondson (Oxford: Oxford University Press, 2015), 341, figure 20.3.
162. Inscription 15 in William M. Ramsay and D. G. Hogarth, "Apollo Lermenus," *JHS* 8 (1887): 376–400, esp. 387–89. I have slightly modified their translation.
163. Ekroth, "Meat," 252.

rifices as well as killing and selling them (*Oeconomica* 2.2.20, 1349b9–14). Animals that had not been sacrificed were even sold in markets. According to Pollux (*Onomasticon* 9.48), there was a shop in Athens where the meat of asses was sold. Furthermore, according to Erotianus (Erotian), the meat of dead animals (χενέβρεια) was sold in an agora called a χενέβρειον (dead animal meat emporium; *Voc. Hippocrat. coll.* 82.12). In short, although meat did have a close connection with sacrifice in the Greek world, it is simply not true that for the Greeks "all consumable meat comes from ritually slaughtered animals" or that there was an "absolute coincidence of meat-eating and sacrificial practice" in Greek thought.[164]

The close association of meat with sacrifice that existed in the Greek world seems not to have been true of the Roman world, where the large domesticated animals principally used for sacrifice "were killed for the food trade without any religious ceremony."[165] Indeed, "in Rome there was no religious requirement that domestic animals killed for food be offered to a god."[166] The contrast between selling an ox for slaughter and selling it for cultic use appears vividly in a passage from Varro, who notes that butchers required sellers to guarantee the soundness of the animal by using a particular formula, and he contrasts this procedure with that followed when animals were sold for sacrifice on the altar: "Butchers [*lanii*] use a somewhat fuller form, following the rule of Manilius, in buying for slaughter [*ad cultrum*]; those who buy for sacrifice [*ad altaria*] do not usually demand a guarantee of soundness in the victim" (Varro, *De re rustica* 2.5.11 [Hooper and Ash, LCL]). As a result of butchers purchasing animals for the meat market, "Roman sacrificial practice . . . [was] far less linked with the everyday diet" than was the case in Greece.[167]

Meat from both domesticated animals and wild game were sold in Roman markets. For example, meat from pigs raised on farms as well as meat from wild boars killed in a hunt were available for purchase, with the pigs slaughtered by a butcher (*lanius*) and the boar meat (a popular luxury item; Pliny, *Nat.* 8.210) prepared and sold in the mar-

---

164. These are the claims of Marcel Detienne, "Culinary Practices and the Spirit of Sacrifice," in *The Cuisine of Sacrifice among the Greeks*, by Marcel Detienne and Jean-Pierre Vernant, trans. Paula Wissing (Chicago: University of Chicago Press, 1989), 3, who also claims that all meat sold in shops came from animals killed in sacrifice. For a rejection of his claim, see Robin Osborne, "Women and Sacrifice in Classical Greece," *The Classical Quarterly* 43, no. 2 (1993): 394–95 n. 11.

165. Dalby, *Food and Drink*, 288.

166. Ibid., 103.

167. Ibid., 288.

ket (*macellum*) by a "market-trader" (*macellarius*) (Varro, *Rust.* 3.2.11).[168] Some vendors seem to have specialized in particular kinds of meat, so that a *bublarius* was a beef-vendor.[169] Some meat that was available in Roman markets was imported from places like Gaul,[170] reflecting the impact of international trade on culinary choices.[171] Depending upon the need, customers could purchase meat either cut up into joints and pieces or an entire animal, including the innards.[172] In the *Life of Aesop*, for example, Aesop buys pigs' tongues in the market (μάχελλον) on two occasions (*Vit. Aesop.* 51, 54), and the tongues bought on at least the first trip come from pigs that have been sacrificed (*Vit. Aesop.* 51).[173]

As the emphasis on sacrificial meat in the Aesop tale implies, both sacrificial and unsacrificed meat were sold in Roman meat markets, and the former appears to have been qualitatively better and/or more esteemed,[174] while the latter would usually have been cheaper. In fact, sacrificial meat is explicitly said to be more expensive by Servius and Servius Auctus, two Latin commentators on Virgil's *Aeneid*, who note the odd wording in *Aen.* 8.183, where Aeneas and the Trojan soldiers are said to feast on "a back of whole beef" (*perpetui tergo bovis*) and the entrails of a sacrificial ox. They explain that "the cuts of meat of this bull sacrificed to Hercules were sold at a greater price for the sake of religion" (*carnes carius vendebantur causa religionis*).[175] In short, as "a highly coveted commodity,"[176] sacrificial meat was more expensive than unsacrificed meat, which also means that it was generally preferred but not always purchased by the frugal or the less affluent. This may be one of the reasons for the fluctuation in the sale of sacrificial animals that Pliny the Younger cites in his famous letter to Trajan regarding the cult of the Christians. In a series of contrasts designed

---

168. As Frayn, "Roman Meat Trade," 107–8, points out, the *macellarius* sometimes functioned as a *lanius* but at other times simply prepared and sold the meat rather than butchering it.

169. Ibid., 110.

170. Corbier, "Broad Bean," 129.

171. Imported meat was salted, cured, or smoked, not fresh. On the sale of meats in Roman and Italian markets, see Joan M. Frayn, *Markets and Fairs in Roman Italy: Their Social and Economic Importance from the Second Century BC to the Third Century AD* (Oxford: Clarendon Press, 1993), 69–72.

172. Ibid.

173. In recension G (the oldest form of the text), he buys sacrificial meat on both occasions. In recension W, he does so on the first trip, but on the second trip nothing is explicitly said about the tongues coming from sacrificial animals. This may imply that they are from unsacrificed pigs. For a discussion, see M. Isenberg, "The Sale of Sacrificial Meat," *Classical Philology* 70, no. 4 (1975): 271–73.

174. Isenberg, "Sale," 272; Frayn, "Roman Meat Trade," 113; and Ekroth, "Meat," 271.

175. Christopher Michael McDonough, "The Pricing of Sacrificial Meat: *Eidolothuton*, the Ara Maxima, and Useful Misinformation from Servius," in *Augusto augurio: Rerum humanarum et divinarum commentationes in honorem Jerzy Linderski*, ed. C. F. Konrad (Stuttgart: Steiner, 2004), 72–73.

176. Ekroth, "Meat," 271.

to show an upswing in recent religious practice, he says that "the sale of sacrificial victims is on sale everywhere, though up till recently scarcely anyone could be found to buy it" (*Ep.* 10.96.10 [Radice, LCL]).[177]

In conclusion, there were a number of complicated issues involving meat in the Greco-Roman world, and this complexity is reflected in the somewhat contorted way in which Paul addresses these issues in 1 Corinthians and Romans. The term that he uses in 1 Corinthians, εἰδωλόθυτον, means simply "food sacrificed to idols"; it includes meat but is not restricted to meat, for other food items, such as cakes, were offered to the gods in sacrifice, and these cakes sometimes included fruit. Since cakes were cereal-based, they were not necessarily expensive.[178] As this fact and the preceding discussion of meat imply, the differences between the strong and weak at Corinth regarding food may well have involved certain socioeconomic factors but they cannot be reduced to them. For Paul, the Corinthian "food fights" were at heart a religious issue, not an economic one.

Finally, there is a certain irony in the fact that Paul uses the terms "strong" and "weak" in discussing the Corinthians and their culinary squabbles, for "strong" and "weak" were in fact used of foods themselves (see, for example, Hippocrates, *Vict.* 2.56). "Strong foods were believed to be most nourishing but hard to digest, weak foods least nourishing but easy to digest."[179] Beef, for example, is classified as a "strong, heavy" food (Hippocrates, *Vict.* 2.46), so that the Corinthian "strong" carnivores would be eating a "strong" food if they consumed beef. And whoever the speaker of 1 Corinthians 10:28 is, the very fact that this person uses the term ἱερόθυτον indicates that the food that is being served has not only been offered in sacrifice to a deity but is a costly dish that was widely regarded in the Greco-Roman world as superior to food items that had not been sacrificed.[180]

---

177. It should be noted, however, that Pliny's text is here the subject of debate and emendation. See A. N. Sherwin-White, *The Letters of Pliny: A Historical and Social Commentary* (Oxford: Clarendon Press, 1966), 709–10.

178. For an overview of cakes, especially sacrificial cakes, see Dalby, *Food and Drink*, 68–71.

179. Grimm, "Food and the Body," 360.

180. In writing this paper, I have benefitted from research done by Jonathan Wilcoxson, a doctoral student at Notre Dame, who is writing his dissertation, "Meat and Identity in Early Christianity."

Select Bibliography

Bekker-Nielsen, Tønnes. "Fish in the Ancient Economy." In *Ancient History Matters: Studies Presented to Jens Erik Skydsgaard on His Seventieth Birthday*, edited by Karen Ascani, Vincent Gabrielsen, Kirsten Kvist, and Anders Holm Rasmussen, 29–37. Analecta Romana Instituti Danici, Supplementum 30. Rome: L'Erma di Bretschneider, 2002.

Berthiaume, Guy. *Les rôles du mágeiros: Étude sur la boucherie, la cuisine et le sacrifice dans la Grèce ancienne.* Mnemosyne 70. Leiden: Brill, 1982.

Corbier, Mireille. "The Ambiguous Status of Meat in Ancient Rome." *Food and Foodways* 3, no. 3 (1989): 223–64.

_____. "The Broad Bean and the Moray: Social Hierarchies and Food in Rome." In *Food: A Culinary History from Antiquity to the Present*, edited by Jean-Louis Flandrin and Massimo Montanari, 128–40. English edition edited by Albert Sonnenfeld. Translated by Clarissa Botsford et al. European Perspectives. New York: Columbia University Press, 1999.

Dalby, Andrew. *Food and Drink in the Ancient World from A to Z.* London: Routledge, 2003.

_____. *Siren Feasts: A History of Food and Gastronomy in Greece.* London: Routledge, 1996.

Detienne, Marcel, and Jean-Pierre Vernant. *The Cuisine of Sacrifice among the Greeks.* Translated by Paula Wissing. Chicago: University of Chicago Press, 1989.

Ekroth, Gunnel. "Meat in Ancient Greece: Sacrificial, Sacred or Secular?" *Food and History* 5, no. 1 (2007): 249–72.

Fitzgerald, John T. "Paul, Wine in the Ancient Mediterranean World, and the Problem of Intoxication." In *Paul's Graeco-Roman Context*, edited by Cilliers Breytenbach, 331–56. BETL 277. Leuven: Peeters, 2015.

Frayn, Joan. "The Roman Meat Trade." In *Food in Antiquity*, edited by John Wilkins, David Harvey, and Mike Dobson, 107–14. Exeter: University of Exeter Press, 1995.

Freidenreich, David M. *Foreigners and Their Food: Constructing Otherness in Jewish, Christian, and Islamic Law.* Berkeley: University of California Press, 2011.

Gallant, Thomas W. *A Fisherman's Tale: An Analysis of the Potential Productivity of Fishing in the Ancient World.* Gent: Belgian Archaeological School in Greece, 1985.

Garnsey, Peter. "The Bean: Substance and Symbol." In *Cities, Peasants and Food in Classical Antiquity: Essays in Social and Economic History*, 214–25. Edited with addenda by Walter Scheidel. Cambridge: Cambridge University Press, 1998.

_____. *Food and Society in Classical Antiquity.* Cambridge: Cambridge University Press, 1999.

Grimm, Veronika E. "On Food and the Body." In *A Companion to the Roman Empire*, edited by David S. Potter, 354–68. Blackwell Companions to the Ancient World. Oxford: Blackwell, 2006.

Jongman, Willem M. "The Early Roman Empire: Consumption." In *The Cambridge Economic History of the Greco-Roman World*, edited by Walter Scheidel, Ian Morris, and Richard Saller, 592–618. Cambridge: Cambridge University Press, 2007.

King, Anthony C. "Diet in the Roman World: A Regional Inter-Site Comparison of the Mammal Bones." *JRA* 12 (1999): 168–202.

MacKinnon, Michael. *Production and Consumption of Animals in Roman Italy: Integrating the Zooarchaeological and Textual Evidence.* Portsmouth, RI: Journal of Roman Archaeology, 2004.

Marzano, Annalisa. *Harvesting the Sea: The Exploitation of Marine Resources in the Roman Mediterranean.* Oxford Studies on the Roman Economy. Oxford: Oxford University Press, 2013.

McDonough, Christopher Michael. "The Pricing of Sacrificial Meat: *Eidolothuton*, the Ara Maxima, and Useful Misinformation from Servius." In *Augusto augurio: Rerum humanarum et divinarum commentationes in honorem Jerzy Linderski*, edited by C. F. Konrad, 69–76. Stuttgart: Steiner, 2004.

Meggitt, Justin J. "Meat Consumption and Social Conflict in Corinth." *JTS* 45, no. 1 (1994): 137–41.

_____. *Paul, Poverty and Survival.* Edinburgh: T&T Clark, 1998.

Rosenblum, Jordan D. *Food and Identity in Early Rabbinic Judaism.* New York: Cambridge University Press, 2010.

Theissen, Gerd. "Social Conflicts in the Corinthian Community: Further Remarks on J. J. Meggitt, *Paul, Poverty and Survival.*" *JSNT* 25, no. 3 (2003): 371–91.

_____. *The Social Setting of Pauline Christianity: Essays on Corinth.* Edited and translated by John H. Schütz. Philadelphia: Fortress Press, 1982.

9

———

Socioeconomic Stratification and the Lord's Supper (1 Cor 11:17–34)

Neil Elliott

Paul's admonition of the Corinthian faithful regarding their practice of the Lord's Supper (1 Cor 11:17–34) has long attracted attention from those interested in the historical origins of the Eucharist.[1] In recent decades, it has become a focus for theologians discussing the theory and practice of the Eucharist in global contexts of socioeconomic disparity and oppression. In this same period, some New Testament scholars have applied social-scientific models to the passage, seeking evidence regarding the socioeconomic status of members of Paul's assemblies (ἐκκλησίαι) and explaining the conflict around the Corinthian supper in terms of socioeconomic stratification within the assembly.

The question of socioeconomic status in the Pauline churches

---

1. See for example, William R. Crockett, *Eucharist: Symbol of Transformation* (Collegeville, MN: Liturgical, 1989); Thomas O'Loughlin, *The Eucharist: Origins and Contemporary Understandings* (London: T&T Clark, 2015).

receives direct attention in other essays in this volume.[2] My interest here is with the conclusions interpreters have drawn from Paul's admonition in 1 Corinthians 11. Those conclusions do not float in their own abstract world, however, and so it is important to describe the wider social and ecclesial context in which they appear.

The Eucharist as a Site of Contestation

The last half of the twentieth century saw dramatic historical developments worldwide. The aftermath of the Second World War, including the plight of millions of displaced and refugee persons and the devastation of European Jews by the Nazis, brought increased attention to human rights, a concern expressed in the formation of the United Nations and the promulgation of the Universal Declaration of Human Rights. The dawn of the nuclear age with the US atomic bombing of Japanese cities and the ensuing arms race with the Soviet Union evoked international concern to slow and reverse the threat of nuclear annihilation. The international rhetoric of democracy and human rights, along with the debilitation of various European powers, fueled decolonization movements that swept through Africa, Asia, and Latin America. The economic and military ascendancy of the United States cast a shadow over all these developments, even as spiraling prosperity for a global minority sharpened the perception of growing economic and political inequality nationally and internationally. For all these reasons, social and political questions of justice and equality were becoming the coin of worldwide interaction.

These dramatic changes were reflected in theological developments, from the foundation of the World Council of Churches to the Second Vatican Council and beyond. In particular, changes in the theological understanding of the Eucharist included the recovery of its original eschatological horizon[3] and of the rich symbolic and narrative repertoire of relevant biblical materials,[4] a shift in emphasis from "ontologi-

2. See also Justin M. Meggitt, *Paul, Poverty and Survival* (Edinburgh: T&T Clark, 1998); Steven J. Friesen, "Poverty in Pauline Studies: Beyond the So-Called New Consensus," *JSNT* 26, no. 3 (2004): 323–61; Steven J. Friesen, "The Blessings of Hegemony: Poverty, Paul's Assemblies, and the Class Interests of the Professoriate," in *The Bible in the Public Square: Reading the Signs of the Times*, ed. Cynthia B. Kittredge, Ellen Bradshaw Aitken, and Jonathan A. Draper (Minneapolis: Fortress Press, 2008); Bruce W. Longenecker, "Socio-Economic Profiling of the First Urban Christians," in *After the First Urban Christians: The Social-Scientific Study of Pauline Christianity Twenty-Five Years Later*, ed. Todd D. Still and David G. Horrell (Edinburgh: T&T Clark, 2009), 36–59.

3. Geoffrey Wainwright, *Eucharist and Eschatology* (New York: Oxford University Press, 1981).

4. *Baptism, Eucharist, and Ministry*, Faith and Order Paper No. 111 (Geneva: World Council of Churches,

cal" questions (e.g., regarding Christ's "real presence" in the Eucharist) and the individual efficacy of the sacrament to its social context and corporate efficacy,[5] and a reorientation of the Eucharist's significance toward questions of human need, especially global hunger.[6] Orthodox theologians emphasized the Eucharist's central and formative role in constituting the church in its authentic missional stance "for the life of the world."[7] Theologians of liberation elucidated its proper role in forming communities dedicated to the project of human emancipation.[8] Early in this period, political theologian Johann B. Metz called the Eucharist a "subversive remembrance."[9] More recently, Andrea Bieler and Luise Schottroff argued that its practice presents an "alternative economy" to the omnivorous neoliberal construction of the human as *homo oeconomicus*, conformed to market demands as consumer or producer in the ubiquitous flow of capital.[10]

This increased emphasis on the social dimension of the Eucharist has been intertwined with the theme of judgment upon social inequality. The World Council of Churches ecumenical statement on *Baptism, Eucharist, and Ministry* (1982) boldly declared:

> The eucharistic celebration . . . is a constant challenge in the search for appropriate relationships in social, economic, and political life. . . . As participants in the eucharist, therefore, we prove inconsistent if we are not actively participating in this ongoing restoration of the world's situation and the human condition. The eucharist shows us that our behavior is inconsistent in the face of the reconciling presence of God in human history: we are placed under continual judgment by the persistence of unjust relationships of all kinds in our society, the manifold divisions on account of human pride, material interest and power politics, and, above

---

1982); *Baptism, Eucharist, and Ministry, 1982-1990: Report on the Process and Responses*, Faith and Order Paper No. 149 (Geneva: World Council of Churches, 1990).

5. Juan Luís Segundo attributes this shift in emphasis to the conciliar documents of Vatican II: *The Sacraments Today*, trans. John Drury (Maryknoll, NY: Orbis, 1974), 124.

6. Examples are Monika K. Hellwig, *The Eucharist and the Hunger of the World* (New York: Paulist Press, 1976); Joseph A. Grassi, *Broken Bread and Broken Bodies: The Lord's Supper and World Hunger* (Maryknoll, NY: Orbis, 1985).

7. Alexander Schmemann, *For the Life of the World: Sacraments and Orthodoxy*, 2nd ed. (Crestwood, NY: St. Vladimir's Seminary Press, 1973); John D. Zizioulas, *The Eucharistic Communion and the World* (London: T&T Clark, 2011).

8. Segundo, *Sacraments Today*; Victor Codina, "Sacraments," in *Mysterium Liberationis: Fundamental Concepts of Liberation Theology*, ed. Ignacio Ellacuría, SJ, and Jon Sobrino, SJ (Maryknoll, NY: Orbis, 1993), 671-72.

9. Johann B. Metz, "The Future in the Memory of Suffering," *Concilium* 6, no. 8 (1972): 19; Johann B. Metz, *Faith in History and Society: Toward a Practical Fundamental Theology* (London: Burns & Oates, 1980), 88-89.

10. Andrea Bieler and Luise Schottroff, *The Eucharist: Bodies, Bread, and Resurrection* (Minneapolis: Fortress Press, 2007), ch. 3.

all, the obstinacy of unjustifiable confessional oppositions within the body of Christ.[11]

Liberation theologians as well understand the Eucharist as a social imperative. So Victor Codina:

> In the eucharist we not only commune with Jesus, but with his Kingdom project; we not only edify the church but anticipate the banquet of the Kingdom. Thus the eucharist is inseparable from the fellowship of love and service. . . . For this very reason a eucharist without real sharing, as occurred in Corinth, "is not the Lord's supper" (1 Cor. 11:20-21). The patristic tradition corroborates this dimension of the eucharist, which is not only ecclesial but social: the offerings of the faithful for the poor; the presence of the slaves and the exhortation for their manumission; the preaching of the Fathers on justice and the defense of the poor; the liturgical excommunication of public sinners, who must be reconciled with the church in order to be readmitted to eucharistic communion.[12]

Or, as J. M. Castillo has put it succinctly, "Where there is no justice, there is no Eucharist."[13]

When theologians and church leaders have drawn such connections between the Eucharist, social justice, and judgment, they have relied on the single biblical text where these themes are combined: the apostle Paul's discussion of the "Lord's supper" in 1 Corinthians 11:17-34. There Paul rebukes the Corinthian assembly because, in his words,

> when you come together it is not for the better but for the worse. . . . When you come together it is not really to eat the Lord's supper. For when the time comes to eat, each of you goes ahead with your own supper, and one goes hungry and another becomes drunk. What! Do you not have homes to eat and drink in? Or do you show contempt for the church of God and humiliate those who have nothing? (1 Cor 11:17, 20-22 NRSV)

Paul goes on to invoke the tradition of Jesus's words at the supper "on the night when he was betrayed," then warns, "whoever, therefore,

---

11. *Baptism, Eucharist, and Ministry*, 14.
12. Codina, "Sacraments," 671. Codina cites the work of J. M. Castillo ("Donde no hay justicia no hay eucaristía," in *Fe y justicia* [Salamanca: Ediciones Sigueme, 1981], 135–71), who discusses the patristic emphasis on public penitence as a condition of eucharistic participation and on the offering presented by the faithful, "two institutions that tended toward the same purpose: to safeguard the necessary connection that pertains between the celebration of the Eucharist and the ethical-social behavior of Christians" (my translation). Castillo relies especially on Ambrose, *De paenitentia* 2.9, 89 (CSEL 73, 198) and 1.2, 5 (CSEL 73, 121), and Tertullian, *De paenitentia* 7.10 and *De carne Christi* 1.333–39, 9.1–6.
13. Castillo, "Donde no hay justicia no hay eucaristía," 135–71.

eats the bread or drinks the cup of the Lord in an unworthy manner will be answerable for the body and blood of the Lord" (1 Cor 11:27 NRSV). He concludes,

> So, then, my brothers and sisters, when you come together to eat, wait for one another. If you are hungry, eat at home, so that when you come together, it will not be for your condemnation. About the other things I will give instructions when I come. (1 Cor 11:33–34 NRSV)

The theme of judgment on social injustice has been developed in an especially acute way by William T. Cavanaugh in his argument for a robust practice of excommunication of the architects of social evil. While the apostle's words appear to refer to social inequality involving "those who have nothing" (NRSV), Cavanaugh has a different subject particularly in view: the practice of torture carried out by military officers and state security officials in Augusto Pinochet's regime—men who continued not only to attend Mass but quite possibly to receive Communion in the company of their victims and their families.[14] Cavanaugh grounds his argument in part in 1 Corinthians 11:17–34.

> Paul would exclude from the Eucharist those who fail to "discern the body," meaning not only Christ's sacramental body but especially his ecclesial body (1 Cor. 11:29). The specific sin Paul addresses in this passage is the "humiliation" of the poor by the rich, who eat their fill when the community gathers while others go hungry (11:21–2). According to Paul this is not simply sin against individuals but "contempt for the church of God" (11:22). The rich bring divisions into the church, and thus threaten the visibility of the body of Christ. Exclusion of the offenders from the Eucharist is meant to restore the church as a sign of reconciliation by leading the offenders to change their conduct (11:31–2). If they do not repent, exclusion from the Eucharist also safeguards the witness of the church by anticipating the Lord's final judgment, when His own will be separated out from the world (11:32).[15]

While Cavanaugh's argument focused on a specific and extreme case, one might reasonably extend the argument to other crimes and other regimes. For example, we might propose that those who committed torture at US military facilities at Abu Ghraib, Guantánamo, or Bagram Air Field should be made excommunicate from any churches of which

---

14. William T. Cavanaugh, *Torture and Eucharist: Theology, Politics, and the Body of Christ* (Oxford: Blackwell, 1998), 260.
15. Ibid., 246.

they are members, along with the architects and apologists of torture programs and those who knowingly permitted their execution through benign neglect.[16] Or, to hew closer to the text's apparent socioeconomic focus, we might propose that those who engineered, then profited from the financial catastrophe of 2007–08 might be considered candidates not only for criminal prosecution but for excommunication, should they refuse to repent and make restitution.[17]

Excommunication generally is understood as an act of grace in an extreme circumstance, intended to move the impenitent sinner to repentance and ultimate reconciliation. Cavanaugh insists that it is also a discipline guaranteeing the integrity of the "body politic" that is the church.

Such a robust understanding of the insoluble connection between the Eucharist and justice stands at some distance from the more sedate solemnities of broad swaths of US church life, as it does from the cerebral reflections of much academic scholarship and even from church-based activism against torture.[18] Indeed, proposing the exclusion from the Eucharist of accused torturers or perpetrators of massive fraud would likely result in the (further) polarization of US churches along political and ideological lines. If some Christians found such proposals compelling, they would no doubt strike others as the misguided politicization of the liturgy. But Cavanaugh's argument suggests that such polarization of the churches would simply reflect the apostle's own theology: "indeed, there have to be factions among you, for only so will it become clear who among you are genuine" (1 Cor 11:19 NRSV).

The question of the Eucharist's relation and relevance to current realities of social injustice is not only theoretical. Direct actions by

16. In April 2003, the Greek Orthodox priest in charge of the Church of the Nativity in Bethlehem barred Iraq War architects George W. Bush, Donald Rumsfeld, Tony Blair, and Jack Straw from entering his church "forever" (reported in the *Jordan Times*, April 4, 2003). In December 2014, after the US Senate's report on torture at military sites was published, a German human-rights group filed war-crime charges against Bush, Rumsfeld, and Dick Cheney ("Should Bush, Cheney, Rumsfeld and CIA Officials Be Tried for Torture? War Crimes Case Filed in Germany," Democracy Now!, December 19, 2014, http://tinyurl.com/zfc76gt). Richard Clark, the top US counterterrorism official under president George W. Bush, declared that their actions "probably" constituted war crimes (Shadee Ashtari, "Former Counterterrorism Czar Richard Clarke: Bush, Cheney Committed War Crimes, *The Huffington Post*, May 29, 2014, http://tinyurl.com/hzvr5y4.

17. Jed S. Rakoff observes that "the Financial Crisis Inquiry Commission, in its final report, uses variants of the word 'fraud' no fewer than 157 times in describing what led to the crisis, concluding that there was a 'systemic breakdown,' not just in accountability, but also in ethical behavior" (*New York Review of Books*, January 9, 2014).

18. The National Religious Coalition against Torture enrolls faith congregations in lobbying efforts to ban torture by US military and government officials; it does not include excommunication of torturers in its agenda (www.nrcat.org).

Christian communities against a wide array of restrictive, militaristic, and punitive social policies include eucharistic celebration as a constitutive element.[19] Actual eucharistic assemblies have proven "subversive," to use Metz's term, as they have challenged systematic oppression. As Cavanaugh reports, in Chile, Christians converged in street Eucharists to mark the buildings where political prisoners were being tortured by the Pinochet regime.[20] In Haiti, priests of *ti legliz*, the "little church," led memorial Masses for victims of the security services that became public demonstrations that eventually rendered Jean-Claude Duvalier's dictatorship untenable.[21] The Eucharist provided Archbishop Oscar Arnulfo Romero a platform to challenge US military support for the murderous junta in El Salvador.[22] US antiwar activists incorporated the Eucharist into their direct action campaigns.[23]

Such practices (and the list could be expanded) have of course been contested. Enthusiastic eucharistic celebrations in Sandinista, Nicaragua, provoked censure by the adamantly anti-Communist Pope John Paul II. Visiting the country in 1983, the pope publicly scolded liberationist priest Ernesto Cardenal for serving in the Sandinista government, warned the Nicaraguan bishops against the ideological "infiltration" he perceived in terms like *iglesia popular*, and used the occasion of a public Eucharist to sternly admonish priests and the people themselves to relinquish any "doctrine or ideology" that set "earthly considerations," such as the preferential option for the poor, above "transcendent" values, which included "*obedience to the bishops and to the pope*"[24]—a value invoked by appeal to the pseudo-Pauline letter to the Ephesians.

---

19. Kellermann offers astute observations about the issues involved: Bill Wylie Kellermann, *Seasons of Faith and Conscience: Kairos, Confession, Liturgy* (Maryknoll, NY: Orbis, 1991), ch. 5.
20. Cavanaugh, *Torture and Eucharist.*
21. Paul Farmer describes one memorial service that sparked a demonstration of some ten thousand protesters: *The Uses of Haiti* (Monroe, ME: Common Courage, 1994), 128–29. Other Haitian priests have described in personal conversation a mass mobilization against the Duvalier régime in the 1980s, centered in the *ti legliz.*
22. Oscar Romero, *Voice of the Voiceless: The Four Pastoral Letters and Other Statements* (Maryknoll, NY: Orbis, 1985).
23. Kellermann, *Seasons of Faith*; John Dear, SJ, *The Sacrament of Civil Disobedience* (Baltimore: Fortkamp, 1994). Both authors place themselves in a larger *communio sanctorum* that includes Philip and Daniel Berrigan, William Stringfellow, Dorothy Day, and many others.
24. John Paul II, "Unity of the Church," *The Pope Speaks* 28 (Fall 1983), 206–10, reprinted in *Liberation Theology: A Documentary History*, ed. Alfred T. Hennelly (Maryknoll, NY: Orbis, 1990), 329–33 (emphasis in original). The pope did not explicitly repudiate the preferential option for the poor (a hallmark of the theology of liberation), but admonished his Nicaraguan audience not to imagine that anyone in the church "has a greater right to citizenship" in the church than anyone else: "neither Jews, nor Greeks, nor slaves, nor freed men, nor men, nor women, *nor the poor, nor the rich*" (330). My italics mark the pope's supplement to Paul's words in Gal 3:28.

Moreover, eucharistic assemblies and ministers have been attacked by state apparatuses. Priests were tortured and murdered in Pinochet's Chile and in El Salvador, where Archbishop Romero was assassinated at the eucharistic table. In Haiti, *ti legliz* priests were threatened and attacked; liberationist priest Jean-Bertrand Aristide was the object of four assassination attempts, including one while he celebrated Mass at the Church of St. Jean Bosco, at which thirteen people were killed by a death squad wearing police uniforms, and another at a memorial mass for other massacre victims at which Aristide was spared only because a would-be assassin's pistol misfired.[25] Notoriously, the architects of these crimes have to date gone unpunished.

In our day, the Eucharist has become a site of ideological contestation, both in terms of theory and of praxis. Paul's voice is claimed on either side of these skirmishes; the interpretation of his words concerning the Lord's Supper in 1 Corinthians seems therefore both relevant and urgent.

The Social-Scientific Interpretation of 1 Corinthians 11:17–34

By contrast, during this same period, discussion of 1 Corinthians 11:17–34 among New Testament scholars has generally been calm and upbeat. Beginning in the 1980s, some scholars applying social-science concepts to the New Testament found a case study in this passage. If previous interpretations of Paul's rebuke focused on religious or theological currents among the Corinthians (Judaism, Gnosticism, "crude sacramentalism," etc.), Gerd Theissen sought to understand the "divisions" and "factions" around the table (so Paul called them: σχίσματα, v. 17; αἱρέσεις, v. 19) not in terms of theological parties but as evidence of social stratification.

This was a degree of social stratification that distinguished the Pauline ἐκκλησίαι from more socially homogeneous Hellenistic associations (θίασοι). "The conflict over the Lord's Supper is a conflict between poor and rich Christians," Theissen proposed. The conflict was caused by "a particular habit of the rich," who had made the common meal possible, yet took part in it on their own, apart, without sharing with others. The fact that some in the assembly went hungry (v. 21) meant in Paul's eyes that the rich had shown contempt for the poor (i.e., those who "have nothing," as Theissen translated τοὺς μὴ ἔχοντας, v. 22).[26]

---

25. The incidents are recounted in Farmer, *The Uses of Haiti*, 136–37. The period comes alive in Amy Wilentz's account, *The Rainy Season: Haiti after Duvalier* (New York: Simon & Schuster, 1989).

In this way, Theissen argued, the wealthier members were reproducing patterns and expectations from the banquets of Hellenistic associations to which they were accustomed, where officers and members who had provided long service to the association would be expected to receive larger portions of better food as a matter of course, if not indeed of bylaw. In those contexts, Theissen wrote, "nobody was in the least offended" by such disparities in the recognition of status. Different shares in the meal were "in fact considered fair and proper."[27] But the socially more disparate Corinthian ἐκκλησία had no such regulations in place. When the wealthier members presumed that they were entitled to reserve more of the common food for themselves—food that they themselves might well have provided—as their "private meal" (ἴδιον δεῖπνον) and to eat it apart, before the common meal began, they gave to lower-status members a degree of offense that their action would never have occasioned in the social circles in which the wealthy more routinely traveled.[28]

Wayne A. Meeks largely followed Theissen's reconstruction of the episode. Meeks proposed that if someone like Gaius, who was a host of the whole ἐκκλησία in Corinth (Rom 16:23), had brought the customs and assumptions of his social class into the common meal—held, after all, in his own dining room—and had "made distinctions in the food he provided for those of his own social level and those who were of lower rank, that would not have been at all out of the ordinary." Meeks observed that just such prevalent practices (or more precisely, their occasional abuse) had offended a few Roman moralists.[29] Paul, Meeks thought, objected to the Corinthian practice "on quite different grounds" than the moralists, however. Steeped in a characteristically Jewish "apocalyptic determinism," Paul regarded divisions in the community as an example of inevitable eschatological testing (1 Cor 11:19).[30]

Jerome Murphy-O'Connor agreed that the Corinthian ἐκκλησία prob-

26. Gerd Theissen, "Social Integration and Sacramental Activity: An Analysis of 1 Cor 11:17–34," in *The Social Setting of Pauline Christianity: Essays on Corinth*, ed./trans. John H. Schütz (Philadelphia: Fortress Press, 1982), 151.

27. Ibid., 156, citing Jérôme Carcopino, *Daily Life in Ancient Rome: The People and the City at the Height of the Empire*, ed. Henry T. Rowell, trans. E. O. Lorimer (New Haven, CT: Yale University Press, 1940), 270–71.

28. Theissen, "Social Integration and Sacramental Activity," 153–55.

29. Wayne A. Meeks, *The First Urban Christians: The Social World of the Apostle Paul* (New Haven, CT: Yale University Press, 1983), 67–70. On this point, Meeks follows Theissen, *Social Setting*, 156–58. Theissen cites Pliny, *Epistulae* 2.6; Martial, *Epigram* 3.60, 1.20, 4.85, 6.11, 10.49; Juvenal, *Satirae* 5. Most of these are expressions of personal indignation at being slighted rather than protests against the principle or practice of social variability at banquets.

ably met in the home of a wealthier member. He went further, relying on archaeological excavations from Corinth and Pompeii to estimate how many individuals might have gathered in the public space of a typical villa. His estimation was that no more than nine guests could have reclined comfortably on the couches in the triclinium, a room furnished for private dining, but that some thirty to forty people might have massed, standing, in the atrium (see fig. 9.1). Murphy-O'Connor speculates that a host like Gaius would have invited "his closest friends, . . . who would have been of the same social class," into the triclinium with himself, while the rest were relegated to the "greatly inferior" space in the atrium. Discrimination via space was compounded by discrimination via time: Gaius and his peers would have gathered earlier to feast at leisure, then joined the poorer members upon their arrival later, after a hard day's work, to share whatever was left—perhaps only "the bread and wine of the Eucharist."[31] The "factions" to which Paul refers seemed vividly apparent.

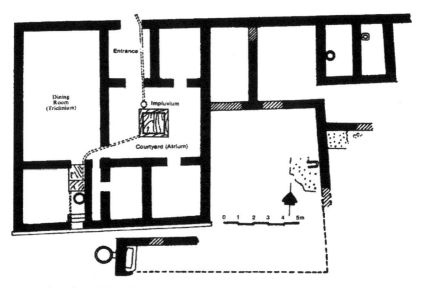

Fig. 9.1. Floorplan of the villa at Anaploga, Corinth, showing the dining room at left and the courtyard at left center; from Murphy-O'Connor, *St. Paul's Corinth*, 154.

---

30. Here, too, Meeks was persuaded by Theissen, *Social Setting*, 164: "the eschatological testing of the congregation."

31. Jerome Murphy-O'Connor, *St. Paul's Corinth: Texts and Archaeology* (Wilmington, DE: Michael Glazier, 1983), 153–61.

These three scholars have provided the components of what has become a widely accepted reconstruction of the situation in Corinth.[32] It bears note that this reconstruction is part of a larger understanding of the social status of members of Paul's assemblies, an understanding hailed already in the late 1970s as a "new consensus."[33] According to that consensus, Paul's churches included a mix of persons holding different social statuses. They were mostly poor but included "middle class" artisans and even a few well-to-do members like Gaius, whom Paul could hail as the "host of the whole church."

Accordingly, Theissen found in 1 Corinthians 11:17–34 an expression of the "ethos of early Christian love-patriarchalism which arose in the Pauline communities."[34] Elsewhere he describes this love-patriarchalism as "a new pattern of integration" that would have been readily adopted by "the society of late antiquity":

> In it [love-patriarchalism] equality of status was extended to all—to women, foreigners, and slaves. . . . At the same time, however, all of this was internalized: it was true "in Christ." In the political and social realm class-specific differences were essentially accepted, affirmed, even religiously legitimated. No longer was there a struggle for equal rights but instead a struggle to achieve a pattern of relationships among members of various strata which would be characterized by respect, concern, and a sense of responsibility.[35]

Paul intended just this strategy of community integration. Theissen grounded that judgment particularly in 1 Corinthians 11:34, which he read as a straightforward instruction: "In fact [Paul] recommends that they celebrate the 'private meal' at home."[36]

> Paul wants to settle the problem of the "private meal" by confining it to private homes. At home everybody may eat and drink in whatever way seems proper. The final result would be a lessening of the role conflict in which the wealthier Christians find themselves. Within their own four walls they are to behave according to the norms of their social class, while at the Lord's Supper the norms of the congregation have absolute prior-

---

32. For example, Gordon D. Fee makes these judgments the basis for his exegesis of the passage: *The First Epistle to the Corinthians*, rev. ed., NICNT (Grand Rapids: Eerdmans, 2014).
33. Abraham J. Malherbe, *Social Aspects of Early Christianity*, 2nd ed. (Philadelphia: Fortress Press, 1983), 31.
34. Theissen, *Social Setting*, 164.
35. Ibid., 109.
36. Ibid., 155.

ity. Clearly this is a compromise. It would be much more consistent with the idea of community to demand that this "private meal" be shared.[37]

On Theissen's influential reading, then, the offense given when some Corinthians met for a private meal (ἴδιον δεῖπνον) before the common meal ("the Lord's Supper," δεῖπνον κυριακόν) was to be ameliorated *by instituting a private meal before the common meal.* If this "solution" appears counterintuitive, Theissen argues the inconsistency lies with Paul, who has "compromised" his values. Furthermore, Theissen regards this capitulation as practically inevitable:

> Paul's compromise, which simply acknowledges the class-specific differences within the community while maintaining their manifestations, corresponds to the realities of a socially stratified congregation which *must* yield a certain preeminence to the rich—even contrary to their own intentions. Within such a community the compromise suggested by Paul is realistic and practical.[38]

The result is an undeniable tension: Paul confronts a social conflict but does not intend finally to resolve it. Rather, "the social tensions between rich and poor Christians have been transposed to a symbolic world transcending the everyday reality. They become part of an eschatological drama" in which divisions between rich and poor constitute an eschatological test as the whole community stands in judgment before the Lord.[39]

Depending in part on Theissen's discussion, Meeks argued that social status was a quite fluid phenomenon in Paul's world. It resulted from a number of factors, including sex, class, family, ethnicity, and status as slave or free, of which relative wealth or poverty was only one. Further, some factors—such as wealth—offered opportunity for "social mobility" to ambitious or enterprising individuals who might climb the social ladder, transcending the conditions of their birth. It followed, Meeks argued, that first-century individuals such as filled Paul's congregations shared a common experience of "status inconsistency" or "status dissonance." Meeks asked, at length, whether such inconsistency would have generated "not only anxiety but also loneliness, in a society in which social position was important and usually rigid?"

---

37. Ibid., 163–64.
38. Ibid., 164 (emphasis added).
39. Ibid.

He suggested that such alienated emotions might have made nascent Christianity all the more appealing.

> Would, then, the intimacy of the Christian groups become a welcome refuge, the emotion-charged language of family and affection and the image of a caring, personal God powerful antidotes, while the master symbol of the crucified savior crystallized a believable picture of the way the world really seemed to work?[40]

Meeks generally follows Theissen's interpretation of 1 Corinthians 11:17–34. In particular, he considers it Paul's advice that the "private suppers" practiced by the Corinthians "ought to be eaten 'at home' (22a, 34)."[41] And where Theissen describes a "compromise," Meeks perceives "some confusion" or inconsistency on the part of the apostle. "For Paul," he writes, "it was a matter of intense concern that *at least one* of the typical instances of reunification declared in the 'baptismal reunification formula' [i.e., Gal 3:28] should have concrete social consequences." That one instance involved the breaking down of distinction between Jew and Greek; Paul was less concerned, however, to insist on equality between male and female or slave and free—the other pairs named in Galatians 3. After all, Meeks observes, Paul "nowhere urges Philemon or other owners to free their slaves."[42] Paul's answer regarding private meals in Corinth is thus of a piece (on Meeks's view) with his broader inconsistency regarding the implication of baptism as a symbol of unity and of the Lord's Supper as a ritual of solidarity. The institution of a second meal, to be eaten at home before the common Lord's Supper, surrendered any opportunity to make the latter an occasion for challenging or weakening social stratification in the assembly.

In the social-science oriented reconstruction of the situation, then, our earliest discussion of the Lord's Supper, which also appears to be the first text to relate the meal to the plight of the poor in the Christian assembly, represents something of an apostolic failure of nerve. Instead of a vital call to social justice, on this reading Paul's text constitutes a ready compromise of ideals.

---

40. Meeks, *First Urban Christians*, 22–23, 191.
41. Ibid., 67.
42. Ibid., 161 (emphasis added). For a different reading of Philemon, see Norman R. Peterson, *Rediscovering Paul: Philemon and the Sociology of Paul's Narrative World* (Philadelphia: Fortress Press, 1985).

Challenging the "New Consensus"

The reading of 1 Corinthians 11:17–34 that I have just sketched has won wide acceptance from a range of scholars. Part of its power may lie in its apparent ability to offer a social-scientific explanation for what has long been perceived as Paul's "social conservatism."[43] There are reasons to question the allure of this reading, however.

1. First of all, we should note that if seeking a social-scientific explanation for the Corinthian correspondence is a modern development, awareness of social disparities at the communal table is hardly a recent discovery. Clement of Alexandria already recognized, on the basis of 1 Corinthians 11, that there were rich and poor side-by-side in the Corinthian assembly. As he read the passage, the wealthy person who "eats without restraint or is insatiable . . . disgraces himself," both by adding to the burden of those who do not have and by laying "his own intemperance bare in front of those who do have." The offense, for Clement, was in part an embarrassing breach of etiquette before one's elite peers.[44]

Later, John Chrysostom knew that "*of course* some were poor, but others rich" in the Corinthian assembly. The disparity was so great, he declared, that the Corinthians simply could not have managed the community of goods that had characterized the first assembly in Jerusalem, so they did only what they could. As Chrysostom imagines the scene, the Corinthians shared a ritual meal "on stated days," then went off to "a common entertainment, the rich bringing their provisions with them, and the poor and destitute being invited by them, and all feasting in common."[45] On this scenario, there were two distinct meals. The Lord's Supper—celebrated first—was not an actual meal, but a ritual one. The "feasting" that was the occasion of "schisms" came afterward, at some (apparently public) entertainment to which the poor had access only as they were "invited" by the rich. The offense was not, for Chrysostom, the deprivation of the poor, but first, the partisanship Paul named at the beginning of the letter (1:26), and second, the sin of immoderate desire. When Paul wrote that "one is hungry, and another is drunken," Chrysostom understood him to mean that the craving of one and the drunkenness of another were both expres-

---

43. On Paul's social conservatism, see Neil Elliott, *Liberating Paul: The Justice of God and the Politics of the Apostle* (Maryknoll, NY: Orbis, 1994), 31–52.
44. Clement of Alexandria, *Paedagogus* 2.13 (ANCL).
45. John Chrysostom, *Homiliae in epistulam i ad Corinthios* 27.1 (NPNF).

sions of excess, that is, alike failures of self-discipline.[46] Economic disparity itself was for Chrysostom inevitable; the point was for members of the upper class not to embarrass themselves or, by shaming the poor or treating them with contempt, to bring public dishonor upon the church.[47] In the bishop's eyes, Paul chose to tread delicately here because he didn't wish to be dismissed by the prosperous in Corinth by appearing to side with the poor.[48]

Both Clement and Chrysostom already presumed that Paul's comments indicated economic stratification within the Corinthian community. Strikingly, without the benefit of sophisticated modern social-scientific analysis, they both managed to attribute to Paul a sort of benevolent paternalism appropriate to members of the upper strata. In contrast to modern social-scientific interpreters, however, for these ancient readers there was no cause to speak of Paul's "inconsistency" or of a "compromise" of his values, since they presumed that Paul simply represented the values of his (and their) own class.

2. Despite the implication of objectivity in the phrase "social-scientific interpretation" it appears that modern exegesis is no less influenced by the political and ideological currents of our own age. In an important essay, Steven Friesen has pointed out that the "new consensus" announced by Abraham Malherbe in the 1970s actually continued a much older habit of interpretation.

Around the turn of the twentieth century, Adolf Deissmann already argued that the Pauline churches included "certain fairly well-to-do Christians," including Gaius, "who offered the hospitality of his house to the whole body of the church" in Corinth and, with Erastus (Rom 16:23), must have belonged "to the middle class."[49] Contrary to the later representation of Deissmann as favoring a "proletarian Christianity," Friesen shows that he had little sympathy for the masses, either in antiquity or in his own day. Concerning the apostle, Deissmann wrote

---

46. Ibid., 27.1, 4 (emphasis added). Note that for Chrysostom, the verb πεινᾶν did not necessarily mean "be hungry" but could refer to experiencing excessive appetite.

47. Recall that Chrysostom took from the Epistle to Philemon the lesson that "we ought not to withdraw slaves from the service of their masters"; he was concerned that Christianity was getting a reputation for solicitude toward slaves, which was tantamount to "the subversion of everything" (Homiliae in epistulam ad Philemonem, Argument; NPNF). Here he is careful to point out that the poor are not so much injured by deprivation of food as they are embarrassed for the church's reputation (Hom. 1 Cor. 27.4).

48. "Further, that he might not seem to say these things on account of the poor only, he does not at once strike into the discourse concerning the tables, lest he render his rebuke such as they might easily come to think slightly of . . ." (John Chrysostom, Hom. 1 Cor. 27.2).

49. Adolf Deissmann, St. Paul: A Study in Social and Religious History, trans. Lionel R. M. Strachan (London: Hodder & Stoughton, 1912), 216–17.

that "the poor folk who made up his churches and who lived on obols and denarii, envious persons who even, as St. Paul once says, 'bite and devour one another,' and who by trooping before pagan judges in their miserable disputes over some mere bagatelle exposed the brotherhood to mockery—these people . . . were not inaccessible to vulgar suspicion and unworthy gossip about a great man" (i.e., Paul).[50] Indeed, on Deissmann's account, Paul recognized among the Corinthians plenty who had formerly been "not too scrupulous" about private property: "'thieves' and 'extortioners,' says St. Paul in plain language." Deissmann is certain Paul is referring here to the unscrupulous poor, though he offers no explanation for that certainty;[51] in fact, to the ancients, avarice (πλεονεξία) was at least as likely to be a vice of the well-to-do.[52]

It appears, then, that Deissmann, an early advocate of views later associated with the social-scientific "new consensus," was hardly a neutral, objective observer. Friesen shows that he was a partisan in the class struggle of his time, seeking to thwart the "dramatic advances" of the Marxist Social Democratic Party in Germany. At an important congress in 1908, Deissmann and Adolf von Harnack gave speeches in which, as Friesen summarizes,

> the social description of Paul's assemblies was intertwined with a determined effort to deny a need for structural change in German society. . . . Most of [the speakers] maintained that the gospel could transform the lower classes without disrupting the status quo because the gospel brought inner enlightenment and peace to individuals. . . . Social stratification was not a problem, [dissenting voices] were told, and poverty was not important. The churches simply needed to do a better job of caring for the souls of individuals in order to win back the hearts and minds of the German working class.[53]

I raise the example of Deissmann to ask (as does Friesen) whether more recent exegetes have escaped the influence of capitalist assumptions and predispositions. In fact, Friesen shows that the celebration of a "new consensus" beginning in the 1970s simply perpetuated Deissmann's characterizations regarding socially mixed assemblies that represented a "cross-section" of society, even as heralds of this new consensus attributed to Deissmann himself a "proletarian" view of early

50. Ibid., 71, citing Gal 5:15; 1 Cor 6:1–11.
51. Ibid., citing 1 Cor 6:10.
52. G. Delling, "πλεονέκτης, κτλ.," *TDNT* 6:266–74.
53. Friesen, "Poverty in Pauline Studies," 330–31.

Christianity that he never in fact held.[54] Elsewhere, Friesen reviews a series of twentieth-century US textbooks on the New Testament that reveal that during the same period that social-science critics have been exploring status ambiguity, "poverty and economic inequality have not been important topics in Pauline studies."[55] As Friesen described the situation, "Instead of remembering the poor, *we prefer* to discuss upwardly mobile individuals and how they coped with the personal challenges of negotiating their ambivalent social status."[56]

Friesen perceives an "unacknowledged bias" at work here on the part of social-scientific interpreters: "our preoccupation with 'social status' is the very mechanism by which we have ignored poverty and economic issues."[57] That preoccupation, and the tendency of textbook authors to "portray the Roman Empire with a booming economy" so that poverty has been marginalized as a topic,[58] fit well in the atmosphere of higher education in the industrial and post-industrial United States, where "the primary function of the American professoriate" has been "to train members of the professional-managerial class." In short, Friesen declares, "higher education taught future professionals to accept and to overlook economic inequality, and Pauline studies did so as well."[59] (Indeed, one prominent textbook on the Mediterranean culture of the New Testament goes so far as to deny any relevance at all to the terms "poverty" or "the poor.")[60]

3. It is one thing, of course, to posit (as does Friesen) a correlation between the values of industrial capitalism and the sort of broad generalizations about the ancient world that appear in textbooks and are hallmarks of the "new consensus." It is another to revisit the sources on which those generalizations have been made. In fact, an important stream of scholarship by classicists challenges the trend that Friesen has identified. These scholars have focused attention precisely on the question of the poor and poverty in the Roman world. As Friesen points out, the measure of wealth "is, after all, the most important component

---

54. On the mistaken attribution of a "proletarian" picture to Deissmann, see ibid., 326.
55. Friesen, "Blessings of Hegemony," 121.
56. Friesen, "Poverty in Pauline Studies," 332–35 (emphasis in original).
57. Ibid.
58. Friesen, "Blessings of Hegemony," 123.
59. Ibid., 125–27.
60. "We simply cannot get any idea" what New Testament authors meant when they referred to "the poor," declares Bruce J. Malina (*The New Testament World: Insights from Cultural Anthropology,* 3rd ed. [Louisville, KY: Westminster John Knox, 2001], 99). On the broader denial of first-century poverty and realities of class in Malina's work, see Neil Elliott, "Diagnosing an Allergic Reaction: The Avoidance of Marx in Pauline Scholarship," *The Bible and Critical Theory* 8, no. 2 (2012): 6–9.

of social status," even if it is "the one least likely to be addressed systematically by New Testament scholars."[61] In 1974—before the announcement of a "new consensus" in New Testament studies—classicist Ramsay MacMullen had described the Roman world in terms of a "steep social pyramid," with a few fantastically wealthy people at the top and the poorer masses at the bottom.[62] The breathtaking inequality and exploitive nature of the Roman economy was described, masterfully, by G. E. M. de Ste. Croix,[63] as well as by others.[64] Justin J. Meggitt criticizes the credulous acceptance on the part of New Testament scholars of the picture provided by elite sources from the Roman period, in which the poor play little role at all. These sources were the products of "a very tiny clique." The more appropriate approach should be to read such sources "against the grain."[65] He argues that in the preindustrial, agrarian Roman economy, "almost everyone lives near the level of subsistence," except for a tiny and extraordinarily powerful elite. Friesen agrees: "There is no economic middle class" in the Roman world because there are no economic structures for amassing surplus wealth.[66]

4. Meggitt and Friesen have led the charge in particular against the "new consensus" regarding the members of Paul's churches. Meggitt objects to the broad tendency to generalize about all Paul's churches from the particular circumstances and tensions in Corinth when, in fact, "we have no reliable information about individuals from most of the churches [Paul] founded." The poor are therefore "doubly afflicted": by their own poverty and by their neglect in Paul's letters, which—except for the passage under discussion here—generally leave them in silence.[67] The members of Paul's churches—and Paul him-

---

61. Steven J. Friesen, "Prospects for a Demography of the Pauline Mission," in *Urban Religion in Roman Corinth: Interdisciplinary Approaches*, ed. Daniel N. Schowalter and Steven J. Friesen (Cambridge, MA: Harvard University Press, 2005), 362, 364. Similarly, classicist Greg Woolf observes that in the Roman world, access to wealth was "one of the most explicit and formal measures of an individual's social standing and a key component of his [sic] public identity." "Writing Poverty in Rome," in *Poverty in the Roman World*, ed. Margaret Atkins and Robin Osbourne (Cambridge: Cambridge University Press, 2006), 92.

62. Ramsay MacMullen, *Roman Social Relations 50 B.C. to A.D. 284* (New Haven: Yale University Press, 1974), 90.

63. G. E. M. de Ste. Croix, *The Class Struggle in the Ancient Greek World* (Ithaca, NY: Cornell University Press, 1981).

64. See, *inter alia*, Keith Hopkins, *Conquerors and Slaves* (Cambridge: Cambridge University Press, 1978); Peter Garnsey and Richard Saller, *The Roman Empire: Economy, Society, and Culture* (Berkeley: University of California Press, 1987); Walter Scheidel, ed., *The Cambridge Companion to the Roman Economy* (Cambridge: Cambridge University Press, 2012).

65. Meggitt, *Paul, Poverty and Survival*, chs. 1–3.

66. Friesen, "Prospects for a Demography," 364, citing Ramsey MacMullen in *Roman Social Relations, 50 B.C. to A.D. 284* (New Haven, CT: Yale University Press, 1974); Meggitt, *Paul, Poverty and Survival*, 6–7.

self—were poor, Meggitt argues at length, probably living just above subsistence level. They practiced a form of economic mutuality that was the principal strategy for survival among the urban poor who could not produce their own food.[68] Friesen has conducted a prosopographical study of all the people named in Paul's letters, concluding that the wealthiest members, like Phoebe (the leader in Cenchrae) and Erastus (the "city steward"), probably had only modest means, enjoying "moderate surplus resources"; others were simply indigent.[69] Bruce Longenecker has offered qualifications of Friesen's scale but agrees that the majority of Paul's congregants were poor and none was fabulously rich. Further, he points out that Paul "expected treasuries for the poor (or their equivalent) to be established within communities that he founded," which Longenecker takes as evidence that the poor were visible members of those communities and that Paul was aware of their need.[70]

5. As to the interpretation of 1 Corinthians 11 in particular, several scholars have challenged the scenario advanced by Meeks, Theissen, and Murphy-O'Connor. I discuss three challenges that cast doubt, from different angles, on the social-science reconstruction of social disparity in the context of a fairly luxurious milieu as described above. These challenges also highlight how much remains uncertain about the situation in Corinth.

In her 1994 study of the apostle's rhetoric in 1 Corinthians, Antoinette Clark Wire argued that the assembly's meals were unlikely to have been on the order of formal cultic banquets in the Roman world but were more probably regular, even daily gatherings, at which lower-status women were more likely to have been responsible for providing food. Paul's reference to each eating their own meal suggests "that the food has been cooked in various homes and carried to a common place," a likely scenario "for a group meeting too regularly in one home to expect full hospitality."[71] Nor does the complaint that "one is hungry while another is drunk . . . prove an orgy," she declares with some hyperbole: it simply shows "that at least occasionally . . . food has

---

67. Friesen, "Prospects for a Demography," 358–61.

68. Meggitt, *Paul, Poverty and Survival*, ch. 5.

69. Friesen locates the two at level 4 or 5 on his Poverty Scale ("Prospects for a Demography," 368); Meggitt, *Paul, Poverty and Survival*, 135–41, 148.

70. Longenecker, "Socio-Economic Profiling," 41; Bruce W. Longenecker, *Remember the Poor: Paul, Poverty, and the Greco-Roman World* (Grand Rapids: Eerdmans, 2010).

71. Antoinette Clark Wire, *The Corinthian Women Prophets: A Reconstruction through Paul's Rhetoric* (Minneapolis: Fortress Press, 1990), 106–7. Peter Lampe has made a similar proposal: "The Eucharist: Identifying with Christ on the Cross," *Interpretation* 48, no. 1 (1994): 36–49.

run out before everyone arrives and this has caused conflict."[72] Since on Wire's view there is no householder/host "in charge" of the meal, Paul's "final solution," his "insistence that hunger be satisfied at home" (1 Cor 11:34), would have had the chief effects of depriving Spirit-filled women of their shared responsibility for providing the community's meal and of sending them back to their homes to prepare household meals, "in traditional roles of female and/or servile subordination."[73] Note that on Wire's reconstruction, there is a single meal; Paul is (as for Theissen and Meeks) instituting a possible second meal, this one in private homes, and by so doing has undermined one of the more egalitarian aspects of the common meal. Wire does not address Paul's charge that the Corinthians are showing contempt for the "have-nots," τοὺς μὴ ἔχοντας, but her discussion implies that no one is being regularly deprived of food.

As part of his argument that the Pauline congregations were largely constituted of poor men and women, Justin J. Meggitt disputes that any of the references in 1 Corinthians 11 signal a disparity of rich and poor in the Corinthian assembly. That some were able to acquire ample amounts of food and drink, or "had homes," hardly requires that they were wealthy, he argues. Furthermore, the Greek phrase τοὺς μὴ ἔχοντας, often translated "those who have nothing" (e.g., NRSV), requires an implied direct object, Meggitt argues, which he identifies as the bread and wine of the Eucharist; this was not, then, Paul's reference to destitute persons. Nor was there a common meal intended for the satisfaction of hunger; rather, Meggitt concludes, some Corinthians were improperly approaching the Lord's Supper, which he identifies with the Eucharist, to satisfy their hunger, so that others were left unable to share in it. The problem appears, on this reading, to have been a case of bad manners among poor Corinthians in the absence of any wealthier members. Paul's "practical advice" was that, "in order to avoid the [eucharistic] elements being treated as food, those that were tempted to do so should consume a real meal before coming together."[74] Again, we see Paul's remark in 11:34 taken as the institution of a second meal, though unlike Wire, Meggitt does not imagine that the "first," common gathering was an actual meal.

David Horrell has challenged Murphy-O'Connor's reliance on the archaeological remains of a "sumptuous villa" at Anaploga. Horrell

---

72. Ibid., 108.
73. Ibid., 109–10.
74. Meggitt, *Paul, Poverty and Survival*, 118–22.

argues that we cannot be sure of the actual use of any particular room in that villa (as a "triclinium," for example), we cannot tell that even a "host of the whole church" like Gaius would have lived in such a villa, and since other, less sumptuous residential spaces have been excavated in Corinth, we cannot say just where or how most of the members of the Corinthian ἐκκλησία lived. It is at least as possible that they would have gathered in much humbler residential spaces on the second or third floor of other buildings (*insulae*, such as those found east of the Corinthian theater), the first floors of which were used commercially. (Since food was prepared in some of these first-floor spaces, presumably for sale, Horrell suggests that congregants might have purchased their food before gathering.) Horrell cites the story in Acts of a young man in Troas who fell from a third-story window as Paul waxed overlong in preaching (Acts 20:7–12) as indirect corroboration that such smaller spaces might indeed have accommodated a Christian assembly.[75]

These arguments all dispute one key aspect of the now-prevalent reconstruction described above: namely, that the Lord's Supper was being eaten in the private house of a wealthy Christian in such a way that disparities between rich and poor were exacerbated to the point of the humiliation of the latter.[76] In this regard, these scholars provide salutary reminders of how little we can say with certainty about the Corinthian situation.

On the other hand, Wire's and Meggitt's arguments effectively minimize any implication that men and women are regularly leaving the assembly hungry, or that this constitutes an actual offense against the destitute (usually perceived in the phrase τοὺς μὴ ἔχοντας). For Wire, any hunger is merely "occasional" and presumably insignificant. It follows that Paul's rhetoric is overheated; it might simply be that the Corinthian women responsible for preparing food simply "were not interested in enforcing more structured patterns of community life," as was Paul.[77] On Wire's reading, the apostle appears as an unreliable source regarding the situation in Corinth. For Meggitt, those who "do

75. David G. Horrell, "Domestic Space and Christian Meetings at Corinth: Imagining New Contexts and the Buildings East of the Theatre," *NTS* 50, no. 3 (2004): 349–69.

76. Robert Jewett's reconstruction similarly entails no high-status host: "Tenement Churches and Communal Meals in the Early Church: The Implications of a Form-Critical Analysis of 2 Thessalonians 3:10," *Biblical Research* 38 (1993): 23–43; see also Robert Jewett, *Romans: A Commentary*, Hermeneia (Minneapolis: Fortress Press, 2007), 64–69. I thank Thomas Blanton for alerting me to the first reference and reminding me of the second.

77. Wire, *Corinthian Women Prophets*, 108.

not have" are being deprived on occasion of the bread and wine of the Eucharist, nothing more; they are not actually going hungry.

In this regard, these authors have allowed their larger arguments—concerning the different social experience of the Corinthian women prophets (Wire) or the general poverty of the Pauline congregations (Meggitt)—to eclipse the possibility of tensions caused by actual socioeconomic disparity in the assembly. We may readily concede that Paul's description of what happens at the common meal—"one goes hungry, and another becomes drunk" (v. 21)—may involve exaggeration, but it is deliberate exaggeration, meant to drive home the accusation that some in Corinth have given offense to their disadvantaged neighbors. In Paul's heated language, they have shown contempt for the church by humiliating "those who have nothing" (καταισχύνετε τοὺς μὴ ἔχοντας). These accusations are not instrumental to some other, extrinsic purpose: they are made to achieve a reversal of the behavior that Paul finds offensive. It is not plausible that he means simply "those who do not have a share in the Eucharistic elements" (contra Meggitt); the meal being shared is evidently a substantial meal at which the satisfaction of hunger is an important expectation, not an occasional aberration.[78] Indeed, Andrew McGowan has recently argued that there may not have been a "token" or "symbolic" meal of bread and wine, distinct from a shared supper, at this point. Paul's invocation of Jesus's action at the Last Supper may be directed to describe the ethos that should infuse the common meal, not to provide an "institution narrative" for a (purely ceremonial) "Lord's Supper."[79]

We should exercise appropriate caution regarding the precise scenario addressed in Corinth, or regarding the precise circumstances of the parties involved. But socioeconomic disparity—and the indifference of some in Corinth to the sensibilities of their social inferiors—are clearly the factors behind some incident (or incidents) of affront that have so provoked the apostle. As Richard A. Horsley judiciously frames the matter, "Judging from Paul's rhetoric, it is impossible to determine just what the schisms at the assembly meals were." Nevertheless, social disparities allowed a "few well-off members" to repeat at the common meal practices of recognizing hierarchy and rank that were abundant

78. On the meal as a real supper, see Hans Conzelmann, *1 Corinthians*, trans. James W. Leitch, Hermeneia (Philadelphia: Fortress Press, 1975), 194–95; Theissen, *Social Setting*, 147–53; Wire, *Corinthian Women Prophets*, 102–10.

79. Andrew McGowan, "The Myth of the 'Lord's Supper': Paul's Eucharistic Meal Terminology and Its Ancient Reception," *CBQ* 77, no. 3 (2015): 503–21.

in the environment. "Paul insists that they break with those hierarchical patterns" as they gather for the common meal.[80]

Attending to Paul's Irony

It is surprising, especially given Wire's focus on a rhetorical-critical reading of 1 Corinthians, that both Wire and Meggitt read parts of Paul's admonition as rhetorically neutral. They thus perpetuate a particular weakness of the reconstruction proposed by Theissen, Meeks, and Murphy-O'Connor.

As we have seen, the latter authors read v. 19 without a hint of irony. When Paul declares that "indeed, there have to be factions among you, for only so will it become clear who among you are genuine," he is (in their view) giving straightforward expression to his "eschatological" viewpoint. Again, all these scholars read v. 34, Paul's declaration that the Corinthians should "eat at home," as plainly practical advice. It is (in their view) a simple "recommendation" or "suggestion" or "solution" that effectively removes the satisfaction of hunger from the sacred context of the assembly and relocates it, at least for those who can manage it, to a second meal, to be eaten at home prior to gathering for the "Lord's Supper." The result of this flattened reading is that Paul has "privatized" the satisfaction of hunger in order to retain a reduced and superficial collegiality at what now has become a purely ritual meal. As we have seen, reading v. 34 in this way leads to the rather paradoxical conclusion that Paul has attempted to resolve what he at first saw as a problem ("each one" eating a private meal) by encouraging everyone to "eat at home" before gathering. Advocates of this scenario recognize this paradoxical aspect but attribute it to Paul himself: Theissen speaks of Paul's "compromise" of his own ideals and Meeks, of Paul's "inconsistency."

These are remarkable failures to recognize the texture of Paul's rhetoric. In contrast, other scholars have recognized that a tone of ironic censure permeates this passage.

The irony begins with the *litotes* in v. 17 ("I do not commend you" = "I rebuke you"), repeated in v. 22.[81] Margaret M. Mitchell holds that Paul's declaration, "when you come together it is not for the better but

---

80. Richard A. Horsley, *1 Corinthians*, ANTC (Nashville: Abingdon, 1998), 164–65.
81. *Litotes* is a figure of speech using an understated negative to express a positive, favored for example by the author of Luke-Acts: David E. Aune, *Westminster Dictionary of New Testament and Early Christian Literature and Rhetoric* (Louisville, KY: Westminster John Knox, 2003), 280.

for the worse" (v. 17, cf. 18, 20), plays on the possible double meaning of συνέρχεσθε, an important term in Hellenistic political discourse. Paul means that they do not come together "in the good sense of the term," by being united, but merely assemble.[82] His "mock disbelief" that there are factions among the Corinthians (v. 18) is a rhetorical tactic: Mitchell shows that mock disbelief was used on occasions of grave censure when divisions had undermined the concord expected of a community.[83]

Paul's declaration that there "have to be [δεῖ] factions among you, for only so will it become clear who among you are genuine" drips with irony; he has already, at the start of the letter, rejected the legitimacy of "divisions" and "quarrels" among them (σχίσματα, ἔριδες; 1:10–13). Further, the manifestation of the "genuine" among them would clearly *not* mean the recognition of those who consider themselves socially superior, whom Paul accuses of showing "contempt for the church of God and humiliat[ing] those who have nothing" (v. 22 NRSV). As Horsley summarizes the point, Paul's comment "should be taken as irony, even sarcasm."[84]

Whatever the specifics of the activity surrounding the meal—as we have seen, no single explanation compels universal acceptance—Paul is clearly concerned that some are being disadvantaged, and in a way that publicly humiliates them. It is possible that this is his overheated reaction to a slight that others in Corinth may not have perceived (so Wire), but (as Wire also recognizes) Paul's perception of a fundamental wrong in the Corinthian assembly permeates the whole letter. Paul is clearly incensed that the action of some has jeopardized the sanctity of the entire assembly: "or do you despise the church of God and humiliate those who have nothing?" The point of Paul's declaration that when the Corinthians gather, it is "not to eat the Lord's supper," as well as of his extended discussion of divine judgment manifest in the meal (11:23–32), is that their practice has nullified the meal's very purpose as a common *and consecrated* meal.[85] It would therefore seem not simply to be a prudent "compromise" but to be an extraordinary capitulation for Paul to declare at last, in v. 34, that the very purpose of assembling for the Lord's Supper should be abandoned.

---

82. Margaret M. Mitchell, *Paul and the Rhetoric of Reconciliation: An Exegetical Investigation of the Language and Composition of 1 Corinthians* (Louisville, KY: Westminster John Knox, 1991), 153–56.

83. Ibid., 151–52, with citations of ancient orators.

84. Horsley, *1 Corinthians*, 158–59. Chrysostom discusses the rebuke at some length (*Hom. 1 Cor.* 27.1).

85. See Luise Schottroff, "Holiness and Justice: Exegetical Comments on 1 Corinthians 11:17–34," *JSNT* 79 (2000): 51–60.

That purpose was not (to use the anachronistic categories of later Christianity) primarily "sacramental." So, for example, we cannot accept Hans Conzelmann's judgment that Paul summons the Corinthians "to separate satisfaction of hunger and the community Supper . . . to separate the *sacrament* from satisfaction of hunger."[86] The purpose of the supper is best gleaned, rather, by restoring it to its first-century context. This requires examining the broader phenomenon of associations (θίασοι) in the Hellenistic world.

Recent research into Hellenistic associations has emphasized the centrality of convivial meals for constituting those associations and the space provided in those meals for "social experimentation" in subtle divergence from, and tension with, the hierarchical and status-conscious values of Hellenistic and Roman imperial culture. Relying on that research, Hal Taussig has argued that "early Christian congregations were almost certainly modeled on associations." Comparison with associations, about which we have a wealth of literary and, even more important, epigraphic information, suggests that early Christian gatherings, too, "were not an elite assembly but most likely included—perhaps even predominantly—many laborers with few resources, women of similar means, and slaves."[87] One important task of association meals was to embody a measure of equality across unequal classes in an atmosphere of liminality, in which ordinary observances of social distance were suspended or lessened.[88] My point in invoking the analogy is not to argue that Paul's initial foundation of the Corinthian ἐκκλησία was an egalitarian paradise but that any impulse in an egalitarian direction (which was constitutive of the association phenomenon in general) would immediately have been neutralized by the surrender of its chief medium, sharing food at a common meal. But just such surrender is what Theissen, Meeks, and others allege Paul to have proposed in 11:34.

We should press the point further. Paul was in no place to restructure the Roman economy, but that hardly means that we should imagine him suddenly abandoning the thrust of his own rhetoric in this passage out of a sense of leaden necessity. (Recall here Theissen's language of inevitability, "the realities of a socially stratified congrega-

---

86. Conzelmann, *1 Corinthians*, 195.
87. Hal Taussig, *In the Beginning Was the Meal: Social Experimentation and Early Christian Identity* (Minneapolis: Fortress Press, 2009), 98, 100. Taussig depends on the rich and important work of Philip Harland, *Associations, Synagogues, and Congregations: Claiming a Place in Ancient Mediterranean Society* (Minneapolis: Fortress Press, 2003). See also John Kloppenborg's essay in this volume.
88. Taussig, *In the Beginning*, 122–23.

tion" requiring the Corinthians, and Paul, to "yield a certain preeminence to the rich" as a "realistic and practical" response.)[89] Such an understanding fails to take full measure of Paul's rhetoric and of the larger purpose it served, summoning individuals into congregations that practiced a measure of socioeconomic equality. The point has been made in terms of individual virtue, that is, that Paul sought to encourage "generosity to the poor as a key component of 'righteousness.'"[90] But we cannot understand Paul's rebuke in this part of the letter without setting it in the larger context of his endeavor to promote a communal practice in his assemblies.

Luise Schottroff makes a related observation, setting 1 Corinthians 11:17–34 in the wider practice of common property in the early Christ movement. "What is presumed in 1 Cor. 11:17–34 is a law of possessions that we also find in Acts 2:42–45 and 4:32–5:11. The congregation is a community sanctified by God, with a common property consecrated to God (*koina*, Acts 2:44; 4:32)." Private property is the opposite of common property; it becomes common property as it is consecrated to the community's use. Thus, "the wealthy in Corinth could have eaten at home (1 Cor. 11:22, 33), *but in doing so they would have withdrawn from the congregation and its holiness.*"[91] It is highly unlikely that this was Paul's intent in 1 Corinthians 11:33.

Lawrence L. Welborn argues that this passage must be interpreted alongside Paul's subsequent appeal to the Corinthians to participate in his collection for "the poor among the saints in Jerusalem," an appeal that Paul grounds in the astonishing claim that the obligation of equality (ἰσότης) requires the redistribution of abundance to meet the needs of others (2 Cor 8:13–14); he later tells the Romans that the Christ-associates in Macedonia and Achaia have "entered into partnership with the poor in Jerusalem because 'they *owed it to them*'" (Rom 15:26–27). Where Justin J. Meggitt finds the practice of economic "mutualism" as a "survival strategy" among the poor,[92] Welborn finds a "structural strategy" on the apostle's part, "one in which the *rudiments* of a consciousness of belonging to a class are operative and which seeks to affect the relationship between classes of people in a society. . . . Paul sought to devise and implement strategies that would change social

89. Theissen, "Social Integration," 64.
90. Longenecker, *Remember the Poor*, 314.
91. Schottroff, "Holiness and Justice," 54; also Bieler and Schottroff, *The Eucharist*, 120. Emphasis added.
92. Meggitt, *Paul, Poverty and Survival*.

relationships in accordance with his understanding of the new being 'in Christ.'"[93]

Despite the limitations of our knowledge about specific circumstances in Corinth, Paul clearly has genuinely disadvantaged people in view in his rhetoric. The "have-nots" in 11:22 echo the "nothings" (τὰ μὴ ὄντα) named at the beginning of the letter, in 1:28—a peculiar phrase but one apparently meant to invoke the members of the Corinthian assembly who were not "wise . . . powerful . . . well-born" (1:26), but were "weak" or powerless (τὰ ἀσθενῆ; 1:27).[94] Paul rebukes the distinctions made by some Corinthians with harsh rhetorical questions in 4:7 ("For who sees anything different in you?" etc.), then admonishes them with sarcastic praise: "Already you have all you want!" (lit. "are satiated," κεκορεσμένοι); "already you have become rich! Quite apart from us you have become kings!" (4:8). He cannot mean to level this accusation against all the Corinthians, only against a few better-off individuals. In contrast, the apostles are weak (or powerless), hungry and thirsty, and so on (4:9–13).[95]

Even if the details of the common meal at last elude our scrutiny, then, it is clear enough that differences in status have created tensions in Corinth and that Paul seeks repeatedly to address the higher-status members by taking the side of the poor—indeed, by insisting that God has taken their side (cf. 1 Cor 1:27–31).[96] Whatever the slight to the poorer members, it constitutes, in Paul's eyes, "contempt for the church of God" (11:22).

In this light, we should read the rhetorical question in v. 22 as a stinging rebuke. The NRSV expresses this tone fittingly (if not precisely) by the addition of an exclamation: "What! Do you not have

---

93. L. L. Welborn, review of *Remember the Poor*, by Bruce W. Longenecker, *RBL* 7 (2012). I thank Ray Pickett for reminding me of this important review essay. Welborn has presented a fuller argument for his view that Paul's purpose was "radical": "the equalization of resources between persons of *different* social classes through voluntary redistribution." L. L. Welborn, "'That There May Be Equality': The Contexts and Consequences of a Pauline Ideal," *NTS* 59, no. 1 (2013): 73–90. We eagerly await his forthcoming monograph by the same title in the Paul in Critical Contexts series from Fortress Press.

94. Theissen (*Social Setting*, 71–72) adduces similar phrases from classical literature using the *topos* of "nothingness" as a social denigration. I thank Thomas Blanton for bringing Theissen's discussion to my attention.

95. Pseudo-Libanius's discussion of epistolary styles describes the ironic style, εἰρωνική, as "that in which we feign praise of someone at the beginning, but at the end display our real aim." His example is a letter of censure: "I am greatly astonished at your sense of equity, that you have so quickly rushed from a well-ordered life to its opposite—for I hesitate to say wickedness." Paul's ironic praise ("Already you have everything you want!") is similarly employed in censure. See Abraham J. Malherbe, "Ancient Epistolary Theorists," *Ohio Journal of Religious Studies* 5 (1977): 3–77.

96. As Fee (*First Epistle*, 594) notes, "The perspective is clearly 'from below,' taking the side of the 'have-nots.'"

homes to eat and drink in?" The double negative μὴ γὰρ οἰκίας οὐκ ἔχετε expects an affirmative answer.[97] But the question is ironic. Of course Paul knows they have houses; he is not asking for information on which to predicate his solution ("oh, you *do* have houses? Then I suggest you simply eat at home"). His question is an example of the aggressive invective that Peter Lampe finds throughout 1 and 2 Corinthians, involving suggestive questions, indirect and direct accusations, irony, and "sarcastic shaming" of opponents.[98] The questions that follow continue the tone of rebuke.[99] Horsley neatly brings out the antagonistic force of these questions: "Those obsessed with their own dinner can banquet in their own houses some other time!"[100]

These arguments suggest that we cannot take Paul's simple declaration in 11:34 at face value, either. The NRSV's paraphrase, "If *you* are hungry, eat at home," is already a distortion of Paul's words in the direction of a general rule for the congregation (reading "you" as a plural). But the Greek uses the indefinite pronoun τις: "if *anyone* is hungry, let that person eat at home." The NIV translation, "if anyone is hungry, he *should* eat at home," flattens Paul's arch comment into sincere advice. In v. 22, the prospect of satisfying hunger at home was not a matter of simple practicality but was characterized as a gesture of contempt for the church and scorn for the poor, shown by some in the assembly. It hardly seems likely, then, that εἴ τις πεινᾷ in v. 34 is meant to refer generally to hunger or that eating at home is now presented as a solution, for v. 22 clearly suggests that some Corinthians, the "have-nots," are not able to satisfy hunger by simply "eating at home." The common view that Paul is encouraging a second, prior meal before the common gathering seems in this light worse than paradoxical.

Neither is it possible, then, that v. 34 is advice directed to the same "hunger" referred to in v. 21. Richard A. Horsley is no doubt closer to the sense of Paul's words with his paraphrase, "if you are hungry (i.e., want a more sumptuous dinner), eat at home."[101] Similarly, Gordon Fee writes that the phrase εἴ τις πεινᾷ "almost certainly means, 'if anyone wants to gorge.'" "Those who want to glut at the common meal are being told to do so at home, as it were."[102] But this means that v. 34

97. BDF 220–21.
98. Peter Lampe, "Can Words Be Violent or Do They Only Sound That Way? Second Corinthians: Verbal Warfare from Afar as Complement to a Placid Personal Presence," in *Paul and Rhetoric*, ed. J. Paul Sampley and Peter Lampe (Edinburgh: T&T Clark, 2010), 226–27.
99. The particle ἤ (or) marks "a reproachful question": Conzelmann, *1 Corinthians*, 195.
100. Horsley, *1 Corinthians*, 195.
101. Ibid., 163.

is not a piece of prosaic advice; it continues the sarcastic rhetoric of rebuke begun in v. 17. Or, as I suggested in an earlier discussion, Paul's response in v. 34 "is a humiliating sarcasm for any who would display their status in the quality of food they are served at the common meal: 'eat at home' (where no one can see what you eat)!"[103]

It may be important, especially for readers inclined to dismiss this argument as an expression of modern Leftist sensibilities, to note that the perception of irony or sarcasm here is hardly the invention of hypersensitive modern interpreters. Chrysostom, who (whatever his faults) was carefully attuned to matters of rhetorical nuance, declared that Paul's response was meant "to shame" the Corinthian offenders. He understood the ostensible license to "eat at home" as ironic. "By permitting [the eating of private meals at home], he [Paul] hinders it, and more strongly than by an absolute prohibition. For he brings [the offender] out of the church and sends him to his house, hereby severely reprimanding them, as slaves to the belly and unable to contain themselves." Chrysostom read Paul's phrase as an open rebuke, "discoursing as with impatient children; as with brute beasts which are slaves to appetite. Since it would indeed be very ridiculous if, because they were hungry, they were to eat at home."[104]

The premise behind both references to eating at home—the rebuking question of v. 22 and the mock command in v. 34—is that the people being addressed are accustomed to a level of social recognition in their dining "at home," among their social peers, that is inappropriate and offensive in the assembly, where they are gathered together out of (ἐκ-κλησία) their homes.[105] To bring those attitudes and practices to the common meal would be to "come together . . . for your condemnation" (11:34). Condemnation in the common gathering has already been broached in this letter—in the case of a man who "has his father's wife," something unheard of "even among the nations" (1 Cor 5:1–2). Worse, the Corinthians have failed to expel the offender from the assembly; their toleration of him, which Paul attributes to their "arrogance," threatens to contaminate the community (5:6–8). Paul pronounces judgment: "When you are assembled, and my spirit is present in the power of our Lord Jesus, you are to hand this man over to Satan

---

102. Fee, *First Epistle*, 629, 603.
103. Elliott, *Liberating Paul*, 208.
104. Chrysostom, *Hom. 1 Cor* 28.3 (NPNF).
105. An ἐκκλησία (traditionally translated "church") was any "regularly summoned assembly"; formed from ἐκ- (out) and καλεῖν (to call), it described people "called" together "out of" their private preoccupations, a "convocation" (BDAG, s.v. ἐκκλησία).

for the destruction of the flesh, so that the spirit may be saved in the day of the Lord" (5.4–5). A similar tone of astonished rebuke hangs over the exhortation in 11:17–34. Paul probably means something similar in this passage: it is better for the offending few (who "wish to glut") to keep their offensive behavior away from the holy gathering, rather than bring judgment upon them all.[106]

"Eat at home" is not, then, a simple statement of "advice" or Paul's "solution" to what he regards as the abuse of the supper.[107] The irony may be brought out by rephrasing v. 34 in the conditional mood: (33) "Come together to eat, welcoming one another. (34) *If* you came together without discerning the body, you would gather for your condemnation, and it would be better in that case for any who can't contain their appetite to eat at home. *But instead,* receive one another!" (ἀλλήλους ἐκδέχεσθε).[108]

It cannot be an accident that at this point Paul drops argument and invective and seems to put the Corinthians on hold until his arrival: "about the other things I will give instructions when I come" (11:34). We cannot tell what "the other things" (τὰ δὲ λοιπὰ) might be; the fact that he proceeds with other topics ("now concerning spiritual gifts," 12:1) might suggest that he has simply dropped a subject about which he is not convinced that further argument will be persuasive.

Conclusion

At last, the exact practices that so exercised the apostle may forever remain tantalizingly elusive. Their precise estimation depends on other judgments concerning the socioeconomic status of the Corinthians—which includes judging whether or not some of them were as impoverished as the common translation "the have-nots" (v. 22) would imply. The apparent goal of Paul's rhetoric is clearer, however: he wishes to safeguard in the Corinthian assembly a meal practice that embodies a shared mutuality among its participants. We have seen reason to doubt the prevalent view that Paul stood ready to compro-

---

106. I am grateful to Thomas Blanton for pointing out the analogy in 1 Corinthians 5.
107. The point is lost in the NRSV's somewhat casual translation, "so that when you come together," (that is, *after* you have eaten your private meals at home) "it will not be for your condemnation."
108. Just how we should understand what is happening in the Corinthian gatherings depends, in part, on translating the verbs προλαμβάνει (v. 21) and ἐκδέχεσθε (v. 33). Either verb might carry a temporal sense—some are "going ahead" and eating "before" others, and are encouraged to "wait"—or a nontemporal sense—προλαμβάνει might mean "devour," and ἐκδέχεσθε "accept each other" (in normal hospitality). I am more inclined to the nontemporal sense of both phrases but do not see that the question can be definitively answered.

mise that goal as soon as it became difficult: that is, when the pressure of social expectations in a socially stratified Roman colony interfered with its realization.

The tremendous energy expended in the scholarly interpretation of this passage today suggests that interpreters continue to look to it for some insight into the social circumstances of the Pauline communities. There is a wider discussion and practice of the Eucharist, however, described at the outset, in which 1 Corinthians 11 seems to offer some compass bearing for different groups pursuing social justice in our own time. Today, socioeconomic disparity threatens not only the coherence of the church's witness but the survival of millions and the viability of countless communities. It is therefore no accident that Paul's thought has attracted considerable attention not just within ecclesial boundaries but outside them, among radical thinkers of a possible different world.[109]

We may at last doubt whether exegetical exertions will satisfy that search, although we have seen that the general neglect of the subject of poverty in recent scholarship has less to do with its absence from the Pauline texts than with the presuppositions of modern (first-world) interpreters. Recognizing the ironic tone of Paul's rhetoric throughout this passage should at least remove the possibility of co-opting the apostle as a partner in that disinterest. The question before us is the same question that challenged the residents of first-century Corinth: whether another world is possible.[110] Whatever our interpretive methods may establish regarding Paul's rhetoric in 1 Corinthians, we remain responsible for the grave socioeconomic challenges that we face.

109. Continental philosophers, including avowed Marxists and atheists, have embraced Paul as a radical figure despite his theism: see the discussion in Peter Frick, ed., *Paul in the Grip of the Philosophers: The Apostle and Contemporary Continental Philosophy* (Minneapolis: Fortress Press, 2013).
110. The theme of the World Social Forum, http://tinyurl.com/za3k398.

Select Bibliography

Bieler, Andrea, and Luise Schottroff. *The Eucharist: Bodies, Bread, and Resurrection.* Minneapolis: Fortress Press, 2007.

Cavanaugh, William T. *Torture and Eucharist: Theology, Politics, and the Body of Christ.* Oxford: Blackwell, 1998.

Elliott, Neil. *Liberating Paul: The Justice of God and the Politics of the Apostle.* Maryknoll, NY: Orbis, 1994.

Fee, Gordon D. *The First Epistle to the Corinthians.* Rev. ed. NICNT. Grand Rapids: Eerdmans, 2014.

Friesen, Steven. "Poverty in Pauline Studies: Beyond the So-Called New Consensus." *JSNT* 26, no. 3 (2004) 323–61.

_____. "Prospects for a Demography of the Pauline Mission." In *Urban Religion in Roman Corinth: Interdisciplinary Approaches*, edited by Daniel N. Schowalter and Steven J. Friesen, 351–70. Cambridge, MA: Harvard University Press, 2005.

Harland, Philip. *Associations, Synagogues, and Congregations: Claiming a Place in Ancient Mediterranean Society.* Minneapolis: Fortress Press, 2003.

Horrell, David. "Domestic Space and Christian Meetings at Corinth: Imagining New Contexts and the Buildings East of the Theatre." *NTS* 50 (2004), 349-69.

Horsley, Richard A. *1 Corinthians.* ANTC. Nashville: Abingdon, 1998.

Longenecker, Bruce W. *Remember the Poor: Paul, Poverty, and the Greco-Roman World.* Grand Rapids: Eerdmans, 2010.

_____. "Socio-Economic Profiling of the First Urban Christians." In *After the First Urban Christians: The Social-Scientific Study of Pauline Christianity Twenty-Five Years Later*, edited by Todd D. Still and David G. Horrell, 36–59. Edinburgh: T&T Clark. 2009.

McGowan, Andrew. "The Myth of the 'Lord's Supper': Paul's Eucharistic Meal Terminology and Its Ancient Reception." *CBQ* 77, no. 3 (2015): 503–21.

Meeks, Wayne A. *The First Urban Christians: The Social World of the Apostle Paul.* New Haven, CT: Yale University Press, 1983.

Meggitt, Justin M. *Paul, Poverty and Survival.* Edinburgh: T&T Clark, 1998.

Mitchell, Margaret M. *Paul and the Rhetoric of Reconciliation: An Exegetical Investigation of the Language and Composition of 1 Corinthians.* Louisville, KY: Westminster John Knox, 1991.

Murphy-O'Connor, Jerome. *St. Paul's Corinth: Texts and Archaeology.* Wilmington, DE: Michael Glazier, 1983.

Schottroff, Luise. "Holiness and Justice: Exegetical Comments on 1 Corinthians 11:17-34." *JSNT* 79 (2000): 51–60.

Taussig, Hal. *In the Beginning Was the Meal: Social Experimentation and Early Christian Identity*. Minneapolis: Fortress Press, 2009.

Theissen, Gerd. "Social Integration and Sacramental Activity: An Analysis of 1 Cor. 11:17-34." In *The Social Setting of Pauline Christianity: Essays on Corinth*, 145–74. Edited and translated by John H. Schütz. Philadelphia: Fortress Press, 1982.

Wire, Antoinette Clark. *The Corinthian Women Prophets: A Reconstruction through Paul's Rhetoric*. Minneapolis: Fortress Press, 1990.

10

The Economic Functions of Gift Exchange in Pauline Assemblies

Thomas R. Blanton IV

In a volume entitled *Paul and Economics*, one might well ask whether a discussion of gift exchange is germane to the topic. The "economy," after all, is often taken to constitute an autonomous sphere associated specifically with market exchange—quite the opposite of the extra-mercantile sphere of family and friends typically associated with gift exchange.[1] In what sense, then, may gift exchange be understood to perform "economic" functions? In order to answer the question, we

---

1. So for example, Jacques Derrida, "The Time of the King," in *The Logic of the Gift: Toward an Ethic of Generosity*, ed. Alan D. Schrift (New York: Routledge, 1997), 121–47; Marcel Hénaff, "Is There Such a Thing as a Gift Economy?" in *Gift Giving and the "Embedded" Economy in the Ancient World*, ed. Filippo Carlà and Maja Gori, Akademiekonferenzen 17 (Heidelberg: Universitätsverlag Winter, 2014), 71–84, who writes: "It is impossible to use the term ["gift economy"] without some sense of irony, since the association of its two constituents verges on the oxymoronic: it is accepted that rational economy, as we know it, is based on self-interest and cannot be based on gift-giving understood as an unconditional generous gesture. Conversely, such gift-giving necessarily constitutes a break with the rational economy" (71).

first briefly survey the lexical history of the term "economics," indicating the variety of associations—in some cases contradictory—that the term has acquired. This brief lexical survey provides the basis for an analysis of the "economic" system by which goods and services were transmitted within early Christian assemblies. Finally, attention to processual aspects of cycles of production, transmission, and consumption facilitates the construction of a "cultural biography" of early Christian goods and services as they are classified and reclassified alternately as commodities, possessions, or gifts.

Economy: A Brief Lexical History

The usage of the term "economy" can be traced back to its origins in the Greek *oikonomia*. A compound of *oikos* (household/estate) and *nomos* (principle of ordering), *oikonomia* refers to the ordering of social relations and the division of labor within the *oikos*.[2] In his short treatise *Oeconomicus* (Gk. *Oikonomikos*), the fifth–fourth century BCE historian Xenophon of Athens discusses the topic of household management (*oikonomia*; *Oec.* 1.1).[3] Good management is evident above all when the *oikonomos*, or estate manager, is able to pay all expenses and at the same time, through the production of a surplus, to "increase" the estate (*Oec.* 1.4). Expenses are to be kept to a minimum, and the productive capacities of the estate are to be utilized effectively. Xenophon advises the male head of household by suggesting techniques to motivate both wife and slaves to perform their work most effectively (*Oec.* 7.35–43, 12.5–15.1)[4] and to increase the output of cultivated land. Insufficient work decreases the land's output, whereas intensified labor may result in surplus or abundance (*Oec.* 20.21). This surplus may be stored against future hard times or reinvested through the acquisition, improvement, and sale of additional estates (*Oec.* 20.22–29). Thrift and profit seeking appear in Xenophon as complementary aspects of the well-ordered *oikos*.[5]

---

2. The *oikos* itself is composed of the architectural structures of a house, storehouses, and barns, the grounds on which the house is located, including fields and orchards, associated crops, and the biological and adoptive family members who reside there, in addition to associated slaves. See Moses Finley, *The Ancient Economy* (Berkeley: University of California Press, 1999), 18–20.

3. Translations are those of E. C. Marchant, *Xenophon: Memorabilia and Oeconomicus*, LCL (London: Heinemann, 1959).

4. On the primary division of labor based on the classification of sex, see Pierre Bourdieu, *The Logic of Practice* (Stanford: Stanford University Press, 1980), 200–270.

5. In contrast, Chris Hann and Keith Hart take thrift and conservation to constitute the opposite of the profit motive, which demands the growth and expansion of markets, the significant use of

Xenophon's contemporary Aristotle is less sanguine about the prospect of investment for the purpose of returning a profit. In his *Politica*, Aristotle distinguishes two forms of the "art of acquisition" (*chrēmatistikē [technē]*; *Pol.* 1.2.2; 1.3.2, 13): one is natural, the other unnatural. The art of household management (*oikonomikē technē*) is "natural" in that its aim is to produce wealth sufficient for the sustenance of a "good life" (*Pol.* 1.3.8). The aim of the householder is simply to produce enough to satisfy "natural wants"; human need is viewed as both modest and limited. The "economic art" consists in procuring "a supply of those goods, capable of accumulation, which are necessary for life and useful for the community [*koinōnia*] of city or household" (*Pol.* 1.3.8).[6] *Kapēleia* (trade or market exchange) is viewed as unnatural inasmuch as it is associated with the fulfillment of immodest and unlimited wants; unlimited wants generate the desire to pursue unlimited wealth (*Pol.* 1.3.9, 10, 18).[7] Household management, associated with limited desire and the production of limited wealth, is construed as the opposite of market exchange, which involves the "unnatural" pursuit of unlimited wealth for the satisfaction of unlimited desires. By positing a strict opposition between *oikonomia* and market exchange, Aristotle places the latter squarely *outside* the realm of the "economy."[8]

The tradition of associating the term "economy" with the affairs of the household continued unabated until the late eighteenth century. In his *Short Introduction to Moral Philosophy*, first published in 1742, Francis Hutcheson largely followed the ancient Greek tradition, treating household management under the heading "The Principles of Oeconomics and Politics" but treating "property, succession, contracts, [and] the value of goods and coin" under the heading "Elements of

resources, and expenditure; see Chris Hann and Keith Hart, *Economic Anthropology: History, Ethnography, Critique* (Cambridge: Polity Press, 2011), 18–36.

6. Translation from H. Rackham, *Aristotle: Politics*, LCL (Cambridge: Harvard University Press, 1959), 38–39.

7. Aristotle (*Politica* 1.3.12) concedes that barter is a form of trade that is not contrary to nature, since it is organized only to provide for natural wants and is not associated with the unlimited production of wealth.

8. For Aristotle, the "art of wealth-getting" (*chrēmatistikē [technē]*) is "another species of the art of acquisition" (*esti de genos allo ktētikēs [technēs]*), distinct from the *oikonomikē technē* (*Pol.* 1.3.10). Aristotle recognizes, however, that the two "arts" are "not far removed." For discussions, see Dotan Leshem, "The Ancient Art of Economics," *European Journal of the History of Economic Thought* 21, no. 2 (2014): 1–29; Dotan Leshem, "Aristotle Economizes the Market," *Boundary 2* 40, no. 3 (2013): 39–57; Dotan Leshem, "Oikonomia Redefined," *Journal of the History of Economic Thought* 35, no. 1 (2013): 43–61; Karl Polanyi, "Aristotle Discovers the Economy," in *Primitive, Archaic, and Modern Economies*, ed. George Dalton (Boston: Beacon Press, 1971), 78–115.

the Law of Nature."[9] As Moses Finley notes, commercial and financial issues "were evidently not part of 'oeconomics.'"[10]

The situation would change in 1776, when Hutcheson's student Adam Smith penned his treatise *An Inquiry into the Nature and Causes of the Wealth of Nations*. The backdrop of Smith's work is set by mercantilism, a constellation of theories and practices that aimed to concentrate monetary reserves in the form of gold and silver within a given country through a positive balance of trade.[11] The locus of "economic" activity was no longer viewed as the domestic unit of the household, but the nation-state. The goal was not, as Aristotle had opined, the satisfaction of the limited wants of the family and slaves seeking to live a modest but "good" life, but rather the accumulation of monetary resources within the confines of the state, a goal that could only be accomplished at the expense of neighboring nations with which it was engaged in trade.[12] The shift from the household to the nation-state as the constitutive element by which the "economy" would be defined was well underway.

Reflecting the close relation between fiscal policy and national interests, mercantilists employed the phrase "political economy," which Smith defines as follows:

> Political economy, considered as a branch of the science of a statesman or legislator, proposes two distinct objects: first, to provide a plentiful revenue or subsistence for the people, or more properly to enable them to provide such a revenue or subsistence for themselves; and second, to supply the state or commonwealth with a revenue sufficient for the public services. It proposes to enrich both the people and the sovereign.[13]

During the Industrial Revolution, however, the relaxation of international trade barriers coincided with a further shift in terminology. During the latter half of the nineteenth century, the phrase "political economy" was used interchangeably with the simpler designation "economics," which concerned itself with general "principles" or "laws" of

9. Finley, *The Ancient Economy*, 17.
10. Ibid., 17.
11. For a discussion, see Robert B. Ekelund Jr. and Robert F. Hébert, *A History of Economic Thought and Method*, 4th ed. (New York: McGraw-Hill, 1997), 39–65.
12. Ibid., 42: "A number of writers looked upon trade and bullion accumulation as a zero-sum game, where more for country A meant less for countries B, C, and so forth. Given these aims, protection and 'beggar-thy-neighbor' were attractive policies and were thought by many mercantilists to produce the desired increase in wealth."
13. Excerpted in Steven G. Medema and Warren J. Samuels, *The History of Economic Thought: A Reader* (London: Routledge, 2003), 165.

commerce rather than the policies of nation-states. In his book *The Theory of Political Economy* (1871), William Stanley Jevons wrote:

> It is clear that Economics, if it is to be a science at all, must be a mathematical science. There exists much prejudice against attempts to introduce the methods and language of mathematics into any branch of the moral sciences. . . . My theory of Economics, however, is purely mathematical in character. . . . The theory consists in applying the differential calculus to the familiar notions of wealth, utility, value, demand, supply, capital, interest, labour, and all the other quantitative notions belonging to the daily operations of industry. As the complete theory of almost every other science involves the use of that calculus, so we cannot have a true theory of Economics without its aid.[14]

Mercantilism's emphasis on the "state or commonwealth" as the locus of economic activity was replaced by the "industry" of the industrial age. Coinciding with the shift from mercantilism's "political economy" to the industrial age's "economy" is a tendency to theorize the market as an autonomous, self-regulating, mathematically describable system—a system in which an "invisible hand" purportedly guides market interactions.[15]

Some fifty years after Jevons published his *Principles*, economic historian Karl Polanyi argued that the eighteenth and nineteenth centuries' liberal economic construct of a self-regulating market—and corresponding attempts to implement it—represented a "great transformation" in social and economic history.[16] The tenets and assumptions developed by the "classical" economic theorists, he argued, did not apply to the "primitive" and "archaic" societies that constituted the norm throughout most human history.[17] Instead of independent markets operating according to their own internal logic set by the "supply-demand-price mechanism,"[18] Polanyi argued that in most societies,

14. Ibid., 415–16.
15. The idea of the "invisible hand" derives from Adam Smith, whose formulations provided the basis for later theorists (on the "invisible hand," see ibid., 167).
16. Karl Polanyi, *Origins of Our Time: The Great Transformation* (London: Victor Gollancz, 1945), 13–15, 49–51, 73–82; Karl Polanyi, "The Self-regulating Market and the Fictitious Commodities: Labor, Land, and Money," in *Primitive, Archaic, and Modern Economies*, 26–37; Karl Polanyi, "Our Obsolete Market Mentality," in *Primitive, Archaic, and Modern Economies*, 59–77.
17. Polanyi, *Origins of Our Time*, 50: "Previously to our time no economy has ever existed that, even in principle, was controlled by markets. . . . Though the institution of the market was fairly common since the later Stone Age, its role was no more than incidental to economic life."
18. "A market economy is an economic system controlled, regulated, and directed by markets alone; order in the production and distribution of goods is entrusted to this self-regulating mechanism." Polanyi, *Primitive, Archaic, and Modern Economies*, 26.

market exchanges were "embedded" within social networks established by kinship, clan, religion, and other forms of sociopolitical affiliation. He writes:

> The outstanding discovery of recent historical and anthropological research is that man's economy, as a rule, is submerged [or embedded] in social relationships. He does not act so as to safeguard his individual interest in the possession of material goods; he acts so as to safeguard his social standing, his social claims, his social assets. He values material goods only insofar as they serve this end.[19]

Polanyi viewed the "economy" as an "instituted process" that included a number of social elements that exist outside of typical market exchanges:

> Social activities, insofar as they form part of the [instituted] process, may be called economic; institutions are so called to the extent to which they contain a concentration of such activities [involving the movement and circulation of goods and services]; any components of the process may be regarded as economic elements. . . . The human economy, then, is embedded and enmeshed in institutions, economic and non-economic. The inclusion of the non-economic is vital. For religion or government may be as important for the structure and functioning of the economy as monetary institutions or the availability of tools and machines themselves that lighten the toil of labor.[20]

In light of this brief lexical history, clearly the construct of the autonomous and self-contained sphere of the market developed by classical economists cannot be taken as a definitive account of what constitutes the "economy." *Oikonomia* and its derivative, the "economy," have been understood to refer to household management, to the set of financial policies by which international trade was to be conducted, to a purportedly self-regulating market system governed by the profit motive, and to the "instituted process" by which goods and services are produced, transmitted, and consumed. This variety of definitions suggests that "economics"—like "religion" and other terms that posit broad categories for the purpose of classifying, and thereby of constructing "reality" in a particular way[21]—is created by owners

19. Ibid., 7.
20. Ibid., 147–48.
21. On the role of classification, see Bruce Lincoln, *Discourse and the Construction of Society: Comparative Studies of Myth, Ritual, and Classification* (New York: Oxford University Press, 1989), 131–41, 196–98; on the process by which arbitrary socially constructed categories are made to appear "natural"

of estates, merchants, scholars, and other invested parties "for their [material and] intellectual purposes and therefore is theirs to define. It is a second order, generic concept that plays the same role in establishing a disciplinary horizon that a concept such as 'language' plays in linguistics or 'culture' plays in anthropology."[22] Discussions that limit the "generic, second-order" construct of "economics" to market exchanges driven by the profit motive are unduly tethered to the theoretical formulations of classical economists.

If one assumes the formulations of the classical economists of the eighteenth and nineteenth centuries as a point of departure, it follows that the informal networks of gift exchange and reciprocity that characterize households and close-knit communities must be viewed either as noneconomic systems[23] or, in Marcel Hènaff's words, "at most [they] can be a marginal aspect of this economy."[24] But such formulations fail to take into account the original connotations of the term *oikonomia*, in which the household and village—and the social and material reciprocities that characterize them—play a definitive role. For that reason, a conceptual framework such as that pioneered by Polanyi is more suitable,[25] as it is broad enough to include the nonmercantile household economies described by Greek writers; the (largely) nonmarket economies described by anthropologists such as Malinowski, Mauss, Sahlins, and others;[26] and the market economies described in such detail by Smith and Jevons, as well as their heirs.[27] In accordance

and inevitable, see the classic work by Peter L. Berger and Thomas Luckmann, *The Social Construction of Reality: A Treatise in the Sociology of Knowledge* (New York: Anchor Books, 1990); Elisabeth Schüssler Fiorenza, *In Memory of Her: A Theological Reconstruction of Christian Origins* (New York: Crossroad, 1983), 251–59; Pierre Bourdieu, *Language and Symbolic Power* (Cambridge, MA: Harvard University Press, 2001), 163–70.

22. Jonathan Z. Smith, "Religion, Religions, Religious," in *Relating Religion: Essays in the Study of Religion* (Chicago: University of Chicago Press, 2004), 193–94.

23. As does Derrida, "Time of the King," 121–47.

24. Hénaff, "Gift Economy?," 71.

25. However, the stark opposition that Polanyi posits between "primitive" economies, in which markets are "embedded" within social systems, and capitalist economies, in which social systems are embedded within the mechanisms of the market, cannot be maintained; see Keith Hart, "Heads or Tails? Two Sides of the Coin," *Man* 21, no. 4 (1986): 637–56; Stephen Gudeman, *The Anthropology of Economy: Community, Market, and Culture* (Oxford: Blackwell, 2001), 1–24; Stephen Gudeman, *Economy's Tension: The Dialectics of Community and Market* (New York: Berghahn Books, 2008).

26. Bronislaw Malinowski, *Argonauts of the Western Pacific: An Account of Native Enterprise and Adventure in the Archipelagos of Melanesian New Guinea* (New York: Routledge, 2014); Marcel Mauss, *The Gift: The Form and Reason for Exchange in Archaic Societies* (New York: W. W. Norton, 1990); Marshall Sahlins, *Stone Age Economics* (New York: Aldine, 1972).

27. Note, however, that "new institutional economics," like Polanyi, recognizes the significant roles played by social practices and political policies in shaping markets; so, for example, Ronald Coase, "The New Institutional Economics," *American Economic Review* 88, no. 2 (1998): 72–74; Oliver E. Williamson, "The New Institutional Economics: Taking Stock, Looking Ahead," *Journal of Economic*

with Polanyi's approach, any component of the "instituted process" of the circulation and exchange of goods and services may be called "economic."[28] Gifts and other modes of transmission of goods and services, therefore, fall squarely within the framework of the economic system operative within early Christian assemblies—the system that we now turn to consider.

The Economic Structure of Early Christian Assemblies: Market Exchange, Redistribution, and Reciprocity

Polanyi suggests three modes of the transmission of goods and services: market exchange, redistribution, and reciprocity.[29] Although the three modes provide convenient headings under which to organize the data, a caveat is in order: the tripartite scheme introduces etic categories.[30] While Paul himself distinguishes market exchange from gifts (2 Cor 2:17; Rom 4:4) and is familiar with the practice of redistribution (1 Cor 16:1–4), nevertheless, he does not recognize a distinction between redistribution and reciprocity: both are theorized under the single category of gift exchange. Moreover, as Marshall Sahlins points out, redistribution (or, "pooling") often amounts to nothing more than an organization or system of reciprocities.[31] (See figs. 10.1 and 10.2.)

Literature 38 (2000): 595–613; Mark Granovetter, "Economic Action and Social Structure: The Problem of Embeddedness," *American Journal of Sociology* 91, no. 3 (1985): 481–510.

28. It is axiomatic in contemporary economic anthropology that the term "economic" is to be understood in this broad sense; see, for example, George Dalton in Polanyi, *Primitive, Archaic, and Modern Economies*, xlii: "What we call *economic* organization, or *economic* structure, or *economic* institutions are the rules in force through which natural resources, human co-operation, and technology are brought together to provide material items and services, in sustained, repetitive fashion." More recently, see Richard R. Wilk and Lisa Cliggett, *Economies and Cultures: Foundations of Economic Anthropology*, 2nd ed. (Boulder, CO: Westview, 2007), 32–37; Gudeman, *Anthropology of Economy*, 1–12; Hann and Hart, *Economic Anthropology*, 8–9: "Study of the economy in our sense cannot be restricted to anonymous purchases in markets, since political institutions, social customs and moral rules establish the preconditions for market exchange."

29. In Polanyi's analyses, however, the three modes (exchange, redistribution, and reciprocity) are not sufficiently differentiated. For the sake of clarity, I limit Polanyi's general category of "exchange" to *market* exchange, and I restrict "reciprocity" to *extra-mercantile* exchanges in which principles of return, gratitude, and counter-transmission are invoked.

30. Etic categories are those not utilized by a group or culture that constitutes the object of academic study, but are applied by the researcher as useful analytical tools. In contrast, emic categories are those utilized by a group under study.

31. Sahlins, *Stone Age Economics*, 188. See also the discussion of Gregory Alles, "Exchange," in *Guide to the Study of Religion*, ed. Willi Braun and Russell T. McCutcheon (London: T&T Clark, 2009), 110–24.

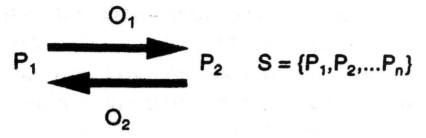

Fig. 10.1: Reciprocity/Gift Exchange (P=person; O=object; S=social group) (From Gregory Alles, "Exchange," 114).

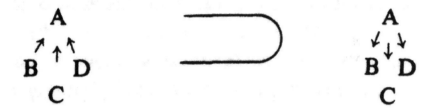

Fig. 10.2: Redistribution (From Marshall Sahlins, *Stone Age Economics*, 188).

Nevertheless, there is an important distinction between the two: "Pooling is socially a *within* relation, the collective action of a group. Reciprocity is a *between* relation, the action and reaction of two parties."[32] While we retain Polanyi's tripartite scheme because it serves useful analytical functions, it is important to recognize that both reciprocity and redistribution may be classified as forms of "gifting."

Market Exchange

Many of the resources available for use in early Christian assemblies likely derived from profits accruing from market transactions. Individuals sold their labor, and households produced and sold goods. Some of the profits that accrued from such ventures, however meager, were used to fund various activities within the assemblies. Market transactions are frequently avoided among family and kinship units,[33] and, as fictive kin,[34] the "brothers" and "sisters" of the assemblies appar-

---

32. Sahlins, *Stone Age Economics*, 188.
33. Ibid., 191–204.
34. On fictive kinship within early Christian assemblies, see Philip A. Harland, "Familial Dimensions of Group Identity: 'Brothers' (Ἀδελφοί) in Associations of the Greek East," *JBL* 124, no. 3 (2005):

ently avoided conducting mercantile transactions with one another, preferring to transmit goods and services on the basis of gift exchange and reciprocity.[35] Market transactions, however, generated revenue, of which a portion could later be put to use within the assembly.

The Sale of Labor and Other Commodities

1. In 1 Thessalonians 2:9, Paul indicates that he "worked night and day so as not to burden" any of his addressees within the early Christian assembly in Thessalonica. According to Acts 18:3, he worked as a leatherworker or "tentmaker" (*skēnopoios*).[36] In Corinth as well, it appears that he worked his trade in order to cover at least some of his living expenses (1 Cor 9:1–18; cf. 2 Cor 11:7).

According to Acts 18:1–3, in Corinth, Paul "found" and "approached" Priska (or, Priscilla) and Aquila, Jews with whom "he remained . . . and worked."[37] Jerome Murphy-O'Connor envisions the couple as crafting protective linen awnings for use in the theater, the forum, in the inner courtyards of houses, or outside shops adjoining the street, and leather tents for use by the military, travelers, and visitors to Corinth's biennial Isthmian games.[38] In view of his self-reported poverty (1 Cor 4:11; 2 Cor 11:27), it is unlikely that Paul possessed the capital to invest in raw materials for the enterprise; he probably gained an income through selling his labor services to the couple.[39] This implies that Priska and Aquila possessed sufficient means to acquire raw materials and to hire laborers to assist in the production of goods, which they sold for a profit. Market exchange generated funds subsequently utilized for the

491–513; Philip A. Harland, *Associations, Synagogues, and Congregations: Claiming a Place in Ancient Mediterranean Society* (Minneapolis: Fortress Press, 2003), 31–33.

35. Julien M. Ogereau (*Paul's Koinonia with the Philippians: A Socio-Historical Investigation of a Pauline Economic Partnership*, WUNT 2/377 [Tübingen: Mohr Siebeck, 2014]) has recently offered an impressively detailed philological argument that Paul and the Philippian assembly were united in a business partnership rather than a gift exchange relationship. He points to the financial terminology used in Philippians 4:15–18 (*logon doseōs kai lēmpseōs, apechō, koinōneō*). Ogereau's thesis, however, does not adequately explain why Paul depicts the Philippian *doma* (payment/gift; Phil 4:17) as a sacrifice to God (Phil 4:18) or why Paul indicates that God would reciprocate the gift by "fulfilling every need" of the Philippians (Phil 4:19), likely in the form of material or "spiritual" benefactions (cf. 2 Cor 9:10–11). The *do ut des* paradigm remains the best explanation for Paul's exchange relationship with the Philippian assembly.

36. On Paul's labor, see Ronald F. Hock, *The Social Context of Paul's Ministry: Tentmaking and Apostleship* (Minneapolis: Fortress Press, 2007); Jerome Murphy-O'Connor, "Prisca and Aquila: Traveling Tentmakers and Church Builders," *BR* 8, no. 6 (1992): 40–51, 62; L. L. Welborn, *An End to Enmity: Paul and the "Wrongdoer" of Second Corinthians*, BZNW 185 (Berlin: de Gruyter, 2011), 355, 392.

37. On the couple, see Murphy-O'Connor, "Prisca and Aquila."

38. Ibid., 43–45, 48.

39. So also ibid., 48.

benefit of early Christian assemblies in Corinth and Rome: Paul, whose labor earned him a minimal livelihood, preached his gospel "free of charge" in Corinth (1 Cor 9:18), and Priska and Aquila, whose sale of commodities earned them surplus income, opened their household for common use during assembly meetings (1 Cor 16:19).[40]

2. In 1 Corinthians 16:1–4, Paul briefly instructs members of the early Christian assembly in Corinth to collect funds to later be transmitted to the assembly's counterpart in Jerusalem: "Let each of you lay aside some of your own resources, saving up whatever extra you earn."[41] These instructions assume profits (however meager) derived from the sale of labor and/or other commodities. Craftsmen and day laborers similar to Paul, struggling to remain at subsistence level,[42] would have been hard pressed to "save up" much in the way of a surplus; contributions from such individuals, if they came at all, would likely have been small.[43] Craftsmen and merchants who could afford to hire labor were probably in a better position to be able to amass surplus earnings.[44]

3. Similar to Aquila and Priska were other merchants such as Lydia, who according to Acts 16:14, was a dealer in purple cloth. Purple dye derived from the murex, a marine mollusk, was expensive to produce, as large numbers of murex were required to make a small amount of dye.[45] According to the Acts narrative, Lydia extended hospitality to Paul for a period of time in Philippi (16:14–15). Since Acts' information concerning Lydia cannot be corroborated, however, it is difficult to assess the reliability of the report.

---

40. Murphy-O'Connor (ibid., 48–50) opines that the couple lived in a rented room above their workshop rather than in a *domus*.

41. NRSV modified. The phrase, "whatever extra you earn" (*ho ti ean euodōtai*; lit. "in that in which you have prospered/been successful") is capable of a broader application and, in addition to profits from market exchanges, may include donations such as the *peculium* of slaves, the *sportula* of clients, and other extra-mercantile sources of income.

42. For a discussion of economic status among early Christians, see the essay by Timothy Brookins in this volume.

43. L. L. Welborn, "'That There May Be Equality': The Contexts and Consequences of a Pauline Ideal," *NTS* 59, no. 1 (2013): 78 writes: "But for the majority of the Corinthians, who lived at the subsistence level, this could hardly have been more than the widow's two mites." However, Philip A. Harland (*Associations, Synagogues, and Congregations: Claiming a Place in Ancient Mediterranean Society* [Minneapolis: Fortress Press, 2003], 38–44) cautions against the assumption that craftspeople formed an economically homogeneous group.

44. Various crafts guilds were able to expend resources on honorific and dedicatory inscriptions (e.g., *Associations in the Greco-Roman World: A Sourcebook* [Waco, TX: Baylor University Press, 2012], 33–34; hereafter *AGRW*) and grave markers (e.g., *AGRW* 37, 40, 56). On the potential difficulties involved with donations from craftworking households, see Peter Oakes, *Reading Romans in Pompeii: Paul's Letter at Ground Level* (Minneapolis: Fortress Press, 2009), 116–18.

45. See "Tyrian Purple," Wikipedia, accessed July 21, 2016, http://tinyurl.com/hag8qga; Mark Cartwright, "Tyrian Purple," *Ancient History Encyclopedia*, July 21, 2016, http://tinyurl.com/goopm4k.

4. It is quite possible that other individuals, such as Stephanas, whose household "devoted themselves to the service of the saints" (1 Cor 16:15 NRSV); Gaius, who is generally understood to have extended hospitality to Paul and to have hosted the "whole assembly" (Rom 16:23);[46] Philemon, who may have put a slave at Paul's disposal (Phlm 1–22); and others who provided him with travel funds, derived some surplus from mercantile activity. The point is uncertain, however, as the extant texts reveal nothing about the sources of these persons' wealth.

In summary, proceeds derived from mercantile activity involving the sale of labor and other commodities in some cases provided financial resources that subsequently were utilized on behalf of the early Christian assemblies. This pattern may have been more widespread than the sources reveal, but the data are sparse.

Redistribution

Polanyi's second category of exchange, redistribution, occurs when goods are transmitted to a central location, stored, and subsequently reallocated. Although Paul was familiar with the practice of redistribution, he tended to conceptualize it under the rubric of gift exchange. The category is nevertheless of analytical utility, since it allows the researcher to distinguish transmissions involving the collective pooling and reallocation of resources from those that do not involve collective pooling.

The Collection for Jerusalem

The "contribution" or "collection" that Paul organized in various regions and local communities for delivery to the relatively prestigious early Christian assembly in Jerusalem falls into the category of redistribution.[47] Donations were presumably collected in the form of currency rather than perishable foodstuffs or other commodities, which would have been more expensive to transport. Individuals retained their own surplus, which was to be gathered within each local community by

---

46. A cautionary note is in order: Richard Last has recently argued that the term *xenos* in Romans 16:23 means not "host," but "guest"; see Last, *The Pauline Church and the Corinthian* Ekklēsia: *Greco-Roman Associations in Comparative Context*, SNTSMS 164 (Cambridge: Cambridge University Press, 2016), 62–71.

47. On the collection, see the essay by John Kloppenborg in this volume.

appointed agents and then transmitted en masse to Jerusalem (1 Cor 16:1–4).

Although Paul uses a variety of concepts to describe his collection effort, the terminology and praxis of gift exchange are salient among them. In 1 Corinthians 16, he writes, "And when I arrive, I will send any whom you approve with letters to take your gift [*charis*] to Jerusalem." The use of *charis* language places the endeavor firmly within the purview of ancient gift giving. In 2 Corinthians 8, in what Hans Dieter Betz has argued is an independent letter to Corinth,[48] Paul uses the terminology of "fellowship" or "partnership" (*koinōnia*; v. 4),[49] "ministry" or "service" (*diakonia*; v. 4), and "favor" or "gift" (*charis*; vv. 4, 6). This set of terms—particularly the use of *charis* language—highlights the voluntary nature of donations to the collection, which Paul explicitly denies is to be understood as an "obligation," "command," or "imposition" (*epitagē*; v. 8). On the other hand, Paul's occasional use of terms denoting compulsory payment, such as *logeia* (1 Cor 16:1–2), which may refer to the collection of taxes,[50] and *leitourgia* (2 Cor 9:12), which may refer to an imposed levy to cover the expenses of a public service,[51] introduce an element of ambiguity concerning the voluntary character of the donation to Jerusalem. As Marcel Mauss noted, although gifts are technically given voluntarily, in practice they are often accompanied by elements of social constraint and compulsion.[52] Paul's collection was no different.

In what may have originally been another independent administrative letter to the assembly at Cenchreae (2 Corinthians 9),[53] Paul describes the collection in similar terms: it is a "ministry" or "service to the saints" (*diakonia eis tous hagious*; v. 1), a "blessing" or "bountiful gift"[54] (*eulogia*; v. 5), and a "public service" (*leitourgia*; v. 12). Paul suggests two distinct motivations for the Achaians' giving, both of which are thoroughly entrenched in the praxis of gift exchange. First, he sug-

---

48. Hans Dieter Betz, *2 Corinthians 8 and 9: A Commentary on Two Administrative Letters of the Apostle Paul*, ed. George W. MacRae, Hermeneia (Philadelphia: Fortress Press, 1985), 3–36.

49. See now the extensive survey of the use of the term in papyri by Ogereau, *Paul's Koinonia*.

50. LSJ, s.v. *logeia*.

51. On the *leitourgia*, see Matthew R. Christ, "Liturgy Avoidance and *Antidosis* in Classical Athens," *Transactions of the American Philological Association* 120 (1990): 147–69; Naphtali Lewis, "Leitourgia Papyri: Documents on Compulsory Public Service in Egypt under Roman Rule," *Transactions of the American Philological Association* 53, no. 9 (1963): 1–39.

52. Mauss, *The Gift*, 3.

53. So Betz, *2 Corinthians 8 and 9*, 3–36, who views 2 Corinthians 9 as an independent letter to Achaia; the addressees are indicated in 9:2. Besides Corinth, the only known Achaian assembly was that of Phoebe in Cenchreae (Rom 16:1).

54. So translates NRSV.

gests that the Achaians are engaged in a contest for honor with the Macedonians.[55] To give abundantly, Paul suggests, would bring them honor, in part through Paul's own boasting about them, whereas to fail to give lavishly would result in their humiliation, as well as Paul's, in the eyes of the Macedonians. He writes: "if Macedonians should come with me [to Cenchreae] and find you unprepared, we—not to mention you—would be put to shame in this venture" (2 Cor 9:4).[56] The accrual of honor and prestige on the basis of liberal giving and the converse, the loss of prestige due to the failure to give liberally, are well-attested cross-cultural norms.[57] Second, in an appeal to the Achaians' self-interest based in an agrarian metaphor, Paul indicates that if they give lavishly, they will be rewarded lavishly by Israel's god: "the one who sows sparingly will also reap sparingly, and the one who sows bountifully will also reap bountifully. . . . God loves a cheerful giver" (2 Cor 9:6–7 NRSV). Paul interprets the collection for Jerusalem using the language and practices of gift exchange. As both Julien Ogereau and Larry Welborn have pointed out, the values of koinōnia ("solidarity"; 2 Cor 8:4, 9:13) and isotēs ("equality"; 2 Cor 8:13–14), as well as the desire to see the needs of fellow assembly members met (2 Cor 8:14, 9:12), are additional motivations that Paul adduces for the collection.[58]

In addition to the Jerusalem collection, the Lord's Supper may be mentioned as a possible instance of redistribution. The current consensus view, developed among others by Gerd Theissen and Jerome Murphy-O'Connor, entails aspects of patronage and hospitality, whereby a wealthier individual opened her household to the gathered assembly and provided food and drink.[59] A competing view proposed by Peter Lampe holds that food was to be brought by each individual or household and collected before being redistributed equally among all those present in an eranos-style meal.[60] In a forthcoming article, John Klop-

---

55. For a discussion of the competition for honor associated with *epidoseis*, see the essay by John Kloppenborg in this volume.
56. My translation.
57. See Mauss, *The Gift*, 33–43; Christopher A. Gregory, "Gifts to Men and Gifts to God: Gift Exchange and Capital Accumulation in Contemporary Papua," *Man* 15, no. 4 (1980), 626–52; so, too, in Paul's Romanized context, see Thomas R. Blanton IV, *A Spiritual Economy: Gift Exchange in the Letters of Paul of Tarsus*, Synkrisis (New Haven, CT: Yale University Press, 2017), 27–40.
58. Welborn, "That There May Be Equality," 73–90 (see also Welborn's contribution in this volume); Julien M. Ogereau, "The Jerusalem Collection as Κοινωνία: Paul's Global Politics of Socio-Economic Equality and Solidarity," *NTS* 58, no. 3 (2012): 360–78.
59. Gerd Theissen, "Social Integration and Sacramental Activity: An Analysis of 1 Cor. 11:17–34," in *The Social Setting of Pauline Christianity: Essays on Corinth*, ed. and trans. John H. Schütz (Philadelphia: Fortress Press, 1982), 145–74; Jerome Murphy-O'Connor, *St. Paul's Corinth: Texts and Archaeology* (Wilmington: Michael Glazier, 1983), 153–61. On the eucharistic meal, see also the essay by Neil Elliott in this volume.

penborg criticizes both views and proposes that, by analogy to communal meals in *collegia* and assemblies in the Greco-Roman milieu, the Lord's Supper may have been financed by regular dues paid by members of early Christian groups.[61] We need only note here that two of the three proposed scenarios—those of Lampe and Kloppenborg—involve redistribution. In contrast, the current consensus view suggests that the meal operated according to principles of reciprocity and patronage, themes to be examined presently.

Reciprocity / Gift Exchange

Of Polanyi's three categories of exchange, reciprocity appears to have been the preferred vehicle for the transfer of goods and services within early Christian assemblies. To avoid overlap between the categories, we limit reciprocity to extra-mercantile exchanges in which principles of return, gratitude, and counter-transmission are invoked; it is thus coterminous with gift exchange[62] and refers to that which is "given" or "donated" rather than "sold," "bartered," or "traded."[63] The dominant forms of reciprocity attested in the Pauline literature include hospitality, the donation of travel funds, and donations of labor time.

Hospitality

Hospitality—the provision of room and board to travelers without pay—falls into the category of reciprocal exchange. Tesserae, or "tokens," were sometimes prepared to mark the initiation of a hospitality relation;[64] guest and host were expected to offer each other

60. Peter Lampe, "Das korinthische Herrenmahl im Schnittpunkt hellenistisch-römischer Mahlpraxis und paulinischer *Theologia Crucis*," ZNW 82, no. 3–4 (1991): 183–213; Peter Lampe, "The Corinthian Eucharistic Dinner Party: Exegesis of a Cultural Context (1 Cor. 11:17–34)," *Affirmation* 4 (1991): 1–15.

61. John S. Kloppenborg, "Precedence at the Communal Meal in Corinth," NovT 58 (2016): 167–203.

62. For a working definition of "gift exchange," see Blanton, *Spiritual Economy*, 8–11.

63. On the distinction between gift and "sale" (or market transaction), see James Carrier, "Gifts, Commodities, and Social Relations: A Maussian View of Exchange," *Sociological Forum* 6, no. 1 (1991): 119–36; James Carrier, "The Gift in Theory and Practice in Melanesia: A Note on the Centrality of Gift Exchange," *Ethnology* 31, no. 2 (1992): 185–93; James Carrier, "Emerging Alienation in Production: A Maussian History," *Man* 27, no. 3 (1992): 539–58. On the fuzziness of the line that sometimes separated the two, see Gretchen Herrmann, "Gift or Commodity: What Changes Hands in the U. S. Garage Sale?" *American Ethnologist* 24, no. 4 (1997): 910–30; Blanton, *Spiritual Economy*, 41–60.

64. John Nicols, "The Practice of *Hospitium* on the Roman Frontier," in *Frontiers in the Roman World: Proceedings of the Ninth Workshop of the International Network Impact of Empire (Durham, 16–19 April 2009)*, ed. Olivier Hekster and Ted Kaizer (Leiden: Brill, 2011), 325; see also John Nicols, "*Hospitium* and Political Friendship in the Late Republic," in *Aspects of Friendship in the Graeco-Roman World*, ed. Michael Peachin (Portsmouth, RI: Journal of Roman Archaeology, 2001), 99–108; Nicols, "Hospital-

social and legal support.[65] In some cases, gifts were given, either to the host[66] or to the visitor.[67] In the early Christian context, guests could respond to their hosts' largesse by providing linguistic offerings: in the Synoptics, Jesus's disciples pronounce a blessing of "peace" over the hosting household (Matt 10:13; Luke 10:5-6). In light of the fact that Paul viewed "material things" and "spiritual things" as existing in a relationship of exchangeability within a system of reciprocity (Rom 15:27),[68] it is possible that hospitality was construed as a response to Paul's "gift" of the gospel. In defense of his "right" to be provided with food and drink (1 Cor 9:1-18)—presumably within the context of hospitality—Paul asks, "If we have sown spiritual good among you, is it too much if we reap material benefits?" (1 Cor 9:11 NRSV). Moreover, the inter-assembly linkages facilitated by hospitality fall into Claude Lévi-Strauss's category of "generalized reciprocity,"[69] popularly designated by the phrase "pay it forward": a sometime host could expect to be hosted herself—although not necessarily by the same individual she had previously hosted—when visiting early Christian assemblies in distant cities.[70]

Claiming the authority of Mosaic law (1 Cor 9:8-12, citing Deut 25:4), Paul asserts that traveling apostles reserved the right to be provided "food and drink," presumably in the context of hospitality (1 Cor 9:4). Although the narrative in Acts likely exaggerates the extent to which Paul enjoyed hospitality during his travels, he is depicted as "staying with" no fewer than eight different hosts in as many cities (Philippi, Thessalonica, Corinth, Ptolemais, Caesarea, Malta, Puteoli, and an undisclosed location between Caesarea and Jerusalem).[71] By his own account, Paul enjoyed the hospitality of Gaius in Corinth (Rom 16:23)[72] and requested that Philemon prepare him a "guest room" (Phlm 22), presumably in the latter's household in Colossae. In his letter recom-

---

ity among the Romans," in *The Oxford Handbook of Social Relations in the Roman World*, ed. Michael Peachin (Oxford: Oxford University Press, 2011), 422-37.

65. Nicols, "The Practice of *Hospitium*," 323.

66. Nicols, "Hospitality among the Romans," 426.

67. So John T. Fitzgerald, "Hospitality" in *Dictionary of New Testament Background*, ed. Craig A. Evans and Stanley E. Porter (Downers Grove: InterVarsity Press, 2000), 522: "The establishment of this pact of guest friendship was cemented and symbolized by a gift that the host bestowed on the departing guest (Homer *Odys.* 1.311-13)."

68. So Blanton, *Spiritual Economy*, 15-26.

69. Claude Lévi-Strauss, *The Elementary Structures of Kinship* (Boston: Beacon Press, 1969), 233-54, 445.

70. For early Christian injunctions to offer hospitality, see 1 Peter 4:9; Hebrews 13:2; see also the dispute over hospitality in 3 John 9-10.

71. Acts 16:11-15, 34; 17:1-9; 18:1-4; 21:7-8, 15-16; 28:7, 14.

72. See, however, the caveat above in n. 46.

mending Phoebe to the early Christian assembly in Rome (Rom 16:1–2), he requests that the addressees "receive her worthily in the Lord and provide her with whatever she might need from you"—implying a request for hospitality.[73] The request for a reception "in the Lord" suggests that hospitality was based not on ethnicity or kinship but on common religious affiliation as members of the "body of Christ" (Rom 12:4–5; 1 Cor 12:12–27).[74] The practice of hospitality both extended the effective range of early Christian missionaries and facilitated the development of inter-assembly relations.[75]

Lord's Supper (à la Theissen, Murphy-O'Connor)

Without presuming that it is necessarily the most compelling reconstruction—Lampe's and Kloppenborg's dissenting opinions have already been noted—we point out here some implications of the current consensus view that patronal figures hosted the Lord's Supper, indicating the ways in which the meal functioned within the context of reciprocity. The consensus view holds that the Lord's Supper was hosted within the household of wealthier members of the assembly. Paul rarely styled such economically well-endowed hosts as patrons—the one possible exception being Phoebe, who is called a "patroness of many" (*prostatis*; Rom 16:2).[76] The economic disparity between the wealthier host and many of his less affluent guests would nonetheless be evident during communal meals, inviting comparison with typical patron-client relations in Rome and its provinces.[77] Whereas elite patrons were typically honored by their clients, that is, the recipients of their largesse, through the construction of statues or inscriptions,[78] the members of early Christian assemblies, typically living close to subsistence level, were in no position to honor their hosts in such a manner. Paul made a point, however, of recognizing such patronal figures by thanking them or otherwise mentioning them

---

73. So, for example, James D. G. Dunn, *Romans 9–16*, WBC 38B (Dallas: Word Books, 1988), 888.
74. Fictive kinship, however, likely also played a role (e.g., Rom 1:13, 14:10; 1 Cor 1:10).
75. On the importance of travel for the maintenance of inter-assembly connections, see the essay by Cavan Concannon in this volume.
76. On the term, see Peter Lampe, "Paul, Patrons, and Clients," in *Paul in the Greco-Roman World: A Handbook*, ed. J. Paul Sampley (Harrisburg, PA: Trinity Press International, 2003), 498–99.
77. So, for example, Murphy-O'Connor, *St. Paul's Corinth*, 178–85; Gerd Theissen, "Social Integration and Sacramental Activity: An Analysis of 1 Cor. 11:17–34," in *Social Setting*, 145–74; Thomas Schmeller, *Hierarchie und Egalität: Eine sozialgeschichtliche Untersuchung paulinischer Gemeinden und griechisch-römischer Vereine* (Stuttgart: Katholisches Bibelwerk, 1995), 66–73.
78. See, for example, Frederick W. Danker, *Benefactor: Epigraphic Study of a Graeco-Roman and New Testament Semantic Field* (St. Louis, MO: Clayton Publishing House, 1982).

in his correspondence; a papyrus letter was a much more economical means of honoring benefactors than a marble inscription or statue (1 Cor 16:15–18; cf. Rom 16:1–4, 5, 19; Phlm 2). In this way, the typical pattern by which patrons offered material aid, and in return received linguistic counter-gifts in the form of praise and thanksgiving,[79] was maintained despite the constraints of a severely limited budget among the early Christian "clientele."[80]

The ritual aspect of the Lord's Supper also deserves consideration, as it involves gift-exchange motifs. In a letter to Corinth, Paul recounts a eucharistic tradition that he had received in which Jesus broke bread, blessed it, and stated, "This is my body that is for you. Do this in memory of me" (1 Cor 11:23–26 NRSV). The body of Jesus, commemorated in the Lord's Supper, is said to be "for you"—that is, "for" the participants in the ritual meal. The terse formulation is elaborated in other Pauline passages, where Jesus is said to have "given" himself as a sacrifice to remove the guilt associated with breaches of covenantal norms (Rom 3:24–26; 5:15, 17; 2 Cor 5:21–6:1; Gal 2:19–21)—associations also indicated in the reference to the "new covenant" in 1 Corinthians 11:25. This entails not only the idea that Jesus's death was voluntary (Phil 2:8) but also the notion that he stripped himself of the heavenly power and glory with which he was invested prior to his earthly existence (Phil 2:5–8): "For your sakes he became poor, so that by his poverty you might become [spiritually] rich" (2 Cor 8:9 NRSV). Such musings likely lead Paul to exclaim: "thanks be to God for his indescribable gift" (2 Cor 9:15). God "gave" his own son (Rom 8:32), who in turn "gave" himself (Gal 1:4, 2:20): Jesus's death on the cross is, for Paul, the "spiritual gift" par excellence. Jesus's gift of himself is memorialized not in a statue or durable inscription but through the ephemeral performance of the ritual meal, which is lent permanence to the extent that it is reiterated "until he comes," as Paul would have it (1 Cor 11:26); the meal constitutes its participants as a living memorial to their heavenly benefactor.[81]

---

79. See Carolyn Osiek, "The Politics of Patronage and the Politics of Kinship: The Meeting of the Ways," *BTB* 39 (2009): 143–52; Blanton, *Spiritual Economy*, 27–40.

80. I thank John Kloppenborg for pointing out that similar "low budget" forms of showing honor were practiced in other Greco-Roman associations: acclamation in the assembly and the bestowal of a crown of olive leaves.

81. On the memorialization of exemplary actions—as Paul takes Jesus's death to be—see Matthew B. Roller, "Exemplarity in Roman Culture: The Cases of Horatius Cocles and Cloelia," *Classical Philology* 99, no. 1 (2004): 1–56; Matthew B. Roller, "The Exemplary Past in Roman Historiography and Culture," in *The Cambridge Companion to the Roman Historians*, ed. Andrew Feldherr (Cambridge: Cambridge University Press, 2009), 214–30.

Travel Funding

In addition to receiving and providing hospitality, members of early Christian assemblies made regular appeals to the communities within which they were active to provide them with funds for travel. Such requests, however, were euphemized in polite expressions, as in Paul's letter to the assembly at Rome: "I hope to see you when I pass through, and to be sent on my way [to Spain] by you, once I have enjoyed your company for a little while" (Rom 15:24 NRSV modified). Paul employs the passive verb *propemphthēnai* (to be sent on one's way) regularly in polite appeals for travel funding. He makes such appeals not only on his own behalf (1 Cor 16:6; 2 Cor 1:16; Rom 15:24), but also on behalf of his protégé, Timothy (1 Cor 16:11). The costs of travel funding may have been borne by wealthier "patronal" members of the assemblies, as Zeba Crook plausibly suggests.[82] Another possibility is raised by a second century inscription from Lanuvium (*AGRW* 310 = *CIL* XIV 2112 = *ILS* 7212), in which functionaries of a cultic association of Diana and Antinoüs are allotted a "round trip travel allowance of twenty sesterces each" (l. 29) when on out-of-town trips to bury deceased members.[83] The travel allowance was apparently drawn from association funds, collected on the basis of regular dues and fees. If this method pertained in early Christian assemblies, then travel funds were transmitted through redistribution rather than reciprocity.

Labor Time

In addition to travel funds, members donated their own labor time pursuant to assembly affairs. Working as a craftsman in Corinth to support himself, Paul devoted his remaining energies to the service of the city's local assembly "free of charge" (1 Cor 9:18). His associate Timothy volunteered his services in the same city (1 Cor 4:17, 16:10–11; 2 Cor 1:19), as in Thessalonica (1 Thess 3:1–6) and Philippi (Phil 1:1, 2:19–23). Silvanus also devoted labor time in the service of the Pauline ministry in Corinth and Thessalonica (2 Cor 1:19; 1 Thess 1:1).

The members of the household of Stephanas "tasked themselves to the service of the saints" by contributing their "work" and "labor" in carrying out assembly affairs (1 Cor 16:16). In return for their diligence, Paul gives them official recognition in his letter and urges his

---

82. See Crook's essay in this volume.
83. *AGRW* 196.

Corinthian addresses to "be subject to" and (publicly) "recognize" such people (vv. 16, 18), service is construed as an avenue to achieve enhanced authority and status. Stephanas, Fortunatus, and Achaicus traveled to Ephesus, where they may have provided material assistance to Paul (1 Cor 16:17–18), as Gerd Theissen tentatively suggests.[84]

"Sister Phoebe," whom Paul describes as a "patroness" and "functionary [*diakonos*] of the assembly in Cenchreae" (Rom 16:1–2), traveled to Rome as a representative of the Achaian assembly, perhaps bearing Paul's letter to be delivered upon arrival. As a representative of the assembly in Philippi, Epaphroditus traveled to visit Paul, who was imprisoned in Rome or Ephesus, to deliver needed supplies (Phil 4:18). Epaphroditus is described as a "brother," "fellow worker," "fellow soldier," and one who "provided for [Paul's] need" (*leitourgon tēs chreias mou*; Phil 2:25). Paul urges his addressees to "hold in esteem" (*kai tous toioutous entimous echete*) those who serve the assembly in such a capacity (Phil 2:29–30). Andronicus and Junia, impounded with Paul as "fellow prisoners" (Rom 16:7), are recognized as "distinguished among the apostles" (Rom 16:7). In each case, service within early Christian assemblies provided an avenue whereby honor and prestige could be accrued, and Paul himself was instrumental in recognizing assembly functionaries: his letters served as vehicles through which honor was apportioned.

Unlike those of Paul, Timothy, Stephanas, Phoebe, and other assembly functionaries whose donations of labor time appear to have been voluntary, the labor services of slaves, clients, and retainers were offered on an involuntary or partially voluntary basis. It is possible that the slave Onesimus orchestrated his own visit to Paul in a Colossian prison in order to appeal to him as an *amicus domini* (friend of the master)[85] to persuade his owner, Philemon, to forgive him for harming Philemon's financial interests (Phlm 18–19). On the other hand, Sara Winter has argued that Onesimus had been tasked by his owner, Philemon, to provide for Paul's needs in prison.[86] If Winter is correct, then Onesimus serves as an example of one whose labor services were offered involuntarily, by order of his master. Since Paul construed the

---

84. Gerd Theissen, "Soziale Schichtung in der korinthischen Gemeinde: Ein Beitrag zur Soziologie des hellenistischen Urchristentums," *ZNW* 65 (1974): 250.

85. So Peter Lampe, "Keine 'Sklavenflucht' des Onesimus," *ZNW* 76 (1985): 135–37.

86. Sara C. Winter, "Paul's Letter to Philemon," *NTS* 33 (1987): 1–15; Sara C. Winter, "Methodological Observations on a New Interpretation of Paul's Letter to Philemon," *Union Seminary Quarterly Review* 39 (1984): 203–12. Ulrike Roth ("Paul, Philemon, and Onesimus: A Christian Design for Mastery," *ZNW* 105, no. 1 [2014]: 102–30) has recently argued that Paul's *koinōnia* language indicates a business partnership between Paul and Philemon (i.e., they were joint owners of the slave).

labor of the slave as a substitute or proxy for that of the master (Phlm 13), merit accrued to the master, not to the slave (Phlm 4–7, 14, 20).[87]

Likewise, the "people" in Ephesus who, under Chloe's authority, reported to Paul internal strife within the Corinthian assembly may have included slaves, clients, or retainers (*hoi Chloēs*; 1 Cor 1:11).[88] In the case of clients or retainers, service to the assembly was technically voluntary but nevertheless performed under a degree of compulsion: one does not lightly refuse the requests of one's patron or employer. Slaves, of course, had little choice but to accede to the requests of their owners. In this case as well, any honor that accrued from such service accrued to Chloe, whose "people" remain anonymous. When slaves or retainers were utilized, labor time in service of the assemblies apparently was construed as the donation of the owner or employer who financed their service.

Early Christian Goods and Services: A Cultural Biography

Although Polanyi's three categories of market exchange, redistribution, and reciprocity provide convenient rubrics, they obscure processual aspects of the transmission of goods and services within early Christian assemblies. The elements of time and process are highlighted as central analytical categories in the work of Igor Kopytoff, who argues that particular goods may pass into and out of situations in which they are classified as "commodities," "possessions," or "gifts."[89] Only by following an object over time, as it is either temporarily possessed or transmitted through various mercantile and extra-mercantile contexts, can the researcher begin to construct a "cultural biography" of the object or good in question. Tracing the trajectories of the goods and services transmitted through the three modes of market exchange, redistribution, and reciprocity illustrates the dynamic processual quality that constitutes their "cultural biography," as indicated in the following charts.

---

87. Roth ("Paul, Philemon, and Onesimus," 121) writes, "slave agents were understood as (physical) extensions of their masters on whose behalf they acted." On early Christian exploitation of slave labor, see also Roth's essay in this volume.

88. Theissen, *Social Setting*, 93: "probably slaves or dependent workers."

89. Igor Kopytoff, "The Cultural Biography of Things: Commoditization as Process," in *The Social Life of Things: Commodities in Cultural Perspective*, ed. Arjun Appadurai (Cambridge: Cambridge University Press, 1986), 64–94. Appadurai elaborates Kopytoff's insights in the introduction to the same volume ("Introduction: Commodities and the Politics of Value," 3–63).

Temporal Sequencing of Modes of Exchange: Two Trajectories
Trajectory 1: Redistribution

Locus of Exchange or Transmission:	Extra-assembly	Inter- or inner-assembly	Extra-assembly
Mode of Exchange or Transmission:	Market Exchange ⟶	⟶ Redistribution ⟶	⟶ Market Exchange
	labor/goods sold on market (= commodities) ⟶ profits ⟶	Jerusalem collection (Social function: to effect inter-assembly solidarity in theory and practice) ⟶	[purchase food, clothing, other goods]
	labor/goods sold on market ⟶ profits ⟶	Travel funding (?)[1] ⟶	Market Exchange (purchase foodstuffs, pay for transportation, lodging)
	labor/goods sold on market (=commodities) ⟶ profits ⟶	Lord's supper (?)[2] (Social function: to effect inner-assembly solidarity in theory and practice)	

Key:
Arrow → indicates temporal sequencing
Square brackets [] indicate hypothetical or contrary-to-fact-projection

[1] If allocated from assembly funds collected by member dues and fees.
[2] If supper is "potluck"/eranistic, or is funded by member dues and fees.

Fig. 10.3.

Temporal Sequencing of Modes of Exchange: Two Trajectories
Trajectory 2: Reciprocity/Gift Exchange

Locus of Exchange or Transmission:	Extra-assembly	Inter- or inner-assembly	Extra-assembly
Mode of Exchange or Transmission:	Market Exchange ————→	Reciprocity/gift ————	→ Market Exchange
	labor/goods sold on market (= commodities) ——→ profits —→	Hospitality (Social functions: to effect inter- and inner-group solidarity; extend effective range of functionaries)	
	labor/goods sold on market ——→ profits —→	Lord's supper (?)[1] (Social function: to effect inner-assembly solidarity in theory and practice)	
	labor/goods sold on market ——→ profits —→	Travel funding (?)[2] —→	Market Exchange (purchase foodstuffs, pay for transportation, lodging)
	labor/goods sold on market ——→ profits —→	Labor time (Social functions: internal assembly affairs: maintain institutional base; missionary activity: augment institutional base)	

Fig. 10.4.

[1] If supper is distributed by patronal figures.
[2] If funds provided largely by patronal figures.

301

We may make the following observations based on the charts:[90]

1. Much of the funding for activities conducted within early Christian assemblies may have originated in market exchanges—that is, through the sale of labor or other commodities—although the relevant data are sparse. Other possible sources of income, such as large bequests or patronal donations, booty from war, and the seizure of properties through legal instruments, generally presuppose a level of affluence and imperial political connection not typically associated with early Christian assemblies and therefore seem unlikely. Smaller endowments may have been within reach; Jinyu Liu notes that endowments to associations that are as small as eighty sesterces are recorded.[91] Other possibilities may also be considered: slaves may have controlled a limited *peculium* derived from tips,[92] and clients may have been able to draw on the *sportulae* provided by patrons. There is no direct evidence, though, to indicate whether these potential sources of funding were utilized in service of the assemblies.

2. A temporal sequence is noted in which profits from the sale of commodities, passing into usage within the assembly, were subsequently redistributed or donated among members, largely in transmissions associated with the language and norms of reciprocity and gift exchange.

3. In some instances, transmissions of goods and services terminated in assembly activities: the food from the Lord's Supper was consumed, as were any comestibles transmitted under the rubric of hospitality, and labor time was expended in service of the community. Goods and services whose "cultural biographies" terminate in assembly activities represent the "cost" of maintaining the sociopolitical unit that consti-

---

90. Note that in fig. 10.3, the square brackets enclosing the second or terminal market exchange mode indicate the hypothetical or counterfactual character of the final disposition of the funds to be transmitted to Jerusalem in Paul's collection effort. It is not known whether or not the Jerusalem assembly accepted the donation. Although there is a strong presumption that the collection for the poor members among the Jerusalem assembly would have been used to purchase food and other supplies for those individuals and households, the uncertainty as to whether the collection was accepted renders this aspect of the chart hypothetical. It indicates what likely would have been the disposition of the funds had they been accepted. Moreover, in both figures, brief notes are included regarding the salient potential social functions of transmissions listed under the rubric of reciprocity or gift exchange. This listing indicates potential social functions without assuming that in any given case those potential effects were realized in practice.

91. Jinyu Liu, "The Economy of Endowments: The Case of Roman Associations," in *Pistoi dia tèn Technèn: Bankers, Loans and Archives in the Ancient World; Studies in Honour of Raymond Bogaert*, ed. Koenraad Verboven, Katelijn Vandorpe, and Véronique Chankowski-Sable, Studia Hellenistica 44 (Leuven: Peeters, 2008), 231–56.

92. On the *peculium*, see now Andreas M. Fleckner, "The *Peculium*: A Legal Device for Donations to *personae alieno iuri subiectae*?" in Carlà and Gori, *Gift Giving*, 213–39. See also the essay of Roth in this volume on the possible use of *peculium* by slaves in early Christian assemblies.

tuted the "body of Christ." Even "spiritual" associations require material support.[93]

4. In other instances, reciprocal or redistributive transmissions within the purview of assembly matters constituted only an intermediate phase within a sequence of exchanges. The collection for Jerusalem's poor, had it succeeded, likely would have been poured back into the market to purchase food, clothing, and other necessities for destitute members. The funds that Paul and other functionaries received to cover travel expenses undoubtedly were expended to secure means of travel, lodging, and food and drink during the journey. In such cases, currency derived from market exchanges was transformed into a gift and subsequently transformed again into a commodity to be traded for other commodities.

5. Market exchanges were suppressed within inner- and inter-assembly transmissions of goods and services and appear to have been conducted largely outside the purview of assembly affairs. This is in keeping with the characteristics of market transactions, which are generally avoided within family and kinship units. Assembly members construed themselves as fictive kin: "brothers" and "sisters" in the "body of Christ"—a relation more conducive to gift exchange than to buying and selling.

6. Note that Polanyi's three modes of transmission of goods and services, although they provide useful heuristic categories with which to organize the data, nonetheless distinguish transactions that Paul collapses under the rubric of gift exchange: the Jerusalem collection, under Polanyi's classificatory system a form of redistribution, is distinctly conceived as a form of gift exchange for Paul, guided by principles of reciprocity. Similarly, as we have seen, the extension of hospitality, donations of travel funds and labor time, and possibly the hosting of the Lord's Supper were construed according to the norms of gift exchange. In many cases, donations of funds, material goods, and labor services were recompensed through the bestowal of honor and public recognition; often this occurred or was enjoined within Paul's letters themselves.

93. The view, derived from Descartes, that posits the "spiritual" (a term used in this essay as a synonym for "religious") as standing in opposition to the "material," and the related view that "religion" is concerned with nonmaterial or transcendent matters opposed to the "material" concerns of "the world," cannot be maintained.

Summary and Conclusions

The "economic" system governing the production, transmission, and consumption of goods and services within early Christian assemblies associated with Paul differed both from the household *oikonomia* described by Aristotle and Xenophon and from that described by "classical" economists. Although it likely relied on the household economy as a basic unit of production, it united assembly members drawn from multiple households within a given locale and facilitated translocal linkages by involving a network of assemblies in the collection project. It differed from the "economic" systems theorized by classical economists such as Smith and Jevons in that it included not just market exchange—although that constituted a significant component—but also systems of reciprocity and redistribution. Paul tended to theorize "economic" relations among members and groups within the early Christian assemblies by adapting the language and practices of gift exchange. By incorporating market exchange, reciprocity, and redistribution into a single system under the aegis of fictive kinship in the "body of Christ," a "spiritual economy" was organized,[94] facilitating the transmissions of currency, goods, and services that both maintained and augmented the social infrastructure of the early Christian assemblies. The phrase "spiritual economy" is not an oxymoron; the collocation is indicative of the necessary—albeit often repressed—material and economic aspects of religion.

The religious ideals that posited early Christian groups as fictive kin united within the "body of Christ," as well as the notion that Israel's god and his son, Jesus, had given, and therefore the believer ought to give in return (e.g., 2 Cor 8:7-12, 9:6-15; cf. 1 Cor 9:11; Phil 4:17-20; Phlm 19-20), are ideals that engendered material consequences, as they motivated the transmission—often in the form of gifts and donations—of food, currency, and labor services. Paul's "spiritual" discourse was crafted to produce tangible *material* effects. The religious ideologies of early Christian communities were both catalysts for and reflec-

---

94. The phrase "spiritual economy" is used as a shorthand to indicate two of the salient features on which the foregoing analysis was based, "religion" and "economy" (on the former category, see the discussion above, 284–85 and n. 22). Neither "religion" nor "economy" are treated here as self-evident categories of human experience; both are scholarly constructs—albeit constructs of considerable heuristic value. Concerning the ideological tenets on which the early Christian economy was predicated, see Blanton, *Spiritual Economy*, 15–26; on the "double structural game" involved in "religious" economies, see Pierre Bourdieu, *Practical Reason: On the Theory of Action* (Stanford: Stanford University Press, 1998), 92–123.

tions of their material and economic infrastructures: "religion" and "economy" were two sides of a single coin.

Select Bibliography

Alles, Gregory. "Exchange." In *Guide to the Study of Religion*, edited by Willi Braun and Russell T. McCutcheon, 110–24. London: T&T Clark, 2009.

Barclay, John M. G. *Paul and the Gift*. Grand Rapids: Eerdmans, 2015.

Betz, Hans Dieter. *2 Corinthians 8 and 9: A Commentary on Two Administrative Letters of the Apostle Paul*. Edited by George W. MacRae. Hermeneia. Philadelphia: Fortress Press, 1985.

Blanton, Thomas R., IV. *A Spiritual Economy: Gift Exchange in the Letters of Paul of Tarsus*. Synkrisis. New Haven, CT: Yale University Press, 2017.

Bourdieu, Pierre. *Practical Reason: On the Theory of Action*. Stanford: Stanford University Press, 1998.

Briones, David E. *Paul's Financial Policy: A Socio-Theological Approach*. LNTS 494. London: Bloomsbury T&T Clark, 2013.

Carrier, James. "Gifts, Commodities, and Social Relations: A Maussian View of Exchange." *Sociological Forum* 6, no. 1 (1991): 119–36.

Crook, Zeba A. *Reconceptualising Conversion: Patronage, Loyalty, and Conversion in the Religions of the Ancient Mediterranean*. BZNW 130. Berlin: de Gruyter, 2004.

Engberg-Pederson, Troels. "Gift-Giving and Friendship: Seneca and Paul in Romans 1–8 and the Logic of God's *Charis* and Its Human Response." *HTR* 101, no. 1 (2008): 15–44.

Gouldner, Alvin W. "The Norm of Reciprocity: A Preliminary Statement." *American Sociological Review* 25, no. 2 (1960): 161–78.

Gregory, Christopher A. "Gifts to Men and Gifts to God: Gift Exchange and Capital Accumulation in Contemporary Papua." *Man* 15, no. 4 (1980): 626–52.

Gudeman, Stephen. *The Anthropology of Economy: Community, Market, and Culture*. Oxford: Blackwell, 2001.

Hann, Chris, and Keith Hart. *Economic Anthropology: History, Ethnography, Critique*. Cambridge: Polity Press, 2011.

Hénaff, Marcel. "Is There Such a Thing as a Gift Economy?" In *Gift Giving and the "Embedded" Economy in the Ancient World*, edited by Filippo Carlà and Maja Gori, 71–84. Akademiekonferenzen 17. Heidelberg: Universitätsverlag Winter, 2014.

Joubert, Stephan. *Paul as Benefactor: Reciprocity, Strategy, and Theological*

Reflection in Paul's Collection. WUNT 2/124. Tübingen: Mohr Siebeck, 2000.

Kopytoff, Igor. "The Cultural Biography of Things: Commoditization as Process." In *The Social Life of Things: Commodities in Cultural Perspective,* edited by Arjun Appadurai, 64–91. Cambridge: Cambridge University Press, 1986.

Mauss, Marcel. *The Gift: The Form and Reason for Exchange in Archaic Societies.* New York: W. W. Norton, 1990.

Ogereau, Julien M. "The Jerusalem Collection as Κοινωνία: Paul's Global Politics of Socio-Economic Equality and Solidarity." *NTS* 58, no. 3 (2012): 360–78.

_____. *Paul's Koinonia with the Philippians: A Socio-Historical Investigation of a Pauline Economic Partnership.* WUNT 2/377. Tübingen: Mohr Siebeck, 2014.

Polanyi, Karl. *Origins of Our Time: The Great Transformation.* London: Victor Gollancz, 1945.

_____. *Primitive, Archaic, and Modern Economies: Essays of Karl Polanyi.* Edited by George Dalton. Boston: Beacon Press, 1971.

Sahlins, Marshall. *Stone Age Economics.* New York: Aldine, 1972.

Welborn, L. L. "'That There May Be Equality': The Contexts and Consequences of a Pauline Ideal." *NTS* 59, no. 1 (2013): 73–90.

Wilk, Richard R., and Lisa Cliggett. *Economies and Cultures: Foundations of Economic Anthropology.* 2nd ed. Boulder, CO: Westview, 2007.

11

Paul's Collection for Jerusalem and the Financial Practices in Greek Cities

John S. Kloppenborg

Scholarship on the "collection for the poor of the saints," mentioned in 1 Corinthians 16:1–4, Galatians 2:10, 2 Corinthians 8–9, and Romans 15:25–28, has focused on the understandings of the collection, respectively, by the Jerusalem group and by Paul. At least five rationales for the collection have been offered, which I will survey without much commentary.[1] The most straightforward solution is that the collection was simply to relieve the distress of the poor in Jerusalem.[2] After all,

1. David J. Downs, *The Offering of the Gentiles: Paul's Collection for Jerusalem in Its Chronological, Cultural, and Cultic Contexts*, WUNT 2/248 (Tübingen: Mohr Siebeck, 2008), 3–26, offers a helpful schematic analysis, which is adapted considerably and expanded here. Throughout this essay I use standard epigraphical abbreviations; in addition, GRA I = John S. Kloppenborg and Richard S. Ascough, *Greco-Roman Associations: Texts, Translations, and Commentary: I. Attica, Central Greece, Macedonia, Thrace*, BZNW 181 (Berlin: de Gruyter, 2011); GRA II = Philip A. Harland, *Greco-Roman Associations: Texts, Translations, and Commentary: II. North Coast of the Black Sea, Asia Minor*, BZNW 204 (Berlin: de Gruyter, 2014).

Paul refers to the collection as a κοινωνίαν . . . εἰς τοὺς πτωχοὺς τῶν ἁγίων τῶν ἐν Ἱερουσαλήμ (Rom 15.26), and in 2 Corinthians 8:14, Paul depicts the collection as something that is a matter of "your present abundance and their need" so that there might be ἰσότης. Yet, this view sidesteps two issues: the first is that the earliest mention of the collection in 1 Corinthians 16:1–4 says nothing about the relief of poverty as the motivation for the collection, and when this rationale is mentioned in 2 Corinthians 8 and 9, it is part of Paul's impassioned and highly rhetorical attempts to revive the Corinthians' flagging interests in the collection. Second, this approach makes the collection Paul's initiative and leaves unexamined what understanding and interest, if any, the Jerusalem group had in the collection, the relation of the collection to Galatians 2:10, and why in Romans 15:25–28 Paul seems anxious that the Jerusalem group would accept the collection.

2. Karl Holl emphasized the political aspects of the collection, at least from the perspective of the Jerusalem group of Christ followers. He conjectured that the collection was effectively a tax imposed by the leaders of the Jerusalem group, which had assumed a leadership and supervisory role vis-à-vis all other Christ groups.[3] Part of Holl's argument was predicated on the assumption that οἱ πτωχοί and οἱ ἅγιοι were monikers for the Jerusalem group itself and that, accordingly, the injunction to "remember the poor" in Galatians 2:10 amounted to a requirement of support for the Jerusalem group imposed upon Paul. Holl's view also implied that there was a disconnect between Jerusalem's view and Paul's representation of the agreement, since he treated the collection not as a tax but as a free gift, flowing from the fact that gentiles had received "spiritual benefits" from them.[4]

3. Johannes Munck objected to Holl's juridical interpretation and to the inference that Paul had fraudulently misrepresented a legally mandated collection to his gentile groups as a free offering. Munck insisted that it was in fact a free offering, taking 2 Corinthians 8:7 and 9:7 at face value and not as Paul's desperate attempts to appeal to the Corinthians' generosity in order to persuade them to continue the collection project. Munck's main contribution, however, was the suggestion that Paul's motivation for the collection was "ecumenical,"[5] evok-

---

2. David G. Horrell, "Paul's Collection: Resources for a Materialist Theology," *Epworth Review* 22, no. 2 (1995): 76, 78.

3. K. Holl, "Die Kirchenbegriff des Paulus in seinem Verhältnis zu dem der Urgemeinde," in *Sitzungsberichte der preussischen Akademie der Wissenschaften. Jahrgang 1921* (Berlin: Verlag der Akademie der Wissenschaften, 1921), 940–41.

4. Holl, "Kirchenbegriff des Paulus," 938.

ing the idea of the eschatological pilgrimage of gentiles to Jerusalem that would serve as a demonstration to the Jerusalem group of the impending eschatological age[6] and even as a "provocative" act to spark the conversion of Israel.[7]

4. Josef Hainz revived some aspects of Holl's view, suggesting that differences existed between the original agreement mentioned in Galatians 2:9–10, the interpretation that the Jerusalem group put both upon the agreement and on the collection, Paul's understanding of what had been agreed upon, and the understandings of his gentile Christ groups. The original agreement was the recognition of different expressions of one gospel and the collection was the means by which this recognition was expressed. But Hainz noted that there was a tension latent in the agreement.[8] Paul's formulation, εὐδόκησαν γὰρ Μακεδονία καὶ Ἀχαΐα κοινωνίαν τινὰ ποιήσασθαι (Rom 15:26), underscores that when writing to the Roman Christ groups, Paul depicted the collection as an initiative that rested with his gentile groups, not with either himself or Jerusalem. The collection was a matter of a free decision of those groups, not a legal imposition of the Jerusalem group. Moreover, κοινωνία τις amounted, in Hainz's view, to an intentional "restriction" of possible claims of Jerusalem, limiting the warrants of the collection to "the realm of fraternal solidarity" and removing it from "the sphere of the legal claims of Jerusualem."[9] For Paul, the collection was "a work of love" and recognition of the preeminent position of Jerusalem, but preeminence was freely recognized and not legally enforceable.

5. Finally, Stephan Joubert understands the dynamics between Paul, his Christ groups, and the Jerusalem group within the framework of reciprocal exchange. The initial agreement, described by Paul in Galatians 2:9–10, involved recognition of Paul's law-free gospel by the "pillars" (James, Peter, and John), a benefit that placed Paul in the debt of the Jerusalem group and put him under an obligation to reciprocate. The reciprocation asked of Paul and of the Antiochene group was material support for the poor members of the Jerusalem group.[10] This is not

---

5. Johannes Munck, *Paul and the Salvation of Mankind*, trans. Frank Clarke (Richmond, VA: John Knox, 1959), 290.

6. Munck, *Paul*, 299–308; Keith F. Nickle, *The Collection: A Study in Paul's Strategy*, SBT 48 (London: SCM Press, 1966), 138–39.

7. Munck, *Paul*, 301; Dieter Georgi, *Remembering the Poor: The History of Paul's Collection for Jerusalem* (Nashville: Abingdon, 1991), 118–19.

8. Josef Hainz, *Koinonia: "Kirche" als Gemeinschaft bei Paulus*, Biblische Untersuchungen 16 (Regensburg: Pustet, 1982), 123–51.

9. Ibid., 149.

10. Stephan Joubert, *Paul as Benefactor: Reciprocity, Strategy and Theological Reflection in Paul's Collection*,

a matter of a tax but rather of the moral obligations created by bene-faction.

According to Joubert, the breakdown in Paul's relationship with Antioch and Barnabas, and hostility to his cause from some factions in Jerusalem, led to a shift in his own representation of the collection. In appealing to the gentile groups in Macedonia and Achaea, he did not refer in the first instance to the economic plight of believers in Jerusalem, still less to an agreement with Jerusalem, "but rather *the repayment of their own debts* to the mother church."[11] Since gentiles would not ordinarily have considered care for the poor as a moral priority, Paul emphasized balanced reciprocity: "not only did they joyfully embrace their role as debtors, but their generous contributions was also proof of their striving to surpass the gift from their benefactors in Jerusalem in deed and spirit."[12] Paul even encouraged the agonistic nature of euergetism, whereby benefactor and beneficiary would exchange roles in a continued game of gift and counter-gift.[13] This presentation of the nature of the collection obscured entirely the original rationale present in Galatians 2:9–10 and any notion of subservience to the Jerusalem group, emphasizing instead the free nature of the gentiles' undertaking.

The sophistication of Joubert's account lies not only in his use of anthropological theory of gift-exchange but in the attention to the complex and shifting ways in which Paul represents his relationship with Jerusalem (and his gentile groups). In Galatians, he treated the relationship with the "pillars" within the framework of reciprocity:

WUNT 2/124 (Tübingen: Mohr Siebeck, 2000), 114–15. See also G. W. Peterman, "Romans 15.26: Make a Contribution or Establish Fellowship?," *NTS* 40, no. 3 (1994): 457–63.

11. Joubert, *Paul as Benefactor*, 132n31 (emphasis original). The term "mother church" is rather unfortunate, since it seems rather doubtful that Paul regarded the Jerusalem group as a "mother church" given his comments in Galatians 1 and even his somewhat disparaging references to οἱ δοκοῦντες στῦλοι in Gal 2:6, 9. Nevertheless, Rom 15:25–30 indicates that Paul saw the importance of acknowledgement by the "pillars."

12. Joubert, *Paul as Benefactor*, 139.

13. Steven J. Friesen, "Paul and Economics: The Jerusalem Collection as an Alternative to Patronage," in *Paul Unbound: Other Perspectives on the Apostle*, ed. Mark D. Given (Peabody, MA: Hendrickson, 2010), 48, is critical of Joubert for holding that Paul and the Corinthians could be both benefactor to, and beneficiary of, the Jerusalem group, arguing that this violates basic definitions of patronage and benefaction. Joubert, however, is careful to distinguish patronage from euergetism. It is not that the Corinthian group aims to become the "patron" of the Jerusalem groups, its erstwhile patron. Joubert's point, moreover, might be explained more clearly by observing that Paul does not represent the relationship with Jerusalem in a single and consistent manner, and that the representation changes depending on Paul's correspondents. To the Corinthians in 2 Corinthians 8–9, he stresses the free initiative of the Macedonians and thus casts to them an euergetic role. To the Romans, he stresses both free undertaking of gentile groups and their balanced exchange with Jerusalem, while constructing himself as an agent of *diakonia*.

they had conferred a benefit, which he and Barnabas were obliged to reciprocate. In 2 Corinthians 8–9, it is not Paul's own obligation to Jerusalem that is mentioned, but the enthusiasm and, in fact, insistence of the Macedonians to participate in a reciprocal exchange, and their free undertaking in doing so. A more complex picture is offered in Romans, since Paul again underscores the initiative of the gentile groups in engaging in the collection (15:26) and articulates the balanced reciprocal nature of the exchange (15:27), ignoring entirely his own obligations. Nevertheless, he also represents the collection as his διακονία rather than as their gift.[14] The anxiety he expressed about the reception of the collection nevertheless betrays the fact that his honor and standing are at stake in the exchange.[15]

With a few exceptions, the discussion of Paul's collection has been conducted without attention to the financial practices known from the Greek and Roman world.[16] If any analogy to other collections is drawn, it is usually the didrachma tax imposed on Judean males.[17] Yet the collection, maintenance, and distribution of communal funds were extremely common throughout the ancient Mediterranean world, and many of the practical issues that Paul's groups had to face find close parallels in other small groups and in the administration of Hellenistic *poleis*.

In what follows, I do not intend to propose that these "influenced" the collection for the poor, or that either Paul or the Jerusalem group "borrowed" practices from the Hellenistic world. It would be impossible to demonstrate such a genealogical relationship in any case, short of Paul admitting that he was copying another practice, which, of course, he does not admit. Moreover, in the twenty-first century, all kinds of collections are taken up without us having to suppose that they are all borrowed from a "common source," ancient or modern. My point, instead, is that we know much more about Hellenistic fiscal practices than we do about the Pauline collection, and knowledge of

---

14. This ambivalence is also expressed in 2 Cor 8:19–20, where he refers to the "gift that is being administered by us" (ᾗ χάριτι ταύτῃ τῇ διακονουμένῃ ὑφ' ἡμῶν) but also as their χάρις (2 Cor 8:6, 7).

15. Downs (*Offering of the Gentiles*, 35–36 n. 2) argues that Paul's trepidation about the reception of the collection would be hard to explain if he were merely carrying out the wishes of the Jerusalem group. Yet, this ignores the profound difficulties that Paul encountered with parts of the Jerusalem group in the subsequent Antioch incident and in his dealings with the Galatian Christ-group. Clearly the terrain had changed since Gal 2:10.

16. Exceptions are Verlyn D. Verbrugge, *Paul's Style of Church Leadership Illustrated by His Instructions to the Corinthians on the Collection* (San Francisco: Mellen Research University, 1992); Joubert, *Paul as Benefactor*; Downs, *Offering of the Gentiles*; and Bruce W. Longenecker, *Remember the Poor: Paul, Poverty, and the Greco-Roman World* (Grand Rapids: Eerdmans, 2011).

17. Nickle, *The Collection*, 74–99.

how other groups collected and disbursed funds, and the problems that were involved in these practices, will help us to see the Pauline collection in a different light, to understand better the kinds of problems and challenges that his collection may have generated, and to raise questions about the collection that would have occurred to most Greeks but have not occurred to exegetes of Pauline literature. That is, my interests are heuristic, not genealogical, and I do not want to fall into the apologetic trap of deciding where Paul's primary "influences" lay.[18]

Four aspects of fiscal practice offer possible analogies to the Pauline collection: the management of common funds with special interest in security, the according of due recognition for largesse, available *comparanda* for euergetic donations for public projects, and the ideology at work in such collections.

Financial Administration: Security and Audit

It is mostly uncontroversial that the Corinthians wrote to Paul inquiring about the collection and that 1 Corinthians 16:1–4 addresses their questions.[19] It has, unfortunately, been common to suppose that the Corinthians were unpracticed in collecting funds, and accordingly, they inquired as to how to organize the collection. Yet it infantilizes the Corinthians to suppose that they were somehow so naïve that they needed instructions on how to collect funds. We have good epigraphical evidence from Achaia, the Isthmus, and the Peloponnese that groups of handworkers and resident aliens (metics)—that is, precisely

18. David Frankfurter, "Comparison and the Study of Religions of Late Antiquity," in *Comparer en histoire des religions antiques. Controverses et propositions*, ed. Claude Calame and Bruce Lincoln (Liège: Presses Universitaires de Liège, 2012), 93–94, helpfully describes the role of comparison in the study of ancient religions: "My procedure then largely follows the method that Smith laid out: (a) to understand that anomaly as part of a *system*, (b) to *describe* it tentatively, (c) to ask of what phenomenon it might be an *example*, (d) to describe it according to some *critical terminology*, (e) to ask or seek out what might be a *fuller or richer* example; (f) to articulate, on the basis of both proximate *comparanda* with limited context and distant *comparanda* with richer context, a plausible social *context* in which the datum makes sense, the anomaly familiarized—a context that may require abandonment or adjustment with further primary data; and finally (g) to propose some broader observations about the *pattern*, the phenomenon, on the basis of this new data." For the purposes of this essay, my procedure is similar—not genealogical (to discover the "source" of Paul's collection) but rather analytic: to propose Hellenistic fiscal practices of which Paul's collection might be an example, to describe those practices using critical terminology (security, recognition, analogy, and ideology), and without seeking more distant *comparanda*, to articulate a social context for the collection.

19. This assumes that περὶ δὲ τῆς λογείας τῆς εἰς τοὺς ἁγίους in 1 Cor 16:1 is a letter response formula, referring to a question raised in the Corinthians' letter to Paul. See John C. Hurd, *The Origin of 1 Corinthians* (London: SPCK, 1965), 200–206. Hurd rightly argues that the Corinthians were likely concerned about the nature of the delivery of the collection, but as will be clear from what follows, they have additional concerns about security and credit.

the kinds of people who made up the majority of Pauline groups—had been engaged in collecting funds for at least four hundred years before Paul arrived in Corinth.[20] Besides, the idea of collecting money for a common project is hardly a conceptually or practically challenging notion.

The issues for the Corinthians, which they expressed in their letter to Paul, were not about how to collect funds, but concerned collecting funds for a nonlocal group (the *ekklēsia* in Jerusalem), how to ensure that such funds collected for that purpose would be delivered to their intended recipients, and how an accounting of the full amount would be guaranteed. That is, the concerns that the Corinthians expressed derived not from not knowing how to collect money but from the anomalous nature of the collection and the peculiar fiscal problems that such a collection presented.

One of the most commonly recurring elements in private association inscriptions pertaining to the management of funds is the insistence on adequate audit procedures. A single example will suffice. In early second century CE Attica, an association of Herakleiastai whose activities included sacrifices and banquets was funded through an endowment, the purchase of priesthoods, entrances fees, member contributions, and various fines. The treasurer was enjoined not to expend more than three hundred drachmae on dinners;[21] if he did, he would incur a fine of three times the sum in excess of three hundred drachmae (SEG 31:122.13–15). Likewise, a former treasurer, having been discovered through audits to have purloined funds for his own use, would be subject to a similar fine (ll. 15–16). Those deputed to purchase wine and meat for the banquets who did not deliver the goods were to be fined twice the value of what they were to supply. The treasurer was required to provide an account of his income and expenses, and auditors were appointed to scrutinize this.

Each of these regulations points to a deep concern that the association's funds would be secured against theft and misuse. That careful auditing of the work of the treasurers and secretaries and scrutiny of their accounts were normal practices in associations is indicated by

---

20. See, *inter alia*, the collection of inscriptions in *GRA* I.

21. At a 6 percent draw on the investment, this would represent an endowment of 5,000 drachmae, well within the typical range of endowments (see Joshua Sosin, "Perpetual Endowments in the Hellenistic World: A Case Study in Economic Rationalism," [PhD diss., Duke University, 2000], passim). For investment returns, see Richard Duncan-Jones, *The Economy of the Roman Empire: Quantitative Studies*, rev. ed. (Cambridge: Cambridge University Press, 1982), 364–65. Sosin uses the figure of 6–10 percent.

the frequency with which former treasurers and secretaries are commended δικαιοσύνης ἕνεκα ("on account of their honesty").[22] Concern about the disposition and integrity of common funds was simply a standard part of associative life.

There is very little, if any, data on the mechanisms by which private associations assembled members' contributions, although in the case of public subscriptions (*epidoseis*, discussed below) more is known. Contributions might have been made in some ritualized form or simply delivered to the secretary or treasurer at each meeting, or at some specified time during the month. Or associations might have used the system of initial pledges of an entire sum followed by periodic delivery of portions of this, as in the case of *epidoseis* discussed below.[23] What is abundantly clear is that associations kept careful records of contributions, endowments, extraordinary gifts, fines, and other income, as the following inscriptions illustrate:

> The dues [*phora*] must be brought to the treasurer (so that) loans can be made. Whoever does not pay shall be fined a double amount. Whoever does not pay at all shall be expelled from the association [*exeranos*]. (SEG 31:122 [*GRA* I 50]: a *synod* of Herakleiastai).

> None of the Iobakchoi who has not paid (the contributions) for either the meetings on the ninth (of the month) or the annual festival is permitted to enter into the gathering, until it has been decided by the priests whether he should pay the fee or be allowed to enter (anyway). (*IG* II2 1368 [*GRA* I 51]: the *Iobakchoi* of Athens).

22. See the commendations in *IG* II2 1256.8 (*GRA* I 5): two members; *IG* II2 1263.22 (*GRA* I 11): a secretary; *IG* II2 1278.11–12 (*GRA* I 17): a treasurer, supervisor, secretary, comptroller, and a record-keeper; *IG* II2 1284.30–31 (*GRA* I 22): a secretary. David Whitehead ("Cardinal Virtues: The Language of Public Approbation in Democratic Athens," *Classica et Mediaevalia* 44 [1993]: 67–68) notes: "Rendered 'righteousness'. . . , *dikaiosynē* is better understood in an epigraphic context as something like 'honesty', the behavior—financial and otherwise—of someone who has been in a position to feather his own nest but has not (detectably) done so. It was thus a virtue which, unlike some of the ones we examined earlier (such as *eunoia*), was from the outset of its use regarded as at least as suitable for Athenian citizen honorees as for noncitizens, and it was a common choice for both the demos as a whole and its subdivisions to apply to the conduct of those who had discharged service in an official capacity."

23. An inscription from Ionia lists the goods promised and delivered to a Dionysiac association: "[. . .] pro|vided [παρέξειν] sufficient wine; | previously [. . .] he had | promised [προεπηγγείλατο] [. . .] *metrētai*. . . . || [. . .]goras son of Protamachos | provided sufficient wine; . . . | he had promised one hundred *metrētai*; | Dionysios son of Dionysios provided | sufficient wine and cooks || and musicians | for banquet and [. . .] *choinikes* of bread." (SEG 31:983.3–11, Söke, Ionia). Because one hundred *metrētai* (3,900 liters) is obviously far too much for a single banquet, we should conclude that the alternation between προεπηγγείλατο (promised) and παρέξειν (to provide) indicates there was an initial subscription of one hundred *metrētai* and that this was then divided among several banquets. Note that ellipses enclosed in brackets indicate missing or illegible text, while ellipses not enclosed by brackets indicate an open space (*vacat*) in the extant inscription.

Although the procedure for payment of dues is not described, the two-stage penal procedure of SEG 31:112 suggests that there was a point at which payment was expected and that after some period of grace, free-riders were expelled.[24] IG II2 1368 suggests that in this case, dues were expected prior to the monthly meetings and yearly festival and that records were kept so that free-riders could be identified and prohibited from participation.[25] Papyri from Egypt containing club accounts illustrate the careful bookkeeping practices of various associations, documenting income from dues, members who had paid in full, members who were in arrears, members who were dues-exempt (ἀσύμβολος), and the expenses incurred for each banquet.

There is no reason to suppose that the Corinthians were any less invested in the solvency of their group or the management and security of funds that they collected. In the case of the funds used for normal operations (i.e., the providing of monthly or weekly banquets), there were presumably procedures in place analogous to what are widely reported in other associations.[26] A more complicated situation existed in the management of funds collected for a special project, such as the collection for the Jerusalem group.

The situation that Paul addressed in Corinth in 1 Corinthians 16:1–4 was one of a collection that he assumed would take several months to complete, but was to be ready by the time of his arrival in Corinth so that the Corinthian funds could be added to those from Macedonia. 1 Corinthians 16:2 implies that Paul imagined that most would be unable to produce a full and final contribution on the spot and would have to accumulate smaller contributions over a period of several months. Hence, his advice that "on the first day of the week let each of you lay aside whatever you can." That these presumably smaller weekly sums should not immediately be given to the ekklēsia but be kept individually (παρ' ἑαυτῷ) meant only that the bookkeeping connected to the collection could be kept separate from whatever other funds the ekklēsia administered. And it would mean that upon Paul's arrival, the full contribution of each member would be known immediately. In the other

---

24. On disaffiliation in associations, see John S. Kloppenborg, "Disaffiliation in Associations and the ἀποσυναγωγός of John," HvTSt 67 (2011): 159–74.

25. See other examples of the recording of contributions: IG II2 1301.14–16 (GRA I 30): [ἀναγρά]||[ψαι δὲ τόδ]ε τὸ ψήφισμα τοὺς [ἐπιμελητὰς εἰς τὴν στή]|[λην ἐν εἶ το]ὺς ἐπιδεδωκότας] ("The supervisors shall inscribe this decree on a stele, on which (are listed) those who have made contributions"); IG II2 1335 (GRA I 43): a list of fifty-one contributors.

26. I have argued elsewhere that the funding of communal meals in Corinth was likely either by a mechanism of member contributions or rotating liturgies. See John S. Kloppenborg, "Precedence at the Communal Meal in Corinth," NovT 58, no. 2 (2016): 167–203.

collections, the final tallies were important if a donor list was to be created. Paul's main concern, however, is not in the size of each donation but rather that the collection not be started only when Paul arrived. His recommendation about the mechanism for collection is reasonable given his belief about the financial resources of at least some of the Corinthian Christ followers and his interest in having a final collection when he arrived.

Paul addresses three other topics in 1 Corinthians 16:1–4: the security of the collection against theft and misappropriation, the delivery instructions, and the issue of due acknowledgement. Paul's statement in 16:3 addresses two critical topics (actually three, the third to be discussed below): first, it assures the Corinthians that the collection will be delivered by οὓς ἐὰν δοκιμάσητε; second, he indicates that they will travel with a letter from Paul, presumably explaining the collection, its sources, and its intended recipients.

As is obvious in the case of funds that are raised and being transported to a different locale, there is always a danger of loss and misappropriation. For this reason, envoys approved by the Corinthian group would assume responsibility for the honest conveyance of the collection. The term Paul uses, δοκιμάζειν, is well attested in both civic and association contexts, signifying the vetting of prospective citizens, candidates for office, and candidates for membership in an association.[27] The point for Paul is that honorable and reliable envoys *of the Corinthians' choosing* will deliver the collection. Holmberg's characterization of the entourage in Acts 20:6, which included representatives from Beroea, Thessaloniki, Derbe, and Asia (and no doubt from Corinth), as "(*unnecessarily*) large"[28] fundamentally misses the point of such a delegation: every Christ group that had contributed had a stake in guaranteeing that their funds would be secure from theft and fraud and would be delivered to the intended recipients.[29]

---

27. See John S. Kloppenborg, "The Moralizing of Discourse in Greco-Roman Associations," in *"The One Who Sows Bountifully": Essays in Honor of Stanley K. Stowers*, ed. Caroline Johnson Hodge, Saul M. Olyan, Daniel Ullucci, and Emma Wasserman (Providence, RI: Brown Judaic Studies, 2013), 216–19; and more generally, T. E. Rihll, "Democracy Denied: Why Ephialtes Attacked the Areiopagus," *JHS* 115 (1995): 93–97; Christophe Feyel, *Dokimasia: la place et le rôle de l'examen préliminaire dans les institutions des cités grecques*, Études anciennes 36 (Nancy: Association pour la diffusion de la recherche sur l'antiquité, 2009) (on the vetting of officials); and Gabriel Adeleye, "The Purpose of the Dokimasia," *GRBS* 24, no. 4 (1983): 295–306 (on the vetting of prospective citizens).

28. Bengt Holmberg, *Paul and Power: The Structure of Authority in the Primitive Church as Reflected in the Pauline Epistles*, ConBNT 11 (Lund: Gleerup, 1978), 38 (emphasis added).

29. Fraud and misappropriation were constant dangers. Thus in the third century BCE, an *epidosis* decree from Chios warns that anyone who attempts to alter the purpose of the collection or to divert it to another use will be fined three thousand drachmae; see Louis Robert, "Sur des

An additional indication that the security of the collection was at stake, both for the Corinthians and for Paul, is Paul's comment in Romans 15:28—"having completed this [the collection] and having certified [σφραγισάμενος] this 'fruit' for them"—where the use of σφραγίζω underscores the importance of a formal authentication or "sealing" of the gift that Jerusalem is to receive. The verb, found often in connection with the delivery of letters or the production of copies of documents, carried a nuance that care has been taken to guard against fraud and deception.[30]

This also implies that all of the funds collected would have to be accounted for at some point. Commenting on the "unusually large" group of envoys accompanying the collection (Acts 20:4), Munck assumes that part of the collection would have been used to defray their travelling expenses.[31] This might have been so, but if we were to assume that fiscal procedures were in place analogous to those of the movement of other envoys, there would be a strict limit placed on how much of the collection, if any, could be expended for travel. More likely, if we take seriously analogous situations where envoys of one group or city travelled to make a petition or otherwise interacted with authorities elsewhere, they would have travelled ἐκ τῶν ἰδίων (at their own expense).[32] In this way, the full amount of the collection would reach Jerusalem and receive a proper accounting when the envoys returned.

The second issue is both practical and rhetorical: Paul, at least at the time of 1 Corinthians, underscores that he is diffident as to whether

---

inscriptions de Chios," *BCH* 57 (1933): 505–17, no. 1.5–9. Five centuries later, a former *stratēgos* in Alexandria is told by the emperor that the *epidosis* that he proposed to offer relief to the farmers in Oxyrhynchus who are suffering economically is approved, but its funds cannot be turned to a different use (*P.Oxy.* 4.705.62–63; Oxyrhynchus, 200–202 CE). A little later, an official from Oxyrhynchus reports that the city treasurer has left the city and perhaps Egypt altogether, and that only a portion of the *epidosis* that was collected in support of the sacred Capitoline games is available (*P.Oxy.* 63.4357.12–13 [317 CE]). It is not clear from this whether only sixty talents were collected from the *epidosis* of the councillors, or whether only sixty talents remain after the departure of the treasurer.

30. See J. Albert Harrill, *The Manumission of Slaves in Early Christianity*, HUT 32 (Tübingen: Mohr Siebeck, 1995), 133 (I am indebted to Bert Harrill for drawing this to my attention).

31. Johannes Munck, *Paul and the Salvation of Mankind*, trans. Frank Clarke (Richmond, VA: John Knox, 1959), 303.

32. Ambassadors normally travelled ἐκ τῶν ἰδίων; see *TAM* V/2 1002 (Thyateira, Lydia, undated): "The leather-cutters [σκυτοτόμοι] honoured T. Flavius Alexandros son of Metrophanes of the tribe of Quirine, who had served as *agoranomos* for six months in a vigorous and extravagant manner, superintendent [*curator*] of the company [*conventus*] of Romans, ambassador to the emperor in Rome three times acting as an advocate at his own expense [δαπά[ναις] ἰδίαις] in the matters that were brought concerning Attaleians, and priest of Artemis in a manner displaying piety and love of honour" (trans. Harland, *GRA* II, modified slightly).

he will even go to Jerusalem. For this reason, a letter of introduction would be essential to ensure the delivery of the collection, for if Paul were to accompany the collection, no such letter would be needed. But his conditional statement, "but if it is suitable for me also to go, they will go with me" and the diffidence he expresses are ways to signal that he would not be in a position to misappropriate the collection, either because he might not be going to Jerusalem at all or because, in any case, he would be accompanied by those whose task it was to ensure the proper delivery of the collection.

Hence, Paul's comments in 1 Corinthians 16:1–4 have nothing to do with the Corinthians' inexperience in collecting money, either for themselves or for some other purpose. Instead their questions reflect the typical concerns that arose in virtually all associations concerning financial propriety. Paul's statements are intended to assure the Corinthians that their contributions will not fail to arrive in Jerusalem and that Paul himself, even though he had initiated the collection, does not stand to benefit financially from this enterprise.

Recognition of Largesse

A consistent feature of Greek donative inscriptions is that due recognition of the benefactor or patron was essential. This was simply part of the nature of exchange, whereby a patron or group of benefactors provided a benefit to the *polis* or to an association, and the *polis* or association in turn recognized this largesse in some public form. This type of exchange provided benefits to the *polis* or association and symbolic capital to the donor or donors.[33]

There is plenty of evidence that the recognition of largesse was critical. A standard provision in an honorific decree was the requirement that the supervisor or secretary of the association arrange for the crowning of those who had demonstrated largesse and that the crowning be announced, usually at the next meeting. Not only that, but it was usual to threaten anyone who would obstruct the act of honoring the benefactor with a fine.

We should, accordingly, imagine that the envoys, when they arrived in Jerusalem, carried not only coin but also a parchment list of the names of those who had contributed or, at the very least, the names of each of the gentile groups involved and perhaps even the amounts

---

33. On symbolic capital, see Pierre Bourdieu, "The Economy of Symbolic Goods," in *Practical Reason: On the Theory of Action* (Cambridge: Polity Press, 1998), 92–126.

each contributed.[34] Paul, as it would turn out, was also positioned to gain social capital from ἡ διακονία μου, as he calls it in Romans 15:31, since he was acting as a broker of a benefit and, at least as far as the Jerusalem group was concerned, as a partner fulfilling his part of an agreement.[35] But that should not obscure the likelihood that each of the Christ-groups represented by the collection would expect to be credited as well.[36]

Extra-Civic Finances and Collections for Common Purposes

There has been resistance to the notion that Paul and his groups traded in the practice of patronage—which typically was a relationship between one wealthy person and a client (an individual or a group, or even a city). It can readily be agreed patronage is not easily mapped onto the collection. If it were the case that this was the only possible model for understanding Paul's practice, it might be right to conclude that Paul was resisting or rejecting the practice of patronage, as Steve Friesen has suggested.[37] But it is not. Other redistributive practices are

---

34. This is perhaps a shocking conclusion, and one that contradicts the supposition that members of Christ-groups typically favored anonymous donations and cared little for recognition. (Of course, Paul cared a great deal for recognition, as Rom 15:25–28, 31 indicates.) On the other hand, as Angelos Chaniotis observes, "In Greek antiquity there is no such thing as the noble spender who wants to retain his anonymity. Financial contributions for the city were visible, transparent, and, above all, very loud." "Public Subscriptions and Loans as Social Capital in the Hellenistic City: Reciprocity, Performance, Commemoration," in *Epigraphical Approaches to the Postclassical Polis: Fourth Century BC to Second Century AD*, ed. Paraskevi Martzavou and Nikolaos Papazarkadas, Oxford Studies in Ancient Documents (Oxford: Oxford University Press, 2013), 91.

35. John N. Collins, *Diakonia: Re-Interpreting the Ancient Resources* (New York: Oxford University Press, 1990), 220, makes the important point that the term διακονία here refers to Paul's role as an envoy: "Paul has used the words in this passage to indicate that he is acting in an official capacity as the appointed courier of the churches. His responsibilities are primarily technical and it is these that he urges in order to explain his delay in visiting Rome, and the instances of the verb and abstract noun at 15:25 and 31 speak directly and exclusively of his commitment to this charge from the churches in Macedonia and Achaia. This has an important bearing on the identity and role of 'God's people' in the earlier translation: 'an errand to God's people', that is the people in Jerusalem. These are rather to be understood as the people of the churches who have commissioned Paul so that we should translate: 'on a mission from God's people.'"

36. A possible objection might be that the thrust of Paul's engagement with the Corinthians in 1 Corinthians is to oppose the self-exertions of the so-called "strong" who have exhibited status through displays of speech, elite eating, and virtuoso performances of charismatic speech. While it is true that Paul wishes to limit such performances, certain forms of *epidoseis* in fact deliberately limited status displays by leveling contributions or by setting a maximum gift (see below, p. 322) and thus focused on "communitarian" values rather than individual self-assertion (see below, pp. 323–25), values that are completely in agreement with Paul's own views. This, however, did not obviate the need for recognition of those who had contributed to the collection.

37. Steven J. Friesen, "Paul and Economics: The Jerusalem Collection as an Alternative to Patronage," in *Paul Unbound: Other Perspectives on the Apostle*, ed. Mark D. Given (Peabody, MA: Hendrickson, 2010), 27–54.

attested in the Greco-Roman culture, none of them a matter of patronage in the sense that Friesen uses the term.

Epidoseis (Public Subscriptions)

Public subscriptions are attested in Athens, other parts of Greece, the Aegean islands, Asia Minor, Cyrenaica, Sicily, and Egypt, and from the fourth century BCE to well into the imperial period.[38] They were used for a wide variety of purposes: for the construction or repair of city walls, the construction or repair of sanctuaries, the construction or repair of public buildings, the support of sacrifices and religious festivals, support for games, the purchase of grain, ransom for the return of prisoners and victims of piracy, and the purchase of oil for the gymnasium. These were normally not ongoing collections but raised for special needs; as Chaniotis observes, Greek cities had relatively sophisticated fiscal systems in place to take care of routine expenses, but for heterogeneous and less predictable expenses, they turned either to external assistance (loans from foreign benefactors) or to "the financial contribution of citizens and foreign residents in the form of extraordinary taxes [εἰσφοραί], organized contributions [ἐπιδόσεις], and voluntary donations [δωρεαί, εὐεργεσίαι]."[39] The (yearly?) collections undertaken by Hellenistic synagogues thus resembled, in some respects, the *epidoseis* of Greek cities but seem to be imagined as ongoing projects.

Although the point of *epidoseis* was to raise funds for specific projects, the administration of the contributions varied significantly. SEG 50:1050, an inscription from Cos (third century BCE) concerning funds for the repair of a temple, is unusually helpful for illuminating the mechanism for the collection of funds:

> For good fortune, let it be decided that the *neopoiai* shall pay 2000 drachmae to the men elected from the funds of the god, and that individuals

---

38. Léopold Migeotte, *Les souscriptions publiques dans les cités grecques*, Hautes études du monde gréco-romain (Genève: Librairie Droz, 1992) is the major collection of ἐπιδόσεις, but others are also attested. See Chaniotis, "Public Subscriptions and Loans"; Aneurin Ellis-Evans, "The Ideology of Public Subscriptions," in Martzavou and Papazarkadas, *Epigraphical Approaches*, 107–25. Léopold Migeotte ("Les souscriptions dans les associations privées," in *Groupes et associations dans les cités grecques [IIIe siècle av. J.-C.-IIe siècle ap. J.-C]. Actes de la table ronde de Paris, INHA, 19-20 juin 2009*, ed. Pierre Fröhlich and Patrice Hamon, Hautes études du monde gréco-romain 49 [Genève: Librairie Droz, 2013], 113–27) discusses ἐπιδόσεις in private associations and collects more than a dozen subscriptions, most for repairs to temples.

39. Chaniotis, "Public Subscriptions and Loans," 91.

from among members of the deme and the other citizens and resident aliens who are willing to pledge no less than 30 drachmae for the construction of the temple; they should make the pledge within a year at the meetings which occur in the deme, beginning with the month of Dalios in the term of Philotas, and they should make the payments of the money to the men elected in three installments, paying the first straightaway after the making of the pledge, the next within six months, and the remaining one in the same way. And in order that there may be a record . . . [here the inscription breaks off].[40]

While the mechanism for collecting funds in many associations is unknown, here the process is clear: prospective contributors would announce (ἐπαγγείλασθαι) amounts in the regular deme meeting and then pay that amount in three installments over the course of a year. The minimum contribution was set at thirty drachmae and no maximum was prescribed.[41] Thirty drachmae was the price on Cos of a full-grown sheep and thus not beyond the means of most contributors,[42] who, as the inscription indicates, included not only demesmen but other citizens and resident aliens.

Of course, the donor's announced promise of a contribution could be an occasion for theatricality, affording wealthier donors the opportunity to display their largesse (and for the miserly to be publicly heckled).[43] Coupled with various epigraphical practices of highlighting the name of the first to contribute,[44] arranging the contributions in descending order by the amount contributed, or flushing the amounts to the right margin of the inscription, making it easy to compare one donor with another,[45] this type of collection allowed donors to gain considerable symbolic capital.

40. Robert Parker and Dirk Obbink, "Aus der Arbeit der 'Inscriptiones Graecae' VIII. Three Further Inscriptions Concerning Coan Cults," *Chiron* 31 (2001): 253–65. The English translation is that of Parker and Obbink.

41. *IG* II2 791 (Athens, 244/3 BCE) sets the lower limit at 50 drachmae and the upper limit at 200 drachmae. Migeotte, *Les souscriptions publiques*, 316–19, suggests that in the absence of specific limits on contributions, minimums and maximums can be derived from the donor list itself. *Epidosis* lists attest ranges from 10–30 drachmae, 100–300 drachmae, 50–500 drachmae, and 100–500 drachmae, but there are contributions to some *epidoseis* as low as 4 drachmae and one list with no contribution greater than 10 drachmae (*IG* VII 3191–92; Orchomenos, Boeotia).

42. Parker and Obbink, "Aus der Arbeit der 'Inscriptiones Graecae,'" 262.

43. E.g., Plutarch's (*Alcibiades* 10.1) description of Alcibiades's contribution to an Athenian *epidosis*; Ellis-Evans, "Ideology of Public Subscriptions," 109.

44. Migeotte, *Les souscriptions publiques*, 93–96 no. 34 (partially reproduced); Yves Béquignon, "Études Thessaliennes: VII. Inscriptions de Thessalie," *BCH* 59 (1935): 36–51 no. 1, face 2.32–38: "they will inscribe on a stone stele the names of everyone who has promised (a contribution), along with their patronym, according to what they promised, the first to promise first, and then the others according to the amount."

45. Ellis-Evans, "Ideology of Public Subscriptions," 119, citing SEG 44:1219a, 48:1343.

Yet other practices are attested that had the effect of rendering status less visible. Some *epidoseis* set a minimum and a maximum contribution, thus preventing the super-rich from entirely outshining those with more modest resources.[46] The arranging of the list simply in the order in which the contributions arrived[47] or listing of names in alphabetical order[48] had a slight levelling effect. Other *epidoseis* had contributors all give the same—usually quite small—amounts.[49] For example, an *epidosis* from Tanagra (Boeotia) raised in order to relocate the sanctuary of Demeter and Kore has ninety-five donors, all of whom are women, with all but the last six contributing five drachmae.[50] Eleven of the eighteen contributors to the renovation of a synagogue in Berenikē (Cyrenaica) in 56 CE contributed ten drachmae, and a further four (including two women) gave five drachmae.[51] In contrast to the practice of variable contributions that made visible status differences, these more communitarian practices, as Aneurin Ellis-Evans observes, rendered less visible "the vast disparities of wealth and power that characterized polis life . . . and the succession of similar sounding sums suggested to the audience that the act of giving, rather than the amount given, was what mattered."[52]

It was not only from citizens that contributions were elicited, but from resident aliens and even foreigners. An *epidosis* inscription from Kos calls on contributions from all:

---

46. E.g., *IG* II2 791.19–20 (Athens, 243 BCE) sets the minimum contribution at fifty drachmae and the maximum at two hundred. Migeotte, *Les souscriptions publiques*, 316–17, observes apropos of *IG* II2 791, "les 83 montants encore lisible sur la pierre confirment non seulement que les donateurs ont respecté la directive, mais que la plupart ont donné le maximum." He also points out that in the case of *IG* II2 2332 (Athens, 183/2 BCE), all of the contributions are either five or ten drachmae (presumably the minimum and the maximum, respectively), and that in *IG* II2 2334 (Athens, second century BCE), an *epidosis* for the building of a theatre in the Piraeus, the contributions are all between five and twenty drachmae.

47. E.g., *Tituli Calymni* 85 (late third century BCE): contributions in the range of 15 (N=66), 20, 30, 40, 50, and 60 drachmae. Chaniotis ("Public Subscriptions and Loans," 94–95) suggests that the list was simply determined by the order in which the donations arrived.

48. SEG 48:1103 (Cos, ca. 200 BCE).

49. *The Inscriptions of Cos* 387 (late third century BCE): contributions to a temple of Aphrodite; forty donors each contributing five drachmae; *The Inscriptions of Cos* 404 (ca. 200 BCE): forty-two donors to an unknown cause, each giving twenty-three drachmae.

50. SEG 43:212(A) = Franciszek Sokolowski, *Lois sacrées des cités grecques* (Paris: Éditions de Boccard, 1969), no. 72 (SEG 25:67, 159, 160, 167, 173–175, 197) (Tanagra, late third / early second century BCE) (the last six contributed less than five drachmae). Other examples of all-female *epidoseis* are discussed by Ellis-Evans, "Ideology of Public Subscriptions," 111.

51. Gert Lüderitz and Joyce M. Reynolds, *Corpus jüdischer Zeugnisse aus der Cyrenaika* (Wiesbaden: Ludwig Reichert, 1983), no. 72.

52. Ellis-Evans, "Ideology of Public Subscriptions," 111.

> It was resolved that those who so wish shall contribute: citizens, women citizens, bastards, resident aliens, and foreigners.[53]

As noted in connection with the *epidosis* (SEG 50:1050) cited above, the use of the verb ἐπαγγέλλεσθαι is noteworthy since it points to the practice in subscriptions of the contributor "announcing" or "promising" the value of his or her contribution and, at some point in the future, delivering it. The gap between promise and fulfilment—marked with συντελεῖν—accounts for the repeated phrases such as one finds in an *epidosis* inscription from Lindos:

> They promised to give freely of their money . . . and they kept their promise according to what they had promised.[54]

Those who reneged on their promises were remembered and, as a speech in Isaeus shows, their names were inscribed on a list of defaulters.[55] Both the public display of contributor lists and the display of defaulters point to the importance of the social capital that was generated from contributions.

Ideological Features of Contributions

Epidoseis were powerful instruments of social formation because they called not only upon the wealthy but upon all residents—citizens, metics, and even foreigners—to contribute to a common project and thus to "perform" their membership in the *polis*.[56]

---

53. *Inscriptions of Cos* 10 (202/1 BCE) = Migeotte, *Les souscriptions publiques*, no. 50. Similarly, Ioulis: Migeotte *Les souscriptions publiques*, no. 56.1-4: [τῶν πολ]ιτῶν καὶ τῶν πολιτ[ίδων καὶ τῶν ἄλλων τῶ]ν ἐν τεῖ πόλει κα[τοικούντων] (late fourth / early third century BCE); *IG* XII/4 94A.17–18 (Halasarna, 250–225 BCE): τῶν δὲ δαμοτᾶν καὶ τῶν ἄλλων πολιτᾶν καὶ παροίκων; *IG* XII/4 314.2 (third century BCE); 320.11–12 (late second century BCE); *SEG* 48:1111 A.48–9; *IG* II2 791.15–17 (Athens, 248–7 BCE): τοὺς βουλομένους τῶ[ν πολιτῶν καὶ τῶν ἄλ]λων τῶν οἰκούντων ἐν τῆι πόλει ἐπιδιδό[ναι εἰς τὴν σωτηρία]ν τῆς πόλεως καὶ τὴν φυλακὴν τῆς χώρας ἐ[παγγείλασθαι.]

54. *ILindos* II 252.3, 6 = Migeotte, *Les souscriptions publiques*, no. 40.

55. Isaeus, *Dicaeogenes* 37–38 (trans. Forster, LCL): "Though so many extraordinary contributions for the cost of the war and the safety of the city have been made by all the citizens, Dicaeogenes has never contributed anything, except that after the capture of Lechaeum, at the request of another citizen, he promised in the public assembly a subscription of 300 drachmas, a smaller sum than Cleonymus the Cretan. [38] This sum he promised but did not pay, and his name was posted on a list of defaulters in front of the statues of the Eponymous Heroes, which was headed: 'These are they who voluntarily promised the people to contribute money for the salvation of the city and failed to pay the amounts promised.'"

56. The role of contributions, even small contributions, in the formation of a social imaginary is documented by anthropologists such as Michael Lambek (*The Weight of the Past: Living with History in Mahajanga, Madagascar*, Contemporary Anthropology of Religion [New York: Palgrave Macmillan, 2002]) who observes of the Sakalava (Malagasy), "It is here that ordinary people most directly

Ellis-Evans puts it this way:

> Public subscriptions sought to encourage members of the *polis* community
> to reproduce civic values by publicly acting them out. Through the serial-
> ization of communitarian acts of generosity, both the initial performance
> and the subsequent epigraphic monumentalization promoted a specific
> set of values as normative for the inhabitants of a *polis*. Since, in the politi-
> cal imaginary of the *polis* of Tanagra, the women of Tanagra should be par-
> ticularly concerned for the temple of Demeter and Kore, the *polis* makes
> them act out this ideal when it holds a public subscription. Because *polis*
> ideology imagines that all parts of the population, citizen or otherwise,
> would want to defend their home, at the Koan war subscription we wit-
> ness otherwise politically disfranchised individuals, who would usually be
> passive observers or altogether absent from a subscription, making con-
> tributions alongside citizens. The reverential place allotted to the man
> who promises first romantically imagines the surge of emotion a wealthy
> patriot feels when a subscription is announced.[57]

Epidoseis, insofar as they frequently received contributions from noncitizens and in some instances solicited contributions *exclusively* from
noncitizens,[58] served as ways for metics and ξένοι—that is, persons who
were formally excluded from the *polis*—to demonstrate their commitment to the *polis* and, at least fictively, to be brought into the city.
Such service brought with it the reasonable expectation that the *polis*
would reciprocate, sometimes with the conferral of the title εὐεργέτης,
or grants of the status of ἰσοτέλεια (i.e., exempt from metic taxes) or
πρόξενος, or even with a grant of citizenship.[59]

Public subscriptions, then, mobilized simultaneously the value of
cooperation and civic pride that had become part of Greek society and
the competitive instinct for honor. An example of both cooperation
and competition functioning together is provided by such Athenian
epidosis inscriptions as a commendation of Apollas son of Tharrhymon,
a noncitizen from Sikyon, for having contributed to an Athenian *epi-*

experience their own participation (their will, intentionality, and agency) and identification with
the ancestral system, which can thrive only through their commitment to service" (ibid., 143).
"Each act of giving is formally *received* with thanks, clapping, speeches, and the like, and the
reception constitutes a form of recognition. Acts of giving take place in a sociable context, with
music, drink and warm fellowship. Everyone appears to have a stake in the maintenance and
reproduction of the politico-religious system; they are proud to have the honor to participate"
(ibid., 162). See also Jean Comaroff, *Body of Power, Spirit of Resistance: The Culture and History of a South
African People* (Chicago: University of Chicago Press, 1985), 235–36.

57. Ellis-Evans, "The Ideology of Public Subscriptions," 112.
58. See Migeotte, *Les souscriptions publiques*, 402 (index, s.v. étrangers).
59. Chaniotis, "Public Subscriptions and Loans," 99–104.

dosis "without having been asked," and for having contributed *first*. He also gave the *most* that was allowed by the terms of the *epidosis*. Thus, Apollas is said to have "*competed* with the citizens."[60] The function of the inscription is obvious: both to commend a foreigner for exemplary behavior and also to stir Athenians to action, provoked by civic pride and competition for honor.[61]

Public subscriptions thus served multiple functions: first, to afford those without sufficient financial resources to function as single *euergetai* the chance to participate collectively in acts that benefitted their cities. In many cases, contributions were very small. *Epidoseis* allowed contributors, whether citizens or nonresident aliens, to "perform" their loyalty to the *polis* and, in the case of nonresidents, to achieve through reciprocity even close affiliation with the *polis*. These subscriptions simultaneously engaged by cooperation and competition and allowed for a spectrum of practices, from those that blatantly encouraged agonistic, even "heroic" competition among the wealthy and powerful, to other forms that deliberately masked status differences and created a model in which communal ideals took precedence over competition for honors. Yet even in the latter form, the competitive aspect resides not in how much one contributed but in whether or not one contributed, since it was immediately known who did and who did not contribute. "Extraordinary" contributions by metics and foreigners stood out in particular.

The Pauline Collection and the Fiscal Practices of Greek Poleis

What do these fiscal practices have to do with the Pauline collection? There are some obvious differences between the *epidoseis* discussed above and Paul's collection. The Pauline collection, although it resembled in significant ways Greek *epidoseis*, was novel in at least three important respects. First, we have no evidence of any *epidosis* organized for the benefit of members of a community other than that of the donors themselves, with the possible exception of the collections that occurred in Hellenistic synagogues. We do have evidence of noncitizen groups supporting a civic project, as in the case of the "former resi-

---

60. See the comments of Chaniotis, "Public Subscriptions and Loans," 103–4. Because of his largesse, Apollas was granted *proxenos* status and the right to buy property (*enktēsis*).

61. A similar instance of a foreigner from Salamis in Cyprus contributing to an Athenian *epidosis* is attested in *IG* II² 283, on which see Michael B. Walbank, "Notes on Attic Decrees," *ZPE* 139 (2002): 63 (no. 5).

dents of Judaea" contributing to a civic project in Erythrai, or Apollas of Sikyon contributing to an Athenian *epidosis* (see above, p. 325).

Second, it is also true that *epidoseis* were not normally framed as relief for "the poor." It is widely acknowledged that support for the poor qua poor is likely the result of transformations that occurred in late antiquity.[62] Indeed, the idea of a special collection for the πτωχοί would probably have struck many Greeks as a curiously counterintuitive undertaking.[63] *Epidoseis* were typically framed more abstractly, with the formulae ἐπέδωκαν . . . εἰς τὴν σωτηρίαν / ἐπισκευήν / κατασκευήν / σιτομετρίαν, although a few inscriptions expressly name the *dēmos* as the recipient of the funds.[64] The "poor" as such were rarely the express object of such undertakings, even if the *dēmos* in times of need was.

Third, Paul's collection was framed not only as a collection for the "poor" but as a collection for members of a different ethnic group. As Welborn has aptly observed,

> it must be emphasized how anomalous Paul's appeal to the principle of "equality" between Jews and Greeks would have seemed. A careful examination of edicts and petitions, together with the relevant passages in Philo and Josephus, provides no grounds for thinking that Jews enjoyed equal rights identified with citizens in any of the Greek cities of the Roman east.[65]

---

62. Peter Brown, *Poverty and Leadership in the Later Roman Empire* (Hanover, NH: University Press of New England, 2002); Greg Woolf, "Writing Poverty in Rome," in *Poverty in the Roman World*, ed. Margaret Atkins and Robin Osborne (Cambridge: Cambridge University Press, 2006), 84; Peter Brown, *Through the Eye of a Needle: Wealth, the Fall of Rome, and the Making of Christianity in the West, 350-550 AD* (Princeton: Princeton University Press, 2012); Ilana F. Silber, "Neither Mauss, Nor Veyne: Peter Brown's Interpretative Path to the Gift," in *The Gift in Antiquity*, ed. Michael L. Satlow (Malden, MA: Wiley Blackwell, 2013), 202-20; Lucia Cecchet, "Gift-Giving to the Poor in the Greek World," in *Gift-Giving and the "Embedded" Economy in the Ancient World*, ed. Filippo Carlà and Maja Gori, Akademiekonferenzen 17 (Heidelberg: Universitätsverlag Winter, 2014), 157-79; Lellia Cracco Ruggini, "From Pagan to Christian Euergetism," in Carlà and Gori, *Gift-Giving*, 203-12.

63. See K. J. Dover, *Greek Popular Morality in the Time of Plato and Aristotle* (Oxford: Basil Blackwell, 1974), 177; Alex Gottesman, "The Beggar and the Clod: The Mythic Notion of Poverty in Ancient Greece," *Transactions of the American Philological Association* 140, no. 2 (2010): 287-322; and Aristotle, *Ethica nicomachea* 4.2 1122a (trans. Rackham, LCL): "the term μεγαλοπρέπεια is not applied to one who spends adequate sums on objects of only small or moderate importance, like the man who said 'Oft gave I alms to homeless wayfarers' [Homer, *Odyssea* 17.420]; it denotes someone who spends suitably on great objects. For though the munificent man is liberal, the liberal man is not necessarily munificent." But see Anneliese Parkin, "'You Do Him No Service': An Exploration of Pagan Almsgiving," in Atkins and Osborne, *Poverty in the Roman World*, 60-82, for a balanced account of charity.

64. E.g., *IG* XII/5 135 (Paros, early first century BCE): ἐπὶ Ἀπελλοῦς Θαργηλιῶνος [ὑσ]τέρου | τετράδι ἱ[σ]ταμένου | οἵδε ἐπέδωκαν τῶι δή|[μ]ωι εἰς τὴν σιτομετρίαν.

65. L. L. Welborn, "'That There May Be Equality': The Contexts and Consequences of a Pauline Ideal," *NTS* 59, no. 1 (2013): 83.

Paul's efforts, at least in 2 Corinthians 8 and 9, to ground the appeal for the collection in the notion of ἰσότης (equality) should be seen in the context of other attempts at the articulation of equality, in particular the failed struggle, only a decade before, for *isopoliteia* between Judeans and Greeks in Alexandria, and the periodic eruptions of conflict between Judeans and gentiles in Caesarea over the same issue that would become one of the events leading to the First Revolt. Paul's notion of equality in 2 Corinthians 8:14 is not one of equal civic rights[66] but of sharing economic resources.

As I have indicated above, my goal is not to seek the "source" of Paul's practice or to argue that he "imitated" or was "influenced" by the practices of Greek cities, but instead to use the practices about which we know quite a lot to raise heuristic questions about Paul's collection (about which we know little) and to understand better the appeal of a collection and the challenges it raised.

The main issue from which the concerns of the Corinthian group flowed had to do with the fact that a collection was being assembled to serve the needs of not Corinthian Christ followers but the Jerusalem group. Although none of the *epidoseis* that are attested provides close parallels to this situation, a number of dynamics integral to those collections do have a bearing on the Pauline collection.

First, the *epidosis* offers an analogy for a community-based fund-raising project rather than a model based on reliance on the largesse of the elite. While some *epidoseis* imposed no upper limit on contributions and allowed for theatrical offers by the elite (thus making these *epidoseis* a site of the performance of status), it is also the case that others limited the contributions and even restricted them to a given—usually very modest—sum, thus taking the focus from status display and placing it on communal benefaction. Since Paul evidently could not rely on elite benefactors to contribute large sums, the more "democratic" practice, like that of the *epidosis*, commended itself as a viable model.

---

66. The meaning of *isopoliteia* itself is disputed. Joseph Modrzejewski (*The Jews of Egypt: From Rameses II to Emperor Hadrian*, trans. Robert Cornman [Princeton: Princeton University Press, 1997]) argued that in Alexandria it was a quest for citizenship, but Aryeh Kasher (*Jews and Hellenistic Cities in Eretz Israel: Relations of the Jews in Eretz-Israel with the Hellenistic Cities during the Second Temple Period (332 BCE–70 CE)*, TSAJ 21 [Tübingen: Mohr Siebeck, 1990], 256) thinks that Judeans in Alexandria were pursuing the status of a *politeuma*, a separate and autonomous political body, with rights equal to the *polis* but not dependent upon it. The goal of *isopoliteia* is even less clear in Caesarea, but the simmering conflict between the Judean and gentile populations of the city was longstanding; see John S. Kloppenborg, "Ethnic and Political Rivalry at Caesarea Maritima," in *Religious Rivalries and the Struggle for Success in Caesarea Maritima*, ed. Terence L. Donaldson (Waterloo, ON: Wilfrid Laurier University Press, 2000), 227–48.

Moreover, some *epidoseis* allowed for amortized contributions, dividing even the relatively modest sum of thirty drachmae into three install ments spread over a year (see above, p. 321. Paul clearly has something like this in mind in 1 Corinthians 16:2.

Second, the gap between promise and delivery is something that troubled Paul as it did the organizers of public subscriptions. Nothing in the tone of Paul's letter in 1 Corinthians 16:1–4 suggests that the Corinthians rejected the proposal for a collection out of hand; they were concerned, on the contrary, with the details of its security and delivery. Whether they had already "promised" certain sums prior to 1 Corinthians is unknowable. But by the time of 2 Corinthians 8 it appears that the collection had broken down; hence, the rhetoric of Paul in this letter is to encourage the collection, which was also the point of sending Titus and "the brother" to Corinth to complete it.[67] Even later, in 2 Corinthians 9,[68] Paul says that he has boasted that the Corinthian collection was complete ἀπὸ πέρυσι, but it is clear from his anxiety that he is unsure that he believed this to be the case.

Given the fact that *epidoseis* employed peer pressure and the possibility of the public shaming of those who refused to contribute as motivations for action,[69] Paul's statement in 2 Corinthians 9:4 is unexceptional: he threatens in a not-too-subtle way that the imminent arrival of Macedonians in Corinth who have contributed will put to shame Corinthians who have not. Paul here is relying on the agonistic instincts of his addressees and an appeal to their civic pride.[70] While

---

67. Margaret Mitchell ("Paul's Letters to Corinth: The Interpretive Intertwining of Literary and Historical Reconstruction," in *Urban Religion in Roman Corinth: Interdisciplinary Approaches*, ed. Daniel N. Schowalter and Steven J. Friesen, HTS 53 [Cambridge, MA: Harvard University Press, 2005], 327–33), building on a sensitive reading of rhetorical echoes between 1 Corinthians 16 and 2 Corinthians 8, has suggested that Paul in 2 Cor 8:22 (συνεπέμψαμεν δὲ αὐτοῖς τὸν ἀδελφὸν ἡμῶν ὂν ἐδοκιμάσαμεν ἐν πολλοῖς πολλάκις σπουδαῖον ὄντα) is going back on this undertaking in 1 Cor 16:3 that the Corinthians will be responsible for choosing envoys to accompany the collection. She suggests, further, that this change of heart was the cause of anger and distrust reflected in Paul's defense of himself that he was not "peddling the word of God" (2 Cor 2:17) and that he was in fact behaving in a guiltless way (2 Cor 4:2) (assuming that 2 Cor 2:14–7:4 minus 6:14–7:1 follows 2 Corinthians 8). Such a change of heart would undoubtedly have caused consternation and distrust, but it is difficult to see how Paul could have blundered into such a counterproductive suggestion given the general anxiety that all had about the security of communally collected funds.
68. I follow Hans Dieter Betz, *2 Corinthians 8 and 9: A Commentary on Two Administrative Letters of the Apostle Paul*, Hermeneia (Philadelphia: Fortress Press, 1985) in thinking that 2 Corinthians 8 and 2 Corinthians 9 are separate letters.
69. See Chaniotis, "Public Subscriptions and Loans."
70. Richard S. Ascough, "The Completion of a Religious Duty: The Background of 2 Cor 8:1–15," NTS 42, no. 4 (1996): 584–99, has shown that Paul's use of ἐπιτελεῖν in 2 Cor 8:1–15 (three times, 6, 11 *bis*) is used in connection with the completion of a cultic duty. Since the verb is frequently connected with the completion of θυσίαι and μυστήρια, it would appear that Paul is attempting to link the collection with a cultic duty.

epidosis practices could avail themselves of the threat of the public shaming of noncontributors by placing the names of deadbeats on a public list, Paul did not have this option open to him. No public inscription would be cut, but in the small face-to-face world of associations and *ekklēsiai* all would know who had contributed and who had not.

Third, although the Pauline collection for the "poor" is anomalous in the context of Greek *epidoseis* in the sense that it was a collection for a group in a locale far removed from that of the contributors, a similar ideology undergirds both kinds of projects. In a culture in which honor was a key and critical value,[71] euergetism was a powerful tool in the construction of personal and corporate self-esteem. The providing of benefits to the *polis* or to the group was, to be sure, an important way to address real hardships and challenges that faced the *polis* and to demonstrate the loyalty of citizens (and noncitizens) to the *polis*, but the quid pro quo in this exchange was the public recognition of largesse, demonstrated by lists of donors that could be read out and inscribed in public space. It was a performance of citizenship. This is true whether the contribution was large or a mere five drachmae. And as I have mentioned above, some of the *epidoseis* were even structured to level status differences and focus on the communitarian aspects of the contribution. Participation in an *epidosis* did not constitute the donor as a patron, but it did constitute him or her as a true citizen.

Paul's appeal employs an analogous logic: he begins in 2 Corinthians 8 by citing the Macedonians' insistence on their participation in this collective event, thus appealing to competitive urges among the Corinthians; if "poor" Macedonians were eager to demonstrate their largesse, then better-off Corinthians should do even more. He then swiftly turns to praising the Corinthians for an array of virtues: πίστις, λόγος, γνῶσις, σπουδή, and ἀγάπη, expressing the hope that they will add χάρις to their accomplishments (2 Cor 8:7). This is plainly an appeal to something analogous to the civic virtues that were celebrated in public decrees and to competitive outlay characteristic of *polis* ideology.[72] It was not the needs of the *polis* of Corinth to which the Corinthians were expected to contribute, but τὸ ἐκείνων ὑστέρημα of the Jerusalem group (2 Cor 8:14). In making this contribution, they would constitute

---

71. J. E. Lendon, *Empire of Honour: The Art of Government in the Roman World* (Oxford: Clarendon Press, 1997); Carlin A. Barton, *Roman Honor: The Fire in the Bones* (Berkeley: University of California Press, 2001).

72. David Whitehead, "Competitive Outlay and Community Profit: φιλοτιμία in Democratic Athens," *Classica et Mediaevalia* 34 (1983): 55–74.

themselves as a group that existed within a larger political network or fictive translocal polity.

Finally, I have suggested above that the role of the envoys of the gentile Christ-groups was not only to ensure that the collection was delivered to its intended recipients and not diverted to other uses, but also to ensure that credit was given to those who had contributed. This would be entirely in accord with donative practices in the Greek world; anonymous donations had not yet become a cultural practice. Whether credit took the form of a list of the names of individual contributors, comparable to many of the *epidosis* lists that we have, or a list of the ἐκκλησίαι that had contributed is a matter of speculation; both forms of lists are attested.[73]

I should not end without commenting on the novel aspects of Paul's project. As I have noted above, his collection was for a nonlocal cause; it was for the πτωχοί—not the poor generally but for a specific group of πτωχοί in Judaea—and it was a collection taken up in Greek cities for persons who in the first century (and even much later) did not enjoy *isopoliteia* in most Greek cities. It is an exaggeration to call Paul's project "subversive," as some have claimed. Subversion was simply beyond Paul's reach, since he lacked the political power and influence to bring about significant change. His collection was hardly an effective challenge to prevailing forms of power and domination. It is doubtful that Paul's collection would be noticed by those outside the narrow circle of Christ followers. If it were, it is hard to imagine that a Roman prefect would consider Paul's collection as anything other than a quaint and benighted practice by an insignificant artisan.[74] Certainly it was nothing to worry the elite or threaten the status quo, since it challenged no one's power or interests.

A better characterization of Paul's project is "transgressive."[75] His

---

73. *ILindos* II 252 (115 BCE) is an *epidosis* list of persons who had both promised to contribute and did contribute to a collection to provide crowns for Athena Lindia, Zeus Polieus, and Nike. The list is mainly the names of individuals, sometimes mentioning wives and sons as associated contributors, but also lists seven *koina*, all associated with a citizen, Timapolis. Similar lists from Rhodes that combine individual donors and associations (*koina*) are found in *IRhodPC* 4 = *IKamiros* 159a and *IKamirosSupp* 157b.

74. Compare Pliny the Younger's (*Epistulae* 10.96) report of his interrogation of Christians sixty years later: by that time Christian numbers in Bithynia-Pontus had grown to the level that their non-participation in local temples had economic impact; hence, one might claim that Christ followers were engaging in a "subversive" practice vis à vis local temples and their priestly apparatus. Yet Pliny seemed to treat Christian nonparticipation in the imperial cult not as a clear and present danger to the empire but only as a test to determine who was a Christian. The Christians, in his view, were largely harmless, if benighted: *nihil aliud inveni quiam superstitionem pravam et immodicam.*

75. See especially J. Albert Harrill, "Paul and Empire: Studying Roman Identity after the Cultural

rationale for the collection transgressed the boundaries of several kinds of cultural practices current in the Greek world, in particular the promotion of an *epidosis*-like collection for an extra-local, non-Greek group. At the same time, as this essay has shown, the project was deeply committed to the mechanisms and ideology of Greek *epidoseis*: the broad appeal to gentile groups to maximize participation operated by the same logic as Greek *epidoseis*, and Paul's collection, at least as he presented it, functioned as a way for individuals and individual groups to "perform membership" in a broader identity. This is hardly subversion, since it threatened no one, all the more so if the results of the collection were paltry, as Paul seems to have feared in his comments indicating the possibility that the collection may not be found "acceptable" in Jerusalem. Only two or three centuries later, when ecclesiastical powers took control of almsgiving and directed it toward the urban poor, can one begin to imagine a practice that subverted the earlier practices of civic patronage by the elite. But such was far beyond Paul's means to effect or, likely, even to imagine.

Without arguing that Pauline Christ-groups borrowed from or were "influenced by" the practices of the many small face-to-face associations that dotted the Mediterranean cityscape or the practices of cities themselves, this paper has shown how a knowledge of those practices can throw into sharper relief the issues that faced Paul's collection and how it would have been viewed by its participants and others.[76]

Select Bibliography

Downs, David J. *The Offering of the Gentiles: Paul's Collection for Jerusalem in Its Chronological, Cultural, and Cultic Contexts.* WUNT 2/248. Tübingen: Mohr Siebeck, 2008.

Joubert, Stephan. *Paul as Benefactor: Reciprocity, Strategy and Theological*

Turn," *Early Christianity* 2, no. 3 (2011): 281–311, for a compelling critique of the notion that Paul was engaged in a "subversion" of Roman imperialism. "*Transgressive* means violating the cultural norms or rules, whereas *subversive* means actually changing the cultural norms and rules." Ibid., 292 (emphasis original).

76. I would like to thank Richard Ascough, Giovanni Bazzana, Philip Harland, J. Albert Harrill, and Arjan Zuiderhoek for suggestions and critiques of this paper.

Reflection in Paul's Collection. WUNT 2/124. Tübingen: Mohr Siebeck, 2000.

Kloppenborg, John S., and Richard S. Ascough. *Greco-Roman Associations: Texts, Translations, and Commentary: I. Attica, Central Greece, Macedonia, Thrace*. BZNW 181. Berlin: de Gruyter, 2011.

Lendon, J. E. *Empire of Honour: The Art of Government in the Roman World*. Oxford: Clarendon Press, 1997.

Longenecker, Bruce W. *Remember the Poor: Paul, Poverty, and the Greco-Roman World*. Grand Rapids: Eerdmans, 2010.

Martzavou, Paraskevi, and Nikolaos Papazarkadas, eds. *Epigraphical Approaches to the Postclassical Polis: Fourth Century BC to Second Century AD*. Oxford Studies in Ancient Documents. Oxford: Oxford University Press, 2013.

Migeotte, Léopold. *Les souscriptions publiques dans les cités grecques*. Hautes études du monde gréco-romain. Genève: Librairie Droz, 1992.

Verbrugge, Verlyn D. *Paul's Style of Church Leadership Illustrated by His Instructions to the Corinthians on the Collection*. San Francisco: Mellen Research University Press, 1992.

Welborn, L. L. "'That There May Be Equality': The Contexts and Consequences of a Pauline Ideal." *New Testament Studies* 59, no. 1 (2013): 73–90.

Whitehead, David. "Cardinal Virtues: The Language of Public Approbation in Democratic Athens." *Classica et Mediaevalia* 44 (1993): 37–75.

Zuiderhoek, Arjan. *The Politics of Munificence in the Roman Empire: Citizens, Elites, and Benefactors in Asia Minor*. Greek Culture in the Roman World. Cambridge: Cambridge University Press, 2009.

A longer version of this paper will appear as "Fiscal Aspects of Paul's Collection for Jerusalem," *Early Christianity* 8, no. 2 (2017).

12

Economic Aspects of Intercity Travel among the Pauline Assemblies

Cavan Concannon

As he made his way to Nicomedia to take up the governorship of Pontus-Bithynia in 111 CE, Pliny the Younger found himself stymied by the late-summer weather patterns of the Aegean Sea. After crossing Cape Malea on the southern end of the Peloponnesos, Pliny's entourage made straight for Ephesos (*Epistulae* 10.15). From there, Pliny would need to move north up the coast toward the Black Sea. He decided to make the voyage partly by boat along the coast and partly by carriage near the coastline. His choice of an eclectic means of travel was dictated, he says, by the excessive heat of overland travel and the arrival of the Etesian winds, which blow to the south in the northern Aegean from May to September.[1] Unfortunately for Pliny, he was taken

---

1. J. Donald Hughes, *Environmental Problems of the Greeks and Romans: Ecology in the Ancient Mediterranean*, 2nd ed. (Baltimore: Johns Hopkins University Press, 2014), 10–11.

with a fever during his initial overland carriage trip, which meant that he had to stop in Pergamon to recover (*Ep.* 10.17a). After this, he switched to coastal vessels, though these were hampered by the prevailing southerly winds. As a result, he arrived in Bithynia on September 17, later than he had initially planned.[2]

Pliny's ability to choose his means of travel is a function of his wealth, but we can see that even for the wealthy, it could be hard to move efficiently, quickly, and easily between cities in the Mediterranean. Fernand Braudel famously referred to this as the "tyranny of distance" in his studies of the Mediterranean.[3] For a traveler who did not happen to be a senator or governor, one can imagine the difficulties, indignities, and challenges that would be faced daily on the road.[4] Because they were not traveling by imperial courier or in the train of a Roman senator, we have to imagine that Paul, his letters, and those who bore them struggled mightily against the tyranny of distance as they traversed the land- and seascapes of the eastern Mediterranean.

It is this struggle against distance that I want to focus on under the rubric of travel. The topic of travel is not commonly taken up as an organizing framework for studying the Pauline assemblies; however, I think that this offers us a useful opportunity to redescribe what typically is called the Pauline mission or the spread (and eventual victory) of early Christianity. Questions about travel, in their own way, skirt around the edges of Pauline studies, and by attending to the discursive role travel plays, we can see some of the subterranean investments of the field. In what follows, I pay attention to travel, by which I really mean movement, the movement of bodies, resources, and letters over geographic space, and the connectivity that mediates and is sustained by such embodied movement. Rather than trying to solve certain traditional questions in Pauline studies, I want to dwell on travel to model a historiography of contingent and fragile possibilities. By putting travel and movement at the center of our reconstructions of early Christian networks, we can see how early Christianity was com-

---

2. His letters indicate that his first stop was Prusa, where he looked into the city's finances (Pliny, *Epistulae* 10.17a–b).

3. Fernand Braudel, *The Structure of Everyday Life*, vol. 1, *Civilization and Capitalism, 15th-18th Century* (Berkeley: University of California Press, 1992), 428–30.

4. On travel more generally in the ancient world, see Lionel Casson, *Travel in the Ancient World* (Baltimore: Johns Hopkins University Press, 1994); Colin Adams and Ray Laurence, eds., *Travel and Geography in the Roman Empire* (New York: Routledge, 2001); Jaś Elsner and Ian Rutherford, eds., *Pilgrimage in Graeco-Roman and Early Christian Antiquity: Seeing the Gods* (Oxford: Oxford University Press, 2005); and Catherine Hezser, *Jewish Travel in Antiquity*, Texte und Studien zum antiken Judentum 144 (Tübingen: Mohr Siebeck, 2011).

prised of tenuous and shifting networks, rather than a single, if at times fractious, "movement."

Typically, we find discussions of movement dispersed into what I would call four general areas of Pauline studies: Pauline chronology, the components of the Pauline missional organization, the psychology of travel, and the discourse of travel. I will begin by looking briefly at each of these four areas that touch on questions of travel between and among Pauline assemblies. I will then conclude with an examination of the association of Jesus followers in Philippi as an example of how to deploy movement and connectivity to frame a more fragile and contingent mapping of the linkages between assemblies in the Pauline network.

The Fantasy of the *Pax Romana*

Before I dig into these four areas, I want to dwell briefly on what I think is a prevailing set of occluded fantasies that underlie the study of travel among the Pauline assemblies. First, many of us are familiar with the trope of the *Pax Romana*, the idea that the peace brought by Rome created a political, cultural, and structural context in which Christian ideas could spread easily.[5] While we meet the beginnings of this investment in the beneficent function of the Roman imperial system in Acts and Eusebius,[6] its prominence in introductory works to Paul and to early Christianity more generally belies a modern neoliberal and colonial investment in the dream of a frictionless landscape of globalized commerce.[7] Even as many modern scholars attempt to articulate

---

5. For a standard example of how scholars describe the peace brought by Rome to the Mediterranean and its effects, see Fernand Braudel, *Memory and the Mediterranean* (New York: Alfred Knopf, 2001), 297–315. On the *Pax Romana* as a mere "benign presence," see David Abulafia, *The Great Sea: A Human History of the Mediterranean* (Oxford: Oxford University Press, 2011), 210.
6. On how Acts constructs Christians as loyal citizens of a beneficent Roman Empire, while also casting aspersion on Jews, see Lawrence Wills, "The Depiction of the Jews in Acts," *Journal of Biblical Literature* 110, no. 4 (1991): 631–54. Eusebius's *Historia ecclesiastica* represents a more robust attempt to continue Luke's project of showing how Christianity fits within the Roman imperial world.
7. One can see this, for example, in Deissmann's glowing descriptions of his own colonial travels through the East and the ways in which he conflates those experiences with those of Paul. See Adolf Deissmann, *Paul: A Study in Social and Religious History* (New York: Harper, 1957), 27–51. On Deissmann's investment in conjuring Paul in this way, and its affinities with that of Heidegger, see Ward Blanton, *Displacing Christian Origins: Philosophy, Secularity, and the New Testament*, Religion and Postmodernism (Chicago: University of Chicago Press, 2007), 105–28. Deissmann was one of many Europeans who romanticized the ancient and biblical worlds to which they traveled, beginning in the nineteenth century and continuing today. See Brian Yothers, *The Romance of the Holy Land in American Travel Writing, 1790–1876* (Aldershot: Ashgate, 2007). Scholars are aided in this romanticizing of the landscape by Acts, which, though it does often recount the harrowing adventures of its protagonists, also tends to treat movement between geographic spaces in rather friction-

an anti-imperial Paul, their own vision of the ancient world involves a fascination with modern forms of colonial capitalism.[8] This trope of imperial mobility is further intertwined with the terminology of germ theory and conquest. Within this favorable landscape, we are told that Christianity *spreads* like a virus, virtuous or not (depending on whether or not we ask Gibbon), it *expands*, it *rises*, or it *conquers* like an army.[9] It is no wonder that Eckhard Schnabel, in his massive study of the early Christian mission (note his use of the singular) draws theoretical inspiration from the military strategist Clausewitz.[10] The spread and conquest of Christianity is visible in the maps that are so common in our textbooks, where color-coded sections are meant to convey the spread of small urban associations as if they were the vanguard of an empire (or perhaps a kingdom of God).

What is not always apparent to the scholars who appropriate these images of expansion and conquest is the underlying anti-Semitism of these descriptors, to say nothing of the overtly militaristic and imperial resonances. In his monumental study of the mission and expansion of Christianity, Adolf von Harnack pondered the "universal spread" and "world-wide expansion" of Christianity and its causes. To explain Christianity's spread, Harnack deployed tropes that remain common in modern explanations: the Hellenization of the Mediterranean after Alexander, Roman political unity and infrastructure building, and religious toleration and the popularity of "eastern" religions.[11] Harnack also saw Judaism and, in particular, forms of Judaism in diaspora as

less ways: "So being sent out by the Holy Spirit, they went down to Seleucia; and from there they sailed to Cyprus. When they arrived in Salamis, they proclaimed the word of God. . . . When they had gone through the whole island as far as Paphos. . ." (Acts 13:4–6); "After this Paul left Athens and went to Corinth" (Acts 18:1); "When he had landed at Caesarea, he went up to Jerusalem and greeted the church, and then went down to Antioch" (Acts 18:22). One can see a similar sense of the speed of movement in the Greek romances, such as Xenophon's *Ephesiaka*.

8. One can see this in the ways in which scholars use a variety of literary and visual pieces of ancient evidence to construct the concept of "Roman imperialism" and then place this construct alongside a reconstruction of Paul's theology. A good example of this is John Dominic Crossan and Jonathan L. Reed, *In Search of Paul: How Jesus's Apostle Opposed Rome's Empire with God's Kingdom* (San Francisco: Harper, 2004). The driving concern of the book is to show the reader that the Roman Empire of the past is equatable with the American Empire of the present (ibid., 412–13). This tendency is also visible in the many attempts to make Paul's gospel into a "counter-imperial" message, as in N. T. Wright, *Paul in Fresh Perspective* (Minneapolis: Fortress Press, 2005), 59–79, though many others could be cited.

9. On Gibbon and early Christianity, see W. H. C. Frend, "Edward Gibbon (1737–1794) and Early Christianity," *Journal of Ecclesiastical History* 45, no. 4 (1994): 661–72.

10. Eckhard J. Schnabel, *Early Christian Mission*, 2 vols. (Downers Grove, IL: InterVarsity Press, 2004), 1:499–517.

11. Adolf von Harnack, *The Mission and Expansion of Christianity in the First Three Centuries*, 2 vols. (Gloucester, MA: Peter Smith, 1972), 1:19–23.

paving the way for Christian expansion. But here Harnack included a key distinction: Judaism before the emergence of Christianity was a "national" religion that had only just begun the process of trans forming itself into a "universal" religion by reducing itself to a set of "central principles."[12] Ultimately, it is Christianity that takes up the potential universalism of diasporic Judaism, while Judaism proper follows the rabbis into ethnic particularism.[13] This characterization of Christianity's universalism and Judaism's particularism is part of Harnack's supersessionist reading of Christian history, wherein Christianity's universalism abrogates and supplants Judaism's ethnic particularity.[14] Indebted to F. C. Baur's importing of Hegelian philosophy into early Christian historiography and to taxonomic categorizations of religions by scholars like Max Müller and Abraham Kuenen, Harnack sees the "spread" of the "universal mission" as the result of Christianity's supersession of Judaism.[15] Scholars who frame the history of early Christianity as one of spread, conquest, and expansion should be aware of the ways in which this paradigm fits within a longer history of Christian anti-Semitism and its rendering of Judaism as an abrogated form of national, particular religion in the face of an (eventually) imperially backed institutionalized church.[16]

We might do better imaging the movement of Christianities across the eastern Mediterranean by imagining nonlinear networks that emerge, endure, and fall apart, thinking, in Deleuzian terms, *rhizomatically*.[17] The edges of these networks traced out tenuous and contingent

---

12. Ibid., 1:15–16.

13. Ibid., 1:16–18.

14. On Harnack's supersessionism, see Adolf von Harnack, *Outlines of the History of Dogma* (Boston: Beacon Press, 1957), 42.

15. On the connections between Harnack, Baur, and Kuenen, see Cavan W. Concannon, *"When You Were Gentiles": Specters of Ethnicity in Roman Corinth and Paul's Corinthian Correspondence*, Synkrisis (New Haven, CT: Yale University Press, 2014), 3 7. For the history of the development of the categories of national and universal religions, see Tomoko Masuzawa, *The Invention of World Religions, Or, How European Universalism Was Preserved in the Language of Pluralism* (Chicago: University of Chicago Press, 2005).

16. An alternate, and perhaps slightly transgressive, way of conceptualizing the "spread" of Christianity outside of the framework of military conquest or supersession might be Deissmann's use of the spread of olive cultivation as the key indicator of mapping Paul's missionary travels: "Without the provision of olives, moreover, Paul's journeys would be inconceivable; the fruit of the olive-tree will have played the same rôle on his sea-voyages that it does to-day on the Levantine steamers and sailing vessels, especially for the sailors and deck-passengers. A handful of olives, a piece of bread, and a drink of water—the Levantine traveller requires no more than that! The world of Paul the world of the olive-tree! There is a map showing the distribution of the olive in the Mediterranean world. When I first saw it, without noticing its title, it appeared to me to be a map of the Jewish or primitive Christian dispersion. . . . The olive-tree zone almost exactly coincides also with the map of Paul's missionary journeys." Deissmann, *Paul*, 39–40.

17. Gilles Deleuze and Felix Guattari, *A Thousand Plateaus* (Minneapolis: University of Minnesota Press,

lines of connections across the Mediterranean landscape, like cracks in a fading fresco, rather than the shaded areas of flat maps in our textbooks that mimic the expansion of the Roman Empire. Lacking a central command structure or clear lines of transmission, rhizomatic diagrams of early Christianity disrupt what Gilles Deleuze might call the weaponized war machine that is militarized by our historiography of spread and conquest.[18]

Pauline Chronology

Turning to sites where travel figures in Pauline studies, I begin with the study of Pauline chronology. Generally, the study of chronology is concerned with sorting out *when* Paul (as well as to some extent his associates) was *where*.[19] Chronology involves collating and arranging New Testament texts so that they can be linked together into a narrative chain. The goal is to produce an objective accounting of Paul's life and mission that can be folded into the larger story of the development of Christianity and also perhaps help in the interpretation of Paul's letters. The central and most controversial aspect of this sorting process is whether or not to include material from the canonical Acts as part of the fabric of linked texts.[20] Once assembled, the chain becomes an outline of movements over time, often deploying a common set of historical anchors like the Gallio inscription from Delphi.[21] Individual routes in the chain can often be further linked to archaeological sources, creating a further sense of solidity and allowing the reader to feel as if

1987), 21. For an example of a rhizomatic approach to early Christianity, see Cavan W. Concannon, "Early Christian Connectivity and Ecclesial Assemblages in Ignatius of Antioch," in *Across the Corrupting Sea: Post-Braudelian Approaches to the Ancient Eastern Mediterranean*, ed. Cavan W. Concannon and Lindsey Mazurek (London: Routledge, 2016).

18. Deleuze and Guattari, *A Thousand Plateaus*, 351–422.

19. Among some of the major attempts to offer a chronology of the Pauline mission, we could include: Robert Jewett, *A Chronology of Paul's Life* (Philadelphia: Fortress Press, 1979); Gerd Lüdemann, *Paul, Apostle to the Gentiles: Studies in Chronology* (Philadelphia: Fortress Press, 1984); John Knox, *Chapters in a Life of Paul* (Macon, GA: Mercer University Press, 1987); Eckhard J. Schnabel, *Paul the Missionary: Realities, Strategies and Methods* (Downers Grove, IL: InterVarsity Press, 2008), 39–122; Douglas A. Campbell, *Framing Paul: An Epistolary Biography* (Grand Rapids: Eerdmans, 2014).

20. For a description of the debates about the historicity of Acts, current to the early 1990s, see Paul Trebilco, "Itineraries, Travel Plans, Journeys, Apostolic Parousia," in *Dictionary of Paul and His Letters*, ed. Gerald F. Hawthorne and Ralph P. Martin (Downers Grove, IL: InterVarsity Press, 1993), 452–55. There is also the slightly less controversial question of whether the disputed Pauline Epistles (Ephesians, Colossians, 2 Thessalonians, 1 and 2 Timothy, and Titus) may be layered into the diagram of Pauline movements.

21. For a good example of how Gallio is used as an anchor for Pauline chronology, see Klaus Haacker, "Paul's Life," in *The Cambridge Companion to St. Paul*, ed. James D. G. Dunn (Cambridge: Cambridge University Press, 2003), 20. See also the more exhaustive reconstruction of the Gallio inscription in Deissmann, *Paul*, 261–86.

she is seeing "what Paul saw."[22] These "solid" anchor points share their solidity with the chronological chain onto which they are linked. Conceptually, this fabric of texts can then be laid over a geographic map of the eastern Mediterranean, as in the ubiquitous maps of Paul's missionary journeys that are found in nearly every Bible. These maps tend to be based upon the narrative of Acts, meaning that they are partisans in the larger battle over whether Acts is itself a reliable source of historical information. The ubiquity of these maps renders a partisan mapping of Pauline movements as trustworthy, even to seemingly critical biblical scholars.[23]

Pauline chronology, as a whole, aims at providing an objective historical timeline that either confirms the account in Acts, often for unstated theological reasons, or offers a mirror version. While the debate over Acts is often seen as a clash between conservative and liberal scholars, what is often missed is that both sides of the debate share the aim of providing a historically objective accounting of Paul's movements. Thus, even scholars who sideline Acts or who subject it to a process of ideological sifting do so as a means of creating a counter-Acts mapping of Paul's mission. Acts' narrative has so thoroughly shaped the field that even in rejecting its objectivity or utility, scholars hope to replace or refine it.[24] While many scholars chase the dream of Acts' geographic pretensions, I think that the quest for precision, facticity, and objectivity is itself a misguided quest given the nature of our limited, rhetorically charged evidence, and one which can and should be avoided.[25]

---

22. A good example of this is David W. J. Gill, "Paul's Travels Through Cyprus (Acts 13:4–12)," *Tyndale Bulletin* 46, no. 2 (1995), 219–28. Here a milestone discovered in 1966 is used as the anchor for an exploration of the route that Paul and Barnabas would have taken between Salamis and Paphos. The milestone, and the road that it thus indicates, creates an opportunity for Gill to describe other points on the route between Salamis and Paphos that are not mentioned in Acts 13:4–12 and to hint that these had some sort of effect on the traveling apostles. What Gill hints at can occasionally become assertions about how travel between two points on Acts' map can have a psychological effect on Paul, a point to which I will return.

23. A final rhetorical move in some of the studies of Pauline chronology is the way that they can loop back to address issues of sourcing, particularly in regards to the value of Acts. So, for example, in his monumental study of the early Christian mission, Schnabel (*Early Christian Mission*, 1:24) argues that Luke's geographic precision is a rationale for accepting his validity as a historical source in other respects. Why Luke's so-called geographic precision is evidence for his trustworthiness as a historical source for the first and not the second or third centuries has never been clear to me, but one regularly encounters this claim in studies of Pauline chronology. This line of argument also falters when paired with the consensus that Luke had a rather weak knowledge of the geography of Palestine; see Helmut Koester, *Introduction to the New Testament*, 2 vols. (Philadelphia: Fortress Press, 1982), 2:314.

24. Knox's *Chapters in a Life of Paul* is the classic example of a reconstruction that aims for the solidity of Acts by privileging evidence from Paul's letters.

Components of the Pauline Organization

A subset of studies that focus on Pauline chronology are those that explore aspects of Paul's organizational apparatus and its functioning. Here travel is discussed as it relates to the functioning of this machine via its constituent parts.[26] Typically we see travel emerge around four issues: travel fundraising, Paul's travel itineraries, the organization of the collection for Jerusalem, and the role of Paul's coworkers and messengers. In order to be brief, and because there is an excellent chapter on Paul's collection in this volume, I will focus my discussion here on the role of Paul's coworkers and messengers.[27] Perhaps the most prominent set of agencies in the network are Paul's coworkers, such as Timothy, Titus, and Sosthenes, among others.[28] These coworkers tend to become visible in the addresses of Paul's letters, thus being available to us in the context of the movement of the letter and in descriptions of their travels on Paul's behalf. A number of interesting scholarly studies have explored the role of Paul's coworkers as messengers, among them Margaret Mitchell's excellent article on the subject.[29] Attention to figures like Timothy and Titus is useful for exploring the broader functioning of the Pauline network. On the one hand, Paul tends to present their movements as the result of his own initiative (1 Cor 4:17; 16:10–11; 2 Cor 8:6, 23; 12:18). This should remind us of the ways in which studies of Paul as an anti-imperial figure often ignore the fact that Paul presents himself as one whose travels bring progress (προκοπή) to those who need it and as one who can commission people to travel on his behalf.[30] On the other hand, attention to the move-

---

25. This does not mean that we have to reject questions of literary and temporal relationships in our historical reconstructions. It is clear, for example, that there are some markers of chronological relationships in some of Paul's letters, notably Paul's descriptions of his travels and mentions of other letters. What I am suggesting is that we give up the presumption of a thorough and objective accounting of Paul's movements.

26. Meeks nicely folds travel into the fabric of other kinds of connections that shaped the Pauline collectives: Wayne Meeks, *The First Urban Christians: The Social World of the Apostle Paul* (New Haven, CT: Yale University Press, 1983), 25–32.

27. On the collection, see the essay by John Kloppenborg in this volume.

28. On their work in negotiating just the relationships between Paul and the Corinthians, see 1 Cor 1:1; 4:17; 16:10; 2 Cor 1:1, 19; 2:13; 7:6, 13–14; 8:6, 16, 23; 12:18.

29. Margaret M. Mitchell, "New Testament Envoys in the Context of Greco-Roman Diplomatic and Epistolary Conventions: The Example of Timothy and Titus," *JBL* 111 (1992): 641–62. For an exhaustive study of Paul's use of secretaries in writing his letters, see E. Randolph Richards, *Paul and First-Century Letter Writing: Secretaries, Composition and Collection* (Downers Grove, IL: InterVarsity Press, 2004).

30. Joseph A. Marchal, *The Politics of Heaven: Women, Gender, and Empire in the Study of Paul* (Minneapolis: Fortress Press), 44–46.

ments and the agency of Paul's coworkers helps us to critically assess assumptions of Paul's centrality to the movement, which is itself a fiction created to serve Paul's own interests (and also maintained by those whose own interests involve maintaining Paul's centrality).[31]

The Psychology of Travel

Travel is often invoked as a means of explaining features of Pauline psychology, identity, and mission. Like the pursuit of an ephemeral Pauline chronology, these projects collate evidence from New Testament texts, ancient literary sources, and archaeology not to plot a route on a map but to open up Paul's inner life. Often this grouping of materials is framed by problematic ethnoracial assumptions. An example of this kind of project is Thomas Davis's work on Paul in Cyprus.[32] Davis draws on archaeological materials to reconstruct Paul's route through Cyprus according to Acts 13; however, Davis takes a further step in layering an ethnocultural grid onto the landscape. While Paul and Barnabas are in Antioch at the outset of the narrative, they are in what Davis calls their "comfort zone," a phrase that is meant to indicate an eastern-oriented cultural context in which a Jew like Paul would feel comfortable. Cyprus is initially gridded as outside of Paul's comfort zone.[33] Yet as the article continues, Cyprus is divided into eastern- and western-oriented geographic spaces, with Salamis oriented to the east and Paphos to the west. Davis then uses this cultural gridding of space to imagine Paul's experience of moving through this space and its effect on Paul's sense of mission. Arriving in Paphos, Paul enters for the first time into a cultural zone that is completely unfamiliar, and his encounter with this foreign cultural zone leads him, according to Davis, to reorient his sense of mission to the gentiles. Travel here becomes a vehicle for exploring Paul's psychological response to

---

31. Elisabeth Schüssler Fiorenza, *Rhetoric and Ethic: The Politics of Biblical Studies* (Minneapolis: Fortress Press, 1999); Cynthia Briggs Kittredge, *Community and Authority: The Rhetoric of Obedience in the Pauline Tradition*, Harvard Theological Studies 45 (Harrisburg, PA: Trinity Press International, 1998); Elizabeth A. Castelli, "Interpretations of Power in 1 Corinthians," *Semeia* 54 (2006): 197–222. Specific studies of components of the Pauline network are useful and important because by focusing on particular agents, interactions, and movements and thoroughly situating them, they offer us a better accounting of the possibilities at each of these particular moments. However, these projects can also be co-opted by the larger project of Pauline chronology, ultimately becoming too concerned with the reconciling of textual problems rather than the exploration of possibilities.
32. Thomas W. Davis, "Saint Paul on Cyprus: Archaeology and the Transformation of an Apostle," *Perspectives on Science and Christian Faith* 64, no. 4 (2012): 230–41.
33. Davis draws on Braudel's notion of "permanent values" that form over the *longue durée* to grid Cyprus as a distinct cultural zone.

a foreign culture and offers Davis the opportunity to claim that he has discovered the hidden, yet world historical moment where Paul turns fully to the gentiles.[34]

While Davis's cultural mapping presumes a Paul that is thoroughly "eastern" in orientation, other studies use Paul's travels as a way of marking out ethnic spaces within Paul's own sense of identity. Paul's facility with travel and his use of Roman provincial geographic terminology in his letters can be offered as proof of Paul's "Roman" identity.[35] This understanding is further supported by those who view as credible Acts' claim that Paul was a Roman citizen. Of course, Paul cannot be "wholly" a Roman, so his identity is further bifurcated into Jewish and (often) Greek or Hellenistic compartments.[36] Travel then becomes a means by which Paul's multiple, yet discrete, identities are diagrammed.

A final form in which travel is said to have an impact on Paul's psychology is through the return of the frictionless geography of the empire. Here Paul's movements through the Roman landscape are said to convey to him a sense of Roman universalism. The argument is usually made by assembling a collection of texts, like Vergil's *Aeneid*, and monuments, like the *Ara Pacis* or the Priene inscription, that would have been inaccessible to Paul but are accessible to the modern scholar.[37] By moving through the frictionless landscape of the Roman Empire described in Roman propaganda, Paul's articulation of a theological universalism relating to the salvific death of Jesus becomes the result of his experience of movement.[38] Paul's mission and its theo-

---

34. For a contrasting view, we might look to Deissmann. Himself enamored of the ways in which archaeological study and travel in the Mediterranean can open up access to the "footsteps" of Paul, Deissmann (*Paul*, 231–33) still locates the psychology of Paul's missionary motives in a personal sense of calling.

35. As in, for example, William M. Ramsay, *St. Paul the Traveller and the Roman Citizen*, 3rd ed. (London: Hodder & Stoughton, 1897), particularly 30–31. See also the recent work of Ksenija Magda, *Paul's Territoriality and Mission Strategy: Searching for the Geographical Awareness Paradigm behind Romans*, WUNT 266 (Tübingen: Mohr Siebeck, 2009).

36. Richard Wallace and Wynne Williams, *The Three Worlds of Paul of Tarsus* (London: Routledge, 1998); Wright, *Paul*, 3–12.

37. For a critique of this assemblage of historical evidence as a context within which to read Paul, see S. R. F. Price, "Response," in *Paul and the Roman Imperial Order*, ed. Richard A. Horsley (Harrisburg, PA: Trinity Press International, 2004), 175–83.

38. One can see this, for example, in the listing of the external conditions for the "world-wide expansion" of Christianity given by Harnack. Harnack (*Mission and Expansion*, 1:19–21) begins by noting the unity of the Mediterranean as a result of Hellenization in the wake of Alexander, then notes the role of Rome in bringing political unity to the region, coupled by its creation of safe and efficient travel routes. This produces a collective sense among Mediterranean inhabitants of an "essential unity of mankind" that then makes it possible for the Christian message of a universal humanity stripped of all particularities to find an audience.

logical underpinnings become a mirror of a constructed theology and mission of the Roman Empire by virtue of Paul's negotiation of a geographic space.

The Discourse of Travel

A final way in which travel is discussed in relation to the Pauline assemblies relates to the discourse of travel, by which I mean the ways in which Paul's descriptions of travel, both real and metaphorical, participate in a larger discursive context shared by Paul and his audience. Travel is thus linked to a broader discursive context that Paul navigates by the rhetorical deployment of travel in his letters. Perhaps the classic study of this type is Robert Funk's isolation of the rhetorical form of the apostolic *parousia*.[39] Funk explores the role that letters play in mediating Paul's absence from his audiences. Another important contribution to this question comes from Joseph Marchal's work on Paul's letter to the Philippians. Marchal's intersectional study argues that we cannot address questions relating to travel, gender, politics, and colonialism separately but should see these issues as braided with one another.[40] One of the questions that must be asked of an ancient text is, "Does this text encourage travel to distant and inhabited lands and how does it justify itself?"[41] By paying attention to how Paul speaks about his travels and those of his associates, Marchal shows that Paul's rhetoric about travel mimics imperialistic logics, indicating that Paul may be anti-Roman only in the sense that he hoped to replace the empire with a different imperialist system.[42]

The best iteration of scholarship that focuses on the discourse of travel in Paul is the recent work of Timothy Luckritz Marquis, who offers a sophisticated exploration of various types of travelers that figured in ancient discourse.[43] Luckritz Marquis shows that travelers were viewed ambivalently in antiquity and that travel could be figured

---

39. Robert W. Funk, "The Apostolic *Parousia*: Form and Significance," in *Christian History and Interpretation: Studies Presented to John Knox*, ed. W. R. Farmer, C. F. D. Moule, and R. R. Niebuhr (Cambridge: Cambridge University Press, 1967), 249–68. For critical appraisals of Funk's work, see Mitchell, "New Testament Envoys," 641–43; and Lee A. Johnson, "Paul's Epistolary Presence in Corinth: A New Look at Robert W. Funk's Apostolic Parousia," *CBQ* 68, no. 3 (2006): 481–501.

40. Marchal here follows Musa Dube, *Postcolonial Feminist Interpretation of the Bible* (St. Louis: Chalice Press, 2000), 201.

41. Marchal, *The Politics of Heaven*, 45–48.

42. Ibid., 54. This is also the thesis of Dieter Georgi, *Theocracy in Paul's Praxis and Theology* (Minneapolis: Fortress Press, 1991).

43. Timothy Luckritz Marquis, *Transient Apostle: Paul, Travel, and the Rhetoric of Empire*, Synkrisis (New Haven, CT: Yale University Press, 2013).

rhetorically in a number of ways. He then shows how Paul plays with these rhetorical tropes in 2 Corinthians 1–9 as a means of negotiating Corinthian perceptions of Paul as a wandering traveler. Following Luckritz Marquis's lead, I want to come back to the actual movements between and among the Pauline assemblies while also attending to the ways in which these movements are mediated to us through Paul's rhetorical context. In what follows, we will focus on Philippi as a node in the Pauline network.

Paulinism and the Speculative Possibilities of Travel

To cycle back through the materiality of movement, let me pose a seemingly simple, practical question: How do you get a letter from wherever Paul is staying to Philippi and vice versa? Too often that question is elided in studies of early Christians and their letters, literature, and ideas. Because Pauline scholars tend to focus on the meaning of the things that Paul says, we tend to skip over all of the logistical practicalities, financial costs, and social and institutional networks that had to be navigated to get a few sheets of papyrus from one place to another. In what follows, I dwell on these negotiations, which will always be speculative given the available historical evidence. I do this not because I want to offer a material "background" to give some color to a reading of Paul's letters; rather, I would argue that speculative description of the connectivity between early Christians allows us to think about assemblages of agents, objects, and movements that were more fundamental to the production and maintenance of early Christianity and its varieties than the ideas conveyed in the letters and literature of the earliest Christians.[44]

To get us started, I'd like to focus on a particular aspect of letter writing that is not generally discussed by modern scholars: possibility. Prior to picking up reed and papyrus, prior to the formation of the ideological or rhetorical content of a letter, there must first exist the possibility of writing. By the possibility of writing, I mean that one has to have a sense of whom to write to and how to get the letter there. In what follows, I'd like to reflect on the possibility of writing and how it might relate to the study of Philippi within Paul's network.

To think about the possibility of writing, we have to foreground

---

44. On the problems of using archaeological materials as "background" to Paul's letters, see Cavan W. Concannon, "The Archaeology of the Pauline Mission," in *All Things to All Cultures: Paul among Jews, Greeks and Romans*, ed. Mark Harding and Alanna Nobbs (Grand Rapids: Eerdmans, 2013), 57–83.

the costs, both in terms of capital expenditures and in terms of the time, effort, and risk taken up by bodies moving across geographic space. As Bruno Latour reminds us, possibilities are not free: "Producing possibilities is as costly, local, and down to earth as making special steels or lasers. Possibilities are bought and sold like everything else. They are not different by nature. They are not, for example, 'unreal.' There is no such thing as a free possibility. The files of consultants are expensive—ask those who went bankrupt because they produced too many possibilities but did not sell enough."[45] To account for these costs, we have to think about the interrelated issues of geographic fragmentation and connectivity.[46] The possibilities for writing to and from Philippi emerged out of and within a broader topography of intersecting networks.[47]

So how might we speak about Philippi as a node within a topology? Fernand Braudel famously spoke of the "tyranny of distance" in the ancient Mediterranean, by which he meant the limitations put on connectivity by the combination of geography and transportation technology.[48] In their own update of Braudel's work, Peregrine Horden and Nicholas Purcell argue that the Mediterranean is a fragmented geography of microregions knit together by short-range cabotage. Rather than possessing some essential "urban variable," an ancient city was "an occasional manifestation of densening in the network of connectivity or a patch of marked turbulence in the eddies of mobility."[49] Horden and Purcell emphasize a plurality of "short distances," a multitude of movements that connects microregions together.[50] Along these short distances, there were always choices to be made on the fly,

45. Bruno Latour, *The Pasteurization of France* (Cambridge, MA: Harvard University Press, 1988), 174.

46. These interrelated aspects of the Mediterranean are central to the work of Peregrine Horden and Nicholas Purcell, *The Corrupting Sea: A Study of Mediterranean History* (Oxford: Blackwell, 2000). Horden and Purcell's vision of the Mediterranean helps to shape much of what I do in this paper. Their work seeks to engage the seminal work of Fernand Braudel, *The Mediterranean and the Mediterranean World in the Age of Philip II*, 2 vols. (New York: Harper & Row, 1972).

47. In their theoretical work on networks, Galloway and Thacker make a similar point with regard to the agency of nodes in a network: "What matters, then, is less the character of the individual nodes than the topological space within which and through which they operate as nodes. To be a node is not solely a causal affair; it is not to 'do' this or 'do' that. To be a node is to exist inseparably from a set of possibilities and parameters—to function within a topology of control." Alexander R. Galloway and Eugene Thacker, *The Exploit: A Theory of Networks*, Electronic Mediations 21 (Minneapolis: University of Minnesota Press, 2007), 40.

48. Braudel, *Structure of Everyday Life*, 1, 428–30. His *Annaliste* predecessor Lucien Febvre was said to have remarked upon reading Braudel's massive *The Mediterranean and the Mediterranean World in the Age of Philip II*: "Routes and cities, cities and routes." Braudel, *The Mediterranean*, 277n1, cited in Horden and Purcell, *The Corrupting Sea*, 89.

49. Horden and Purcell, *The Corrupting Sea*, 43.

50. Ibid., 150–52.

"routes within routes—multitudes of them."[51] Routes and cities thus become the effects of a plurality of forces acting to knit together the fragmentation of the landscape.[52] In the Mediterranean, connectivity was about stringing together a multitude of these short distances.

The possibility of writing was produced, then, by a sense, a mental map, of how one might fashion a sheet of papyrus to an assemblage of routes, objects, persons, and landscapes.[53] In a forthcoming article, I have endeavored to explore what it might look like to construct such a mental map for the average Philippian, by which I mean the sense of how one might imagine stringing together a set of short distances to move to and from Philippi.[54]

A Philippian geography must begin with the view from the Philippian acropolis, because it is this view of the immediately accessible landscape that forms the basis for a sense of Philippi's place in the networks of the Mediterranean.[55] From the Philippian acropolis, looking south from the mountain spur against which the city is nestled, one would see a mixture of marsh and farmland stretching out to the Pangaion mountain range. Following the line of hills to the left, a tiny gap in the hills shows the path through which the Via Egnatia passed on its way to the port of Neapolis. On a clear day, the mountainous island of Thasos looms in the distance. Every Philippian could theoretically climb to the acropolis, look out over the landscape, and see the same geography, though they could each imagine different ways to cross it that were not visible from this stunning vista. To think about the connections that might be imagined from Philippi, we have to look for evidence that points us to how Philippians might have connected with places that were out of their line of sight. Evidence from Philippian inscriptions, pottery imports, and building materials indicates that Philippi's highest levels of connectivity were clustered around the northern Aegean, between Macedonia and Asia Minor.

---

51. Ibid., 14.
52. Ibid., 97.
53. On mental maps, see Peter Gould and Rodney White, *Mental Maps* (New York: Routledge, 1986).
54. Cavan W. Concannon, "'Let Us Know Anything Further Which You Have Heard': Mapping Philippian Connectivity," in *Philippi: From colonia augusta to communitas christiania: Religion and Society in Transition*, ed. Steven Friesen and Daniel N. Schowalter (Leiden: Brill, forthcoming).
55. As Horden and Purcell rightly note: "Fields of perception and their foci are characteristic ingredients in the definition of Mediterranean microregions. . . . The chains of perceptibility created by looking from one vantage point to the next serve both to express the relationship of individual localities to one another and . . . to make sense of the wider world." Horden and Purcell, *The Corrupting Sea*, 125.

Fig. 12.1. Philippian Geography.

In figure 12.1, I have laid out a map of Philippian connectivity and will briefly describe what sorts of connections are mapped here. The circles on the map indicate places that are mentioned in Philippian inscriptions or places where Philippians are said to have visited or lived. The circles also represent the locations of Italian *negotiatores*, trading families operating in the Greek East, who share the same *nomen* as inhabitants of Philippi. The circles arc larger depending on the number of times the place pops up in the data. The shaded area on the west coast of Asia Minor marks the major source for imported pottery to Philippi and Macedonia more generally, an indicator of trading activity between the two regions. I will briefly discuss each of these data sets before exploring what this mapping might mean for studies of travel between Philippi and other Pauline collectives.

Inscriptions from Philippi and elsewhere give us an indication of the places to which Philippians could imagine traveling and the places from which they might have come.[56] In some instances, these traces mark someone's place of origin, as in the epitaph of the retired soldier L. Calventius Bassus from Eporedia in Gaul,[57] or a city where a Philippian held priesthoods, as in the case of the C. Antonius Rufus,[58] or locales mentioned in military dossiers and civic *cursus*.[59] All in all, I have found forty-eight places that mark traces of connectivity.[60] Figure 12.1 shows a clear clustering of these sites along the coasts of the north Aegean.[61]

Included on the map are communities where we find Italian *nego-*

---

56. I have used Peter Pilhofer's catalogue for this data set: Peter Pilhofer, *Philippi II: Katalog der Inschriften von Philippi*, 2nd ed., WUNT 119 (Tübingen: Mohr Siebeck, 2009). There are still inscriptions that have not yet been published from Philippi that could change the contours of this set. References to inscriptions in what follows will follow Pilhofer's numbering (e.g., *Philippi II*, no. 123). The French School at Athens is currently publishing the complete corpus of inscriptions from the city, as in the recent collection of Cedric Brelaz, *Corpus des inscriptions grecques et latines de Philippes. Tome II. La colonie romaine. Partie 1. La vie publique de la colonie*, Études épigraphiques 6 (Athènes: École française d'Athènes, 2014). In my own sorting of the data, I have excluded places that were mentioned prior to the building of the Via Egnatia, because I assumed that the construction of this road fundamentally reshaped Philippian connectivity in the wider Mediterranean. Another way of demarcating time would have been to exclude inscriptions from the period prior to Philippi's refounding as a Roman colony, a suggestion made to me in private correspondence by Cedric Brelaz.

57. *Philippi II*, no. 389.

58. *Philippi II*, nos. 700–703.

59. I have excluded the Philippian *vici* from the data set, since these are generally places lying within Philippi's line of sight. For a list of the *vici*, see Fanoula Papazoglou, *Les Villes de Macédoine à l'époque Romains*, BCH Supp. 16 (Paris: École Française d'Athènes, 1988), 411.

60. I have also included places that Philippians could imagine visiting, as in the mention of Paphos in a poem found near Agios Athanasios and what may have been a picture of Mount Olympus painted on the wall of the Association of Silvanus, at a cost of fifteen denarii (*Philippi II*, nos. 439, 164, respectively).

61. The bulk of the peripheral sites that appear on the map (Africa, Gaul, Noricum, Dalmatia, and Moesia) are epitaphs for Philippians who died serving abroad in the legions. As one example, we can take the epitaph of C. Graecinius Firminus, dated to the first or second century CE (*Philippi II*, no. 718). Graecinius's epitaph was found in Thessaloniki, but he served as a decurion and quaestor at Philippi, alongside offices in the province of Africa. Rome also appears on the map largely because of Philippians serving in the military (*Philippi II*, nos. 30, 705, 705a). Vienne, Alexandria, and Rhodes only appear as points on a portable bronze sundial found in the excavations of the

tiatores that share the same *nomen* as inhabitants of Philippi.[62] As Gary Reger has pointed out, merchants are important links in ancient social networks that cross geographic regions because they are themselves dependent on the connections that they possess.[63] In all, I have found forty-three family *nomina* in Philippi from Jean Hatzfeld's list in Peter Pilhofer's catalogue.[64] It is difficult, given the available evidence, to determine whether any of these Philippians would have been connected to one of these trading families, but it is likely that at least some of them were.[65] The presence of *negotiatores* in Philippi would suggest that the Via Egnatia may have functioned as a catalyst for the spread of these trading families east.

Philippi's connectivity can also be glimpsed by its trading partners,

city (*Philippi II*, no. 326). See Mario Arnaldi and Karlheinz Schaldach, "A Roman Cylinder Dial: Witness to a Forgotten Tradition," *Journal for the History of Astronomy* 28 (1997): 107–30.

62. On *negotiatores*, see the classic studies by Hatzfeld: Jean Hatzfeld, "Les italiens résidant a Délos," *BCH* 36 (1912); and Jean Hatzfeld, *Les trafiquants italiens dans l'Orient hellénique*, Bibliothèque des écoles françaises d'Athènes et de Rome; fasc. 115 (Paris: E. de Boccard, 1919). For more recent work on these trading families, see Alan John Nisbet Wilson, *Emigration from Italy in the Republican Age of Rome* (New York: Barnes & Noble, 1966); Antony Spawforth, "Roman Corinth: The Formation of a Colonial Elite," in *Roman Onomastics in the Greek East: Social and Political Aspects: Proceedings of the International Colloquium Organized by the Finnish Institute and the Centre for Greek and Roman Antiquity, Athens, 7-9 September 1993*, ed. A. D. Rizakes, Meletemata 21 (Athens: Kentron Hellenikes kai Romaikes Archaiotetos Ethnikon Hidryma Ereunon, 1996), 167–82; Athanasios Rizakis, "L'émigration romaine en Macédoine et la communauté marchande de Thessalonique: perspectives économiques et sociales," in *Les Italiens dans le monde grec, IIe siècle av. J.-C.-Ier siècle ap. J.-C.; Circulation, Activités, Intégration*, ed. C. Müller and C. Hasenohr, BCH supp. 41 (Paris: de Boccard, 2002), 109–32; and Concannon, *When You Were Gentiles*, 56–63.

63. Gary Reger, "On the Road to India with Apollonios of Tyana and Thomas the Apostle," in *Greek and Roman Networks in the Mediterranean*, ed. Irad Malkin, Christy Constantakopoulou, and Katerina Panagopoulou (New York: Routledge, 2009), 253.

64. For the list of *nomina* at Philippi, see Pilhofer, *Philippi II*, 1119–31. Alongside Hatzfeld's data, I have included in the map recent work that notes the presence of *negotiatores* at Mygdonian Apollonia, at Amphipolis, and at Thessaloniki (Rizakis, "L'émigration romaine," 109–32). We also know of Roman merchants from Acanthus (*SEG* 1.282; John S. Kloppenborg and Richard Ascough, *Greco-Roman Associations: Texts, Translations, and Commentary. 1. Attica, Central Greece, Macedonia, Thrace*, Beiheft zur Zeitschrift für die neutestamentliche Wissenschaft 181 [New York: de Gruyter, 2011], 297–98).

65. Finding identifiable Philippian connections to these families is difficult. As Lolos notes, some of these *negotiatores* were involved in the slave trade, which means that the traces of their economic connections would not be visible in the archaeological record; see Yannis Lolos, "Via Egnatia after Egnatius: Imperial Policy and Inter-Regional Contacts," *Mediterranean Historical Review* 22, no. 2 (2007): 280–81. Rizakis ("L'émigration romaine," 126n80, 128) has suggested that we might also find connections among the Philippian Herennii and the Novellii. We might also find evidence for *negotiatores* by looking at voluntary associations in the city. For example, the membership lists of the Association of Silvanus contain sixteen of the family names on Hatzfeld's list, which should tell us something about the kinds of connections that intersect among the members of this group (*Philippi II*, nos. 163–66; Kloppenborg and Ascough, *Greco-Roman Associations*, 315–24; Richard S. Ascough, *Paul's Macedonian Associations: The Social Context of 1 Thessalonians and Philippians*, WUNT 2/161 [Tübingen: Mohr Siebeck, 2003], 51, 54, 64–65; Joseph H. Hellerman, *Reconstructing Honor in Roman Philippi: Carmen Christi as Cursus Pudorum*, SNTS Monograph Series 132 [Cambridge: Cambridge University Press, 2005], 100–108).

traces of which remain in the imported ceramics that made their way to the city. Though studies of imported pottery at Philippi have not been done, we can extrapolate a bit from Vaitsa Malamidou's work on pottery imports in Macedonia.[66] At a broad level, Malamidou shows that the market for fine wares in Macedonia was dominated by the forms coming out of workshops in western Asia Minor, notably Eastern Sigillata A (ESA) and Eastern Sigillata B (ESB)[67] and then, by the end of the first century, Çandarli ware from Pergamon.[68] Malamidou's work shows that pottery imports in Macedonia were dominated by trade with the west coast of Asia Minor and that there was a near complete absence of evidence indicating trade with Italy, where fine Italian sigillata was produced and regularly shipped to the Greek East. This suggests that there was (1) a limit to the eastern spread of Italian sigillata, and thus certain kinds of trade with Italy, during this period, even as Dyrrachium, at the western end of the Via Egnatia, emerged as a major facilitator of goods moving east;[69] and (2) that the cities of this region looked to the east to Asia Minor for their major trading partners. Because pottery was often parasitic on other, more lucrative forms of trade, this may be an indicator of the direction and intensity of trade in the region.[70]

While Philippi was connected to a robust network of trade in the

---

66. Vaitsa Malamidou, *Roman Pottery in Context: Fine and Coarse Wares from Five Sites in North-Eastern Greece*, British Archaeological Reports Series 1386 (Oxford: John & Erica Hedges, 2005). Malamidou examines five sites in Macedonia (Amphipolis, Philippi, Kepia, Abdera, and Thasos) and compares their pottery assemblages with those at Stobi and Berenice. Her sample from Philippi, taken from excavations in the northern part of the Theater, yielded only coarse ware; see ibid., 20–21.

67. ESA generally was produced somewhere in western Syria during the first centuries BCE and CE, while ESB was produced in the area around Tralles and Ephesos from the first to the second centuries CE. For a description of ESA and ESB, see John W. Hayes, *Handbook of Mediterranean Roman Pottery* (Norman: University of Oklahoma Press, 1997), 52–59.

68. Malamidou, *Roman Pottery in Context*, 111, table 31.

69. Lolos, "Via Egnatia after Egnatius," 280.

70. Cedric Brelaz, "Philippi: A Roman Colony within Its Regional Context," in *L'hégémonie romaine sur les communautés du Nord Égéen (IIe s. av. J.-C.—IIe s. ap. J.-C.): entre ruptures et continuités*, ed. J. Fournier and M.-G. G. Parissaki (Athens: École française d'Athènes, forthcoming), takes a similar position on the extent of Philippian involvement with other regions. Malamidou's study comes with several caveats. First, these findings are generalities for the region. Ancient trade was, in many ways, idiosyncratic at the local level, depending on the kinds of connections that could be forged via cabotage. Second, as Yannis Lolos has pointed out, we may not be able to completely rule out a market for Italian fine wares in the region, since there is some evidence for Pompeian red ware, produced in Campania, at Amphipolis and at Thessalonike (Lolos, "Via Egnatia after Egnatius," 280; Malamidou, *Roman Pottery in Context*, 104, table 18). While there was certainly some trade with Italy making its way to Philippi, the intensity of trade around Philippi was dominated by Asia Minor, as we can see in the dominance of eastern sigillata and Çandarli ware in Malamidou's study. Finally, Malamidou's study intentionally ignores the huge amount of amphorae fragments in the assemblages from northeast Greece (Lolos, "Via Egnatia after Egnatius," 280). Study of these fragments could indicate other patterns of economic exchange in the region.

northern Aegean, we should not overestimate the extent to which the city relied on interregional networks. For example, when we look at the materials that Philippians used to build their public buildings, we can see that local sources dominated.[71] Philippian buildings that made use of marble in the period after the refounding of the city as a Roman colony largely used local marble that was quarried off the side of the Philippian acropolis, or perhaps at other sites in the nearby area.[72] The finer white marbles that could be found on the more expensive buildings were imported from Thasos, an island just off the coast of Philippi's harbor at Neapolis.[73]

To summarize, the inscriptions of Philippi show a robust set of connections across the northeastern Aegean, with more far-flung connections largely the result of Philippian soldiers abroad. The ceramic imports also suggest stronger trading connections between northeast Greece and Asia Minor. As a node on the Via Egnatia, Philippi likely had a small population of Italian *negotiatores* who would have brokered local and contingent trading relationships along their networks. Marble use was mostly a local affair, though new information might allow us to extend the network further. Philippi was thus a city that was connected to regions outside of its immediate, visible landscape, notably with other cities in Macedonia along the Via Egnatia and across the Aegean to Asia Minor; however, Philippi was not a major hub in trading networks that moved much further afield from these more local interactions.

This mapping of Philippian connectivity becomes visible in a different way when we factor in the costs and the travel time from Philippi. In figures 12.2 and 12.3, I have plotted maps that measure travel from Philippi using ORBIS, a mapping platform developed by Walter Scheidel at Stanford University.[74]

---

71. On the stone trade in the Roman world, see Ben Russell, *The Economics of the Roman Stone Trade*, Oxford Studies on the Roman Economy (Oxford: Oxford University Press, 2014).

72. According to Ben Russell's database of active Roman quarries (http://tinyurl.com/z5ftla5), the closest quarries to Philippi are at Agios Pneuma to the west, Drama to the north, Abdera to the east, and the various quarries on Thasos to the south. While the quarries on Thasos and Abdera produced white and white-grey marble, the quarry at Drama produced dark-grey or black marble. Of these sites, only those at Thasos were exported outside of the region.

73. In a personal communication, Michalis Lychounas was kind enough to confirm this for me.

74. orbis.stanford.edu. This platform culls together information about ancient roads, prices, modes of travel, geography, wind patterns, and sea currents and allows users to map various kinds of routes between a large number of ancient cities, using criteria such as time of year, speed, price, and mode of transport. It is important to note that the numbers that ORBIS provides are not meant to be accurate and precise measurements of distance, time, and cost. As Scheidel notes, "Computed travel costs do not (and inevitably cannot) capture the experience of any given trip but instead seek to approximate mean outcomes for an infinite number of trips taken on a given route with a

Fig. 12.2. Isochrome Map Measuring Distance from Philippi by Time.

given mode of transport in a given month, under the simplifying assumption that these trips used the best available path and were continuous. In so doing, the results reflect structural conditions in two ways, by providing orders of magnitude for actual time and price cost and by allowing us to relate them in a consistent manner to those for other routes. The ultimate goal is to establish the real cost involved in connecting imperial centers to particular regions." Walter Scheidel, "The Shape of the Roman World," *Princeton/Stanford Working Papers in Classics*, 2013, 4.

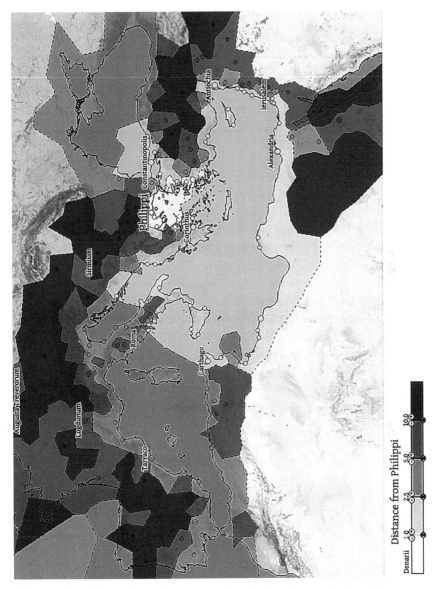

Fig. 12.3. Isochrome Map Measuring Distance from Philippi by Cost (in denarii).

In figure 12.2, we see a zone map that measures distance in time, while figure 12.3 represents distance as a measure of the cost (in denarii) of moving a kilogram of wheat. Note that these maps are actually quite different; however, both cohere with the patterns I have already noted, namely that the fastest and cheapest connections to Philippi cover its proximate neighbors in Macedonia and sites along the Aegean coast of Asia Minor.

1. Paul in Philippi (Phil 4:15)
2. Aid comes to Paul in Thessaloniki more than once (καὶ ἅπαξ καὶ δίς) from Philippi (Phil 4:16)
3. Epaphroditus brings another gift to Paul (Phil 4:18)
4. Philippians hear of Epaphroditus's illness (Phil 2:26)
5. Paul and Timothy write and send Philippians
6. Timothy will come to Philippi later (Phil 2:19–24)
7. Paul, in Ephesos, tells the Corinthians he will pass through Macdonia on his way to Corinth (1 Cor 16:5, 8–9)
8. Unnamed Macedonians may come with Paul to pick up collection in Corinth (2 Cor 9:4)

Fig. 12.4. Philippi in Paul's Network.

Keeping the preceding and following maps in mind, let us try to put Philippi into the Pauline network. In figure 12.4, you can see the movements to and from Philippi in Paul's letters, to which I have added the references to the "Macedonians" in 2 Corinthians 9, since it is not clear who exactly is meant here. For the sake of simplicity, I have chosen to treat Philippians as a single letter, though that is by no means a certainty.[75] One of the things we notice in this list is that Paul's interactions with the Philippians are most intense and frequent when he is in close proximity, as during his time in nearby Thessaloniki when he receives several gifts of money from them (Phil 4:16). After Paul receives their most recent gift (Phil 4:18), news of the messenger Epaphroditus's illness goes back to Philippi before Paul's letter is dispatched (Phil 2:26), suggesting that Paul is perhaps operating in close proximity to the region. That Paul also can easily envision traveling to Philippi from Ephesos makes sense given that the trip could be made in under a week (1 Cor 16:5, 8–9). But, on the other hand, we should also pay careful attention to the fact that Paul must have deployed a tremendous amount of resources and effort to sustain a connection between Ephesos and Philippi 692 kilometers apart (figure 12.5). Prox-

75. For partition theories of Philippians, see Koester, *Introduction to the New Testament*, 2:53–54; Philip Sellew, "*Laodiceans* and the Philippians Fragments Hypothesis," HTR 87 (1994): 17–28; Günther Bornkamm, "Der Philipperbrief als paulinische Briefsammlung," in *Geschichte und Glaube 2*, ed. Günther Bornkamm (München: Kaiser, 1971), 195–205.

imity is one thing, but maintaining a connection takes work, resources, and a little bit of miracle.

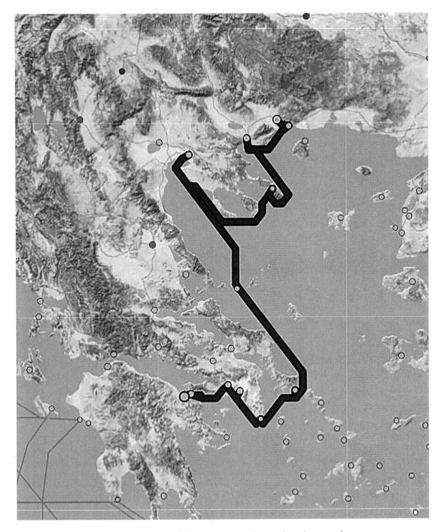

Fig 12.5. The *fastest* journey from Philippi to Corinth in July takes 8.2 days, covering 1,105 kilometers. Prices in denarii, based on the use of a faster sail ship and a civilian river boat (where applicable), and on these road options: wheat (by donkey): 1.89/kg; wheat (by wagon): 2.19 kg; per passenger in a carriage: 228.14.

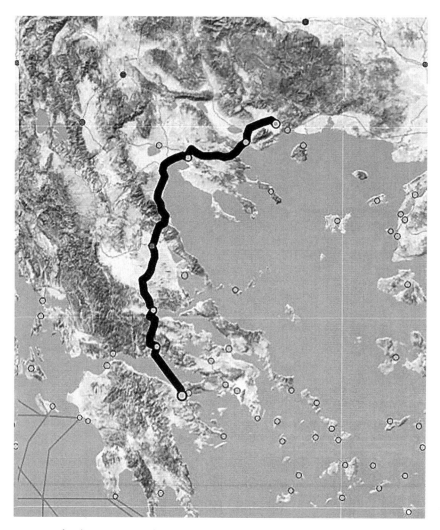

Fig. 12.6. The *shortest* journey from Philippi to Corinth in July takes 16.6 days, covering 560 kilometers. Prices in denarii, based on the use of a faster sail ship and a civilian river boat (where applicable), and on these road options: wheat (by donkey): 13.61/kg; wheat (by wagon): 17.01 kg; per passenger in a carriage: 664.65.

We might see something of this by paying attention to the connection that Paul fosters between Corinth and Macedonia. Here the distance between the two sites is much greater, either by sea or by land, making it much harder to deliver on preplanned travel itineraries and to maintain connections over time (figure 12.6). As regards the former, given what Luckritz Marquis has shown with regard to the suspicion that was often directed at travelers in antiquity, it is no surprise that Paul's failure to follow through on his plans to visit Corinth via Macedonia caused the Corinthians to question his broader intentions with regard to the collection, as we see them doing in Paul's defensive rhetoric throughout 2 Corinthians.[76]

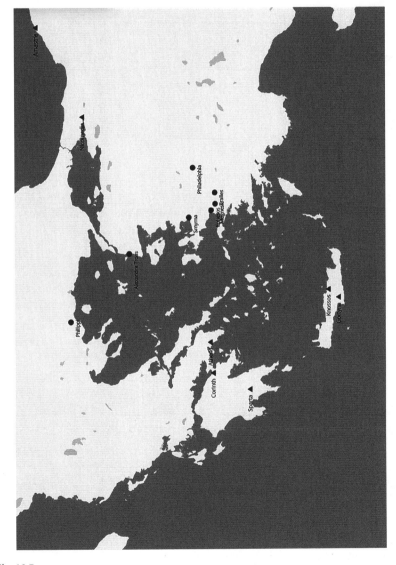

Fig. 12.7.

76. On Paul's tense interactions with the Corinthians, see Concannon, *When You Were Gentiles*, 147–50.

As to the latter, it is interesting to see that by the second century, Philippi and Corinth have been linked into different early Christian networks, one connected to Dionysios of Corinth and another that is visible in the letters of Ignatius (figure 12.7). I have used circles to plot the assemblies connected to Corinth in the letter collection of Dionysios of Corinth in the latter half of the second century. Triangles mark the communities linked to Ignatius of Antioch during his travels through the region, many of which were already linked together as the seven churches of revelation or later as the network of Asian churches that spurred the Quartodeciman controversy in the late second century. Because of the distance between them (notice that Corinth sits outside of the fastest and cheapest zone from Philippi on figures 12.2 and 12.3), it was difficult in practical terms to maintain connections between Corinth and Philippi, meaning that once Paul ceased to function as an organizer, mediator, and funder of such connectivity, these locales would naturally disconnect. While most scholarship on early Christianity is enamored of the trope of Christianity's spread and success and often tacitly assumes that the "Pauline churches" remained networked together, we should be perhaps more attentive to the natural tendency for tenuous networks of assemblies to fall apart rather than stay together.

By focusing on connectivity, and the possibilities that it afforded, I am pushing scholars of early Christianity to pay careful attention to tenuous and shifting networks, made up of people, letters, boats, and wind patterns, and the work, cost, and contingency that made them possible.[77] Unless we find ways to account for the costs of connectivity, an accurate picture of the diffuse and shifting networks of early Christians will elude us. As Latour rightly notes, "If there are identities between actants, this is because they have been constructed at great expense. If there are equivalences, this is because they have been built out of bits and pieces with much toil and sweat, and because they are maintained by force. If there are exchanges, these are always unequal and cost a fortune both to establish and to maintain."[78] Of any kind of sociality, we always have to ask, "how many people maintain it and how much it costs to pay them" and then add that to the bill.[79]

---

77. Rarely is this cost accounted for in studies that focus on particular early Christian letters or letter writers. This is not to say that they do not exist. One classic example is Ramsay's *St. Paul the Traveller*. Ramsay knew firsthand the difficulties of traveling across the Mediterranean in the nineteenth century, though his analysis of these places and their local cultures is replete with orientalist sentiment.

78. Latour, *Pasteurization of France*, 162.

Select Bibliography

Abulafia, David. *The Great Sea: A Human History of the Mediterranean.* Oxford: Oxford University Press, 2011.

Adams, Colin, and Ray Laurence, eds. *Travel and Geography in the Roman Empire.* New York: Routledge, 2001.

Braudel, Fernand. *The Mediterranean and the Mediterranean World in the Age of Philip II.* 2 vols. New York: Harper & Row, 1972–73.

Casson, Lionel. *Travel in the Ancient World.* Baltimore: Johns Hopkins University Press, 1994.

Concannon, Cavan W. "The Archaeology of the Pauline Mission." In *All Things to All Cultures: Paul among Jews, Greeks and Romans,* edited by Mark Harding and Alanna Nobbs, 57–83. Grand Rapids: Eerdmans, 2013.

_____. "Early Christian Connectivity and Ecclesial Assemblages in Ignatius of Antioch." In *Across the Corrupting Sea: Post-Braudelian Approaches to the Ancient Eastern Mediterranean,* edited by Cavan W. Concannon and Lindsey Mazurek, 65–90. London: Routledge, 2016.

_____. "'Let Us Know Anything Further Which You Have Heard': Mapping Philippian Connectivity." In *Philippi: From colonia augusta to communitas christiania: Religion and Society in Transition,* edited by Steven J. Friesen and Daniel N. Schowalter. Leiden: Brill, forthcoming.

_____. *"When You Were Gentiles": Specters of Ethnicity in Roman Corinth and Paul's Corinthian Correspondence.* Synkrisis. New Haven, CT: Yale University Press, 2014.

Elsner, Jaś, and Ian Rutherford, eds. *Pilgrimage in Graeco-Roman and Early Christian Antiquity: Seeing the Gods.* Oxford: Oxford University Press, 2005.

Funk, Robert W. "The Apostolic *Parousia*: Form and Significance." In *Christian History and Interpretation: Studies Presented to John Knox,* edited by W. R. Farmer, C. F. D. Moule, and R. R. Niebuhr, 249–68. Cambridge: Cambridge University Press, 1967.

Haacker, Klaus. "Paul's Life." In *The Cambridge Companion to St. Paul,* edited by James D. G. Dunn, 19–33. Cambridge: Cambridge University Press, 2003.

Harnack, Adolf von. *The Mission and Expansion of Christianity in the First Three Centuries.* 2 vols. Translated by James Moffatt. Gloucester, MA: Peter Smith, 1972.

79. Ibid., 221.

Hezser, Catherine. *Jewish Travel in Antiquity*. Texte und Studien zum antiken Judentum 144. Tübingen: Mohr Siebeck, 2011.

Horden, Peregrine, and Nicholas Purcell. *The Corrupting Sea: A Study of Mediterranean History*. Oxford: Blackwell, 2000.

Hughes, J. Donald. *Environmental Problems of the Greeks and Romans: Ecology in the Ancient Mediterranean*. 2nd ed. Baltimore: Johns Hopkins University Press, 2014.

Jewett, Robert. *A Chronology of Paul's Life*. Philadelphia: Fortress Press, 1979.

Knox, John. *Chapters in a Life of Paul*. Macon, GA: Mercer University Press, 1987.

Luckritz Marquis, Timothy. *Transient Apostle: Paul, Travel, and the Rhetoric of Empire*. Synkrisis. New Haven, CT: Yale University Press, 2013.

Lüdemann, Gerd. *Paul, Apostle to the Gentiles: Studies in Chronology*. Philadelphia: Fortress Press, 1984.

Meeks, Wayne. *The First Urban Christians: The Social World of the Apostle Paul*. New Haven, CT: Yale University Press, 1983.

Mitchell, Margaret M. "New Testament Envoys in the Context of Greco-Roman Diplomatic and Epistolary Conventions: The Example of Timothy and Titus." *JBL* 111, no. 4 (1992): 641–62.

Ramsay, William M. *St. Paul the Traveller and the Roman Citizen*. 3rd ed. London: Hodder & Stoughton, 1897.

Richards, E. Randolph. *Paul and First-Century Letter Writing: Secretaries, Composition and Collection*. Downers Grove, IL: InterVarsity Press, 2004.

Schnabel, Eckhard J. *Early Christian Mission*. 2 vols. Downers Grove, IL: InterVarsity Press, 2004.

Trebilco, Paul. "Itineraries, Travel Plans, Journeys, Apostolic Parousia." In *Dictionary of Paul and His Letters*, edited by Gerald F. Hawthorne and Ralph P. Martin, 446–56. Downers Grove, IL: InterVarsity Press, 1993.

13

Marxism and Capitalism in Pauline Studies

L. L. Welborn

Because Paul explicitly comments on the social status of his converts (1 Cor 1:26–28),[1] and because Paul directly intervenes in a conflict between the "haves" and the "have-nots" at Corinth (1 Cor 11:17–34),[2] and, most of all, because Paul devoted his energies for many years to a collection for the poor among the saints at Jerusalem (Gal 2:10; 1 Cor 16:1–4; Rom 15:25–28),[3] and, in that connection, developed an argu-

---

1. For the interpretation of the descriptive terms in 1 Cor 1:26–28 ("wise," "powerful," "nobly born," "foolish," "weak," "low and despised," etc.) in a social sense, see Gerd Theissen, *The Social Setting of Pauline Christianity: Essays on Corinth*, ed. and trans. John H. Schütz (Philadelphia: Fortress Press, 1982), 70–73; contra Richard A. Horsley, *Wisdom and Spiritual Transcendence at Corinth: Studies in First Corinthians* (Eugene, OR: Cascade Books, 2008), 14–15, 32, 126, 130, 134–36, who insists that these terms must be understood in a "spiritual sense," denying the relevance of the social and political usages of these terms in Greek literature from Aristotle to Josephus.
2. Wayne A. Meeks, *The First Urban Christians: The Social World of the Apostle Paul* (New Haven, CT: Yale University Press, 1983), 68: "the phrase 'the have-nots' is to be taken absolutely, that is, the poor." See also Theissen, *Social Setting*, 145–74, esp. 148; Thomas Schmeller, *Hierarchie und Egalität: Eine sozialgeschichtliche Untersuchung paulinischer Gemeinden und griechisch-römischer Vereine* (Stuttgart: Katholisches Bibelwerk, 1995), esp. 60, 71.
3. Dieter Georgi, *Remembering the Poor: The History of Paul's Collection for Jerusalem* (Nashville: Abingdon, 1992); Petros Vassiliadis, "The Collection Revisited," *Deltion Biblikon Meleton* 11 (1992): 42–48;

ment for "equality" (ἰσότης) as the presupposition and the goal of economic relations between Christ believers (2 Cor 8:13–15),[4] one might suppose that Paul's letters would be the focus of attention for Marxist scholars seeking to discover the antecedents of the social revolution that was expected to come.[5] But there are surprises in the history of Pauline studies, and poignant ironies. For example, the most prominent Marxist historian of antiquity, G. E. M. de Ste. Croix, pronounced the Pauline abolition of a distinction between slave and free in Galatians 3:28 (cf. Col 1:11) as unworthy of serious attention by the historian: "these passages have a purely spiritual or eschatological meaning and relate only to the situation as it is 'in the sight of God', or 'in the next world'; they have no significance whatever for this world, where relations in real life between master and slave are not affected in any way."[6] By contrast, E. A. Judge, no Marxist, argued that "Paul conducted a head-on personal assault on the status system which supplied the ideology of the established order," and asserted that "Paul would have found much in common with the restless, argumentative and single-minded apostle of revolution [Karl Marx]—like him a son of Israel turned to the Gentiles, and committed to showing the whole world its true destiny."[7]

Explaining how these ironies arose, that is, why Paul was long discounted as a resource for Marxist theory and revolutionary praxis, must be one object of this essay. But beyond this postmortem examination, the essay will expound how the appropriation of the insights of Marx by social scientists produced ideological interpretations of Paul that transformed Marx's basic intention into its opposite.[8] Then, the

Julien Ogereau, "The Jerusalem Collection as Κοινωνία: Paul's Global Politics of Socio-Economic Equality and Solidarity," *New Testament Studies* 58 (2012): 360–78.

4. L. L. Welborn, "'That There May Be Equality': The Contexts and Consequences of a Pauline Ideal," *New Testament Studies* 59, no. 1 (2013): 73–90.

5. The idea of investigating past eras, especially the period of the decline and fall of the Roman Empire, with the aim of discovering historical parallels to the imminent socialist revolution is already implicit in "The Communist Manifesto" of Karl Marx and Friedrich Engels (1848), reprinted in Karl Marx, *On Revolution* (New York: McGraw-Hill, 1971), and is clearly articulated by Karl Kautsky in "Social Reform and Social Revolution" (1902), reprinted in Karl Kautsky, *The Social Revolution: Reform and Revolution, the Day after the Revolution*, translated by A. M. Simons (Whitefish, MT: Kessinger Publishing, 2010).

6. G. E. M. de Ste. Croix, *The Class Struggle in the Ancient Greek World: From the Archaic Age to the Arab Conquests* (Ithaca, NY: Cornell University Press, 1981), 107–8; similarly, 419.

7. E. A. Judge, "Cultural Conformity and Innovation in Paul: Some Clues from Contemporary Documents," *Tyndale Bulletin* 35 (1984): 3–24, reprinted in *Social Distinctives of the Christians in the First Century: Pivotal Essays by E. A. Judge*, ed. David M. Scholar (Peabody, MA: Hendrickson, 2008), 159–60.

8. Not only the works of "moderate functionalists" such as Theissen (*Social Setting*, esp. 163–68) and Meeks (*First Urban Christians*, esp. 6–7) but also the sociological interpretations of David E. Briones, *Paul's Financial Policy: A Socio-Theological Approach* (London: Bloomsbury T&T Clark, 2013), esp. 17;

essay will explore how, after the collapse of the Soviet system, disillusionment with the Marxist utopia precipitated interpretations of Paul from the perspective pauperism as the promoter of economic mutualism among the dispossessed.[9] In the face of the "evidence" of capitalism's triumph all around us, some interpreters have recently presented Paul as the apostle of charity, who knew how to negotiate the margins of choice left to those who were determined to "remember the poor."[10] And just when it seemed that the funeral of the radical Paul was being planned, fresh Marxist readings of Paul emerged, applying classic Marxist concepts such as the theory of surplus value, the commodification of labor, and ideology as an instrument of social reproduction to crucial Pauline texts.[11] The essay will conclude by looking forward, in an effort to identify several Marxist approaches that may illuminate Paul's thought and practice: the messianic materialism of Walter Benjamin, the structural Marxism of Louis Althusser, and the radical egalitarianism of Jacques Rancière.

Before proceeding, a few disclaimers must be made. First, the essay will treat Pauline scholars, rather than the philosophers or sociologists whose theories they employ. Reference may occasionally be made to Marxist theory, in order to clarify assumptions (e.g., the function of religion)[12] or to comprehend developments (e.g., in the theory of ideology),[13] but the task of analyzing the critical theories that have illuminated, or may illuminate, the subject of Paul and economics has been left to others, especially to Ward Blanton in the present volume.[14]

---

and Thomas R. Blanton IV, *A Spiritual Economy: Gift Exchange in the Letters of Paul of Tarsus* (New Haven, CT: Yale University Press, 2017), appealing to the sociology of Pierre Bourdieu.

9. E.g., Justin J. Meggitt, *Paul, Poverty and Survival* (Edinburgh: T&T Clark, 1998).

10. E.g., Bruce W. Longenecker, *Remember the Poor: Paul, Poverty and the Greco-Roman World* (Grand Rapids: Eerdmans, 2010).

11. Jorunn Økland, "Textual Reproduction as Surplus Value: Paul on Pleasing Christ and Spouses, in Light of Simone de Beauvoir" in *Marxist Feminist Criticism of the Bible*, ed. Roland Boer and Jorunn Økland (Sheffield: Sheffield Phoenix Press, 2008), 182–203; Neil Elliott, "Ideological Closure in the Christ-Event: A Marxist Response to Alain Badiou's Paul" in *Paul, Philosophy, and the Theopolitical Vision*, ed. Douglas Harink (Eugene, OR: Cascade Books, 2010), 135–54; L. L. Welborn, "Towards Structural Marxism as a Hermeneutic of Early Christian Literature, Illustrated with Reference to Paul's Spectacle Metaphor in 1 Corinthians 15:30–32," *The Bible and Critical Theory* 8 (2012): 27–35; Laura Salah Nasrallah, "'You Were Bought with a Price': Freedpersons and Things in 1 Corinthians" in *Corinth in Contrast: Studies in Inequality*, ed. Steven J. Friesen, Sarah A. James, and Daniel N. Schowalter (Leiden: Brill, 2014), 54–73.

12. Delos B. McKown, *The Classical Marxist Critiques of Religion* (The Hague: Martinus Nijhoff, 1975); "Christianity, Origins of" in *Marxism, Communism and Western Society: A Comparative Encyclopedia*, ed. C. D. Kernig (New York: Herder & Herder, 1972), 409–22; Roland Boer, *Criticism of Heaven: On Marxism and Theology* (Leiden: Brill, 2007).

13. Jan Rehmann, *Theories of Ideology: The Powers of Alienation and Subjection* (Leiden: Brill, 2013).

14. See Ward Blanton's essay in this volume, "A New Horizon for Paul and the Philosophers: Shifting from Comparative 'Political Theology' to 'Economic Theology.'"

Second, no attempt will be made to present a comprehensive account of Marxist interpretations of Paul; rather, representative interpreters have been chosen for analysis. Much less will capitalist interpreters of Paul be surveyed in any detail, since, as Steven Friesen has correctly observed, "capitalist criticism" has been the mainstream of Pauline scholarship and still is.[15] Rather, capitalist interpreters will be treated in what follows only as they recoil from Marxist criticism or when they follow the lure of post-Marxist sociologists into the game of converting economic into symbolic capital. Third, the essay will make no strong distinction between explicit and implicit operations of economic philosophies in the interpretation of Paul's epistles; indeed, interpreters may be more strongly influenced by Marxist theory or by capitalist ideology when they are not fully conscious of the views to which they subscribe.[16] Fourth, and finally, the scope of the essay will be restricted to the letters of Paul that are recognized by a critical consensus to be authentic;[17] pseudonymous writings such as Colossians, Ephesians, and the Pastoral Epistles will be considered only in cases where a naïve acceptance of these texts as genuinely Pauline led early Marxist interpreters astray.

Next, some definitions are in order. For the purposes of this essay, we define a Marxist interpretation of Paul as one in which the logic of class is operative, that is, one in which history is conceived as a struggle between the classes, "freeman and slave, patrician and plebian—in a word, oppressor and oppressed—[which] stood in constant opposition to one another, [and] carried on an uninterrupted, now hidden, now open fight."[18] As the quotation from the Manifesto makes clear, Marx conceived of class as a relation between groups in society, not a position on an economic scale. True to Marx, the historian G. E. M. de Ste. Croix defines class as "the collective social expression of the fact of exploitation, the way in which exploitation is embodied in a social structure."[19] Thus, a Marxist interpretation recognizes the his-

---

15. Steven J. Friesen, "The Blessings of Hegemony: The Preferential Option for the Rich in Pauline Studies" in The Bible in the Public Square: Reading the Signs of the Times, ed. Cynthia Briggs Kittredge, Ellen Bradshaw Aitken, and Jonathan A. Draper (Minneapolis: Fortress Press, 2008), 117–28. Friesen first employed the term "capitalist criticism" in his essay "Poverty in Pauline Studies: Beyond the So-called New Consensus," Journal for the Study of the New Testament 26 (2004): 336.

16. Cf. Dale B. Martin, The Corinthian Body (New Haven, CT: Yale University Press, 1995), xiv–xv, on the operation of ideology in general and in the interpretation of Paul's letters specifically.

17. Günther Bornkamm, "Appendix I: Authentic and Inauthentic Pauline Letters" in Paul (New York: Harper & Row, 1971), 241–44; the authentic letters are 1 Thessalonians, 1 Corinthians, Galatians, 2 Corinthians, Philippians, Philemon, and Romans. Helmut Koester, Introduction to the New Testament, Volume 2: History and Literature of Early Christianity (Berlin: de Gruyter, 1987), 52.

18. Marx and Engels, "The Communist Manifesto" in On Revolution, 81.

torical reality of the subordination of the laboring class to the propertied class, which permits the extraction of surplus value.[20] This fundamental tenet has corollaries, some of which have been important in Pauline studies, such as the use of ideology to reinforce the asymmetrical social relations of power.[21] With a view to the question of Paul's social intentions, a second qualification must be made: a Marxist interpretation is one that contests the assumption that the exploitative relation between the classes is inevitable, and argues that a different collective organization is possible, one that would eliminate the inequality of wealth.[22]

A capitalist interpretation, by contrast, is one that ignores or rejects the category of class (defined by relation to the means of production) as irrelevant to an understanding of Paul[23] and prefers a less precise category, such as "status," as more applicable to Roman society.[24] Further, we may stipulate that a capitalist interpretation implicitly assumes or explicitly argues that Paul sought to implement no structural strategies to eliminate inequality between the classes, but merely sought to alleviate social conflicts through promoting affection and charity.[25]

To begin at the beginning: it is often forgotten that Karl Marx characterized religion as the "groan of the oppressed creature" (*Seufzer der bedrängten Kreatur*),[26] a formulation that clearly echoes Paul's declaration in Romans 8:22, "We know that the whole creation groans and suffers labor-pains until now."[27] But it was Marx's collaborator, Friedrich

---

19. De Ste. Croix, *Class Struggle*, 41.
20. Ibid., 59. Cf. Dale B. Martin, "Ancient Slavery, Class, and Early Christianity," *Fides et Historia* 23 (1991): 105–13; Martin, *Corinthian Body*, xvi–xvii.
21. Martin, *Corinthian Body*, xiv–xv; Welborn, "Towards Structural Marxism," 27–29.
22. Alain Badiou, "The Communist Hypothesis," *New Left Review* 49 (2008): 29–42, esp. 34–35.
23. E.g., Longenecker, *Remember the Poor*, 41. Cf. Steven J. Friesen, "Paul and Economics: The Jerusalem Collection as an Alternative to Patronage" in *Paul Unbound: Other Perspectives on the Apostle*, ed. Mark D. Given (Peabody, MA: Hendrickson, 2010), 30–32, listing the characteristic assumptions of "capitalist criticism": (1) that "religion has no integral connection to economy," (2) "that Christianity was not generated by economic factors," (3) "that religion operates according to market principles," and (4) that "poverty is irrelevant in the interpretation of Christian origins."
24. E.g., Meeks, *First Urban Christians*, 53–55; Bengt Holmberg, *Sociology and the New Testament: An Appraisal* (Minneapolis: Fortress Press, 1990), 21–24. Note the attempt to develop a distinction between "rank" and "status" by E. A. Judge, *Rank and Status in the World of the Caesars and St. Paul* (Christchurch: University of Canterbury, 1983), reprinted in Judge, *Social Distinctives*, 137–56.
25. E.g., Theissen, *Social Setting*, esp. 163–68; Longenecker, *Remember the Poor*, esp. 107, 121, 300; Briones, *Paul's Financial Policy*, passim.
26. Karl Marx and Friedrich Engels, *Werke I* (Berlin: Dietz Verlag, 1961), 378. I have translated *Seufzer* here as "groan," because the customary rendering of *Seufzer* as "sigh" prevents readers from recognizing the Pauline origin of Marx's phrase.
27. Cf. Brigitte Kahl and Jan Rehmann, "Warum Paulus für die Linke(n) von Bedeutung ist," *Luxemburg* 19 (2014): 27.

Engels, who first treated Christianity at length as a precursor of the modern working-class movement.[28] Engels asserted: "The history of early Christianity has notable points of resemblance with the modern working-class movement. Like the latter, Christianity was originally a movement of oppressed people: it first appeared as the religion of slaves and emancipated slaves, of poor people deprived of all rights, of peoples subjugated or dispersed by Rome."[29] Reflecting upon the points of resemblance between early Christianity and modern socialism, Engels endorsed the statement of Ernst Renan: "When you want to get a distinct idea of what the first Christian communities were, do not compare them to the parish congregations of our day; they were rather like the local sections of the International Working Men's Association."[30]

Karl Kautsky, the editor of the journal in which Engels's most substantial essay on early Christianity was published,[31] contributed the first book-length account of Christian origins from the perspective of a materialist conception of history.[32] Kautsky regarded early Christianity as a movement of the urban proletariat and argued that a primitive "communism of consumption" (as opposed to "production") characterized the thought and practice of the first Christians.[33] Kautsky's treatment of Paul is brief but consistent with his general thesis. Thus, Paul's advice to avoid marriage (in 1 Corinthians 7) is taken as evidence of hostility toward the traditional family.[34] Paul's concession of the right of women to appear as prophetesses (in 1 Corinthians 11) is proof of the freedom of proletarian women to exceed the narrow confines of the family.[35] The little paragraph in 1 Corinthians that seeks to silence women in the assembly (1 Cor 14:33b–36) is fearlessly identified as

28. Friedrich Engels, "On the History of Early Christianity (1894–1895)" in *On Religion*, by Karl Marx and Friedrich Engels (Moscow: Foreign Languages Publishing House, 1957), 313–32.

29. Ibid., 313.

30. Friedrich Engels, "The Book of Revelation (1883)" in Marx and Engels, *On Religion*, 204.

31. Kautsky became acquainted with Engels in London in 1885; he founded *Die Neue Zeit* in Frankfurt in 1890, a monthly journal that he edited for more than thirty years. Engels entrusted Kautsky with the publication of Marx's manuscript on the theories of surplus value.

32. Karl Kautsky, *Der Ursprung des Christentums: eine historische Untersuchung* (Stuttgart: J. H. W. Dietz, 1908); Karl Kautsky, *Foundations of Christianity: A Study in Christian Origins*, 1st English ed. (London: George Allen and Unwin, 1925); translated a second time by Henry F. Mins as Karl Kautsky, *Foundations of Christianity* (New York: Russell & Russell, 1953). Kautsky had previously discussed early Christianity in one section of his *Die Vorläufer des neueren Sozialismus: Erster Band, erster Theil: Von Plato bis zu den Wiedertäusern* (Stuttgart: J. H. W. Dietz, 1895); cf. Roland Boer, "Karl Kautsky's *Forerunners of Modern Socialism*," *Chiasma: A Site for Thought*, issue 1, posted 2014, PDF, http://tinyurl.com/zejk66k.

33. Kautsky, *Foundations of Christianity*, xi–xx, 272–84, 350–57.

34. Ibid., 294–96.

35. Ibid., 300.

an interpolation by a later redactor,[36] and the Pastoral Epistles, which attempt to force women back into the circle of the family and the role of childbearing (esp. 1 Tim 2:15), are declared to be forgeries of the second century.[37] Paul's concern for the poor in Jerusalem (Gal 2:10) and his exhortation to mutual assistance (2 Corinthians 8 and 9) are recognized as constitutive elements of Paul's ministry.[38] Most importantly, Kautsky reckoned Paul to be one of the "'saints' or 'perfect ones' [within the Christian community] who carried out communism radically, renouncing all possessions and individual marriage, and giving all they possessed to the community."[39] Because of his radical communism, Paul was obliged to depend upon the communities that he founded for material support.[40]

In the most thorough Marxist analysis of Greco-Roman antiquity, G. E. M. de Ste. Croix discusses Paul repeatedly but in consistently negative terms.[41] Paul is held responsible for the "unhealthy attitude toward sex and marriage," which, according to de Ste. Croix, characterized early Christianity in general, referencing passages in 1 Corinthians 7 (esp. 7:2 and 7:9).[42] Paul is also blamed for the subjection of wives to their husbands, concentrating upon 1 Corinthians 11:3 and Ephesians 5:22-24.[43] Although de Ste. Croix concedes that this attitude was firmly rooted in the Old Testament and strongly emphasized by Philo and Josephus, he makes Paul responsible for extending the regime of male dominance to Greek and Roman converts to Christianity.[44] Similarly, de Ste. Croix insists that the exhortation in Ephesians 6:5 ("Slaves, obey your earthly masters with fear and trembling, in singleness of heart, as you obey Christ") had "sinister implications" that were fully brought out in later Christian writings, which appealed to "the *apostolica auctoritas* of St. Paul" to argue for a willing submission of slaves to their masters that exceeded anything in pagan literature.[45] Finally, de Ste. Croix asserts that it was Paul who persuaded Christians to accept the Roman emperor as God's chosen representative by promulgating "the disastrous principle" that "the powers that be are ordained of God" (Rom

---

36. Ibid.
37. Ibid.
38. Ibid., 330.
39. Ibid., 365.
40. Ibid., 365-66, citing 1 Cor 9:1-12 and 2 Cor 11:8-9 in evidence.
41. De Ste. Croix, *Class Struggle*, 103-10, 398, 400, 419-20, 432-33, 439, 440, 447, 455-56, 458, 462, 498.
42. Ibid., 103-4.
43. Ibid., 104-5.
44. Ibid., 106-7.
45. Ibid., 419-20.

13:1–7).[46] Summing up, de Ste. Croix concludes that Pauline doctrine was principally to blame for the fact that "early Christianity so signally failed to produce any important change for the better in Greco-Roman society."[47]

It is surprising that de Ste. Croix's reading of Paul is so relentlessly negative, given the constructive appropriation of Paul by Engels and Kautsky, of which de Ste. Croix makes no mention. The ire of the great Marxist historian is obviously directed at passages in the Pauline epistles that enjoin submission upon wives, obedience upon slaves, and acquiescence to governmental authorities upon all Christians. But de Ste. Croix shows himself fully aware of the critical consensus that Paul himself was not the author of the texts in which these injunctions are found (e.g., Col 3:18; Eph 5:22–24, 33; 6:5; 1 Tim 2:11–14; 6:1–2; Titus 2:5, 9–10).[48] De Ste. Croix even knows that the little paragraph in 1 Corinthians enjoining silence upon women in the assemblies (1 Cor 14:33b–36) is regarded by many New Testament scholars as an interpolation by a redactor.[49] Yet de Ste. Croix persists in holding Paul responsible for these retrograde instructions, explaining, finally: "As it happens, I am myself far less interested in the views of Paul himself than in what I may call 'Pauline Christianity,' which is mainstream early Christianity, basing itself upon all the epistles attributed to Paul."[50] It is difficult to resist the impression that an animus against Paul is revealed in de Ste. Croix's writings, an animus rooted in his upbringing as the only child of a widowed, fundamentalist mother, vividly recounted in his lecture on "Sex and St. Paul."[51]

Dimitris Kyrtatas, the Marxist protégé of de Ste. Croix, continues the trajectory of his mentor's interpretation of Paul, focusing upon the social position of the first Christians.[52] Kyrtatas argues that Paul recruited the majority of his converts not among the poor and the slaves but from the ranks of the prosperous freedmen and the artisans in the cities.[53] Like de Ste. Croix, Kyrtatas concludes that Paul's teaching posed no challenge to the social order of the Roman Empire but replicated that order within Christian communities.[54] Comparing

---

46. Ibid., 398, 400, 432–33.
47. Ibid., 438–39, again referencing Rom 13:1–7.
48. Ibid., 105, 419.
49. Ibid., 556n16.
50. Ibid., 105.
51. Cited by Robert Parker, "Geoffrey Ernest Maurice de Ste. Croix 1910–2000," *Proceedings of the British Academy* 111 (2001): 448.
52. Dimitris J. Kyrtatas, *The Social Structure of the Early Christian Communities* (London: Verso, 1987).
53. Ibid., 73, 755–76, 121.

Seneca's advice to slave owners with Paul's admonition to slaves, Kyrtatas concludes that Paul actually strengthened the ideological justification for slavery:[55] whereas Seneca called for milder treatment of slaves, Paul summoned slaves to voluntary submission.[56] This conclusion depends heavily upon the interpretation of an ambiguous phrase in 1 Corinthians 7:21, μᾶλλον χρῆσαι, which Kyrtatas translates "Even if you can become free, remain rather a slave."[57] More recently, however, New Testament scholars have argued that the brachylogy μᾶλλον χρῆσαι should be taken in an adversative sense, translating 1 Corinthians 7:21 "If you can indeed become free, make use of freedom instead."[58] In any case, Kyrtatas regards the unambiguous statement of Ephesians 6:5 ("Slaves, obey your earthly masters") as normative for the Pauline tradition, even if the epistle was not written by Paul himself.[59] Kyrtatas observes that the small number of slaves who are mentioned in Paul's epistles, such as "Chloe's people" (1 Cor 1:11) and Onesimus (Phlm 10), are the slaves of Christian masters, and concludes that whatever slaves existed in Pauline communities came into the church in consequence of ownership.[60]

Kyrtatas devotes most of his energy to an attempt to demonstrate that the Pauline Christians were not members of the oppressed classes, whether slave or free poor, but persons of substance—artisans, prosperous freedmen, merchants, and members of the *familia Caesaris*.[61] Kyrtatas accepts without quibble the report of Acts (18:3) that Paul and his associates Aquila and Prisca were "tentmakers," and argues that some artisans were socially mobile.[62] Examining the names mentioned by Paul in the greetings of Romans (16:3–16), Kyrtatas concludes that the names belonged to freedmen rather than slaves, while conceding that all of the names were common slave names.[63] Kyrtatas infers that Lydia of Thyatira was "a wealthy convert," from the description of her occupation as "a dealer in purple fabric" (Acts 16:14).[64] Finally, Kyrtatas

---

54. Ibid., 32–33, 63.
55. Ibid., 33, citing de Ste. Croix, *Class Struggle*, 420, in support of this conclusion.
56. Kyrtatas, *Social Structure*, 32–33.
57. Ibid., 33.
58. For arguments in support of this translation, see J. Albert Harrill, *The Manumission of Slaves in Early Christianity* (Tübingen: Mohr Siebeck, 1995), 76–121, esp. 108–121; cf. Joseph A. Fitzmyer, *First Corinthians: A New Translation with Introduction and Commentary* (New Haven, CT: Yale University Press, 2008), 309; Nasrallah, "You Were Bought," 63–64.
59. Kyrtatas, *Social Structure*, 32.
60. Ibid., 45–46.
61. Ibid., 73, 75–76, 79, 83, 85, 97, 121, 128–31, 134.
62. Ibid., 121–23.
63. Ibid., 73, appealing to Meeks, *First Urban Christians*, 58–59.

adduces Paul's greeting from saints who belonged to "the emperor's household" in Philippians (4:22) as evidence that believers were to be found among members of the imperial civil service.[65] Kyrtatas asserts that the households of Aristobulus and Narcissus, to whom Paul sends greetings in Romans (16:10–11), should be identified with members of the imperial *familia* in Rome.[66]

If one asks why a historian, whose position is "thoroughly Marxist,"[67] should offer an interpretation of Paul that fails to recruit Paul to the cause of the oppressed and that is deaf to the empathy with the poor that is expressed in a number of Pauline passages (e.g., 1 Cor 11:22; Gal 2:10; Rom 15:25–27), then the answer, in this case, is evidently not resentment over the historic role of certain deutero-Pauline texts in coercing submission from wives, obedience from slaves, and resignation from the working poor, but something more subtle and theoretical: the influence of sociology. One cannot fail to notice the praise that is lavished upon Wayne Meeks's *The First Urban Christians* in the introduction to Kyrtatas's book, where he sets forth the principles and scope of his study: "Meeks has clearly demonstrated that, even in the age of Paul, Christianity, far from being a movement of the destitute and the most oppressed, represented a cross-section of urban society."[68] Elaborating upon the consequences of Meeks's sociological analysis, Kyrtatas explains: "Furthermore, a number of the first converts are shown to have had 'high status inconsistency,' a fact which probably made them more sensitive to religious experiences than others."[69] At crucial points in his argument that Paul's converts were drawn not from the lower class but from the relatively prosperous inhabitants of the cities, Kyrtatas cites Meeks as his authority.[70]

It is disconcerting to watch a Marxist historian invoke Meeks as the authority for his interpretation of Paul, since Meeks forthrightly describes his position as that of a "moderate functionalist" in terms of sociological theory.[71] As a functionalist, Meeks is primarily concerned

64. Kyrtatas, *Social Structure*, 121, appealing to Meeks, *First Urban Christians*, 62.

65. Kyrtatas, *Social Structure*, 76.

66. Ibid., 55, 73, 76.

67. Ibid., xi.

68. Ibid., 14.

69. Ibid.

70. Ibid., 41, 71, 86, and esp. 121, citing Meeks, *First Urban Christians*, 65, for the conclusion that an analysis of Paul's language in reference to his converts "would fit the picture of fairly well-off artisans and tradespeople as the typical Christians."

71. Meeks, *First Urban Christians*, 7, 198n15, appealing to Ernest Gellner, "Concepts and Society" in *Sociological Theory and Philosophical Analysis*, ed. Dorothy Emmet and Alasdair MacIntyre (New York: Macmillan, 1970), 115–49.

with how religion, specifically Pauline Christianity, contributed to the stability of the whole society.[72] To be sure, Meeks allows that religion's function is not always integrative: "In fact, it may be disruptive or, paradoxically, integrative for a disruptive movement."[73] But as a functionalist, Meeks assumes that "the sort of questions to be asked about the early Christian movement are those about how it worked"[74] within a structure whose hierarchies he does not challenge. Accordingly, Meeks analyzes the rituals operative in the Pauline assembly (coming together, singing hymns, instruction, admonition, initiation, table fellowship, etc.) in terms of what they contributed to the solidarity of the group.[75] Similarly, the tenets of Pauline theology promote "unity and harmony within the sect."[76] Even Paul's use of apocalyptic language encourages the solidarity and stability of the congregations by providing "relief from cognitive dissonance, by offering a new or transformed set of fundamental images of the world and of relationships."[77] When Meeks examines conflict in the Pauline *ekklēsia*, it is under the twin rubrics of "dealing with conflict" and "controlling deviance."[78]

Meeks allows that Marxist historians have made contributions to an understanding of early Christianity by exploring the complex dialectic between social structures and belief structures.[79] But Meeks judges that Marxist interpretations are ultimately "reductionist,"[80] and prefers to follow the lead of Max Weber,[81] whose sociology of religion sought to rationalize the relation between social stratification and religious ideas.[82] Surely, Meeks knew that Weber rejected the view of Christian

---

72. Meeks, *First Urban Christians*, 6–7. Functionalism has its roots in the works of Emile Durkheim, as developed by Herbert Spencer and Talcott Parsons, among others. See esp. Talcott Parsons, *The Social System* (London: Routledge, 1951); Talcott Parsons, *Theories of Society: Foundations of Modern Sociological Theory* (New York: Free Press, 1961).

73. Ibid., 6, criticizing Geertz's diagram of how sacred symbols contribute to the synthesis of a "world view" in Clifford Geertz, *The Interpretation of Cultures* (New York: Basic Books, 1973), 126–41.

74. Meeks, *First Urban Christians*, 7.

75. Ibid., 140–63.

76. Ibid., 164–70.

77. Ibid., 173–74.

78. Ibid., 111–31.

79. Ibid., 3. Referencing essays by Heinz Kreissig, "Zur sozialen Zusammenstezung der frühchristlichen Gemeinden im ersten Jahrhundert u. Z.," *Eirene* 6 (1967): 91–100; and G. E. M. de Ste. Croix, "Early Christian Attitudes to Property and Slavery" in *Church, Society, and Politics*, ed. Derek Baker (Oxford: Blackwell, 1975), 1–38.

80. Meeks, *First Urban Christians*, 3, with specific reference to Karl Kautsky's *Foundations of Christianity*.

81. Meeks, *First Urban Christians*, 5–6, 53. Weber's influence upon Meeks was mediated through the moderate functionalist Talcott Parsons, who translated Weber's *Grundriss der Sozialökonomik* under the title *Theory of Social and Economic Organization* (New York: Free Press, 1947).

82. Max Weber, *Gesammelte Aufsätze zur Religionssoziologie*, 3 vols. (Tübingen: Mohr Siebeck, 1963). For

origins expressed by Engels and Kautsky, as epitomized in the following quotation from Weber's essay on the agrarian sociology of antiquity:

> It is not only mistaken, it is absolute nonsense to maintain theories such as that Christianity was the result of "social" conditions or was a product of ancient "socialist" movements. It is enough to point out that, like every redemptive religion, Christianity held that worldly aims were dangerous.... Indeed it was just because of the belief in the permanence of Roman rule until the end of time that men felt it was hopeless to strive for social reform and therefore rejected all class struggles; and this was the source from which flowed Christian love—purely ethical, charitable, and transcendental.[83]

The most instructive example of an interpretation of Paul that paradoxically transforms Paul's social intention into its opposite, under the influence of the sociology of Max Weber, is Gerd Theissen's essay on social integration and sacramental activity in 1 Corinthians.[84] In keeping with functionalist theory, Theissen assumes that Paul sought to lessen conflict between "the haves" and "the have-nots" in the *ekklēsia* at Corinth without actually calling for a redistribution of resources. Thus, Theissen suggests that Paul proposed a "compromise" between the class interests of his converts: the rich were permitted to behave in accordance with their own social norms within the privacy of their homes, while the norms of the community were to have priority when believers assembled to eat the Lord's Supper. The communal meal established a "symbolic" equality between the rich and the poor, "transcending the everyday reality," as believers participated in an "eschatological drama."[85] Theissen asserts: "Paul's compromise, which simply acknowledges the class-specific differences within the community while minimizing their manifestations, corresponds to the realities of a socially stratified congregation, which must yield a certain preeminence to the rich."[86] Theissen judges: "Within such a community, the

---

insightful analysis and critique of Weber from a Marxist perspective, see Jan Rehmann, *Max Weber: Modernisation as Passive Revolution. A Gramscian Analysis*, trans. Max Henninger (Chicago: Haymarket Books, 2015).

83. Max Weber, *The Agrarian Sociology of Ancient Civilizations* (London: Humanities Press, 1976), 258–59.

84. Gerd Theissen, "Social Integration and Sacramental Activity: An Analysis of 1 Cor. 11:17–34" in *The Social Setting of Pauline Christianity: Essays on Corinth*, ed. and trans. John H. Schütz (Philadelphia: Fortress Press, 1982), 145–74. In his programmatic essay "The Sociological Interpretation of Religious Traditions: Its Methodological Problems as Exemplified in Early Christianity," Theissen writes: "Still unexcelled in the historical sphere are Max Weber's works in the sociology of religion." *Social Setting*, 195n1.

85. Theissen, *Social Setting*, 163–64.

compromise suggested by Paul is realistic and practical," which is to say, above all, "functional."[87]

It is important to understand how the limits of Theissen's sociological method, bound, as he acknowledges, by "the functional context of social action,"[88] obscure the purpose of Paul's advice on the Lord's Supper at Corinth. In 1 Corinthians 11:17–34, Paul is clearly concerned about the unequal distribution of food and drink at the communal meal, which has resulted in the "humiliation" of "the have-nots" (οἱ μὴ ἔχοντες; 1 Cor 11:22).[89] Paul advises the Corinthians "to wait for one another" (ἀλλήλους ἐκδέχεσθε) and to eat together (1 Cor 11:33). Only if someone is too hungry to wait is he to eat at home (1 Cor 11:34). Now, because Theissen assumes that Paul aims to resolve the conflict within the existing class structure, he is largely deaf to the biting irony of Paul's challenge to the rich in 1 Corinthians 11:22: "What! Do you not have houses to eat and drink in?"[90] Theissen concludes: "Paul wants to settle the problem of the 'private meal' by confining it to private homes."[91] Further, Theissen is at a loss to explain Paul's reference to some at Corinth who have failed to "discern the body" as they ate and drank the Lord's Supper (1 Cor 11:29), and suggests, implausibly, that "body" (σῶμα) refers to animal meats that the Corinthians had introduced into the communal meal.[92] Theissen cannot see that the "body" which the Corinthians have failed to discern is the "body of Christ," specifically the needs of poor members of the Corinthian body, who were living below the subsistence level (1 Cor 11:21–22) and for whom the communal meal was a vital source of nourishment. As Paul explains, because of this failure of discernment, "many have become weak and sick, and some have even died" (1 Cor 11:30).

Theissen concludes that Paul does not call upon the rich to question the behavioral norms of their socioeconomic class. Nor, Theissen states, should we raise "moralistic objections" against the conduct of the rich; after all, the communal meal was made possible by their contributions, and the rich had to consider the opinion of their social peers.[93] Theissen judges that Paul's compromise—the creation of a rit-

---

86. Ibid., 164.
87. Ibid.
88. Ibid., 168; these are the last words of Theissen's essay.
89. Cf. Meeks, *First Urban Christians*, 68: "the phrase οἱ μὴ ἔχοντες is to be taken absolutely, 'the have-nots,' that is, the poor."
90. For a sense of the high irony of 1 Cor 11:22a, see Johannes Weiss, *Der erste Korintherbrief* (Göttingen: Vandenhoeck & Ruprecht, 1910), 293.
91. Theissen, *Social Setting*, 163–64.
92. Ibid., 159.

ual of "symbolic" equality—"offers a good example of the ethos of early Christian love patriarchalism which arose in Pauline communities and which we encounter most clearly in the household codes of the deutero-Pauline letters (Col. 3:18ff.; Eph. 5:22ff.)."[94] The concept of "love-patriarchalism" is derived from Ernst Troeltsch, whom Theissen cites approvingly.[95] According to Troeltsch, who was influenced by Weber's conception of sociology,

> the basic idea of love-patriarchalism is the willing acceptance of given inequalities, and making them fruitful for the ethical values of personal relationships. . . . The great must care for the small, . . . the little ones must submit to those who bear authority . . . , inner religious equality is affirmed and the ethical dimension is enlarged by the exercise of the tender virtues of responsibility for and of trustful surrender to each other. It is undeniable that this ideal is perceived dimly by Paul, and only by means of this ideal does he desire to alter given conditions from within outwards, without touching their external aspect at all.[96]

It is ironic that Wayne Meeks's student and successor, Dale Martin, should be responsible for the revival of "class" as a viable category for the analysis of the Pauline epistles.[97] In *The Corinthian Body*, a work that has attained the status of a classic in Pauline studies, Martin asserts that class is an essential concept for understanding the conflicts between various groups in the church at Corinth.[98] Invoking de Ste. Croix's definition of class, Martin stipulates: "Since class is a relation, those who live off the surplus labor value of others (no matter how wealthy or otherwise) are members of the propertied, or upper, class, whereas those whose labor provides the surplus value that supports the livelihood of others are members of the exploited class or classes."[99] Moreover, Martin forthrightly employs the concept of "ideology" to explain the relation between language (especially symbolic language) and social structures of power.[100] To be sure, Martin distin-

---

93. Ibid., 160–61.
94. Ibid., 164.
95. Ibid., 167–68.
96. Ernst Troeltsch, *The Social Teaching of the Christian Churches*, trans. Olive Wyon (London: George Allen & Unwin, 1931), 78.
97. The incongruity is lessened when one recalls that Weber's sociology was developed in hidden but constant debate with Marx. As Jan Rehmann (*Max Weber*, xi) observes, "Weber, who set out to overcome Marx's historical materialism, nevertheless absorbed so much of it that his conservative opponents accused him of thinking in terms of class struggle like a Marxist."
98. Dale B. Martin, *The Corinthian Body* (New Haven, CT: Yale University Press, 1995), xvi–xvii.
99. Ibid., xvi.
100. Ibid., xiv–xv.

guishes his use of ideology from "some older Marxist users of the term . . . [who] equate ideology with 'false consciousness,' as against something called 'truth.'"[101] Martin prefers what he regards as the more flexible and self-conscious concept of ideology in the works of the sociologists John Thompson and Anthony Giddens.[102] Martin allows that he is able to conceive of "liberating 'counter-ideologies' employed by subordinated groups to oppose the oppressive ideologies of the dominant class."[103] But, for the most part, Martin's usage of the concept of ideology refers to "the system of symbols that supports and enforces the power structure of the dominant class."[104]

In Dale Martin's hands, the category of class, defined as a relationship of dominance and exploitation, powerfully illuminates the conflict between "the Strong" and "the Weak" in the church at Corinth. Martin argues that the theological debates recorded in 1 Corinthians arose from different ideological constructions of the body, which correlate with different socioeconomic positions in the class structure: "the Strong," who enjoyed "a relatively secure economic position and a high level of education," emphasized "the hierarchical arrangement of the body and the proper balance of its constituents"—an ideological construction that mirrored and supported the power structure of Greco-Roman society;[105] "the Weak," by contrast, who were poor and less well educated, "saw the body as a dangerously permeable entity threatened by polluting agents."[106] In this conflict, Paul took the side of lower-class believers, as a demagogue of sorts.[107] As an analysis of the way in which class conflict and its attendant ideological constructions shaped the development of an early Christian community, Dale Martin's *The Corinthian Body* qualifies as the most thorough Marxist interpretation of a Pauline epistle to date.

Yet, with respect to the second criterion of a Marxist interpretation—that it should contest the inevitability of the exploitative relation

---

101. Ibid., xv. Martin does not specify which "older Marxist" theorists he has in mind, but one notes the absence here (and throughout *The Corinthian Body*) of reference to the seminal essay of Louis Althusser, "Ideology and Ideological State Apparatuses (Notes towards an Investigation)" in *Lenin and Philosophy and Other Essays* (London: New Left Books, 1971), 127–86.

102. Martin, *Corinthian Body*, 253n4, referencing John B. Thompson, *Ideology and Modern Culture: Critical Theory in the Era of Mass Communication* (Stanford: Stanford University Press, 1990); and Anthony Giddens, "Four Theses on Ideology," *Canadian Journal of Political and Social Theory* 7 (1983): 8–21.

103. Martin, *Corinthian Body*, xv.

104. Ibid., xv.

105. Ibid., xv, xviii.

106. Ibid., xv.

107. Ibid., xv–xvi, xviii. For Paul as demagogue, see Martin's earlier work *Slavery as Salvation: The Metaphor of Slavery in Pauline Christianity* (New Haven, CT: Yale University Press, 1990).

between the classes—Martin's position is equivocal. In the postscript, Martin confesses to the hope that Paul did not win all his arguments with "the Strong" at Corinth,[108] despite his recognition that Paul is the spokesman and defender of the lower class throughout 1 Corinthians. If one asks why Martin withholds his support for "the communist hypothesis," as Alain Badiou terms it, then the answer is partly a concern that Martin clearly shares with de Ste. Croix for the oppressive legacy of Paul's advice on sex, marriage, and the status of women.[109] But is it more than this? One notes Martin's reluctance to "speculate" about Paul's motives in taking the side of the oppressed, contenting himself with the observation, "But, for whatever reason, his [Paul's] view of the body is more in harmony with views generally held by lower-status, less-educated members of Greco-Roman society."[110] Martin's reticence on this point is remarkable, since Paul explicitly grounds his proclamation of the "crucified Christ" in the fact that *God has chosen the foolish, . . . the weak, . . . the lowborn of the world and the despised*" (1 Cor 1:26–27), a divine choice that has drastic consequences for Paul and his colleagues, who are henceforth associated with the dregs of society, the scum of the earth (1 Cor 4:9–13).[111] In any case, Martin states, looking back over his argument, that his purpose was not to "change anyone's stance" in respect to the conflicts he has described but "to argue that religious language must be analyzed ideologically" and to promote examination of "the often unrecognized implications of our own constructions of the bodies of ourselves and others."[112] As an interpreter of Paul and the early history of a Pauline community, Martin positions himself above the fray, as a cultural anthropologist rather than a contestant for a different collective organization of power and resources.

The dissolution of the Soviet Union in 1991 and the rise of neoconservatism in the West brought a sense of disorientation and depression to thinkers on the Left and provoked much soul searching about the past and future of Marxism.[113] In 1992, Francis Fukuyama proclaimed "the end of history," by which he meant the end of the class struggle and ideological evolution, and the universalization of liberal democracy and free market capitalism as the final forms of government and

---

108. Martin, *Corinthian Body*, 251.
109. Ibid., 198–228, 229–49, 251.
110. Ibid., xvi.
111. L. L. Welborn, *Paul, the Fool of Christ: A Study of 1 Corinthians 1–4 in the Comic-Philosophic Tradition* (London: T&T Clark, 2005), 50–86, 147, 249, 252.
112. Martin, *Corinthian Body*, 251.
113. Benjamin Kunkel, *Utopia or Bust: A Guide to the Present Crisis* (London: Verso, 2014).

economy.[114] It is in this context that we must place Justin Meggitt's monograph *Paul, Poverty and Survival* in order to understand its most perplexing feature: the ambivalent attitude toward Marxism on the part of one who passionately seeks "to give voice to the lived reality of the poor" in Pauline communities.[115] On the one hand, Meggitt strongly disavows the principle that "economic factors are the prime determinants of human social life, in some Marxian sense."[116] But on the other hand, Meggitt invokes E. P. Thompson, a Marxist historian, in support of his attempt to construct an appropriate context for the interpretation of the Pauline epistles, so as "to rescue the lives of the non-elite from 'the enormous condescension of posterity.'"[117] Moreover, in his reconstruction of the lives of the poor who responded to Paul's gospel, Meggitt repeatedly has recourse to the Marxist historian of antiquity, G. E. M. de Ste. Croix.[118]

Meggitt's book vigorously challenges the so-called "New Consensus" among Pauline scholars (whose principal representatives were Abraham Malherbe, Gerd Theissen, and Wayne Meeks), which held that the Pauline communities incorporated persons from different socioeconomic levels.[119] By contrast, Meggitt argues that "Paul and his followers should be located among the 'poor' of the first century."[120] Along with 99 percent of the Roman Empire's population, the Pauline Christians lived "at or near the subsistence level,"[121] in "abject poverty."[122] At points, Meggitt reveals an awareness that the social level to which he assigns the Pauline Christians resembles that which was posited by early Marxist interpreters. Meggitt quotes Karl Kautsky's statement that "die christliche Gemeinde ursprünglich fast ausschließlich proletarische Elemente umfaßte und eine proletarische Organisation war."[123] But Meggitt takes care to distinguish his own perspective from

---

114. Francis Fukuyama, *The End of History and the Last Man* (New York: Free Press, 1992).

115. Justin J. Meggitt, *Paul, Poverty and Survival* (Edinburgh: T&T Clark, 1998).

116. Ibid., 5.

117. Ibid., 14, and again 179, citing E. P. Thompson, *The Making of the English Working Class* (London: Victor Gallancz, 1963), 12. Meggitt also cites approvingly the work of Eric Hobsbawn, a Marxist historian of the rise of industrial capitalism and nationalism, who sought to reconstruct "the world of an anonymous and undocumented body of people"; see E. J. E. Hobsbawm and G. Rudé, *Captain Swing* (Harmondsworth, UK: Penguin, 1973), 12.

118. Meggitt, *Paul, Poverty and Survival*, 43, 57, 58, 60, 82–83, 166, 185, 186.

119. Abraham J. Malherbe, *Social Aspects of Early Christianity* (Baton Rouge: Louisiana State University Press, 1977), 31–59; Theissen, *Social Setting*, 69; Meeks, *First Urban Christians*, 51–53.

120. Meggitt, *Paul, Poverty and Survival*, 179.

121. Ibid., 4.

122. Ibid., 50.

123. Ibid., 102, citing Kautsky, *Ursprung des Christentums*, 338.

that of Marxist historians, denying that his focus of attention *"in any way presumes to privilege 'economic' reality."*[124]

Meggitt's book has been harshly, and rightly, criticized, not only for the extremity of its thesis but also for the tendentiousness of its use of ancient sources and for the rhetoric of its argumentation.[125] Meggitt is able to portray *all* Pauline Christians as poor only by systematic distortion of the evidence. The mechanism of this distortion is the denial that words and phrases in Paul's epistles and Acts have their lexical meanings as established by usage. So, for example, the term ἀρχισυνάγωγος (synagogue president), which designates the office held by Crispus prior to his conversion (in Acts 18:8; cf. 1 Cor 1:14),[126] does not retain, in Meggitt's hands, the meaning that is attested on numerous inscriptions recording the donation of buildings to the Jewish community, along with the repair and decoration of such buildings.[127] The inscriptions make clear that the role of the ἀρχισυνάγωγος was that of benefactor and patron, and entailed significant financial responsibilities.[128] But Meggitt alleges that the epigraphic evidence is "peculiar," and is not dispositive, arguing, tautologically, that the inscriptions reveal "a bias towards recording involvement in funding building work."[129] Similarly, Meggitt asserts that the terms σοφοί, δυνατοί, and εὐγενεῖς, by which Paul characterizes a few, if only a few,[130] of the Christians at Corinth, do not have the meanings that are well established in a wide range

---

124. Meggitt, *Paul, Poverty and Survival*, 6 (his emphasis).

125. Dale B. Martin, "Review Essay: Justin J. Meggitt, *Paul, Poverty and Survival*," *Journal for the Study of the New Testament* 84 (2001): 51–64; Gerd Theissen, "The Social Structure of Pauline Communities: Some Critical Remarks on J. J. Meggitt, *Paul, Poverty and Survival*," *Journal for the Study of the New Testament* 84 (2001): 65–84; Gerd Theissen, "Social Conflicts in the Corinthian Community: Further Remarks on J. J. Meggitt, *Paul, Poverty and Survival*," *Journal for the Study of the New Testament* 25 (2003): 371–91.

126. It is hardly possible to doubt the identity of the Crispus of Acts 18:8 as the same man named by Paul in 1 Cor 1:14. Cf. Anthony J. Blasi, *Early Christianity as a Social Movement* (Toronto: Peter Lang, 1988), 56–59. On the historical reliability of the tradition preserved in Acts 18:8, see Gerd Lüdemann, *Early Christianity According to the Traditions in Acts: A Commentary* (Minneapolis: Fortress Press, 1989), 203–4.

127. E.g., Jean-Baptiste Frey, *Corpus Inscriptionum Judaicarum: Jewish Inscriptions from the Third Century B.C. to the Seventh Century A.D.* (New York: KTAV Publishing, 1975), nos. 548, 722, 1404; Baruch Lifschitz, *Donateurs et fondateurs dans les synagogues juives* (Paris: Gabalda, 1967), nos. 1, 79. Cf. Tessa Rajak, "Appendix I: Archisynagogoi as donors" in *The Jewish Dialogue with Greece and Rome: Studies in Cultural and Social Interaction* (Leiden: Brill, 2002), 393–430, with the summary observation on 416: "Archisynagogoi are found as donors of whole synagogue buildings, restorers of buildings, or donors of parts of buildings: mosaic floors, a chancel screen, columns. These Jewish benefactors operate essentially like Greco-Roman benefactors within a 'euergistic' framework of giving benefits and receiving honors."

128. Rajak, *Jewish Dialogue*, 417: "The *archisynagogos* was a patronal figure. With his wealth, his standing, and the advantage of a title which the outside world could recognize instantly, he had the wherewithal to act as mediator for the community."

129. Meggitt, *Paul, Poverty and Survival*, 143.

of authors (Aristotle, Philo, Josephus, Plutarch, and Dio Chrysostom, among others), where the terms denote the advantages of members of the upper class—education, wealth, and birth[131]—but are "substantially more equivocal than has been assumed."[132] Relativizing the meaning of these terms, Meggitt continues: "As emotive labels, . . . they were open to ongoing appropriation and 'transgressive re-inscription' (the process by which vocabulary can be radically adapted, and even subverted, upon entering the lexical arena). . . . Each term gathered to it a broad and dynamic range of possible meanings and the designations became essentially *relative*."[133]

Examples of such legerdemain are found throughout the fourth chapter of Meggitt's book, where he seeks to challenge the interpretation of the so-called New Consensus among Pauline scholars.[134] But rather than multiplying examples, it is important to understand the motive for these distortions, which may be reasonably inferred from their effects. The underlying motive emerges most clearly in Meggitt's discussion of 1 Corinthians 11:17–34, where Paul addresses the problem of divisions that appeared when the Christ believers at Corinth gathered to eat their communal meal, the "Lord's Supper."[135] Paul speaks of some who are "hungry" and others who are "satiated" (literally, "drunken"; 1 Cor 11:21). Paul is outraged at the inequity in the distribution of food and drink, which has resulted in the "humiliation" of "the have nots" (οἱ μὴ ἔχοντες; 1 Cor 11:22). Now, Meggitt denies that the phrase οἱ μὴ ἔχοντες is meant to be taken in an absolute sense, as "a synonym for the destitute."[136] Rather, Meggitt suggests that the implied object of the participle ἔχοντες is "*the bread and wine of the eucharist*."[137] Paul's censure of the Corinthians is aimed at "ridiculing

---

130. On the litotes in 1 Cor 1:26 (οὐ πολλοί for ὀλίγοι), see E. A. Judge, *The Social Pattern of the Christian Groups in the First Century* (London: Tyndale Press, 1960), 59.

131. E.g., Aristotle, *Rhetorica* 2.12.2; Philo, *De virtutibus* 187; Plutarch, *Moralia* 58E; Dio Chrysostom, *Or.* 15.29. Cf. Dieter Sänger, "Die Dynatoi in 1 Kor 1,26," *Zeitschrift für die neutestamentliche Wissenschaft* 76 (1985): 285–91; Andrew D. Clarke, *Secular and Christian Leadership in Corinth: A Socio-Historical and Exegetical Study of 1 Corinthians 1–6* (Leiden: Brill, 1993), 43–45; L. L. Welborn, *Politics and Rhetoric in the Corinthian Epistles* (Macon, GA: Mercer University Press, 1997), 21–22.

132. Meggitt, *Paul, Poverty and Survival*, 103.

133. Ibid., 104.

134. For detailed analysis of the defects in Meggitt's argument, see Martin, "Review Essay: Justin J. Meggitt," 51–64, esp. the summary judgment on the rhetoric of Meggitt's argumentation (61): "If one were to grant Meggitt the exact phrasing of many of his objections to the popular consensus, it would be impossible to refute his points. In fact, by an indiscriminate use of qualifying terms, Meggitt renders many of his claims non-falsifiable by normal historiography."

135. Meggitt, *Paul, Poverty and Survival*, 118–122.

136. Ibid., 119.

137. Ibid., 120 (his emphasis).

those congregants who gorged themselves on the elements."[138] Not surprisingly, this interpretation necessitates some adjustment in the primary meanings of the verbs denoting "hunger" and "drunkenness" (in 1 Cor 11:21): in an appendix, Meggitt explains that πεινάω "has a breadth of meaning and can refer to the hunger for something other than actual physical sustenance" and that μεθύω can describe persons who "exhibited the kind of unrestrained behavior which accompanied the consumption of alcohol, even if they had, in fact, imbibed very little."[139] In sum, Meggitt challenges the widely held view that the Lord's Supper at Corinth was a real meal, and instead proposes that it consisted in "the consumption of the elements alone."[140]

One catches a glimpse of the place from which Meggitt's interpretation emerges in the introduction and conclusion to his discussion of the divisions at the Lord's Supper. Meggitt aims to refute the notion that 1 Corinthians 11 reflects "a clash between poor and rich members of the community."[141] Meggitt summarizes the results of his interpretation: 1 Corinthians 11 gives the New Testament historian "no direct evidence at all about social divisions in the early Church."[142] One may surmise that despair over the successful outcome of the class struggle, which swept over so many Leftist thinkers in the 1990s, animates Meggitt's project from beginning to end. His relentless effort to prove that no members of the Pauline communities came from the higher levels of first-century society has the effect of eliminating class conflict from the Pauline church.[143] But if the class struggle is eliminated as futile, then what remains, especially for one who wishes to give voice to the oppressed? What remains is the practice of "mutualism" as a survival strategy among the poor. This is Meggitt's own hypothesis regarding the principle of economic relations between Pauline Christians.[144]

Bruce Longenecker's *Remember the Poor* goes a step beyond Meggitt in accommodating Paul to the existing order of things. Longenecker expresses the hope that his book will "encourage the poor" and promote "spirited generosity" among the rich, or among any who have something to give.[145] To that end, Longenecker describes the urban

---

138. Ibid., 121.
139. Ibid., 191.
140. Ibid., 190.
141. Ibid., 118.
142. Ibid., 122. It is telling that Meggitt nowhere addresses Paul's use of the term σχίσματα to describe the conflict.
143. Ibid., 118, 122.
144. Ibid., 155–78.

Christ-groups established by the apostle Paul as "miniature oases of eschatological refreshment amid the harsh economic conditions of the Greco-Roman world."[146] Longenecker argues that it was Paul's general practice to promote "generosity to the poor as a key component of 'righteousness' before Israel's deity."[147]

At the center of Longenecker's enterprise is a controversial interpretation of Galatians 2:10.[148] Longenecker argues that "the 'poor' of Gal. 2:10 is a [general] reference to the needy who were indigenous to the geographical areas that Paul's gentile mission was to infiltrate,"[149] rather than a specific reference to "the poor among the saints in Jerusalem" (Rom 15:26), which is the way in which virtually all interpreters take Paul's avowal of eagerness to "remember the poor" (Gal 2:10). Why should Longenecker insist that Paul's own usage of the term "the poor" in Romans 15:26 is irrelevant to the referent of "the poor" in Galatians 2:10[150] and that "it is important to differentiate between remembrance of the poor and the collection effort"?[151] In any case, Longenecker pays scant attention to Romans 15:26, offering no extended discussion of the verse containing the crucial phrase "the poor among the saints in Jerusalem,"[152] an astonishing omission in a work on the subject of Paul and poverty. As a result of the occlusion of Romans 15:26, Longenecker does not confront one of Paul's most provocative statements about economic relations between Christ believers: the Macedonians and Achaians entered into partnership with the poor in Jerusalem because *they owed it to them*; for if the Gentiles partook in their spiritual benefits, they are obligated to render services [literally, "pay liturgies"] to them in fleshly [that is, financial] matters" (Rom 15:26–27).

Nor is 2 Corinthians 8 given more consideration. Indeed, at the conclusion of his discussion of "care for the poor in Pauline communities," Longenecker seeks excuses for "the fact that Paul does not devote

145. Bruce Longenecker, *Remember the Poor: Paul, Poverty and the Greco-Roman World* (Grand Rapids: Eerdmans, 2010), v, 121.
146. Ibid., 300.
147. Ibid., 314.
148. Ibid., ix, 300, where the importance of his interpretation of this verse is conceded.
149. Ibid., 183.
150. Ibid., 161–62, where Longenecker begins his search for meaning of "the poor" in Gal 2:10 not with Paul's own proximate usage in Rom 15:26 but with Tertullian's usage in the third century.
151. Ibid., 188.
152. The crucial phrase "the poor among the saints in Jerusalem" (Rom 15:26) is echoed only once in 365 pages, at the beginning of chapter 8, but without citation of chapter and verse (ibid., 183). Otherwise, Rom 15:26 appears only in Longenecker's citations of the works of other scholars (ibid., 145, 159, 175, 179, 208) and in parenthetical references to the collection (ibid., 184, 186, 187, 312).

whole chapters of his extant letters to the issue of care for the poor,"[153] evidently forgetting about 2 Corinthians 8 or judging that care for the poor was not the purpose of Paul's appeal for partnership in the collection—the one alternative as remarkable as the other. Second Corinthians 8 is discussed only in passing, for the example that Paul provides (in 2 Cor 8:9) of the generous self-giving of Jesus. But Paul invokes the memory of Jesus in this passage not as an illustration of charity but as an archetype of change in social and economic status: "he became poor [ἐπτώχευσεν], even though he was rich [πλούσιος]" (2 Cor 8:9). Nor is the goal of Paul's argument in 2 Corinthians 8 to encourage the acceptance of "generosity to the poor as a key component of 'righteousness.'"[154] Rather, Paul spells out a rudimentary theory of economic relations between Christ believers, articulated around the idea of "equality" (ἰσότης): "In the now time, your abundance should be for their lack, in order that their abundance should be for your lack, with the result that there may be equality" (2 Cor 8:14). Paul buttresses this radical principle with an amended quotation of Exodus 16:18: "The one who has much should not have more, and the one who has little should not have less" (2 Cor 8:15). Again, it is astonishing that there is no discussion of this text in a book on Paul's concern for the poor.

It is not difficult to identify the cause of the omissions and lacunae in Longenecker's work. Longenecker is opposed to the idea that Paul devised or implemented strategies of structural change in the relationship between the classes in order to ameliorate poverty.[155] Longenecker reserves his harshest criticism for proponents of this idea, who are explicitly identified as Marxists.[156] So, Peter Brown is criticized for depicting Paul as "one who advocated the 'leveling out' or 'equalizing' ... of resources between the brethren."[157] Longenecker comments: "language of this sort endangers a proper conceptualization of socio-economic relationships and responsibilities within urban Jesus-groups."[158] Earle Ellis is commended for resisting the notion that Paul's concern for the poor verged upon "a social gospel" or "Marxist revolution."[159] Wayne Meeks is lauded for "the broad canvas of status complexity" embodied in his work, because it discourages "the view

---

153. Ibid., 155.
154. Ibid., 314.
155. Ibid., 107.
156. Ibid., 205, 222, 287.
157. Ibid., 287.
158. Ibid., 287.
159. Ibid., 205.

that the early Jesus-movement was part of a 'class struggle' of a kind favored by Marxist analysis."[160] And the work of Dieter Georgi on Paul's collection for the poor is dismissed with the observation that "it is unproductive to consider whether Paul hoped that his collection would help to establish improved long-term economic structures among the Jerusalem Jesus-followers, along the lines that Dieter Georgi follows. . . . For Paul, the collection was symbolic."[161]

The source of Longenecker's resistance to seeing Paul as a reformer of the class structure may well be the latent capitalism that Steven Friesen has diagnosed in the contributors to the so-called New Consensus.[162] However that may be, it seems clear that Longenecker has despaired of the possibility of the structural reform of society, both in antiquity and today. As is the case with many, Longenecker has heard and believed Fukuyama's dysevangel about the "end of history" and the futility of the class struggle.[163] In what is simultaneously the most poignant and the most flawed paragraph of the book, Longenecker writes:

> It needs to be recognized that anything that might qualify as a structural strategy for offsetting poverty in the ancient world was out of reach of all but the tiniest minority of people in the ES1 through ES3 economic levels. Structural reform could not have emerged from the 97 percent of the ancient urban population that fell below ES3, simply because of the realities of ancient power. And, of course, the examples of elite attempts at structural change are exceedingly few and far between. . . . If the elite were not going to change the structures, the sub-elite *could not*. It was simply not feasible for those at lower economic levels to even contemplate anything more than a charitable posture towards the needy.[164]

Given the impossibility of structural strategies, Longenecker concludes that there remained only "charitable initiatives," which "must have been seen (and probably should still be seen) as laudable, honorable acts that were worthy of commendation."[165]

Recently, young scholars such as David Briones have had recourse to the concept of "symbolic capital" developed by the social theorist

---

160. Ibid., 222.
161. Ibid., 315n38.
162. Friesen, "Blessings of Hegemony," 117–28.
163. The term "dysevangel" was used by Nietzsche in "The Antichrist" to refer to Paul's gospel, not as "good news," but as "evil tidings."
164. Longenecker, *Remember the Poor*, 107. The designations ES1 and ES3 refer to an elaborate "economy scale" that Longenecker develops to replace the "binary" model of class analysis.
165. Ibid.

Pierre Bourdieu in order to illuminate economic aspects of Paul's ministry within a society structured by an exchange of benefits and obligations.[166] Bourdieu uses the term "capital" broadly as a synonym for power,[167] distinguishing four generic types of capital: economic, cultural, social, and symbolic.[168] While one might assume that Bourdieu's notion of capital is derived from Marx, it is not, in fact, related to Marx's theory of surplus value extracted through the exploitation of the working class.[169] Rather, Bourdieu recognizes that classes do not reproduce themselves by economic means alone, and thus seeks to analyze the subtle ways in which the class structure is reinforced and maintained by broadening and differentiating the operation of capital in each field of social life.[170]

Since Paul viewed "material things" and "spiritual things" as commensurate in the relationship between Christ believers (Rom 15:27), Bourdieu's concept of "symbolic capital" has proven irresistible to some Pauline scholars. So, for example, David Briones invokes Bourdieu's notion of "symbolic capital," in opposition to the consensus of Pauline scholars who present the Pauline groups as functioning within the patron-client structures of Roman society.[171] With Bourdieu in hand,[172] Briones counters: "But does giving money make a person a patron? Assuming that it does so denies the fluidity of 'symbolic capital'. Money does not always exist as the higher-value commodity. Spiritual goods in the divine economy carry a higher value than material payments (cf. 1 Cor. 9:11. 14; Rom. 15:27). So it cannot be that money necessarily represents patronage. It functions within other gift-exchange relationships in contradistinction to the patron-client bond."[173]

The problem with Briones' appropriation of Bourdieu is that Bourdieu does not sever symbolic capital from economic capital in the way

---

166. David E. Briones, *Paul's Financial Policy: A Socio-Theological Approach* (London: T&T Clark, 2013).

167. Rehmann, *Theories of Ideology*, 226.

168. Pierre Bourdieu and Loïc Wacquant, *An Invitation to Reflexive Sociology* (Chicago: University of Chicago Press, 1992), 118–19.

169. David Schwartz, *Culture and Power: The Sociology of Pierre Bourdieu* (Chicago: University of Chicago Press, 1997), 74–75. For Bourdieu's complex relationship to Marx, see his own statements in "The Forms of Capital" in *Education, Globalization and Social Change*, ed. Hugh Lauder, Phillip Brown, Jo-Anne Dillabough, and A. H. Halsey (New York: Oxford University Press, 2006), 105–18.

170. Rehmann, *Theories of Ideology*, 226.

171. E.g., Martin, *Slavery as Salvation*, 138–39; Martin, *Corinthian Body*; John Chow, *Patronage and Power: A Study of Social Networks in Corinth* (Sheffield: Sheffield Academic Press, 1992); L. L. Welborn, *An End to Enmity: Paul and the "Wrongdoer" of Second Corinthians* (Berlin: de Gruyter, 2011).

172. Briones, *Paul's Financial Policy*, 17, citing Pierre Bourdieu, *The Logic of Practice* (Cambridge: Polity, 1990) 112–21.

173. Briones, *Paul's Financial Policy*, 17.

that Briones's theological interpretation suggests. To be sure, the different forms of capital in Bourdieu's theory have a relative autonomy within the field that each occupies and structures.[174] But, for Bourdieu, economic capital has the greatest weight and determines the other forms of capital in the last instance.[175] The parties to the exchange can only play the game of conversion of different forms of capital into one another by concealing from themselves the truth of their practice—namely, that relations of domination control the game of reciprocity.[176] As Jacques Rancière observes: "The more the law of economic capital imposes itself, the more does this truth as well: the symbolic game is reserved for the rich and is merely the *euphemizing* of domination."[177] Because Briones is aware that Bourdieu's theory of gift exchange involves "a 'common misrecognition' of the gift's logic, . . . as givers and receivers deceive one another and themselves,"[178] he ultimately discards Bourdieu, in favor of a theological interpretation in which Paul is the "broker" of divine grace.[179] As for Paul's economic relations with his churches, Briones finds a similarity between Paul's understanding of gift exchange and Seneca's philosophy of "benefits."[180] Briones seems innocent of any ideological reading of the billionaire Seneca, with no regard for the possibility that it is in the self-interest of Seneca to mask the relations of domination by the language of reciprocity.

The global economic crisis of 2008 exposed the defects of capitalism and its destructive consequences for 99 percent of the population.[181] In this context we may place the fresh Marxist readings of Paul that have emerged, employing concepts such as ideology as an instrument of social reproduction and the commodification of labor. We take as an example Neil Elliott's essay of 2010 on ideological closure in the Christ event.[182] Elliott argues that Paul's proclamation of the crucified and

---

174. Rehmann, *Theories of Ideology*, 226–27.

175. Schwartz, *Culture and Power*, 79–80.

176. Pierre Bourdieu, *The Logic of Practice*, trans. Richard Nice (Stanford: Stanford University Press, 1990), 98–111.

177. Jacques Rancière, *The Philosopher and His Poor*, trans. John Drury (Durham: Duke University Press, 2003), 183.

178. Briones, *Paul's Financial Policy*, 154.

179. Ibid., 218–24.

180. Ibid., 41–57.

181. Joseph Stiglitz, *The Price of Inequality: How Today's Divided Society Endangers Our Future* (New York: W.W. Norton & Company, 2012).

182. Neil Elliott, "Ideological Closure in the Christ-Event: A Marxist Response to Alain Badiou" in *Paul, Philosophy, and the Theopolitical Vision*, ed. Douglas Harink (Eugene, OR: Cascade Books, 2010), 135–54.

risen Christ was an "ideological gesture" of defiance against Roman imperialism.[183] Applying a Marxist understanding of the modes of production to the Roman Empire, Elliott observes that the economy of the empire in the time of Paul was in transition from an agrarian mode of production to an economy increasingly reliant upon slave labor.[184] The ideology, or symbolic system, required to support and enforce such a power structure was complex. Elliott sketches the codes and rituals through which, in the Roman era, clear distinctions were established and maintained between noncitizens and citizens, slaves and free persons, conquered and conquerors—that is, between those who could and those who could not be tortured.[185] Elliott summarizes:

> In the Roman Empire, the careful distinction of bodies that could and could not be tortured went hand in hand with an elaborate ideological representation of the emperor as benevolent monarch, a supreme patron, father, and priest; that is, the symbolization dominant in an agrarian mode of production overlapped with and in part was used to routinize and legitimize the symbolization dominant in a slave mode of production.[186]

Elliott suggests that Paul's proclamation of a crucified and risen Christ becomes fully understandable only in the context of the oppressive ideology of Roman imperialism.[187] Elliott focuses upon Paul's statement that Christ took "the form of a slave" and "became obedient to the point of death—even death on a cross" (Phil 2:7–8). Elliott observes that this verse "has traditionally been taken to refer to Christ's appearance as a human being" but insists that it "surely refers more pointedly to the manner of his death, the shameful subjection to a *slave's* death by crucifixion."[188] Elliott explains: "Such a death publicly re-inscribed on certain bodies the status of slave/conquered and thus reinforced the routinization of the symbolic cultural dominant."[189] Drawing the consequences, Elliott asserts:

> For Paul to proclaim that just such a body, inscribed in death as a slave by the power . . . of the Empire, had been raised from the dead by God, and that this divine act established the true filiation of a free people regardless

---

183. Ibid., 143–44, 150–54.
184. Ibid., 144, referencing the discussion of "the question of the mode of production" by Roland Boer, *Marxist Criticism of the Bible* (Sheffield: Sheffield Academic, 2003), 229–46.
185. Elliott, "Ideological Closure," 144.
186. Ibid., 145.
187. Ibid.
188. Ibid.
189. Ibid.

of their ascribed status in the Roman symbolic economy—this was inherently and irreducibly subversive.[190]

> Paul's proclamation of Jesus' resurrection means, inevitably, that the biopower of the state is *not* sovereign, that its totalizing claims can be resisted.[191]

Nevertheless, Elliott holds that Paul's subversive gesture was constrained and contorted by the dominant ideology of Roman imperialism, from whose grasp Paul was unable entirely to free himself.[192] In this judgment, Elliott is influenced by the Marxist literary critic Fredric Jameson, who argues that the liberating impulses arising from the collective imagination, or "political unconscious," are limited and channeled by the dominant ideology of the power structure. Jameson urges that it is the task of a Marxist interpreter to identify the places in a text where the dominant ideological forces constrain human imaginative strivings toward freedom.[193] Applying this framework to Paul's epistles, Elliott asserts that Paul's vision of a coming "lord" ($\kappa\acute{u}\rho\iota\varsigma$) who "rises to rule the nations" in Romans 15:12 (where Paul cites Isa 11:10) merely replaces the "bad kyriarchy" of Roman rule with the "good kyriarchy" of "a *benevolent* lord," without breaking free of the structure of kyriarchy itself, to a new collective organization that would have no need of a monarch.[194] Elliott locates a second instance of textual torsion in Paul's apocalyptic assertion that the creation has been "subjected to futility" and "bondage to decay" by God, so that "the whole creation has been groaning in labor pains until now," longing for "the glorious liberation of the children of God" and waiting for "the redemption of our bodies" (Rom 8:19–23).[195]

One might object that Elliott has underestimated the capacity of Paul's paradoxical conception of the Christ event to subvert and overthrow the categories and formulae appropriated from the dominant culture. In the very text cited by Elliott in evidence of Paul's bondage to kyriarchy, Paul describes the one who "rises to rule" as a "servant" (Rom 15:8), the one he elsewhere calls a "slave," who suffered a slave's death on the cross (Phil 2:7–8). Paul's "lord" Jesus "became poor" and

---

190. Ibid.
191. Ibid., 147.
192. Ibid., 151–54.
193. Fredric Jameson, *The Political Unconscious: Narrative as a Socially Symbolic Act* (Ithaca, NY: Cornell University Press, 1981), 17–102.
194. Elliott, "Ideological Closure," 152.
195. Ibid., 152–53.

experienced "beggarly poverty" (πτωχεία; 2 Cor 8:9). Judith Butler has emphasized the "performative force [that] results from the rehearsal of conventional formulae in non-conventional ways."[196] Butler asserts: "The appropriation of such norms to oppose their historically sedimented effect constitutes the insurrectionary moment of that history, the moment that founds a future through a break with the past."[197] Moreover, one might suggest that the apocalyptic language of Romans 8, in which Elliott detects an "unconscious tension" generated by the constraint of Roman imperial ideology,[198] is better understood as an instance of Walter Benjamin's "dialectics at a standstill": the inward groaning of those who await liberation is "the immediate messianic intensity of the heart" which, through suffering the transience and futility of worldly existence, augments and hastens the coming of the messianic kingdom.[199]

A second example of a recent Marxist interpretation of Paul is Laura Nasrallah's essay exploring Paul's references to human beings as "commodities" in the system of slavery and manumission of the Roman Empire.[200] Nasrallah focuses on three passages in 1 Corinthians: in two places, Paul evokes the new condition of believers in Christ with the words "You were bought with a price" (1 Cor 6:20, 7:23); in a third, Paul explains that a person who may have been a slave when "called in the Lord" is henceforth a "freedperson of the Lord," employing the technical term for a "freedperson," ἀπελεύθερος (1 Cor 7:22). Nasrallah argues that Paul's language of being "bought with a price" and of being a "freedperson" would have had a particular resonance at Roman Corinth, a city where the local magistrates were often freedmen[201] and where a large slave trade seems to have developed.[202] The purpose of Nasrallah's essay is to invite New Testament scholars to reflect upon the multiple ways in which members of the assembly at Corinth

196. Judith Butler, *Excitable Speech: A Politics of the Performative* (New York: Routledge, 1997), 147.
197. Ibid., 159.
198. Elliott, "Ideological Closure," 153.
199. Walter Benjamin, "Theologico-Political Fragment" in *Reflections: Essays, Aphorisms, Autobiographical Writings*, ed. Peter Demetz, trans. Edmund Jephcott (New York: Harcourt Brace Jovanovich, 1978), 312–13.
200. Laura Salah Nasrallah, "'You Were Bought with a Price': Freedpersons and Things in 1 Corinthians" in *Corinth in Contrast: Studies in Inequality*, ed. Steven J. Friesen, Sarah A. James, and Daniel N. Schowalter (Leiden: Brill, 2014), 54–73. Nasrallah does not explicitly identify her interpretation as Marxist; her use of Marxist concepts is implicit.
201. Ibid., 55, 60–61, appealing to Benjamin W. Millis, "Local Magistrates and Elite of Roman Corinth" in Friesen, James, and Schowalter, *Corinth in Contrast*, 38–53.
202. Nasrallah, "You Were Bought," 61, appealing to Harrill, *Manumission of Slaves*, 72–73. Cf. H. A. Stansbury, "Corinthian Honor, Corinthian Conflict: A Social History of Early Roman Corinth and Its Pauline Community" (PhD diss., University of California Irvine, 1990), 163.

would have heard Paul's statements about slaves and freedpersons.[203] Acknowledging the difficulty of reconstructing the full transcript of Paul's discussion with the Corinthians, Nasrallah nevertheless asserts that "1 Corinthians 7 gives evidence of deliberation and debate over whether to replicate or revolutionize relations of domination natural-ized by slavery and manumission practices in the 1st-century Roman Empire."[204]

Nasrallah is conscious of the constraints imposed upon our under-standing of human beings as commodities in the Greco-Roman world by the lacuna in the literary and archaeological evidence. She cites the conclusion of the Roman social historian Walter Scheidel that "at least 100 million people—and probably many more—were seized and sold as slaves throughout the Mediterranean and its hinterlands" dur-ing the period of the Roman Empire.[205] Nasrallah uses what evidence exists to estimate the price of slaves and the cost of manumission, fol-lowing historians Monika Trümper and Keith Hopkins, who conclude, on the basis of studies of inscriptions, that "a young adult slave with moderate skills would be worth . . . slightly more than three years' sur-vival income for a peasant family at subsistence level,"[206] and that the cost of full manumission doubled in the case of male slaves from the second century BCE to the first century CE.[207] With respect to slaves in the Pauline assemblies, Nasrallah asserts: "It is clear in 1 Corinthi-ans 7 and implicit elsewhere in the letter that slaves were participants in the assembly in Christ."[208] As evidence, she adduces Paul's refer-ences to "those of Chloe" in 1 Corinthians 1:11 and to the "household of Stephanas" in 1 Corinthians 1:16, concluding that "such references may indicate a few with wealth within the early Christian *ekklesia* and that male and female owners and their slaves participated together within the community."[209]

In answer to the question of how Corinthian readers would have understood Paul's injunctions regarding slaves and freedpersons, Nas-

---

203. Nasrallah, "You Were Bought," 55.

204. Ibid., 56.

205. Ibid., 55, citing Walter Scheidel, "The Roman Slave Supply" in *The Cambridge World History of Slav-ery*, vol. 1, *The Ancient Mediterranean World*, ed. Keith Bradley and Paul Cartledge (Cambridge: Cam-bridge University Press, 2011), 309.

206. Nasrallah, "You Were Bought," 66–67, referencing Monika Trümper, *Graeco-Roman Slave Markets* (Oxford: Oxbow Books, 2009), 22–23.

207. Nasrallah, "You Were Bought," 67, citing Keith Hopkins, *Conquerors and Slaves* (Cambridge: Cam-bridge University Press, 1978), 161.

208. Nasrallah, "You Were Bought," 61.

209. Ibid., 61–62n37.

rallah urges: "We have no reason to assume that eschatological thought rendered Paul, his co-workers, and the ekklēsiai to which he wrote unconcerned about the reality of slavery—that their emphasis upon an imminent end made them accepting of social inequalities."[210] Playing out the modalities of reception, Nasrallah suggests:

> The letter's reference to the freedperson and its insistence that one is "bought with a price" demands that those who had risen in status despite being ex-slaves recall the price of freedom; those in the assembly who might own slaves are asked not only to consider the work of their slaves, but also to consider themselves as potential slaves; those who were slaves might recall their price and calculate the cost of manumission.[211]

In sum, all, "whether slave or free or freedpersons, are asked to imagine themselves as things or commodities."[212] Nasrallah concludes with a provocative possibility: "finally, and most radically, some Corinthians may have heard the text as demanding that free and slave and freedperson alike think about the slave owner as commodity. What is s/he worth? You, too, the letter insists, are bought with a price. What is the value of the thing that you are?"[213]

The power of Nasrallah's reading, and the means by which it surpasses other recent Marxist interpretations, whether based upon Bourdieu or Jameson, is its capacity to imagine how Paul's appropriation of the language and symbols of the dominant ideology, which support and reinforce the most appalling slave economy, and whose toll in human suffering was colossal and unimaginable, turns the tables on the distinctions by which class and status were maintained, destabilizing all subject positions. Nasrallah comprehends how Paul's speech resists and confounds the structures and norms by which Roman society was regulated. Here, at last, we have Butler's "insurrectionary moment" in a reading of Paul.

We conclude by looking forward in order to identify Marxist approaches that may be fruitful in the study of Paul. First, we consider the messianic materialism of Walter Benjamin. Since the publication of the transcript of Jacob Taubes's Heidelberg seminar on the political theology of Paul,[214] it has been evident that the works of the philoso-

---

210. Ibid., 55–56.
211. Ibid., 56.
212. Ibid., 59.
213. Ibid., 73.
214. Originally published as Jacob Taubes, *Die Politische Theologie des Paulus* (München: Wilhelm Fink Verlag, 1993); English trans.: Jacob Taubes, *The Political Theology of Paul*, ed. Aleida Assmann and

pher and critical theorist Walter Benjamin would be significant for scholars seeking a deeper understanding of Paul's theology.[215] Taubes's interpretation of Paul was fueled by Benjamin's "Theologico-Political Fragment," the only text cited and expounded by Taubes in its entirety. Taubes sees Benjamin as the truest exegete of Romans 8:19–23, finding an "astonishing parallel" between Paul's description of the "futility" of creation and Benjamin's account of "worldly existence" as leading to "an eternity of downfall, transitory in its totality," and related to the Messianic "by reason of its passing away."[216] In detecting the influence of Paul upon Benjamin, Taubes was the forerunner of Giorgio Agamben, who eventually discovered and documented Pauline citations in Benjamin's final statement of his messianic conception of history.[217] Specifically, Agamben demonstrated that a passage in Benjamin's "Theses on the Philosophy of History," in which he speaks of "a *weak* Messianic power," is an allusion to 2 Corinthians 12:9–10, where Paul reveals the paradoxical weakness of Christ's power.[218] More importantly, Agamben argued that Benjamin's notion of "messianic time" as the *Jetztzeit* illuminates, retrospectively, Paul's concept of "the now time" (ὁ νῦν καιρός) of the Christ event.[219]

One may venture to hope that the intuitions of an affinity between Paul and Benjamin by the philosophers will lead on to detailed historical and exegetical studies. In my own monograph on Paul's discussion of the "neighbor," the "*kairos*," and the "awakening" in Romans 13:8–14, I have sought to show that the elements of Paul's mature theology may be illuminated when read through crucial passages in Walter Benjamin.[220] From such a reading, the constellation of Paul's ideas emerges as a summons to awareness of the implications of the

Jan Assmann with Horst Folkers, Wolf-Daniel Hartwich, and Christoph Schulte, trans. Dana Hollander (Stanford: Stanford University Press, 2004).

215. In his philosophical commentary on Paul's epistle to the Romans, Giorgio Agamben (*The Time That Remains*, trans. Patricia Dailey [Stanford: Stanford University Press, 2005], 1–3) asserts that the publication of Taubes's *Political Theology of Paul* "marks an important turning point" in the project of restoring Paul's letters "to the status of the fundamental messianic text for the Western tradition."

216. Taubes, *Political Theology of Paul*, 72, citing Benjamin, "Theologico-Political Fragment," 312–13.

217. Agamben, *Time That Remains*, 138–45.

218. Ibid., 139–40, referencing Walter Benjamin, "Theses on the Philosophy" in *Illuminations*, ed. Hannah Arendt, trans. Harry Zohn (Glasgow: William Collins Sons, 1979), 256.

219. Agamben, *Time That Remains*, 62–68, 143–46, referencing Benjamin, *Illuminations*, 261–64.

220. L. L. Welborn, *Paul's Summons to Messianic Life: Political Theology and the Coming Awakening* (New York: Columbia University Press, 2015), drawing upon Benjamin's "Theses" for the notion of "messianic time" and upon Benjamin's treatment of the concept of "awakening" in Convolute K "Dream City" in Walter Benjamin, *The Arcades Project*, trans. Howard Eiland and Kevin McLaughlin (Cambridge, MA: Harvard University Press, 1999), 382–92.

messianic event that, as Benjamin wrote, "is characteristic of the revolutionary classes at the moment of their action" to liberate the oppressed.[221]

Second, we consider the structural Marxism of Louis Althusser. It seems clear that Althusser's analysis of the way in which ideologies constitute individuals as subjects will continue to generate insightful readings of Paul,[222] despite the criticisms to which his theory has been subjected. Invoking Paul's speech before the philosophers in Acts ("As St. Paul admirably puts it, it is in the 'Logos,'" meaning in ideology, that we 'live, move and have our being'"[223]), Althusser repudiated the capitalist notion of the subject as a self-conscious agent endowed with inalienable rights and insisted, rather, that subjectivity is imposed upon individuals by the structure of society and is recognized by individuals as "inevitable" or "natural," in a reaction that ideology serves to produce. Unlike traditional Marxism, where economic relations in the base rigorously determine the superstructure, Althusser allowed that the ideological apparatuses of the superstructure—the religious, the educational, the domestic, the legal, the political, the cultural—are semiautonomous and variously interpellate individuals as subjects, as they reproduce both the means and the relations of production.

Althusser's theory of the constitution of subjects has been criticized by Pierre Bourdieu as a "pessimistic functionalism" that merely explains the stability of the power structure, but does not take sufficient account of "the resistance, the claims, the contention . . . of the dominated."[224] Jacques Rancière criticized Althusser for overlooking the way in which ideological forms "are not simply social forms of representation" but "the forms in which a struggle is fought out."[225] Althusser responded to these criticisms by emphasizing the primacy of the class struggle and by introducing the concept of a "proletarian ideology," which recruits individuals as militant subjects, in opposition to the ruling class.[226] Thus, Althusser's theory of ideology leaves room for

---

221. Benjamin, *Illuminations*, 261.
222. Louis Althusser, "Ideology and Ideological State Apparatuses" in *Lenin and Philosophy and Other Essays* (London: New Left Books, 1971), 127–86.
223. Ibid., 171.
224. Bourdieu and Wacquant, *Reflexive Sociology*, 102; cf. Rehmann, *Theories of Ideology*, 152.
225. Jacques Rancière, *Althusser's Lesson*, trans. Emiliano Battista (London: Continuum, 2011), 151–52; originally published in 1974 as *La Leçon d'Althusser*.
226. Louis Althusser, "Remarks on the Ideological State Apparatuses" in *Essays in Self-Criticism*, trans. Grahame Lock (London: New Left Books, 1976); Louis Althusser, *Sur la reproduction* (Paris: Presses Universitaires de France, 1995), 312–13. To be sure, it must be acknowledged that Althusser himself did not develop the analytical tools to conceptualize the resistance against hegemonic interpellations.

the possibility of liberating counter-ideologies employed by oppressed groups to fight the ideologies of the state apparatuses.[227]

The potential of Althusser's program of structural Marxism to provide a resonant hermeneutic of Paul's epistles has been demonstrated by Alain Badiou, who draws upon Althusser's theory of the relative autonomy of the practices in the superstructure and Althusser's concept of interpellation, in order to argue that Paul's message of the resurrection functioned as a liberating counter-ideology, with the power to extract subjects from the "situated void" of death constructed by the ruling class of the Roman Empire.[228] In her *Galatians Re-Imagined*, Brigitte Kahl employs Althusser's theory of the constitution of the subject to analyze the mechanism of subjection in Roman imperial ideology and religion.[229] In my own study of Paul's spectacle metaphor in 1 Corinthians 15:30–32, I have sought to show how Paul and the Cynic philosopher Diogenes (in Dio Chrysostom's essay *De virtute*) were similarly constituted as embattled subjects by the power structure of Greco-Roman society but responded differently in the way in which each imagined his relationship to the transpersonal reality in the superstructure, God.[230] In another essay, "The Culture of Crucifixion and the Resurrection of the Dispossessed," I have sought to imagine how persons of different classes in the church at Corinth might have responded to Paul's "message about the cross," in accordance with the subject positions to which they were assigned by the ideology of the Roman Empire.[231] Most recently, K. Edwin Bryant has drawn upon Althusser's concept of interpellation to analyze how Paul offered slave readers subversive and liberating ways to imagine existence apart from Roman power in Romans 6:12–23.[232]

Finally, we consider the radical egalitarianism of Jacques Rancière. In a series of writings, Rancière has deepened understanding of the

---

227. Rehmann, *Theories of Ideology*, 178.

228. Alain Badiou, *Saint Paul: The Foundation of Universalism*, trans. Ray Brassier (Stanford: Stanford University Press, 2003), 68–73.

229. Brigitte Kahl, *Galatians Re-Imagined: Reading with the Eyes of the Vanquished* (Minneapolis: Fortress Press, 2010), 116, 146, 188, 195.

230. L. L. Welborn, "Towards Structural Marxism as a Hermeneutic of Early Christian Literature, Illustrated by Reference to Paul's Spectacle Metaphor in 1 Corinthians 15:30–32," *The Bible and Critical Theory* 8 (2012): 27–35.

231. L. L. Welborn, "The Culture of Crucifixion and the Resurrection of the Dispossessed: The Interpellation of the Subject in the Roman Empire and Paul's Gospel as Truth Event" in *Paul and the Philosophers*, ed. Ward Blanton and Hent de Vries (New York: Fordham University Press, 2012), 127–40.

232. K. Edwin Bryant, *Paul and the Rise of the Slave: Death and Resurrection of the Oppressed in the Epistle of the Romans* (Leiden: Brill, 2016). Bryant builds, in part, upon the seminal essay of Luise Schottroff, "Die Schreckensherrschaft der Sünde und die Befreiung durch Christus nach dem Römerbrief des Paulus," *Evangelische Theologie* 39 (1979): 497–510.

principle of "equality" that is at the base of the communist hypothe-sis.[233] Rancière traces the emergence of the idea of "equality" to the birth of democracy in fifth-century Athens, when the common people, the *dēmos*, asserted that any speaking being—any artisan or shopkeeper or laborer whatsoever—is counted as taking part in the affairs of the city as an equal.[234] The assertion of equality was (and is) scandalous, because Aristotle, reflecting the opinion of the rich, tells us that the indistinct mass of free poor, who were doomed to the anonymity of work and reproduction, "had no part in anything."[235] In Athens, for the first time, "the *dēmos* attributes to itself as its proper lot the equality that belongs to all citizens."[236] Thus, the *dēmos* is not merely one party or faction alongside others. The *dēmos* represents the radical claim of "the part of those who have no part."[237] This claim is the beginning of "politics" as such, according to Rancière: politics is based upon a rad-ical, heterogenous assumption, "an assumption that, at the end of the day, demonstrates the contingency of the order of power: the equality of any speaking being with any other speaking being."[238]

It is not difficult to imagine how Rancière's theorization of "equal-ity" might illuminate one of Paul's most radical arguments: his appeal for partnership in the collection for the poor, on the basis of "equality" (ἰσότης) in 2 Corinthians 8:13–15. In the new economic order that Paul wishes to implement among Christ believers, "equality" is not merely the goal of redistributive action but also the ground. In 2 Corinthians 8:13, Paul states that the contribution that he solicits is ἐξ ἰσότητος (on the basis of equality). And in 2 Corinthians 8:14, Paul urges the shar-ing of abundance ὅπως γένηται ἰσότης (that there may be equality). Here, Paul anticipates the radical premise of Rancière's argument that equal-ity is not merely a social goal, "a fanciful dream of fools and tender souls," but the hidden presupposition of inequality itself: "It is this intrication of equality in inequality that the democratic scandal makes manifest."[239] Engagement with Rancière may finally make it possible

233. Jacques Rancière, "Plato's Lie" in *The Philosopher and His Poor*, ed. Andrew Parker, trans. John Drury (Durham: Duke University Press, 2003), 3–56; Jacques Rancière, *Dis-Agreement: Politics and Philoso-phy*, trans. Julie Rose (Minneapolis: University of Minnesota Press, 1999); Jacques Rancière, "Pol-itics, or the Lost Shepherd" in *Hatred of Democracy*, trans. Steve Corcoran (London: Verso, 2014), 33–50.
234. Rancière, *Dis-agreement*, 7.
235. Ibid., 9, citing Aristotle, *Athēnaīn politeia* 2.
236. Ibid., 8.
237. Ibid., 9, 11.
238. Ibid., 30.
239. Rancière, *Hatred of Democracy*, 48.

to reclaim from the clutches of capitalist interpreters the Pauline text that, from the beginning, has held the greatest promise for Marxist interpreters.[240]

Select Bibliography

Briones, David E. *Paul's Financial Policy: A Socio-Theological Approach*. London: Bloomsbury T&T Clark, 2013.

De Ste. Croix, G. E. M. *The Class Struggle in the Ancient Greek World: From the Archaic Age to the Arab Conquests*. Ithaca, NY: Cornell University Press, 1981.

Elliott, Neil. "Ideological Closure in the Christ-Event: A Marxist Response to Alain Badiou's Paul." In *Paul, Philosophy, and the Theopolitical Vision*, edited by Douglas Harink, 135–54. Eugene, OR: Cascade Books, 2010.

Engels, Friedrich. "On the History of Early Christianity." In *On Religion*, by Karl Marx and Friedrich Engels, 313–32. Moscow: Foreign Languages Publishing House, 1957.

Friesen, Steven J. "The Blessings of Hegemony: The Preferential Option for the Rich in Pauline Studies." In *The Bible in the Public Square: Reading the Signs of the Times*, edited by Cynthia Briggs Kittredge, Ellen Bradshaw Aitken, and Jonathan A. Draper, 117–28. Minneapolis: Fortress Press, 2008.

Kahl, Brigitte. *Galatians Re-Imagined: Reading with the Eyes of the Vanquished*. Minneapolis: Fortress Press, 2010.

Kautsky, Karl. *Foundations of Christianity*. Translated by Henry F. Mins. New York: Russell & Russell, 1953.

Kyrtatas, Dimitris J. *The Social Structure of the Early Christian Communities*. London: Verso, 1987.

Longenecker, Bruce W. *Remember the Poor: Paul, Poverty and the Greco-Roman World*. Grand Rapids: Eerdmans, 2010.

Martin, Dale B. *The Corinthian Body*. New Haven, CT: Yale University Press, 1995.

Meeks, Wayne. *The First Urban Christians: The Social World of the Apostle Paul*. New Haven, CT: Yale University Press, 1983.

Meggitt, Justin J. *Paul, Poverty and Survival*. Edinburgh: T&T Clark, 1998.

Nasrallah, Laura Salah. "'You Were Bought with a Price': Freedpersons and Things in 1 Corinthians." In *Corinth in Contrast: Studies in Inequal-*

---

240. For a start in this direction, see Welborn, "That There May Be Equality," 73–90.

ity, edited by Steven J. Friesen, Sarah A. James, and Daniel N. Schowalter, 54 73. Leiden: Brill, 2014.

Rehmann, Jan. *Theories of Ideology: The Powers of Alienation and Subjection.* Leiden: Brill, 2013.

Theissen, Gerd. *The Social Setting of Pauline Christianity: Essays on Corinth.* Edited and translated by John H. Schütz. Philadelphia: Fortress Press, 1982.

Welborn, L. L. *Paul's Summons to Messianic Life: Political Theology and the Coming Awakening.* New York: Columbia University Press, 2015.

_____. "'That There May Be Equality': The Contexts and Consequences of a Pauline Ideal." *New Testament Studies* 59, no. 1 (2013): 73–90.

_____. "Towards Structural Marxism as a Hermeneutic of Early Christian Literature, Illustrated by Reference to Paul's Spectacle Metaphor in 1 Corinthians 15:30-32." *The Bible and Critical Theory* 8 (2012): 27–35.

14

———

A New Horizon for Paul and the Philosophers: Shifting from Comparative "Political Theology" to "Economic Theology"

Ward Blanton

Earlier philosophical discussions of Paul were dominated by questions of "political theology," in which Paul appeared as a kind of repressed touchstone within apparently secular conceptualizations and practices of the political.[1] Economic crises since 2000, however—and particularly those crises emerging since 2008, with the aftermath of the subprime mortgage debacle—have produced more recently a wide-ranging philosophical fascination with the possibility of addressing similar structures of political life by way of a comparative and genealogical

1. For a useful overview and analysis of this literature, see Ward Blanton and Hent de Vries, eds., *Paul and the Philosophers* (New York: Fordham University Press, 2013).

exploration of "economic theology." The philosophical examples tell the tale of this shift in focus. If earlier philosophical explorations of political theology were steeped in allusions to American exceptionalism, the preemptive invasion of Iraq, and the emergency suspension of laws prohibiting torture or the detentions at Guantanamo Bay, then more recent discussions of "economic theology" are similarly steeped in references to the massive proliferation of student and consumer debts, the European Union's dramatic enforcement of austerity measures against the democratic will of individual member states, and the political implications of publicly funded US and European bailouts of banking corporations.

As we will see, the shift in language from the political to the economic is a shift only in emphasis, an effort to understand the ways in which sovereignty (or the real capacity to create and enforce salient political distinctions) seems to be migrating from spheres of inherited representational politics into more globalized or diffusely international zones of "the economy."[2] This essay will provide a basic sketch of some of these philosophical trends in relation to this migration of sovereignty from the political to the economic, showing how these trends transform and intensify some of the earlier philosophical discussions of the Pauline legacy. Finally, since the comparative consideration of Paul is so essential to these recent philosophical negotiations of economic sovereignty, the essay will conclude with suggestions about some politically and intellectually significant ways in which biblical scholars—capitalizing on new work on the historical Paul in the ancient economy—might blaze new paths in relation to

---

2. With all the recent talk of Paul and gift, it is crucial that biblical scholars develop more extensive genealogies of the way readings of Paul and understandings of economy evolved alongside each other. To date, precious little analysis has been done on the evident links between modern European understandings of law, calculation, and the absolvent freedom of the noncalculating. There is no major work, for example, about the integral comparative links between, say, European discussions of the ancient religious past and the emergence of modern capitalism. The modern histories of interpretation of these integrated fields is beyond my purview here, though one should note useful starting points in the work of Roland Boer, *The Sacred Economy of Ancient Israel* (Louisville, KY: Westminster John Knox, 2015), 1–52; and Roland Boer and Christina Petterson, *Idols of Nations: Biblical Myth at the Origins of Capitalism* (Minneapolis: Fortress Press, 2014). Other very useful starting points for thinking modern readings of religion and economy together include Gil Anidjar, *Blood: A Critique of Christianity* (New York: Columbia University Press, 2014); Joseph Vogl, *Specter of Capital*, trans. Joachim Redner and Robert Savage (Stanford: Stanford University Press, 2014); Joachim Redner and Robert Savage (Stanford: Stanford University Press, 2014); Tomas Sedlacek, *Economics of Good and Evil: The Quest for Economic Meaning from Gilgamesh to Wall Street* (Oxford: Oxford University Press, 2013); Giorgio Agamben, *The Kingdom and the Glory: For a Theological Genealogy of Economy and Government* (Stanford: Stanford University Press, 2011).

these defining interdisciplinary and, indeed, internationally significant struggles of comparative self-understanding.

Economy and Political Myth: Why Naming a Crisis Is Already Mobilizing a Response

> This book originally aimed at pressing a useful metaphor into the service of elucidating a troubled world; a world that could no longer be understood properly by means of the paradigms that dominated our thinking before the Crash of 2008. . . . The metaphor crept up on me.[3]

We are hermeneutic creatures: metaphors, names, and echoes creep up on us as we struggle to orient collective understanding in the situations in which we find ourselves. Recent memories congeal into old myths, and sometimes their union constitutes an unexpected guiding light and powerful new form of collective orientation or attention. Such has been, to take one example, Yanis Varoufakis's hitting on the "global minotaur" as a figuration, a nomination, of Wall Street, in this case an ancient myth eliding itself into the more recent icon, perhaps an icon no less mythical, in fact. In the end, this potential for historically vibrant repetition—in this case, the return of the "minotaur" in new garb—is also the governing backdrop for the recent return of Paul as the philosophical name for a way of being amidst a very contemporary series of economic and social pressures. For hermeneutic creatures, the time of the contemporary is necessarily comparative or, famously, "out of joint."

At the start of our sketch of new philosophical movements and their comparative appropriations of Paul, we should begin by noting how it is difficult to overestimate the effects of economic crises since 2000 on the self-understanding of continental philosophy, particularly those crises associated since 2008 with the aftermath of the subprime mortgage disaster. These effects, registered in the specific comparative pressures expressed in the philosophical readings of Paul, have tended to amplify earlier discussions of the economic aspects of the philosophical Paul. The economic backdrop of these philosophical discussions was ever present in earlier conversations about "political theology," but never so highlighted as it has been since recent economic crises.[4]

---

3. Yanis Varoufakis, *The Global Minotaur: America, Europe and the Future of the Global Economy* (London: Zed Books, 2015), xiii.

4. To take up the issues here is beyond the purview of my discussion. Nevertheless, it may be recalled that the discussions since Carl Schmitt were already driven by the desire to save "political

We should remember, moreover, that the "philosophical Paul" has emerged from generations of philosophers steeped in philosophical engagement with Marxist critiques of political economy (a topic that, while obvious enough, is surprisingly underdeveloped to date).[5] Nevertheless, philosophical work since these economic crises, and perhaps especially since the European Union's dramatic enforcements of austerity measures against its own member states (and sometimes in direct contravention of democratic decisions within those states), have provoked new levels of engagement with questions of economy (see below). They have also led to a renewal of philosophical fascination with Pauline topics of debt and gift, "spirit" as a name for liberty that secedes from or exceeds the various spheres of law as a form of calculation, and myths of the so-called "*katechon*" or agent of the suppressions of chaos, that violent maintenance of normality.

One philosopher who relies on Pauline references with surprising frequency throughout his own prolific work on a contemporary political problem of "biopolitics" is the Italian thinker Roberto Esposito. Esposito goes so far as to say that there has been, since the crisis, a clear "economic turn" discernible within continental thought, with a major topic shifting from post-secular reflection on sovereignty as a veiled "political theology" to a new kind of awareness of the mysterious functioning of what he calls "sovereign debt."[6] What he means

sovereignty" from the "neutralizing" effects of the emerging global economy. See, for example, Carl Schmitt, *The Concept of the Political* (Chicago: University of Chicago Press, 2007), especially "The Stages of Neutralization and Depoliticization," pp. 80–96; Jacques Derrida, *Politics of Friendship* (London: Verso, 2005), especially, "Oath, Conjuration, Fraternization," pp. 138–70; Paul W. Kahn, *Political Theology: Four New Chapters on the Concept of Sovereignty* (New York: Columbia University Press, 2011). For me, Kahn is essential for showing crucial links between the earlier European discussions and the American experience.

5. I have developed some of the genealogical links between the philosophical turn to Paul and the vicissitudes of post-Marxist thought in Ward Blanton, *A Materialism for the Masses: Saint Paul and the Philosophy of Undying Life* (New York: Columbia University Press, 2014). There I emphasized particularly the rise of contingency as an essential post-Marxist category, as well as post-Marxist efforts to think about the essential but, properly speaking, imaginary nature of political solidarity. These are some of the philosophical interests that, we might say, select for a renewed fascination with Paul as a figure of an emancipatory movement.

6. Integrally related to his earlier discussions of the "debts" of community, sovereign debt emerges as a specific term in Roberto Esposito, *Communitas: The Origin and Destiny of Community*, trans. Timothy Campbell (Stanford: Stanford University Press, 2010), 9–19; Roberto Esposito, *Two: The Machine of Political Theology and the Place of Thought*, trans. Zakiya Hanafi (Stanford: Stanford University Press, 2015), 203–10. In ways not frequently discussed (in part because some philosophers find them perplexing), there are in Esposito's writings crucial formal conceptual issues being negotiated by way of a reading of Pauline figures. See, for example, Roberto Esposito, *Immunitas: The Protection and Negation of Life*, trans. Zakiya Hanafi (Cambridge: Polity Press, 2011), 52–79; Roberto Esposito, *Living Thought: The Origins and Actuality of Italian Philosophy*, trans. Zakiya Hanafi (Stanford: Stanford University Press, 2012), 217–77.

is that secular Italian philosophy—which had been for some time fascinated with a consideration of secular politics as a repressed form of biblical and theological *topoi* and dynamics (generally glossed as the question of "political theology")—was increasingly feeling a need to explore repressed "theologies" in Europe not only as odd mirrors for the realm of political sovereignty but also for the realm of the economic.[7] For example, remarking on the fascinating transformation of discourse about the ownership and obligation of national debt since the recent economic crises in the European Union, Esposito writes:

> Compared to this dynamic in the publicization of debt, the recent qualification of "sovereign" in lieu of "public" may appear somewhat incongruous. All the more so since, in the current economic crisis, it refers to state bodies that are increasingly devoid of effective decision-making capacity with respect to transnational subjects, such as the financial markets, which are destined to replace them in formulating economic policies. Thus, a term that is highly politically charged like sovereignty ends up being used to ratify a process of depoliticization. Unless, instead of using the expression "sovereign debt" with its current meaning of "national debt," we adopt the much more semantically charged one of "debt sovereignty," of the transfer of sovereignty from the national government to global finance. If this were the case—if, rather than vanishing into nothingness, sovereignty had actually passed into other hands—then instead of talking about the end of political theology, we should be talking about its transformation into an economic theology, one that is itself endowed with political attributes, including the supreme one of deciding on the possible survival of subjects.[8]

It is this sublimation, so to speak, of political sovereignty—at the very moment of its neutralization—which seems to yield a kind of ghostly or more abstract "return" of the older power of the sovereign, a kind of ascension or resurrection of the old state sovereignties in more ethereal but generalizable forms.

No doubt, recent shocks about the apparently unquestionable power of "economy" to subjugate democratic self-determination in a place like Greece (see Douzinas below) or Puerto Rico are palpable in lines like these. And, just empirically, Esposito seems certainly to be on solid ground here in his announcement of a shift in focus within phi-

---

7. For an excellent introduction to the tradition of political theology, see de Vries's substantial introduction to Hent de Vries and Lawrence E. Sullivan, eds., *Political Theologies: Public Religions in a Post-Secular World* (New York: Fordham University Press, 2006), 1–90.
8. Esposito, *Two*, 204.

losophy, inasmuch as many of the agenda-setting figures of Italian philosophy are writing increasingly about "economic theology" as an essential topic for comparative self-understanding in current debates about indebtedness, austerity, and internationalism (e.g., Mario Tronti, Giorgio Agamben, Gianni Vattimo, Davide Tarizzo, Elettra Stimilli, Massimo Cacciari, Lorenzo Chiesa, and Esposito himself).

It is also very clear that, if earlier discussions of "political theology" (sovereignty as exceptionalism, the power to declare a state of emergency in order to abrogate normal laws) were keyed to American intervention in Iraq after 9/11, the metamorphosis of "political theology" into "economic theology" is an effort to address recent economic crisis and the rise of what Maurizzio Lazzarato diagnoses as the new geopolitical mode of "governing by debt."[9] Are the mysterious opacities of contemporary forms of sovereignty, often exerted in the name of an apparently transcendent "economy," usefully susceptible to analysis through histories of religion, debt, and sin? Indeed, are these alleged detours into the theological tradition not in some sense necessary in order to grasp the functioning of economy, whether as a process, an academic science, or a political mode of management? Do we not, for example, understand the current functioning of economy better now than before Varoufakis unleashed his "global minotaur"? If so, then we are indeed hermeneutic creatures for whom the time of the contemporary is, so to speak, out of joint, suspended in a comparative zone as if waiting to be actualized as a form of collective self-understanding. Or, perhaps ours is a moment when we need a new Hans Blumenberg (*Legitimacy of the Modern Age*), a new Horkheimer and Adorno (*Dialectic of Enlightenment*), as with economy (as in scientific enquiry and political organization) we need fresh thinking about how to negotiate analogical similarity or possibly constitutive differences operating between contemporary "economy" and earlier modes of thinking embodied in "economic theology."[10]

---

9. See Maurizio Lazzarato, *Governing by Debt*, trans. Joshua David Jordan (South Pasadena, CA: Semiotext(e), 2013); Maurizio Lazzarato, *The Making of the Indebted Man: An Essay on the Neoliberal Condition*, trans. Joshua David Jordan (Los Angeles: Semiotext(e), 2012).

10. I mention these two classics not only because of the ingenious modes in which they navigated the vexed or "out of joint" comparative spaces of the ancient and modern, but also because of the remarkable ways in which they deployed new readings of old myths in order to do so. Biblical scholarship must continue to endeavor to be at the cutting edge of discussions of such magnitude and creative reorientation of perspective.

Mobilizing Myth: Student Debt and the Solidarities of Sin

Significantly, Esposito's own engagement with our current experiences of political power as an effect of a new/ancient "economic theology" concludes with an evocation of Paul (a consistent touchstone in Esposito's work) and also the biblical myth of a Jubilee year. To paraphrase, if the sublimated sovereignty of a transnational or imperial "political theology" of the economy itself now exerts itself as a regime of austerity measures enforcing a massive redistribution of debt ownership, then what new and old myths might indicate to us enlightening images of contemporary thought and action? If we live in a moment of the reduction of representative democratic leaders to the role of debt managers, then for a start—Esposito urges—we need to experiment with our basic cognitive mapping of the current state of affairs, just as Varoufakis was doing with his "minotaur" of Wall Street. What are we, where are we, and indeed *when* are we in struggles like the ones we are in? How do we name ourselves at a moment like this?

Esposito relies, too, on hermeneutics as a comparative enterprise in search of new names of who and what we are. As he describes our relation to the global economy, "in order to gain a way out from something that has no outside, even before changing life, we would need to change the way we interpret it—the conceptual language that we have inherited from an extremely long tradition."[11] Rummaging through the rag and bones shop that is the inherited archives of religion, the quest for newly enlightening comparative images of thought and action therefore replaces two alternatives. One the one hand, this archival sifting for illuminating comparative models of contemporary thought and action replaces what might be imagined as a more straightforward or positivistic statement of the contemporary situation, as if our proximity to this situation as a "now" makes that situation easily readable, comprehensible, or (simply) "present" to us. On the other hand, Esposito seems here also to be distancing the role of the comparative archivist-activist from a simple Marxist story about the point of thinking being not to understand but to change the world. The very capacity of either option to make sense would hinge on a more fundamental moment of interpretation, for which creative leap we need comparatively to collect ourselves. No doubt, for Esposito's

11. Esposito, *Two*, 208.

call for a new comparativeness and a new self-understanding, the hermeneutic time seems to be out of joint.

If Esposito's *Living Thought: The Origins and Actuality of Italian Philosophy* ends with a section called "the return of Italian philosophy"—a return he describes, significantly, through Italian philosophy's new wrestling with the Pauline legacy—so too his book *Two: The Machine of Political Theology and the Place of Thought* ends on a similarly consequential evocation of the figure of Paul. In this latter case, Esposito invites us to reflect on the potential solidarities—indeed, the potential political struggles—we might foment were we, in light of the history of economic theology, to differently identify with indebtedness, indeed to overflow through excessive identification the usual registers (and the usual private ownership) of debt as a kind of justly attributable guilt. Rather than directly face "sovereign debt" as that newly sublimated version of older political sovereignty, Esposito suggests,

> what we can do, as far as sovereign debt is concerned, is reverse its meaning. Instead of trying to stop what is by now an unstoppable dynamic, we can speed it up, pushing it to its limit point, until it implodes. The fact that we are all debtors, or are becoming ones, means that there are no more real creditors. Every creditor is a debtor to another, in a chain whose first link has been lost. The problem we are facing is to transform this oppressive chain into a circuit of solidarity.[12]

In this context, Esposito goes on to mention a renewed myth of Jubilee explicitly. But for those who read his other work, it is also immediately recognizable that the philosopher is inviting us to reenact what he understands as a Pauline moment in which oddly subversive solidarities emerge when communities identify with sin/debt in such a way that this identification scrambles inherited codes of territorialized or proprietorial identity. On this occasion, Esposito invites us, for example, to interpret the massive proliferation of student debt as a scapegoat mechanism whereby the larger educational economy, broadly conceived, maintains its expansionistic (i.e., indebted) horizons by transferring debts onto students in new ways. Consider, for example, the recent new levels of privatization of the costs of a university education in the United Kingdom. In a word, Esposito is inviting us to wonder about the ways we might understand the present through the allegedly distant and ancient. Have students become, so to speak, "sin for us,"

12. Ibid., 208–9.

on our behalf, as if being sacrificed such that other forms of economic accumulation can normalize themselves through this sacrificial ritual?

The genealogical or comparative invitation of Esposito is, therefore, that we consider ourselves as part of a tableau whereby normalization of community is acquired and maintained through sacrifice. The invitation to see ourselves within this ancient structure, however, is at the same time a form of mobilization in its transformative subversion. What new religious event will occur, so to speak, if our own redistributions of sin-debt—from the student debt to austerity measures in Greece—are refused or, more to the point, overloaded with an excess of identification such that the system that relies on them "implodes"? If a comparative and hermeneutical approach seemed without risk, therefore, it probably does so no longer, as talk of implosion is presumably more than a little precise as a projection of what would happen in a moment when students refuse to play the role of sinner-scapegoat, even as the rest of society identifies, in trust, with the sacrificial victims of economic theology. This identification would be transformative, not a mere repetition of the ready-made substances of contemporary identity (in which, say, I am certainly no longer a student). Instead, the shareable substance of identity would emerge through debt as a kind of lack that separates us from ourselves. Precisely this pressing nonidentity, this zone of separation that is not currently "owned" by our identities, would then be the potential fund of a peculiar new sphere of the common and communal. On this note, Esposito's interpretive struggle concludes. This is my body, say the students, given for you, and our participation in the return of the ancient myth of sacrifice renders inoperative the sacrificial logic itself. For Esposito, like Varoufakis's minotaur, the evocation of the ancient analogy congeals into the inauguration a new form of communism or collective solidarity, one that "implodes" the current form of governance through redistribution of debt.[13]

What should be clear is that, far from a straightforward valorization of a biblical figure, philosophical encounters with Paulinism of this sort are rather an invitation to a form of risky collective experimentation in the very "interpretation" of the economic and political situation in which we find ourselves. There is every chance, in other words, that

13. Without being led astray into discussions we do not have space for here, what I am flagging up is the way Esposito's Pauline gesture in relation to the student debt crisis is yet another articulation of that new and peculiar form of communism that Esposito also finds in Georges Bataille, Jean-Luc Nancy, and Giorgio Agamben.

all the "conceptual language that we have inherited from an extremely long tradition" will be transformed in the process of translation and mysterious actualization. Remember that Esposito describes this transformation of past and present coordinates as a necessarily paradoxical exodus "from something that has no outside." Any success or failure in this venture would emerge from the event itself rather than some imagined guarantee about the preestablished truth of a given state of affairs, whether economic or political or religious, whether past or present or future. This is the potential of a return of Paul within a philosophy of becoming.

Pistis, or, Who Funds a Politics of Friendship?

While a great deal could be said about the various modes in which the archive of Paulinism and messianic *pistis* (trust) return to actuality at a moment of crisis within finance capitalism, we will limit ourselves to a few more examples, including the one indicated by recent discussions of philosophers Slavoj Žižek and Jean-Pierre Dupuy. In a provocatively entitled book, *Economy and the Future: A Crisis of Faith*, Dupuy situates his diagnoses of current economic crises also at the remarkable recent migrations of sovereignty from the political to the economic realm. On the one hand, Dupuy argues, even when it is at its best or most effective, the political today seems everywhere to be reduced to a form of economic managerialism:

> Every time the political class avows its determination to take on the markets and congratulates itself for having avoided the worst, at least for the moment, authority places itself on the same level as managerialism: whether it wins or loses does not matter, for it has already debased itself, and will go on debasing itself, by virtue of its very willingness to fight, like a teacher who lowers himself to trade blows with unruly students.[14]

On the one hand, then, political sovereignty seems to have lost itself in the face of economic management. On the other hand, Dupuy continues, academic and public economists seemed to him incapable of evaluating evident failures, crises, and gross inequities within the current economic machinery, understanding these as mere nothings or, even worse, as states of affairs emerging from the introduction of heteronomous obstructions to the market, obstructions fantasized as the

---

14. Jean-Pierre Dupuy, *Economy and the Future: A Crisis of Faith* (East Lansing, MI: Michigan State University Press, 2014), xi.

cause of current crises within the otherwise apparently self-regulating and endlessly fecund market operations themselves. As if speaking in the name of that sublimated "political" sovereignty that has migrated into the more ethereal sphere of "economy," the scientists of economy name the obstruction of the market's capacity to yield increasing levels of collective prosperity, indeed often naming it "politics" itself. As an example of what he understands as a kind of dogmatic blindness among his economist colleagues, Dupuy mentions the way his "shame" over the current state of affairs

> intensified on learning that two American economists who had recently been awarded the Nobel prize took the opportunity provided by this honor to lecture Europeans. One of them made a point of insisting that "there are no new questions *for economic theory* regarding Europe and the euro." Well, then, one might ask, if the solution to the problem is known, why has it not been put into effect? "Resolving the sovereign debt crisis in the Eurozone is child's play," answered the other laureate. "From an economic point of view at least. The stumbling block is politics."[15]

In a way comparable to Esposito's radically hermeneutical approach to the question of "theology" and "economy," Dupuy's analysis raises the same disconcerting question. In what way is the very question of "religion" and "economy" already a question of competing mythemes or fundamental hermeneutical stances such that any argumentative gesture toward a sure and given ground for debate would always already refer, rather, back to the more originary opening to understanding made possible by a commitment to the mytheme in question? That would also be the provocative suggestion of recent "spectrologies" of economic theory such as we get in Jacques Derrida's *Specters of Marx* or, more recently, Joseph Vogl's *Specter of Capital*.[16] The implications of a vision of the conjuration and exorcism of divinities or ghosts without a given "outside" to this struggle to name "economy" are of course massive for our understanding of the Pauline legacy in relation to contemporary political debates about the economy.

In keeping with a long tradition of talk about a crisis of European spirit, the recent high-profile standoff between political self-determination and the demands of economy appears characterized by mutual

---

15. Ibid., xi-xii.
16. Jacques Derrida, *Specters of Marx: The State of the Debt, the Work of Mourning, and the New International* (New York: Routledge, 1994); Joseph Vogl, *Specter of Capital* (Stanford, CA: Stanford University Press, 2014).

blindness: naming the current crisis. It is, therefore, just like clockwork that in this tradition, Dupuy would go on to take up religious traditions in an effort to find names for the repressed mediating links uniting these otherwise polarized zones of relational economics and self-reliant self-determination. Politics cannot seem to do anything besides managing the economy, a characteristic that was already an essential part of what Michel Foucault diagnosed as the emergence of a regime of biopower and that Esposito speaks about in terms of a migration from "political theology" to "economic theology."

The very naming of a crisis is already to have solicited a mobilizing political myth (in the broadest sense) that might provide some remedy against it. In Dupuy's case, he explores the modes in which—as a structure of self-transcendence and the future as risk—the economy must be read in light of inherited notions of providential predestination, a sense of calling, and atoning sacrifice. And, as we might expect given the delineation of the issues this way, in the end Dupuy urges a drawing of strong political distinctions between (as Martin Buber once put it) two types of faith.

One cannot suppress the theological (and in fact Pauline) echoes—as Žižek will not in his conversations with Dupuy. After analyzing the structures of relatedness to the future and the paradoxes of collective self-production in economic terms, Dupuy strikes a pose as a new Paul delivering a new letter to the Romans. In this iteration, Dupuy will declare of this strangely post-secular economism that has absorbed the political that in it (compared to earlier modes of thinking), "the immutable and eternal decision of God has been replaced by the unpredictable and capricious judgment of the crowd. We have therefore exchanged a sublime conception of human purpose and worth for a ridiculous one."[17] This exchange is, moreover, a fateful one: "we have passed . . . from truth to falsehood, from life to death," leaving us to wonder how we might, in fact, be transformed back into that state we have apparently lost.[18] One must be clear to see the full drama of his gesture. Dupuy is by no means simply preaching a religious jeremiad about the secular economy. His philosophical quest is, rather, to articulate what he calls a "faith—a secular faith, what is commonly, but obscurely, called confidence in the future," which can secede from the structure of "bad faith" to which the exchange (of a truly sublime opening onto the future for the idolatrous image) has consigned us as

---

17. Dupuy, *Economy and the Future*, 124.
18. Ibid., 125.

neoliberal economic actors, as if the best we can do is to hope our private lottery tickets come up the proverbial aces.[19] The promise of the project—its "problematic" we might say—is therefore, that, secularized to be sure, a reconceptualized archive of religion might operate as a diagnosis of the current function of economy in relation to the political, and this in a way that reveals to us a stance of *pistis* (trust) or faith that feels to us as the very difference between life and death, freedom and slavery, a true divinity from the idol. As in Esposito, here is a contest of economic theologies indeed.

In the dramatic conclusion of his massive book, *Less than Nothing: Hegel and the Shadow of Dialectical Materialism*, Slavoj Žižek highlights some of the political implications of the way Dupuy's work is integrally part of a longer discussion of sacrifice as a model of ideologies supporting the maintenance of current social hierarchies. As Žižek describes Dupuy's refusal to naturalize the sacrificial demands of "economy" in relation to debt: "Once the innocence of the sacrificial victim is *known*, the efficacy of the entire sacrificial mechanism of scapegoating is undermined: sacrifices become hypocritical, inoperative, fake."[20] Linking Dupuy's critique of political economy to Giorgio Agamben's revival of that "messianic experience" he finds in a reading of 1 Corinthians 7 through Walter Benjamin and Gershom Scholem, Žižek also urges us to explore the potentials that emerge when we suspend, ignore, or elude our cultural (and indeed economic) mechanisms of sacrifice. Sacrifice, after all, is easily read as a mechanism for the suppression of chaotic upheavals within a currently normalized state of affairs, including our currently naturalized or normalized economic hierarchies.

Žižek, reading Dupuy and Agamben, is effectively enacting the same strategy as Yannis Varoufakis, who named the Greek myth of the minotaur for a period of finance capitalism driven by Wall Street. The iteration of the ancient myth in Varoufakis's evocation is clear in terms of its contemporary demand: will the Greeks (once again, as it were) somehow refuse the naturalization of the foreigners' demand for sacrifice? In the case of Žižek (or Dupuy or Agamben), the situation is the same: the question is whether we will refuse a "bad faith" that trusts in a perpetuation or maintenance of the current regime, and indeed whether we can hit upon—in this refusal—another faith (Žižek

---

19. Ibid.
20. Slavoj Žižek, *Less than Nothing: Hegel and the Shadow of Dialectical Materialism* (London: Verso, 2012), 975.

also speaks of "another grace"), indeed another "messianic suspension" of regnant laws whether written or just generally assumed. Here we should note that at the end of his decades of *Homo Sacer* studies, Agamben, too, turns back to Paul as a kind of capstone of what it looks like to enact the philosophical way of life he feels his studies demand (see epilogue of *The Use of Bodies*).[21] The evocation by all these authors of "messianic moments" and apocalyptic or catastrophic scenarios is here essential, in the sense that what is being suspended in the suspension of sacrificial demands of the economy (Dupuy), or the current regime's (*katechontic*) suppression of chaos (Agamben), or the structural violence of contemporary capitalism (Žižek), is the dialectically imagined, hypocritical peace of a current empire of economy. Naturally, this empire secretes its own sense of trust, solidarity and, indeed, sinful obstruction. The question is whether, on beginning to believe that we are caught in an "economic theology" of the current regime, this experience might also inspire a contrary movement and, in fact, a counter-imperial experience. As we might put it in this hermeneutic or ancient/new contest of ideologies: "at the very moment when the economic managers say *pax et securitas*, the messianic destruction will appear" (cf. 1 Thess 5:3).

This is an important point for understanding the contemporary philosophical fascination with Paul. It is clear enough that the specter of a philosophical Paul in these texts comes not to bring peace but a sword, even if that sword is—as it tends to be in these texts—the call for a decision about whether it is acceptable for us (indeed, *to* us) to naturalize the sacrifices, those stochastic irruptions of deprivation or violence that punctuate our current economic and political orders. Paul returns, therefore, as a kind of myth about our ambiguous relationship to the question of the maintenance—or the transformation—of political economy itself. We might even say that the role of "religion" or "theology" or "Paul" in these philosophical calls to the philosophical life is to provide a tableau that seems appropriately evocative of the intensity of the experience hoped for—an existential reorientation that goes hand in glove with the implosion of the current regime of political economy. The myth of Paul, in other words, seems somehow more appropriate to the hoped-for event than to the language of "political economy." In the new quest for an irruption of a nonprofane, unordinary time of change, no wonder philosophers are casting a compar-

---

21. Giorgio Agamben, *The Use of Bodies* (Stanford: Stanford University Press, 2016).

ative eye onto the biblical legacies. The quest is, quite simply, to hit upon a kind of hyperreal element within our political experience, a kind of sacred carnival capable of interrupting our busy maintenance of the profane economies in which we find ourselves.

Whose *Katechon*? Which *Kairos*?

Put this way, the contemporary philosophical function of Pauline references is an explicit invitation to take up a dramatic stance in relation to that open question: will we, in the end, have continued to maintain our current economic order or will some other order break through? Without question, among the philosophers many are keen to mobilize Pauline *topoi* in the name of an unscripted—or at least improvisatory—rebellion against the present order, hoping to conjure out of the many dispersed crises, transformations, and disenchantments a larger, even global, new movement. Costas Douzinas is a useful indication of this much larger philosophical pattern when he diagnoses the current situation in his *Philosophy and Resistance in the Crisis*:

> Identity politics and humanitarian campaigns dominated the 1990s and early 2000s. This changed after the collapse of the financial system in 2008 and the imposition of austerity policies. Mass resistance returned to public spaces and marks the politics of the twenty-first century. A series of protests, spontaneous insurrections and occupations, and the desire for radical change broke out everywhere. They include the Paris *banlieues* riots in 2005, the Athens December 2008 uprising, the Arab spring, the Spanish *indignados* and the Greek *aganaktisemnoi* occupations, Occupy Wall Street, Occupy London, and similar occupations around the world.[22]

Douzinas's intuition is therefore that it is the global economic crises that are giving rise to new social movements with the potential to affect much more than other recent (and ostensibly more localized) forms of political action. Many other philosophers, Alain Badiou for example, regularly say as much when they look to the same social movements as the "rebirth of history" in a grand manner after a period when the apparent triumph of global capitalism over any really existing alternative seemed to consign us to a more limited role of more or less effective management of economy.[23] The "rebirth of history"

22. Costas Douzinas, *Philosophy and Resistance in the Crisis: Greece and the Future of Europe* (Cambridge: Polity Press, 2013), 8.
23. Alain Badiou, *The Rebirth of History: Times of Riots and Uprisings*, trans. Gregory Elliott (London: Verso, 2012).

appears therefore against the backdrop of what Francis Fukuyama (following Alexandre Kojève) had of course famously nominated as a triumphant neoliberalism's "end of history."[24] In that vision, the empire of neoliberalism and the market economy had emerged, and while there may be blips in the history of this empire, its fundamental status as the empire without limit in space or time is sure.

Whether or not the recent economic crises and protest movements turn out to have instigated new forms of political creation remains to be seen, of course. By the same token, even to frame things the way Douzinas does echoes earlier discussions of European history, the freedom of European "spirit," and the relationship between normal/linear time and the stochastic break of a "messianic" moment, all of these old conversations whereby the European intellectual tradition (just for a start) attempted to come to grips with itself and its potentials by way of a rereading of its scriptural and theological traditions.[25] Since Marx at least, economic crises have always been the philosophical material of a potential new political mobilization, and analyses of the sort Douzinas provides have exploded, as if in revenge for the confident affirmations that the empire of neoliberal economics had become an empire without end, effectively capable of suppressing the chaos that might subvert or revolutionize it.

Similarly, philosopher Alain Badiou's *Rebirth of History* may usefully be read as a kind of intellectual cookbook with recipes for transforming local riots and uprisings (he is thinking of the same ones as Douzinas) into a global "idea" capable of engaging directly the political transformation of contemporary capitalism. The metamorphosis of local outburst into global transformation is, in fact, the "rebirth of history" out of the apparent world-without-end of exploitative capitalism, a form of extraction that, Badiou argues, controls the state, reducing state politics to a policing on behalf of the continuation of global markets generally and specific neoliberal policies at the national level. With his

---

24. Francis Fukuyama, *The End of History and the Last Man* (London: Penguin, 2012). Recall that Alexandre Kojève's declarations about the end of history occur in lectures on the philosophical eschatology, so to speak, of Hegel, and that these declarations were likewise shaped by Kojève's early research on theological traditions of wisdom. Once again, the question of "economy" is in no sense here a given outside of the history of reflection on religion. They evolve alongside each other, or perhaps even better, inside each other. Incidentally, Fukuyama's most intriguing defense can be found in Peter Sloterdijk, *Rage and Time: A Psychopolitical Investigation*, trans. Mario Wenning (New York: Columbia University Press, 2012), 1–43.

25. See for example Jacob Taubes, *Occidental Eschatology*, trans. David Ratmoko (Stanford: Stanford University Press, 2009); Reinhart Koselleck, *Futures Past: On the Semantics of Historical Time* (New York: Columbia University Press, 2004).

characteristic wry smile and trenchant criticism, he describes a new trinity of sovereignty that demonizes, criminalizes, and suppresses the transformative "chaos" of real transformation. Badiou calls the trinity POL:

> What are these celebrated values [in the name of which we demonize the rioters in the Paris *banlieues*]? We all know. They are called Property, Occident, Laicism. This is the dreadful POL, the dominant ideology in all countries that make themselves out to be civilized. In the name of POL, "public opinion" will demand "zero tolerance" of our fellow citizens in the so-called *banlieues*. Note, by the way, that while there is "zero tolerance" for the young black who steals a screwdriver, there is infinite tolerance for the crimes of bankers and government embezzlers which affect the lives of millions.[26]

We must remember that Badiou has done perhaps more than anyone else to inspire large scale international philosophical discussions about the Pauline legacy (cf. *The Incident at Antioch*; *Saint Paul: The Foundation of Universalism*). We should also notice that a wide-ranging and eager reception of Badiou's work, say, in North America, was initially inspired in turn by his readings of the Pauline legacy in the *Saint Paul* book. Will Paul "return" in a movement that will also have been our own? Slavoj Žižek preached during Occupy Wall Street that it was important that people realized that real Paulinism was not that of the Fundamentalist Christians and their fake patriotism but, rather, that of an egalitarian community of believers pursuing freedom.

> What is Christianity? It is the holy spirit. What is the holy spirit? It's an egalitarian community of believers who are linked by love for each other and who only have their own freedom and responsibility to do it. In this sense, the holy spirit is here now, and down there on Wall Street there are pagans who are worshiping blasphemous idols. So all we need is patience. The only thing I'm afraid of is that we will someday just go home. And then we will meet once a year, drinking beer, and nostalgically remembering what a nice time we had here. Promise ourselves that this will not be the case. We all know people who desire things who don't really want them. Don't be afraid to really want what you desire![27]

Whose *kairos* or which *katechon* indeed!

26. Badiou, *Rebirth of History*, 18–19.
27. Slavoj Žižek, "We Are the Awakening!," YouTube video, 18:39, from a speech given to Occupy Wall Street, posted by "Slavoj Zizek Videos," May 8, 2014, http://tinyurl.com/jpxxlpr.

A key issue for these discussions has to do with the way that the "sovereign" mirrors tales of divine sovereignty in earlier influential discussions (above all, those in Carl Schmitt and Walter Benjamin) because, like the divine, the decisionism—and hence the "political" nature—of the sovereign act subtracts itself from the usual realm of calculating behavior. For this Schmittian tradition, sovereignty is in that sense transcendent. What is important here for discussions closer to our own time, however, is the way that a "transcendent" decisionism blurs over into the category of the "autonomous" zone of the political. One may detach the dictatorial "sovereign" from the Schmittian tradition, but the question remaining with many of the more recent genealogists of the theologico-political tradition is whether the political is an autonomous category and, if so, in what sense. Consider Žižek's tableau (following Hegel, following Joachim of Fiore) that the "age of the spirit" is one in which an egalitarian community, grounding themselves on nothing but self-reliance, love, or fidelity to their freely projected cause, move forward together as the very picture of autonomy.

Finally, I would like to point out how this question affects another hot-button issue always floating around the philosophical discussions of Paulinism, namely, the question of "biopolitics." Following Michel Foucault, there is a growing tradition of philosophers who articulate the problem of the "immanence" of power through the language of biopolitics, or a politics keyed specifically not to traditional representational forms but rather more directly—more immanently—to the measurable qualities of pre-political "life" itself.[28] For our purposes, the formal structures of these discussions fit well with the question of whether "economy" names a form of power and control that eludes modern discussions of representational politics even as this form of power is oddly more invasive to everyday life, public and private, than it was before. Very simply put, this basic issue of the possibility that economic power both eludes and exceeds those forms of power tied to representational political discussion produces an ambivalent philosophical response. Some we have considered obviously lament the incapacity of inherited representational political forms (say, national and democratic) to grapple directly with the issues of "economy" in ways that would allow them to exert their own sovereignty against it.

---

28. For much more extended discussions of the role of "immanence" in the philosophical fascination with Paul, see Blanton, *Materialism for the Masses*, where this issue is explored throughout. More general overviews of "biopolitics" include Vanessa Lemm and Miguel Vatter, eds., *The Government of Life: Foucault, Biopolitics, and Neoliberalism* (New York: Fordham University Press, 2014).

For others, the trauma of new forms of global or international economic sovereignty brings with it an unexpected invitation for activists to struggle directly with "economy" without worrying about the mediating apparatus of state structures.

The question of whose *katechon* or which *kairos* continues here. Do we read the sublimated escape of "economy" from the sphere of national politics to indicate the instauration of a new form of sovereignty "from above," indeed from a sphere even more untouchably transcendent than earlier national forms of governance? Alternatively, does this transfer of sovereignty from the national to the global-economic indicate instead a profound resource whereby our actions are more directly able to inscribe themselves on a global economy without being tempered or muted by the slower machinations of parliamentarian or representative democracies? Is there a break with the norm that might also emerge "from below"?

How one responds to the question of autonomy in the political realm, therefore, in some sense determines whether one opts for some kind of new vitalism of a (good) biopolitical affirmationism (power "from below"), or whether one imagines sovereignty as a power, as it were, reigning "from above" and beyond the mere effects of the diffuse gestures, patterns, energies—the materialities (even if broadly conceived) of our everyday lives. One very interesting example should suffice to clarify some of the issues, the powerful effort of Antonio Negri and Michael Hardt to invent an affirmative or in some sense vitalist biopolitics of the "multitude" against, precisely, the usual ways of thinking about the forming political power of those pretending to be in charge. Hardt and Negri make a strong distinction between political theories keyed to an affirmative trust in our common productive experimentations and those keyed to a sense of the basic "evil" of humanity and the subsequent need to imagine politics as providing "conceptual tools necessary to confront and restrain evil."[29] The authors assert that Paul was, for them, on the wrong side of this great divide:

> Evil is posed by some in religious terms as transcendent (sin, for example) and by others as a transcendental element (a radical evil that marks the limit of human society). Saint Paul manages to grasp these two formulations in a single verse: "I would not have known sin except through the law" (Romans 7:7).[30]

29. Michael Hardt and Antonio Negri, *Commonwealth* (Cambridge, MA: Belknap Press, 2009), 190.

The philosophers return to the basic distinction further on when they "return to the pessimistic political anthropologies" that reify evil and thus demand that power be imagined as a necessary repressive or *katechontic* force:

> Even among those authors whose work is very close to ours, we recognize a recent tendency to link a notion of evil as an invariant of human nature to a politics aimed at restraining evil. One fascinating occasion for developing this line of reasoning is a passage in Paul's epistles that proposes the figure of the *katechon* (the one that restrains). The *katechon*, Paul explains, restrains the "lawless one," a satanic figure, and thus holds off the apocalypse until its proper time (2 Thessalonians 2:1–12).[31]

In this way, Hardt and Negri distinguish their own affirmative and, in some sense, vitalist ontology against those who ontologize the need for defense and restraint of a naturalized evil inclination by reference to the old myth of the *katechon*. Over against what they read in this tradition, their own tradition is marked by trust, affirmation, and a willingness to experiment: "Since evil is secondary to love, we are not limited to external containment but have access to [evil's] inner mechanisms."[32] Rather than guarding one's private property or merely local self-interests, the affirmative ontology of Hardt and Negri invites us to consider that a form of processual affirmation and desire—a love—allows us to undercut a politics of the sovereign restrainer because it plugs us in more directly to the real nature of being. It is for this reason that they can declare: "Love [rather than formal mechanisms of restraint of a natural evil inclination] is the battlefield for the struggle against evil. . . . What it means, though, is that the battle is ours to win."[33]

The distinction, working through their rejection of the fascination with the *katechon* myth in other philosophers who are "in other respects quite close" to them, is essential for their larger project. After all, the "empire" that has returned is one in which various mediating thresholds between governance and economy (e.g., the threshold of the nation state, the threshold between work and leisure or public and private life, the threshold of material and immaterial labor) no longer provide firm coordinates within which to imagine the nature of

30. Ibid.
31. Ibid., 197.
32. Ibid., 198.
33. Ibid., 198.

the political. The gamble of Hardt and Negri is that one can undercut the new "biopolitical" empire—its immanence to what were before imagined as noneconomic territories—through their vitalist affirmation of the potentials of the same, and that is a gesture premised on a refusal of the externality, indeed transcendence, of political decisionism and the "restraint" of evil in the Schmittian story. While they are very different in their readings of philosophy and also of Paulinism, it is worth comparing Hardt and Negri on this score to Jacob Taubes's intriguing fascination with the idea that Paulinism may signal a kind of anti-Schmittian sovereign break with normalcy proceeding not "from above" (as in Schmitt) but "from below."[34]

Similarly, Jeffrey Robbins also takes the project of Hardt and Negri to have set a challenge—namely, a kind of integration of the tradition of "political theology" with a thought of politics, as it were, from below—from their sources in a kind of vitalist materialism that is not overshadowed or captured by its representational forms of sovereignty. As Robbins writes:

> What Hardt and Negri provide is a way to conceive a political theology apart from the priority it gives to the concept of sovereignty and consistent with democratic theory. In the place of Schmitt's political theology, which follows from the idea of a sovereign and transcendent God, what I am proposing here is an immanent political theology predicated on the constituent power of the multitude.[35]

As Hent de Vries points out (and as Robbins notes), however, the very thought of the replacement of sovereign transcendence (sovereignty "from above" so to speak) with a vital materialism or multitude of constituent power "from below" immediately brings with it the question about whether there is, in the immanent sphere, a return of the exceptional, subtractive, or indeed transcendent zone of Schmittian sovereignty:

> To articulate all this . . . means rewriting a certain idea of transcendence (the notions, dimensions, or experiences with which "religion" and the "theologico-political" are most often identified) in the language of immanence, associated with the history of atomism, materialism, naturalism,

---

34. See Jacob Taubes, *The Political Theology of Paul*, ed. Aleida Assmann and Jan Assmann, trans. Dana Hollander (Stanford: Stanford University Press, 2004), 103.

35. Jeffrey W. Robbins, *Radical Democracy and Political Theology* (New York: Columbia University Press, 2013), 84.

and pantheism. The latter traverses the history of thought as a heretical countercurrent, of sorts. Yet this rewriting also implies interrogating the historical and systematic pertinence of the very distinction and opposition between transcendence and immanence as well.[36]

Or, in terms closer to our own interests here, if the rise of "empire" has something to do with the way an imagined immanence of global economy (compared to earlier modes of anti-capitalist political resistance) does not bring with it new experiences of the "sovereign exception" that irrupts not from "above" in some external realm of "politics" but rather within economic "life," imagined as the generative or constituent matrix of eventually constituted political structures. Whose *katechon*, which *kairos*? Everywhere the philosophers are seeing, through Paul (one way or another), an implicit answer to a vexing problem of how to conceptualize power, and the power of transformation, in the contemporary geopolitical scene.

Conclusion: Apparatuses of Divine Economy

Such are some basic maps situating recent philosophical interest in Paul as a comparative touchstone through which to attempt to name economic effects and to orient ourselves therein. No doubt these maps could be used in multiple ways to indicate crucial comparative stories that Pauline scholars should introduce to the larger debates concerning political economy. By way of a conclusion, I would like to name several comparative issues we biblical scholars could insinuate into the larger interdisciplinary and international discussions. One (of many) significant ways forward is for us to focus on the formal philosophical question of the repetition, maintenance, normalization, or regularity of time in relation to transformative, utopian, or revolutionary gestures. Naturally, the function of the word *katechon* in 2 Thessalonians may not be as comparatively interesting as the philosophers—in their reduction of this word to a formal mytheme about the struggle for the normalization of temporal experience—tend to assume. As I have tried to make clear, however, historians should not misinterpret such reductions as a mere absence of historical information. Such reductions to forms, to formulae, to ideas—in the end—are in fact endemic to the philosophical enterprise. In fact, as we pointed out, reductive mythemes may in fact be endemic to naming "economy" as such. The

36. Ibid.

shrewd move here is not simply to play the historically detailed over against the formal but, rather, to consider how in comparative conversations across disciplines we might contribute to the useful transformation of the reductions, images, icons, forms, or formulae that are orienting contemporary thought. In other words, far from an obstruction, the formal questions dominating philosophical reception of something like the *katechon* reference is a fascination historians can use to good effect—in this case, perhaps by pulling the formalization into a different historical archive than the ones tending to inform philosophers. Historians, in a word, should participate in, rather than withdraw from, the contemporary intellectual and political ferment around economy and biblical legacies.

How, historically (and therefore comparatively), did Paul and the communities with which he associated experience temporal newness or breaks in temporal continuities in relation to transformations or intensifications of certain economic practices? Were there threshold events that became, in multiple spheres of experience perhaps, emblematic of a difference that could then likewise be sublimated into a grand discourse of temporality or epochal shift, whether personally, ethnically, or in terms of empires? One of the poignant comparative links between many of the current philosophers of Paulinism and ancient Pauline communities involves the way both groups are decided minorities trying, so to speak, to suture some emblem of economic exchange to a discourse of temporal break and transformation. Naturally, the suturing effect is sometime absurdly overreaching or out of keeping with the economic exchanges in question.

One hears the tension of the struggle to link local ruptures in usual practice to some large scale—much less epochal—temporal transformation, in Alain Badiou's proclamation that we are living at a moment of the "rebirth of history," the end of the static (apparently eternal) empire of neoliberal governance—even as it seems we are (somehow, nevertheless, counterfactually) seeing the French youth of the Paris *banlieues* paying dearly for a stolen hammer while the truly exorbitant economic demands of the bank bailouts become a debt readily forgiven by the same state machinery. With such tragicomic experiences, Badiou's "revolution" appears blazingly, poignantly, as a minority position whose future looks like the proverbial long shot. No wonder Badiou, in his other work, has been profoundly attracted to the idea of a Pauline minority that has given up on centralized state-like institutions in order to turn to the loose affiliations and economic sharing of a nonstate network grounded or secured only by the weakness of a common *pistis* or trust.

Remember, too, that in this respect, the poignancies of a minority community's efforts to suture economic and temporal emblems are also interestingly operative in the philosophical communities. Sometimes this effort to conjure convincing linkages between grand epochs and everyday practices occurs as it does in the Cynic epistle of Anarchasis to Croesus, where the Cynic's vagrancy or refusal to participate in the economy of work-and-wage signals a return to that lost utopia in which everything was owned in common.[37] Sharing resources with the otherwise jobless and homeless teacher, in fact, was the major emblem (alongside the redistribution of resources currently territorialized into the temple networks) signaling one's participation in the new and old utopianism of the countercultural economy of nature. The salient point to make is that we could construct comparative maps of minority communities trying to conjure convincing links between sometimes the most minor of tweaks within everyday economic practice (and the protocols and hierarchies flowing therefrom) and the most grandiose proclamations of (or protreptic invitations to) collective epochal shifts.

In light of philosophical readings of Paul, but also of the many readings of Paul as a (usually quasi-Barthian) "apocalyptic" thinker, we might be tempted to say, therefore, that what we need is a new (and perhaps deflationary) exploration of the minutiae of economic practice that are often the occasioning emblems, even the convincing "special effects," of an imagined participation of a grand temporal shift.[38] The sublime comedy of these ancient minorities is, after all, more relevant to contemporary anti-capitalist movements than most feel comfortable enough to admit. In each case, the question of the special effect or emergence of a collective "apparatus" of experience is a question of the way in which small continuities or ruptures in everyday life become, effectively and repeatedly, signals or indications of an imagined grand collective story, whether as energizing (or sublimated) little indications of a better world that might just appear, or as enervating annoyances also taken as effects of some fall into the economy of the idol (Paul), the territorialized/privatized common of nature (Cynic), or, more recently, the vampiric and enslaving demands of a contemporary

---

37. Cf. Anacharsis to Croesus 9.9–25, in Abraham J. Malherbe, ed., *The Cynic Epistles: A Study Edition* (Atlanta: Society of Biblical Literature, 2006), 47.

38. I borrow the logic of the "special effect" from Hent de Vries, this topic being an analytic tool for the consideration of social organization very similar to that of the "apparatus" in Agamben and Foucault. See Blanton, *Materialism for the Masses*, 14, 18–20, 31–35, 103–7.

regime of "capital." To take up the nominalist challenge of Foucault, Deleuze, and Agamben to chart the unpredictable emergence of "apparatuses" organizing our collective experience, historians of the ancient materials should be at the vanguard of charting the shifting and often surprising ways in which early Jewish and Christian groups attempted to suture their own cultural and countercultural visions onto everyday practices of exchange.

Select Bibliography

Agamben, Giorgio. *The Kingdom and the Glory: For a Theological Genealogy of Economy and Government*. Stanford: Stanford University Press, 2011.

_____. *The Use of Bodies*. Stanford: Stanford University Press, 2016.

Anidjar, Gil. *Blood: A Critique of Christianity*. New York: Columbia University Press, 2014.

Badiou, Alain. *The Rebirth of History: Times of Riots and Uprisings*. Translated by Gregory Elliott. London: Verso, 2012.

Blanton, Ward. *A Materialism for the Masses: Saint Paul and the Philosophy of Undying Life*. New York: Columbia University Press, 2014.

_____, and Hent de Vries, eds. *Paul and the Philosophers*. New York: Fordham University Press, 2013.

Boer, Roland. *The Sacred Economy of Ancient Israel*. Louisville, KY: Westminster John Knox, 2015.

_____, and Christina Petterson, *Idols of Nations: Biblical Myth at the Origins of Capitalism*. Minneapolis: Fortress Press, 2014.

Derrida, Jacques. *Politics of Friendship*. London: Verso, 2005.

_____. *Specters of Marx: The State of the Debt, the Work of Mourning, and the New International*. New York: Routledge, 1994.

Douzinas, Costas. *Philosophy and Resistance in the Crisis: Greece and the Future of Europe*. Cambridge: Polity Press, 2013.

Dupuy, Jean-Pierre. *Economy and the Future: A Crisis of Faith*. East Lansing, MI: Michigan State University Press, 2014.

Esposito, Roberto. *Communitas: The Origin and Destiny of Community*. Translated by Timothy Campbell. Stanford: Stanford University Press, 2010.

_____. *Immunitas: The Protection and Negation of Life*. Translated by Zakiya Hanafi. Cambridge: Polity Press, 2011.

_____. *Living Thought: The Origins and Actuality of Italian Philosophy*. Translated by Zakiya Hanafi. Stanford: Stanford University Press, 2012.

_____. *Two: The Machine of Political Theology and the Place of Thought.* Translated by Zakiya Hanafi. Stanford. Stanford University Press, 2015.

Fukuyama, Francis. *The End of History and the Last Man.* London: Penguin, 2012.

Hardt, Michael, and Antonio Negri. *Commonwealth.* Cambridge, MA: Belknap Press, 2009.

Kahn, Paul W. *Political Theology: Four New Chapters on the Concept of Sovereignty.* New York: Columbia University Press, 2011.

Koselleck, Reinhart. *Futures Past: On the Semantics of Historical Time.* New York: Columbia University Press, 2004.

Lazzarato, Maurizio. *Governing by Debt.* Translated by Joshua David Jordan. South Pasadena, CA: Semiotext(e), 2013.

_____. *The Making of the Indebted Man: An Essay on the Neoliberal Condition.* Translated by Joshua David Jordan. Los Angeles: Semiotext(e), 2012.

Lemm, Vanessa, and Miguel Vatter, eds. *The Government of Life: Foucault, Biopolitics, and Neoliberalism.* New York: Fordham University Press, 2014.

Malherbe, Abraham J., ed. *The Cynic Epistles: A Study Edition.* Atlanta: Society of Biblical Literature, 2006.

Robbins, Jeffrey W. *Radical Democracy and Political Theology.* New York: Columbia University Press, 2013.

Schmitt, Carl. *The Concept of the Political.* Chicago: University of Chicago Press, 2007.

Sedlacek, Tomas. *Economics of Good and Evil: The Quest for Economic Meaning from Gilgamesh to Wall Street.* Oxford: Oxford University Press, 2013.

Sloterdijk, Peter. *Rage and Time: A Psychopolitical Investigation.* Translated by Mario Wenning. New York: Columbia University Press, 2012.

Taubes, Jacob. *Occidental Eschatology.* Translated by David Ratmoko. Stanford: Stanford University Press, 2009.

_____. *The Political Theology of Paul.* Edited by Aleida Assmann and Jan Assmann with Horst Folkers, Wolf-Daniel Hartwich, and Christoph Schulte. Translated by Dana Hollander. Stanford: Stanford University Press, 2004.

Varoufakis, Yanis. *The Global Minotaur: America, Europe and the Future of the Global Economy.* London: Zed Books, 2015.

Vogl, Joseph. *Specter of Capital.* Translated by Joachim Redner and Robert Savage. Stanford: Stanford University Press, 2014.

Vries, Hent de, and Lawrence E. Sullivan, eds. *Political Theologies: Public*

Religions in a Post-Secular World. New York: Fordham University Press, 2006.

Žižek, Slavoj. *Less than Nothing: Hegel and the Shadow of Dialectical Materialism*. London: Verso, 2012.

Index